WINDOWS 2000

Design & Migration

About the Author. . .

Rand H. Morimoto, MCSE, is president of Inacom Oakland. He has been in the industry for over 20 years and is an internationally known speaker and author in the fields of desktop computing, electronic messaging, wide area network implementation, and remote and mobile computing. Rand is a member of the Microsoft Dealer Advisory Board and participates in strategy recommendations and technology reviews of Microsoft's products and solutions.

Rand's firm, Inacom Oakland, has over 50 full-time consultants and technical experts specializing in wide area network and messaging infrastructure design, implementation, end user and administrator training, and network management services. Microsoft recognized Inacom Oakland in 1996 as one of the Top 3 Solution Providers in the world in Windows NT design and implementation.

Rand is a Microsoft MCSE and Novell Master CNE with an undergraduate degree in Electrical Engineering and an MBA in Strategic Planning and Business Management from UC Berkeley.

WINDOWS 2000

Design & Migration

RAND MORIMOTO

Osborne/**McGraw-Hill**

Berkeley   New York   St. Louis   San Francisco
Auckland   Bogotá   Hamburg   London   Madrid
Mexico City   Milan   Montreal   New Delhi   Panama City
Paris   São Paulo   Singapore   Sydney
Tokyo   Toronto

Osborne/**McGraw-Hill**
2600 Tenth Street
Berkeley, California 94710
U.S.A.

For information on translations or book distributors outside the U.S.A., or to arrange bulk purchase discounts for sales promotions, premiums, or fund-raisers, please contact Osborne/**McGraw-Hill** at the above address.

Windows 2000 Design & Migration

1234567890 AGM AGM 019876543210

ISBN 0-07-212205-6

Publisher
Brandon A. Nordin
Associate Publisher, Editor-in-Chief
Scott Rogers
Acquisitions Editor
Wendy Rinaldi
Project Editor
Carolyn Welch
Acquisitions Coordinator
Monika Faltiss
Technical Editor
Chris Amaris
Contributing Writers
Chris Amaris
Joe R. Coca, Jr.
Chris Doyle, MCSE
Lynn Langfeld
Colin Spence
Kevin Tsai
James V. Walker
Mark E. Weinhardt

Copy Editors
Andy Carroll
Dennis Weaver
Proofreader
Jo Grissom
Indexer
Meg McDonnell
Computer Designers
Jani Beckwith
Jean Butterfield
Dick Schwartz
Illustrators
Robert Hansen
Brian Wells
Beth Young
Series Design
Peter F. Hancik
Cover Design
Matthew Willis

This book was composed with Corel VENTURA ™ Publisher.

To my wife Kim and my daughter Kelly.

AT A GLANCE

CONTENTS

Part II

Designing and Planning the Migration to Windows 2000

Part III

Deploying Windows 2000

ACKNOWLEDGMENTS

Numerous people have been instrumental in helping to get this book to print. Kathy Ivens and Chris Amaris ensured that the content and technical aspects were accurate. The Osborne/McGraw-Hill team, including Monika Faltiss, Carolyn Welch, and Wendy Rinaldi, worked behind the scenes to produce this book. Special thanks, also, to Jani Beckwith, Dick Schwartz, and the entire Osborne Production staff; these folks are the best in the business.

I would also like to acknowledge the efforts of the Microsoft Windows 2000 development team. With their assistance and support, they gave my company and me the technical resources for gaining expertise in Windows 2000 long before the product was publicly available. They also provided us with the opportunity to work with some of the largest organizations in the country and thus gain experience in designing, planning, prototyping, implementing, and supporting Windows 2000—experience vital to the knowledge base that has become the foundation of this book.

And finally, I would like to thank Inacom Oakland senior consultants, account executives, and system engineers Brian Peladeau, Chris Amaris, Chris Doyle, Colin Spence, James Walker, Joe Coca, Joe Pennetta, Kevin Tsai, Kimber Edwards, Lynn Langfeld, and Mark Weinhardt for their part in working with our clients on Windows 2000 projects. Thousands of hours have been spent in working with the Windows 2000 solutions summarized in this book. It is my hope that the lessons learned by many people before you will enrich your experience with this product.

There is another group of people who have made this book possible. To my parents, my loving thanks for giving me life. I hope I have made you proud. To Richard, Mike, Lee, and Joseph, who helped me gain the wisdom to write this book, and to Johnny Huffman, for all his words of switching wisdom and fine photography, thanks. To Craig Dunton and Mary Beth Lesko, for their additional edits and comments. To Harry Newton and his Telecom Dictionary—it never hurts to have a second opinion. To Creative Labs, Pinnacle Software, Vivo, Voice Information Systems, Teltone, and ACS for providing insider information about the industry. And finally, my thanks to anyone whom I may have forgotten.

INTRODUCTION

Windows 2000 is so much like Windows NT, yet so different. You who are working with the product will find similarities to Windows 95, Windows 98, and Windows NT that will make using and learning Windows 2000 somewhat familiar. However, new technologies such as Active Directory, Remote Storage, Intellimirror, Terminal Services, and Group Policies will be completely new to all users and administrators.

What I've set out to accomplish in this book is not to rewrite an installation guide or general product information manual, but rather to draw from a couple years of practical experience with the Windows 2000 product family (back from its original start as Windows NT 5) to highlight things that organizations around the world are doing to leverage the capabilities of the product—thus improving the way they do business.

As with any product, there are a number of "gotchas" in planning, implementation, and support that you may not recognize until you head down the wrong path—and then must work around the problems. I hope that the information in this book, compiled from hundreds of installations of Windows 2000, will help prevent you from making mistakes and guide you through the planning and implementation of a highly functional networking infrastructure.

HOW THIS BOOK IS STRUCTURED

Part I of this book provides valuable background information, including what's new for those who are already familiar with Windows NT, and explanations of the DNS and Active Directory technologies that make up the core structure of Microsoft Windows 2000.

Part II focuses on planning a successful implementation or migration to the Windows 2000 environment. Far too often have I seen organizations start from an idea and jump straight into prototyping or testing an installation without giving much thought to what the final solution would entail. It's very tempting to just insert the Windows 2000 CD and let the Upgrade wizard convert an old Windows 95 or Windows NT system to Windows 2000. However, every successful installation or migration that I have participated in has begun with investing significant time detailing every component of the current implementation, as well as the company's needs, so that when the project was completed, it met the goals and expectations of the organization. Part II highlights the key success factors in preparing a successful installation.

Part III covers the actual steps involved in installing or migrating to Windows 2000 as a server, workstation, or domain controller in a networking environment. Here I describe not only the installation of the core operating system, but also the key add-in components that provide automated software installation (Intellimirror), thin-client technologies (Terminal Services), high availability, and fault tolerance (Clustering and Network Load Balancing). For organizations that are currently running Windows NT 4 or Novell Netware, Part III explains the process involved in migrating a network environment to Windows 2000.

After an organization has installed Windows 2000, routine tuning, optimization, and management of the installation are crucial to making the system run efficiently and effectively. I take the approach of supporting individual users and the entire enterprise network through system optimization and configuration modifications. Maintaining the Windows 2000 environment is critical to maximizing the product's capabilities.

There is a lot covered here. However, the Microsoft Windows 2000 product is a robust network infrastructure environment. I hope you will be able to use the information in this book to get the most out of the product as you plan, design, migrate to, deploy, maintain, and support your own Windows 2000 network.

PART I

Windows 2000: Understanding the New Paradigm

Windows 2000 is more than just a new operating system—it introduces a completely new method of communication between desktop systems and computer networks. If you've used previous versions of the Windows NT operating system, you'll notice similarities in many of the day-to-day file and print features of the product, but the design and implementation of the Windows 2000 infrastructure are completely different.

The first part of this book focuses on the terminology used in Windows 2000, concentrating on the new Active Directory naming and security structure, as well as the implementation of the Domain Name System (DNS). It also discusses the new administration tools. These first five chapters will provide you with the background necessary to understand the core features and functions of this new operating environment.

CHAPTER 1

The Windows 2000 Environment

Throughout this book, you'll find a lot of discussion of the core components of the Windows 2000 products, so let's start by defining those components and the terminology you'll see.

THE WINDOWS 2000 FAMILY OF PRODUCTS

The Windows 2000 product line is made up of four versions. Unlike previous versions of Windows NT, which typically only differed between server and workstation versions, the Windows 2000 family has significant inclusions and exclusions of features among the various versions of the product.

▼ **Windows 2000 Professional**   The Windows 2000 Professional edition is the desktop or workstation version of the product line. It includes all the security functions, mobile user features, system reliability components, and network integration components necessary for a workstation or laptop to integrate into a Windows 2000 environment.

■ **Windows 2000 Server**   The Windows 2000 Server edition provides four-way symmetrical multiprocessing for small and medium enterprise workgroup, application server, or branch office environments. It includes all the internetworking components needed to provide the server-level and network management connectivity of a Windows 2000 environment.

■ **Windows 2000 Advanced Server**   The Windows 2000 Advanced Server edition provides up to eight-way symmetrical multiprocessing for more powerful enterprise, departmental, and application server purposes. With enhanced memory access capabilities, integrated two-way clustering, and load-balancing support, the Advanced Server edition provides better support for scalable network server needs.

▲ **Windows 2000 Datacenter Server**   The Windows 2000 Datacenter Server edition supports up to 32-way symmetrical multiprocessing and up to 64 gigabytes (GB) of physical memory. It provides both four-way clustering and load-balancing capabilities for the most robust scalable and mission-critical enterprise needs.

THE CORE COMPONENTS OF WINDOWS 2000

The Windows 2000 family of products is made up of servers, domain controllers, and client desktop systems. This may seem the same as in previous versions of the operating system, but the definitions of these components have changed—thus, the way you'll implement these elements is slightly different. (See Chapter 5 for more details on the hardware requirements and suggested configurations of the servers, domain controllers, and desktop systems.)

Servers (Application and File Servers)

The first component in any network is a *file server*. The term "file server" is a historical term that refers to the main system in a network that manages files. However, in today's networking environment, the file server is more commonly just called a server because of the varying uses of server systems. A *server* today can be either a centralized storage system for files in the traditional sense, or it can be an application server.

It's common to use application servers for business productivity or line-of-business applications. Some examples are SQL databases, electronic messaging applications, human resource systems, web server information, and company intranet systems. These application servers manage program information and application data instead of merely providing individual files for users. Users have access to all of the structured, stored information.

Domain Controllers

You'll need to set up *domain controllers* to authenticate users and to grant secured access to the networking environment. The domain controller is usually a separate dedicated system acting as an application server, and its sole function is as a domain controller. Of course, domain controller services could be added to the functions of any other file or application server, creating a dual-function machine.

Windows 2000, unlike previous versions of Windows NT, lets you make the decision about using a computer as a domain controller at any time. You don't have to make this determination when you install the operating system, because any member server can be promoted to a domain controller. (Chapter 9 has detailed discussions on the placement of the domain controllers.)

Client Systems

The final component of a network is the *client*. Clients have traditionally been personal computers with lots of memory and high desktop-processing speeds. Windows 2000 offers a wide range of options for client connectivity.

Windows 2000 systems can use standard PCs (for instance, an Intel *x*86/Pentium computer), Apple Macintosh computers, or the new thin-client technology workstations (terminals with very modest processing capabilities). The Windows Terminal Services technology is embedded in the operating system, allowing a server to share its processing capabilities with the client. (See Chapter 14 for a discussion of desktop client options, including thin-client technologies.)

ORGANIZATIONAL COMPONENTS

Windows 2000 introduces a new series of terms based on the directory management system called the *Active Directory*. The Active Directory is a new method of managing users, groups, and network resources in a hierarchical structure. This section covers some of the important terms you need to know about the organizational structure of this environment. (See Chapter 6 for a full discussion of the Active Directory and the design and implementation processes.)

Active Directory

The Active Directory is a new hierarchical administration and management system that's been integrated into the Windows 2000 family of products. One of the side benefits you'll notice immediately is an improvement in your ability to distribute management roles for the organization's security system. Instead of granting either full administrative rights or limited user security rights, the Active Directory provides a virtually unlimited number of levels of security. You can delegate administration and management of any portion of the enterprise hierarchy. The substructures are called *organizational units,* and you can arrange them in any way you wish—for example, by business unit or site.

Organizational Units

An organizational unit can be any segment of your organization. You could use department grouping (such as Finance, Manufacturing, and Marketing), or geographical grouping (such as San Francisco, New York, and Tokyo). In fact, you can deepen the segmentation, perhaps by breaking down a site organizational unit into its departmental groupings. Each layer of the organization that is designated an organizational unit can be separately administered and managed. You can allocate resources to an organizational unit, as well as create a security policy that limits users to those resources.

Furthermore, you can permit administrators to delegate administrative tasks for suborganizations (creating a group of subadministrators). This is an organized and logical way to control which individuals have access to which resources within the organizational structure. In other words, you can build levels of delegation rights that administrators can use to assign administrative tasks to other users within the organizational unit.

Sites

Windows 2000 also has a formal designation known as a *site.* The organizational units designate levels of security and user administration boundaries, and the site designates the boundaries for the replication of security information within the organization. If your organization is physically distributed across multiple locations, you can create sites to manage user authentication and directory replication. The computers (both workstations and servers) in a single site should be connected by high-speed lines.

It may be that your organization refers to a city as a site (for example, your offices in Tokyo are a site). However, if you have multiple office buildings spread across that city and they're connected by low-speed frame relay connections (56K lease lines or ISDN connections), you should consider each location as an individual site. Your Windows 2000 sites may be Tokyo-North, Tokyo-South, and Tokyo-West.

The method you use to create sites determines how the Active Directory is partitioned into multiple segments and how user authentication is distributed across various locations. You would not want a single domain controller in one site authenticating users in each of the other sites if the sites are connected by low-speed lines. By designating three separate sites and placing a domain controller in each of them, you'll have a more efficient method of logon authentication.

Domains

Forget your definition of a *domain*. Windows 2000 brings a new meaning to the word. A domain is no longer defined as an authentication group where domain controllers validate users. In Windows 2000, a domain is a separate physical site or zone within the organization. Domain names are now based on the general Internet Domain Name System (DNS) structure. (You'll learn more on DNS in Chapter 2.) Domain names designate the public view of the organization, its sites, and any organizational units, starting with the master (or root) domain name.

In fact, there's even a method of assigning multiple root domains, which is useful for companies that operate under more than one business name (even though those business names are frequently administered and managed centrally). Of course, it's common for the different named entities to share resources, so trusts can be created between the domains to allow resources to be accessible across the domains.

Domains that exist high up in the Active Directory are *parent* domains, and domains below parent domains are *child* domains. Security, administration, and management flows from the parents to the children. (Helpful information on domain naming and designing multiple-domain structures can be found in Chapters 2 and 7 of this book.)

Figure 1-1 shows an organizational structure based on domains, distributed by sites, and broken down further by organizational units. This figure illustrates how a variety of components create the basic structure of the Active Directory.

Trees and Forests

For each domain in an organization, there is a tree that has branches that represent organizational units. Security rights are delegated to the branches for administrative purposes, but all of the branches are defined as a single, master administered organization, which is called the *tree*.

In previous versions of Windows NT, you probably created certain domains in order to provide secured (restricted) access to sensitive organizational units, such as payroll or human resource information. Now, using the Active Directory, you can safely collapse multiple NT 4 domains into a common tree and assign extremely high levels of secured access to specific resources within any branch of the tree. (Read Chapter 3 for more information about security in Windows 2000, and Chapter 6 for detailed information about designing the Active Directory.)

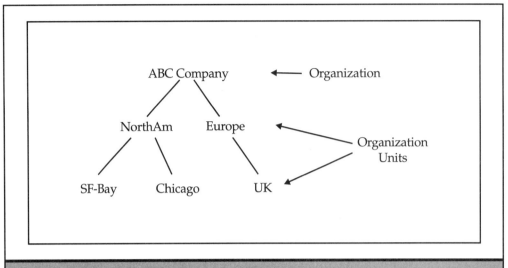

Figure 1-1.   An Active Directory, including domains, sites, and organization units

NOTE: The initial release of Windows 2000 does not support the ability to merge or split trees once you create them, nor will you be able to merge multiple types of tree schemas together. Chapters 2, 6, and 7 define trees, schemas, and other Active Directory terminology as well as help you understand how to design your DNS namespace and Active Directory so that you create the right tree structure from the beginning.

Some organizations require more than one tree. For instance, you may administer a large company that operates with a single set of administrative resources but actually operates (and is known to the public) as more than one entity. Or, each division of your organization may operate as a separate company (perhaps you separate products from services).

When you have multiple trees, you have a *forest*, and that's the terminology Windows 2000 uses. A forest shares trusts as well as common schemas between the trees, so resources can be shared among all the individual trees. However, the naming structures and delegation structures can be completely unique for each tree.

A forest allows multiple organizations to retain their individual domain names (like ABC Company and XYZ Company) while being administered by a single IT organization. The individual organizations can share certain business functions (such as a common accounting organization or common human resources organization), so they need to have a common naming and administrative structure. Figure 1-2 shows parallel Active Directory trees of two completely different organizations that together can form a forest for centralized administration.

Early designs and deployments of Windows 2000 have shown that a forest isn't always sufficient. Organizations that have separate IT administration units need clusters of forests. That's because a forest, by definition, requires the trees to share the same schema.

If your organization has separate IT units administering individual entities, you'll want to delegate administration on a per-IT-unit basis. But suppose now you find you still need to share certain business functions (again, like a common accounting or human resource organization). In this case, you'd create explicit trusts among the organizations, each of which is structured in separately designed forests. The administrators of each forest can design and manage their own schemas and groups of trees, and share common resources within the organizational structure.

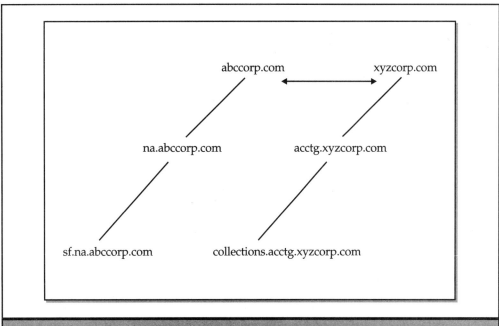

Figure 1-2. A forest shares organizational resources

> *NOTE:*   In the initial release of Windows 2000, you will be able neither to move resources between forests nor to merge different schemas. This means that when you create clusters of forests, you must be certain that you have no intention of redesigning and consolidating the organizational structure back to a single forest or single tree design. Chapters 6 and 7 discuss the design of trees, forests, and clusters of forests so you can get an idea of how to plan the appropriate structure for your organization.

Groups

Windows 2000 also adds new terms to the definition and concept of user groups, by adding a new group called the *universal group*. Of course, if you consider the new paradigm of organizational units, trees, and forests, the concept of a universal group is quite logical.

The universal group in a native Windows 2000 domain is a group that can be moved anywhere within a tree or forest in an organization. Local domain users or global domain users are specific to certain branches in your organizational units or sites.

A *group* is essentially a centrally managed organizational unit. A *local group* (belonging to an organizational unit) or a *global group* (belonging to a tree) can be a list of users that share common characteristics and needs. However, it's frequently unnecessary to administer this group separately by naming an administrator. You can even simplify administration (such as delegating security privileges) by selecting a group rather than individual user or resource names.

Group creation and management is critical in the migration to Windows 2000. Many of the administrative and management utilities you'll use to migrate users work best if the users in an existing NT 4 domain are managed as universal groups. Chapter 16 has detailed discussions on this topic.

Trusts

Trusts are a core feature in previous versions of Windows NT, allowing users to access resources in other domains within your organization. However, in Windows 2000, trusts are a feature you'll use to enhance security and administration, rather than a mandatory component to facilitate resource sharing. The three types of trusts in Windows 2000 are transitive trusts, explicit trusts, and explicit trusts within a tree.

▼ **Transitive trust**   A *transitive trust* is the default level of creating secured communications between domains in an organization. When multiple domains or zones are created in Windows DNS, child domains by default are assigned their trust levels from their parent domain in the tree. Trusts flow up and down through the domain structure. Therefore, as shown in Figure 1-3, sf.na.abccorp.com must go through na.abccorp.com to get to abccorp.com before going down to europe.abccorp.com to get to uk.europe.abccorp.com.

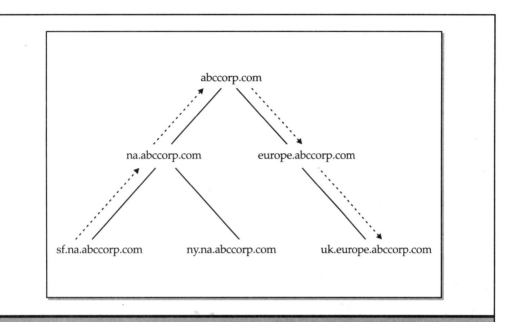

Figure 1-3.   Transitive trusts flow up and down through a domain

- ■ **Explicit trust**   An *explicit trust* is designed to connect two trees, each of which has a unique namespace. This differs from a transitive trust, which only links domains within a common namespace. When you create a forest, you link its multiple trees through the use of explicit trusts. As shown in Figure 1-4, domains abccorp.com and xyzcorp.com are explicitly defined to trust each other based on the security rule at the top of the two trees.

- ▲ **Explicit trust within a tree**   You can bypass the default upward and downward flow of trusts within a tree by assigning an explicit trust between branches of a tree. As shown in Figure 1-5, this feature means that sf.na.abccorp.com doesn't have to use transitive trusts to go up and down the entire tree to get to the uk.europe.abccorp.com domain. Instead, an explicit trust is created directly between the sf.na.abccorp.com branch and the uk.europe.abccorp.com branch. This provides instant secured access to another portion of the tree.

NOTE: You can also limit explicit trust access to members of the current branch of the tree and inhibit child-level pass-through use of the explicit trust.

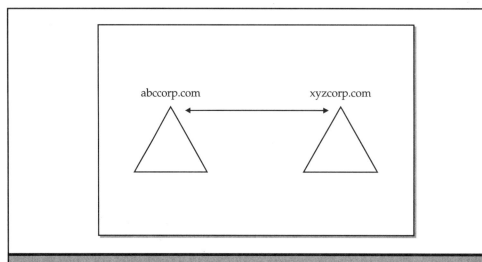

Figure 1-4. Create explicit trusts to connect trees

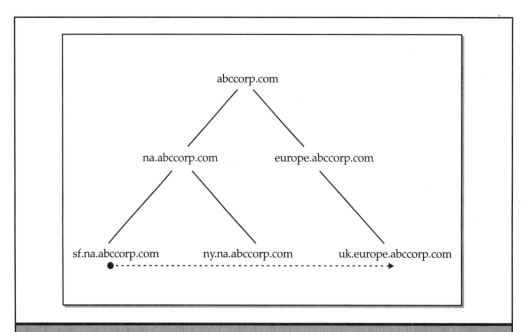

Figure 1-5. For frequently used access, create an explicit trust within a tree

OPERATIONAL COMPONENTS

The operational components of Windows 2000 include storage management functions, desktop deployment, and network management features that are new to the operating system.

Storage Management Improvements

Windows 2000 greatly improves storage. It provides support for new storage media, better tools for managing the information, and improved fault-tolerance features.

Multilevel Storage Capabilities

Managing and administering the files stored on your servers is a significant chore. One big challenge is storing information that is no longer actively required. Users always feel they require access to their files regardless of how long the files have been stored on the network. Windows 2000 supports storage systems that provide fast access with disk fault tolerance for files that need to be immediately accessible and protected against loss, along with secondary and tertiary storage systems that store files for archived long-term storage on lower-cost media. The lower-cost media could be magneto-optical storage systems, CD-ROM, DVD, or sequential streaming tape.

Called *hierarchical storage management* (HSM), this is a method of using different levels of storage. Users continue to see their files stored in the same place as they had originally saved the information, and the network administrator can manage the files by setting limits on files and directories. After a specified period, files are automatically migrated from the primary storage system to a secondary system, then to a tertiary storage system, and so on. Each time the information is transferred, the organization can minimize the cost of storage by using lower-cost storage media.

Information is automatically migrated from storage system to storage system based on either the creation date of the file(s) or based on the last time the information was accessed. For example, if no user has accessed a file in the past six months, the administrator of the network could flag the file system to automatically migrate the information to a secondary storage system. If after another six months no one has accessed the file from the secondary storage system, it could then be automatically migrated to the tertiary system. Figure 1-6 shows how information can flow from high-availability servers to general data warehouse servers, improving disaster-recovery processes and file-management systems.

NOTE: Windows 2000 provides hierarchical storage management for two levels (primary to secondary), and any migration thereafter will be provided by third-party add-in products.

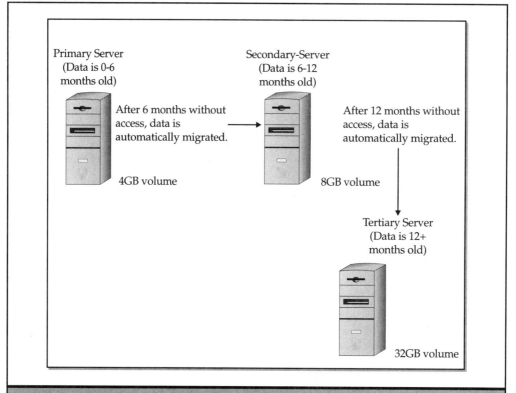

Figure 1-6. Leveraging hierarchical storage management

Some organizations are using the hierarchical storage management system not only as an archiving tool, but also as a data management system to help the organization better manage huge data store systems that are difficult, if not impossible, to administer. While disk storage systems have gotten relatively inexpensive and the creation of large data servers storing 30GB, 50GB, or 100GB are not uncommon, the problem with large data servers is the ability of the organization to back up and restore the information effectively in the event of a system failure. Although an organization can do incremental backups to a large data server, if the server were to crash, it could take the organization days or weeks to restore the information from tape. Through the creative implementation of HSM, you could store a manageable 3–5GB of information on a primary/active information server that users access frequently. It could, for example, store information created in the past seven days. Any information that is between seven and 30 days old can be migrated to a secondary storage system, and information older than 30 days can be migrated to a tertiary storage system, and so on. In the event of a primary server failure, you can easily restore the most current files (3–5GB) within minutes. In the event of a secondary or tertiary server failure, chances of users requiring information from that source are less likely, giving you time to restore the servers without drastically affecting the overall operations of the business.

Hardware RAID Drive Management

Microsoft has worked very closely with hardware vendors to create integrated solutions that minimize the number of separate applications, tools, and tasks required to administer the Windows 2000 family of products. The result is the integration of a number of the tools necessary to manage RAID drive subsystems. The tools needed to check the status of the hardware RAID configuration, validate that all disk partitions are operational, and conduct recovery of a failed RAID dataset are now in the Microsoft Management Console utility. These management tools are part of the core network operating system.

Distributed File System (DFS)

Windows 2000 enhances the *distributed file system* (DFS) that provides a logical array of storage space in a network when physical storage is distributed across multiple servers. Each file is visible from a single centralized logical drive somewhere on the network, although the information may actually be stored on any of multiple physical drives on multiple servers. This means you can distribute files across multiple servers for load balancing or to assist your fault-tolerance scheme. DFS gives you a simple view of multiple directories and file volumes within a single logical directory tree.

You benefit from the ability to distribute files across multiple file servers, while users access only a single logical volume when they need files. A single server failure can put dozens of gigabytes of information offline; with the distributed file system, you can have a dozen servers, each with 12–16GB of storage, all organized as a single Windows 2000 DFS volume, as shown in Figure 1-7.

Several disk file indexing solutions, including the Microsoft Index Server product, let you index all the files on a physical disk volume or in a large distributed file system volume. Thus, anything you need is located in the index of files on the system. Between DFS and file indexing, you can easily store, access, and manage all the information on your network. More information about DFS is in Chapter 12.

Dynamic Volume Management

Now that information can be stored on multiple servers, with a single logical pointer for users, the logical next step is a way to relocate data when there's an emergency. *Dynamic Volume Management* means that information can be migrated from a failing server to another server while users are logged on to the network. The files are migrated in the background, and a new physical pointer is created to the source of the information. To the user, the information remains in the same location; the logical distributed file system tree stays the same.

TIP: Use Dynamic Volume Management as part of your disaster recovery and fault-tolerance recovery system plans. By designating hot data relocation backup servers, you can ensure that a network server volume is always available to users, regardless of whether the primary drive volume is being upgraded or serviced, or has crashed.

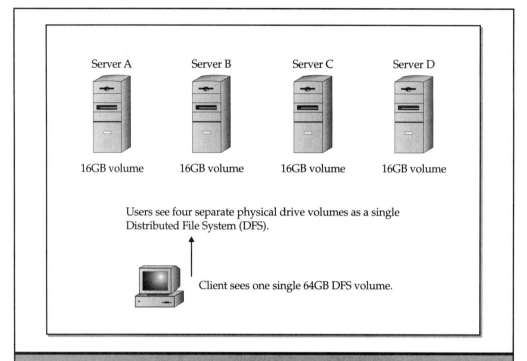

Figure 1-7.   A single directory name actually points to multiple physical data locations

Windows 2000 Server Media Services

Windows 2000 includes a new feature called Windows 2000 Media Services. Windows 2000 Media Services provides a consistent method for accessing a variety of storage media, including fixed storage, random storage, and sequential storage subsystems. This is a real improvement over previous versions of the operating system, which handled CD-ROM information and tape backup information differently, creating occasional difficulty in managing data.

With Windows 2000 Media Services, the various storage media look and operate similarly. This means you can use a variety of storage systems more easily. Information can be archived to a writable CD-ROM drive or to a magneto-optical WORM drive. Tape drives are no longer just disaster-recovery devices—they're another form of hard drive where information can be archived on a regular basis. This frees up the more dynamic access capabilities of the fixed or random storage for data demands that require fast information access.

As part of the overall media storage-management capabilities of Windows 2000, features such as creating, extending, or mirroring a volume set can be conducted online without shutting down the server or interrupting user access to the operational resources. With a common interface for mounting and dismounting any form of media, you have better control of your information.

Enhanced Backup Capabilities

Windows 2000 provides enhanced backup capabilities that extend the abilities of the backup system. One of the major enhancements is the ability to back up and restore information while the network continues to be in operation. Windows 2000 includes a preemptive file access process that allows files to be accessed while in use. You can provide 24 × 7 service to users without sacrificing the importance of backing up.

Media Mirror

An extension to the new media services provided by Windows 2000 is the Media Mirror, which provides fault tolerance for the sequential write tape backup subsystems. All of us know the uneasiness that comes from using a tape drive as the ultimate crash-and-burn disaster-recovery savior. There's always a concern about whether the tape is flawed when you write to it, or whether it becomes damaged during a restore operation.

The Media Mirror, as shown in Figure 1-8, means you can set up mirrored tape drives. Information is simultaneously written to two tape drives, providing a level of comfort that you've backed up within the definition of a fault-tolerant scheme. It's like RAID for tape!

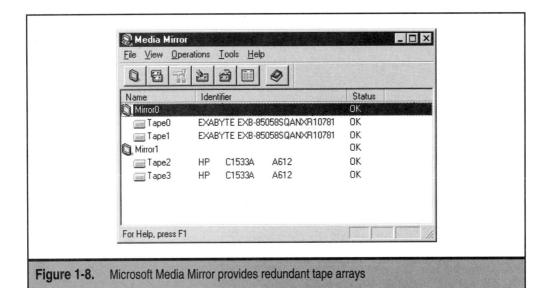

Figure 1-8.   Microsoft Media Mirror provides redundant tape arrays

Attributed File Support System

The new attributed file support system provides multiple levels of volume security. You can set access rights for the disk volume, the logical file volume, a directory, or a file. Attributes can be set by user, by group, or as a default for the entire organization. This gives you an incredibly rich set of controls as you manage information.

Integrated Volume Defragmentation

Instead of relying on third-party add-ins, you now have a built-in disk integrity scanning and file defragmentation utility. When files are written to disk, the information is written as quickly as possible to the first available disk space found on the drive subsystem. While this is the most efficient immediate write system available, over time the inefficiencies caused by defragmented files causes deterioration in the network file system. The built-in disk defragmentation in Windows 2000 can improve file access speeds by two to three times.

Disk defragmentation is a snap-in tool in the Microsoft Management Console (see Figure 1-9). You can schedule it for automatic launching, or defragment whenever you feel it's necessary. Of course, regular disk defragmentation means the job is performed more quickly each time.

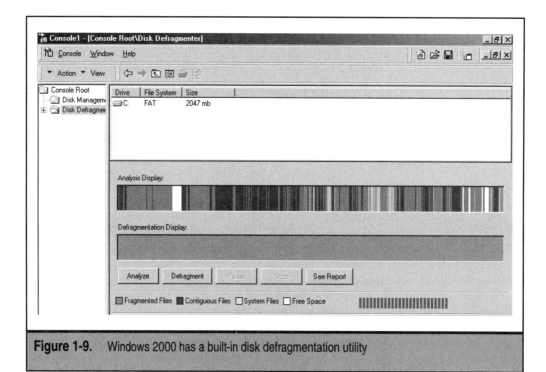

Figure 1-9. Windows 2000 has a built-in disk defragmentation utility

TIP: Schedule defragmentation right before the tape backup. This provides the fastest backup speed to tape in addition to optimizing system performance.

Simplified Desktop Deployment and Management

Instead of having a separate operating system for the server (like Windows NT 4 Server) and a separate operating system for the desktop (like Windows 95), Windows 2000 provides a single operating system family (Windows 2000 Server or Advanced Server for file servers, Windows 2000 Datacenter or Advanced Server for application servers, and Windows 2000 Professional for desktops). This integrates desktop management capabilities into the core network operating environment.

Stricter Rules for Shared Components

One of the biggest challenges for administrators in managing application installation and loading on the desktop is the conflict of software drivers, commonly known as *DLLs* (dynamic link libraries). These files can have the same name, even though they're provided by different software vendors and may provide different functions or services. There's also the ongoing problem of mismatched DLLs based on the age of the set of files installed at the time an application is installed on the system. For some DLLs to work properly, a series of DLLs must all match in date or version number. As new applications are installed, certain DLLs are installed from a different set of files, causing a mismatch of files that creates an unstable desktop system.

With Windows 2000, Microsoft is requiring stricter adherence to shared file standards along with a unified advertisement and application state declaration process that will try to achieve better operational support for the installation and operation of applications. Applications that will be Windows 2000 certified would share common DLLs only published by Microsoft from the initial distributed build of Windows 2000 or from regularly scheduled service packs that adhere to the published standards. An application does not receive Microsoft Windows 2000 certification if it attempts to write files to the System32 directory of the server.

When applications adhere to strict standards—applications registering with the operating system with their name, size, version number, and date of the files installed, and reporting their state of operation back to the operating system—there is better control over software distribution or just in time (JIT) application distribution and execution.

With better management of the files stored on the desktops, the desktops remain more stable, and the installation of applications does not cause the system to become less stable over time.

 NOTE: The integrated defragmentation tool in Windows 2000 is not the best solution available. While it does basic file defragmentation, it has no file access or data access analysis, both of which are required for optimizing a server. Also, the tool provides no maintenance or optimization of application server databases or data stores, so you should evaluate third-party add-ins for data optimization and file defragmentation.

Integrated Desktop Tools in Windows 2000

Windows 2000 has tools that maintain a more stable desktop environment for the initial installation and the ongoing management of applications on the system. The tools install an initial template of programs and configuration files on the system. The template can be updated on a regular basis through application scripting. When configured properly, a brand-new computer is set on the desktop, a template is cloned onto the system, and any unique user information is automatically scripted on the system.

SYSPREP   The Sysprep utility creates an exact duplicate of a drive image of a system for faster and more standard desktop deployments. Similar to the Ghost program available for previous Windows systems, Sysprep makes a full image of a system that can be stored on a hard drive partition, on a network server, or on a writable CD-ROM. In the process shown in Figure 1-10, the image can be exploded on the hard drive of a different system.

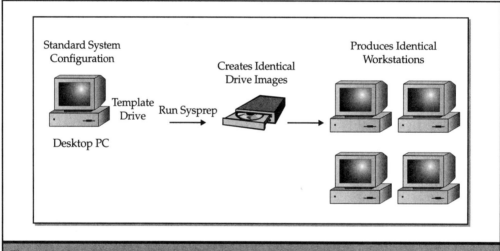

Figure 1-10.   Sysprep can create a new desktop computer in minutes instead of hours

Previous versions of cloning software faced problems when the components inside a computer system were different in the new cloned system from the original master system. If the original system had a different hard drive controller type (SCSI as opposed to EIDE), or a different network adapter (3Com network adapter as opposed to an Intel network adapter), then the clone would either require minor maintenance or in some cases not work at all. However, with Windows 2000, because the operating system includes plug-and-play as a core hardware detection system, new hardware is easily detected the first time the system is booted. Windows 2000 automatically assists the user in configuring the new hardware. If the new hardware has auto-configuring PCI devices, the devices are automatically configured and require no user intervention on boot-up, drastically simplifying user interaction.

Additionally, Windows 2000 has a maintenance bootup mode that permits a safe mode boot if you press F8. Then you can configure the key devices on the system before fully booting Windows 2000.

Several other Windows 2000 utilities, such as Netafx, are designed to help you make changes in property components of a network configuration object. Rather than going into the control panel on each system individually to make changes in a networking protocol setting, or defining DHCP versus static IP addressing, utilities like Netafx allow you to make command-line modifications. Through the use of scripted configuration changes, you can more easily deploy Windows 2000 to the desktop, have plug-and-play update the hardware configuration, and script property configuration changes all in a single pass through the system installation or reconfiguration.

These features of Windows 2000 make cloning systems from system to system much easier to do. (The step-by-step operation of Sysprep is discussed in Chapter 14.)

INTELLIMIRROR   The Intellimirror suite of technology tools provides a different method of installing a new desktop. These tools run a complete installation script that starts with formatting the desktop hard drive, installs a clean copy of Windows 2000 Professional, and installs applications onto the system using a scripted installation procedure. Through the use of remote boot technology a desktop system can boot directly to a Windows 2000 server through the use of a diskless boot ROM chip installed on the desktop systems network adapter. With the diskless boot ROM installed, the system boots to a Windows 2000 DHCP server to get an IP address, then boots to a remote host partition to begin the installation of a clean Windows 2000 desktop configuration.

If you've implemented roaming user profiles under Windows 2000, desktop configuration items such as screen-savers, backgrounds, special application folders, or icons automatically appear on the new desktop setting. As part of a life-cycle management process, Intellimirror provides a complete end-to-end solution for replacing an old desktop system with a new desktop system.

WINDOWS SCRIPTING HOST (WSH)   After a base template has been installed on a desktop system (either by Sysprep or by Intellimirror), you may want to make minor changes to the desktop, such as changing icons or even adding software components. Windows 2000 includes a utility called the Windows Scripting Host (WSH) that provides scripted installation of applications or scripted changes to the desktop. WSH can automate tasks such as connecting network drives, creating desktop shortcuts, adding a printer, or installing a software application. The Windows Scripting Host software supports scripts created in Visual Basic or Java. WSH can be invoked by a logon of a user to a system, or it can be automatically invoked on the system without user intervention.

There are two versions of the WSH utility. Wscript.exe runs from a centralized NT-based scripting host. Cscript.exe runs from the command line and is used for individual system script installation. Additionally, scripts can be launched from a web server, by use of an HTML document that has scripts embedded into the web page.

Scripts drastically minimize the time it takes to install software on multiple systems. With the advances noted earlier in this section on registered DLLs that prevent accidental overwriting of conflicting information for the system, the pushing of information to a desktop actually works. (You'll find a detailed description of the Windows Scripting Host application in Chapter 14.)

Secure Desktop

Key to the Microsoft Windows 2000 strategy is the ability to create a secured networking environment. Windows NT 4 used the individual user logon to give access to resources, and that logon and password was really the only level of security integrated into the system.

With Windows 2000, CryptoAPI is the built-in programmers' interface that provides encrypted access between the workstation and the server. After a user has been validated and has gained access to the system, an encrypted file system provides even more security for the files stored in the file system. Enhanced auditing tools can track user access and file access. System control logging keeps a tight watch over unauthorized access.

Temporary Elevated User Security

We've all seen the problem that ensues when a user tries to execute a command that requires administrative privileges. Of course, if the user can't perform the task, the administrator has to do it, adding to his or her workload. Now you can grant temporary elevated user security for a specific process. For example, there may be a component of an installation process, contained within a script, that requires administrative privileges. Working in an elevated privilege state, the script can update the system, make system changes, or process information as if an administrator were performing the function.

Integrated Installer Technology

Windows 2000 has an integrated installer for applications called Windows Installer, and it unifies the installation and configuration of application software on all Windows 2000 desktops and servers under the Software Installation snap-in. In previous versions of operating systems, the installation utility for software was a third-party tool with a number of variations in how it managed the installation of new software on the systems. Instead, the Windows Installer and the Software Installation snap-in provide a common method and controlled process for installations.

The Windows Installer provides a standard package format that handles the installation, repair, removal, and tracking of installed components on any Windows 2000 system. The tracking system monitors the files installed, files replaced, modifications to the registry, folders added, and icons and shortcuts added to the NT environment. Because of the level of tracking and logging conducted when software is installed onto a system, Windows 2000 provides a method for safely uninstalling the software and a method of tracking version revision numbers for subsequent application upgrades and updates.

Additionally, the integrated installer provides a method for just in time (JIT) installation of applications. Perhaps a user needs to work with a document from an application that is not installed on the local system. The operating system knows what files should be installed on the system (from the packaged application script), and the system can dynamically install the necessary files on demand and execute the application. JIT launching of applications can be set as a policy-based component within the operating system in which an application is advertised on the system through the system policy of the network. The software is installed based on need.

Integrated Networking Enhancements

TCP/IP and DNS have become networking standards in Windows 2000, but there are a number of other enhancements that improve networking as well as network administration tasks. You'll need to create a plan to update your protocols and communications standards. Some of these new components include:

▼ **TCP/IP as the default protocol**   Using TCP/IP as the default protocol will simplify the communications between Windows 2000 desktops, servers, and external resources such as the Internet. The TCP/IP standard is only the beginning, as functions based around TCP/IP networking such as TCP/IP printing to network printers, DHCP for automatic IP address allocation, DNS for name resolution, SMTP for standard messaging communications, and SNMP for standard network management communications also become common in the new Windows 2000 enterprise. (More information about the network infrastructure is found in Chapter 9.)

- **Dynamic DNS** Dynamic DNS, adhering to industry standards, helps to minimize the work involved in managing DNS name servers on the network. Unlike standard DNS that requires a table to be created and updated with new names and IP addresses of devices on the network, dynamic DNS automatically adds new names and IP addresses of devices to the dynamic DNS table. For small or large networks, this drastically minimizes the amount of time spent manually updating the DNS tables for the network as new devices are added to the network.

- **Automatic Private IP Addressing** Dynamic Host Configuration Protocol (DHCP) is used in Windows 2000 to distribute IP addresses to devices added to the network that meet the segment configuration of the organization. However, for those devices that fail to connect to a valid DHCP host, Windows 2000 provides Automatic Private IP Addressing (APIPA) for the system to enable the device to complete a valid boot process. When a DHCP server becomes available, or an IP address becomes available on the DHCP server to be leased to the workstations on the network, the workstation replaces the temporary auto address with a fully qualified DHCP address for the network. The process of acquiring a DHCP address and attaching itself to the network is automatic and does not require a reboot (previous versions of NT did require a reboot). Also, if a DHCP server is not added to the network and the system acquires an automatic address, the network administrator can replace the automatically assigned IP address with a static IP address at any time, also without having to reboot the system.

- **Plug-and-play networking for mobile users** Windows 2000 includes some advanced plug-and-play hardware support for mobile users. There is a key enhancement to plug-and-play networking that automatically handles logon and logoff to the network. This feature can sleep and wake up the network configuration settings to connect and disconnect from the network. Users can log on to the network with a PCMCIA network card in their system and have full access to network resources, then log off and disconnect the PCMCIA card from the system. When the PCMCIA card is removed from the system, the workstation immediately acknowledges it has been disconnected from the network. If the user tries to log on to the desktop off of the network, he or she will get an error noting that the domain is not found. However, a networking cache authenticates the user so that he or she has access to the resources stored on the laptop. The user can log off the local system and plug in the network adapter to re–log on to the network. This time the insertion of the network adapter is acknowledged automatically, and the user is reattached to the network just as if the system had been cold-booted from scratch.

  Similarly, if a user powers off a laptop system while connected to the network, the network will put a sleep state on the user's connection. When the laptop is powered on again, the adapter will wake up and reestablish a connection without any need to log on again.

■ **Routing and remote access**   Windows 2000 integrates Routing and Remote Access Services (RRAS) into the operating system. This provides the ability to route and manage both TCP/IP and IPX through the operating system. With RRAS you can enable or disable routing across multiple adapters in a single server, or do protocol and address transactions across a single server. Additionally, RRAS provides the ability to have profiles and policies for remote users stored in the Active Directory as group profiles to enable or disable user access to the network from a remote location.

For protocol translation, Windows 2000 can act as a proxy server to translate internal IPX traffic into a single IP external connection for an organization, using a combination of NT and NetWare servers within the organization. Additionally, through Network Address Translation (NAT) Windows 2000, you can use internal private addressing (using the 10.*x.x.x* Class A addressing space), and then, through a server, display the server to an external segment as a single registered IP address. NAT gives you the flexibility of designing an IP scheme without limits imposed by limited IP addresses available from the InterNIC. (More on network addressing and interactions with the general Internet is in Chapter 2.)

■ **Remote access**   In keeping with industry standards, the remote access capabilities of Windows 2000 support standards such as the extensible authentication protocol (EAP) and the bandwidth allocation protocol (BAP). The EAP allows for third-party authentication services to integrate with Windows 2000 for devices such as cardkeys, SecurID cards, and authentication modules to plug into RRAS for point-to-point communications validation. The BAP allows the dynamic addition and deletion of multilink connections to increase or decrease bandwidth to a remote site based on use of the link. Using technologies like ISDN, an organization can add or delete ISDN lines almost instantly based on the demands of the users of the organization, thus optimizing the communication link between sites.

■ **Quality of Service (QoS)**   QoS allows you to set up device reserve bandwidth across a communication link and establish priority for the transmission of information across that link. This is used for communication that's sensitive to delays, such as video or audio transmissions, or even time-sensitive datasets that need prioritization on a connection link to transmit an entire dataset in an evening. QoS is part of the Windows 2000 admission control service (ACS) that will permit QoS-aware applications to reserve bandwidth and transmit information within the maximum limits of the network.

▲ **Windows ATM Services**   Windows 2000 includes services that support Asynchronous Transfer Mode (ATM) on the network. The Windows ATM services allow you to manage ATM virtual circuits (VCs). The system determines the quality of service required of a data stream and streams the data, voice, or video information through each VC. Windows ATM services also provide the encapsulation of TCP/IP within an ATM stream to operate more efficiently across ATM VCs. For data streams that support direct streaming based on the raw channel access filter, ATM virtual circuits are created to enhance Win32 data streams within the ATM environment. ATM is also extended to remote sites through the support of PPP tunneling through dial-up networking to facilitate remote Windows support across an ATM wide-area network backbone.

MANAGEMENT COMPONENTS

A number of components in Windows 2000 help administrators manage and administer the resources in the organization. Unlike previous versions of Windows NT that required a different administration tool or a series of tools to conduct even the simplest tasks, Windows 2000 has consolidated functions and automated routine administrative tasks to minimize the time and effort it takes to manage the resources of the organization.

Microsoft Management Console

The first tool that consolidates resource administration in Windows 2000 is the Microsoft Management Console (MMC). In Windows NT 4, there were separate administration tools to manage the network, such as the User Manager for Domains to add/modify users, Server Manager to manage servers, RAS Administrator to administer remote users, WINS Administrator to manage name resolution, Event View to check the network error log, and so on. Some tools limited you to working on the server that contained the tool, meaning you had to physically move to another server that needed your attention.

The MMC is a single application that works with multiple snap-ins, which you can add to the MMC interface to provide a single point of administration. You can use these snap-ins to add and modify users, validate resource names, configure logging, and manage local and remote resources. The snap-in model extends beyond just the normal network administration tasks, including administration tools for Microsoft Backoffice products like Microsoft Exchange, SNA Server, and Internet Information Server. In fact, you can use the MMC to manage third-party products such as tape backup software, virus detection software, or global enterprise management tools. Figure 1-11 shows an example of the Microsoft Management Console with multiple windows open. You can see it's easy to view and administer network resources from a single application.

MMC snap-ins extend beyond just administration components and can be full system-management applications that provide network policy management or security administration and management. Snap-ins such as the group policy editor or the security configuration editor are two such examples.

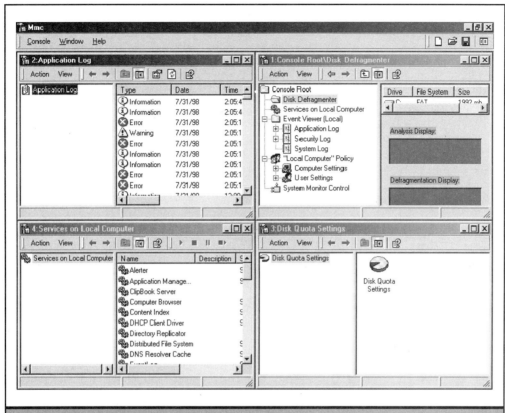

Figure 1-11.   The MMC makes it easier to manage all sorts of network resources

Group Policy Editor

The group policy editor (GPE) is a snap-in to the MMC that manages user and group policies as they are distributed across multiple sites, domains, and organizations within the
Active Directory tree of your organization (see Figure 1-12). Unlike the policy editor in
Windows NT 4 that focused on locking down functionality of the desktop or setting user
desktop customization settings for things like screen-savers or system settings, the GPE
uses a series of Visual Basic scripts that are run by a computer during startup, shutdown,
network logon, or network logoff. The GPE can also identify files that need to be installed
onto a desktop system, distribute applications, and publish application services.

Setting policies involves a distinct scheme of parsing through a series of policies. You
can remember it as DSOU: the parsing starts at the domain level, then the site level, and finally at the organizational unit level. Group policies, however, can be set to be exclusive
or explicit policies to resources in the organization by just noting the policy role on the
policy properties page.

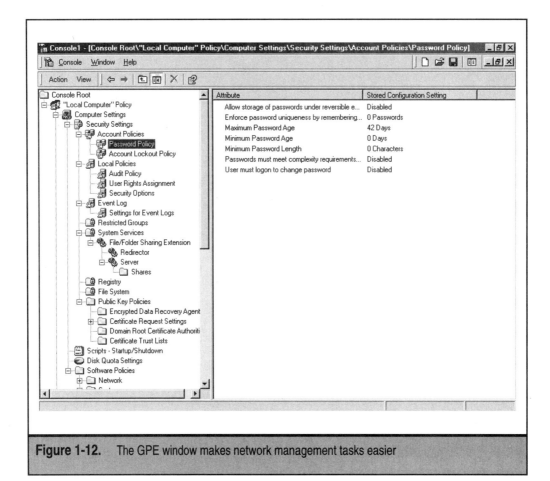

Figure 1-12. The GPE window makes network management tasks easier

Security Configuration Editor

The security configuration editor snap-in manages the overall system security configuration as well as ongoing security analysis. This includes auditing all changes to registry settings, validating and auditing access controls on files and on registry keys, and performing security configuration of system services. The security configuration editor allows the security administrator to configure the security of local and remote Windows 2000 base systems (servers and desktops). Some of the components of the security configuration editor include the ability to set system security policy for the organization. Using the editor, the security administrator can set access policies on the system (such as when users can log on to the network), specify password restrictions, configure auditing, and define domain policies.

The security configuration editor also manages user accounts and system services specific to security components. You can assign group privileges and user rights, configure network services, configure file-sharing security, and manage printer access services. The security configuration editor also deals with modification of the security values of the system registry, as well as modification of security parameters for file volumes and for the directory trees.

You can create templates that include the security attributes for all the modifiable security components that can then be applied to users and groups. The templates are text-based INF files, so a simple text editor can modify the configuration information. Windows 2000 comes with a series of sample templates. They are stored in \winnt\security\templates on the Windows system drive at the time of installation.

Device Manager

The device manager snap-in to the MMC gives you the ability to configure devices and resources on a computer. Typically, this is used to manage hardware parameters such as interrupts, I/O addresses, or the various states of the devices. When a device doesn't work, you can use the device manager to solve the problem, either installing the proper driver, or reconfiguring the hardware parameters.

File Service Manager

The file service manager snap-in is used to create shares, manage sessions, and manage connections. Shares can be based on physical drive partitions, or across multiple physical drive partitions (taking advantage of the DFS). You can use the session and network connection components of the file service manager to administer user access to shares.

System Service Manager

Use the system service manager snap-in to start, stop, pause, and resume services on a network system. While it might sound as if this is no different from the Services applet in the Control Panel, what's exciting is that the new system service manager works on both the local and remote systems. This is truly a centralized management system. You can also set recovery states on the service controls that determine if a service has failed, and track the process flow the operating system uses to reinitiate the failed service. This means you don't have to spend a lot of time managing noncritical faults, because they take care of their own recovery.

Disk Quotas

Storing virtually unlimited amounts of data on a distributed file system volume seems appealing, but it's not really a good idea. It's far easier to manage information if it's in manageable chunks. Windows 2000 provides the ability to put quotas on the amount of information users can store. Disk quotas can be established by user or by group. You might set a default quota for all members of the organization of 50 megabytes (MB) of personal files, and then set specific limits for individual users or groups. It usually works well to limit some users to 20MB of storage space, giving other users almost unlimited space.

Disk quotas can be set either on a server volume, or across a distributed disk volume set (if DFS is enabled). Figure 1-13 shows an example of disk quota configuration.

TIP: You can configure a warning notification for a user when the storage size is approaching the limit. This gives the user a chance to do some housekeeping. However, it will probably mean a request to raise the quota. You'll have to establish some policies for this problem.

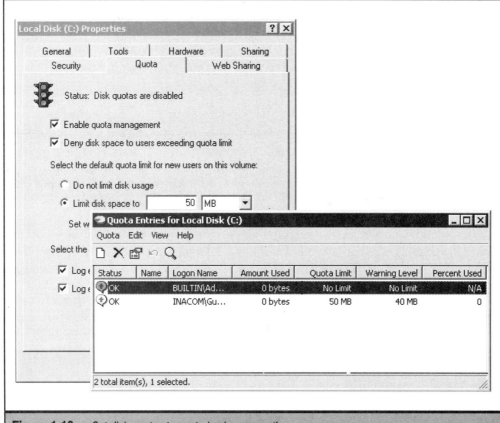

Figure 1-13. Set disk quotas to control volume growth

CHAPTER 2

Overview of Active Directory and DNS

Active Directory and the industry standard DNS provide a whole new way of administering and managing a network. Active Directory changes the way we view the organizational and administrative structures of a network. In previous versions of Windows NT, we put servers, workstations, and printers into physical sites and domains. We then managed those individual systems using the concept of trusts. But with the Active Directory, we can now expand our definitions. A user in San Francisco can print to a printer in Tokyo; spreadsheet data can be shared across the Internet using secured virtual private networking instead of dedicated and private WAN links; and network resources can include physical devices that are managed and maintained by other organizations. It is the flexibility built into Active Directory that makes Windows 2000 a true enterprise networking operating environment.

INTERNETWORKING COMPONENTS

In the Windows 2000 Active Directory, the organizational internetworking components include the organization name, the organizational unit, the site names, the domain controllers, and the global catalog. These components define the initial tree structure of the organization, and you use them to manage the administration and resource authentication process of the organization.

Organization Name

In the Active Directory, the organization name is the very top of the Active Directory tree, and all other components of the tree cascade down from there. The organization name is usually the same as the name of the company, or at least is something similar and recognizable.

NOTE: Use alphanumeric characters for the organization name to ensure that users who employ interfaces that don't support nonalphanumeric characters can access your network.

Organizational Units

Within a domain, directory service objects are organized into organizational units, called OUs. OUs in the Active Directory are administrative boundaries.

NOTE: Don't confuse OUs for AD with OUs in X500—they're not the same.

Use OUs to organize users and resources into administrative groups that can be administered effectively.

Sites

With the OU designating the administrative boundary for the domain, the site in AD defines a series of subnets in a physical topology. The site is created for the purpose of directory access and replication, and it's assumed that all objects within a site are physically connected through a high-speed connection (typically 256K or faster). Because high bandwidth is assumed, the communication (such as replication) between servers within a site is bandwidth-intensive.

For example, if you have multiple offices in a city connected by a 56K frame relay connection (for example, Tokyo North, Tokyo South, Tokyo West), the communication isn't speedy enough for efficiency. Therefore, you'd want to create a discrete site for each office. However, you can put all of the cities into one OU (the Tokyo Organizational Unit) to create one administrative unit.

Domain Controllers

A domain controller in the Active Directory holds a copy (replica) of the AD that is both readable and writable in a native Windows 2000 environment. The specific portion of the AD contained in the domain controller is typically based on the proximity and usage of the validation of the objects to the domain controller. For example, users and resources in a European cluster would authenticate to a domain controller in Europe, while users and resources from the Asian operations authenticate to a domain controller in Asia.

The Asian users and resources aren't stored on the European domain controller, which minimizes the management of transferring, updating, and administering objects that are not relevant to the administrators in the European office.

Global Catalog

The global catalog maintains the full directory, storing all the information from all the domain controllers in the organization. The global catalog is used to manage the partitioning of the directory to various domain controllers throughout the organization. It's also used to manage replication and synchronization of directory information. There is only one global catalog in an organization.

ACTIVE DIRECTORY CONCEPTS

It's helpful to understand the concept of directory services, both generically and in terms of the Windows 2000 Active Directory. Let's start by defining what directory services in general provide to organizations. A directory service provides these features:

▼ Manages the distribution of the directory across an organization

■ Replicates the directory in a manner that provides fault tolerance as well as distributed access to users and resources throughout the organization

■ Partitions the directory to improve the efficiency and effectiveness of distribution and replication to multiple sites in the organization

▲ Provides security

The Windows 2000 Active Directory is designed to meet these goals. In addition, AD is designed to provide a view of the network that simplifies the number of directories, namespaces, and organizational structures. This, of course, eases the administration of the network.

In fact, the Active Directory was developed for scalability. You can use AD for a network that has a single server providing services to dozens of users and resources, or for a network that has thousands of servers providing services to millions of users and resources. Regardless of where your company falls in this scale, you administer your network with the same set of tools as every other administrator who has the advantage of AD.

How Active Directory Builds on a Domain Structure

The Active Directory builds by creating a single copy of the directory store for each domain in the organization. This copy holds objects that apply only to that domain. If multiple domains are interrelated, they are linked together to form a tree. This means the AD is built by creating small, easy to administer pieces. As more pieces are added, the tree gets fuller, but each piece is discrete so it can be administered and managed without great difficulty.

Replicas of the individual portions of the tree are also easily administered, managed, and synchronized. Changes made to a portion of the tree are replicated to other portions of the tree in a hierarchical manner.

The global administrator of the tree sees a unified network of all of the pieces of the organization, linked to each other in a logical manner. This means that high-level administrators won't be overwhelmed with the responsibility of setting complicated policies and security privileges at the top of the tree, hoping that the inherited rights flow properly all the way down the tree structure. Instead, administrators down the line can take on the responsibilities of maintaining policies.

When designing an Active Directory (covered in depth in Chapter 6), the global administrator of the network just has to plan for each domain grouping of the organization and then piece those domains together to form the organizational tree that makes up the whole organization.

Tree vs. Forest

Some people have a hard time understanding the difference between a *tree* (also called a *domain tree*) and a *forest* in the Active Directory structure.

A tree is a series of domains that are interconnected, and this results in a hierarchical directory structure. The tree starts with a single domain, then grows to link other domains together (to form a domain tree). The way you link domains depends on security issues, as you can create both explicit and implicit trusts between domains. The sample tree shown in Figure 2-1 has three domains that have individual trusts with each other, and then the three domains have trusts among themselves.

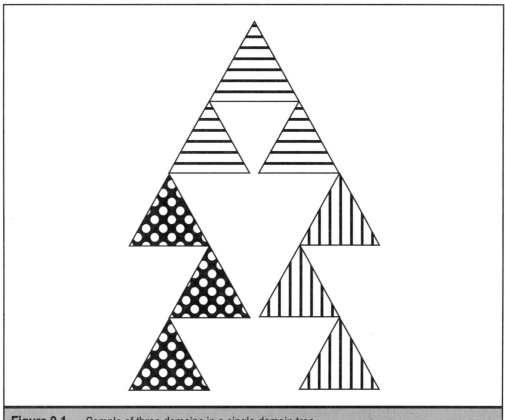

Figure 2-1. Sample of three domains in a single domain tree

If you don't require security links between the domains, you can split the domains into independent trees. These trees can all belong to the same organization structure (the forest). Because the domains are not directly connected, security between them is inherently switched off (although you could create an explicit trust if you think it's necessary).

From an organizational point of view, the multiple domains are independently administered and managed, but centrally viewed and maintained. Figure 2-2 shows how the same three domains can be set up as three completely separate trees, with their own independent security structures.

Lightweight Directory Access Protocol (LDAP)

The Lightweight Directory Access Protocol (LDAP) is an Internet standard (RFC-1777) for accessing directory services. This is what Windows 2000 uses for directory lookups, directory synchronization, and directory management throughout the Active Directory structure.

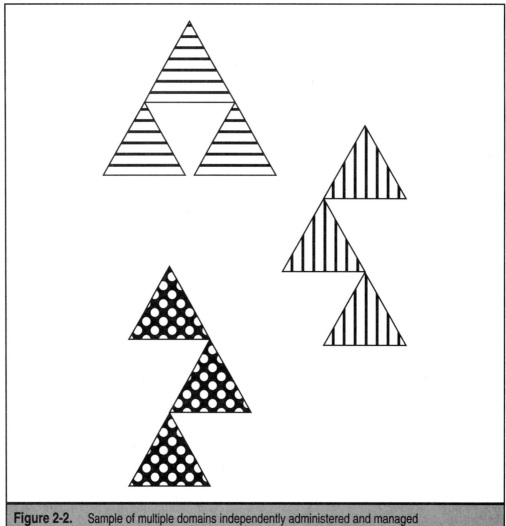

Figure 2-2. Sample of multiple domains independently administered and managed

LDAP was developed as a simpler alternative to the X.500 Directory Access Protocol (DAP). An LDAP URL names the server where Active Directory services are contained, and also uses the X.500 naming convention called *attributed naming*. For example, my URL would be LDAP://orgserver.company.com/cn=rand,ou=corp,o=company,c=us

Active Directory Is Not X.500

By now you realize that Active Directory is not the same as X.500 directory services. X.500 defines several protocols:

▼ Directory Access Protocol (DAP)

■ Directory System Protocol (DSP)

■ Directory Information Shadowing Protocol (DISP)

▲ Directory Operational Binding Management Protocol (DOP)

As noted earlier, the Active Directory uses LDAP as the access protocol because it has full support for X.500 information, but does not require all of the systems to host the entire X.500 overhead. Active Directory does not implement the full X.500 information model because X.500 is dependent on OSI networking, instead of the TCP/IP networking that Windows 2000 is built under. OSI is not efficient over a TCP/IP network, and the performance degradation would be undesirable.

Active Directory does support a variation of DAP (LDAP) for the directory access, taking advantage of the most important functions in both DAP and DSP. LDAP works well over TCP/IP natively without the need to encapsulate itself within OSI.

In order to maintain X.500 interoperatability, Windows 2000 supports the implementation of connectors. You'll be able to exchange directories between the Active Directory and any standard X.500 directory system.

Active Directory Namespace

The Active Directory *namespace* is the bounded area where any Active Directory object is resolved to a corresponding physical device or object. In simpler terms, the namespace is where the name of an object in the directory is resolved to the object itself.

The AD object is a named set of attributes, representing a user, a printer, a server, an application, or any other element on your network. The attributes hold the data that describes the directory object. For example, the attributes of a user in the namespace would include things such as first name, last name, email address, and so on.

Active Directory Name

A *name* is used to identify every object in the Active Directory. There are two different types of names: the distinguished name, and the relative distinguished name.

The Distinguished Name (DN) identifies the domain that holds the object, including the entire path to the object. As an example, my DN is /O=Internet/DC=Com/DC=Company/CN=Users/CN=Rand Morimoto. This DN identifies Rand Morimoto as a user object in the Company.Com domain.

The Relative Distinguished Name (RDN), is the part of the name that is an attribute of the object itself. Using the previous example, the RDN of the Rand Morimoto user object is CN=Rand Morimoto. The RDN of the parent object is CN=Users (CN is the common name of the Active Directory name).

Active Directory Container Security

The administrator of the Active Directory grants permissions to users based on the scope of the functions the users must perform. Administrative scopes can include an entire domain, a single OU, or a subtree of an OU within a domain.

When a user account is created, it is initially associated with a specific domain, but it could be placed in any organization unit as well. Therefore, permission to create users in an OU can be delegated to allow an administrator to manage and administer the users of the organizational unit.

Value of a Virtual Container

The Active Directory can also have virtual containers within the tree. A virtual container allows any LDAP-compliant directory to be accessed from the Active Directory and then have the contents of the foreign directory stored in an Active Directory container.

The information is actually external data that is replicated from (and potentially synchronized with) the external information source. However, to users, the objects are part of the Windows 2000 Active Directory.

Active Directory Services Interface (ADSI)

Microsoft developed ADSI to simplify access to the Active Directory, as well as foreign LDAP-enabled directories, when you need to exchange information. ADSI is a set of extensible, easy-to-program interfaces that can be used to write applications to access and manage the Active Directory and the foreign LDAP-based directory (including Novell's NDS directory). ADSI also provides a single set of directory service interfaces for managing network resources. Those common objects found in network directories include two types of objects: standard container objects and standard leaf objects.

The standard container objects include the following:

▼ Namespace
■ Country
■ Locality
■ Organization
■ Organizational unit
■ Domain
▲ Computer

Standard leaf objects include the following:

▼ User

■ Group

■ Alias

■ Service

■ Print device

■ Print queue

■ Print job

■ File share

■ File service

■ Session

▲ Resource

This standardization of objects between the Active Directory and other directory services greatly simplifies the development and administration of distributed applications across multiple directory systems.

ACTIVE DIRECTORY VERSUS THE DOMAIN MODEL

Windows 2000 includes the hierarchical Active Directory structure. A small organization with a single location and single administrator found Windows NT 4 to be a very easy operating environment to work with since you were either a user or an administrator of the network.

However, for organizations that had multiple locations or wanted to distribute the administration of the network to multiple administrators, the single domain concept of Windows NT required setting up parallel user domains and parallel resource domains into master domains. Administrators would be granted security and management access over their domain to add users, groups, and network resources, and special security trusts were created between these master domains to create continuity between the domains to work as a single master entity.

In addition to the difficulty of designing a large domain environment with the proper security trusts needed to administer the network, the wide area network (WAN) traffic caused large resource drains. Entire careers were built around the expertise required to set up the proper trusts and the analysis of bandwidth requirements between trusted domains.

With the Active Directory environment of Windows 2000, multiple administrators can be assigned to different parts of the Active Directory tree, providing each administrator the rights to add, delete, and modify resources for the portion of the directory they have been assigned.

The Active Directory also logically splits up the network into zones, which can minimize the communication traffic between portions of the organization.

Remove Registry Restrictions on Users

One of the limitations of the Windows NT 4 domain model was the size of the administration database known as the Security Account Manager (SAM). The SAM contains information on users, groups, and resource security, and is a flat file extension of the registry information stored on the domain controllers of the network. Because the file is a flat file, it's limited to approximately 100,000 objects or about 26,000 users. For organizations with a large number of users, or sophisticated security protocols even without a large number of users, this limitation means multiple master domains are needed to manage the users and resources of the organization. Besides creating difficulties in configuring a domain design, the large flat file domain databases are prone to data corruption as they reach their size limits.

Windows 2000 uses a database built around the extensible storage engine (ESE) standard introduced in Microsoft Exchange Server version 5.5. The database stores user, group, resource, and security information for the Active Directory. This means a single data store can hold over ten million objects, a drastic extension in capability over Windows NT 4. You can create even larger organizational trees by establishing trusts between directories.

In addition, the ESE is a relational database that provides redundancy capabilities. The database and the objects within it can be replicated and stored in smaller subcomponents for faster access, easier management, and greater flexibility.

DNS over WINS

Although Windows Internet Name Service (WINS) is being supported in Windows 2000 to provide backward compatibility, you shouldn't consider it a supported element in the operating system. Windows 2000 uses Domain Name System (DNS) directory name service.

Both DNS and WINS provide translation between a device's IP address and its common name. For example, it's a lot easier to remember the name EXCHSRVR than it is to remember the address 10.1.3.119, just as it's easier to remember www.inaoak.com rather than 204.31.169.77.

In Windows NT 4, the common names and the IP addresses are translated using WINS, which is proprietary to Windows NT networks running a WINS server. If you want to translate WINS addresses with the Internet, your WINS system has to integrate with a DNS server somewhere on the network.

In Windows 2000, DNS becomes the standard domain name resolution system for both the internal Windows 2000 network as well as with the general Internet. See the section "Understanding DNS" later in this chapter.

Multimaster Replication

Primary domain controllers (PDCs) and backup domain controllers (BDCs) are replaced in Windows 2000 with a simpler notion of domain controllers (DCs). In a PDC-BDC environment, you place a single read/write copy of the domain information on the PDC, and then replicate read-only copies to the BDCs.

In Windows 2000, all DCs contain a read/write copy of domain information. Additionally, a domain controller can contain all the domain information, or only a portion of the information. This means you can partition information so that replication schemes are designed to minimize network traffic and so that you distribute the control of objects around the organization.

This means you're working with a *multimaster replication model*. Changes can be made to any domain controller in the domain and then replicated to all the replication partners established for that DC.

The consistency and integrity of the DC information is managed through a sophisticated algorithm based on an update sequence number (USN). The USN keeps the partitioned copies of the Active Directory synchronized. The Active Directory does not depend on time stamps for detecting and managing synchronization, as do many other directories service systems that live and die by the perfection of absolutely accurate time and date synchronization. Instead, USN updates are tracked each time a change is made to an object in the directory. When a change to the directory occurs, the update sequence number is incremented and written to the property and to the object. Changes are monitored, and replication partners compare USNs. When the property and/or object USN is greater than the partner machine's USN, an update occurs so that the property with the higher USN replaces the property of the lower USN object. Only properties with higher USNs are updated. If two objects both have advanced their USNs, causing a conflict, the time stamp is the tiebreaker and latest change wins.

UNDERSTANDING DNS

With DNS as the core infrastructure naming system for Windows 2000, you should have a solid understanding of how DNS works before you begin designing your Active Directory structure. A big challenge facing Windows NT administrators is the "UNIX-speak" terminology needed to plan DNS successfully. A number of the terms and conventions introduced in this section stem from UNIX.

The DNS Tree Structure

The Domain Name System tree is actually an inverted tree with branches at the bottom, all coming to a single point at the top of the tree, as shown in Figure 2-3. The top of the tree

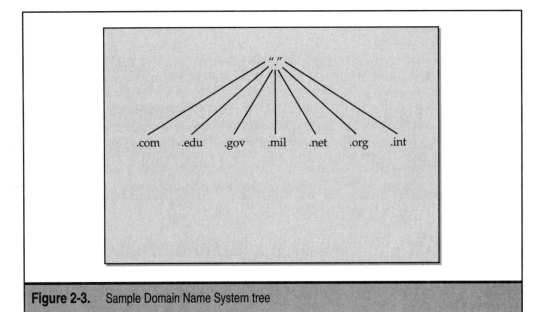

Figure 2-3.   Sample Domain Name System tree

is named with a null label " " and written as a single dot ("."). This is called the root of the Internet domain tree, and it's managed by the Internet Network Information Center, commonly called the InterNIC (http://www.networksolutions.com).

Top-Level Domain or First-Level Domain

Immediately below the root are the top-level domains (also called first-level domains). These are the extensions used for email addresses and Web addresses. Currently, there are seven top-level domains. In RFC-1591, these seven top-level domains were outlined to clarify the type of organization that fits into one of the seven categories as noted in Table 2-1.

There's one other series of domain name suffixes that you may have seen—suffixes that are specific to countries. These suffixes are based on the ISO-3166 two-letter country code (.us for the United States, .jp for Japan, .uk for the United Kingdom, .fr for France, and so on). See Appendix A for a list of all the ISO-3166 country codes.

The two-letter country code was created to provide a naming convention for non-United States–based organizations. Because the Internet was created in the United States for the Department of Defense, the early naming schemes were built around U.S. organizational designations like businesses, nonprofit organizations, and the like. However, international organizations are able to use the two-letter country code within the naming scheme because the three-letter suffixes have no meaning in many countries (or have an entirely different meaning). Some countries have adopted the three-letter suffix of .com or .edu, so you may see intel.com.hk for the Hong Kong office of Intel, or inacom.com.mx for the Mexican operations of Inacom.

Extension	Description
.com	Commercial businesses (such as microsoft.com, intel.com, hp.com)
.edu	Four-year degree institutions (such as berkeley.edu, harvard.edu)
.gov	U.S. government agencies (such as whitehouse.gov, irs.gov)
.mil	U.S. military organizations (such as army.mil, navy.mil)
.net	Network-related organizations (such as psi.net, att.net)
.org	Noncommercial organizations (such as iana.org)
.int	International organizations (such as nato.int)

Table 2-1. Top-Level Internet Domains

Some countries have created a two-letter trailer that includes .co for a company and .ac or .ai for an academic institution. This creates domain names like chuo-u.ac.jp, or bbc.co.uk. Even in the United States, some organizations that do not fit the top-level domain designations may take on the .us two-letter country code. Since the .edu site must be a four-year degree qualifying institution and .gov must be a United Stated Federal government site, you will see domain names like oakland.k12.ca.us for the Oakland Unified School District in California, or co.alameda.ca.us for the County government offices in Alameda, California.

However, with all the rules in place, the .com, .org, and .net domain name suffixes are no longer monitored or verified. When the Internet was much smaller and the managing body for domain names handled far fewer requests for domain name registrations, they had more time to verify organizations' validity in a specific designation. Today, except for the .edu and .gov registrations, which are monitored and verified before a domain name is issued, the suffixes aren't checked.

An additional top-level domain is the in-addr.arpa domain. The in-addr.arpa is a special domain that does a reverse-address lookup by going from address to domain name. Rather than a flat file table system that holds all of the addresses for all of the domain names and searches the table, the in-addr.arpa works as a reverse tree, first looking at the first octet of the address and then working its way down the address tree until it finds the domain name. As shown in Figure 2-4, the lookup of an address for 204.31.169.77 starts with the 204 branch, then goes down to the 31 branch, then the 169 branch, and finally the 77 branch. The final branch links to the name of the host server. In-add.arpa naming works backwards when written out because the address scheme works backwards to resolve the host name. The final lookup would be 77.169.31.204.in-addr.arpa, which will resolve the name www.inaoak.com.

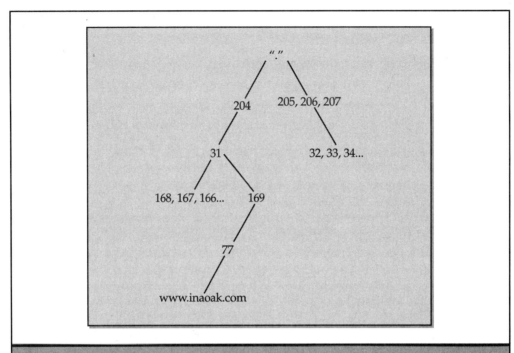

Figure 2-4. Reverse lookup from IP address to domain name

Root Servers

On the Internet, 13 servers contain the authoritative data for the very top of the Domain Name System hierarchy. These servers are distributed around the world in the United States, Japan, the United Kingdom, and Sweden. The root servers know which nameservers contain authoritative data for the first-level servers (.com, .edu, .uk, .us, and so on).

Second-Level Domain Names

Second-level domain names are children of the top-level domain name. For the domain name co.alameda.ca.us, .us is the first level, .ca is the second level, .alameda is the third level, and so on. This means you know who owns the branch of the tree in which the authority of the domain resides. The .us domain owns authority over all subdomains represented by various states of the Union. The .ca.us domain owns authority over the California portion of the .us domain, but not authority over the subdomains of any other state in the Union, and so forth.

You may find reference to upper-level domains or lower-level domains. This is just a relative reference to your particular position within the domain structure. If you are in the alameda portion of co.alameda.ca.us, then both .ca.us and the .us are considered upper domains. Likewise, if you are at microsoft.com, then Windows 2000dev.microsoft.com is a lower domain than your current position in the hierarchy.

Understanding DNS Master Nameservers

There are master domain servers that are considered primary nameservers, and there are servers that are considered secondary nameservers. These servers make up the hierarchy for the information they hold, based on the authority granted to them.

Primary and Secondary Nameservers

A primary nameserver holds the valid information for the portion of the domain over which it has authoritative rights. A secondary nameserver receives its information from a primary nameserver and assumes the primary nameserver has valid information (which means that the primary nameserver is *authoritative*). Placing a series of primary and secondary nameservers throughout the domain provides both fault tolerance and load balancing.

Understand, however, that the secondary nameserver could be the primary nameserver for a second-level domain. While it is the primary nameserver for a first-level root domain, it can also be authoritative for a portion of the domain at the second level and downward. A secondary nameserver for this portion of the domain can receive information from the primary domain server, creating a series of primary and secondary domain servers that constantly replicate the information on the Internet. Figure 2-5 illustrates the hierarchy of nested primary and secondary nameservers that maintain a *top-down* structure of information distribution. This is a continuation of the original design for the Internet, which was to create a system that minimizes the chance for a single point of failure. It's also a continuation of the original design for the DNS system, where multiple devices can be authoritative for information throughout the organizational structure.

Zones

While primary and secondary nameservers manage the distribution of information from server to server, a zone is an administrative unit for the Domain Name System. A zone does not necessarily encompass a branch of a tree and everything below it; it can be a subset of branches. Such a zone is created specifically to be an administrative unit of a portion of a tree. As primary and secondary nameservers are added to the domain to create distributed storage and authentication of information between servers, the zone administrator manages a portion of that information. The administrative portion is based on the zone administrative authority that's been granted. Zone administration rights are shown in Figure 2-6.

Zone Transfers

The method of transferring authoritative information among servers is called a *zone transfer*. In this process, a server requests information from an authoritative source and then transfers it. What is transferred is a zone file, and it is through these zone transfers that information is disseminated throughout the Internet. After a change is made to the

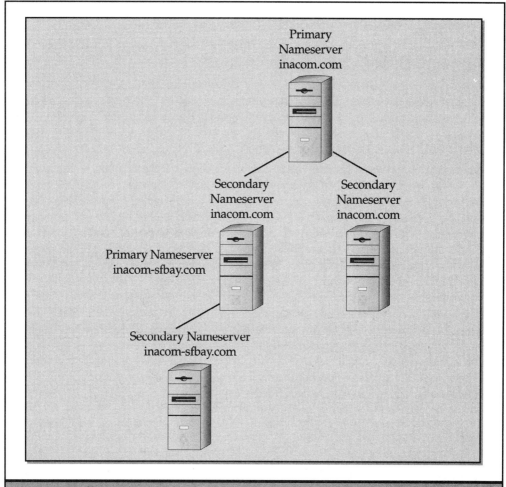

Figure 2-5. Nested primary and secondary name hierarchy

primary zone file, the new information is transferred from server to server, eventually reaching every nameserver on the Internet. This takes time, and it may be a couple of days before the information makes its way down to every one of the thousands of nameservers on the Internet.

Secondary Master Nameservers

While primary nameservers are the primary source for authoritative information, there is an important role for the second tier of nameservers, called *secondary master nameservers*.

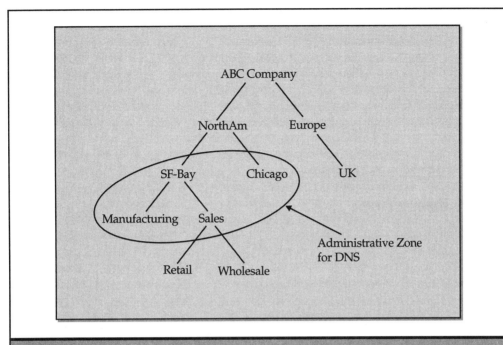

Figure 2-6.   Zone administration rights

These secondary systems provide a number of important functions, which are described in this section.

DISTRIBUTION OF LOAD   Millions of users on the Internet need name resolution services, so the scalability of address authentication is extremely important. Allotting name resolution services to multiple second-level systems distributes the workload. It works because the secondary nameservers have authoritative information directly from the primary master nameserver. In effect, the secondary systems become authoritative hosts.

FAULT TOLERANCE   Multiple secondary master nameservers throughout the Internet receive each change that's made to the information on the primary master nameservers. As the information is distributed down to multiple secondary master nameservers, it creates a backup system in the event that the primary master domain controller fails, or if any one of the secondary master domain servers becomes inaccessible.

MAINTENANCE OF REMOTE LOCATION PERFORMANCE LEVELS   Some of the secondary master nameservers reside in remote locations, where they're accessed with slower data links. Users on the remote segment will have faster access to the secondary master nameserver on their local segment than trying to reach the primary nameserver over the slower WAN connection.

Forwarders

When the DNS process needs to resolve a name for an internal namespace and cannot find the requested host, the internal nameserver tries to query an external nameserver to attempt a resolution. Communication between an internal server and an external resource presents a potential security problem. To limit these internal-to-external communications, DNS provides a way to establish specific DNS servers as forwarders, and only servers designated as forwarders can communicate externally. All the other DNS servers must forward their DNS lookup requests to one of the forwarder servers. Administrators of the internal network can monitor, administer, and manage the forwarder servers for security and management purposes.

DNS Name Resolution

When a name needs to be resolved, a client system (a *resolver*) identifies an initial nameserver to provide the resolution. As seen in Figure 2-7, a system can use multiple DNS servers to resolve the query, including both internal and external DNS servers.

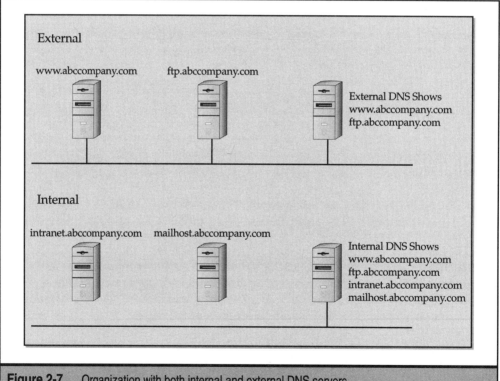

Figure 2-7.   Organization with both internal and external DNS servers

Because it's a security risk to publish a list of internal servers to the general Internet, administrators need an internal DNS server that accesses public servers in a manner that takes advantage of the safety built in to the organization's firewall. It's also important to have a backup DNS server in the naming list.

When a user enters a name in a Web browser or an FTP file transfer query, he or she may be asked to enter the fully qualified domain name (FQDN). The FQDN is similar to the usual entry (such as www.microsoft.com), but requires a dot at the end of the entry (www.microsoft.com.).

The importance of the FQDN becomes apparent when you realize that addresses are relative to the FQDN. For example, if I were inside the microsoft.com network, I could request access to a server named Windows 2000dev. Because my context is already set to microsoft.com, the Windows 2000dev server is available without the need to enter the domain name. Typing **test.windows2000dev** takes me to that relative name address. Had I started at a different location, I'd need to identify the target server explicitly, by typing **test.windows2000dev.microsoft.com**.

FQDNs are common when using utilities like NSLOOKUP, where the movement between nameservers and the trees within nameserver lists is accomplished relative to the user's current location in the tree.

Recursion

When seeking the FQDN, the resolver puts the responsibility for name resolution on the nameserver. This is called a recursive request, and a response is expected directly from the target nameserver.

Iteration (or Nonrecursive)

For iterative, or nonrecursive, name resolution, the resolver requests a name of a nameserver. If that nameserver can't find the name, it passes an iterative resolution request to the next nameserver. If that nameserver has the information, it returns the answer; otherwise, it returns a pointer to a server that may be closer to the answer.

The iterative request can travel to all servers, and if the request makes it all the way up to the primary master with no resolution, the system finally returns an error.

In Figure 2-8, you will see instances of both recursion and iteration requests being used to resolve an address from a name.

Caching

If a server had to find information in a database table every single time a request arrived, or had to refer requests to other servers, the delays would prevent the DNS name resolution system from responding to millions of requests on a regular basis.

The process works because nameservers use caching. When a query is made to a nameserver (as shown in Figure 2-9) and the server has previously found an authoritative nameserver for the response, it caches the response for future reference. When it attempts to resolve a name and fails, it stores that information as well. Caching both the positive and negative response information creates a form of artificial intelligence that the

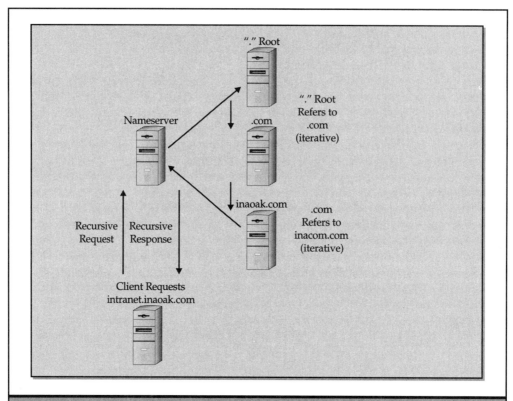

Figure 2-8. Recursion and iteration requests in a query

nameservers apply when queries arrive (and, of course, this also reduces the number of iterative requests made to a nameserver).

Caching means that the NSLOOKUP utility can receive both authoritative responses and nonauthoritative responses to the same request. An authoritative response means the nameserver actually checked with a server of authority that knew for a fact the information you requested is true. If you repeat your request, you'll probably receive a nonauthoritative answer, which means that the last time a request was sent for this information an authoritative answer was received, but this time the server is relying on its cache to provide the information.

Time to Live

Cached information has a designated time to live (TTL), which is the default amount of time that a system can cache information about the positive and negative responses to queries.

```
C:\WINNT.0\System32\cmd.exe - nslookup                                    _ □ ✕

> inaoak.com
Server:  pri1.dns.psi.net
Address:  38.8.94.2

inaoak.com        nameserver = pri1.dns.psi.net
inaoak.com        nameserver = pri2.dns.psi.net
inaoak.com        nameserver = pri3.dns.psi.net
> server 38.9.224.2
Default Server:  sw2.res.dns.psi.net
Address:  38.9.224.2

> inaoak.com
Server:  sw2.res.dns.psi.net
Address:  38.9.224.2

Non-authoritative answer:
inaoak.com        nameserver = PRI2.DNS.PSI.NET
inaoak.com        nameserver = PRI3.DNS.PSI.NET
inaoak.com        nameserver = PRI1.DNS.PSI.NET

PRI2.DNS.PSI.NET          internet address = 38.8.95.2
PRI3.DNS.PSI.NET          internet address = 38.8.96.2
PRI1.DNS.PSI.NET          internet address = 38.8.94.2
>
```

Figure 2-9.   Authoritative and nonauthoritative responses

Although cached information is generally valid, if a server moves, an IP address changes, or servers are added and deleted, the information in the cache is incorrect. The purpose of the TTL is to maximize caching to improve performance while minimizing the chance of sending incorrect information.

For some types of information, the TTL may be a matter of seconds, while the TTL for other types of information could be extended to minutes or hours. For the general Internet, information is stored and flushed at least several times a day, which provides a good performance level for the variety of information types needed.

When you build your own DNS server, you have the option of setting the TTL to match your own needs. If your environment is relatively static, experiencing few changes on a regular basis, your internal TTL may be set relatively high. This gives you maximum use of the cache, which improves the response speed.

However, if your environment has a large number of temporary users (such as laptop systems or remote dial-up systems), this more dynamic environment would benefit from a shorter TTL.

Using the NSLOOKUP Utility

The NSLOOKUP utility that comes with Windows 2000 provides access to DNS records on nameservers. You can query the DNS database to gain information about the nameservers that provide authoritative information about an organization's servers.

NSLOOKUP is a command-line utility, and there are quite a few commands available. Check your Windows help file system for a detailed list.

Querying Records with NSLOOKUP

The information available from the resource records of a nameserver includes the manner in which email messages are routed to the organization (found in the mail exchange [MX] record), or the resolution of aliases (using the CNAME record).

Debugging DNS Implementations with NSLOOKUP

DNS implementations that are incorrectly designed and configured are a serious and prevalent problem. Sometimes, though, the problems are created and propagated on the Internet, and are outside of your control.

For example, I recently ran into a situation where email messages from one company were intermittently being sent to the mail server of another company. I used NSLOOKUP to validate the fact that the problem was caused by an error in a DNS routing table on the East Coast of the United States. When this routing table was used, the mail messages were forwarded to the wrong target company. Bringing this error to the attention of the administrator of the DNS server caused a correction. Without the information I gained through the use of the debugging tools in NSLOOKUP, the problem may not have been identified so easily. (See Chapter 18 for more on problem solving and debugging Windows 2000 DNS problems.)

Understanding the Content in the Resource Records

Zone files contain information above and beyond the name and IP addresses of the hosts within the authority of a nameserver. There are resource records that hold pertinent information about the contact person, location of other nameservers, mail system locations, and other useful information specific to each address within the database.

Service of Authority (SOA)

The service of authority (SOA) record is the first record in the database and is the information management record for each host. The SOA contains the following data:

▼ **Source host**   This is the host that stores the original file.

■ **Contact email**   This is the Internet email address for the person responsible for the domain's database information. The name is displayed with dots between the segments (for instance, hostmaster.microsoft.com). You must replace the first dot with an at symbol (@) to create the valid email name (hostmaster@microsoft.com).

■ **Serial number**   This is the version number of this database file, and it is increased each time the file is modified. This provides a method of validating changes across multiple servers.

- ■ **Refresh time**   This is the elapsed time (in seconds) that a secondary server should wait before it checks the master server to see if the file has changed and whether a zone transfer is necessary.

- ■ **Retry time**   This is the elapsed time (in seconds) that a secondary server should wait before retrying a failed zone transfer.

- ■ **Expiration time**   This is the elapsed time (in seconds) that a secondary server should try to download a zone's information. After this time expires, old zone information will need to be discarded.

- ▲ **Time to live (TTL)**   This is the elapsed time (in seconds) that a DNS server is allowed to cache resource records from the database file.

Nameserver (NS)

The nameserver (NS) record lists the servers that are permitted to look up names in your domain. These additional servers extend the reach of information of the domain by advertising the names of these additional servers as resources.

You can use NSLOOKUP, setting the resource record lookup type to NS, to access a list of the nameservers that have authority over the resource records for the domain. If the server has been queried for the information previously, the response comes from the cache. The nonauthoritative response informs you that the information has been verified within the limits of the time-to-live timeout value and should be valid information. Here's an example of a session for an NS record query:

```
C:\>nslookup
Default Server:  sw3.res.dns.psi.net {this line will vary based on
your DNS setting}
Address:  38.9.234.2 {this line will vary based on your DNS setting}
> set type=ns
> microsoft.com
Server:  sw3.res.dns.psi.net {this line will vary based on your DNS
setting}
Address:  38.9.234.2 {this line will vary based on your DNS setting}
Non-authoritative answer:
microsoft.com    nameserver = dns1.microsoft.com
microsoft.com    nameserver = dns2.microsoft.com
microsoft.com    nameserver = dns3.nwnet.net
microsoft.com    nameserver = dns4.nwnet.net
dns1.microsoft.com       internet address = 131.107.1.7
dns2.microsoft.com       internet address = 131.107.1.240
dns3.nwnet.net   internet address = 192.220.250.7
dns4.nwnet.net   internet address = 192.220.251.7
>
```

The session information indicates that four nameservers hold the microsoft.com name for authoritative responses, and lists dns1.microsoft.com, dns2.microsoft.com, dns3.nwnet.net, and dns4.nwnet.net. The second section of this record provides the actual IP addresses for each of these nameservers, so a query can be made to either the nameserver or the IP address of the nameserver.

Mail Exchange (MX)

The mail exchange (MX) record reports the host that processes mail for the domain. In many cases multiple MX records exist, so the resolver will contact the mail servers in order of preference from the lowest value number (which has the highest priority designation) to the highest value number (or lowest priority designation).

Using the NSLOOKUP utility, you set the resource record lookup type to MX in order to query the nameserver. In the sample MX query here, the mail host resolution for johnsmith@microsoft.com sends the mail message to johnsmith@mail1.microsoft.com first. If the attempt fails, it sends the message to johnsmith@mail2.microsoft.com, and so on. From the MX record information, we also know that the host mail1.microsoft.com has a physical IP address of 131.107.3.125. Therefore, if we send email to johnsmith@microsoft.com, we are in fact sending the message to johnsmith@131.107.3.125. But unlike sending a message to a single IP address, DNS MX records provide us a series of hosts, so that if mail1.microsoft.com is nonoperational, the MX record instructs us to try mail2.microsoft (or IP address 131.107.3.124) and so forth until the message is transmitted.

```
C:\>nslookup
Default Server:  sw3.res.dns.psi.net {this line will vary based on
your DNS setting}
> server dns1.microsoft.com

Default Server:  dns1.microsoft.com
Address:  131.107.1.7

> set type=mx
> microsoft.com
Server:  dns1.microsoft.com
Address:  131.107.1.7

Nonauthoritative answer:
microsoft.com   MX preference = 10, mail exchanger =
mail1.microsoft.com
microsoft.com   MX preference = 10, mail exchanger =
mail2.microsoft.com
microsoft.com   MX preference = 10, mail exchanger =
mail3.microsoft.com
microsoft.com   MX preference = 10, mail exchanger =
```

```
mail4.microsoft.com
microsoft.com    MX preference = 10, mail exchanger =
mail5.microsoft.com

microsoft.com    nameserver = dns3.nwnet.net
microsoft.com    nameserver = dns4.nwnet.net
microsoft.com    nameserver = dns1.microsoft.com
microsoft.com    nameserver = dns2.microsoft.com
mail1.microsoft.com      internet address = 131.107.3.125
mail2.microsoft.com      internet address = 131.107.3.124
mail3.microsoft.com      internet address = 131.107.3.123
mail4.microsoft.com      internet address = 131.107.3.122
mail5.microsoft.com      internet address = 131.107.3.121
dns3.nwnet.net  internet address = 192.220.250.7
dns4.nwnet.net  internet address = 192.220.251.7
dns1.microsoft.com       internet address = 131.107.1.7
dns2.microsoft.com       internet address = 131.107.1.240
>
```

In this example, you can see that Microsoft has five email servers that receive company messages. The servers are listed with both their host names and their IP addresses. As mail is sent to Microsoft, it is first sent to mail1.microsoft.com at IP address 131.107.3.125, and then goes to each subsequent server in the list until the message is accepted. Notice that the MX listing also displays the DNS servers that hold the authoritative information for the nameservers.

The preference designator in the MX record designates the priority (from low number to high number) for the preference server.

NOTE: If you change your ISP, you may want to have multiple IP addresses and host names in your Internet profile. If the first server with the first ISP is down, an attempt is made to redirect the transmission to the second server and/or the second ISP. This round-robin process can be used in a variety of ways to improve reliability (by having multiple paths to the organization's network) or to provide a migration process from one ISP to another.

Host Record (A)

Host records are used to statically associate host names to IP addresses within a zone. For all servers, nameservers, mail hosts, print devices, or other systems that require static mapping, this file retains the entries for all the hosts that require these static mappings.

Using NSLOOKUP, set the resource record lookup type to A in order to query the nameserver.

```
C:\>nslookup
Default Server:  sw3.res.dns.psi.net {this line will vary based on
your DNS setting}
Address:  38.9.234.2 {this line will vary based on your DNS setting}
> set type=a
> microsoft.com
Server:  [38.9.224.2]
Address:  38.9.224.2 {this line will vary based on your DNS setting}

Name:    microsoft.com
Addresses:  207.46.130.139, 207.46.130.149, 207.46.130.150,
            207.46.131.15, 207.46.131.16, 207.46.131.135,
            207.46.177.21, 207.46.130.14, 207.46.130.15
```

In this example, the host record for microsoft.com is managed by 9 servers, each of which is noted with its IP address.

CNAME (CNAME)

The CNAME record (CNAMEs are sometimes called aliases) are technically known as canonical name entries. These records are used when more than one name points to a single host in a multihomed system.

Using NSLOOKUP, set the resource record lookup type to CNAME in order to query a nameserver for the various aliases a server may use.

TRADITIONAL DNS DOMAIN STRUCTURE

In a traditional DNS domain structure, there is a series of both internal and external servers in the organization. External servers are the Web servers or FTP servers providing World Wide Web or file transfer capabilities to clients or members of the Internet in general. Internal servers include file and print servers, or intranet servers that are used by employees of the organization while they are logged on to the organization's network. For security purposes, you don't want external users to have access to internal servers, but you usually do want internal users to have access to both internal and external servers.

External Namespace

The external namespace is the domain-naming scheme used by an organization to address the servers that are available to the general Internet. This is the public domain name such as microsoft.com, or hp.com, or inacom.com. The external namespace is used to gain access to the organization's Web servers, or to address email.

Internal Namespace

The internal namespace is the domain-naming scheme used for servers that are internal to the organization. The domain name may be the same as the external name, or you can elect to have a different internal name (such as msoft.com, hpinternal.com, or inac.com). The internal namespace is used to log on to the organization's network, so an internal user logs on as, for example, fredjones@msoft.com. There are pros and cons to consider about each approach, and you can learn more about naming strategies in Chapter 7 of this book.

Using Subdomains

Within an internal or external namespace, you can have multiple subdomains. These subdomains become multiple administrative zones, and they're used as part of a network management strategy. Subdomains provide several advantages:

- ▼ They facilitate the access services needed when remote locations must be brought online to join the network.
- ■ They distribute the management of security and administration.
- ▲ They make it easier to change the administration procedures (there are no complicated trusts or reconfiguration of resources, just granting or denying authorization to a branch of a tree).

Assigning IP Addresses

When you create a TCP/IP-based network, you need to assign IP addresses. (If you requested IP addresses in the past, and received them without charge, consider yourself lucky.) You can learn how to procure IP addresses by contacting the Internet Assigned Number Authority (IANA) at http://www.iana.org. IANA distributes the responsibility for IP number management by location:

- ▼ **United States**   American Registry for Internet Numbers (http://www.arin.net)
- ■ **Asia**   Asia Pacific Ripe NCC (http://www.apnic.net)
- ▲ **Europe**   Reseaux IP Europeens (http://www.ripe.net)

If you don't have assigned IP addresses, or if you've run out of them, you can buy them (IANA's Web page displays sources). However, you may want to opt to use proxy servers and handle IP addressing through network address translation (NAT).

Using Proxy Servers

Typically, a proxy server is positioned between the general Internet and your internal network, acting as a gateway between the two environments. Externally, the proxy server can be a firewall, limiting the inbound traffic from the Internet. The proxy server uses filters to screen external information, stopping anything that fails to meet the criteria of the filters. For example, you can screen out all but authenticated remote users, provide limited access to a specific server, or reject all forms of communication except incoming email traffic.

A proxy server can also manage internal-to-external communications. You can use filters to screen internal information before passing it on to the external environment. You can limit the transmissions to specific individuals, specific times of day, or specific destinations. And, you can log the communication traffic in order to track who is accessing what information at what time of day.

Network Address Translation (NAT)

A proxy server can provide translation functions between internal IP addresses and external IP addresses. This means you can use a series of IP addresses internally, even though they aren't registered IP addresses. At the moment, additional IP addresses are not available, so you must use unregistered IP addresses internally. The proxy server translates those IP addresses so that the unregistered IP addresses do not pass from the internal network to the Internet. This is the process known as network address translation (NAT).

IANA has allocated three blocks of IP addresses reserved for universal use by any organization using NAT, as shown in Table 2-2.

Supporting a Multihomed Server

A proxy server can also provide multiple Internet addresses or multiple domain names that are routed to a single server or a single network segment. For instance, you may want to have a single server appear as multiple servers on the network. Multihoming is useful when several small departments that are sharing a single server want to appear completely separate to their users. In addition, each department can maintain its own distinct resources, such as printers and workstations. Users see a single entity (assuming the server is assigned only to them), while the server is actually serving multiple organizations simultaneously. Multihoming also lets you use one server that presents one server name to external users and a different server name to internal users. Multihoming eliminates the expense of managing multiple servers, multiple backup systems, and so on.

Class	Starting Reserved Address	Ending Reserved Address
Class A	10.0.0.0	10.255.255.255
Class B	172.6.0.0	172.31.255.255
Class C	192.168.0.0	192.168.255.255

Table 2-2. Reserved IP Addresses for Network Address Translation

CHAPTER 3

Security

Security is of paramount importance in today's highly connected information age. If stolen, human resource information, payroll, corporate secrets, financial information, and other highly confidential data can blunt an organization's competitive edge or even result in bankruptcy. On the other hand, there is an ever increasing demand for access to outside information, in the form of high-speed Internet connections for internal use, remote access to mobile and home-office users, authorized access for customers via the Internet, and extranet links to key suppliers.

The technologies integrated into Windows 2000 allow organizations to provide information to personnel while keeping the information secure. That optimum balance is struck through effective security planning.

A good security plan outlines a vision of security and the specific policies that flow from that vision. It should also contain a roadmap for implementation so that security concerns are addressed at each critical stage. This should include vision statements like the following:

▼ **Access**   This includes statements such as "Access will be provided to corporate computing resources from 6 A.M. to 6 P.M. every weekday" or "All access to corporate computing resources will be validated."

▲ **Privacy**   This includes statements such as "All data within the corporate computing environment belongs to the corporation and is subject to monitoring and review at any time."

These vision statements should be developed with support at the executive level and from the legal department.

SECURITY IN THE ORGANIZATION

Windows 2000 provides a wide variety of tools to maintain a secure environment. The tools include authentication protocols, access control lists, security groups, group policy, secret key encryption, cryptography, public key encryption, single sign-on authentication, nonrepudiation, code authentication, and auditing.

Authentication

The basis of a security system is ensuring that the users, services, or computers requesting access are who they say they are. Authentication is the process of confirming the identity of a user, server, or service. The goal of authentication is to ensure that the identity is correct and not that of an imposter.

Kerberos

Windows 2000 uses the Kerberos v5 authentication protocol, which was developed at MIT over 10 years ago. The Kerberos protocol is more secure, flexible, and efficient than the standard Windows NT NTLM protocol, and is the preferred authentication protocol for Windows 2000.

Kerberos allows the identification of the user and the network resources for mutual authentication. A hacker cannot impersonate a user, nor can a hacker-installed resource impersonate a network resource.

When a user requests authentication by entering their username and password combination as credentials, Windows 2000 uses the Active Directory and a Kerberos authentication service to validate the credentials. After validating the credentials, the Kerberos service issues a ticket to the user. This initial ticket is then used transparently by Windows 2000 to request authentication to other network resources, saving users the trouble of entering username and password combinations again.

NTLM

The Windows NTLM protocol was the default for the Microsoft Windows NT 4.0 operating system and is implemented in Windows 2000 mainly to provide backward compatibility. Its use allows access to older Windows NT 4.0 resources, and allows older clients, such as Windows 3.11, Windows 95/98, and Windows NT 4.0, to access Windows 2000. While NTLM is available in Windows 2000, it is important to minimize or eliminate its use, as more clients become Kerberos-capable. Kerberos has the following benefits when compared to NTLM:

▼   **Efficiency**   With Kerberos, the servers do not need to contact a domain controller to validate credentials. With the NTLM protocol, each request must be validated by contacting a domain controller. Kerberos reduces the load on the domain controllers and on the network infrastructure.

■   **Flexibility**   Kerberos allows both mutual authentication and delegation of authentication, for which there are no NTLM equivalents. Mutual authentication allows the client to verify the identity of the service that it is accessing, which allows the client to make sure that the service is who it says it is. Delegation of authentication allows the service, with the proper authorization, to act as a user on behalf of that user.

▲   **Interoperability**   Because Kerberos is based on the Internet Engineering Task Force (IETF) standard, it will interoperate with any other standard implementation of Kerberos, such as UNIX-based systems. This allows organizations to create enterprise-wide security systems, including single sign-on to non-Microsoft platforms.

Two-Factor Authentication

Two-factor authentication requires a password and a physical object that uniquely identifies the user. These physical objects could be objects given to users, such as cards or keys, or they could be biometric objects, such as fingerprints, hand scans, or retinal scans. The best-known example of a two-factor authentication is an automated teller machine (ATM), which requires a personal identification number (PIN) as the password and a unique card as the physical object. The two-factor authentication is more expensive to deploy and maintain, but provides a greater measure of security, because it means the hacker must also steal a physical object from the user.

The most widely used two-factor technology for Windows 2000 is smart-card technology, which functions very much like the ATM. A smart-card enabled workstation has a card reader through which a user passes a card in order to log on to the network. The network then prompts the user for a password. The card contains information stored in a security certificate that identifies the user, eliminating the need for the user to type in a logon name. The certificates usually include the user's private key and logon information, and a public-key certificate.

Since two-factor mechanisms increase the security of access to network resources, they are an excellent choice for high security environments. The issues that need to be thought through and decided on in advance include:

▼ **Security vs. deployment**   Does the cost-benefit ratio make sense for the organization? Are the security risks such that improved security will justify the costs of deployment and maintenance?

■ **How many users**   How many users will participate in the smart-card program? Should it be only a subset of the organization or the entire organization?

■ **Initial issue of smart cards**   Should the users present ID? Should there be a security review or background checks? Should there be mandatory training on security awareness and use of the cards?

■ **Lost or forgotten smart cards**   Can users use a temporary card? Should they have to go back home if they left it there, or should they get a temporary card?

▲ **Location of readers**   Should there be a reader on every desktop or only on key security desktops?

The decisions and policies you set will affect the deployment costs, ease of use, and long-term support costs for maintaining the smart cards.

Authorization for Access

Authenticated users of a corporate system are authorized to access certain corporate resources. Corporate resources can include file systems, network shares, file shares, print shares, Active Directory resources, and databases. The rights a user has will depend on the implementation of access rights (no access, read-only access, and read/write access). Windows 2000 provides a number of features to control access to resources.

Access Control Lists

The mechanism that Windows 2000 uses to control access is Access Control Lists (ACLs). These lists describe the users and groups who have rights to access specific objects and what those access rights are. The users and groups access control rights are maintained in the Active Directory, as are the access control rights information of resource objects. ACLs are present on almost all resources, allowing permissions to be granted or denied at an extremely fine level of detail.

Many objects have default rights assigned to the Everyone group by their ACL. It is important to restrict this access to specific groups that need access, rather than to assume that Windows 2000 will automatically secure all resources. Evaluate how resources will be used and explicitly assign rights on that basis.

In some cases, even the knowledge that a particular resource exists can compromise security. Seeing that a resource exists on the network (such as a share called PAYROLL or STAFF REDUCTION) can be an invitation to attempt to break into it. In those cases and in general, even the viewing of resources should be restricted to authorized personnel. Windows 2000 allows administrators to restrict who sees what resources.

Security Groups

In Windows 2000, users and other domain objects are logically organized into groups within the Active Directory. This simplifies administration of access permissions and helps ensure the consistency of security. Groups are added to the ACLs, and users are added to the appropriate groups depending on the access they need.

There are several group types within Windows 2000:

▼   **Domain Local Groups**   These groups are typically used to grant access to file-system or print resources. Domain local groups can contain members from either the same domain or from outside of the domain.

■   **Global Groups**   These groups are used to aggregate users who share a common security need within a domain.

■   **Universal Groups**   These groups are used in multidomain organizations to grant access to groups of users in different domains. Typically, the members of universal groups would be global groups from the respective domains.

▲   **Computer Local Groups**   These groups are used primarily for local administration, because computer local groups are not recognized by any entity other than the local machine.

Security groups are very useful in managing security. Users with similar security profiles can be included in a security group, and permission can be assigned to the group, rather than to each individual. This helps administrators visualize the security model, and it also makes security easier to administer. If a user no longer fits a security group profile, simply removing the user from the group also removes all of those group permissions assigned to the user.

Default Security Groups

The Windows 2000 operating system creates and assigns access rights to several key groups by default. These default access rights are slightly different in Windows 2000 than in Windows NT 4.0.

▼   **Everyone and Users**   The members of these groups do not have the broad access rights they did in Windows NT 4.0. Their rights are restricted for the most part to read-only, with read/write access being granted only in individual profile directories. This limits these groups' ability to install applications. In addition, users cannot log on interactively to domain controller systems, which is the same as in Windows NT 4.0.

■ **Power Users**   These rights have not changed from Windows NT 4.0—these users have both read and write access to most of the system. Power users can install applications with few or no restrictions.

■ **Administrators**   These rights have not changed in Windows 2000. Members of the Administrators group have total control of the system.

▲ **Operators**   These groups include the Account Operator, Print Operator, and Server Operator groups. These groups retain the same levels of access rights that they had in Windows NT 4.0.

Group Policy

One of the core elements for administering security within Windows 2000 is the group policy. Group policy is a collection of settings, which includes an extensive profile of security permissions and parameters. These are mainly settings for domain-level policy assignments and computer-level policy assignments, though there are some user aspects, as well. Group policy complements security groups, because it can be applied to multiple groups and users.

A sample of group-policy security setting includes:

▼ **Account Policies**   This includes areas such as account lockout policy, the Kerberos policy, and the password policy. This group policy is applied domain-wide.

■ **Public Key Policies**   This includes a list of trusted certificate authorities, automatic certificate requests, and encrypted data-recovery agent information. This group policy is also applied domain-wide.

■ **Event Log Policies**   This includes maximum log sizes, log retention, and overwrite parameters. This group policy can be applied at the organization-unit level.

■ **Registry Policies**   Restrictions on registry keys are set within this group policy, including access and auditing of keys. This sets policies on what keys users can view or modify. This group policy can be applied at the organization unit level.

▲ **File System**   This group policy can be used to configure security for files and folders, as well as to control the auditing of files and folders. This is where access to the system folder is restricted. This group policy can be applied at the organization-unit level.

Group policy objects are assigned to organizational units within the Active Directory and are applied to all computers stored in that organizational unit. Some policies, such as the account and public-key policies, are applied only at the domain level. Multiple group-policy objects can be assigned to a single organizational unit, which can lead to conflicts that are resolved automatically via the group-policy precedence.

Reduce Exceptions

Access is best allocated at the group level, because it provides the easiest level of management.

Exceptions occur when different rights are allocated to handle special circumstances or conditions. An example of this is granting access to a sensitive Accounting Department resource to someone who is working on a particular document. The security risk is that once this transitory access right is no longer needed, that individual might not be removed from the access rights list. By defining security rights by groups, the administrator can better track individualized access rights in the network.

Another example is a Human Resources data pool to which all users within the Human Resources Department, and also all directors, need access. Rather than assigning rights to all the directors as individuals, it would be better to create a group called Directors, add the individual directors to that group, and assign access rights to the group. Then if there is a change of directors, the group's membership can be changed and the access rights would change accordingly.

Confidentiality and Integrity

Underlying the security model are technologies that ensure the confidentiality of the data being accessed. These technologies prevent unauthorized users from accessing the information, even when that unauthorized user has access to the physical hardware (for example when a laptop is lost with replicated data) or the physical medium (for example when an intruder can run a packet capture on the network).

Encryption

Encryption technologies are very useful for protecting data confidentiality and integrity. Windows 2000 has a number of features that take advantage of encryption technologies to secure and protect data.

The Encrypting File System (EFS) is a prime example of a technology that helps protect data within Windows 2000. Any data written to an EFS-enabled directory is kept both confidential and complete by encrypting it as it is written. This technology uses public-key encryption extensively (discussed later in this chapter).

Another encryption technology is Internet Protocol Security (IPSec), which protects network traffic. This technology encrypts data packets as they leave the source, and decrypts the packets as they arrive at the destination, ensuring a secure end-to-end connection. This activity occurs at the transport layer, which is completely transparent to the application and to the network layers of the OSI model. This makes this technology particularly useful for securing traffic between applications that are completely security-unaware.

IPSec comes with a performance penalty, because some computer performance is sacrificed to encrypt and decrypt packets. This can range from 10 to 30 percent, depending on the volume and nature of the traffic. The encryption algorithm being used can also have a substantial effect. Computers can be set with a group policy to always communicate using IPSec, to accept IPSec communications initiated by another computer, to initiate communications using IPSec, or to never communicate using IPSec.

Cryptography

Cryptography is the science of protecting data to ensure its confidentiality. Some of the original forms involved the basic concept of substituting numbers for letters, based on a previously agreed pattern. The pattern was used as a basis for scrambling and unscrambling the text.

The elements in cryptography include the plaintext (the message), encryption keys (the pattern), a cryptographic algorithm (the process of substitution) and the ciphertext (the scrambled message). This process is the same today, although it is now much more sophisticated.

Plaintext and Ciphertext

Plaintext is the original unencrypted text that can be easily read, and it needs to be protected. Once the text is protected, it is called ciphertext. The process of protecting the text is called encryption. The process of turning ciphertext back into plaintext is *decryption*.

Encryption Key

The encryption key is the secret key needed to either lock or unlock the text. In some forms of cryptography, there is only one key used to both encrypt and decrypt the text. In other forms of cryptography, there is a key to encrypt and a different key to decrypt. These keys are ideally very long, to make them difficult to guess.

Cryptographic Algorithm

The cryptographic algorithm is the mathematical formula or technique used on the plaintext, in conjunction with the key, to transform the plaintext into encrypted text, and vice versa. These mathematical formulas are very complex, which makes it difficult to reverse the process without the correct key.

Some examples of cryptographic algorithms include Data Encryption Standard (DES), Rivest-Shamir-Adleman (RSA), Elliptic Curve Cryptography (ECC), and Diffie-Hellman (DH). Each algorithm has its advantages and disadvantages, leading to their use in particular areas of cryptography and their different levels of security.

Transformation

Ideally, the transformation process should be extremely difficult to reverse. This is typically accomplished by making it computationally very difficult to reverse the encryption process without the key. The level of difficulty is typically expressed as a span of time over which the encryption could be broken at today's computing power, as in "A message encrypted with the DES encryption could be cracked in 10 years at today's computing power."

Secret-Key Encryption

Secret-key encryption is fast and effective, relying on a shared secret key. It is used extensively by Windows 2000. Some examples of uses in Windows 2000 include Encrypting File System (EFS), Internet Protocol Security (IPSec), Layer 2 Tunneling Protocol (L2TP), and Secure/Multipurpose Internet Mail Extensions (S/MIME).

Single Key

There is only a single key in secret-key encryption, which is different from public-key encryption. Both parties to the transaction must share this single key. This can lead to some logistical difficulties in sharing the key in advance, which public-key encryption is useful in surmounting.

Encryption and Decryption

The single key is used for both encryption and decryption. For this reason, this encryption technique is often known as symmetric-key encryption, because the key works both ways. This is illustrated in Figure 3-1.

Fast Performance

The mathematical transformations are simpler with the symmetric-key encryption, so the technique is less computation-intensive and yields faster performance than some other techniques. This can be 100 to 1000 times faster than public-key encryption, which is a sig-

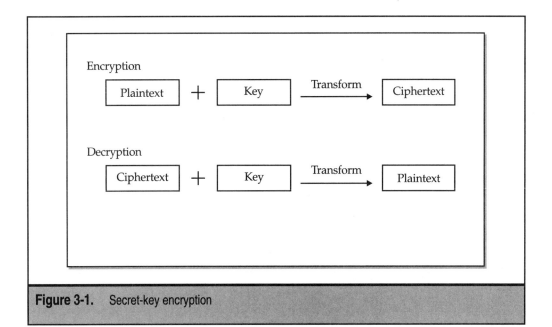

Figure 3-1. Secret-key encryption

nificant difference. Anything requiring large quantities of data to be encrypted, referred to as bulk encryption, should use a symmetric key for performance.

Used Internally

This method of encryption is most commonly used internally, when it is safe to have a common, shared, secret key. It is also used in conjunction with public-key encryption to provide both portability and performance.

Public-Key Encryption

Encryption algorithms that use two different keys—one for encrypting and one for decrypting—are using public-key encryption. The name refers to the ability to have one of the keys publicly available, while still allowing a variety of security strategies.

Two Keys

Public-key encryption uses a private (secret) key and a public key. These two keys are complementary. Text that is encrypted with the public key can only be decrypted with the private key, as shown in Figure 3-2. In some, but not all, cases, data that is encrypted with the private key can only be decrypted with the public key.

With these two keys, the need for a shared secret key (and thus the need for a method of exchanging keys) is eliminated. Public-key encryption provides a method of exchanging data securely over open public networks. It also facilitates security concepts such as

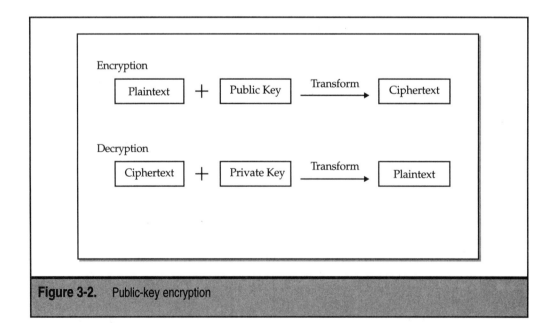

Figure 3-2. Public-key encryption

authentication and nonrepudiation. Authentication allows parties to mutually verify their identities, and nonrepudiation ensures that the sender of information cannot deny having originated information.

Public-key encryption can also be combined with symmetric-key encryption to provide high performance and secure technologies. Using public-key encryption to securely transmit the shared secret key needed for symmetric encryption does this. The actual text encryption is then done with the symmetric key.

Public-Key Infrastructure

To effectively utilize public-key encryption on a scalable basis, there must be a public-key infrastructure (PKI). This provides the services, technologies, protocols, and standards that are the components required to implement the technology. Some of the components include digital certificates and certification authorities.

The Windows 2000 public-key infrastructure is based on the recommendations of the Public Key Infrastructure X.509 (PKIX) working group of the Internet Engineering Task Force (IETF). Because the Windows 2000 PKI is based on standards, it interoperates fully with other third-party PKIs that follow the PKIX standard.

Single Sign-on

One of the top ease-of-use complaints from users is the need to sign on multiple times when accessing corporate computing resources. In a typical complex computing environment, users need to authenticate themselves to the workstation when they arrive in the morning to access their mail system and mainframe services and, potentially, when they need to access business applications.

Ease of Use

Different resources typically use different name and password logon combinations, making it difficult for users to remember and use the correct combination. To make matters worse, services can have different length and complexity requirements for passwords, and different password-change intervals.

Security Risks

When users have to remember a number of different passwords, they tend to try to optimize their time and effort. They may write down all the pesky username and password combinations and post the lists at their desks. Worse, they may create the lists with a word processor or spreadsheet application, storing the document with the helpful filename "passwords" or "My Passwords."

This behavior leaves the system wide open to several different types of breaches. More important, it indicates an environment that has become lax about password security. Frequently, users who can't remember one of their passwords call the help desk and are given a new password. Users become accustomed to discussing passwords with the help desk over the phone, making them susceptible to a call from a hacker impersonating the help desk to "verify" the user's password.

Login Once

The solution to these problems is to have users authenticated once per session, using a single username and password combination. This one-time authentication is referred to as single sign-on. A session is typically a contiguous work period, perhaps starting when the user arrives at work in the morning and continuing until mid-day when the user leaves for lunch. After the initial sign-on, access to other systems is granted automatically through either the presentation of cached credentials or through delegation of authority.

With a single username and password combination, users are far less likely to forget the combination and won't need to contact the help desk or write down authentication information. With fewer incidents of lost passwords, more stringent password recovery procedures can be put in place, such as requiring users to go to a security officer and present identification. The users will also have a much easier time using the systems if they are granted access automatically as a result of the initial login, thus increasing the use of the systems.

Data Confidentiality and Integrity

Data needs to be protected from unauthorized viewing, modification, and damage. Protecting the data from viewing is called confidentiality. Protecting data from unauthorized changes is called data integrity. Unauthorized users should not be able to delete, overwrite, or edit files, or to view files for which they do not have viewing permissions. Data should also be protected from unauthorized viewing or modification while traveling over the network.

Through the use of file encryption and file security permissions, information on the network can be kept confidential and secure.

Code Authentication

Today's environment consists of daily outbreaks of viruses, exacerbated by downloading code in the form of ActiveX controls, Java applets, scripts, and macros. Virus scanners help, but they lag behind the outbreaks. Viruses can either be hidden as stowaways in code written by a reputable organization, or they can be written from whole cloth.

Code authentication technologies were developed to prevent this problem. With these technologies, code is "digitally signed" after development is completed. Users can choose whom they trust as reputable sources of code, and they will also know whether the code has been tampered with after it was signed. Any code with no signature that originates from an untrusted source, or that has been modified after the signature, can be rejected.

Auditing

Auditing takes two forms within the computing context. One is the automatic generation of an electronic trail of user activity, from logon to logoff. This could include unsuccessful attempts to access resources or to perform an operation. The audit information is typically stored in logs.

The second form of auditing is the review, or audit, of logged information. This human process monitors and reviews all the captured information, detecting unauthorized attempts to violate data confidentiality or integrity.

In addition, the logging of the electronic trail poses a security barrier for a hacker, in that the hacker is forced to take the log into account. If a sophisticated hacker breaks into the system, he or she will need to spend time dealing with the logging.

The audit logs could also provide legal evidence for the prosecution of intruders who are apprehended.

Physical Security

Physical security is of critical importance and is frequently overlooked, especially in smaller organizations. Physical security can often eliminate risks that would be difficult to avoid otherwise.

Brute Force

A simple example of a risk that would be difficult to counter is a sledgehammer. If a malicious intruder has physical access to systems, very few computers could withstand a few blows from a sledgehammer.

Complete Access

Most security systems for servers are designed to withstand attacks from the network, but not from physical access. Given access to the server console, an intruder could read data or damage the system.

Environmental

Another potential source of attack, albeit often accidental, is environmental. If the ambient temperature is too low or too high, network resource equipment can fail. Excessive humidity, a fire, or earth tremors can also affect the equipment adversely.

Secured Premise

Network resource equipment should reside in locked facilities with restricted access. The equipment should be secured in earthquake-resistant racks. These facilities should be environmentally controlled and monitored.

SECURITY OVER THE INTERNET

Security over the very public Internet is of paramount importance. Organizations want to use the Internet to reach their customers, provide low-cost, worldwide access for their mobile users, and download updates for rapidly evolving applications. PKIs help implement these technologies while maintaining strong security.

Microsoft Windows 2000 provides a platform for a comprehensive PKI, using an integrated suite of services and tools for creating, deploying, and managing public key– based applications.

What Is PKI?

A public-key infrastructure (PKI) provides a platform for building strongly secured and scalable solutions. It is used in conjunction with other security services to allow parties to communicate over public networks without fear of other parties snooping.

Shared-Secret Constraint

Public-key encryption is a solution to establishing a shared secret between two parties who wish to communicate securely. By implementing a public-key infrastructure, the two parties can establish a shared secret securely via a public key.

System of Digital Certification

Public-key infrastructure also provides a mechanism for establishing mutual authentication in a way that is not susceptible to repudiation. This mechanism for digitally signing both the authentication information and the data allows parties to accept sensitive communications with confidence over public networks.

This system extends not only to the enterprise, but also to the greater public as well, through the use of third-party certificate authorities with the Windows 2000 standards.

Electronic Transactions

With an infrastructure for establishing security across public networks, electronic transactions become very reliable and easy to use. This is rapidly becoming the backbone of electronic commerce over the Internet.

Understanding PKI

This section examines the core components of a PKI, covering the different components and their interactions. The Windows 2000 model is used, though there are other third-party models for implementing a PKI. See Figure 3-3 for an overview of the components.

Public-Key Encryption

The public-key infrastructure facilitates and uses public-key encryption. Using both a public and private key, methods have been developed to communicate securely, and the public-key infrastructure delivers that in an easy-to-use and scalable manner.

Digital Signatures

Using public-key encryption, digital signatures can be created and validated with the use of a mathematical transformation to combine the private key with data. This enables three aspects of digital signatures:

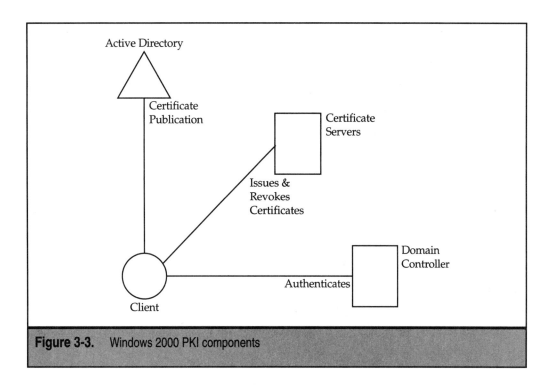

Figure 3-3.   Windows 2000 PKI components

▼   Only the holder of the private key could have created the digital signature, so the origin of the data being signed can be verified.

■   Anyone can use the public key to validate the digital signature, and thus the data.

▲   Any change to the signed data will render the signature invalid, so no changes can be made that will not be detected.

The signature itself is just a sequence of data, so it can be appended and transported with the data without fear of tampering.

Certificates

A certificate is a digital mechanism for establishing and validating the relationship between a public key and the holder of the private key. It is a digitally signed statement from an issuer. The certificate may also contain other information, such as the name of the holder.

The most common form of these certificates, and the one used by Windows 2000, is the X.509 certificate.

Certificate Authority

An issuer of certificates is known as a certificate authority (CA). The CA issues certificates and acts as a guarantor of the validity of the certificates it issues.

Microsoft Windows 2000 includes a certificate authority, Microsoft Certificate Services. Microsoft Certificate Services supports issuance and revocation of certificates, and it is integrated into the Active Directory. The Active Directory publishes the certificates and also the revocation information. Microsoft Certificate Services supports X.509 version 3 certificates.

In addition to the Microsoft-provided CA, there are third-party certificate authorities. An example of a third-party CA is VeriSign.

Certificate Hierarchies

Certificate authorities can be organized in a hierarchical model, which is very scalable, easier to administer, and integrates well with third-party certificate authorities. The hierarchical model takes the form of an inverted tree, with parent CAs certifying child CAs. The topmost CA in the hierarchy is called the root CA (there can be multiple root CAs).

The advantages of having multiple CAs include:

▼ **Performance**   Multiple CAs provide better performance geographically or in high-usage environments.

■ **Usage**   Certificate authorities might be dedicated to specific functions.

▲ **Organization**   Certificate authorities might operate at different levels of security or have differing policy requirements in different parts of the organization.

Enterprise Certificate-Authority Strategies

Enterprise certificate authorities support the internal operations of an organization, whereas an external certificate authority supports public or extranet applications. Microsoft's PKI provides support for both enterprise and external CAs. An organization can mix and match as dictated by its business requirements.

Some of the issues to consider when deploying an enterprise certificate authority include the following:

▼ **Host server**   The certificate services can run on any Windows 2000 server. The best location for services depends on existing and expected load, physical security, connectivity, and other factors.

■ **Naming**   The CA name is integrated into the certificates that it issues, so the name cannot change without invalidating the certificates that have been issued. The name should be chosen carefully.

■ **Active Directory integration**   A CA object is created in the Active Directory when the CA is installed.

■ **Issuing policy**   The installation of a CA automatically creates and configures a policy module for the CA. This should be modified according to the certificate-issuing policies of the organization.

▲ **Fault tolerance**   The CA is a critical component, in that the loss of the issuing CA can prevent certificates from being validated. It is important to keep up to date backups, to build in fault tolerance for the server, and to have a viable disaster-recovery plan.

Applications of PKI

Public-key infrastructure is a very interesting technology, but without useful applications it is just a waste of resources. Fortunately, there are a host of interesting and practical applications for the technology.

Email

Standard email based on the Simple Mail Transfer Protocol (SMTP) is sent completely unsecured over the Internet. Given that mail is typically forwarded through a number of hosts en route to its destination, this can be a major security risk. A hacker could intercept sensitive mail, impersonate a user, or even modify the contents of a message, all completely undetected.

Secure/Multipurpose Internet Mail Extensions (S/MIME) was developed by the IETF as an open standard to address these concerns. The S/MIME standard enables digital signing and encryption of mail. Email clients that support S/MIME can exchange messages securely over the Internet, as the messages can be both authenticated and encrypted. Microsoft's Outlook 98 messaging client supports S/MIME.

Clients with S/MIME use public-key infrastructure and industry standard X.509 version 3 digital certificates to secure mail. See Figure 3-4 for an overview of the process.

Web Services

Standard Web traffic that uses the HTTP protocol, the telnet protocol, or file transfer protocol (FTP) are not secure because they transfer information in plaintext over the Internet. Information transmitted with these protocols can be intercepted, read, and modified unless additional security measures are applied. Additionally, Web sites can be impersonated and can publish illegitimate information without detection by client systems.

A variety of secure Web communication standards that use public-key encryption have been developed, such as Secure Sockets Layer (SSL) and Transport Layer Security (TLS). Secure Web communications requires the use of certificates for both the client and the server. SSL and TLS provide the following core services:

▼   **Authentication**   Both client and server are mutually authenticated, based on their certificates. Either specific external or enterprise certificate authorities can issue these certificates.

■   **Confidentiality**   The communication between client and server is encrypted using a combination of public-key encryption and secret-key encryption. The server generates a random secret key for encrypting the data, encrypts it using the client's public key, and transmits it to the client securely over the Internet. The client decrypts the secret key using its private key, and then subsequently uses the secret key for secure communications with the server.

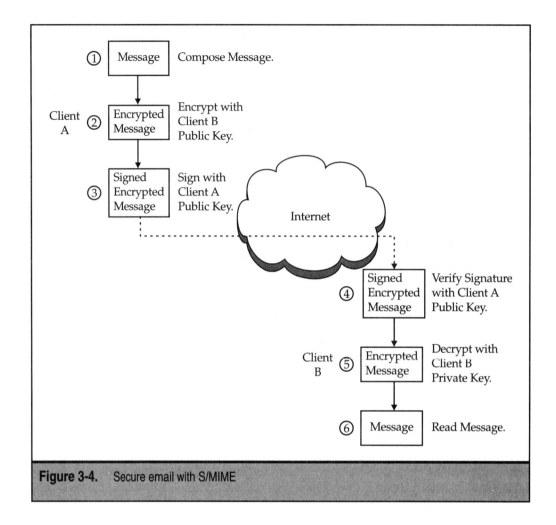

Figure 3-4.   Secure email with S/MIME

▲ **Data integrity**   A hacker cannot modify the communications between the client and the server, as each packet of data is digitally signed using the certificates.

The Microsoft Windows 2000 Public Key Encryption Infrastructure uses the Microsoft Certificate Services to issue both client and server certificates. Both Microsoft Internet Information Server (IIS) and Microsoft Internet Explorer take full advantage of the SSL and TLS secure Web communications standards.

Digital Signatures

Software downloaded from the Internet can contain viruses that are intended to damage the client computer or breach security. To make matters worse, many times the software is downloaded automatically and transparently as an ActiveX control or Java applet.

Microsoft developed a technology to allow developers to digitally sign code using X.509 certificates. This technology is called Authenticode. There are other third-party code-signature technologies that also use X.509 certificates. This digital signing of code allows users to verify the origin of the code being downloaded, as well as the integrity of the code.

Code signatures for software distributed over the Internet typically use a third-party certificate authority, as the public is more likely to trust a reputable third-party certificate authority. For internal software distribution, an enterprise certificate authority provides more flexibility.

Encrypting File System

Even when secure communications are used throughout the enterprise, there are circumstances where sensitive data can be in jeopardy. For example, a traveling laptop user could have the laptop stolen, or corporate offices could lose servers to burglars. In these cases, hackers with complete physical access to the systems could potentially use sector editors or other tools to access sensitive data.

Windows 2000 implements the Encrypting File System (EFS) to address this potential security breech. Files are encrypted as they are saved to disk, thereby protecting them from being deciphered even if read from the disk with a sector editor.

The EFS encrypts files using a combination of secret-key encryption and public-key encryption using the following processes:

1. Generates a random secret key.
2. Encrypts the file using the secret key.
3. Encrypts the secret key with the user's public key.
4. Attaches the encrypted secret key to the file.

This process ensures that Windows 2000 provides bulk encryption by using symmetric-key encryption to encrypt the files, yet it provides ease of access by using public-key encryption to secure the symmetric key.

Managing Security

Once security has been defined and implemented, it is critical to manage it on an ongoing basis. Your security plan should not be a static document or design, but rather one that evolves over time as changes arise.

Administrative Granularity

An important element in managing security is the delegation of authority. This might include delegating to other members of the administrative staff, or to the human resource group, or to managers. It is important to grant only the level of access that is necessary to perform the tasks, in order to ensure security. Windows 2000 facilitates this through its administrative granularity.

Monitoring

While the network infrastructure is running, it is important to monitor the performance and metrics. This could involve a comprehensive network and system-management routine, or the built-in tools such as Performance Monitor, or even a daily checklist conducted manually.

In the course of monitoring, trends can be viewed and problems identified before they affect the user community. From a security perspective, some things to monitor include failed logon attempts, hours of access, excessive data transfers, and other security events.

There should also be management reports generated from the system, identifying trends, events, and assessments of the overall health of the security infrastructure. These might be produced on a monthly or quarterly basis, depending on the needs of the organization.

Audits

The audit logs should be reviewed periodically for any security issues. This ensures that the security services are fully operational and continue to provide the same level of protection as when freshly implemented.

Security Reviews

It is also important to conduct periodic reviews of the security plan and infrastructure to ensure that the design continues to meet the needs of the organization. As organizations evolve, their security needs change and the security infrastructure should change accordingly.

Documentation

Whenever you make changes or delegate authority, it is important to update and revise any relevant documentation. Network administration documents should be considered living documents that grow and change over time, as the network infrastructure evolves.

SECURITY RISKS

The following is a rogue's gallery of security risks. Your organization may not face all of these risks, and every company must develop its own list of likely risks. This assessment will help you develop the strategies you need to deal with the risks specific to your organization.

Identity Interception

An intruder can gain access simply by obtaining a username and password combination. This can be accomplished with technical skills, using a protocol capture of a user's logon session, or by using brute-force password-cracking programs. However, phony ID access can also be accomplished through softer means, such as finding a password written at a careless user's desk or by watching the keyboard as a user types in a password.

Impersonation

Also known as "spoofing," impersonation is accomplished by an intruder assuming the IP address of a trusted system and gaining its access rights. Impersonation might occur midstream in a session that the impersonated system is having with the target resources.

Replay

Replay captures a valid user session, using a protocol analyzer and later playing it back to gain access to the target resources. Assuming the session was successful, it contains a valid username and password combination.

Interception

Data accessed by a valid user can be captured by an intruder without the knowledge of the user or target resource. This is possible if the information is transmitted across the wire as plaintext (without any encryption).

Manipulation

Transmitted data can be modified in transit, changing the results. For example, an intruder could capture a user's banking session and modify the amount and destination of a payment. A malicious internal user could manipulate a payroll transaction to increase the amount of his or her own paycheck.

Denial of Service

A denial of service attack seeks to prevent legitimate use of a resource. This is accomplished by flooding the target resource with fake requests, or by initiating a sequence of actions that trigger a failure of the target resource. Denial of service attacks frequently take advantage of software bugs.

Virus

"Virus" is the general term for malicious code that includes virus programs, macro viruses, Java applets, ActiveX controls, and other programs that intend to harm the target system. Viruses can be written from scratch or by modifying existing code.

Abuse of Privilege

Abuse of privilege describes the actions of a user who knowingly violates corporate policies to access or modify corporate data. This could include copying data to local media and moving it offsite, or granting other unauthorized users access to sensitive resources.

CHAPTER 4

Familiarizing Yourself with Windows 2000 Tools

Windows 2000 contains many tools that you can use to manage, administer, and support a Windows 2000 environment. Many of the tools you use in Windows 2000 are built on the Microsoft Management Console (MMC). Also, as in all Windows environments, the Control Panel plays an important part as the central location for other system utilities and services. Additionally, the event viewer provides a way to view problems that were logged by the operating system.

For readers migrating to Windows 2000 from Windows NT, I'll also explain where to find the common administration tools and functions in Windows 2000 from the perspective of a Windows NT network administrator.

THE MICROSOFT MANAGEMENT CONSOLE

The Microsoft Management Console (MMC) is the core utility under which all Windows 2000 administration tools run. The MMC is a common interface for the administration components known as *snap-ins*, which add specific functionality to the system. Snap-ins are included with Windows 2000 for functions such as adding users, setting site-to-site security, configuring DNS configurations, or monitoring system performance.

The MMC replaces the individual administrative applications in Windows NT, such as User Manager, RAS Administrator, Performance Monitor, and the like. You can now work in a single unified management tool, instead of loading dozens of individual applications for different management functions. Additionally, the MMC provides the ability to distribute administration tasks to other administrators. The MMC can be limited to only run selected components when you want to delegate administrative tasks.

Windows 2000 comes with a series of built-in administrative tools that make it easy to conduct configuration and administration tasks. However, you may prefer to customize the console screens for functions specific to your own organization.

It's a good idea to use the built-in tools until you become familiar with their functions and capabilities. Then you can create your own tools. You can add more snap-in components or create highly customized tools that you can distribute to other administrators.

Using the Built-in Administrative Tools

The built-in tools are not special or unique, and after you become familiar with the MMC, you can create a tool in a matter of minutes. The built-in tools just provide a quick way to begin administering and managing your Windows 2000 environment.

To view the built-in administration tools, select Start | Programs | Administrative Tools to see the list of programs shown in Figure 4-1.

Making Major and Minor Modifications to the Settings

You can use the built-in configuration tools to make major and minor modifications to a tool's behavior. Minor modifications include adding a new column to a view screen or

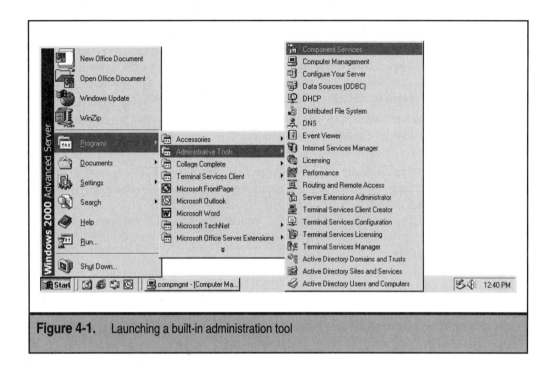

Figure 4-1.   Launching a built-in administration tool

deleting an unnecessary toolbar. Major modifications include adding additional servers to be monitored or defining new branches of the Active Directory tree.

When you make modifications to the built-in settings of the MMC, the changes are automatically saved. Note, however, that the built-in tools only allow you to maintain one set of configuration options. If you wish to switch between different sets of configuration options, you need to customize your own MMC, which permits you to configure and save multiple settings for specific administration tools.

What the Tools Do

Here's an overview of some of the administration tools that Microsoft has built into Windows 2000:

▼   **Active Directory Domains and Trusts**   Use this tool to manage a local domain and other domains in the organization. Domains are linked together through trust security, which is also defined, administered, and managed through this built-in tool. This tool can also link domains together to form interlinked directory trees and forests.

■   **Active Directory Sites and Services**   Use this tool to create new sites, or to link existing sites to new sites to form a multisite Active Directory tree. You can also create the necessary security to delegate administrative tasks to other administrators.

■ **Active Directory Users and Computers**   This tool creates new users in the domain, modifies user privileges, adds computers, and provides administration and management tools for these resources.

■ **Component Services**   Use this tool to add, delete, or modify the component objects installed on the server. Components in Windows 2000 include services such as COM+ and DCOM.

■ **Computer Management**   This tool provides a number of functions for configuring and managing the hardware and services on the computer. This includes managing disk drives (partitioning, formatting, and defragmenting drives), starting and stopping Windows 2000 services, viewing and modifying system devices, monitoring error events, and monitoring system performance.

■ **Configure Your Server**   This tool provides a menu and online help for a number of server services, such as invoking DNS administration, creating a domain controller, and administering add-in services.

■ **DHCP**   If you have DHCP loaded on your system, the DHCP administrator appears in the Administrative Tools submenu. The DHCP administrator controls the creation of DHCP scopes that dynamically provide IP addresses to computers on the network.

■ **Distributed File System**   The Distributed File System (DFS) tool provides the ability to create, modify, and administer DFS on the network.

■ **DNS**   If you have installed Domain Name System (DNS), the DNS administrator appears in the Administrative Tools submenu. The DNS administrator is where you create name servers on the network so that users can resolve names to IP addresses, and IP addresses to names.

■ **Event Viewer**   The Event Viewer provides a view of the error logs on the system. The event logs are organized into categories, which makes it easier to find the information you need.

■ **Internet Services Manager**   This tool provides the ability to administer and manage Web Services on your network. This includes creating virtual Web sites, creating folders below the main Web page, or configuring security for pages and folders managed by Web Services.

■ **Licensing**   The Licensing administration tool provides license controls.

▲ **Performance**   The Performance tool is used to monitor and analyze the operation of a server or servers on the network.

Creating Your Own Administrative Tools

While the built-in administration tools are quick and simple to launch and use, after a while, most administrators create tools that are specific to their needs. By customizing an administration tool, you can view multiple servers on a single screen, for instance. This centralization provides a quick view of all the systems you're responsible for. Other customizations can permit you to launch a single tool with all of the administration snap-ins loaded.

Centralizing Management in a Single Tool

The first task many administrators perform is to centralize management functions into a single console tool. The built-in administration tools were created to administer and manage only one server and one service at a time, but most administrators need to view, monitor, and manage multiple servers simultaneously.

UNDERSTANDING THE MMC CONSOLE   To begin customizing a single tool for administration, launch the basic Windows 2000 Microsoft Management Console program by selecting Start | Run and entering **mmc**. This launches the basic MMC console screen, as shown in Figure 4-2.

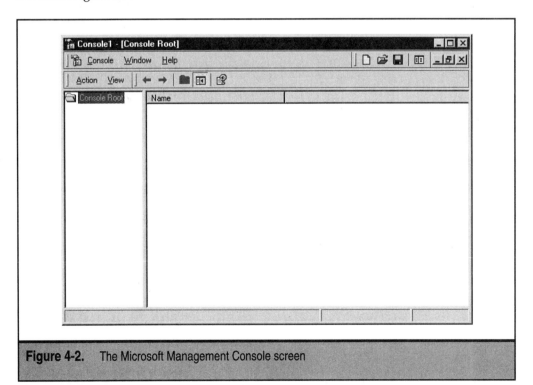

Figure 4-2.   The Microsoft Management Console screen

The main console screen displays two frames, a toolbar, and buttons:

▼ **Console frame**   The console frame is the frame around the entire MMC application. The console frame has pull down menus including Console, Windows, and Help.

■ **Console screen**   The console screen is the window within the console frame. This screen is where the administrative tools appear when they are installed in the MMC program.

■ **Standard menu**   The console screen contains the menu items, such as Action and View.

■ **Standard buttons**   Buttons provide navigation assistance when you are working with objects. These are the standard buttons.

▲ **Console tree**   The console screen is typically split into a right and left pane, and the console tree is the left pane.

CREATING A CENTRALIZED MMC CONSOLE   To design your own centralized MMC console, you need to add snap-ins to the console screen. To do so, choose Console | Add/Remove Snap-In. When the Add/Remove Snap-In screen appears, click Add to display the Add Standalone Snap-In window shown in Figure 4-3. Select the snap-ins you want to

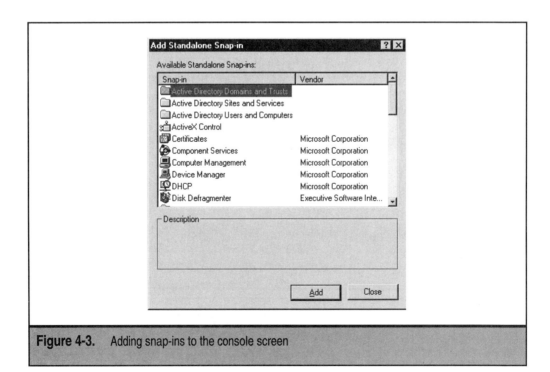

Figure 4-3.   Adding snap-ins to the console screen

add to your console screen, clicking Add as you select each one. You can add as many snap-ins as you wish.

Some of the snap-ins display an additional screen when you click Add. This additional screen typically asks whether you want to monitor the local computer or browse the entire network, in which case you can select another computer to monitor or manage. When you are administering a number of different computers for the same function, you have the ability to add multiple computers with the same snap-in function to a single MMC console screen.

When selecting multiple computers to manage, you can either add the snap-in multiple times (each time individually selecting a server to manage), or select the "Allow the selected computer to be changed when launching from the command line" checkbox. By selecting this checkbox, you only need to load a single instance of the snap-in, and right-click the snap-in at any time to select "Connect to another computer." If you don't have a lot of servers on your network, it's probably easier to load the snap-in multiple times to cover all the servers.

SAVING THE CENTRALIZED MMC CONSOLE FOR ADMINISTRATIVE USE   After you've added all of the snap-ins and servers you wish to manage or monitor, save your settings. Select Console | Save As and enter a filename for this tool (the system adds the .msc extension). Name the file descriptively, such as "Administer All DNS Servers," or "Performance Monitor for All North American Servers."

You can save the file to any location, but there are a few places that tend to be more strategic:

▼ **Desktop**   If you save the tool directly on your desktop, it is always available. To save to the desktop, select \Documents and Settings\{username}\Desktop\{filename} where {username} is your network logon name and {filename} is the descriptive name you are giving this console view.

■ **Personal Start menu**   You can save your administration tool to your Start menu. Select \Documents and Settings\{username}\Start Menu\{filename}.

▲ **Administrative Tools folder/menu**   You can save your administration tool to the Administrative Tools folder on the system you are logged on to, which is where all of the built-in tools are located. To save to the Administrative Tools folder on the local system, select \Documents and Settings\All Users\Start Menu\Programs\Administrative Tools\{filename}.

Distributing Management to Others

When you create an administrative tool that you want to distribute to others, you should limit the functions the target administrator can access. The following section discusses creating a limited MMC tool.

CREATING A DISTRIBUTED MMC CONSOLE   To create a console for distribution, launch the MMC utility with Start | Run and enter **mmc**, then press OK. Now you need to add the appropriate snap-ins, which you do by selecting Console | Add/Remove Snap-in. When the Add/Remove Snap-in window appears, click Add to bring up the Add Standalone Snap-in window. Choose the snap-ins you want to delegate to another administrator, and click Add to list them in the console. (Some snap-ins display an additional screen that offers options.)

If you wish to delegate administrative rights for multiple servers, select the appropriate server and add the snap-in again for additional servers.

SAVING THE DISTRIBUTED MMC CONSOLE FOR SPECIALIZED USE   After you create the new console, you can limit the MMC options for the delegated administrators:

▼ **Hiding the console tree**   If the administrator will only be managing a certain piece of a snap-in, you can limit access to the console tree. For example, if the administrator will only be viewing and managing the Services piece of the Computer Management snap-in, select the Services object in the console tree. The details for the Services object will appear in the right pane of the Console. Select View | Console Tree to deselect the console tree, leaving only the right pane with the services view active.

■ **Creating console taskpads**   You can limit a view even more by creating a new taskpad that allows you to select specific properties for administration. To create a console taskpad, select Actions | New Taskpad on the Console screen. This launches the Taskpad Creation Wizard. You can choose either a single item (which shows a list of properties to monitor or manage, as well as the details), or you can choose Standalone (which displays only the tasks). The Standalone option is much more limiting. Enter a name and description for this taskpad, and then select the Task Creation Wizard. You are prompted to choose between launching a shortcut menu or running an MS-DOS command (the common choice is a shortcut menu). A shortcut-menu command screen displays all the features of the snap-in. If you've selected a single item, you will have a series of options to choose from. If you've selected Standalone, you can only choose one item to delegate. You can add an icon to the option you selected, and then you can run the wizard again to add another stand-alone task. When you finish, the limited taskpad screen shows you the properties the administrator will be able to manage (see Figure 4-4).

■ **Hiding standard menus and buttons**   You can limit a delegated administrator's power by hiding the standard menus and buttons. Choose View | Customize and uncheck the box labeled Standard Menus (Action and View) and then uncheck Standard Toolbars to eliminate these elements. However, the administrator can still right-click any of the options to execute a command. See the console mode options to eliminate access to other commands.

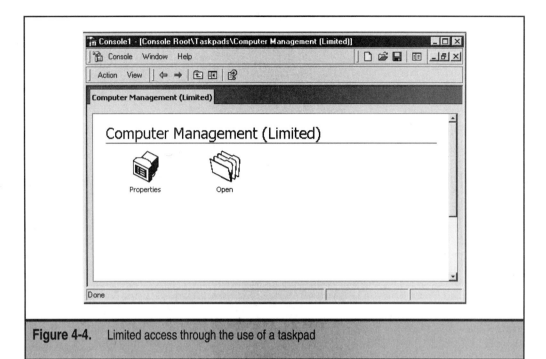

Figure 4-4.   Limited access through the use of a taskpad

▲ **Console mode**   The console mode is the final step to limiting a delegated administrator's access to management console functions. There are four options:

■ **Author mode**   Author mode provides access to all MMC functions, including the ability to add and remove snap-ins, create new windows, and navigate through the entire console tree.

■ **User Mode—Full Access**   The full-access user mode provides full access within the console screen of the MMC, including full control of the console tree and all objects in a snap-in. Users cannot add or remove snap-ins, nor perform console administration tasks, such as saving the console under a different name.

■ **User Mode—Limited Access, Multiple Window**   This option limits the user by removing the user's ability to open new windows and access areas of the control tree that were not visible when the console file was saved. Multiple child windows are allowed, but the user cannot close the windows.

■ **User Mode—Limited Access, Single Window**   This option limits the user to a single window. Any part of the console tree that was not visible when the console was saved is inaccessible to the user.

To set the console mode, select Console | Options and go to the Console tab. Select the appropriate option from the Console Mode list, and then save the console with a new name. Copy the file to the delegated administrator's desktop, Start menu, or Administrative Tools folder.

EVENT VIEWER

The Event Viewer lets you look at the log files of a computer. Most administrators usually wait until they have a problem before examining the Event Viewer. However, if you're not familiar with the tool, you will not know whether the information you are looking at is pertinent to your problem or not. Common events are logged regularly, and they are not indicative of a problem. You should learn how to use the Event Viewer and gain an understanding of the common events before you experience your first system problem. That way you will be able to distinguish the common events from the problem events.

Familiarizing Yourself with the Event Viewer

The first thing to do when working with the Event Viewer is to familiarize yourself with the Event Viewer information. When you launch the Event Viewer (select Start | Programs | Administrative Tools | Event Viewer), you will see a screen similar to the one shown in Figure 4-5.

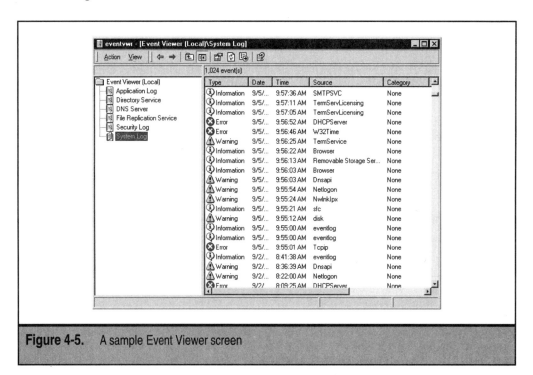

Figure 4-5. A sample Event Viewer screen

The Event Viewer logs different types of events, such as warnings, errors, and notes, into three or more log files. The severity levels of events logged by the application, and the details of the events of the error, can frequently be controlled by setting parameters in the application program. Not all applications log levels of severity the same way, so it takes some practice to determine whether a significant event in one application is as severe as an informational event in another application.

Levels of Severity

Within applications, you can usually set a debugging level for logging specific events. It is up to the application to determine whether an event is severe or not and to determine how that information is posted in the log. The application also determines where it places the event—whether it posts the event into the application log, security log, system log, or into a specific application log file accessible by the Event Viewer. Most of these parameters are not defined by the administrator, so you must know where to look for the information.

In addition to the levels of severity specified by an application, there are different categories of events, including errors, warnings, information, and audits.

▼ **Error**   An error event denotes a significant problem. Perhaps a service did not start or an application failed to launch.

■ **Warning**   A warning event denotes a significant event, but not a serious failure. Perhaps a user has typed a password incorrectly or disk space is running low.

■ **Information**   An information event denotes that something has occurred (typically successfully) and the information was simply noted in the logs. Informational events include notices that the event logs have started or that an email message successfully transferred from one server to another.

▲ **Audit**   Audits can be enabled and disabled by system-level security, and are focused on tracking information requested by the administrator. There can be audits placed on successful events or on failed events. For instance, you can audit a printer, recording events when a user is able or unable to attach to the printer (or both).

Log Files

There are at least three different logs in the Event Viewer: the Application Log, the Security Log, and the System Log. Unlike previous versions of Windows NT, where all events from all applications were written to one of these three logs, Windows 2000 creates additional, specific logs to make it easier for administrators to find information. Some of the additional log files created include the Directory Service, the DNS Server, and the File Replication Service logs.

APPLICATION LOG   The Application Log contains events logged by application programs. The events include notifications of email message transfers, database read and write activities, or Web server query events.

As noted previously, the Application Log only receives the information designated by the applications. It is up to the administrator to set logging or debugging levels high enough that the appropriate events are tracked.

SECURITY LOG   The Security Log contains events that affect the security of the server or the network, such as a successful or failed logon. The events that are logged can be specified by the administrator.

Security events are typically configured within security administration components to log, audit, and track events on the network. For example, you may be concerned that someone is attempting to log on to the network as an authorized user. To audit successful as well as failed logon attempts, enable audit logging with the following steps:

1. Select Start | Programs | Administrative Tools | Active Directory Users and Computers.

2. Right-click the Domain Controllers folder, and select Properties.

3. Choose the Group Policy tab.

4. Select the Default Domain Policy group, and then click Edit.

5. Double-click Computer Configuration.

6. Double-click Windows Settings.

7. Double-click Security Settings.

8. Double-click Local Policies.

9. Click the Audit Policy.

A number of audit options will appear, including Audit Account Logon Events, Audit Account Management, Audit Directory Services Access, Audit Logon Events, Audit Object Access, Audit Policy Change, Audit Privilege Use, Audit Process Tracking, and Audit Systems Events.

To track authorized and unauthorized logon events, enable the Audit Logon Events option. Any time a logon event occurs, the information will be logged in the Security Log on the server.

SYSTEM LOG   The System Log contains events logged by the Windows operating system, such as starting the event log, the failure of drivers to load, and so on. The event types logged by the system components in Windows 2000 are predetermined by the Windows operating system. An administrator cannot change what gets logged and what does not get logged.

OTHER LOG FILES   As noted earlier, Windows 2000 now includes additional log files beyond the Application, Security, and System logs. New files, such as the Directory Service,

DNS Server, and File Replication Service logs, are designed to track specific events for these services.

Common Events Seen in the Event Viewer

Key to reviewing and understanding the event logs on a Windows 2000 server is an understanding of what events are common events and what events are indicative of a problem.

Common Application Log Events

Some of the common application log events are as follows:

▼ **"Security policy in the Group policy objects are applied successfully" (Information)**   This is logged when the Group policy has been modified.

■ **"Adapter Type is Ethernet" (Information)**   This is a boot-up notification generated by the system.

■ **"The database engine started" (Information)**   Indicates the boot-up start process on the Active Directory.

■ **"The database engine is initiating recovery steps" (Information)**   Indicates common maintenance to the Active Directory database, and it is typically followed by the next event in this list.

■ **"The database engine has successfully completed recovery steps" (Information)**   The Windows 2000 Active Directory maintenance completed its normal update and maintenance; this typically follows the preceding event.

■ **"Service Start" (Information/Source: defined)**   The specified source has started. This is common for application services that start and stop on the server.

■ **"Product: {productname}—Installation operation completed successfully" (Information)**   The defined product completed installation successfully.

▲ **"Microsoft Exchange System Attendant has Started. Microsoft Exchange Server System Attendant, service startup complete" (Information)**   The Microsoft Exchange server system attendant service started successfully; this type of notification is quite common for most applications that are loaded on servers.

Common Security Log Events

By default, the Security Log is disabled, so you may find that when you go into the Security Log, the log is empty. To enable security logging, open the MMC and use Group Policy to select the Security Audit Policy. Some of the common Security Log events are as follows:

▼ **"Successful Network Logon" (Success Audit)**   This notifies you that a user (ID specified in the message) has successfully logged on to the network.

■ **"Special privileges assign to new logon" (Success Audit)**   This notifies you that the group policy has been edited.

■ **"A trusted logon process has registered with the Local Security Authority. This logon process will be trusted to submit logon requests" (Success Audit)** This informs you that a local security process known to the server has completed successfully.

▲ **"Object Open…" (Success Audit)** This notifies you that an object (as specified in the body of the log message) has successfully opened. You will receive many of these for objects and applications as they are loaded and launched.

Common System Log Events

Some of the common System Log events are as follows:

▼ **"Event Log Service was Started" (Information)** This event indicates the last time that the server was booted and started.

■ **"Event Log Service was Stopped" (Information)** This event tells you when the server was last shut down successfully.

■ **"The browser has forced an election on the network…because a Windows NT Server (or domain master) browser is started" (Information)** This informs you that an Active Directory synchronization has begun.

■ **"SMTP service has been started" (Information)** This informs you that a system service has been started. You will see many of these types of service notifications when modifications are made to the system.

▲ **"IPSec Policy agent started successfully" (Information)** This informs you that IPSec security is operational.

Problem Events Seen in the Event Viewer

It is not simple to define and outline problem events in the Event Viewer, because many error and warning events are simply informational events with some level of severity if the event affects other components of the network. Each organization needs to evaluate these error and warning events with respect to their own organization.

When an error occurs, information is sent to the event logs. Sometimes an error is a notification that a particular service failed to start, but the service may not be needed. In that case, it may be effective to disable the service so that an error does not appear in the Event Viewer the next time the system is started.

Finding Information Easily

As the networking environment gets larger, and more events are monitored and logged, the event logs can get very large very quickly. In some heavily logged environments, the event log can have hundreds of logged events in just a 10–15 second interval. With that many transactions, it is nearly impossible to find the information you need to determine whether the system is running properly or not.

You can get control over the logs in a variety of ways, such as by filtering events, sorting events, or exporting the information to a program like Microsoft Excel.

Filtering Events

Events can easily be filtered in the event log, based on any of a number of criteria. To filter events, select View | Filter to see a screen similar to the one shown in Figure 4-6. The log information can be filtered based on a starting and ending date, or even a starting and ending time of day. Events can be filtered for type (information events, error events, warning events, or audit events). If you know the source, category, user, computer, or event ID, you can filter on any of those criteria to narrow the information.

Sorting Events

You can arrange the information so that the newest information is displayed first (the default) or the oldest information is displayed first. Sometimes when you are trying to track down a system problem, it's more effective to sort the event log so that the oldest information is first. This shows the events in chronological order. To sort events, choose View | Newest First or View | Oldest First.

Exporting Information to Excel

Some administrators find managing information in the Event Viewer to be a very challenging experience and prefer to use a more familiar information tool, such as Microsoft

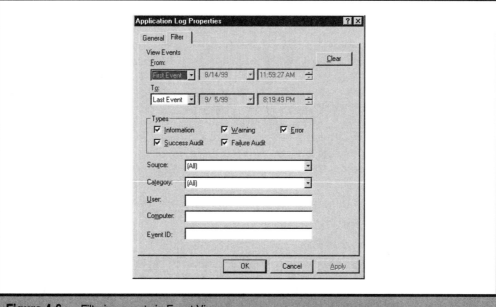

Figure 4-6.   Filtering events in Event Viewer

Excel. Information in the event logs can be exported to an Excel file by means of the following steps:

1. In the left pane of the Event Viewer, select the log file you wish to export.
2. Choose Action | Export List.
3. Enter a filename for the exported file.
4. Set the Save As type to be "Text (Comma Delimited)."
5. Select the directory in which you want to save the file.
6. Click Save to save the file.

After you save the file, launch Microsoft Excel or any other spreadsheet application you wish to use. Open the file you just saved by specifying the filename. Make sure to specify a .csv filename extension, because the file will be stored in a comma-delimited file format.

When you have the file on screen, you can sort or manipulate the data just as you would with any other spreadsheet file.

Error Events That Are Not Logged

Sometimes a system fails but an error event is not registered in the event logs. This commonly happens when there is such a catastrophic error that the system did not have time to write the error to the event log. Typically when a system locks up or fails, and the event is not registered in the event log, the problem is hardware specific.

When a system "bluescreens," causing a system failure where the dump code and error report is displayed on screen, the error is typically logged in the event log, because software or operating system controls have caused the system to fail while the system was able to display an error report.

THE WINDOWS 2000 CONTROL PANEL

Windows 2000 includes a Control Panel, shown in Figure 4-7, just like all previous versions of the Windows operating system. Some of the tools and utilities are new to Windows 2000. This section covers the key utilities for the administration and management of Windows 2000.

Common Control Panel Options

Some of the more common Control Panel options remain the same as in previous versions of Windows. Since the options are familiar, I will only briefly list them and their functions:

▼ **Accessibility Options** Accessibility options are alternative keyboard, sound, display, and mouse functions designed for people with motor skill, auditory, or visual impairments.

- **Date/Time**   The Date/Time option sets the time and date, and also sets the regional time zone.

- **Display**   The Display option configures the desktop, screen saver, and display resolution (640×480, 800×600, 1024×768, and so on), as well as the number of colors displayed on screen.

- **Folder Options**   The Folder Options set associations between file extensions and applications (which ensures that the correction loads when you double-click a file). You can also configure user interaction with the desktop, such as requiring single or double clicks to launch applications, folder-browsing options (opening multiple windows versus replacing windows), and enabling offline folders to synchronize information with a remote computer.

- **Fonts**   The Fonts option installs screen and print fonts.

- **Game Controllers**   The Game Controllers option configures joysticks or game controllers.

- **Internet Options**   The Internet Options set configuration options for the system browser, including the home page, security settings, connection to a proxy server, HTML editor, and email program.

- **Keyboard**   The Keyboard setting configures repeat-key settings, cursor-blink rates, and the type/language of the keyboard.

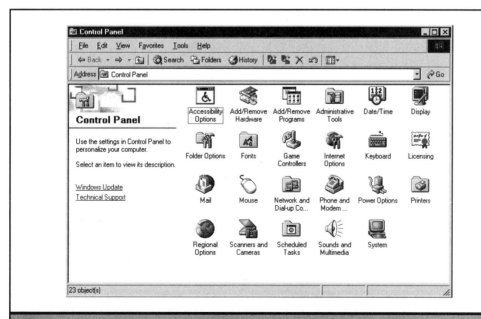

Figure 4-7.   The Windows 2000 Control Panel

- **Licensing**   Licensing tracks the Windows 2000 Server licenses (either per seat or per server).

- **Mail**   The Mail option configures support for electronic messaging (for Microsoft Exchange or an Internet service provider), including profiles and address book defaults.

- **Mouse**   The Mouse option configures the mouse, including changes to a left-handed mouse, the double-click speed, and selection of pointers.

- **Phone and Modem Options**   The Phone and Modem Options (which were separate options in previous versions of Windows) configure modem settings and dial-up locations.

- **Power Options**   The Power Options configure power schemes, including the ability to turn off the hard drive or monitor, or to hibernate the system after a period of inactivity. Additionally, there are extensive configuration options for laptops.

- **Printers**   The Printers option adds and configures printers.

- **Regional Options**   The Regional Options configure the locale, which affects the characteristics of numbers, currency, times, and dates.

- **Scanners and Cameras**   Scanners and Cameras options set the computer to work with these devices.

- **Scheduled Tasks**   Scheduled tasks can be configured to launch software and utilities on an unattended basis.

▲ **Sounds and Multimedia**   Sounds and Multimedia (which were separate options in previous versions of Windows) configures the sounds that are played at system events and also configures the audio and CD-ROM properties for playing multimedia files.

New or Modified Options in Windows 2000

Some of the Control Panel options in Windows 2000 are new to the system or have had significant modifications from previous versions of Windows.

Add/Remove Hardware

The Add/Remove Hardware option launches a wizard that walks an authorized user through the process of adding, removing, or troubleshooting a device. (Because Windows 2000 supports plug-and-play technologies, many devices are added automatically during the next boot-up and don't require the wizard.)

Add/Remove Programs

The Add/Remote Programs option allows an authorized user to install or delete software. You can also change the installation configuration, add or remove components, or remove an application entirely. In addition, you can add and remove Windows components.

Administrative Tools

The Administrative Tools option shows all of the built-in administration components available on Windows 2000. This includes utilities such as Computer Manager, Performance Monitor, Event Viewer, DHCP and DNS Administrators, and the like. (See "Using the Built-In Administrative Tools" earlier in this chapter.)

Network and Dial-Up Connections

The Network and Dial-Up Connections option is used to add, modify, or delete a network connection or a dial-up connection. Adding or modifying a network connection involves installing a network adapter and then configuring the communication protocol (TCP/IP, IPX/SPX, or NetBEUI). For dial-up connections, this option creates and configures connections to dial-up services such as a PPP dial-up service to a RAS server, or a Telnet or SLIP connection to a dial-up communication service.

System

The System option has a number of subcomponents for hardware, devices, and the computer environment.

NETWORK IDENTIFICATION   The Network Identification section of the System option is where an authorized user can change the name of the computer and change the workgroup or domain that the computer joins. You cannot change the name of a domain controller. However, you can demote a domain controller to be a stand-alone server and then change its name. See Chapter 13 for information about DCPromote.

HARDWARE   The Hardware tab on the System option controls a series of options, including adding and removing hardware from the system. You can also specify whether you require authentication of drivers.

▼   **Hardware Wizard**   The Hardware Wizard option launches the Add/Remove Hardware Wizard on the Control Panel.

■   **Driver Signing**   The Driver Signing option configures the system to require software applications to be validated (or signatures to be verified) before the application is installed. For organizations adhering to a strict "Windows 2000 certified application" environment, the option should be set to block the installation of any application not signed and authorized by Microsoft.

■   **Device Manager Tool**   The Device Manager tool allows the properties of a device to be viewed and modified. This includes changing the IRQ, Port Address, Memory Address, or configuration of the device manually.

▲   **Hardware Profiles**   Hardware profiles are useful when you need variations in the devices that are enabled during boot-up (such as laptops that occasionally connect to a docking station).

USER PROFILES   The User Profiles option in the Windows 2000 System properties displays the properties for users on the system. These properties can be copied to network shares so that a user can begin using roaming profiles, or to other specific computers.

ADVANCED   The Advanced tab on the System properties provides configuration options for performance, environment, and startup and recovery procedures.

  ▼   **Performance Options**   You can specify whether the system should be optimized for foreground application functions or for background application services and tasks. You can also change the size of the paging file.

  ■   **Environment Variables**   You can change the locations of system folders such as the temp folder, the location of the cmd.exe program, the folder where drivers are stored, and the folder where the Windows application program resides.

  ▲   **Startup and Recovery Options**   You can specify the number of seconds that elapse without a user choice before the operating system is loaded automatically at startup. Also, you can configure recovery options, such as where memory dump files are stored, and whether the computer automatically reboots after a fatal system error.

WINDOWS 2000 ADMINISTRATION FOR NT 4 ADMINISTRATORS

Nothing is more frustrating for a seasoned user of an operating system than to have options moved around. This section is dedicated to those of you who know how to administer and manage a Windows NT 4 environment and want to know where the familiar functions reside in Windows 2000.

System Hardware Configuration

The following are system hardware configuration options in Windows NT 4 and where to find the options in Windows 2000:

  ▼   Changing a server name or the domain in which a server resides (formerly done through the Control Panel | Networks option) is now done in the Control Panel | System | Network Identification tab. You can now demote a domain controller to be a member server and promote a member server to be a domain controller (see information on the DCPromote utility in Chapter 13).

  ■   Devices (formerly Control Panel | Devices) is now in the Control Panel | System | Hardware tab | Device Manager option.

  ■   Disk Administrator (formerly diskadm.exe) is now executed by launching the Computer Management snap-in by choosing Start | Programs | Administrative Tools | Computer Management | Storage | Disk Management.

- Hardware Wizard (formerly Control Panel | Hardware Wizard) is now in the Control Panel | System | Hardware tab option.

- Modems (formerly Control Panel | Modems) is now accessed from Control Panel | Phone and Modem Options on the Modems tab.

- MSInfo (formerly the msinfo.exe program) is now executed by launching the Computer Management snap-in by choosing Start | Programs | Administrative Tools | Computer Management | System Tools | System Information.

- Multimedia (formerly Control Panel | Multimedia) is now in the Control Panel | Sounds and Multimedia option under the Advanced Properties tab.

- Networks (formerly Control Panel | Networks) is now in Control Panel | Networks and Dial-Up Connections.

▲ Services (formerly in Control Panel | Services) is now executed by launching the Computer Management snap-in by choosing Start | Programs | Administrative Tools | Computer Management | System Tools | Services.

User and Group Administration

The following are User and Group Administration options in Windows NT 4 and their new locations in Windows 2000:

▼ Policy Editor (formerly poledit.exe) is now the Group Policy Editor. The Group Policy Editor is launched by selecting Start | Programs | Administrative Tools | Active Directory Users and Computers. Right-click on the domain, site, or organizational unit for which you wish to set policy, and select Properties. Click the Group Policy tab and select the Default Domain Policy. Click Edit and set group policies for Computers or Users.

- User Manager for Domains (formerly the usrmgr.exe program for the domain) is now the Active Directory Users and Computers snap-in. You can launch this snap-in by choosing Start | Programs | Administrative Tools | Active Directory Users and Computers.

▲ User Manager for Local Users and Groups (formerly the msrmgr.exe or usrmgr.exe program for the local computer) is now accessed by launching the Computer Management snap-in by choosing Start | Programs | Administrative Tools | Computer Management | System Tools | Local Users and Groups.

Network Administration

The following are Network Administration options in Windows NT 4 and their new locations in Windows 2000:

▼   Event Viewer (formerly the eventvwr.exe utility) is now accessed by launching the Computer Management snap-in by selecting Start | Programs | Administrative Tools | Computer Management | System Tools | Event Viewer, or by selecting the Event Viewer snap-in directory by selecting Start | Programs | Administrative Tools | Event Viewer.

■   Performance Monitor (formerly the perfmon.exe utility) is now accessed by launching the Computer Management snap-in by selecting Start | Programs | Administrative Tools | Computer Management | System Tools | Performance Logs and Alerts, or by selecting the Performance snap-in directory by selecting Start | Programs | Administrative Tools | Performance.

▲   Server Manager (formerly the svrmgr.exe program) is now accessed by launching the Active Directory Sites and Services snap-in by selecting Start | Programs | Administrative Tools | Active Directory Sites and Services. Double-click Sites, and either edit the site or double-click a specific site to get to the servers within the site.

Add-in Components

DNS (formerly dnsadmin.exe), DHCP (formerly dhcpadmn.exe), RAS Administrator (formerly rasadmin.exe), all from Windows NT 4, are now MMC snap-in programs in Windows 2000. They are found in Start | Programs | Administrative Tools. If you want to run a component that is not listed in the Administrative Tools submenu, start **mmc** from the Run command, and select Console, Add/Remove Snap-In. Then select the snap-in for the component you wish to administer.

CHAPTER 5

Windows 2000 Hardware

W indows 2000 provides new and important features for supporting hardware components. In this chapter, I cover hardware on two levels: standard hardware (CPU, RAM, hard drive, and LAN adapter) and the hardware enhancements in Windows 2000 (plug-and-play, USB, I₂O, and Fibre Channel).

HARDWARE COMPONENTS OF WINDOWS 2000

The standard hardware components of a system (CPU, RAM, disk, and network adapter) are important considerations as you plan your migration to Windows 2000. If you spend some time thinking through the Active Directory, security, and migration components of your Windows 2000 system, the number and size of servers can be planned in a methodical manner.

Microprocessor

The processor is one of the most important determinants of system performance. Generally the faster the processor, the faster the server. Systems are sold with 1, 2, 4, 8, or 16 processors.

The relationship between the number of processors and server performance is not as linear you may think. For example, on a file and print server there is a point at which little performance is gained by additional CPUs, because the CPU is not used very much for these tasks. Bottlenecks usually arise from the I/O components, such as hard drives or drive controllers. LAN adapters can also affect performance.

Application servers benefit from multiple processors as long as the applications have been designed for multithreaded execution. The type and architecture of the CPU can also impact the server's performance. In the Intel arena, Pentium II and Xeon processors are the chips of choice. Xeon chips have support for higher clock speeds and more Level 2 cache.

NOTE: You need Windows 2000 Advanced Server to take advantage of eight-way symmetrical processing, and you need the DataCenter version of Windows 2000 to take advantage of more than eight-way multiprocessing.

Microsoft's recommendations are 200MHz CPUs—Pentium Pro or better. Symmetric multiprocessing (SMP) is supported, but is not required. (For enterprise class servers, the system should support expansion to additional processors so that in the future you can add more processors if your server demands increase.) A minimum of a 256K Level 2 (L2) cache is recommended. (For Enterprise class servers with a single processor installed, the recommendation for L2 cache size is 512K or greater.) All multiprocessor systems typically have the equivalent of a minimum of a 256K L2 cache for each processor, and the L2 cache cannot be shared between processors in a multiprocessor system. (The caching requirement does not apply to processors that can achieve equivalent performance without an L2 cache.) If the L2 cache can be configured for either write-back or write-through mode, choose write-back cache mode to get the most system performance. Write-back cache means the cache controller responds immediately to the CPU and later writes the transactions to the main memory, rather than writing out transactions before signaling the CPU. Write-back technology prevents the cache from slowing down the system during high bus traffic.

NOTE: Multiprocessing systems must meet ACPI 1.0 specifications and Intel's Multiprocessor Specification (MP Spec) v1.4 or later. Most systems today will meet the specification, but systems that are a few years old will not.

There are a number of processor and system configuration options that allow an organization to scale their Windows 2000 servers as shown in Figure 5-1.

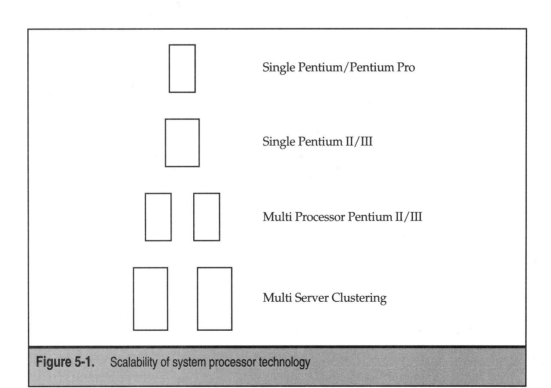

Figure 5-1.   Scalability of system processor technology

The Intel Pentium Server

When Intel released the Pentium processor in 1994, the ability of a file server to conduct multiple tasks simultaneously grew substantially. As the Pentium processor evolved from a 60MHz version to 200MHz or faster, multitasking application servers became possible for workgroups as large as 50–150 users.

The Pentium Pro Server

The Intel Pentium Pro processor has the ability to process even more information on a single processor, while still maintaining full compatibility with existing Intel-based software applications. A single-processor Pentium Pro server can easily manage application server needs of workgroups of up to 150–250 users.

The Pentium II and III Servers

In the late 1990s, Intel released a number of different processors, including the Pentium II and the Pentium III processor chips. These chips have significant improvements in processor performance over previous chips, and produce clock speeds in excess of 500MHz. A single-processor Pentium II or III server can easily manage application server needs of workgroups with up to 250–500 users.

Multiprocessor Servers

When you outgrow the capabilities of a single-processor Pentium (Pro, II, or III) system, consider a multiprocessor system. Unlike many previous network operating systems that either never supported multiple processors or produced limited gains in performance with 2–3 processors, Windows 2000 provides support for 16 or more processors with near linear scalability. Many computers and servers only support a single processor (or two at most), so when you're selecting your file server, look for multiprocessor support.

Server Clustering

If even a series of file servers that balance the load of the network is inadequate, consider clustering Windows 2000 servers to take advantage of server-to-server scalability. Server-to-server scalability gives you multiple servers that provide resource distribution that is far more efficient than any group of single servers. The server clustering process distributes the demands of the workgroup across multiple servers simultaneously. The cluster can access and manage resources at performance levels higher than ever achieved in a single-server environment.

Taking the Microsoft recommendations for minimum power into consideration, and adding some real-world experience, here are my recommendations for CPU sizing scenarios:

▼   **For heavy workloads**   1–4 capable Pentium III Xeon CPUs (400MHz, 512K–1MB cache). A powerful Intel/Microsoft solution using Pentium Pro and Pentium II architectures with full-speed cache, faster bus, better I/O systems.

- **For light workloads** 1–2 capable Pentium II or III CPUs (400MHz, 512K–1MB cache).

▲ **For DC and future expansion** 1–2 capable Pentium II or III CPUs (400MHz, 512K–1MB cache).

RAM

Another important component for Windows 2000 is random access memory (RAM). When the system runs out of RAM, it uses the hard disk for virtual memory, which is much slower and less efficient. Swapping causes a significant degradation in system performance and should be avoided at all costs. Your Windows 2000 system should have enough memory to prevent disk swapping. Let's take a look at what suggested minimums are from Microsoft and then some of my recommendations for basic servers, workgroup servers, and enterprise servers.

Windows 2000 Professional workstations must have a minimum of 64MB of RAM, with a suggested minimum of 96MB of memory. Workgroup servers, typically used for file and print and client/server applications, should have a minimum of 128MB for RAM. Enterprise, application, or multiprocessor servers should have a minimum of 256MB RAM. As you get further into high-availability enterprise application servers, you typically require significantly more memory to meet the caching requirements of the application. With Windows 2000, there's no longer a 2GB or 4GB limit on RAM. Windows 2000 can address and manage several gigabytes of memory, both for application access as well as system cache.

Error-correcting code (ECC) RAM, designed specifically for servers, is typically more costly than standard RAM memory chips, but for enterprise and mission-critical environments it is worth it. ECC memory provides high-availability capabilities because it can detect and correct common memory errors without bringing the server down with a memory error.

NOTE: Multiprocessor systems must have a minimum of 256MB of RAM for each processor installed.

The more users and storage a server supports, the more RAM you will need. Unfortunately there's no simple formula that says if you have 100 users accessing the server for file and print servers that you need to have a certain amount of RAM per user.

I've created an initial suggestion for RAM and disk storage for a standard server configuration in Table 5-1 as a reference.

Remember that as you add more services (Web services, DNS services, index services, etc.) to Windows 2000 servers, the demand on file server RAM is also increased.

If your system runs mission-critical applications, RAM becomes even more important. Because of recent advances in the manufacturing of chips, and the densities of chips themselves, most enterprise application servers can hold 2GB or 4GB of RAM out of the box. Standard RAM, ECC (error-correcting code), and EDO (extended data out) memory

Users per Server	File and Print Only	Application Server (Exchange / SQL)
20 users	Pentium/Pentium Pro, 96MB RAM, 4GB disk	Pentium II, 192MB RAM, 16GB disk memory
50 users	Pentium/Pentium Pro, 128MB RAM, 8GB disk	Pentium III, 256MB RAM, 32GB disk
100 users	Pentium II, 192MB RAM, 16GB disk memory	Dual-processor Pentium II or III, 512MB Ram, 64GB disk
200 users	Pentium III, 256MB RAM, 32GB disk	Three-processor Pentium II or III, 768MB RAM, 96GB disk
500 users	Dual-processor Pentium II or III, 512MB RAM, 64GB disk	Four-processor Pentium II or III, 1GB RAM, 128GB disk
750 users	Three-processor Pentium II or III, 768MB RAM, 96GB disk	Four-processor Pentium III Xeon, 1GB RAM, 128GB disk
1,000 users	Four-processor Pentium III Xeon, 1GB RAM, 128GB disk	Six-processor Pentium III Xeon, 1.5GB RAM, 160GB disk
1,500 users	Six-processor Pentium III Xeon, 1.5GB RAM, 160GB disk	Eight-processor Pentium III Xeon, 2GB RAM, 256GB disk

Table 5-1.   Sample "per Server" Configurations for Windows 2000

all cost about the same (SDRAM costs slightly more), so get the error correcting and the fastest RAM possible.

Storage

Of course, the way you use a server has a direct relationship to the amount of storage you'll need on that server. On an application server, disk storage may be greater for application services functions that manage data (such as a SQL Server or Exchange Server), but for some application services like DNS or remote access services, the storage demands are not as extensive.

Sizing the Required Disk Storage

To measure your disk storage needs, tracking the growth of disk storage demands on the current system can help you determine the storage demands for the future. For example, if your existing server storage demands grow over a 30-day period by 100MB, and you want to keep up to three years of files available to users, 36GB of storage space will be able to handle the projected storage needs.

There are many factors that either increase or decrease this storage demand estimate. There are a variety of causes for the variations. Factors that could increase your storage needs include the following:

▼ Implementation of knowledge management systems (such as forms, contact management, document imaging, audio/video, or faxing).

■ Increase in the number of users accessing and storing information (through business growth or acquisition/merger).

▲ User shift from nonelectronic methods of storage (such as paper, microfiche, audiotape) to electronic storage.

Factors that may decrease your storage needs, include the following:

▼ Use of file compression, which is supported by Windows 2000.

▲ Automatic file archiving, also known as hierarchical storage management (HSM), which is supported by Windows 2000. HSM lets you migrate files to other servers for temporary or permanent storage. (You'll find more information on HSM in Chapter 9.)

Storage can be just as important on an enterprise application server as on traditional file and print server implementations. In most cases, high-capacity, non-ISA, low latency (low access and seek times), high-speed devices (20 Mbps to 40 Mbps data transfer rates) with full SCSI-3 support is a must. On many server systems, the system board itself has an embedded SCSI adapter. There are a number of variations in SCSI adapters, and in the devices the adapters support. For instance, you can use differential SCSI, automatic and built-in termination, start/stop support to decrease power consumption, and external SCSI-2 connections. For the fastest performance, look for drive subsystems that have the highest level of throughput (minimum of 40 Mbps), taking advantage of some of the latest ultra 2 low voltage differential (LVD) implementation-capable disk subsystem devices that can support burst transfers up to 80 Mbps. Disks that spin at 10,000 rpm will also help with throughput. Table 5-2 is a summary of various hard drive technology specifications.

Fibre Channel is even faster than SCSI. It's based on the same protocol as Gigabit Ethernet and supports data transfer rates of up to 100 Mbps, full duplex. It's expected that the speed will reach 400 Mbps in a few years.

ISA-based IDE is not recommended for use in servers. If you must use IDE, the specifications for compliance are ATA-2, dual-PCI IDE adapters, support for drives larger than 528MB, support for bus mastering, and fulfillment of the self monitoring analysis and reporting technology (S.M.A.R.T) standard.

CD-ROM specifications for Windows 2000 are similar to those in NT 4 or other networking environments. Use drives with a minimum speed of 8X, and the ability to boot

Controller Technology	Performance Specification
IDE	Limited transfer speeds; 528MB limit
EIDE	Faster transfer speeds; limited to two drives per channel
SCSI	5MB transfer, 8-bit bus, 8 devices per channel
Fast SCSI	10MB transfer, 8-bit bus, 8 devices
Fast-Wide SCSI	20MB transfer, 16-bit bus, 16 devices
Ultra SCSI	20MB transfer, 8-bit bus, 8 devices
Wide Ultra SCSI	40MB transfer, 16-bit bus, 16 devices
Wide Ultra SCSI	40MB transfer, 8-bit bus, 8 devices
Wide Ultra-2 SCSI	80MB, 16-bit bus, 16 devices
Fibre Channel	100MB+, 32-bit, 32+ devices

Table 5-2.   Disk Controller Technology Specifications

directly from the CD-ROM drive (for easier software installation). DVD drives should support direct memory access, bus mastering data transfers, and universal disk format. For Windows 2000 Professional, you may want drives that support audio and video from CD-ROM or DVD, a high-speed bus supporting multiple data formats, sustained transfer rates of 12 Mbps, and support of video playback standards such as MPEG-2.

Every server system should include a tape drive for backup, restore, and archiving purposes. SCSI-based tape drives that hold at least 4GB of data and can attain throughput speeds of 20 Mbps are a minimum recommendation for basic servers. For enterprise servers, the tape capacity should be at least 8GB.

Network Interface Cards (NICs)

The network adapter in a Windows 2000 server is the portal of communication between the clients and the server. On a small network (less than 50 users), all users, file servers, and printers are typically connected to a single segment. However, if your organization or workgroup exceeds 50–70 users, you may elect to split the network's physical connections so that the number of users on the network is limited. Rather than have 100 users vying for the single port connection on a file server, split the network into two separate segments of 50 users each.

ISA or PCI?

The introduction of Peripheral Component Interconnect (PCI) and multiple expansion bus slot types have expanded the considerations available to you when you're selecting network adapters. Performance, bus sharing, and ease of configuration are three important issues.

Performance should always be your top priority when choosing network interface cards. PCI offers many advantages over ISA. PCI has a bus speed of 33MHz, while the ISA bus speed runs at 16MHz or slower. The bus width between the two is also different—PCI has a bus width of 32 bits, while ISA has a bus width of 16 bits. Because the PCI bus is four times faster and two times wider than ISA, the PCI bus can move two times the data and can move it four times faster than ISA.

Ease of use in configuring PCI cards is a big plus in terms of time and troubleshooting. Integrated peripherals monopolize ISA resources. For example, many system boards come with two IDE channels, a parallel port, a serial port, SVGA, and sometimes a sound card. Unused devices can be disabled, but they still require an ISA configuration utility for BIOS modification and resource allocation. In contrast, PCI resources are assigned automatically, so conflicts are not an issue.

ISA cards are adequate for older machines, but in order to realize the full potential of modern PCI-based personal computers in today's enterprise network environments, PCI is the preferred type of network adapter.

Half-Duplex or Full-Duplex?

There are two modes of operation to consider when looking at NIC communications speed across the network: half-duplex and full-duplex. Half-duplex is a slower, one-way mode of transmission. Full-duplex is a faster, two-way mode of transmission.

Half-duplex is the most common transmission method. It is adequate for most normal workstation and PC connections, since most network drivers and hubs/routers are configured and designed for half-duplex. Many network infrastructures may not support full-duplex request/response connections and are unlikely to benefit (or even operate properly) with full-duplex communication. Half-duplex works optimally when one device transmits and all others receive, as shown in Figure 5-2; otherwise, collisions are likely to occur. If collisions are detected, any devices involved in the collision perform exponential backoff, and then retransmit when the transmission media is clear of collisions. Throughput is therefore limited by the need to retransmit data when collisions occur.

If your network adapter and internetworking infrastructure support full-duplex, it is obviously best to set all devices to take advantage of the significantly higher performing full-duplex capabilities. However, I have seen significant LAN and WAN I/O performance problems caused by attempting to configure a server for full-duplex when all devices on the internetwork do not support (or do not properly support) full-duplex. If you experience network performance problems, or network packet failures, drop your servers down to half-duplex and retry the system operation.

Full-duplex provides dual communication on a point-to-point connection, and simultaneously transmits and receives on a single connection (see Figure 5-3). It is supported only on media that contain separate transmission and reception conductors or fibers such as 10BaseT or 100BaseT. Full-duplex operation is not possible on connections using coaxial (10Base2) or AUI (10Base5) cabling or most hubs. Typical uses for full-duplex are server-to-server, server-to-switch, or switch-to-switch connections.

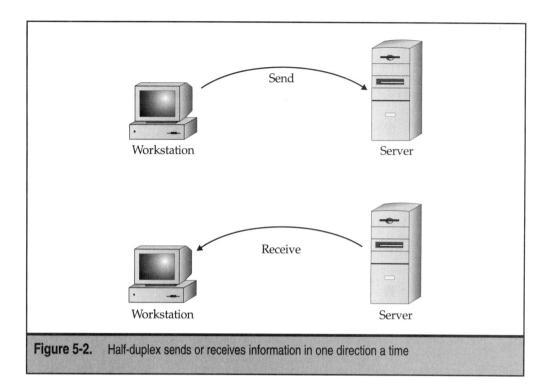

Figure 5-2. Half-duplex sends or receives information in one direction a time

Theoretically, if reads and writes on a full-duplex link are symmetric, data throughput can be doubled. In actual usage, bandwidth improvements are more modest. Even so, full-duplex eliminates collisions and doesn't force a station to wait until another station stops transmitting.

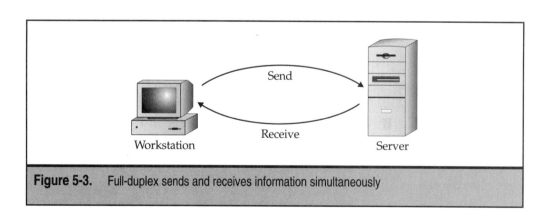

Figure 5-3. Full-duplex sends and receives information simultaneously

Automatic duplex, another feature, negotiates whether or not the attached device is transmitting in half-duplex or full-duplex, and then switches to that mode of operation, maximizing transmission speeds.

Autonegotiation is another feature that improves the effectiveness of dual-speed links that have the capacity to work at either speed (10 Mbps or 100 Mbps) and either duplex mode (half- or full-duplex). This feature eliminates the need to manually configure the speed or mode. The hardware detects the capabilities of devices across the wire, and self-configures itself automatically to use the same technology.

NOTE: With Ethernet and Fast Ethernet, full-duplex is limited to a single connection between two devices (i.e., a server and a switch). For three or more devices attached to the same segment, only half-duplex operation is possible.

WINDOWS 2000 BASIC SYSTEM CONFIGURATION

Beyond the basic hardware requirements and specifications, Windows 2000 has basic disk storage as well as software licensing components.

Hard Drive Space Requirements

The hard drive disk space requirement for Windows 2000 varies depending on the installation components. The basic installation of Windows 2000 requires approximately 270MB of disk space. This includes the core operating system and its associated DLL drivers, configuration files, and executables. Each additional server component takes up 5–25MB, and a full installation of Windows 2000 with all components uses about 450MB.

Most organizations copy the Windows 2000 installation CD contents to the boot drive of the server. This installs new components without having to insert a CD-ROM. If you copy the files from the \I386 directory of the CD-ROM (for Intel-based configurations), add an additional 550MB of storage requirements.

Software Licensing

You are responsible for determining the legal licensing required for your installation. Some administrators aren't sure whether they need to purchase a client license in addition to the core Windows 2000 server license, or whether they need to purchase a license at all (since Windows 9*x* and NT 4 workstations automatically connect to the Windows 2000 server).

You must purchase Windows 2000 Server, Advanced Server, or DataCenter for each server. Each client workstation that attaches to any of the Windows 2000 servers for access to file services or printer services managed by the server needs to have a valid client access license, or CAL. However, if the Windows 2000 server is only acting as an application server (such as an Exchange mail server, SQL database server, IIS Web server, or the like), then licenses for the application need to be purchased, but not client licenses for accessing the server. You only need a client license when the client accesses the server for reading and writing to the server's hard drive.

For Windows 2000 Professional, any desktop or laptop system with Windows 2000 Professional installed requires a Windows 2000 Professional software license.

HARDWARE ENHANCEMENTS

Windows 2000 provides better hardware functionality than previous versions of NT. The new technologies include plug-and-play, the Windows Driver Model (WDM), the universal serial bus (USB), and wider product support for devices such as DVD drives, Intelligent Input/Output (I_2O), and Fibre Channel. These new features in Windows 2000 are technology enhancements that can greatly improve the performance you get from your implementation of Windows 2000.

Plug-and-Play

Windows 2000 now supports plug-and-play, a combination of hardware and software support that enables a computer to recognize and automatically adapt to hardware changes without user intervention or system rebooting. With plug-and-play (PnP), a user can add or remove devices dynamically, without awkward and often confusing manual configuration, and without intimate knowledge of a computer's operation. For example, a user can dock a laptop computer and use the docking station's Ethernet card to connect to the network and its resources. The user undocks the system later and uses the same laptop with an internal NIC, and connects to the network without making any configuration changes.

A new Hardware Wizard and Device Manager (as shown in Figure 5-4) makes it easier to install, configure, and troubleshoot new hardware such as peripherals, CD-ROMs, NICs, and hard drives. These features reduce the need for server reboots and software reinstallation.

Plug-and-play and power management have slowly evolved since their introduction in Windows 95. Tightly integrated with this growth has been the OnNow initiative, which includes Advanced Configuration and Power Interface (ACPI). This specification defines a new system board, plug-and-play BIOS, and Advanced Power Management (APM). ACPI is independent of the CPU or operating system and enhances system design flexibility.

Unlike PnP in Window 9x, Windows 2000 PnP implementation does not depend on an APM BIOS or a plug-and-play BIOS. These two implementations were developed in the early implementations for support of PnP and power management. They are maintained in Windows 2000 for backward compatibility only, and ACPI provides both of these services in Windows 2000.

One design goal of Windows 2000 and plug-and-play is to enhance the existing Windows NT infrastructure in support of PnP and power management while maintaining

New Hardware Found

Bus Toaster - PCMCIA SCSI Host Adapter (Alternate)

Windows is installing the software for your new hardware.

Figure 5-4.   The Windows 2000 Hardware Wizard and Device Manager

support for industry standards for PnP. Another goal is to achieve common device driver interfaces that support PnP and power management for multiple device classes in Windows 2000 and future operating systems.

PnP is optimized for laptop, workstations, and server computers that support ACPI system boards and provides support for device classes provided within the Windows Driver Model (WDM).

NOTE: Windows 2000 will support some legacy Windows NT drivers. However, those drivers will have no plug-and-play or power management functionality. Responsibility for creating new driver sets lies with individual hardware manufacturers.

Beyond just recognizing new devices in your system, plug-and-play in Windows 2000 also includes enhancements to networking functionality called disconnect, sleep, and wake-up modes.

In previous versions of Windows plug-and-play, even though the laptop or desktop recognized system changes and installed the appropriate driver, you needed to reboot the system (sometimes a complete cold boot) to use the new device.

In Windows 2000, when you install a driver for a new network adapter, Windows 2000 invokes a wake-up command that enables the adapter, and then automatically attempts to log the user on to the network, as shown in Figure 5-5. If the user has not entered a proper logon name or password, a screen pops up to allow the user to complete the authentication process.

When a Windows 2000 system is disconnected from the network by a plug-and-play disconnect (such as a PCMCIA laptop network adapter ejected from the slot, or a laptop ejected from a desktop docking station), Windows 2000 will automatically disconnect and log the user off the network. The laptop operating system will recognize that the system is disconnected from the network, and so will know not to attempt to access network resources like drive letter attachments, network printers, or other (unavailable) network devices. When the system is reconnected to the network, the system is reauthenticated to the domain, and devices become available to the user once more.

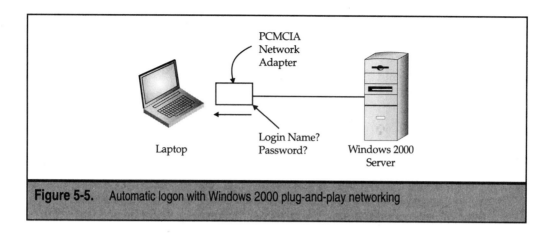

Figure 5-5. Automatic logon with Windows 2000 plug-and-play networking

Finally, with Windows 2000 plug-and-play networking, if the system (laptop or desktop) is put into a sleep mode (which is common in "green" energy-conserving or battery power management-conserving systems), the network connection is put into a sleep state. In previous operating systems, this sleep state would frequently cause the system to drop its connection to the network, but Windows 2000 flags the connection as sleep/dormant. When the system is activated again, the connection is validated for security, and the user is authenticated to the network automatically.

Windows Driver Model

The Windows Driver Model (WDM) is designed to provide a common architecture of services and device drivers for both the Windows 9x and Windows NT operating systems. In previous versions of Windows 95 and NT, there were driver incompatibilities between the operating systems. In Windows 2000, the WDM means hardware vendors can write one driver to run on both Windows 9x and 2000 operating systems. The new model provides a binary-compatible driver that should increase the number of drivers available to Windows 2000 administrators and allow them to use a greater array of add-on hardware. The WDM provides support for a variety of devices. Input drivers support DirectX, keyboards, mice, and joysticks. The universal serial bus (USB) supports cameras, modems, and audio. Imaging is included with support for still image and scanner via parallel, USB, and SCSI. Multimedia is enhanced via a new audio stack. The new Institute of Electrical and Electronic Engineers (IEEE) 1394 specification, an offshoot of Apple Computer's Firewire Initiative, is for interconnecting high-speed devices such as cameras and storage. Windows 2000 compatibility with Windows 9x brings NT out of isolation, a feature that will benefit companies that run both Windows operating systems.

The WDM adds several other features not currently available in NT device drivers, such as power on now and plug-and-play. As mentioned earlier, plug-and-play allows hardware to be added to a system with little or no configuration required. Power on is now part of the power management feature set in WDM. This allows powering down of devices not in use to achieve the most efficient power usage. It also eliminates startup and shutdown delays by taking a snapshot of the system's working state (both virtual and physical) before entering hibernation mode. That information is written to an image file on the hard disk. When the system is powered on, the image file is read and the operating system is returned to its state before hibernation. WDM is a combination of hardware and software that allows greater system flexibility and control.

Universal Serial Bus (USB)

The new USB technology provides a dramatic increase in communication speed between devices and the computer. A USB port can functionally replace the communication ports found on the back of computers. Using a single cable/port, USB allows connection of 127 peripherals to the computer, and can support a cable distance as long as 5 meters (more than 15 feet). USB also allows hot-swap insertion and removal—similar to plug-and-play as found in the Windows 95/98 operating systems—without powering down or reconfiguring the computer. When a device is added or removed, the system automatically detects the change and then loads or unloads the appropriate driver.

The USB communication channels put more information through the cable than just data; it also supplies a 5V power line to power the connected devices. This means you can do away with many of the connector cables, power cables, and power supplies that are needed for current devices.

In comparison to parallel and serial ports, USB ports are incredibly fast. USB has two data speeds: 1.5 Mbps for lower-end devices such as mice or keyboards, and 12 Mbps for higher-end devices such as scanners, printers, monitors, or modems (12 Mbps is comparable to the speed of a 10BaseT network)!

While not all of the devices the USB can handle are available in the market, there are many current uses for USB:

▼ Input devices, such as keyboards, mice, and joysticks

■ Communication devices, such as telephones and modems (both analog and digital)

■ Output devices such as monitors and printers

■ IEEE 1394 (Firewire) digital cameras

■ WDM digital audio such as MP3, Liquid Audio, and Multimedia

■ DVD movie playback

■ WMD still image capture such as scanners and printers

▲ WDM video capture

DVD

Windows 2000 includes built-in support for DVD devices. The driver support is included within WDM. Windows 2000 supports DVD movie playback as well as DVD-ROM as an optical storage device. DVD is a natural enhancement of CD-ROM and will provide the next generation of optical storage technology for an unforeseen number of future computing devices.

DVD provides digital data storage that spans audio, video, and computer data. It has the potential of replacing current storage media such as laser disc, audio CD, CD-ROM, and VHS video. In fact, DVD was designed for multimedia applications. Because of the compression technologies currently used (MPEG-2 and AAC-3), over two hours of audio and video can be stored on a single disk.

Windows DVD support is provided through the following components:

▼ Windows Driver Model–based DVD driver with full support for universal disk format (UDF) file system version 1.5

■ Windows Driver Model Streaming Class Driver

■ DirectShow

■ DirectDraw hardware abstraction layer (HAL) with video port extensions (VPE)

■ Copyright protection

▲ Regionalization

Intelligent Input/Output (I_2O)

CPUs in today's high-performance server systems often spend too much time idle, waiting for data to arrive, or acting as managers of the I/O processes. The I2O Special Interest Group developed and established the open input/output architecture that handles the demands of the current and future Intel microprocessors.

In terms of server throughput, I/O has become the bottleneck. Great leaps in CPU and memory performance have outpaced the increase in I/O processing requirements. A fast CPU is undermined by the intense amount of asynchronous interrupt required by I/O processing. The interrupts bog down the processor, so few resources are available for application processing. I_2O relieves the CPU from the burden of processing asynchronous interrupts.

The I_2O architecture includes three parts: an I/O processor dedicated to handling I/O requests, a split driver that features both OS and device driver interfaces, and a peer-to-peer communication layer that streamlines communication between hardware devices. The architecture is designed to facilitate Intelligent I/O systems, and increase system scalability and availability. This means more users can be supported on a single server. The Intelligent I/O subsystems allow interrupts (network and storage transactions) to be handled by the I/O subsystem, freeing the CPU to perform application tasks. I_2O architecture enables the I/O subsystem to scale with CPU power, increasing overall system performance.

I_2O is a software spec that is being implemented into server, adapter card, and OS products. Versions 1.0 and 1.5 of the specification address LAN and storage subsystem peripherals; version 2.0 encompasses hot-plugging PCI technology, clustering, Fibre Channel, ATM, and WAN support. The I_2O driver model includes two parts: OSM (OS services model) which interfaces with the host operating system, and HDM (hardware device module) that interfaces with the device, media, or server the driver must manage. The modules interface through a communication system composed of two layers: the message layer, which establishes the communication session, and the transport layer, which defines how to share information.

PCI hot plug will provide support for server tot plugging features in the I_2O architecture, and 64-bit addressing will give I/O devices the ability to address more than 4GB of memory. Enhanced PCI transport reduces main processor accesses across the PCI bus and allows direct memory access for better performance. Peer-to-peer technology allows peer cards to talk to each other on the PCI bus. The I/O traffic bypasses the host CPU, memory, and system bus, freeing resources for applications processing. Potential applications for this technology could include video files, online storage, and remote storage backup.

The best application of I_2O will initially be targeted for I_2O products in enterprise computing environments, which face the largest I/O bottlenecks. Future uses of I_2O may include desktop and workstation implementations. Due to increasing interest from industry and private sectors to achieve higher throughput with graphical applications, workstations may be the next implemented platform.

I_2O is creating a paradigm in the PC server industry by creating a common approach for managing and scaling I/O in server systems. IT managers benefit financially as manufacturers provide better, more cost-effective server solutions, with more bandwidth to handle future demands. I_2O is becoming the industry standard interface for I/O functions in server computing systems.

Fibre Channel

Fibre channel is the solution for enterprise systems that need reliable, cost-effective information delivery and storage. With development beginning in 1988 and ANSI standard approval in 1994, Fibre Channel (FC) is a safe solution for high-speed communications. Today's enterprise architecture and technology explosion provides unprecedented challenges in data warehousing, imaging, audio video integration, network storage, collaborative projects and products, and computer aided design and engineering.

Fibre channel is a cost-effective solution for storage and networks, because it provides versatile connectivity with scalable performance. FC ensures the reliability of communications, because it is capable of sustained delivery of information. FC has support for gigabit bandwidth now, with even better bandwidth possibilities in the future. It also supports multiple topologies: dedicated point to point, shared loops, and scaled switch technologies, and multiple protocols: SCSI, TCP/IP, raw data, or video.

FC supports environments from single point-to-point links, to enterprises with hundreds of servers, all with high efficiency. It is congestion-free, using credit-based flow control that delivers data as fast as the data is buffered and received, all with low overhead. Most important, the Fibre Channel protocol is specifically designed for highly efficient hardware operation.

Fibre Channel is ideal for applications such as:

▼ High-performance storage

■ Large databases and data warehouses

■ Storage backup systems and recovery

■ Server clusters

■ Network-based storage

■ High-performance workgroups

■ Campus backbones

▲ Digital audio/video networks

FC is being offered as a standard disk interface by many hardware vendors and RAID manufacturers. Fibre Channel loop and redundant loops are integrated into server backplanes, providing 100-Mbps full-duplex input/output operation, hot-swap storage drive capability, and eliminating SCSI problems of distance, bandwidth, scalability, and reliability. Storage devices (disks, RAID arrays, tape backup units, etc.) can be implemented on a totally separate network of their own, using Fibre channel arbitrated loop (FCAL), also referred to as a storage area network (SAN). Data is delivered to servers anywhere on the network, and backed up during working hours with little or no increase in traffic, which is a real benefit in today's distributed network.

PART II

Designing and Planning the Migration to Windows 2000

As I highlighted in the first part of the book, Windows 2000 adds a number of new technologies and features to the desktop and server operating environment. While it is tempting to begin installing the software already, it is important to methodically design and plan the migration or implementation to minimize the potential for problems after the network has been installed.

In this second part of the book, I will cover how organizations are designing and planning their migration to Windows 2000 and what lessons they have learned in the process of implementing a Windows 2000 environment. The first couple of chapters will cover how to design an Active Directory and DNS infrastructure that will provide advanced security and administration capabilities to the network structure. This part includes a chapter on designing a scalable connectivity infrastructure to support the servers and desktops throughout the organization as well as a chapter on designing key servers to provide the services the organization requires to manage files, printers, and network-based applications. And with thin-client and Web-based information access growing in demand throughout the industry, there is a chapter on designing a thin-client terminals services environment. Last, I will finish this part of the book with a chapter on creating a microcosm that will put all of the plans and designs to a practical test in a prototype lab environment.

CHAPTER 6

Planning Your Active Directory

P lanning your implementation of Active Directory is a time-consuming but necessary task. It's critical to put together a design team to validate and sign off on essential design elements. Although Active Directory allows ongoing configuration for fine-tuning and redesign, this is not an excuse to forego planning and create a sloppy Active Directory structure.

Don't expect the first installation of Active Directory to be perfect. The scenario you face is learn, plan, validate, learn more, plan again, validate again, etc. The more you plan and validate your design at the beginning of the project, the closer to perfect it will be at implementation. Professionals who have experience planning and deploying large Microsoft Exchange Server and Windows NT implementations should be quite familiar with these concepts. It may be comforting to know that Active Directory is more forgiving than Windows NT domains and Microsoft Exchange Server when you have to correct design mistakes.

Spend time prototyping the design in both lab and production environments so you can catch and remove mistakes before they impact your user community and drive your network support staff insane.

PREREQUISITES

Before you can plan your Active Directory implementation, you need to understand the hierarchy and terminology. That means you'll need to conduct needs and risk assessments, document the current environment, and implement DNS.

If you skipped the basic concepts in earlier chapters of this book, hoping to dive into implementation of your Active Directory system, please stop here. Implementing Active Directory is not easy, and this chapter will make more sense after you've read Chapter 2, which covers the hierarchical model of Active Directory as well as an overview of the Domain Name System.

Needs Assessment

The first question you need to consider is why you want to implement Active Directory. Windows 2000 and Active Directory are going to increase your workload during planning and implementation, so you should determine whether the payoff is worth the work. Formally document the problems you hope to correct, or the results you hope to achieve, so you can evaluate whether Active Directory is the correct solution. You may want to get input from stakeholders within the company and assess their needs as you make this decision. The formal documentation makes it easier to assess the success of the project.

Clear and documented goals before beginning this project keep everything in focus and prevent endless work that has no closure. Without clear goals and a focused scope of work, "scope creep" can set in and grow the task to a point where you lose control. Project team members must understand the underlying business reasons that are driving the project, and those reasons must be clearly documented for all members to view.

If you don't have concrete reasons for moving to Active Directory, then you should reevaluate whether or not to pursue the project. If implementing Active Directory is a top-down mandate from the business side of your organization, then the mandate should include the business reasons, or a business case, for moving to Active Directory. If this information was not included with the mandate, the business people should be able to provide it for you.

There is a shift in the industry to bring business people and technical people together, and implementing Active Directory may provide you with a good opportunity to align the technical decisions with your organization's business objectives.

Business people like technology that helps the business reduce costs, increase productivity, and so on. Business people like to discuss technology in business terms, not detailed technical terms. However, as communication continues, each group learns from the other.

Risk Assessment

The initial risk assessment for an Active Directory project should include a time line and a list of the areas the project will impact. Be sure to include input from representatives throughout the organization. These stakeholders can provide information about the way individual departments within the company function. For example, you need to know about peak periods of activity, such as the close of a fiscal cycle or the release of a product. You should understand what employees do on a day-to-day basis, and how they use the network.

This is also a good time to address any issues regarding the confidence of the business unit in the technical staff to complete the project successfully. A little public relations work can go a long way, and it's important to choose an individual with the right combination of people skills and technical skills to handle this portion of the project. Once input has been gathered from the stakeholders you can begin to map stakeholder reservations into your time line. If you see problem areas cropping up, you may want to reorganize and shift tasks in order to accommodate business unit concerns and maintain support for the project.

In some companies it's possible to move ahead without the support of all the stakeholders. You may also find that a stakeholder who pledged full support at the beginning backs out later. A project manager's role is not easy, and it requires constant communication and negotiation to ensure a successful project. There are times when you must pull strings and push forward, and other times when you must back down and reorganize the project. Choose your battles carefully or you could face a revolt during a critical point in the project. If you plan to manage future projects, you may want to err on the side of caution and maintain solid relationships with your business unit contacts.

As you develop the project plan, note and assess the major risks you might encounter. Tasks that involve an extraordinary amount of risk, such as migrating file server data for entire departments, should raise a red flag. Prototype high-risk tasks in a lab environment to offset some of the risk, and document your results. High-risk items should have a contingency plan in order to recover from a failed process without losing data. Test every element in the contingency plan. For instance, building a contingency plan that relies on backup media means you must validate the backup media before beginning the high-risk task.

You can mitigate some of your risk by using an outside consulting firm that has performed a significant number of similar projects. An experienced outside resource can review your design and point out critical high-risk areas that you may have missed.

Documentation of the Current Environment

It's critical to document the existing environment, whether you are migrating to Active Directory from Windows NT domains, UNIX-based systems, NetWare bindery, or NDS. The documentation influences the key decisions you'll make during implementation. For example, documentation helps you decide which elements of the current environment need to be salvaged, what should be migrated first, what should be migrated last, and how to make this a comfortable transition for your end users.

Many organizations are amazed during a migration to discover that they are still using an ancient gateway in a dusty corner of the server room somewhere, and no one in the company is quite sure what the gateway is for or what its function is on the network. With the amount of job turnover in this industry, situations like these are not uncommon. Before people are released from your organization, make sure they document what they were working on. Verbal knowledge transfers usually get lost over time, and the person receiving the verbal instructions could also be the next person in the organization to leave.

Documentation should include at a minimum:

▼ The conceptual design information for the current system

■ Explanations for why it was configured and implemented the way it was

■ Current naming formats for users, groups, servers, etc.

■ Inventory of servers, including location, configuration, and purpose

▲ Inventory of other network devices (printers, plotters, scanners, etc.), including configuration and location, and documentation on major events such as merging NDS trees for an acquisition

It's not always apparent, but an important element in your documentation is what you don't know or understand about your current environment. What you don't know can hurt you. Getting answers to these questions will help you assess the risks you may face. There will always be things that could blindside you, but ignoring what you don't know can affect the success of the project. This is a risk that can be avoided by asking the right questions and doing some research.

Documentation of the Existing Network Infrastructure

You need to understand and document the physical network layout. This is critical in large organizations that segment the infrastructure groups from the server groups. Check with other members of the IT department for diagrams and documentation that detail the physical connections between the network infrastructure components such as hubs, switches, and routers. If the information is not available, take the time to collect the information yourself. This information will be invaluable before and after the Active Directory project. If your organization is short on time and resources, consider contracting someone to collect the information and document the network.

If your organization has a wide area network, you need to know how your locations are physically connected, along with the bandwidth ratings of the media types. Document the utilization levels on your LAN and WAN connections. Having a T1 connection is great, but if the utilization on the T1 is consistently above 70 percent you may have problems replicating Active Directory over that link. If you don't have a protocol analyzer or the internetworking skills to evaluate the condition of your network's WAN and LAN connections, hire specialists to perform a detailed protocol analysis.

DNS Implementation

The Active Directory namespace is built on the DNS namespace, and they cannot exist without each other. DNS terminology and concepts are important to understand when planning and designing an Active Directory structure. (If you need a refresher on DNS, read Chapter 2.)

ACTIVE DIRECTORY DESIGN COMPONENTS

It's important to understand the design rules and options for the components of your Active Directory structure.

Organization Name

Nothing about the organization name is negotiable, iffy, or hard to understand. Here are the rules:

- ▼ There can be only one organization name.
- ■ The name is created during the installation of the first domain controller of the top-level domain.
- ■ The name should contain only alphanumeric characters and spaces.
- ▲ The name can match the company's fully qualified domain name. (See Chapter 2 and Chapter 7 for more information on DNS and internal and external namespaces.)

Organizational Unit

The organizational unit (OU) should be designed for efficiency, with the following guidelines:

- ▼ The primary use of the OU is to delegate administration.
- ■ The recommended use is to map logical structures, such as departments or workgroups, into the Active Directory.

- ■ The hierarchy of an OU applies only to the domain in which it exists.
- ■ The OU can contain computers, users, groups, printers, or other organization elements.
- ■ The OU is the smallest scope in which you can assign group policies or administrative controls.
- ■ Use an OU to minimize the number of domains.
- ■ In large organizations, the central IT organization may opt to design and support only the first-level OU.
- ▲ First-layer organizational units should be standard throughout the organization.

Domains and Domain Controllers

Here are the guidelines for designing the structure of your domains and their domain controllers:

- ▼ Domains are created by installing Active Directory on a Windows 2000 server.
- ■ A domain controller stores the Active Directory information for all the objects in the domain.
- ■ A domain controller is responsible for user logon processes, authentication, and directory searches.
- ■ You should use multiple domain controllers in a domain in order to provide high availability as well as fault tolerance.
- ■ A domain controller requires a DNS domain name for installation.
- ■ Domains can be used to delegate administrative authority or assign group policies.
- ■ Domains can be used to map either the physical network or logical groupings into the Active Directory.
- ■ To scale the Active Directory to meet the needs of large organizations, use domain trees and forests.
- ■ Domain terminology addresses the domains as root, first level, second level and special access.
- ▲ A single domain is usually sufficient for most small and medium-size organizations.

Domain Trees

Here are the guidelines for designing domain trees:

- ▼ Trees are multiple domains that share the same contiguous DNS namespace.

- Domains in a tree trust each other through a hierarchical Kerberos trust.
- Use domain trees to scale the Active Directory to fit the needs of larger organizations, or organizations that span many geographic areas.
- All domains within a domain tree share the same configuration, global catalog, and schema.
- The name of the domain tree is the name of the root domain.
- ▲ Domain trees are sufficient to support Active Directory implementations for large organizations.

Forests

Here are the design guidelines to consider if you are planning on using forests:

- ▼ Forests are domain trees that share the same configuration, global catalog, and schema but do not share a contiguous DNS namespace.
- All trees in the forest are linked by a transitive Kerberos trust relationship.
- A forest does not have a distinct name, and it's referred to by the tree name at the root of the trust.
- Forests are really a combination of pointers that cross-reference objects in the Active Directory, and they have the trust relationships that allow access to those objects.
- Forests can be used to fulfill special needs such as:
  - Linking a business partner (such as an accounting firm) into your Active Directory.
  - Merging the Active Directories of companies joined by an acquisition. The companies may need to share access to certain resources, but can still be managed independently and retain their individual DNS namespaces.

Global Catalog

Your design plans impact the global catalog, so here are some things to keep in mind:

- ▼ The global catalog is automatically created during the installation of the first domain controller.
- The global catalog provides universal group membership.
- The global catalog is used to locate information within the Active Directory, regardless of the domain in which the resource you're seeking resides.
- ▲ If the global catalog is unavailable, users who are not members of the Domain Administrators group are able to log on only to the local machine.

Sites

Your site design should take into consideration the following information about the way sites work:

▼ Sites can be used to control directory replication traffic across slow or saturated network connections.

■ Site boundaries should map the physical structure of your network, and are generally drawn between locations separated by wide area network connections.

■ The user logon process locates domain controllers in the user's home site before trying domain controllers in other sites within the domain.

■ Sites can contain multiple domains, and a domain can contain multiple sites.

■ Sites are connected by a service, and IP and SMTP are the default services.

▲ Replication within the site occurs automatically and uses the USN (update sequence number) for synchronization.

Computers and Users

Your design must provide the following services for computers and users:

▼ Authenticate the identity of the computer or user

■ Authorize access to domain resources

▲ Audit actions performed by the computer or user

Groups

Your design must take into consideration the following facts about groups:

▼ Groups are used to manage user and computer access to shared resources.

■ Groups can contain computers, users, contacts, and other groups (nested groups).

■ You can assign rights to some types of groups on local servers, domains, domain trees, or forests.

▲ Group types are local, global, and universal. (The appropriate use of groups is discussed later in this chapter.)

Servers

Design your servers with the following guidelines:

▼ Even though servers that are not domain controllers are considered to be regular computers within Active Directory, make them a separate design component because they provide services to other computers.

- A server is a leaf object that provides shared network resources and services.
- Your server design must take into consideration the following elements:
    - Consistent object naming standards
    - Placement within the network
    - User access rights to the server's resources
    - Delegating administrative control of the server

Printers

Use the following guidelines as you design the implementation of printing services:

- ▼ A printer is a leaf object for network print services.
- Your server design must take into consideration the following elements:
    - Consistent object naming standards
    - Printer placement within the network
    - Access rights to the printers
    - Delegating administrative control of the printers

NAMING STANDARDS

There's no such thing as the one "right" standard for names, although in most organizations it's easy to agree on what doesn't work. Two design goals to keep in mind are consistency and ease of use.

Your naming standards should be consistent across all containers in the organization. If you are naming your domains based on regional boundaries, then don't add a new domain and name it based on its business function. Consistency contributes to ease of use for both users and administrators.

Ease of use (or easy to understand) is critical for objects that end users interact with. Elements such as logon names, email addresses, servers, printers, and shared resources should be easy to find and understand. If users can't locate resources within the network, you've defeated one of the main purposes for moving to Active Directory in the first place. Keep your naming scheme similar across the entire environment.

NOTE: Windows 2000 calls the logon name the user principal name (UPN).

Mixing Numbers with Letters in Names and Email Addresses

Using numbers in logon names and email addresses doesn't always work properly. For instance, consider the possible confusion between a lowercase L, an uppercase I, and the number 1.

Using three initials seems to work until you hire two people with the same three initials.

Logon and email names that use the first name are generally easier to cope with than last names. Everyone knows how to spell Mark but have difficulty spelling Weinhardt, so MarkW is easier than WeinhardtM.

Email addresses with punctuation (such as an underscore) are inconvenient because of the pesky SHIFT key, and should avoided if possible. Putting a hyphen in a user's name is not a common practice, and should also be avoided.

A common trend is to use only the first name and, as conflicts arise, assign subsequent users characters of the last name. In this standard the first person named John becomes John, the second person becomes JohnS, the third person becomes JohnSm, and so on.

Naming Structures for High-Level Objects

Listed below are a few sample options for naming conventions at the higher levels of the Active Directory.

Organization Name

This is always the fully qualified domain name (FQDN) of the organization as it is registered on the Internet or the registered name for the internal DNS namespace. The organization name is inherited from the installation of the first Active Directory domain. The organization name is also the suffix of UPN for users.

Organizational Unit Name

Organizational units are used to map your organization's logical hierarchy into the Active Directory. Common OU naming standards include business units, such as accounting, development, and sales. Only administrators see the organizational unit structure.

Domain Name

Domains are used to store directory information and to authenticate end users. The domain structure could map your logical hierarchy into the Active Directory, but a more common use of domains is to implement a delimiter. Regional boundaries are one such use of domains, so your naming standard could be NorthAmerica or Europe.

The domain structure may or may not be visible to the end users, based on the configuration decisions made by the administrator regarding the UPN. Naming conventions for domains must be at least three characters so that they do not conflict with the ISO 3166 two-character country code.

Site

A site is the portion of the domain that is used to control replication of directory information. All domain controllers within the site communicate frequently about the status of the directory, and fast links should be used between domain controllers. If you assume that domains are based on regions, then a city can be a site. If you have five buildings in Santa Clara, California, all connected over an unsaturated FDDI ring at 100 Mbps, you can join all five buildings in one site, called SantaClara. Only administrators see the site structures within domains.

Names for Security Principal Objects

Security principal objects include computer accounts, user accounts, and groups. For all three of these objects, the following rules apply:

▼ Names must be unique for the type within a domain.

■ Names can contain up to 20 uppercase and lowercase characters except for these: / \ [ ] : ; | = + * ? < >.

▲ Names cannot be solely spaces or periods.

Computer Names

Consider different naming conventions for workstations and servers. Because end users need to interact with servers, server names should be intuitive and descriptive, referring to the services the server provides.

Your first tendency may be to align the server names with your organizational unit structure. As you familiarize yourself with the ease of creating organizational units and moving objects within the Active Directory, you may find that is not such a good idea, especially in organizations that reorganize frequently. You may be better off aligning your server names with a more fixed attribute that more closely aligns the server with physical rather than logical structures in the Active Directory (such as domains or sites). For example, if I am adding a second domain controller server for Active Directory fault tolerance in the inaoak.com organization in the professional services organizational unit in the WEST domain, I may name this server WEST-DC1. Designers will be glad to know that we can rename servers in Active Directory much easier than we did in Windows NT domains. However, because end users are using the servers' resources, it's a bit more difficult to rename a server without any consequences.

Here are some general guidelines for naming computers:

▼ Don't use the underscore for server names. Although it's currently a popular element in server naming conventions, the underscore is not a valid DNS character according to the RFC specifications. If you must use a character to divide the server name, use a dash.

■ PDC and BDC aren't necessary anymore. Many administrators named domain controllers with either PDC or BDC somewhere in the name. The Windows 2000 multimaster replication of the Active Directory makes the PDC/BDC concept obsolete. If you prefer to advertise domain controller functionality, use the initials DC somewhere in the server name.

▲ Computer accounts for workstations can follow any standard (again, refrain from using the underscore character). Active Directory, like Windows NT, does not support the ability of Windows 95 and 98 machines to register a computer account with the domain.

Users

User accounts should be kept consistent across the Active Directory. You also need to make sure that you have a system for resolving duplicate names. Usually, less than five characters is too short and more than eight characters is too long (unless your naming convention is based on a user's whole name).

A poor naming scheme example would be the first three letters of the first name plus the first five letters of the last name. This forces the user to calculate how many characters of which name they have typed, and does not provide a way to resolve duplicates (consider the problem when the second person named John Williams joins the organization).

One thing to note about security principal objects is that a name is not considered a duplicate if it's in a different domain of the Active Directory tree. You can have two John Williams with a logon of JohnW without conflict if one is in the EAST domain and the other is in the WEST domain. If they are both in the WEST domain, then you could add the second letter of the last name to one user's logon to resolve duplicates (one JohnW and one JohnWi).

Synchronizing the login name with the email address is also a good idea, provided your email addresses follow a standard that is not cryptic or full of special characters. If you are using Microsoft Exchange Server and your Internet mail addresses are cryptic, consider adding a secondary proxy address to the mailboxes and setting the new address as the reply address. Users will be able to receive mail under both addresses, but by marking the secondary proxy address as the reply address, recipients of their messages will reply to them using the new address.

A UPN is an easy to use naming style (it was outlined in RFC 822). A UPN has two parts:

▼ The first part is called the prefix, and it is the user's logon name (the same as Windows NT domains).

▲ The second part is the suffix, and it is a domain name. This is usually the registered DNS domain name, but it is configurable by the administrator.

The prefix and the suffix are joined by the @ symbol. Windows 2000 uses the UPN naming format for logging on to a domain in the Active Directory. Administrators may want to consider changing the suffix of the UPN if the registered domain name for the organization is extraordinarily long or is difficult to type.

Groups

Group names should be descriptive. You can have one naming structure for groups that access resources, and another structure for email distribution lists. Unlike Windows NT domains, the icon that denotes the group type is the same whether the group is a distribution list, a local group, a global group, or a universal group. (Active Directory uses the description field to denote differences in group types.)

For local, global, and universal groups, you may wish to denote the group type in the name of the group to avoid confusion. For example, you might use –L, –G and –U at the end of global and universal group names.

Printers

Most end users don't care what type of printer they are printing to; they only care about where they have to go to retrieve their documents.

Naming schemes for printers are often tough to design, but many administrators include the location of the printer in the name. If you want to tie printers in to their OUs, you could invent a printer name convention that uses both the OU name and the location of the printer, as in MRKT-B1 for a printer in the Marketing group in building 1.

For special interest printers such as color laser printers and plotters, you may want to add either the P for plotter or C for color to the end of the printer name.

DESIGN IMPACTS AND DECISIONS

The way you design the Active Directory impacts the entire structure—and the security—of your system. You have to create a structure that you can secure, and continue to secure, without making it difficult to administer your system. (Detailed information on creating policies for administrative control and the security functionality that Windows 2000 Server provides is covered in Chapter 16.)

Single vs. Multiple Domain Designs and Security

Here are some things to consider when you choose either a single or multiple domain model for Active Directory:

▼ Are you able to control replication traffic?

■ Have you considered the impact the design will have on security?

■ Can changes be made without reengineering the domain structure?

■ Can the design evolve as the needs of the organization change?

▲ Do you really need a large domain tree or forest?

Domain Trees and Hierarchical Domain Structures

Microsoft addresses the domains in a domain tree with the terminology *root domain*, *first-layer domains*, and *second-layer domains*. Smaller organizations may choose to implement only a root-level structure, and possibly a first-level domain structure.

Including second-level domains provides more granular replication, and also limits the reign of domain administrators. With a deep domain structure, very large organizations can set up a small group of global administrators whose rights flow down from the root domain.

The Root Domain

The root domain is the top-level domain and is usually built upon the external DNS namespace, although you could use a registered internal namespace. All other domains within the tree are spawned off the root domain.

For medium-size or large organizations, the internal root domain can be an unpopulated namespace used strictly for core directory and network services. Domain controllers in the root domain should never reside on the public Internet.

First-Level Domains

Domains at the first level should be stable and unchanging, because changes to the underlying domain structure after Active Directory is implemented are time-consuming to implement. The delimiter used to divide the first-level domains should be a large scope, such as a continent or a large geopolitical boundary. One design goal at this layer is to create an environment that will minimize directory service replication.

First-level domains could also contain the organizational units of remote offices that do not have the personnel resources to be managed as separate domains. Defining the remote offices as organizational units provides the option of promoting them to first-level domains if the location grows.

If additional domains are needed, they should be created as child domains off the first-level domains, forming a second-level domain structure.

If you're considering a second-level domain structure, the naming convention for the domains at the first level should be at least three characters. This enables you to use the ISO 3166 two-character country code or U.S. postal codes to name the second-layer domains and organizational units.

Second-Level Domains

The second-level domain structure is recommended only for large or worldwide organizations. Microsoft suggests that domains at the second layer should be created as countries, using the two letter ISO 3166 country codes.

> **TIP:** If you plan to use a structure that includes both domains and organizational units at the same level, be sure to use a naming convention that allows you to promote an organizational unit to a domain with as little user impact as possible.

Large branch offices and sites within a country can be child domains off the country domain. Or, you could divide the country domain into sites, then use OUs for the offices.

If your organization operates entirely within one country, the second-level domain could be a metropolitan area. A large U.S.-based second-level domain structure could use the U.S. postal code to designate the second-level domains with the exception of California, which conflicts with the ISO country code for Canada. Child domains could then be the large offices, any other logical set of sites that control the administration of replication, or an organizational unit of a company.

> **CAUTION:** Don't lock yourself into a structure that can't accommodate mergers or worldwide expansion.

Special Access Domains

Special access domains are domains that do not fit within your root-, first-, or second-level domain structures. Special access domains are owned and managed by your organization but connect to an entity that your organization may not have direct control of. You can use these domains to connect to a business partner, incorporate a tree structure after a merger in which administrative functions will stay separated, or connect an isolated internal group within the company (such as auditors). Separate namespaces join these domains to the rest of your structure in a forest, and contiguous namespaces join them into the domain tree.

Special access domains contain all user accounts and resources that are needed by the group the domain serves. These domains join your Active Directory by explicit one-way trusts or by transitive trusts. Relationships that result from a merger usually warrant a transitive trust, while a special access domain that connects the Auditors group would most likely be an explicit one-way trust.

Don't confuse vendors or contractors with the purpose of special access domains. Contractors are commonly managed within the organizational units for which they are working. Rights and permissions can be granted within the organizational unit and will not require an additional server to handle the directory, authentication, and replication.

When to Form a Domain Tree

An Active Directory domain tree is a hierarchy of Windows 2000 root-, first-, and second-level domains. If the Active Directory domain tree is enterprise-wide, then all Active Directory domains in the enterprise should belong to a domain tree.

To form a domain tree, all domains in an Active Directory tree must form a contiguous namespace. The shape of your tree can also be determined by the trust relationships between the domains of the tree. A child domain's namespace is contiguous by default, and the child domain will inherit the parent's namespace. The distinguished name of every object in a child domain will have the name of the parent domain as a prefix.

When to Form a Forest

Disjointed trees that do not have a contiguous namespace should be joined into a forest if access to resources between the domains in the forest is required. Special access domains that connect business partners are one example of when to form a forest. A forest may also be implemented after a merger or acquisition, when both organizations will retain their independent namespace. The forest will provide access to necessary resources through the explicit trust relationship, and the administration and the majority of the business can remain separate.

Trust Relationships in Active Directory

Two types of trust mechanisms exist in Active Directory. The first type of trusts are transitive Kerberos trusts, which allow a user access to any branch of a single-domain tree without configuring a specific trust relationship between all domains in the tree. A transitive trust means that if A trusts B, and B trusts C, then A trusts C as well. The second type of trust relationship in Active Directory is the explicit trust similar to the Windows NT one-way trust relationships. The explicit trust relationships are necessary in Active Directory to provide backward compatibility with Windows NT domains. Explicit trusts are also used to allow access between Active Directory domain trees. One-way trust relationships are not transitive, so when A trusts B and B trusts C, A does not trust C unless a specific trust is established between A and C. A one-way trust relationship provides a mechanism for limiting the resources that are available to members of the domain linked by the one-way trust. This is especially useful for special access domains, because you can provide access to necessary resources without exposing all of the company's resources to the special access domain users.

Forming Trust Relationships

When a domain is joined to an Active Directory domain tree, a Kerberos transitive trust relationship is automatically established between the joined domain and its parent in the tree. Since the Kerberos trust is transitive, no additional trust relationships are required among tree members. Administrators no longer have to explicitly form and maintain two-way trusts between all of the domains. The root domain of the domain tree is the root of the transitive trust relationship for first-level domains. Second-level domains establish their transitive trust hierarchically from their parent branch of the tree off the root.

Explicit trust relationships can be formed between domain trees within a forest, or to connect to Windows NT domains through the Active Directory Domains and Trusts snap-in to the Microsoft Management console. Explicit trusts are one way, and if two-way access is needed you will have to configure explicit trusts in both domains.

Using Groups to Assign Permissions

Windows 2000 Server retains the local and global group concepts that exist in Windows NT. However, Windows 2000 groups can contain both users and other groups, as well as other objects (such as contacts, computers, and email distribution lists).

There are some changes in the way administrators work with groups in Windows 2000:

▼ Local groups are simply called local groups.

■ A global group can contain another global group.

▲ There is a new group, called a universal group.

To understand why we need a universal group in Windows 2000, it's important to understand a bit more about the other two groups.

Domain Local Groups

Domain local groups can contain users and global groups from any domain in the Active Directory forest. Domain local groups can only be applied to access control lists (ACLs) on objects within the same domain. Domain local groups are used to assign permissions to resources within a single domain.

Global Groups

Global groups can contain users and other global groups. The limitation of the global group is that it can only contain users and other global groups from the same domain that the global group resides in and not from anywhere in the Active Directory forest.

Universal Group

In Active Directory, a universal group is required when permissions are needed across the entire domain tree or forest. Universal groups can contain global groups and users from any domain tree in the forest, and can be used to assign permissions to any object on the ACL.

Using Groups to Control Access

When you design groups to control access within the Active Directory, you need to make sure that rights within the directory flow smoothly (which reduces the administration efforts). Here are some guidelines to keep in mind:

▼   Use global groups to organize your users into a container for ease of administration in each domain.

■   Grant permissions to the domain local group on the ACL of a shared resource where the shared resource resides.

■   Universal groups should be created for access to domain resources across the entire Active Directory and should only contain the global groups from each domain. Do not assign individual users to a universal group.

▲   Add the universal groups to domain local groups to grant permission to shared resources.

By following the above recommendations for implementing groups, you will also help reduce the size of the global catalog, which in turn reduces the amount of information that must be replicated throughout the directory.

▼   Domain local groups do not appear in the global catalog.

■   For global groups, only the group itself appears and not the users.

▲   Universal groups and their membership appear in the global catalog, so by adding only global groups to universal groups you reduce the amount of information that must be replicated.

Domains vs. Organizational Units

One of the toughest decisions you face when designing the Active Directory is whether to use domains or organizational units to segment the directory. (Life is simpler when you don't have a choice and there is only one way to implement a design.) Active Directory puts few controls on designers, providing flexibility and creative license. Either component can be used to designate physical and logical network boundaries, so which one do you use? The answer is easier if you have a clear idea about your goals.

Here are some general guidelines that should help you make your decision:

▼ If your goal is to delegate administrative control over a subset of the Active Directory, the appropriate solution is to create an organizational unit.

■ If your goal is to map the logical structure of the organization's business units and hierarchy into the Active Directory, an organizational unit should be implemented.

■ Organizational units should also be used in unstable organizations that are subject to frequent changes in organizational structure.

▲ If your organization has decentralized administrative processes and separate groups manage different portions of the organization, a domain should be chosen.

Domains should also be used in situations where a designer does not want to replicate the directory across a really slow or saturated network link. Most often, you will be better off upgrading the link and using separate sites to control the replication traffic. However, there may be times when it is not physically possible or cost-effective to upgrade the link.

If you believe a domain is the best decision, consider these additional points to further justify your decision.

▼ Remote offices with two or more data servers are candidates for a domain. (Not domain servers. All domains need at least two domain controllers for performance and fault tolerance.)

■ A domain should have local technical IT support personnel on site.

■ Offices with a staff of more than 1,000 are candidates for a separate domain.

■ Offices that are domains need sufficient network bandwidth to support directory replication.

▲ Do you have the budget to afford another domain?

A domain may be the decision that best fits the needs of the organization, but the benefit of an organizational unit is that there are no replication or hardware costs. If you can't afford the domain at the present time, a possible alternative is to build an organizational unit at the same level the domain would have been, using the same naming structure. Later, you can promote the organizational unit to a domain.

Failing to follow through on the organizational unit promotion may break your original hierarchical design, which can put the Active Directory in a nonuniform state.

Whatever decision you make, the most important rule to follow is to be consistent. Don't use organizational units to delegate control in one portion of the directory and then use domains in another unless it's an extremely temporary solution. Mixing design components in the same directory can have disastrous results and will cost time and money in the long run.

CREATING YOUR ACTIVE DIRECTORY

If you are tasked with the responsibility of creating the Active Directory, you'll probably stare at a blank sheet of paper for a while (that's the normal behavior). It's a daunting task if you approach your Active Directory from a global perspective. You might even (mistakenly) start by mapping out your entire organization chart and get really lost and overwhelmed. Let me simplify the task.

In all of our Active Directory designs, what has worked best is to start small and work your way up through the organization. No matter how large your organization is, starting with one department and building from it gives you a valuable perspective of the organizational structure.

One of the major advantages of Active Directory when compared with other directory services such as Novell Directory Services or pure LDAP implementations is that when you design an Active Directory you have the option to start the design process from the workgroup level. For those of you with prior design experience, especially with Novell Directory Service or Microsoft Exchange Server, this concept may seem foreign. With those directory services, you were always forced to design a structure from the top down.

You do have the option of designing an Active Directory structure in the traditional top-down method, but the flexibility in Active Directory provides a second option. You may want to design the Active Directory from the workgroup up for the following reasons:

▼ Your organization may be subject to frequent acquisitions or expansions.

■ Your organization may be in a state of disarray from a previous acquisition or expansion.

■ Your organization may not have a centralized administration structure.

■ Your organization may be a mesh of multiple network services providing different functionality.

▲ Your organization may cover a wide geographic area with different needs and functions in each geographic region.

Designing from the Workgroup Level

From the workgroup level, you can work your way up to a much larger directory structure if the business needs of the organization change. With other directory services, you had to lock yourself into an organizational unit structure based on physical locations, business function, regions, or some other delimiter. When changes were made to the organization—through acquisition, expansion, or other unforeseen events—the directory structure and partition scheme did not always allow a seamless integration of the change to the business.

Microsoft's networking solutions have always been focused on the way users work; hence, the term *workgroup* within Microsoft networking. While workgroups and domains may have been appropriate for the way end users work, they were only good for administrators while the organization was small. Domains and workgroups don't scale well enough to support and administer larger organizations. Microsoft has taken an extreme amount of criticism within the information technology world for its lack of scalability and administrative control within the domain and workgroup structures. In order for larger organizations to be able to scale their networks and still be able to administer them, they were forced to link domains through a complex network of trust relationships, or move to another top-down focused solution like NetWare and Novell's Directory Services. With Active Directory, we have the best of both worlds. We can allow users to work the way that's best for the business, while providing the scalability and administrative control that's necessary to support the needs of larger organizations.

If you are in the IT department, start there. Identify the users, printers, and IT departmental production servers that get used every day (specifically, production servers—don't confuse this design with test servers, lab servers, or other temporary devices you use).

You probably have a single main administrator who oversees security and user administration. You also probably have private directories for your files. This combination of administration and security provides the basis for developing the security access in your Windows 2000 Active Directory.

Your department may have other sites, and you need to identify the users who need access to the centralized IT servers and printers. Your department may be part of a division that is part of a region. All of these larger structures help you build your Active Directory from a small department perspective into a large global organization with access and relationship design requirements.

When you start the Active Directory from the perspective of a small department and build on it from there, you'll find that the structure for one workgroup (including security, access, and privileges) works for other workgroups. In fact, most of the time you can just copy that structure to other workgroups. After you have defined a number of workgroups, you can link them together to build the basis of the organizational Active Directory.

First Workgroup

Assuming you're implementing a new domain, rather than migrating from a previous operating system, select a workgroup to begin the Active Directory. The steps you took during your needs analysis phase should have helped you decide which workgroup you will install first.

For this example let's take an office of 60 employees in one physical location, with a single DNS namespace. The office has three workgroups: Sales, Service, and Operations. The best design is a single-domain model, with a single site and multiple organizational units that map to the business units. Because this organization is small, we have chosen to configure the root domain as the only domain. The organization is a classic case of how we can design the Active Directory from the workgroup up through the organization. At the end of this process I will provide a few different scenarios that describe business changes to our organization that will require changes to our Active Directory design so you can see what we may have done in a different situation.

The following examples are templates for some sample organizational structures, but should not be assumed to be ready-made Active Directory structures specific for your organization. Each organization is unique, and requires individual evaluation to design a network that will function correctly.

Building the Domain Structure

Before installing the first Active Directory domain, you must complete the following steps:

1. Select the Active Directory domain name.
2. Create the DNS structure to support the Active Directory domain name.
3. Select a name for the Windows 2000 Server.
4. Install a Windows 2000 Server that meets the criteria above with the appropriate hardware and drive configuration to support Active Directory. (For more information on hardware needs and configuration, see Chapter 5.)

In this example, I have created the domain with the DNS namespace of inaoak.com. The domain controller name is INACOM-AD. Once my installation is complete, I can set up my organizational unit structure through the Active Directory and Computers snap-in to the Microsoft Management console.

I first create an organizational unit for the workgroup called Service. Once I have my organizational unit, I will set up my group structures within the OU. I will create global groups for the following: consultants, engineers, managers, and project managers. Once I have the global groups defined, I can create a universal group under the inaoak.com domain called InacomOakland-ALL and a universal group called Inacom-Service and add my four services global groups to the universal group. Next, I will add the servers, workstations, and printers for the Services workgroup to their organizational unit. Once I have the resources defined, I can design my group policies (assigning network resources to groups). After I have my group structures defined, I can define different policies for different groups, or one policy for the organizational unit. I can then build templates for end users, who will be assigned to appropriate groups. Templates can also define the logon name, who they report to, business address, fax number, email address, etc. I can then add the users and apply the template (either manually or by importing a .csv file). I can then delegate administrative control for the organizational unit to one of the network administrators in the administrative structure shown in Figure 6-1. I can use the universal groups for assigning rights to the infrastructure services above the domain level.

Replicating the Structure to the Next Workgroup

The first organizational unit is the toughest to implement. Once completed, it can be copied to the group structures, templates, and policies and applied to the Sales and Operations workgroups, creating an organizational structure as shown in Figure 6-2. I can then implement the other workgroups as organizational units using this same process. When I have completed the organizational unit, I can delegate the administration.

Modifying the Design to Support Business Needs and Changes

Things get more complex when we add other entities, such as multiple domains, sites, domain trees, and forests. Organizations large enough to need domain trees and forests need to plan more thoroughly at the top levels, but the structures at the domain and organizational unit levels can still be built one workgroup at a time.

If our organization expands its operation by opening a new office, we need to incorporate the new office with its engineers, project managers, consultants, account executives, and office manager into the existing Active Directory. Since most of the employees, besides the office manager, will be in the field all the time, all database and mail services will still reside in the main corporate location, but we will add a file server, printers, and workstations to the new office. A leased line connection will connect the new office to the Internet and a secured virtual private network will be configured to provide access to the central database and mail services.

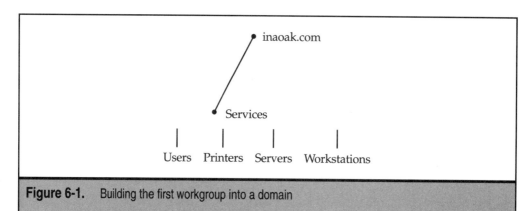

Figure 6-1.   Building the first workgroup into a domain

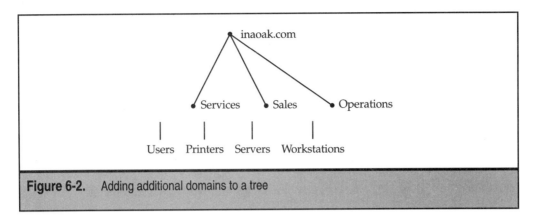

Figure 6-2. Adding additional domains to a tree

The new file server will become a domain controller in the existing domain to validate users and provide access to files on the file server in case the Internet connection is down. With Windows 2000, we can delegate administrative control of the printers and file server for the new office to a technical administrator in the remote office. Since the new office is in the same domain as the main office, the organizational unit structure we created in the first example will apply to the new domain controller server, creating the structure shown in Figure 6-3. We need to add DNS services to the new server as a secondary server for the organization's namespace, and we have to split the domain into two separate sites to control replication over the VPN.

Another variation of the design above would have been to use a root- and first-level domain combination. While that would have increased the complexity of implementing the Active Directory, it would have provided the flexibility to isolate the infrastructure services and incorporate larger changes to the Active Directory. If I had expected the organization to grow to hundreds of employees spread across the country, I might have used this strategy, creating the structure shown in Figure 6-4. The root domain would be

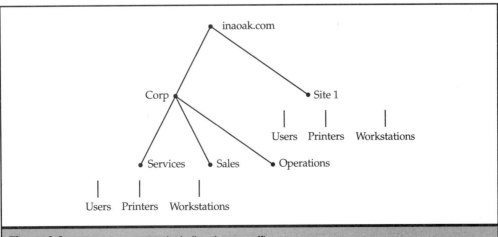

Figure 6-3. Domain structure including the new office

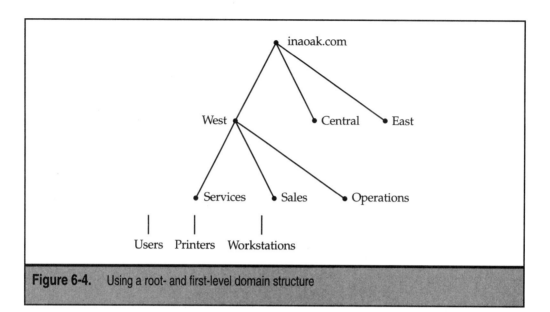

Figure 6-4. Using a root- and first-level domain structure

inaoak.com, and I would create a first-level domain structure. My first-level domains would have been installed in a domain tree off the root domain inaoak.com. I may have named my first-level domains West, East, and Central to cover each area of the country. Second-level domains probably would not be necessary, but I would divide the domains into sites to control replication over the WAN links in each regional domain. My organizational unit structures could be implemented within each domain, and the fact that they are all within the same domain tree would provide the transitive trusts to facilitate access to resources throughout the organization. The business needs would most likely require that the business administration organizational unit be divided into multiple organizational units, which would be an easy modification. With this design I can delegate administration to regional IT support staff at each location and have a small group of global administrators managing the core services in the inaoak.com domain.

If this were a worldwide organization I may have augmented the design by creating a second-level domain structure to further segment the directory by country, creating the structure shown in Figure 6-5. Obviously, my first-level structure's naming conventions would not have been the same as the U.S.-centric example above, and would instead follow the continents or other global delimiters. The need for worldwide information sharing and access to resources would dictate whether I use a forest or a domain tree. Most likely, it would be a domain tree. If it were a forest, I would have to use the explicit trusts to facilitate access between the domain trees.

Notice that in the above examples I haven't used a special access domain. If this office were part of a larger organization, I could implement a special access domain that is in a forest with the local domain tree, linking this organization into the structure as shown in Figure 6-6. Explicit trusts would secure confidential information and allow access to data. Also, the parent company could implement an explicit trust to the local organization to provide access to needed files.

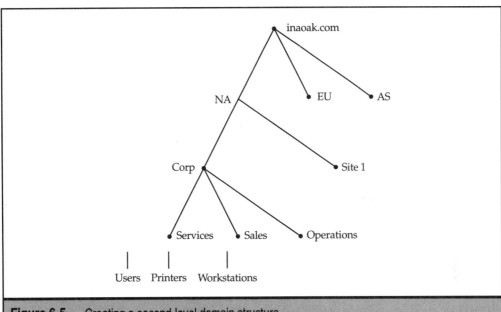

Figure 6-5.   Creating a second-level domain structure

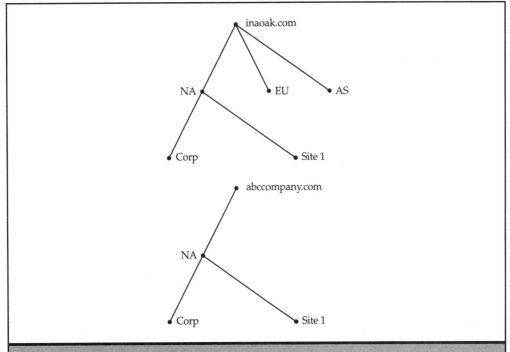

Figure 6-6.   Creating a special access domain

MINIMIZING THE IMPACT OF ACTIVE DIRECTORY ON THE NETWORK

The organizational structure greatly influences the type of design we select for the implementation of our Active Directory. One of the biggest influencing factors is the impact of multiple sites on the design structure. Sites that are connected through slow WAN connections need to be managed and administered differently than resources directly connected to a fast LAN connection.

Sites and Replication

The Active Directory can be broken down into sites to provide localized logon validation. The term used to describe such a portion of the Active Directory is a *replica* of the global catalog. A site is defined as one or more TCP/IP subnets that are "well connected." Administrators can create the sites directly from the TCP/IP subnets to allow a faster client logon process and more control over replication.

During logon, a client always attempts to locate a server within the same site. Active Directory uses site information to locate a domain controller server close to the user. When a workstation boots in an IP based network, it receives a TCP/IP address and a subnet mask from a DHCP server, which also identifies which subnet the workstation is on. If your network uses static addressing on your workstations, you must manually configure the IP address and the subnet mask. Based on the IP address and subnet mask information of the workstation, the domain controller locator service will search for an Active Directory server on the same subnet as the workstation.

Active Directory has drastically departed from the method that Windows NT domains used to replicate changes to the SAM database. Windows NT domains made all their changes to a single server, called the primary domain controller (PDC), and administrators had to connect to the PDC to make changes to the domain. This was also true for users who wanted to change their passwords. Complex networks with WAN connections and slow links required complex registry configurations in order to connect to the PDC. The PDC replicated all the changes to the backup domain controllers (BDCs). Placement of both PDC and BDC servers within the network was a major factor in the ability to replicate the SAM.

In Active Directory, changes are written to any directory server and are replicated throughout the network through *multimaster replication*. Multimaster replication means that all replicas of the partition of the Active Directory are readable and writable. Updates can be applied to any replica of the partition, and Active Directory replicates the changes to all other partitions in the site. Replication is automatic through the replication ring that is formed among all domain controllers within the site.

Replication occurs automatically through the synchronization of the *update sequence number (USN)* of all objects within the Active Directory. For those of you familiar with Microsoft Exchange, the process for replicating changes to the directory within a site is very similar to Active Directory. Within a site, directory replication is performed via remote procedure calls (RPCs). Between sites, replication can be selectively configured to use RPC or messaging. By default, Active Directory replicates between sites via SMTP. By integrating Microsoft Exchange into the Active Directory tree, intersite replication can be transported via Exchange Server X.400 or other connectors.

> **NOTE:** Active Directory defines a site as "one or more IP subnets of the network where connectivity among machines is assumed to be well-connected." *Well-connected* means that the bandwidth between the domain controller servers within in the site is at LAN speed of 10 Mbps. Sites could also span other links such as frame relay, ATM, or other link types, provided they are unsaturated and the appropriate replication settings have been implemented to adjust for tighter bandwidth if the speed rating is below LAN speed.

Planning Sites

Sites are commonly used within a single domain to control replication and improve the speed of the logon process. The site planning process should begin after the tree, domain, and organizational unit planning decisions have been made. Focus on getting the end user validated within the tree and replicating directory changes throughout the Active Directory.

The first step in designing the sites is to map the domain design into the network diagram. This is a simple task with a single domain, but assigning physical locations to each domain with a multiple-domain design may be a much more complex task. Once the domains are mapped into your physical network diagrams, you must decide whether you need multiple sites within the domain. If the locations are well-connected and the average utilization levels do not indicate the link is saturated for the media type being used, then a single site may be acceptable. If the locations are not well-connected, or the average utilization for the media type is high, then you need to implement multiple sites.

Active Directory assumes that all machines in a site share a common high-bandwidth network and it will replicate across the link assuming the Active Directory designers knew what they were doing by locating the server in the same site. In general, you should consider implementing multiple sites if locations are linked by a WAN connection through a frame relay circuit or a leased line. ATM or microwave circuits may have sufficient bandwidth for a single site, but using a multiple-site design may be a better design decision. In a multiple-site design, the administrator has more control over how and when traffic is sent across the link, which can cut down on the traffic.

One example of a site-design decision is an FDDI ring connecting six buildings in one city. You can treat the entire group of buildings as a single domain, but a more difficult decision is whether to use a single or multiple site design. Let's say the FDDI ring average utilization is about 40 percent, which is not too bad. We could implement a single site, because the locations within the city are well-connected. Sometimes the design question for a single or multiple site design comes down to "should I," rather than "could I." A single-site design in this scenario would probably work well.

Suppose, however, the company is growing exponentially and is planning to open two new facilities with 100 employees in each facility. The CIO wants them added to the FDDI ring. The FDDI ring utilization will change drastically. In that case, a multiple-site design would work better.

Don't Divide Well-Connected Segments into Multiple Sites

It's not a good idea to create multiple sites on a well-connected network. By dividing well-connected subnets into multiple sites, you can actually decrease performance. If a domain controller is not available in one of the sites, another site can process user requests. That site can be any other site in the domain, and not the other sites still functioning on the well-connected network.

For example, let's say we have three sites in one domain. Two sites reside on a 100-Mbps switching backbone, and the other site is across a 128-Kbps frame relay connection with a 64-Kbps CIR rate. If we only had one domain controller in each site and we lost one of the domain controllers in one of the high-speed switching sites, user requests may be sent across the frame relay connection for processing. A significant drop in performance would be noticed in this scenario. To avoid this, place all well-connected subnets in the same physical location in the same site.

Server Placement

To facilitate efficient access to the Active Directory, designers have to decide where to place the domain controller. Besides users, application and file servers need access to the domain controller in order to validate user requests for files. A domain controller must be able to respond to user and replication requests in a timely manner to avoid timeouts and sporadic replication results. For best performance, place at least one domain controller in each physical site that contains users or computers connected to that domain. Size the domain controller hardware so that it is capable of supporting the number of objects within the domain.

Domains can scale from several hundred thousand objects to a million objects, so large domains should implement powerful domain controllers. (See Chapter 13 for a deeper discussion of hardware selection and domain controller configuration.)

In general, locations that are separated by a WAN link should have domain controllers on each side of the link, and be in separate sites within the domain. Locations with multiple servers should designate two servers as domain controllers (for fault tolerance and redundancy). If the servers are separated by a WAN link and in a separate site, then one of the servers can be specified as a bridgehead and handle the intersite directory replication. This reduces the replication load on an individual server. If the bridgehead server fails, the other domain controller can become the bridgehead until the primary bridgehead server is recovered.

PARTITIONING THE GLOBAL CATALOG

In a large organizational structure, the Active Directory should be broken apart to facilitate localized access to the directory. This also improves replication and directory management. In Windows 2000, this is handled with a global catalog that includes all of the directory objects, and replicas of the global catalog distributed across the WAN. The partitioning and placement of the Active Directory seems logical, but needs to be detailed to ensure successful Active Directory management.

Centralizing the Global Catalog

A global catalog server must have enough capacity to hold all objects from all domains in the forest. (For more information on sizing your global catalog servers, see Chapter 13.)

The best query performance is obtained when you place a domain controller at a small site, enabling the server to fulfill queries about objects in that site. Adding a domain controller increases the amount of data to be replicated, so you do not want to replicate the entire global catalog to every domain controller. You can achieve a balance between query performance and efficient replication by placing a domain controller in each major site. Major sites can be defined as locations on your WAN that have a large collection of users and resources (such as the center of the star in a star WAN configuration). One global catalog server per Active Directory site is recommended. In multiple-domain configurations where more than one domain resides at a given location, the domains can use the same global catalog to locate resources within the tree.

Remember that universal groups are also contained and replicated in the global catalog. Adding global groups and omitting end users in the universal groups helps minimize the size of the global catalog.

Partitioning the Directory

Since you will not be replicating the entire global catalog to every domain controller, you should select a portion of the global catalog to replicate to other domain controllers. This is called *partitioning* the directory.

The trust hierarchy of the global catalog is stored in *cross-reference* objects. These objects are part of the directory information in the partitions container. The partitions container is a child of the configuration container that contains cross-reference objects. With virtual containers, there may be cross-reference objects outside the main organizational structure, such as printers residing on a client's network that are accessed over the Internet.

When we partition the directory, we want to take into account all the objects that users need. If we partition the directory based on site structure (for example, by continent as shown in Figure 6-7), we need to make sure that the replica in Europe includes all of the European servers, workstations, users, printers, and virtual container objects used. When we distribute this replica to Europe, all the necessary objects will be available for faster logon authentication and access by those users.

The rule of thumb is this: If users at a site don't need access to resources at a different site, then partition the directory so that only the resources at the site are in that partition of the directory.

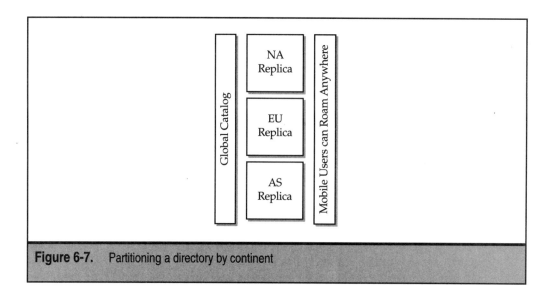

Figure 6-7. Partitioning a directory by continent

If you have three sites in a local region and employees frequently travel to the regional offices, it's more efficient to replicate the entire global catalog. I would probably draw the line at 80 percent, which means that if 80 percent of the users in a location have no need to access objects in other sites, then only replicate a partition.

Mobile or Universal-Access Users

Most organizations have users that travel from site to site and need access to resources anywhere in the organization. Rather than replicating the entire catalog to all domain controllers just to satisfy the needs of these traveling users, we can create a separate partition just for these users and the objects they need to access.

We can partition the directory so that North American users and resources are allocated in the NA partition, European users and resources are allocated in the EU partition, and Asian users and resources are allocated in the AS partition. Create a discrete partition for the users that travel, and replicate that portion of the directory to all locations.

CHAPTER 7

Planning Your DNS Namespace, Domains, and Sites

The Active Directory is built on and integrates tightly with the Domain Name Service (DNS), which is the directory service for Windows 2000. The operating system relies on DNS because it is an open standard, supported on all major platforms. Windows 2000 uses DNS as the name-resolution protocol for accessing the LDAP-based Active Directory, and every domain is represented by a DNS domain name. For a successful implementation of Active Directory, you must have a well-designed and well-planned DNS. Fortunately, DNS planning is easier than Active Directory planning.

PLANNING CONSIDERATIONS AND ISSUES

Windows 2000 requires a DNS server. The Active Directory is mirrored in the DNS namespace, and the structure creates the replication boundaries for the Active Directory, which transfers information to the DNS.

The design of the DNS should facilitate the scaling of the Active Directory. The goal is a flexible, scalable, and understandable DNS design. Some of the administrative design issues include creating a support environment that reduces the total cost of ownership, scaling up or down as the organization changes, and optimizing performance.

NOTE: The Dynamic Update Protocol (IETF RFC 2136) allows clients and servers to register domain names and IP addresses with the name service. This provides automatic updating of the namespace, rather than having administrators process them manually.

Supportability

Administration time and fault tolerance affect supportability. The number of servers, the way the DNS databases are distributed, and the manner in which administration is delegated all affect the supportability. The supportability of a system is a measure of how much support is required (and even whether the system can be supported). This is a critical component for the total cost of ownership.

Service-Level Agreements

The IT department's service-level agreements affect the supportability and design of the DNS infrastructure. If the agreements target 24 × 7 availability, for instance, with 99.98 percent uptime for domain name services, then a robust, redundant, and fault-tolerant design is critical. If the agreements are less stringent, then a less costly implementation can be designed. During the design phase, it is important to identify and document the targeted service level.

Fault Tolerance

To improve supportability, fault tolerance should be built into the infrastructure. This includes implementing the name servers with built-in redundancy, such as RAID disk subsystems, dual redundant power supplies, and dual network cards.

Installing redundant name servers at the application level is also critical, so that redundant systems can process the namespace queries in the event of a server outage. This even extends to placing redundant servers in different geographic regions to survive natural disasters, such as earthquakes, floods, or tornados.

Scaling

The DNS is a distributed database that provides excellent scalability. However, this leads to design issues when distributing DNS information across various DNS systems or geographically distant locations and administering the entire infrastructure. The design of the DNS namespace is important for long-term scaling of the infrastructure. As an organization develops, the design must survive, accommodating new developments and their impact on the namespace.

Organizational Changes

As an organization changes and reorganizes, the namespace must adjust to those changes. A well thought out design that is based on geographic first-layer domains and departmental second-layer domains provides a robust structure.

For example, the Inacom Corporation has selected inacom.com for their root domain, usawest.inacom.com for the western USA and usaeast.inacom.com for the eastern USA. In addition, there are secondary domains based on departments, such as accounting (acct.usawest.inacom.com and acct.usaeast.inacom.com). If, in the future, Inacom Corporation decides to consolidate the accounting department into the western USA, the infrastructure can accommodate the change with minimal administrative effort.

Organizational Growth

As an organization grows, the namespace should grow naturally with it. A structured design facilitates this. As growth occurs, the namespace can be further divided and expanded. Regional domains can have city subdomains, departmental domains can be broken into section subdomains, and even sections can be broken into buildings or floors in very large organizations.

Divestitures

Divestitures or downsizing should pose no problem for a well-designed namespace. If the organization spins off a region or a division, the namespace will accommodate those changes as easily as it did the growth. Clear replication boundaries also provide excellent separation boundaries when the need arises.

For example, if the Inacom Corporation needed to divest itself of the Consulting division, it would simply migrate those domains (consulting.usawest.inacom.com and consulting.usaeast.inacom.com) to newly created name servers belonging to the divested group.

Acquisitions and Mergers

The merger of two organizations, or the acquisition of one organization by another, poses special challenges to a DNS namespace. There might be a completely different design model in one organization that must be integrated with the existing namespace design.

If the design of the newly acquired organization is not very good, then it's easy to make a good case for replacing it with the well-crafted design already in place. However, if the newly acquired organization is well designed and fundamentally different, then the decision becomes more difficult. If both designs are well thought out and documented, then look for size advantages, the level of effort required to make changes, potential separate-but-equal arrangements, or other compromises.

Ultimately, these issues are often settled less on technical or design grounds, and more on political grounds. Typically, the acquiring organization's DNS become the standard.

Performance

Due to the reliance of Windows 2000 on the DNS services, performance is a critical factor. Performance is measured in several ways:

▼ **Query efficiency**   How fast is a query made by a client resolved?

■ **Bandwidth conservation**   How much wide area network (WAN) bandwidth is consumed by queries and zone transfers?

■ **Fault tolerance**   How well does the solution work in the event of WAN outages?

▲ **Local processing**   What resources are required on the local server to resolve requests (a key factor for heavily loaded servers)?

Performance hinges on the server types and where they are placed. The results of these measurements and optimizing the system is discussed in the "Server Model" section of this chapter.

Domain Namespace

Domain names are based on the DNS namespace. Any client or server can have a DNS name, as can any service. The namespace is typically the name that Internet users see when they access the corporate Web page or communicate with the company via email. Internal users also use these names to access corporate resources. As a result, the names should be meaningful, concise, recognizable, and memorable.

The namespace includes both registered and unregistered names, and in a complex environment, it is distributed across several locations. Even though a company has registered names with InterNIC, the use of those names may be either external, internal, or both.

Internal namespaces are those domain namespaces that corporate users use to access internal resources, such as files, services, logons, and private intranet services. External namespaces are those domain names that people external to the company use to access the company extranet servers, to send email, or to access the corporate Internet site. A namespace can also be used for both internal and external purposes.

Separate Internal and External Namespaces

You can elect to have completely separate namespaces to represent the internal and external resources. For example, the Inacom Corporation might have an external namespace with a root of inacom.com and an internal namespace with a root of inacomcorp.com. A user named Fred would log on to the Windows 2000 domain as fred@inacomcorp.com and access intranet servers using http://email.inacomcorp.com. People would send email to Fred at fred@inacom.com and use www.inacom.com to access the Inacom home page.

The advantages to this scheme are the following:

▼   A clear differentiation is made between external and internal resources.

■   Security is cleaner.

▲   Client configurations are simple.

The disadvantages are:

▼   It is confusing for internal users.

▲   Multiple namespaces must be reserved for the company.

Same Internal and External Namespaces

In the previous example, if the internal and external namespaces for the Inacom Corporation are the same, all access is made via inacom.com. Fred logs on to the domain as fred@inacom.com and accesses intranet severs as http://email.inacom.com. Individuals send email to fred@inacom.com and use www.inacom.com to access the home page.

The advantages of this design are as follows:

▼   There is less confusion for corporate users.

▲   A single namespace is reserved for the corporation.

The disadvantages are as follows:

▼   A clear distinction must be made between resources available internally and externally, which can be confusing and complex for internal operations.

■   Resource requests from clients are more complex.

▲ Users may be confused when presented with a differing view of resources depending on whether they are accessing resources internally or externally.

Domain Structure

The domain structure is important for Active Directory integration, both for administration and for performance.

Domains

Domain names are repeatedly used to access resources and to communicate both within Windows 2000 and outside the organization. Domain names contain both resources and other subdomains. The domain name identifies the position of the domain within the domain hierarchy. The number of domains required depends on two primary factors: administrative control and replication overhead. Administrative control is sometimes connected to political boundaries within the organization, such as when competing IT organizations want to maintain control over their own portion of the namespace. Different groups might have different security requirements, requiring the design of multiple domains to accommodate the multiple security models.

Since the DNS namespace is a distributed database, there is replication overhead in moving namespace data from one name server to another. Setting up domains to cover different geographic segments that are joined by relatively fast links is one way of addressing this issue. This allows administrators to configure less frequent replication across slow links, reducing the replication traffic.

Root Domains

The highest-level domain in the namespace is known as the root domain, and it represents the entire organization. All other domain names stem from this domain, so it is important to choose a name that accurately represents the organization. Note that the root domain of a particular namespace may not be (and usually is not), the root domain of the entire tree. It reflects the root of that namespace, which is under the control of one entity.

For example, the Inacom Corporation has several divisions, such as the Hardware division, the Services division, and the Consulting division. A root domain of inacomhardware.com would not be a wise choice. A better choice would be inacom.com or inacomcorp.com, as this more faithfully represents the entire organization.

The root domain is also the domain that is registered with the Internet, so it is both public and static. For planning purposes, plan on a life for the root domain name of at least five years, and very likely longer. The name must be approved at the highest level of the organization and by the legal department, due to its public and ubiquitous nature.

Subdomains

Below the root domain are the subdomains. Subdomains are not required, but they can be created to delegate administration, create replication boundaries, and minimize unnecessary replication.

The first-layer subdomains should be stable and survive reasonable corporate reorganizations. Some examples of first-layer subdomains for the Inacom Corporation are hardware.inacom.com and services.inacom.com, based on corporate divisions within the company. Another approach is to use usawest.inacom.com, usaeast.inacom.com, and europe.inacom.com, based on geographic distribution.

Second-layer subdomains represent specific locations or departments within the domains specified by the first-layer subdomains. For example, hardware.usawest.inacom.com, sfo.usawest.inacom.com, and corp.usawest.inacom.com, represent the western USA portion of the Inacom Corporation's Hardware division, the San Francisco office of the Inacom Corporation, and the corporate headquarters. Setting up a DNS structure with a three-division organization (Inacom Corporation's Hardware, Services, and Consulting division) is shown in Figure 7-1.

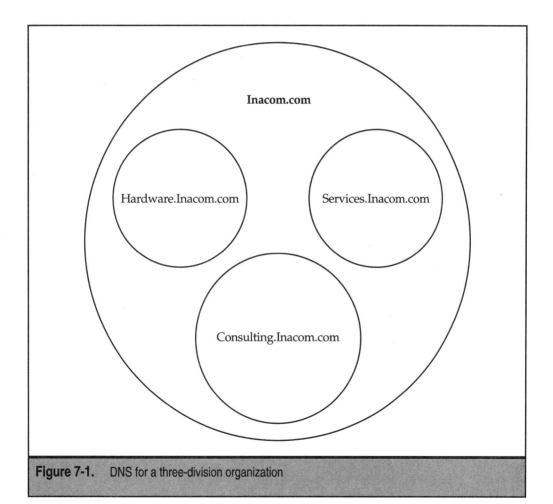

Figure 7-1.   DNS for a three-division organization

The subdomain names are usually approved at the departmental level, rather than the corporate executive level. Domain administrators should set general naming guidelines to ensure consistency in the naming structure. To streamline the planning of the subdomains, create a draft naming scheme that matches the departmental structure or other organizational boundaries.

> **NOTE:**   The naming convention for the first-layer subdomains should be longer than three characters so the names do not conflict with the International Standards Organization (ISO) 3166 two-character country code designations.

Zones

Each zone is anchored in a domain node known as the root domain. For example, Inacom Corporation's inacom.com is an entire zone anchored in the "com" domain. A zone does not have to contain the complete tree of subdomains, as some portion of the domain space may be allocated to other zones, such as usawest.inacom.com. This allows distribution of management to multiple support organizations. It also facilitates efficient replication.

> **NOTE:**   Domain administrators usually select the zones, as they are hidden from users.

Sites

Physical sites are good boundaries for replications via zone transfers, and also for administrative control. You can improve performance and fault tolerance by having servers at every site. If central control is an issue, you can make the site servers secondary name servers.

Server Model

The location of servers, the total number of servers, and the placement of servers, all impact the supportability and performance of the DNS infrastructure. The servers, or name servers, are the actual devices that respond to user queries and replicate the namespace. Careful planning of the server locations can make a dramatic difference in the overall performance of the domain. The options for domain server models are the following:

▼ Single server

■ Multiple servers

▲ Hierarchical servers

The server placement and type within the model chosen are also important planning considerations.

Single-Server Model

A single server is effective only for very small organizations, where the onus of providing both the DNS infrastructure and services is not generally severe. A daily backup provides an acceptable level of fault tolerance.

Multiple-Server Model

For medium-sized organizations, multiple servers can provide the performance enhancements and fault tolerance needed to keep operations running smoothly. The servers can be set up as primary and secondary pairs, using the secondary server as the target for backups of the primary name-server zones, as well as off-loading name-service queries.

Another option for organizations with separate divisions and separate IT administrations is dual primary name servers. These name servers maintain the zone information for their respective divisions, but they also operate as secondary name servers for their sister divisions. This design provides both division-level administration of the DNS namespace and organization-wide fault tolerance. This solution also scales well to more than two divisions.

Using pairs of servers as the repositories for namespace information provides a robust solution, but remember that each name server must contain the entire namespace. This can become unwieldy for large organizations when they add zones. At that point, consider a hierarchical solution, which simplifies maintenance and administration. This is also true for organizations with widely distributed geographical locations because the sites are dependant on the network links to the central office and its name servers.

Hierarchical-Server Model

Large organizations need a hierarchical design, which provides much better scalability, performance, and fault tolerance. Rather than have each name server act as a secondary for the entire organization, the hierarchical model allows lower-layer name servers to forward their requests up to the higher-level name servers. Using Inacom Corporation as an example, the root domain server exists in the corporate headquarters in San Francisco. Regional first-layer domains exist for each region such as western USA, eastern USA, and Europe.

For fault tolerance, the root domain can contain the corporate zone's primary and secondary servers. These servers can also be secondary name servers for each of the regional zones, providing corporation-wide fault tolerance for the namespace. The regional first-layer domains can each have primary and secondary name servers, and they can also provide forwarding designations to the corporate name servers. Additionally, key sites can have either secondary or caching name servers, which improves the performance of namespace queries at each site.

While significantly more complex, this hierarchical structure provides the level of performance and fault tolerance that a large enterprise requires.

Server Placement

If the DNS infrastructure is distributed within a single site, or among several sites with high bandwidth, then geographic performance constraints are likely to be minimal. If the organization is very geographically distributed, with slow links between sites, then the design needs to be tuned.

Since the DNS is a distributed database, the replication of the database can place significant loads on slow links. This is particularly true if the organization is very large (with large zone files) or if a legacy DNS is being used (requiring full zone file transfers, rather than incremental zone file transfers).

Local servers become important in constrained environments, as well, because lookups on centralized name servers consume bandwidth, resulting in lookup delays.

Server Types

Different types of servers have different levels of impact on operation and performance, and it's important that you understand the differences when planning a domain.

▼ **Secondary**   Name servers configured as secondary servers can pull the central domain server information on a regular basis, allowing queries to be completed locally. Secondary servers provide greater query efficiency, bandwidth conservation, and fault tolerance.

■ **Forwarders**   When a name server gets a request, it searches its local database to match the information. If it finds no match, it returns an error to the requestor. To expand the reach of the search, name servers can be configured as forwarders. In that case, after failing to find a match in the local database, the server forwards the request to other authoritative servers. These forwarding requests take some additional time to process, but they eliminate the need for the name server to do zone transfers with a larger number of servers.

■ **Slaves**   A slave name server is a server that has been configured as a forwarder only, so it does not use a local database to resolve queries. Slave name servers automatically forward all requests (there is no local lookup), which may expand the time needed to resolve queries. Slaves do little to improve any of the key performance variables and serve mainly to distribute the server load.

▲ **Cache**   Cache name servers are slave name servers that cache the results that are returned from queries. They contain no local zone information and are not authoritative for any domain. After receiving a request, the cache name server first tries to resolve the request from its local cache and then from the designated forwarder. Initially, the cache name server operates as a slave name server, because there are no entries in the cache. After a period of time, queries can be processed from the cache rather than through the forwarder. Over time, this can improve the query efficiency and conserve bandwidth.

The different server types and their characteristics are listed in Table 7-1.

Forwarding

Forwarding is a useful feature for DNS because it facilitates security and control of the DNS infrastructure. A good domain plan uses forwarding effectively, especially in a complex environment.

▼ **Security**   DNS forwarding lets you limit DNS traffic to only the internal DNS that is handling the forwarding service. All external requests are handled by the designated forwarder DNS, and you can configure your firewall to block any DNS requests that originate from any other systems.

▲ **Control**   Use forwarders to gain control over namespace lookups. You can channel lookups over specific name servers to balance loads, restrict access through firewalls, monitor lookups more effectively, and prevent lookups of banned sites.

Forwarding lets you redirect DNS requests to internal mirrored replicas of external destinations. Instead of providing a separate set of addresses for the internally mirrored Web servers, you can implement a DNS forward that redirects requests to the appropriate mirrored servers or external destinations. Figure 7-2 illustrates a simple DNS forwarding configuration.

Existing DNS Integration

If you have preexisting DNS infrastructures, you can handle them in one of the following ways:

▼ Replace them with the Microsoft DNS services.

■ Integrate them into the DNS needed for Windows 2000.

▲ Supplement them with Windows 2000.

Method	Query Efficiency	Fault Tolerance	Bandwidth Conservation
Primary	High	High	High
Secondary	High	High	Medium
Forwarder	Low	Low	High
Slave	Low	Low	Low
Cache	Medium	Medium	Medium

Table 7-1.   Characteristics of the DNS Server Types

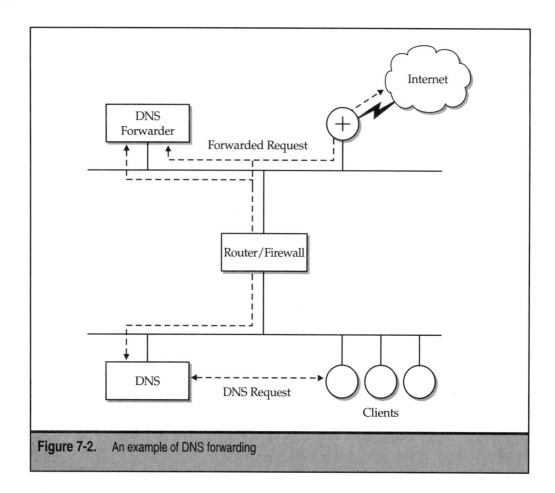

Figure 7-2. An example of DNS forwarding

Your decision will depend on a variety of conditions, including the design of the existing implementations, the specifications of the existing DNS servers, and internal political considerations. If the existing domain infrastructure is a Microsoft Windows 2000 DNS, you should integrate them. If the existing domain infrastructure is a non–Microsoft Windows 2000 variant, then you need to evaluate your options.

Potential Issues

If your goal is to integrate your Microsoft Windows 2000 DNS with the existing DNS infrastructure, you must consider several issues, one of which is the technical feasibility for integration. You must examine the Requests for Comment (RFCs) supported by the current infrastructure. To integrate Microsoft Active Directory, a minimum level of RFC compliance is necessary (this is discussed next). If the minimum level of compliance is not met, it is not possible to integrate the two DNS services, although some workarounds are available.

Request for Comment

There are a variety of RFCs that cover DNS, but several have particular relevance for the Windows 2000 DNS design: the Service Location Resource Record, the Dynamic Update Protocol, and the Incremental Zone Transfer Protocol.

The Service Location Resource Record (RFC 2052) specifies a generalization of the MX record concept that allows servers to advertise similar services. This permits services to be advertised within the DNS. For Windows 2000, the resource records point to domain controllers.

The Dynamic Update Protocol (IETF RFC 2136) allows clients and servers to register domain names and IP addresses with the name service. This allows automatic updates of the namespace, so that administrators don't have to process them manually.

Incremental Zone Transfer Protocol (IETF RFC 1995) allows incremental information to be transferred in the zone transfer process, rather than the entire zone file. For larger zones, this can dramatically reduce the bandwidth demands of replicating the distributed namespace.

Minimum Requirements

The minimum level of RFC compliance required for a DNS to integrate with the Windows 2000 Active Directory is defined in the Service Location Resource Record (RFC 2052). For clients and servers to locate Microsoft Windows 2000 domain controllers within the DNS, the DNS must support this RFC. If the DNS does not comply with RFC 2052, then you must replace the DNS or design a workaround.

Recommended Requirements

In addition to meeting the minimum requirement of Service Location Resource Record (RFC 2052), it is strongly recommended that the DNS comply with the Dynamic Update Protocol (IETF RFC 2136) and the Incremental Zone Transfer Protocol (IETF RFC 1995), and provide for DHCP integration. This reduces the administrative overhead required to manually update the namespace with servers, clients, and IP addresses. It also reduces the bandwidth requirements for maintaining the database replicas across WAN links.

If the recommendations cannot be met with the existing DNS, then seriously consider either upgrading the DNS to support them, or replacing the DNS with Microsoft DNS. Otherwise, you will have to devise a plan that builds in the additional overhead required to maintain the legacy DNS.

Existing DNS Group

If there is an existing DNS group that is responsible for the design and maintenance of the domain service, it is important to integrate with it. There are typically territorial concerns, especially if the existing DNS design requires extensive changes.

In many cases, there are constraints in the technology the existing DNS group is willing to support. For example, many legacy DNS systems are UNIX- based, and this can result in technology concerns if the Windows 2000 team proposes to replace the existing UNIX-based DNS. The process of dynamic updates to the formerly static namespace might prompt extensive discussions and resistance.

One of the key success factors in working with the existing DNS group is including them in the DNS discussions and decision-making process. Failure to include the DNS group and get their agreement on key decisions could result in a less-than-optimal design for the Windows 2000 system.

DNS SERVER OPTIONS

You have three primary options for deploying DNS:

▼ Use the Microsoft DNS server that comes with Windows 2000.

■ Use a compliant third-party DNS.

▲ Use a noncompliant third-party DNS.

There are clear advantages to choosing Microsoft DNS over the others.

Microsoft DNS

Using the Windows 2000 Microsoft DNS server is by far the best design choice. It provides a number of key supportability benefits, as well as the assurance that it has been thoroughly tested to ensure complete compatibility in a Microsoft Windows 2000 environment. If there is no existing DNS or there are plans to replace the existing DNS, use the Microsoft DNS server.

Implementation

The steps for implementing DNS depend on the level of complexity of the organization's domain and Active Directory structure. If Microsoft DNS is replacing an existing DNS, the infrastructure has to be set up in parallel, in order to maintain services. This requires additional effort to integrate, transfer existing DNS records, and train staff, but it reduces the need to reconfigure existing servers and desktops (which are presumably using the existing DNS systems). See Figure 7-3 for a sample design using Microsoft DNS.

If Microsoft DNS is the first DNS service in the enterprise, implementation is much more straightforward. The DNS infrastructure can be deployed along with the operating system, or even deployed in advance. Existing desktops and servers must be modified to reference the new DNS infrastructure.

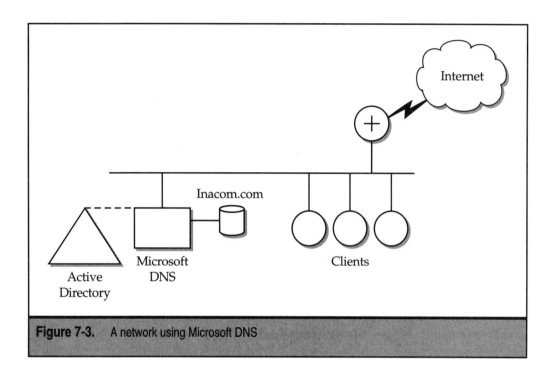

Figure 7-3.   A network using Microsoft DNS

NOTE: This is an excellent opportunity to deploy Dynamic Host Configuration Protocol (DHCP) services, if they are not already deployed. The DHCP services provide automatic IP address assignments and also integrate closely with the Microsoft DNS, reducing administration.

Advantages

The Microsoft DNS server meets all DNS server guidelines, and even has some additional features. The key RFCs are fully implemented in the Microsoft DNS server, including Service Location Resource Record (RFC 2052), Dynamic Update Protocol (IETF RFC 2136), and Incremental Zone Transfer Protocol (IETF RFC 1995). (These RFCs are described in the "Request for Comment" section, earlier in this chapter.)

Additionally, the Microsoft DNS server supports Unicode and is fully integrated with DHCP. This gives you more flexibility for naming conventions, as well as easier administration of dynamically allocated IP addresses.

The Microsoft DNS server has an easy to use graphical interface, along with other features that ease administration tasks and reduce the total cost of ownership.

Finally, the Microsoft DNS server is included with the operating system and is easy to deploy.

Disadvantages

If there is an existing DNS server platform, it may be difficult to justify the effort required to replace it, especially if the existing DNS meets recommended specifications.

Unfortunately, political wrangling can also be a large factor in the decision-making process. If the group controlling the existing DNS is well entrenched, then it might not be possible to replace the DNS. In that case, there are workarounds that can be implemented to continue the project.

Compliant Non-Microsoft DNS

If an existing DNS supports the minimum requirements, you can integrate it with the Windows 2000 Active Directory. You can configure the Active Directory to reference the existing DNS, although you might want to update the records manually.

Be sure to perform extensive testing of the integration of DNS with the Active Directory, and with DHCP, to ensure full functionality. Additional testing may be required to ensure the DNS can support the additional load imposed by the integration of Windows 2000. Assuming there are no upgrades needed to support RFCs, you should not have to make any enterprise-level changes to integrate the DNS with Windows 2000. See Figure 7-4 for a sample design of a compliant non-Microsoft DNS design.

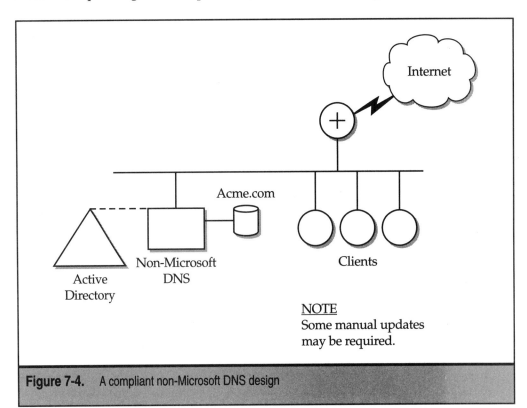

Figure 7-4.   A compliant non-Microsoft DNS design

Advantages

Integrating Windows 2000 with an existing DNS requires less effort than setting up a new DNS, because you merely need to integrate what is already there. Integrating instead of building saves time and expense, and it allows more resources to be dedicated to the deployment of Windows 2000.

Disadvantages

Using a compliant non-Microsoft DNS with Windows 2000 does increase the administrative overhead because of the additional manual data entry, maintenance, and training. If the existing DNS meets only the minimum requirements for supporting service location resource records (RFC 2052), you will have to expend significant administrative effort over the long term, adding records manually and troubleshooting problems. You also face higher bandwidth requirements.

Testing requires more effort, because the existing DNS system is not configured or tested for the integration. Remember also that even if the existing DNS supports the dynamic update RFC (IETF RFC 2136), you will have a single point of failure for dynamic registrations, which can affect fault tolerance.

Noncompliant Non-Microsoft DNS

If there is an existing DNS infrastructure that is not compliant with standard DNS standards, or if the existing DNS infrastructure will not be replaced by the Microsoft DNS, you need to implement a workaround in order to allow the Active Directory to function properly.

The most straightforward workaround is to create a delegated subdomain for the Windows 2000 Active Directory. The main DNS is configured to forward all namespace queries to the designated Windows 2000 name server. This solution provides continuity while providing the benefits of the Windows 2000 DNS server.

To implement the workaround, set up a domain for the Windows 2000 Active Directory. For example, the Inacom Corporation might create an ad.inacom.com subdomain, where "ad" represents Active Directory. This subdomain contains the resource records for the Windows 2000 domains.

After the subdomain is set up, implement the standard configuration of a Windows 2000 DNS server for use with the Active Directory. If this domain will be used for namespace queries, then the name servers should be configured to forward namespace queries to the existing noncompliant DNS to ensure full integration of the namespaces. See Figure 7-5 for a sample design.

Advantages

There is considerably less impact on the existing DNS if you use a delegated subdomain for the Windows 2000 integration. The risk of introducing a new DNS service to replace the existing DNS is neatly avoided, as are the additional effort and political battles.

There is also the benefit of reducing the Active Directory's dependence on the existing DNS and avoiding potential incompatibilities. The process of delegating subdomains is

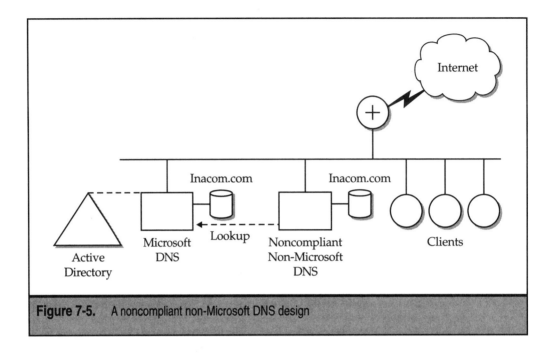

Figure 7-5. A noncompliant non-Microsoft DNS design

well understood and practiced, so there is a low risk of problems arising from this approach. However, Windows 2000 and the Active Directory are new technologies, and integrating them with legacy DNS services means breaking new ground.

Disadvantages

This workaround requires a separate namespace for the Windows 2000 logons, which is slower and may require more user support on a long-term basis. The additional administrative overhead includes management of dual DNS services, as well as training.

PLANNING THE DESIGN CHANGE

To create a plan, review the existing environment, research different vendors, and make a thorough review of available design options. After you have gathered information and created potential design options, document the design and the plan, including the decision-making processes that led to the design.

Reviewing the Existing Environment

It is important to conduct a thorough review of the existing environment prior to initiating a design change. Even if there are preexisting documents, you must verify their accuracy.

Document Review

Review any documents that provide information about existing systems, including as-built reports, topology diagrams, maintenance guides, and other organization-specific documentation. This review will help you develop a context and understanding of what is installed or, more likely, what was originally installed. Systems have a way of changing over time, and documentation is not always maintained. Once you have a clear understanding of what is supposed to be on the ground, verify and update the information.

Discovery

Discovery is the hands-on inspection of systems, network links, software, versions, configurations, and locations of systems. This also includes testing, such as verifying DNS server names and IP addresses. It's important to gather version information and patch histories for all relevant platforms. This is very important for determining whether existing DNS services are compliant with the important RFCs, and it also aids in considering potential problems.

   If possible, gather performance metrics and problem histories, as well. Even if there are no historical performance metrics, gathering the current metrics for a period of a week or a month will help you understand how changes might affect the infrastructure. Gathering recent problem histories is also valuable.

Interviews

Conduct interviews with the existing support staff, architects, and managers to learn how the current environment is performing and to locate any current problems. These interviews should happen after the document review and the discovery phases are completed. If interviews are conducted prior to the document review step, it is difficult to establish a context for the interview, and the interviewer will likely miss key points.

   Also, prepare a list of questions and have a clear understanding of what information needs to be gathered from each interview. Another helpful technique is to have two people conduct the interviews—one to ask the questions and the other to take notes. Both interviewers should be familiar with the project and technology, and with the goals of the interviews.

Research Possible Solutions

After the basic information has been discovered, perform detailed research on the information. Verify compliance and features with vendors, research design options with Microsoft, and search relevant knowledge databases.

Vendors

Contact vendors to verify the features of the installed versions and to learn about upgrade options. This gives you a way to check for potential incompatibilities. It is important to obtain written documentation or statements from vendors to ensure accountability. Vendor

Web sites also offer extensive white papers and product specifications, which are great research tools.

Microsoft

Microsoft provides a large array of resources covering Windows 2000 specifications, design guides, technical references, sample designs, and planning guides. Their staff of solutions providers can bring experience to the project, imparting solid background knowlege of the relevant technologies and processes, along with high-level links to Microsoft.

Knowledge Databases

Search the relevant knowledge databases for sample designs, white papers, tips, tricks, and bug reports. Microsoft Technet, the official Microsoft technical support database, contains hundreds of megabytes of very useful information. Other sources include books (such as this one), user groups, and email lists. Lists are particularly helpful if you have specific questions for which you've been unable to gain answers.

Review the Options

After gathering the environment information, updating it with the current state, and researching the vendors, you can document your options, evaluate them, and make a decision.

Document the Options

It is important to document the options that come out of the review, discovery, and research phases. This is helpful when you have to make your decision, and it is also helpful for defending your decision. After you make your decision, your documentation makes it clear to anyone reviewing your decisions (such as upper management or auditors) that you used clear rationales. The options document need not be very extensive, and can be as simple as a statement of each option with the perceived advantages and disadvantages.

Decision Matrix

Another tool for making defensible decisions is to use a decision matrix. This is a table with a list of criteria on which the various options are weighted. After the options are rated on the criteria, their total score is added up to determine which option scores highest. Figure 7-6 shows a sample weighted decision matrix.

Plan the Implementation

Creating the plan for implementing your design has five key phases: planning, prototyping, pilot implementation, deployment, and closing. These are general minimum guidelines; they can be expanded as the need arises for more complex plans.

CRITERIA	WEIGHT (1-5)	OPTION A: MICROSOFT		OPTION B: X		OPTION C: Y	
		RATED		RATED		RATED	
Cost	4	10	40	5	20	8	24
Compliance	5	10	50	7	35	7	35
TCO	3	8	24	6	18	5	15
Resistance	3	3	9	5	15	8	24
TOTALS			123		88		98

Figure 7-6. A weighted decision matrix

Planning

During the planning phase, the other phases are refined, timelines are detailed, resources are allocated, hardware and software is ordered, and planning documents are prepared. This step is crucial for forming your teams and setting up communications. The planning phase typically takes 5 percent of the total project duration and effort.

Prototyping

The prototype phase is also known as the proof-of-concept phase. In this phase, the concepts that were developed in the design phase are implemented on a small scale to ensure they meet all requirements, including vendor assurances and compatibility. This phase is also used to determine macro-level deployment efforts and to create training guides. Prototypes are generally conducted apart from the actual environment, employing only test users. Feedback from this phase helps you adjust your design. The prototype phase typically takes 5 percent of the total project duration and effort.

Pilot Implementation

The pilot phase allows you to refine the design and implementation plan. The number of users involved is typically increased in several steps, such as 1 percent of the user population, 5 percent of the user population, and 10 percent of the user population. Problems that emerge will affect only a small number of users, and the plan can be further refined in real time. At the end of the pilot phase, you should have 20 percent of the total user population on the new system, and a well-defined process for deploying the balance of the users. This phase typically takes 20 percent of the total project duration and effort.

Deployment

The deployment phase, in which users and systems are moved to the new platform, can be uneventful if the other phases have been executed properly. While it is not exciting, this is the natural outcome of the entire process and typically takes 70 percent of the total project duration and effort.

Closing

The closing phase is a very small, but crucial phase of the project. This is the time to complete your documentation: generate built reports, conduct satisfaction surveys, and hold a post-mortem meeting. This phase winds down the process, making sure that what was done is clearly documented, and the lessons learned are brought into the corporate knowledge base. This phase typically takes less than 1 percent of the total project duration and effort.

Document the Design

After you complete the design and plan, you must communicate the results to the team and the rest of the organization. The detail level and complexity of the DNS design and plan varies by organization and project, but the main components should all be present in some level of detail. In other words, instead of eliminating any key components of the document, you should reduce the level of detail of the components.

The document should include the following components: executive summary, overview, scope (mission statement), background, design options, design decisions, design, plan, and conclusion.

Executive Summary

The executive summary is an overview of the entire document, designed to provide a busy executive an understanding of the results. This is normally a one-page document with an abbreviated overview, scope, and design.

Overview

The overview gives the reader an understanding of the entire project, and is typically a page or two in length. Use the narrative form, and discuss the scope, background, process, and end results of the project.

Scope (Mission Statement)

This is normally a concise description of the overall purpose of the project, along with a prioritized list of goals and objectives. The goals and objectives are typically SMART objectives: specific, measurable, achievable, relevant, and time-bound. These statements are typically one sentence, or at most, one paragraph.

Background

The background section is a detailed description of the history and the problems that have occurred. Include information about previous attempts to solve the problem, business drivers, and other information that might be relevant. This section is usually one or two pages in length, depending on the complexity of the project.

Design Options

The design and planning options section helps the reader understand the alternatives that are available. This could include namespace options, server-placement options, architectural options, and any other alternatives. The options should be presented impartially, with a clear statement of the advantages and disadvantages of each. In some cases, it is useful to include citations from respected sources, such as industry reports and experts.

Design Decisions

The design decisions section clearly states the rationale for your decision. This is critical for defending the decision, as it provides a detailed blueprint of the decision-making process.

Design

The design is documented in this section. Include a narrative description of each of the components and their interconnections, along with architectural diagrams and charts, if possible. For the domain design, the design portion of the document should include:

▼ Domain architecture
■ Naming conventions
■ Servers
■ Server types
■ Replication strategies
▲ Existing DNS integration strategies

Plan

The plan for implementing the design is documented in this section. The plan should include the following components:

- ▼ **Phases**   A description of each phase with key objectives.
- ■ **Milestones**   Key dates, such as end of phases, deployment high points, and other salient dates. This is useful for reporting, checking progress, and motivating the team.
- ■ **Tasks**   The individual tasks that must be completed to successfully implement the design.
- ■ **Timeline**   Overall timeline of phases and milestones, including specific times for tasks. This is normally placed on a Gantt chart.
- ■ **Resources**   Staff, equipment, and space needed to implement the design.
- ▲ **Roles**   Roles and responsibilities for the staff assigned to the project.

Conclusion

The conclusion summarizes the results of the project. This section typically gives an abbreviated discussion of the overview and a description of the design. This is an important element of the report, as it is the last part read and, thus, needs to impress the reader. This section is typically one page in length.

CHAPTER 8

Designing Connectivity

The definition of a network changed as organizations moved to connectivity beyond the traditional cable. Today, designing a network is more than worrying about the performance of file servers and workstations; it includes consideration of the importance of the communication link between the user and server, and between servers.

Additionally, the definition of a network now encompasses an organizational information system structure. That information may be distributed across multiple sites and servers, using a private wide area network or the Internet.

To maintain such a distributed and diverse infrastructure, you must develop standards and processes for communication across diverse systems and over extended distances.

In this chapter we will explore the communication standards, the impact of the hardware, and the importance of adequate bandwidth in the total Windows 2000 communications environment.

STANDARDIZING ON TCP/IP

With Windows 2000, Microsoft has standardized on the Transmission Control Protocol/Internet Protocol (TCP/IP) communications protocol for network communications. In previous versions of Windows NT, Microsoft used the NetBEUI communications protocol with the NetBIOS naming system as the standard.

The change to TCP/IP with DNS as the name resolution system matches the standards used by UNIX systems, the Internet, and other local area and wide area network operating systems. This provides better compatibility with other systems and has the additional benefit of simplifying communications across backbones such as the Internet.

TCP/IP Basics

TCP/IP provides a common physical addressing system and a common communication language that facilitates communications between other TCP/IP systems. The system uses IP addresses that are internationally assigned and registered, which has been envisioned as the way to provide a unique address for every single system in the global TCP/IP network structure.

However, because there are a finite number of addresses, there is a limit to the ability to assign a unique address to every single system. The solution is to find a system that can reuse the same addresses without creating any conflicts across multiple systems. That solution is implemented with network address translation (NAT). The node management and diverse system interoperatability of the Windows 2000 environment are based on the concepts of IP addressing and NAT.

Addressing

While every device (server, workstation, printer, gateway, router, and so on) has a unique IP address, that address is actually a unique node on a unique segment in the TCP/IP addressing system. This can be compared to postal addresses, which are based on a street name and a street number. This allows a mail carrier to find the street, and then find the address. In the TCP/IP addressing system, a segment is similar to a street name, and a unique node address (IP address) is like a street address. Devices on a TCP/IP network find each other by having other devices point to the segment, at which point the device can narrow down the segment to a very specific part of the network (more on the concept of a routing table later in this chapter).

An IP address is based on four octets separated by periods, where an octet is a number between 0 and 255. This permits a range from 0.0.0.0 to 255.255.255.255. However, the range from 0.0.0.0 to 0.255.255.255 is not used, so the first IP segment is actually 1.0.0.0. When an organization is assigned a block of IP addresses, that block includes a range of addresses—for example, from 140.0.0.0 to 140.0.9.255. This allows the organization to have 25,600 different nodes on a single segment.

Segmentation

Organizations typically break their assigned range of addresses into multiple internal segments, making it possible to break down its network into more manageable segments. For example, an organization may want to create ten segments, giving each segment 256 nodes. One segment is assigned the address 140.0.0.*x*, with nodes ranging from 0 to 255 in the last octet position, giving the range 140.0.0.0 to 140.0.0.255. Another segment would be 140.0.1.*x* with its unique 256 nodes on that segment, and so on. It is this segmentation that enables an organization to distribute the traffic across multiple segments of the network, which improves both the performance and the manageability of each individual segment.

Network Address Translation

As I mentioned, with a finite number of IP addresses available, NAT provides a way to expand the number of addresses accessible in the addressing scheme. The way it works is that NAT uses the Internet address space from 10.0.0.0 to 10.255.255.255. The translation process allows an organization to have over 16 million devices within network connections. One single IP address, external to the network, is published to the world (at least the world as described by the Internet).

TCP/IP Management

For an administrator, the management of workstations, services, and devices on a TCP/IP network is accomplished with the Windows 2000 TCP/IP management tools and utilities (DHCP and DNS).

Dynamic Host Configuration Protocol (DHCP)

To assign IP addresses, you can either manually assign each and every device on the network an address or use the automatic address distribution system called Dynamic Host Configuration Protocol, or DHCP. When a system or device in a Windows 2000 network boots without a predefined IP address (or static address), it needs to acquire one. It searches the network for a DHCP server from which it can obtain an IP address.

The DHCP server is configured to hold a range of valid addresses that it makes available to devices. (Installation and configuration of DHCP is covered in Chapter 13.) The DHCP server leases this address to the device for the length of time determined by the network administrator. The advantage of using DHCP is, obviously, that you don't need to track the static addresses of every system and device on your network. Just define the range of addresses that can be used and let the devices grab one of the available addresses within the range.

Not only does DHCP minimize the tracking of individual IP addresses, but it also provides a way to change the segment configuration of the network. As I noted earlier in this chapter, your organization is built on a range of IP addresses that are segmented to improve communications and connectivity performance, and, if needed, to create zones of the network that designate different physical sites of the organization. Sites are the physical segmentations of your network and the site is the unit you use to replicate information, administer the organization, and distribute data.

Domain Name Services (DNS)

Windows 2000 uses DNS, eliminating the previously used Windows Internetworking Naming Service (WINS). Because all addressing is handled by the physical IP address on the network, with logical names assigned to each device, translating names to IP addresses—and vice versa—is accomplished through a lookup table. The lookup table resides on DNS servers strategically placed throughout the organization.

As you plan your network infrastructure, it's important to remember that the closer the DNS name resolution server is to the client workstation, the faster the client system will be able to resolve names and IP addresses.

Converting to TCP/IP

Because TCP/IP is the default protocol for Windows 2000, and DNS is the default name resolution system, your current network will eventually need to be upgraded. (The conversion to TCP/IP and DNS is detailed in Chapter 15 of this book.)

Your current NT system is probably using NetBEUI and NetBIOS, and if you're also running Novell NetWare, you're also running IPX/SPX. Now, you probably want to ask, "If I'm already using NetBIOS, NetBEUI, or IPX/SPX, why wouldn't I just continue to use them?" There are a number of good reasons to migrate to TCP/IP.

Routing Capabilities

TCP/IP is a routable protocol, but NetBEUI is not. This means when you create a wide area network, TCP/IP allows you to segment the network based on the multiple sites you have in your organization. When a packet of information needs to be sent from one segment to the other, the packet knows that the segment does not reside on the local network and that it needs to be routed to another segment. This is an efficient method of moving selected sets of information from one part of an organization to another.

Without a routable protocol, the information is just forwarded throughout your organization's structure until the destination device, which sometimes doesn't work properly, captures the information it's supposed to receive. This method of communication causes excessive traffic and congestion, and isn't an efficient method for getting information to its final destination.

Industry Standards

TCP/IP has become a standard for internetworking. It's used by UNIX systems, mainframe computers, Macintosh systems, Novell networks, the Internet, etc. Having a common protocol makes it easier to exchange information between devices.

It also means you can use DNS name resolution servers to service the name resolution requests from all of the device types on your system. Without TCP/IP, you'd have to have a specific name resolution server for each system type on your network.

Consolidation of Protocols

Standardizing on a common protocol that all your devices can use means you minimize the number of languages being transmitted on your network. This is a more efficient communications process because you don't have the excessive traffic generated by multiple protocols on a single network system.

UNDERSTANDING THE EXISTING SYSTEM INFRASTRUCTURE

The key to designing an efficient environment for a network is to understand both the existing structure (including LANs and WANs) as well as the future communication requirements. Log and analyze your current utilization to develop an appropriate plan for your organization. Of course, if your organization has no existing network, the infrastructure demands of the system will be based solely on the analysis of the expected performance requirements of the organization (a wish list). As you begin, you'll find that diagrams and documentation of the current network infrastructure are extremely helpful.

As you diagram and document the current configuration of your network, you're likely to find inconsistencies between what you think the network configuration is and the way it really is configured. As you plan your Windows 2000 network, including site distribution, DNS, and DHCP, it's important that the port connections and resource distribution are configured as expected. This ensures that name resolution requests are properly distributed among the available DNS servers on the network, traffic is distributed across the various segments on the network, and active directory partitioning is replicated across the correct site segments of the network.

Creating Diagrams of the Infrastructure

There are two types of diagrams, both of which are going to be useful in your planning: physical diagrams and logical diagrams.

Physical Diagrams

Physical diagrams show the actual port-to-port connections of each device in your system, through switches, hubs, gateways, and routers. If a router has two ports, the physical diagram shows where both ports of the router are connected. If a switch has 12 ports, the physical diagram has 12 lines going from the graphic of the switch to each of the physical devices connected to the switch. Figure 8-1 is a representative illustration of a physical diagram.

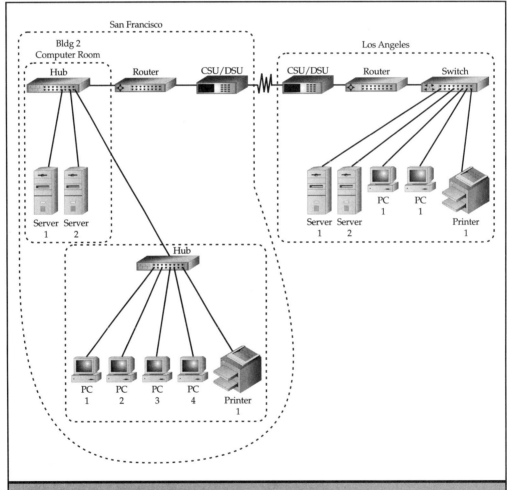

Figure 8-1. Use physical diagrams to represent all the connections on your network

Logical Diagrams

You're probably quite familiar with logical diagrams. The typical logical diagram may show a generic cloud to represent a wide area network, or display a single line with multiple devices branching off the line to represent interconnectivity. As shown in Figure 8-2, logical diagrams show connectivity between devices from a relative connection standpoint rather than a specific connection basis.

Typically, a logical diagram is easier to understand when you need to see the overall configuration of a network at a glance. A physical diagram does a better job of representing the actual port-to-port configuration, which you need to consider when you're determining the actual path of communication between devices.

Documenting the Existing Server Infrastructure

Documenting your existing server infrastructure will make the planning and migration processes to Windows 2000 easier. This section covers the issues you need to document.

Documenting Current Servers

For each server in your organization, you need to document the following information.

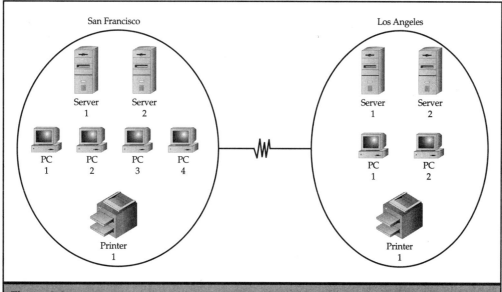

Figure 8-2.   Logical diagrams present an overview of connectivity rather than specific connections

SERVER ROLE   Is the server an application server, a general file server, or a print server? If the server is an application server, document the applications, including versions. This information is useful when you begin creating upgrade and migration plans for the server operating system.

INSTALLED MEMORY   Note the amount of memory in the server, because the available memory is a core component for network server performance analysis.

DISK STORAGE   Document the available space so you know whether the server has enough space to install a system upgrade, a service pack, or an additional server service.

OS VERSION   Note the operating system, including the version number and service pack or patch level. (Different configurations may make upgrade processes different, or may impact license upgrades.)

IP ADDRESSES   Knowing the IP address and the subnet mask on each adapter in the server will help you determine which segments the server is attached to. Additionally, if you use applications that look for servers based on the IP address, when the server is upgraded or replaced, the IP address must be retained. Otherwise, your software may need to be reconfigured.

PROTOCOLS IN USE   Documenting the protocols used by the server is important because many client workstations may be accessing the server over NetBEUI or IPX instead of TCP/IP. During your migration to Windows 2000, you'll need to make a decision—you'll either include all of these protocols or configure the server exclusively for TCP/IP. The latter may require you to update the workstations.

SERVICES IN USE   Note whether the server is a WINS server, a DHCP server, a DNS server, an application server, or any combination. When the server is upgraded, it is important that the server services are still running after the migration. (You can move the services to another server during the migration process.) During a capacity or system performance analysis, it is important to test the load that additional server services add to the workload of the servers. For example, as you reconfigure your network, you may find that the load of a site server may increase (or decrease). Review the impact that site and organizational infrastructure changes place on the network environment.

MEMBER SERVER OR DOMAIN CONTROLLER   It's important to know if a server is acting as a domain controller or as a member server on the network. Domain controllers are usually treated differently during an upgrade or migration process. You need to decide the role of the server during migration, and there are several alternatives available:

▼ The server can temporarily serve as both an NT 4 PDC or BDL, and a Windows 2000 domain controller.

■ The server can be migrated solely to a Windows 2000 domain controller.

▲ The server can be migrated to perform as a Windows 2000 member server.

These decisions are made during the analysis phase, after the load of the domain authentication and replica replication is determined.

ROUTING FUNCTIONS   It is important to know whether the server is acting as a router on the network from a single adapter or across multiple network adapters. Just as protocols are important for client-to-server access, if certain traffic is being converted or diverted at the server across protocols, it's important to know this before the server is upgraded or replaced.

Surprisingly, during a number of our Windows 2000 migrations we found that many of the organizations were unaware how much of their network traffic was using a particular server or a series of servers to route traffic between segments. In fact, in a few instances we found that the administrators wrongly assumed that the routers on their network were handling the traffic instead of servers. Additionally, we found organizations where nobody was aware that external Internet traffic had full access to the LAN through a Windows NT server route.

Table 8-1 presents a simple form you might want to use, or base your own form on, as you document the servers in your network.

Server Name

Location

Description

Server Information

Operating system installed

Version or patch level of NOS

File/print or application server?

Domain controller or member?

Physical Configuration

Processor type and qty

Total RAM memory

Disk Subsystem Information

Total disk space

Available disk space

Fault tolerance configuration

Table 8-1.   Checklist for Documenting Server Infrastructure

Protocol Information

TCP/IP? (IP address/subnet mask)

IPX/NetBEUI/other?

Routing enabled?

Server Applications

WINS enabled?

DHCP enabled?

DNS enabled?

Other services installed

Table 8-1. Checklist for Documenting Server Infrastructure *(continued)*

Documenting the Existing Desktop Infrastructure

Because Windows 2000 is a distributed processing environment, the functions of both the desktops and the servers play an important part in your migration strategy. Just as in the server configuration process, something as simple as a protocol change or server name change can render client access inaccessible, there are a number of other workstation components that affect the overall LAN and WAN connectivity process. Understanding those processes helps you achieve a successful migration to Windows 2000. Here's what you need to know about your existing desktop machines.

Workstation Configuration

You need to document the basic workstation configuration, including processor type, amount of memory, and available disk space. This is important because client access drivers for the new operating system need to be installed, so knowing the configuration ensures that the correct drivers will be installed. If the desktops in your network will also be upgraded to Windows 2000, you need to make sure they have the appropriate memory, disk space, and processing speed to run the new operating system.

Workstation OS Versions

The version of the operating system on the desktop as well as the revision level or update level play an important role in any update or upgrade to the desktop. Since different versions of the operating system upgrade using different tools and utilities, the upgrade process is different based on the current system configuration.

IP Addresses

You must know the IP address and the subnet mask on the workstation adapter so you know which segment on the network the workstation is connected to.

Protocols in Use

If the workstation is currently accessing a server or application with NetBEUI or IPX and you make TCP/IP the new standard, the connection between the client system and the server may fail. You must know how the client currently connects to the server in order to know the breadth of your protocol update processes.

DHCP and Name Resolution Strategy

If your organization has implemented DHCP for dynamic IP allocation, a DHCP server must be available on the workstation's network segment. If you migrate from NT to Windows 2000 and DNS is replacing WINS for the organization's default name resolution, DNS will need to be installed and tested to ensure ongoing operations.

Software Distribution Strategy

If your organization is using software distribution such as Microsoft Systems Management Server (SMS) or a third-party software distribution program, you can use the existing software distribution process to distribute software updates and upgrades to the workstations. In many cases, it is the workstation upgrades that cause bottlenecks in the migration process. When you have a way to quickly and easily upgrade workstations, the complications are greatly minimized.

Table 8-2 is a basic documentation form you can use to analyze the workstations on your network.

Workstation Identification

Workstation name

Location

Description

Workstation Information

Operating system installed

Version or patch level of OS

Table 8-2.   Checklist for Documenting Workstation Infrastructure

Physical Configuration

Processor type

Total RAM memory

Disk Subsystem Information

Total disk space

Available disk space

Communications Information

TCP/IP? (if so, IP address/subnet mask)

IPX/NetBEUI/other?

DHCP enabled?

WINS or DNS in use?

Software Application in Use

Apps installed on a server?

Apps installed on the local system?

Table 8-2.   Checklist for Documenting Workstation Infrastructure *(continued)*

Documenting the Existing LAN/WAN Structure

After you document the existing server and desktop configurations, you need to look at the rest of the network infrastructure. You must document the elements that impact the bandwidth demands and availability, because they affect the performance of the network.

Domain Controllers

Because domain controllers exchange directory information, you need to design your network so the controllers authenticate users as efficiently as possible. Additionally, you must take bandwidth into consideration to maintain the speed with which replication is accomplished.

Time Servers

Information about the location of the time servers around the network needs to be documented (as well as the timing of synchronization between them).

Replication Partners

These are servers that synchronize information across the network by replicating data to other servers. Replication partners include mail servers, intranet data servers, and database servers. Replication brings information closer to the users who need it, and also provides the redundancy necessary for a good fault-tolerance or disaster recovery plan. Document and analyze the placement and performance of the replication partners on the network.

WAN Infrastructure

Documenting the existing WAN infrastructure (routers, bridges, gateways, and network segments) is the way to understand how information flows around the network. When you review WAN configurations, there are a number of processes that you must complete, as follows:

▼ Note the physical placement of routers, bridges, and gateways, and identify the segments they serve.

■ Document the traffic that is supposed to flow between segments (the original plan), then analyze the flow to see what is actually moving between segments.

■ Determine the protocols that are in use to transmit the information around the network.

▲ Analyze the bandwidth and whether it really meets the demands of the information transmitted on the network. This information helps you design the placement of domain controllers and data storage servers on the network.

IP Addresses of All Devices

Record the IP addresses of all devices on the network. Remember that in addition to servers, workstations, and internetworking devices, your printers are part of the system. Printers should always be on the same segment as the users who access them, because moving the constant data produced by printing across routers creates bottlenecks.

Firmware Version of Internetworking Devices

In many cases, the performance or operations of routing communications are impacted by the version of the firmware on the devices. We have seen many installations in which connectivity was troublesome, or didn't work at all, until upgrades were installed for the firmware of the routers on the network.

Protocols Supported by Routers

Some routers (especially those with old firmware) do not support many of the new standards for secured communications or efficient network communications. Support for current TCP/IP protocol standards is especially important. Analyze the routers to make sure they support current communication protocols.

Existing LAN/WAN Speeds

Document the existing LAN and WAN connection speeds to make sure you're getting the speed you expected. The individual connection types (10MB Ethernet, 100MB Ethernet, routed frame relay, Gigabit Ethernet, or ATM) should be analyzed to gain realistic information. On a number of Windows 2000 migrations, we found organizations that thought they had faster bandwidth on the network than they really had. Many problems were caused by autosensing ports and adapters that allowed each device to automatically set its speed on boot-up. If devices on both sides of a connection were set to autosensing, and the devices did not autosync to the faster connection speed, they would both default to a lower speed. This causes many networks to perform significantly slower than the administrator expected. Document the speed of how the link is performing, and then compare it to what your expectations were.

Remote Access Strategies

More and more organizations have users who access the network from remote locations. The larger numbers, combined with the variety of remote access solutions (PPP dial-up connections, VPN Internet connections, remote control into a centralized communications server, or dial-up directly to a workstation PC), mean the remote demands on the network infrastructure are growing exponentially. Document the incoming points of communication, the type of remote connection, the frequency of access from remote users, and the type of information being requested over the remote communication links. You need this information to determine the total communication requirements of your organization.

Table 8-3 is a sample form you may find useful as you set about your documentation of your LAN/WAN configuration.

Domain controllers	Graphically identify the location of all servers acting as domain controllers in the enterprise
Time sync servers	Graphically identify the location of all servers acting as time sync servers in the enterprise
Replication partners	Graphically identify the location of all servers acting as replication partners in the enterprise, the applications being replicated, the amount of information being replicated, and the frequency of replication

Table 8-3. Information You Should Document About Your LAN/WAN System

WAN infrastructure	Graphically identify the location of all routers, bridges, and gateways in the enterprise, including the type of links between WAN connections
IP addresses	Document the IP addresses of all devices (including servers, routers, bridges, gateways, workstations, and printers) in the enterprise
Firmware version	Document the firmware versions of all devices (including servers, routers, bridges, gateways, workstations, and printers) in the enterprise
Protocols supported	Document the protocols used by all servers and workstations in the enterprise, plus the protocols supported by the routers and links between LAN and WAN connections
Existing LAN and WAN speeds	Document the LAN and WAN speeds of all devices on the network, including notation on which devices are autosensing and which devices are fixed-speed connections
Remote access strategies	Document the remote access strategies of the organization, including the number of simultaneous remote connections possible as well as the speed and type of connections for each device

Table 8-3.   Information You Should Document About Your LAN/WAN System *(continued)*

Documenting Existing Line of Business Functionality

You should document the current uses of your information technology system. (Later in this chapter I explain how to look ahead to examine and plan for future business functionality.) The use of your system means the applications being used, how users and workgroups interact, how information is shared between workgroups, and the current culture of the organization to adopt new or different technologies.

Applications Used

The first things to document are the applications being used in your organization. This includes office automation tools such as electronic messaging, word processing, and spreadsheet applications. In addition, it includes specific vertical business applications such as proprietary database applications, accounting programs, human resource applications, and application development utilities. It is helpful to create a table similar to Table 8-4 of the applications in use, the versions of the software being used, the users or workgroups that use the applications, and how the applications are shared between users of the organization.

Server- or Desktop-Based Applications

When you are faced with an upgrade or migration for desktops or servers, it is important to know whether applications and data reside on local hard drives or servers. If application software resides on workstation hard drives, then modifications to the server are less complicated. However, if applications are stored on servers, an upgrade to the server requires that you test the applications for compatibility on the servers (and also test after the upgrade is completed to make sure everything runs as expected).

NOTE: A good rule of thumb is that if an application (such as a word processor or a spreadsheet program) can run on a desktop, but you've elected to install it on a server, you can probably safely back up and restore to a new server operating system since the code is not specific to the operating system. However, if the application is a true client/server application (like Microsoft Exchange Server, or SAP) the server component would typically need to be reinstalled on the new operating system on the server. Any time you have to reinstall software, you need to make sure that the software is compatible with the new operating system.

Application	Sales Group	Engineering Group	Bsmith	Jjones	Kedwards
Microsoft Word 2000	✓			✓	✓
Microsoft Word 97		✓			
Excel 97		✓			✓
Outlook 98	✓	✓			
Internet Explorer 5.0	✓	✓	✓		
Windows 95	✓		✓	✓	
NT Workstation 4.0 SP6	✓				✓

Table 8-4.   A Sample Documentation Form for Applications. Track Down and Document All Information About Application Usage.

Software installed on a desktop system can be more complicated to plan around. You need to confirm whether the software has installed all of its components in the program and data directory of the application, or whether the application has installed components into a shared components directory (like C:\windows\system directory, or C:\Program Files\Common Files directory). If the application has installed some of the components in a shared directory, it is typically harder to pick out the components from the various directories to place the individual components back into the right directories. This is particularly difficult when an application is installed so that some of the application files reside on the server and some reside on the workstation (and some of those files are stored in shared directories). It is important to document the storage locations, and make a backup of all critical server and desktop components before performing an operating system upgrade. Conduct compatibility testing prior to the migration, and then have documentation and backups to debug any application problems after the conversion.

Interaction Between Departments and Workgroups

It's also important to document the manner in which departments and workgroups use applications. Many organizations have their networks structured and organized based on the physical layouts of their buildings, with little or no consideration to the exchange of information between workgroups or departments. If workgroups that share a large amount of information (especially involving large files such as huge graphics or CAD files) are split across multiple segments of a network, the traffic can produce significant bottlenecks. If the switch or router is a shared component on the network across multiple segments of the organization, the entire communications flow across your organization can be negatively impacted by this simple design flaw.

UNDERSTANDING THE EXISTING NETWORK PERFORMANCE STRUCTURE

When designing the connectivity of a network infrastructure, there are two components that need to be analyzed: the LAN performance and the WAN bandwidth demands and capabilities. I discussed the documentation of the existing structure of the organization in the previous section of this chapter, and now it's time to analyze and interpret the actual traffic demand. This is the only way to determine the best design.

Analyzing LAN Performance

LAN performance is the utilization of the bandwidth between desktops and servers, as well as between servers within a networking site. In most organizations, this traffic tends to be bursty as users send information in a batch to a server or printer, then have a period of network inactivity. However, as more and more users are added to the network, the bursts of information from dozens or hundreds of users create a perpetually congested network.

There are a number of tools that can help you analyze the bandwidth usage and demands on your network. Typically, a network sniffer analyzes the traffic on a network segment and reports the utilization of the segment, the top stations utilizing the traffic on the network, and the type of traffic being sent on the network. However, with the implementation of technologies that place each device on a switch on its own segment, the ability to use a sniffer as effectively as before is reduced.

If you use switched or shared backplane technologies to distribute traffic across dozens (or hundreds) of separate collision domains or virtual segments, you need a utility designed to analyze this type of traffic. With the right tools, you can analyze traffic on hubs, chassis, or internetworking devices. Look into tools like Cisco System's CiscoWorks, or Hewlett Packard's OpenView that provide port-by-port performance and communications information.

Use these tools to generate information about bandwidth demands, utilization, traffic patterns, type of communications information, and other statistical information. You need to track time, quantity, and source/destination information about your network transmissions. If the demand for traffic exceeds the available bandwidth of the network, the length of congestion and the source and destination of the congestion needs to be documented. With this detailed information in hand, you can determine whether additional bandwidth is required, whether the connection link between the source and destination can be optimized by consolidating server applications, or whether you just need to bring the information closer to the workstations that require it.

Analyzing WAN Bandwidth Demands and Capabilities

Similar to the bandwidth demands of the LAN between desktops and servers, the WAN bandwidth demands need to be analyzed to determine the amount, type, and speed of traffic between WAN connections. WAN communications are typically easier to analyze than LAN traffic, because most WAN traffic is specific to a remote device (such as a mainframe, electronic mail host, or other singular device). However, if your organization is inefficiently or inappropriately transmitting information across a WAN without the intended purpose of communicating to the remote device, the traffic information is harder to analyze.

The tools you use to analyze LAN traffic are usually also appropriate for analyzing WAN traffic. You should analyze the time, the duration, the type of information, and the quantity of information being communicated between the local and remote devices. As the demands are analyzed, you can determine whether the bandwidth available is adequate for the communications being sent. If not, you need to investigate the type of communications link you need to facilitate those traffic demands.

DETERMINING THE TRUE INFRASTRUCTURE NEEDS OF THE ORGANIZATION

It's possible to get so bogged down in analyzing existing networking structures that you're unable to step back and make a realistic determination about the networking structure that will work best. With the amount of energy you're required expend to develop and maintain the existing system, you usually don't take time to sit down and determine what you would design if you were starting from scratch. It's possible you would be better off in the long run with a new network infrastructure design, instead of trying to convert, manipulate, and migrate your existing design.

Compare the current documented configuration of your infrastructure and see how it compares to the system you would design and implement today. If the difference is drastic, and you see that major modifications have to be made to your current system, then consider an alternate migration plan—what would it take to redesign and replace the existing structure?

You cannot effectively determine your networking needs (whether you're migrating your existing system or designing a new one) until you learn how the personnel in your organization use your system, and also determine and how they would like to use it.

Conducting Interviews of Key Personnel

To get an accurate handle about the way your organization uses the network structure, and what you need to do to provide optimum services, you need to interview key personnel.

The definition of "key personnel" varies between organizations (both in size and type of business), but the general rule of thumb is to interview one or more of the following personnel types:

▼ People who handle the day-to-day network administration and management.

■ Managers of the operations that are involved in line-of-business processes.

▲ Senior managers who know the goals and future plans of the organization.

Getting the Right Information

As you conduct your interviews, you need to focus on the information you need to plan a restructuring or migration process. In this section, I offer some guidelines to assist that effort.

Current Use of the Network

This is really a survey of the type of tasks the people in your organization perform on their computers, and the network elements they access to do so. Tasks, of course, include business productivity functions (word processing, data entry, or department-specialized tasks). The tools the employees use may include databases, spreadsheets, mainframe data entry systems, or financial calculators. It's important that the interviewer focus on the task of documenting and tracking the information without getting too involved in any analysis of the information (that can come later).

You may find that the information you gather about the use of the current structure may prove to be less appropriate and efficient than it could be. For example, some organizations may be employing basic spreadsheet applications to perform important line of business tasks, when specialized applications that integrate information across multiple facets of organization management are available.

Wish Lists

It's important to conduct interviews that include questions focused on what the individuals would like to have in the organization's networking structure. In many cases, employees are aware of application software specific to their industry, or better suited to their needs (perhaps they've used such software at other firms).

An employee with real expertise in a business function can often articulate a list of priorities, functions, and tools (including data sharing across the network) that is helpful. Even without a deep understanding of technology and the ability to translate the wish list to technical functionality, you'll find this person's analysis extremely worthwhile.

Some of your questions should focus on gaining the information you need to analyze future bandwidth demands. This could include the implementation of a unified messaging solution, implementation of a data warehouse to manage information throughout the organization, remote communications and access for mobile users, and general questions focused on Internet and intranet demands.

All this information will help you understand the technology demands that are needed to meet the expectations of individuals in the organization. Table 8-5 presents a sample form you can use for your questionnaire.

General Information

Name

Title

Role in the organization (business
strategy focused, technology focused,
line of business focused)

Current use of technology

Type of computer used

Applications used

Table 8-5.   A Sample Form You Can Use to Kick Off Your Own Questionnaire

Use of the applications

Desired use of Technology

Software individuals think is
appropriate to be used

Business interactions

Who does the individual share
information with?

What type of inbound and outbound
information sharing is conducted

Table 8-5.   A Sample Form You Can Use to Kick Off Your Own Questionnaire *(continued)*

ANALYZING THE RESULTS AND DESIGNING A NETWORK BACKBONE

Having documented the technology that's in place and collected information that can guide you about future needs, you can move on to the analysis stage, then to the design of a network backbone that meets the needs and the demands you've recorded.

Some of the key analysis points are the performance capabilities of the links between clients and servers, the links between workgroups, and the links between sites. Both hardware recommendations and logical workgroup/ workflow recommendations are needed as you design your network connections.

Implementing a Complete TCP/IP Infrastructure

To deploy Windows 2000, one of the first things you need to implement is a LAN and WAN system that is built around TCP/IP. As I've mentioned repeatedly, Windows 2000 uses common TCP/IP structures such as DNS naming, TCP/IP subnets, and IP routing as its core communications structure.

For some organizations, this may require a conversion from previous Windows NT structures based on the NetBEUI or IPX/SPX protocols. Since many organizations are already enabling Internet access to the desktop for users by adding TCP/IP at the desktop level, the migration to a completely TCP/IP environment has already begun.

Planning LAN Performance Connectivity

For LAN performance connectivity, the decision to implement or upgrade the network to 100MB or gigabit technology between desktop servers needs to be based on the type of data throughput demands. Far too many networks are based on limited bandwidth capabilities of 10MB or slower technologies because they were set up with existing hardware (cable and NICs). Your performance plans should be based on the needs of the organization, and if the existing hardware is limiting your communications, you have to upgrade.

As you conduct your analysis, look at information in the following order:

▼ **Current user application tasks**   Which users/desktops are communicating with which servers.

■ **Expected or desired application needs**   Do they use the same (or similar) links between the users/desktops and the servers? If they do, continue with the steps below. If they don't, reconsider the LAN and WAN connections.

■ **Segments**   Are the users/desktops residing on the same segments as the servers they access? If not, how many hops are there between the users/desktops and the servers? Can this be minimized? Are there bottlenecks between the users and the servers? Is the bandwidth sufficient for the type of information being transmitted (large graphics files require more bandwidth than word processing documents)?

■ **Run analysis tests**   If you can manage this, it's a good way to confirm the amount of data, frequency of transmission, and utilization of bandwidth of the servers, desktops, and LAN/WAN connections. This is an efficient way to make sure you have appropriate bandwidth available.

▲ **Assign/reassign bandwidth designations**   Diagram the computers as well as the LAN and WAN bandwidth speed for all communication links in your organization. (Note this on the organization diagram to confirm any upgrade or update you feel is needed.)

A baby step that many organizations have elected to take is the implementation of 100MB technologies for the servers. While it is typically quick and easy to implement 100MB technologies for the servers since they all tend to be located in a single computer room or data center (so cabling behind walls is not a deciding factor), these 100MB server clusters do not address the client/server communications needs.

Also important in the deciding factors for LAN performance capabilities is the decision about implementation of switched technologies for the organization. Switched technology implies that there is a need for parallel communications between the clients and the servers so multiple users can communicate to multiple servers simultaneously. However, if all of the servers are connected to a single 100MB segment and are then connected to the 10MB segments for the desktops, then switched technologies have little or no impact on the overall performance between desktops and servers. The switched technologies require parallel communications; thus, if the servers are on 100MB technology, the desktops should also be using 100MB technologies to take advantage of the bandwidth being made available by the servers. The key to selecting autospeed sensing switched technology solutions is to make sure that there are no bottlenecks from a slow connection point.

Designing Routing Schemes

When analyzing the communications demands of an organization, the way information is routed from site to site is important. You need to ensure that information is not inappropriately being routed across links, because that causes unnecessary traffic over those links.

To test current routing schemes, put traces on communication packets to determine their source and their destination and confirm the route the traffic is taking to get to its destination.

Planning WAN Performance Connectivity

Now it's time to take a look at some performance consideration options for the WAN connectivity on your network. You have many types of links available for WANs, and I'll cover them in this section.

Modem

Dial-up connections using asynchronous modems are the lowest-cost WAN communications available, but they're also the slowest connections. Because of the lack of speed, few organizations use modems as the primary method of WAN connectivity. At most, organizations use dial-up communications to transmit a file or two between offices, or as a method of email transfers to the Internet for small businesses. As data communication becomes more and more important for businesses, and the cost of connectivity decreases due to competing technologies, dial-up asynchronous connectivity will probably become an obsolete option of communications.

ISDN

Dial-up connections based on ISDN technologies are the next best choice after modems, but this technology is also being replaced by other, faster, technologies. ISDN communication offers limited speed (128K maximum), but organizations have used the technology as a backup system. In the event that a higher-speed frame relay or point-to-point connection fails, the system falls back to the ISDN link. However, as the primary links are moved to the higher speeds available today, the speed of ISDN, even as a backup system, is becoming less acceptable and alternatives need to be implemented.

Private Frame Relay and Point to Point

Many organizations utilize some form of frame relay or point-to-point digital communication link to create their WAN backbone. These solutions provide a private and secured communication link, typically with guarantees on bandwidth and uptime. The connections can range from as low as 56K all the way to 1.54MB, but it's common to settle on 256K as the lowest acceptable speed. Incidentally, companies that currently use these technologies are beginning to look at even higher-speed solutions, as well as solutions based on lower-cost shared access technologies.

Virtual Private Networking (VPN) over the Internet

Virtual private networking has become a popular solution for organizations looking to connect selected remote sites. The technology provides high bandwidth at an economical cost. VPN uses the Internet as the backbone for the communications of the organization, and through a series of encrypted and encapsulated transport mediums, you can create a link between sites while maintaining a secured communication over the generally unprotected backbone of the Internet. This gives you high-speed connection links like Digital Subscriber Lines (DSL) at a fraction of the cost of a private frame relay or point-to-point connection link. You can access the Internet at extremely high speeds and low cost, and then encapsulate secured information through a VPN back to your main office. Because the Internet provides no guarantees for throughput or reliability, this solution is being implemented by outlying offices that are not mission critical to the operations of a business.

Virtual Private Networking (VPN) over a Private Network Service Provider

Many people are not aware that there are a number of providers of VPN connections that do not use the general Internet. Since many of the global communication providers like ATT or MCI, or the Internet providers like PSInet or UUnet, own their own fiber links around the world, they can provide communications exclusively over their fiber backbones outside the general Internet. This increases those providers' ability to offer guarantees on data throughput as well as reliability of uptime. The services vary from provider to provider, and with deregulation of communications there are a number of other providers entering the market. This is a solution that is lower in cost than private frame relay or point-to-point communications, but more costly and more reliable than transporting over the general Internet. You'll want to analyze the cost, reliability, and security against your own situation.

Asynchronous Transfer Mode (ATM) Technologies

For organizations that require speeds in excess of the speeds provided by frame or point-to-point technologies, ATM provides a variable rate connection link between sites. Rather than paying the high cost of a DS3 connection (45MB connection) when the organization may only burst to that speed a few times in a day, ATM provides a variable speed link that increases bandwidth when it's needed, and decreases the bandwidth when normal speeds are adequate. The cost of service varies along with the usage of communications, so you only pay for high speed when you need it.

Quality of Service (QoS) Link Communications

Network WAN and communications companies are offering a standard built around quality of service, or QoS communications. QoS allows a destination requester to request bandwidth from a source location for the transmission of information across the wide area link. The information may be video information that requires a steady stream link between connections, or time-sensitive information that requires a minimal transfer time between the source and destination. QoS can ensure that communication between sites maintains a minimum steady stream state, which means there is always adequate bandwidth between links.

While many organizations select connections based solely on the budget, it's more appropriate to determine the requirements for each link. In many cases, doing bandwidth demand analysis results in the knowledge that a majority of sites can use a slower WAN connection, and the savings permit higher-speed connections for the few sites that require it. The use of analysis tools helps you purchase the right connection speed for each need.

Planning Remote Access Schemes

Just a few years ago, when we planned a network, we only considered the devices physically attached to the local area or wide area network. However, as more and more users need access to the network from home or when they travel, the need to add remote access to the network plan has become extremely important.

Remote access users have the same network access needs as users on the LAN: electronic mail, data files, access to databases, and data from line of business information systems.

This traffic needs to be taken into account when you are planning a network infrastructure. In addition to the bandwidth demands of mobile users, you have to plan common access points. Routing of information across the organization's WAN to mobile users needs to be configured to minimize the impact of the communications traffic generated. Also, mobile users need access points to the network that minimize long-distance dial-up phone charges.

Creating the Network Plan

The overall goal of a network design plan is to create an efficient network, and that plan should accomplish a number of individual goals:

- ▼ It identifies the traffic demands and patterns of the users.
- ■ It distributes the users to the segments for direct access to the devices they need.
- ▲ It identifies logical distribution of shared resources (DNS servers, DHCP servers, printers, and so on).

Once the communication links are defined, new physical and logical diagrams have to be created so you can outline the structure of the organization visually. The diagrams will be reviewed and analyzed to ensure the new design is adequate.

The actual placement of servers, creation of sites, and distribution of shared server services are discussed in the next three chapters of this book.

CHAPTER 9

Planning Services

Designing a server requires an understanding of the role the server plays. For instance, if you buy powerful hardware components—such as quad processor machines—for a database server, processing performance may still be slow. Transactional processing performance is dependent on disk I/O, not on processor power.

DETERMINING THE ROLE OF THE SERVER

First, determine the server's function. Servers can provide simple file and print services, run applications, manage hundreds or thousands of email messages, provide data warehouse functions, or manage network services.

File and Print Server

File and print servers are used to save files and access printers. Plan the capacity for files by giving an allotment of space to each user. Print servers need disk space for queues to network printing devices.

Application Server

Application servers are the fastest growing segment of server functionality. Client/server technologies such as SQL databases, Internet Web servers, and electronic messaging servers are gaining popularity. You must determine how you will distribute these specific application service functions.

Databases such as Microsoft SQL Server and Oracle have the database engine running on the server. However, some shared file databases (such as Microsoft Access) allow multiple users to access the data files stored centrally on the server, while the database program itself resides on the client. In that case, the server is not really an application server, but rather a file server.

Domain Controller

When a user logs on to a Windows 2000 domain, a domain controller performs the authentication. Servers and workstations in a domain must also be members of the domain to participate in the domain, and domain controllers contain an account for each of these machines. In essence, domain controllers are the linchpins that hold domains together.

Name Server

A Windows 2000 server can act as a name server, doing name resolution using standard Domain Name System (DNS). In the Windows 2000 native mode, since Windows 2000 machines do not need to use the previous versions of NetBIOS name resolution, it is necessary to have name servers on the network to manage name resolution.

Terminal Services

Terminal Services for Windows 2000 has introduced a new classification of servers. Terminal services provides both the data and the GUI to the remote client system, and it's possible to provide a rich set of applications to distant clients. More on terminal services can be found in Chapters 10 and 17 of this book.

Terminal Services for Windows 2000 is especially appropriate for a highly dispersed organization with many small offices. It's inefficient to have an onsite administrator in every office, and terminal servers allow centralized administration of the applications at a home site.

DESIGNING AND PLANNING SERVERS ACCORDING TO UPTIME EXPECTATIONS

When planning servers, most people only think of the "role" of the server (file and print, client/server applications) and the "size" of the server (number of users). It's just as important to determine the uptime requirements, fault-tolerance needs, the level of high availability mission-critical components, and method of administration.

Uptime for Business Requirements

Is it acceptable for a server to be down for any length of time? Typically, servers fall into one of three categories: business critical, mission critical, or 24×7.

A business-critical server is expected to be online almost all the time, but some unexpected downtime may be tolerated. In most organizations, email systems fall under this category.

Mission-critical servers are expected to be up under all circumstances during business hours, but can afford downtime after those hours. A transactional business database may fit into this category.

The 24×7 servers are expected to be up 24×7, period. Police, medical transports, and other public safety organizations are commonly classified in this category.

It is very important to classify servers appropriately. Some would argue that an email server is 24×7 because the organization relies heavily on electronic communications to conduct business. However, in most companies, if an email server is down between 2:00 A.M. and 3:00 A.M., and email takes an extra hour to go out from or come into the server, the results aren't disastrous. Compare that to a 911 emergency dispatch center where having a server down between 2:00 and 3:00 A.M. would mean that people could literally die at 2:00 in the morning.

Establishing Server Fault Tolerance

Rule of thumb: anything that moves will break. This includes hard drives, cooling fans, CD-ROMs, and floppy drives. You need to determine whether one of these failures will cause significant problems. Obviously, if the floppy drive fails, it more than likely will have little or no impact on the operations of the server.

But what about cooling fans? Power supplies usually fail because the cooling fan fails. If a power supply fails, it takes only about 10 minutes to replace it, as long as you have another one on hand. Replacing a hard disk also takes about 10 minutes, providing you have one.

Today, the common practice is to buy servers with redundant, hot-swapping power supplies, redundant hot-swapping cooling fans, and redundant hot-swapping hard disks (RAID arrays).

Hot-swappable power supplies allow you to unplug one of the (usually two or three) power supplies and replace it without taking the server down. Redundant cooling fans simply slide out. These are features that are important to consider.

If you are trying to achieve a 24×7 server operation because downtime is impossible, redundant, hot-swappable equipment becomes extremely important. If you can afford to bring a server down for a few minutes to swap out a part, the server qualifies as mission critical rather than 24×7.

You can purchase a computer with a CPU that has a heat sink that relies on internal ventilation to cool itself, rather than a fan that is bolted on to the processor. You can improve server reliability with just that little feature. Remember: no fan, no moving parts. No moving parts means less chance of something breaking. And when things have a lesser chance of breaking, downtime is minimized.

RAID Drive Fault Tolerance

Because of the severe downtime that can incur from tape restores if a hard drive fails, RAID arrays are the most important fault-tolerance device for drive subsystems. RAID arrays use mirroring or parity to preserve information, even when one of the drives fails. Hot swapping is a normal feature for RAID arrays.

In addition, many RAID controllers support hot-spare drives. These drives are not a part of the array, but will automatically activate when a drive in an active array fails. With the combination of parity and the information in the remaining drives, the lost drive can be rebuilt online without taking the server down or restoring from tape.

There are various levels of RAID for fault tolerance. The options range from no disk redundancy to a sophisticated disk redundancy system that involves two to three different levels of disk failure protection.

The most common disk redundancy options include the following:

▼ **RAID-1 (disk mirroring)** In a RAID-1 implementation, hard drives in the system are duplicated and information is written to both sets of hard disks simultaneously. In the event that one hard drive or hard drive set fails, the other drive or drive set continues to operate. Disk storage purchase requirements should be double the amount of available disk space desired. Thus, if you require 4GB of disk space, purchase two 4GB hard drives and mirror the drives.

- ■ **RAID-2 (disk duplexing)**   In a RAID-2 implementation, both the hard drives and the hard drive controllers are duplicated in a system. The same double-disk purchase requirements apply as in the disk redundancy above; however, you also must purchase a redundant hard drive controller for the system. In the event of a failure of either a drive or a controller, the redundant set would continue system operations without interruption or loss of information.

- ■ **RAID-5 (disk striping with parity)**   A RAID-5 implementation requires a file server and hard drive controller that support RAID-5 disk redundancy. This is a disk redundancy system comprising at least three hard drives. In an $n+1$ model, the equivalent of one drive in the RAID-5 configuration retains a mathematical representation of the fault-tolerance parity information. This fault-tolerant component is distributed across all of the hard drives in the RAID-5 drive set. In the event that any of the drives in the set fail, the RAID-5 environment continues to run without interruption or data loss. A RAID-5 configuration is more economical than a disk mirror or duplexing system that requires an exact one-to-one relationship between drives. If the subsystem involves three 4GB drives for 12GB of usable disk space, a RAID-5 configuration will require just one extra 4GB drive to meet the RAID-5 $n+1$ specification. However, in a mirror or duplexing scenario, the three 4GB drives would need to be matched with three additional 4GB drives to provide the one-to-one relationship of the mirrored or duplexed configuration.

- ▲ **RAID-6 (disk striping with parity and online spare)**   A RAID-6 configuration is similar to a RAID-5 configuration in which there is an $n+1$ relationship of drives (one extra drive for a series of data drives). However, RAID-6 includes one additional drive, which is an online spare. In the event that one drive in a RAID-5 subsystem fails, the system continues to operate, but if a second drive fails, all data will be lost and recovery would need to be performed from the last tape backup. With an online spare drive, when the first drive in the subsystem fails, the extra online spare drive automatically substitutes for the failed drive and begins recovery of the RAID-5 configuration. Once recovered to a RAID-5 configuration, an additional drive can fail and the system will still be operational, still allowing for the potential of an additional failure. In effect, a RAID-6 configuration can have two drives in the drive set fail before the environment is in a fault situation in which data can be lost.

Figure 9-1 shows the various disk fault-tolerance options.

Hardware vs. Software Disk Fault Tolerance

You can implement disk fault tolerance either through hardware management or software management. Microsoft Windows 2000 provides software disk fault tolerance for

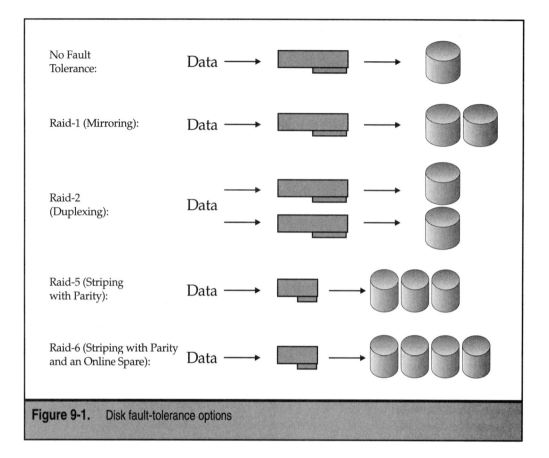

Figure 9-1. Disk fault-tolerance options

disk mirroring and disk striping, whereas a hardware-based solution requires the purchase of a file server and a disk controller that support hardware fault tolerance. Hardware fault tolerance is generally superior to software fault tolerance for the following reasons:

▼ **Faster performance**   Because hardware fault tolerance is managed by a controller card or other hardware device, processing performance is not compromised in order to provide fault tolerance. Software fault tolerance, however, requires resources from the operating system and system processor.

▲ **Error trapping**   If there is a hard drive subsystem failure, software fault tolerance can potentially cause the server to halt network operating system functions. A hardware fault-tolerance system can isolate the disk failure from the operating system functions.

If the file server hardware vendor provides utilities to create fault-tolerant disk configurations for the server, it is best to use these options for disk mirroring, duplexing, or data striping instead of the software options included in the Windows 2000 Management console disk administrator.

Separating the Boot and Log File Drives

For client/server structures, data should be stored on a separate drive from the log files and the page file. For example, give SQL or Exchange Server a separate drive to write error logs, transaction logs, and the server swap file. On a completely separate disk store, the SQL or Exchange Server can write message data and other user information. The boot drive may only need to be 4–8GB in size, with the bulk of the server's disk storage allocated to the data drive.

Designing High Server Availability

If you've worked with Windows NT long enough, you've probably seen a blue screen. In the Novell world, it's the venerable ABEND. No hardware configuration is going to save you from the blue screen, because the reasons it appears include software bugs, an interruption of system processing, poorly written drivers or utilities, and so on. Mission-critical needs demand redundant servers with up-to-the-second mirrored information, ready to activate and take over when the production server fails to operate properly.

There are a number of products that provide this type of high-availability solution, including Microsoft's own Cluster Server. When a primary server fails, the services "fail over" to the backup server. The backup server assumes the identity of the primary server and continues to perform the services of the primary server. Depending on the services that are failed over, this process typically takes one to ten minutes.

Having the Right People to Support Your Servers

It's critical to have a staff that's qualified to support the systems you install. In many organizations, you commonly find a three-tier hierarchy:

Tier 1: Helpdesk

Tier 1 personnel answer phones and provide deskside support to users who need support at the workstation. These staff members need to understand how to troubleshoot common desktop problems as well as network connectivity issues. They also need to know when to escalate problems to the Tier 2 level.

Tier 2: Administration

Tier 2 personnel perform the day-to-day server administration tasks. They monitor server resources, watching for performance bottlenecks and disk space usage, and perform backups and restores. Tier 2 support is crucial to anticipating such impending problems as low disk space, a service that consumes too much processor capacity, or disk arrays with a failed redundant drive in the dataset.

Tier 3: End-of-Line Support

When there's a catastrophic loss, such as a site failure (power failure, fire, flood), the site must be restored in as short a period of time as possible. Tier 3 mobilizes personnel for such functions.

Many organizations are too small to have three tiers of staff, and in some small companies, all three tiers rest in the hands of a single individual. It's important to have a well-defined support policy that indicates who is responsible for which procedures.

NAMING THE SERVERS

Now that we've determined what the server will do (file, print, applications, services) and the level of redundancy we want (RAID, clustering, management), we need to name the server. There are many opinions about how a server should be named; in most cases, server naming is based on a standard begun by the person who installed the first server on the network.

Regardless of your past naming system, during your implementation of Windows 2000, you have an opportunity to devise a logical naming, useful system for your servers.

Keeping the Names Short but Descriptive

With historical autonomy given to the network administrator to select a server naming scheme, some organizations find their servers named after characters from TV shows, movies, or the administrator's childhood pet. While Fido is a nice name for a dog, however, it may not be the most appropriate name for the enterprise messaging server. To the person who names the servers, their functions are very apparent—perhaps not because the names describe the server, but because he or she has installed them. Keep in mind that server names should be short and descriptive of the server's function. Moreover, it is best not to name the server for the product installed on it. While a server providing file and print services, for instance, could use "FP001" indefinitely as a valid server name, a server named NETWARE311 would outgrow its name more quickly.

Limitations

The Windows 2000 naming specification conforms to Internet naming standards of DNS, permitting a maximum of 63 characters for a host name. While a 63-character server name can be very descriptive, it is also very cumbersome trying to enter such a long name from the command line. Furthermore, if you are migrating from NT 4, you're likely to use a mixed-mode operating system before your full cutover. In this case, the limitation is 15 characters, which provides backward compatibility for NetBIOS.

DNS names support only a–z, A–Z, 0–9, and hyphen, so any server names that utilize the underscore (such as FS_01) should be renamed during the migration process to Windows 2000.

Evaluating the Existing Naming Scheme

Examine your current naming protocol. Your server names may already conform to Internet naming schemes, and perhaps they are already short and meaningful. If not, though, you're in the majority. You probably have some characters that are not Internet compliant, such as a server named BIG_SQL. And, of course, all your workstations are configured to find the database server with the underscore in its name.

While a change to a more universally supported DNS name is appropriate, you need a lot of planning and preparation to minimize interruption in user access to your servers. There are a number of options in a name conversion process, including multinaming a server on the network (covered in detail in Chapter 12).

Multinaming provides the simple option of changing a server name and using DNS CNAME aliases. This results in multiple server names assigned to a single server. The server can be migrated with the old name maintaining NetBIOS backward compatibility, and the new name placed in the DNS naming table.

As users are migrated from NetBIOS naming to DNS naming, you can reconfigure the desktops to reflect the new name.

Naming the Distributed File System

Distributed File System, or DFS, is an add-on for Windows NT 4 and an integrated universal file management system in Windows 2000. DFS provides directory-centric resource access as opposed to server-centric resource access. What that means is that instead of looking for files on *servername* on the file-share \files, you can go directly to the DFS location \files and the files will be available regardless of which independent server stores the information. With some files residing on \\server1, some on \\server2, and some on \\server3, users don't have to worry about naming the server, and can head straight to the file-share location.

Implementing DFS in a Windows NT 4 environment while you plan and prepare your full migration to Windows 2000 may not be a bad idea. DFS gives you the ability to change your server names while continuing to represent the network resources with their original names. This is a way to create a structure of network resources that is logical to your users, who don't have to think about the actual physical location of the resource.

SELECTING AND SIZING THE SERVER

Server expenditure is not a cheap proposition. Make sure your hardware is certified in the hardware compatibility list. You may save 10–30 percent on the initial cost of servers by buying an inexpensive clone system, but in the end, you might easily spend much more trying to make the inexpensive clone system work properly.

Microsoft Recommendations

These are the bare minimum specifications that Microsoft recommends for an Intel-based Windows 2000 server:

▼ **Processor**   166 MHz P5

■ **Video**   VGA or higher

■ **Disk**   2GB HD; 500MB free

■ **RAM**   64MB RAM minimum; 128MB recommended

■ **Removable drives**   CD-ROM; 3.5" FDD if CD-ROM is nonbootable

▲ **NIC**   Windows 2000–compatible NIC

My Recommendations

In reality, the minimum recommendations are good enough to load the operating system—but not much more. In Chapter 5, I cover some recommended system configurations based on the number of users and the role of the server. In this section, I detail some guidelines for server planning.

As a rule of thumb, if you will be running a processor-intensive application such as SQL, Exchange Server, or IIS, it's better to use multiple servers to distribute the workload, instead of installing a single large server. Although in many cases, the cost of multiple servers is the same as that of one large server, the performance benefits of multiple servers can outweigh the costs anyway.

File Servers

Assume you'll need 30MB for each user's private directory. If you have 600 users, the server requires 18GB, without including common storage and operating system space. For such a server, plan on about 27GB storage space distributed over 9GB or 18GB drives in a RAID configuration. RAID-5 offers fast read speeds and is more space efficient than most other RAID implementations. You can also use disk quotas—a new built-in feature of Windows 2000—to limit usage on a user-by-user basis.

File servers are usually not processor intensive, since the bottleneck of a file server is typically drive related, so the best area of investment in a file and print server is in the performance of the drive subsystem. Adding RAM helps the file and print server cache directories for faster file lookup.

Application Servers

An application server, on the other hand, is typically very processor intensive, because it runs programs. The application running on the server determines the resource needs. The better you understand how data flows within the application, the better you can configure and optimize core components of the application server.

If you have a highly transactional database, your application will probably heavily rely on committed transactions. Response times of committing transactions are highly dependent on the performance of your transaction log. Unlike databases, transaction logs are written sequentially; one transaction follows the next with little drive head movement. If you place other requirements on the drive where the transaction logs reside, you will experience performance contention, drastically reducing your transaction rates. More RAM may help the general speed, but by definition, a commit is a transaction written to the transaction log on disk.

Further, if the database drive array fails but the transaction log array survives (because it is on a different physical subsystem), you can restore up to the last committed transaction from a tape backup by replaying the transaction logs to restore recent data information. Hence, you should have an array for the database and operating system, and another separate array for the transaction log.

If, on the other hand, your database is decision support, read performance is critical. In order to have fast reads and queries, you need a wide array so that data is spread over many drive heads. Also, you should have a separate array for indexes. (If your indexes are small enough, they may fit into RAM.)

Applications such as Exchange Server and order processing databases are highly transactional in nature. Place the databases and operating system on a RAID-5 array and the transaction logs in a RAID-1 or RAID-10 array. RAID-1 and RAID-10 are faster and more easily recoverable, but are also a more costly investment. Data warehouse applications are query intensive by nature. If the indexes are too big to fit into RAM, you may need to configure a RAID-5 for the databases and operating system and RAID-1 or RAID-10 for the indexes. If your database application has both big indexes and many transactions, consider a RAID-5 for the database and operating system, a RAID-1 or RAID-10 for the transaction logs, and another RAID-1 or RAID-10 for the indexes.

Database applications engines such as Microsoft Access and FoxPro, and mail applications such as MSMail and cc:Mail, are run on the client; the server only serves as a host for the database files. Transactions are written across the network. From the server's point of view, an Access engine modifying an Access database is no different from a user modifying a Word document. If these are your applications, refer to the section on file servers.

Domain Controllers

Where application servers are the busiest during working hours, domain controllers are typically the busiest in the beginning of the workday and after lunch. This makes sense as users log on to the network in the morning and after lunch. One of the most frustrating experiences a user can face is to wait a long time for logon. You can prevent this by making sure you have devoted enough resources to these logon servers.

If you support 4,000 users, all of whom arrive between 8:00 A.M. and 9:00 A.M., the server handles 4,000 logons in 3,600 seconds. There is also a significant amount of network traffic as users pull their profiles and open network applications and data files.

If this is your scenario, you probably already have your network segmented into smaller subnets to distribute traffic across multiple network connections. If you don't already have that, you really should consider doing so (see Chapter 8 on planning and designing connectivity for more suggestions on distributing LAN/WAN traffic). Place a domain controller in each of your network segments.

This domain controller should be a system with fast processor capability and plenty of RAM, since requests from users will need to query the Active Directory replica (which will hopefully be stored in server RAM if there is adequate memory in the server), and the high-speed processor will validate logon authentication. A Pentium II or III system with 256MB RAM should be adequate. Just as with an application server, it is better to have multiple servers distributing the transaction load instead of a single very overloaded system. Disk storage is minimal since the system only stores a portion of the Active Directory. Typically, a 4GB or 8GB drive (plus fault tolerance on the drives) is sufficient. Active Directory transaction logs should be on a separate drive in order to distribute the disk I/O transactions and provide a method of recovery for the directory. If you have one small site, you can use your domain controller as a file and print server, or application server. You should have a minimum of two servers for your domain, making them both redundant Active Directory servers.

If you have many small sites that are geographically dispersed, consider an Active Directory server in each site to allow local logon to the domain, which avoids logon authentication across the WAN connection. To reduce replication traffic, use the site properties to throttle Active Directory replication. (See Chapter 13 on implementing domain controllers on the network.)

If you have a large organization, you can distribute the demands of the network across multiple domain controllers, file and print servers, and application servers with the use of resource distribution. These techniques are covered in more detail later in this chapter as well as in Chapter 12.

DHCP, DNS, and WINS Servers

Except for exceptional circumstances, your servers should use static IP addresses since server devices should remain constantly configured in your domain. Your workstations, however, will probably use DHCP-assigned IP addresses. In order to provide dynamic IP addresses to your workstations using DHCP, you must install DHCP services on a Windows 2000 server.

In sizing the power of your DHCP server, performance demands are processor related; however, the demands on the server are relatively minimal. A workstation typically only makes a DHCP request once during the day, and for organizations that keep their workstations on continuously, the DHCP IP request is not enacted at all.

DNS servers provide Internet standard name resolution. If you're running in Windows 2000 native mode, your servers and workstations rely on the Dynamic DNS, or

DDNS. DDNS allows clients to register their host names and DHCP-given IP addresses as they connect to the network, and release them as they disconnect from the network. This amounts to a more significant resource requirement than those of the traditional DNS servers, which are not dynamic. DDNS servers are not disk intensive, but, rather, CPU and network intensive just like DHCP servers.

WINS servers are used for backward compatibility with NetBIOS naming system networks, including Windows NT 4.0 networks. Most organizations will probably use some combination of browsing and WINS during migration. Since most organizations that are already using Windows NT 4 as a networking environment probably already have WINS servers on the network, those machines can remain on the network throughout the migration process. When the organization finally converts to a full Windows 2000 DNS-based environment, the WINS servers can be taken off the network. Like the DDNS service, WINS is CPU and network intensive. If you migrate your existing WINS servers to Windows 2000, when you are completely migrated to Windows 2000 you can uninstall the WINS service from the Windows 2000 server.

Terminal Servers

Terminal servers are very processor and memory dependent, since all of the processing for each terminal session utilizes the resources of the terminal server. Additional memory does not make the terminal server go faster; it just allows more users to access the same server simultaneously. Most terminal servers have a minimum of 256MB of memory, allowing for 5–10 simultaneous users to access the server using thin client technologies. As more users need to access the system, additional RAM gets added to the system.

Disk requirements for a terminal server are comparable to that of a workstation. You will need storage space for the operating system and the applications. A RAID-1 mirror will do fine.

Terminal servers are tuned differently than application servers. Whereas application servers run services, terminal servers run many instances of desktop applications. Don't make a terminal server a file and print or application server unless absolutely necessary. While the terminal sever could serve as a multipurpose server for a very small environment, the performance distribution would be limiting.

Web, Proxy, and Firewall Servers

Traditional Web servers are nothing more than files servers that respond to TCP port 80 requests with file-based information. Today, many Web applications depend on the processing power of a Web server to generate Web pages dynamically from CGI and ASP scripts, as well as runtime DLLs. Performance and response is dependent on the processing capability of the Web server. By determining the demands of the server (rated in hits made to the server), a Web server can be scaled (or load-balanced to multiple servers) to meet the demands of the requests to the server.

Many organizations today are switching from active scripted page processing to embedded page processing in DLLs. DLLs offer security in that if the code is stolen, it is a compiled code, and must to be reverse-engineered before it can be used.

For enhanced security as well as general administrative control for access to the Internet, many organizations are implementing proxy servers as a layer between the Internet and the company network. With a proxy server, an organization can implement network address translation to provide IP addresses inside the proxy server, and they're hidden from the outside Internet. While this provides security and administrative control for the organization, it does put a translation-processing load on the proxy server.

The proxy server needs to have enough processing ability to do the translation, which means a very fast single-processor Pentium II or Pentium III for small organizations and multiprocessor Pentium II/III systems for large organizations. Since the security implementation splits the network between internal and external, the proxy server needs to have two network adapters.

The last type of Internet-connected server is a firewall. Firewalls vary in complexity based on their protection algorithm and the type of other services the firewall provides. The more the firewall secures, the higher the processing power it needs. Some firewalls do basic packet filtering, which has the least performance demands for a firewall. This requires limited processing requirements to operate, but also provides the lowest level of security of all firewalls. A single-processor Pentium II/III can easily handle simple packet filtering.

For a Checkpoint Firewall-1 system based on the multilayer packet-filtering algorithm, the firewall does everything a packet-filter firewall does and also covers user controls in and out of the firewall. Since the firewall adds capabilities to basic packet filtering, the firewall requires more processing capabilities than a packet-filter firewall. Typically, a very high performance single process server or even a multiprocessor server is suggested.

For the highest level of server-based security, organizations look to application-level filtering found in products like Axent's Raptor Eagle firewall software. The firewall actually strips the packet headers all the way to the application level, validating whether the contents of the packets are what you would expect them to be. By validating the contents of packets, the potential of a hacker submitting malicious code into a series of packets heading into the firewall is minimized. However, this level of security comes at the cost of processing power. This either means multiple servers need to be implemented to distribute the processing load of the network, or some of the fastest server technology needs to be implemented.

Mixing and Matching Server Capabilities

Servers are configured and tuned differently for different roles. Terminal servers, application servers, file servers, print servers, Active Directory servers, and name servers have different demands on processor, RAM, and disk I/O. Spreading these services across multiple machines reduces the impact of a single server failure and also distributes the demand.

CAPACITY PLANNING
FOR THE WINDOWS 2000 ENVIRONMENT

After you take into account the function and role of the Windows 2000 server, along with the fault tolerance and redundancy demands of the system, you can size your servers. Servers should have the right amount of processor speed, the right amount of memory, the right type of drive subsystem, and the right type of LAN/WAN connection.

But what is "right"? There's no definitive answer, so you start with a best guess for configuring your server resources. Once you start using the server in a production environment, there are utilities to help you determine whether your server needs to be tuned by adding more memory or processor capacity to the system to meet the demands of your organization. This is called *capacity planning* and *load testing*.

Capacity planning and load testing in a Windows 2000 environment takes on three different roles during the life of the server. The first occurs prior to the purchase and installation of the Windows 2000 Server software and is used to determine the size and capabilities of the new server. The second occurs after the server has been installed and users are using the system, at which point an analysis is conducted to confirm that the server configuration is adequate for the demands of the environment. And lastly, as the demands of the server change (addition of users, addition of or changes to add-in applications being used, increase in user access to the server), you need to conduct incremental capacity analyses to ensure the server can continue to meet the needs of the organization.

Sizing a New Server Configuration

Before you deploy Windows 2000, you can conduct tests to determine what size server is appropriate. Rather than just guessing wildly about capacity, you can simulate the network environment and test server performance response prior to putting the system into full production. The tests are used to determine what server processor to use, the amount of memory necessary, and the disk storage capacity needed. The tests can also tell you if the LAN/WAN capacity will be adequate. For organizations already using network server technology, much of the historical information of user traffic, file storage, and server demand is already available. Organizations new to networking, or those that will be using some of the advanced application server capabilities of Windows 2000, will have to estimate their usage.

There are a number of third-party utilities available to do performance and capacity analysis of a Windows 2000 environment. The program that I find provides the best analysis for a Windows 2000 server (at the time of this writing) is a product called Dynameasure from Bluecurve Software (http://www.bluecurve.com). Dynameasure makes it possible for an administrator to define options for input and measuring of the information, and to produce graphs, charts, and reports that simulate actual user activity for a given server configuration.

Dynameasure provides user-defined input criteria based on dozens of variable options, as shown in Figure 9-2. Tests are conducted in a controlled state where the administrator can put as much load or as little load on the production server as desired without dramatically impacting the day-to-day usage of the server. However, the advantage of testing against an existing server provides more exact analysis of capacity and capabilities. Additionally, by allowing variable time and duration of testing, an administrator can test the performance of a server at various times during the day. Many utilities will test a server over an extended period of time and average the results throughout time. However, in real life scenarios, system demands vary from morning, to mid-day, to afternoon. It is at these time intervals that testing should be analyzed for server impact.

During any server capacity analysis, the component being tested (in this case, Microsoft Windows 2000) should not be the only environment tested. Just as other applications impact the performance of a Windows 2000 server (like mainframe access, file

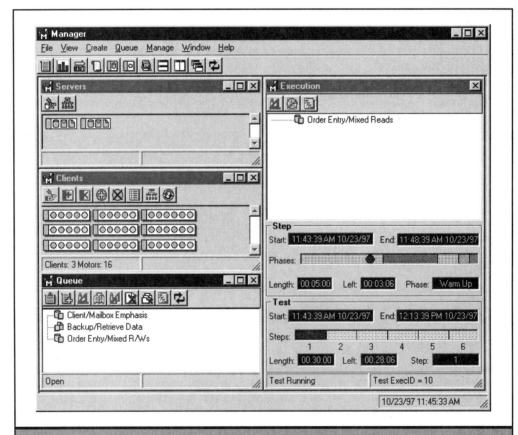

Figure 9-2.   Dynameasure capacity planning and analysis tool

and print access, data warehouse interaction), the implementation or migration to Windows 2000 can have an impact on existing applications. Testing should include other demands on the network, in order to ensure that implementation of a new network operating environment does not negatively impact the performance of the rest of the environment. Dynameasure also analyzes and measures file and print access as well as SQL/database access. These measurements can be conducted independently, or the analysis can be conducted as part of testing the Windows 2000 server. Figure 9-3 shows a sample graphic that provides comparative information about demands on a Windows 2000 server's CPU utilization, disk utilization, and network I/O.

Using Performance Console for Capacity Planning

As you extend the services provided by Windows 2000, or add more users to the organization, you need to determine whether an existing server is running as efficiently as it should be. You need to determine if there is a bottleneck in the network, and if there is, where the bottleneck resides. Obvious bottlenecks include the server processor, memory,

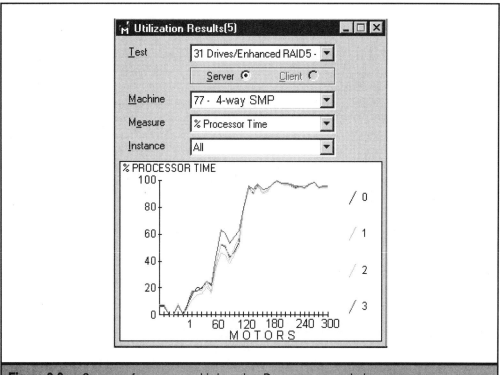

Figure 9-3.   Server performance graphic based on Dynameasure analysis

disk capacity, and network adapter, but also can include WAN connections, third-party add-in applications, and so on.

A utility provided by Microsoft that is included with Windows 2000 is Performance Console, a snap-in to the Microsoft Management console (MMC). Performance Console provides the ability to view current statistics about the operation of a server. Unlike Dynameasure, which simulates network traffic to do pre-implementation performance analysis, Performance Console requires the server to be operational to get appropriate statistical information.

The statistics gathered from the Performance Console tell you the current state of the network server, and whether a problem (or potential problem) exists. You must then use the Performance Console components to identify what object is the root of the problem. In most cases, problems occur in improperly configured or tuned hardware components (like drive configurations, caching, LAN adapter performance, and the like). When properly used, Performance Console can alert you about impending problems.

Planning for Additional Load on an Existing Server

You need to analyze what an increase in the number of users, or other server functions, will do to performance. The goal is to determine if your original guess for server configuration is adequate for the actual demands on the server in production. Additionally, you would want to determine the growth requirements of the organization and then model the growth to determine if the server will be sufficient.

Baseline

A baseline is a level at which you can begin doing comparative analysis of the environment. The best things to baseline in a Windows 2000 Server environment are server processor utilization, server RAM utilization, network LAN and WAN bandwidth utilization, and disk read and write requests. Start by creating a baseline standard of the working environment at different times of the day, since demand loads vary during the day. Then, determine the performance of the server for various levels of system capacity during those times, in order to determine the impact of performance capacity throughout the day. With a baseline taken during normal and stressed periods of the day, week, or month, if there is a problem you can run a performance analysis and compare the current performance with the baseline.

Baselines are dynamic, and should be rerun periodically. If users are added to the network, it means the baseline has changed and new statistical information should be drawn. Additionally, if new applications or services are added to the network, a new baseline should be created and filed.

Modeling Performance Requirements

With a solid, up-to-date baseline in place, if changes are planned, you can model and even project future changes with relative accuracy. For example, if the organization has added 20 new users to the network twice before, and each time a new baseline was taken, if the organization wants to add 20 more users to the network, a comparison could be made using the historical data. For example, if network performance is affected by 3 percent each time 20 new users are added, you can assume that this new addition of 20 users will also impact the network by 3 percent.

To confirm this expectation, performance model tests can be conducted. First, make sure to have a baseline of the existing system performance. Then, determine what the expected additional increase in demand or growth will be on the network. Set up a performance modeling utility like Bluecurve's Dynameasure to model the additional load. The utility will be able to determine the effect of the new load.

CHOOSING A FILE SYSTEM

When installing Windows 2000, you'll have the option of selecting the type of file system you want to install, choosing among FAT16, FAT32, or NTFS. There were a number of different opinions regarding whether to implement FAT or NTFS in Windows NT 4, but with Windows 2000, there are more defining reasons to select one file system vs. the other.

FAT16/FAT32

Unlike Windows NT 4.0, Windows 2000 natively supports both FAT16 and FAT32 file systems. You'll need FAT16 if you want to boot Windows NT 4, Windows 95/98, and Windows 2000 Professional on the same system. FAT16 has a 2GB limit—hardly enough for any significant storage these days—so it would seem that since most systems have 8GB or larger hard drives, you would want to use FAT32 (with its 4TB limit) at a minimum.

The reason many organizations preferred to boot to a FAT partition in Windows NT 4 was to be able to do maintenance on the boot partition of the system. However, with Windows 2000 and the <F8> maintenance mode, an administrator can boot to a command prompt, or to a safe mode version of Windows 2000, and perform maintenance on the Windows 2000 boot partition even if it's not running FAT.

NTFS

Most organizations installed Windows NT 4 with NTFS as the file system for the servers. With Windows 2000 NTFS5, there is now a 64EB (exabyte, 1,000 terabytes) addressable partition space, along with file- and directory-level security, a recovery log, and built-in disk compression. File and directory security is called *discretionary access control*, one of the requirements for C2-level security. Recovery log reduces the chance of data corruption in a dirty shutdown. Compression allows more data to fit on a volume than possible without compression and is conducted during read and write cycles of the system. New to Windows 2000 and NTFS5 is the encryption feature that is available by activating the encrypted file system of the operating system, called Encrypting File System (EFS). With this feature, a user can encrypt a file in a public directory where everyone can see it but cannot read it; only the user with the correct logon can read it seamlessly.

Typically, wherever data files are stored, the file system should be NTFS. NTFS security and better file management provides a better system for data management. You should avoid compression on regularly used servers, because performance degradation is significant as the server compresses and decompresses files on the fly. Use compression on archive servers, where information may be 6–12 months old (or older).

PARTITION PLANNING

Once you select the type of file system you want to install, you need to determine how to partition your drive subsystem. Many administrators purchase multiple drives and create one large RAID configuration on the subsystem, effectively making one large C: drive. In fact, there are good reasons to create multiple partitions on a server, splitting up the bootable operating system, the drive data, and the log files as shown in Figure 9-4.

The OS Partition

The Windows 2000 operating system should be installed on its own partition, not just on the C: drive of a large RAID configuration. The Windows 2000 operating system needs approximately 500MB of disk space, but you should consider also putting the installation files on the drive (the \i386 directory). This partition can be FAT or NTFS, but configuring the boot partition for NTFS provides significantly better security.

The reason to install the operating system on a dedicated boot drive is to completely isolate the operating system from application or data. During an operating system upgrade, update, or service pack installation, if the operating system drive and the data drive are the same, you are effectively modifying the drive that contains your mission-critical data. If your operating system is on a completely separate drive, any maintenance done to that drive is completely isolated from your application and data.

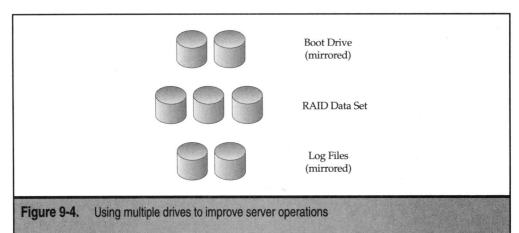

Boot Drive
(mirrored)

RAID Data Set

Log Files
(mirrored)

Figure 9-4. Using multiple drives to improve server operations

Fault tolerance for a boot drive should be mirrored at a minimum. This will ensure that if your primary boot drive fails, there is a secondary drive available to bring your server up.

If you are planning on clustering the server, you need to ensure the boot drive of the server is dedicated only to the operating system, since cluster server boot drives have unique information that is completely separate from application and data information. Applications and data files on a cluster need to be installed on a separate array, which is discussed later in this chapter.

The Data Partition

Data partitions on a server tend to be large and need good security and file administration features, so NTFS or EFS is really your only choice.

You can elect to create logical partitions for your large data store, so you can have applications stored on one logical partition and data stored on another logical partition. However, there is no benefit from a performance perspective, and with proper security configurations, there is no benefit from a security perspective.

For fault tolerance, the data partition is typically RAID-5 at a minimum, providing the highest density of data striping across an additional drive for data integrity. You need a fault-tolerant system that provides redundancy, but not on a one-to-one drive requirement as in drive mirroring or duplexing.

The Transaction Log Partition

Set up a completely separate physical drive for transaction logs. Most organizations put their data files and their transaction logs on the same large RAID drive configuration. The problem with that is anything written to the data store (whether in Microsoft Exchange or SQL Server) writes to both the transaction log and the database store. With both of these files stored on the same drive, there is a contention for writes to two separate files simultaneously. If the transaction logs and the data files are stored on separate physical drives, they can be written to simultaneously. This increases performance dramatically on very busy messaging and database servers.

Additionally, part of the data integrity components of Exchange and SQL is that if a database is lost during the day, a restore of the last backup can take place and the transaction logs can be replayed into the database file to catch the database up. However, if both the data files and the transaction logs reside on the same drive subsystem, if you lost the data file drive, you have also lost your transaction log files. This is why having the two sets of information on different drives is better.

For fault tolerance on the transaction log drive, since the information being transacted is being written to the data files, the transaction logs are backups to the data files. As long as you don't lose both your data drive and the transaction log drive, having fault tolerance on the data drive is sufficient. If you are looking to enhance data integrity, creating a mirror pair or RAID configuration on the log file drive will ensure the log files are protected as well.

DECIDING BETWEEN
AN UPGRADE AND A CLEAN INSTALLATION

For the installation of Windows 2000 on a system that already has an operating system, you must decide whether you upgrade the existing operating system, format the hard drive(s), or install a new hard drive and install from scratch.

With Windows 2000, upgrade utilities are provided to upgrade Windows 95/98 and Windows NT Workstation (v3.51/v4.0) to Windows 2000 Professional, and to upgrade Windows NT Server (v3.51/v4.0) to Windows 2000 Server or Advanced Server. If you have other operating systems, there may be migration utilities to assist with the conversion of user lists and files. Upgrading from Windows 95/98 or Windows NT Workstation to Windows 2000 Professional is covered in Chapter 14 on workstation upgrades.

Upgrading to Windows 2000

There are some advantages to upgrading a server instead of performing a clean install:

▼ If the server is a primary domain controller (PDC), it automatically becomes a Windows 2000 domain controller.

■ If the server is a backup domain controller (BDC), you can choose to make the server a domain controller or a member server.

▲ If the server is a member server, it remains a member server.

After the upgrade, you can change any member server to a Windows 2000 domain controller by running the DCPromo utility provided with Windows 2000 (see Chapter 13 for domain controller upgrades and updates).

Upgrading is the best installation choice if the server already has configuration settings specific to the operation of the system. For example, if you have file-share security allowing user access to specific shares on the server, or if you have a control list for file-level attributes, upgrade the server to maintain those options. If you have an application server, and your application is Windows 2000 compatible, upgrading retains the settings for the application in the registry (such as default database files, log files, transaction settings, and the like).

Clean Installation of Windows 2000

A clean installation of Windows 2000 enables you to make changes to the configuration (such as replacing hardware, striping larger drive sets) and also ensures a clean installation of the operating system on the server. You may have learned from experience how to configure the server more efficiently. If you're running an older version of an application and would like to upgrade the application, this is the perfect opportunity to do so.

PLANNING AND DOCUMENTING SERVER IMPLEMENTATIONS

Now that we've gone through the background of the various decisions that need to be made when implementing Windows 2000, we can formalize the plan and document the implementation steps.

Installation and Configuration Instructions

While planning a Windows 2000 deployment, it's helpful to document the step-by-step set of instructions for the server installation. Regardless of the size of your organization, this won't be the last server you'll install, so a set of installation instructions specific to your organization is a good investment. If you will be sending instructions to nontechnical installers (or just want to ensure the installation procedures are followed perfectly), create a document, including screenshots, to make the installation and configuration process easy.

Your Project Plan

Your plan must state what needs to be done (in what order), how long it should take to complete, and who is responsible for doing the work.

A new single server introduced to your network may or may not impact your users, but a company-wide rollout of servers is certain to be felt.

Your Rollback Plan

In an ideal world, you would have a test lab that could replicate the entire network. You would have unlimited time and money to bring together immaculate instructions and a plan.

In the absence of an ideal world, you're probably not going to be able to cover all the bases and test everything. Therefore, you need a rollback plan so you can roll back to the point of time at which you started the integration of the new operating system. If your integration is going to affect other servers that are currently in production, you'll need to have a plan for them as well. This is your last line of defense.

Prototyping

If your new server is an addition to the existing network and is no more complicated than a file and print server, you can probably go ahead and bring it into your infrastructure. If, however, your installation requires taking down existing network resources, you will be exposing your existing infrastructure to possible loss of availability. You may want to replicate your database server to another server (even if it is only temporary). By doing so, you have a fallback system in case of a system failure.

You can get a better picture of what the ramifications are of an installation or migration process if you spend some time prototyping.

Your Maintenance Plan

After you've spent some time developing the implementation plan and the prototype of the server installation, you will become aware of the need to maintain the server on an on-going basis. Maintenance on a file server typically involves backups and drive defragmentation. Windows 2000 has built in defragmentation that you can schedule. If the volume is very large, you can schedule full defragmentation on the weekends. If the server is a 24×7 server, you might consider file-only defragmentation on a more regular basis. On a monthly basis, include with your backup plan an hour or so to try restoring a random set of files from your backups, preferably from the entire set of tapes you rotate. Backup and verify does not guarantee the data can be restored.

YOUR DISASTER RECOVERY PLAN

Just as essential to the proper installation and configuration of a basic server is the need to conduct disaster recovery planning to minimize network failures and preventable server downtime.

Total Disaster Recovery

The best way to plan for disaster recovery is to assume your server suddenly disappears from the face of the planet. In this very worst case, you'll have to immediately acquire a replacement server to begin system recovery. Before you even restore a byte of data, you have to rebuild the server exactly as you had it before. Did you have 32GB of storage or 64GB of storage? Was this server a domain controller or a member server. This is where all of the documentation we outlined earlier in the chapter pays off. This is also where all of the step-by-step installation instructions become helpful.

Traditional disaster recovery methods require you to install an operating system onto your new server and restore everything from tape. If, however, your hardware is different, you have to be very careful of the boot device. The restore must also include the device driver of the boot device. For example, if your old system was configured with a two-year-old version of a hard drive controller (that is no longer made today), doing a tape restore of the boot drive information would cause the system to fail with the new hard drive controller in the replacement system.

Incremental Disaster Recovery

If you always have to follow the plan for total disaster recovery, a set of missing files would take hours to recover. You need contingency plans. If a set of data files gets corrupted, recovery may be as simple as running a restoration from your backup software. If you need to restore a dozen mailboxes to your Exchange email server, but you have been using a tape backup software that does not allow you to restore individual mailboxes, you have a problem that is going to be very difficult to recover from after the fact. Part of addressing disaster recovery planning is to think about every detail.

Establishing an Alternate Site

No matter where your data center resides, natural disasters occur. Whether resulting from earthquakes in California, hurricanes in North Carolina, snow storms in New York, or extended power failures anywhere in the world, a data center failure can bring an entire network down. If you need to be operational at or near 24 hours a day, 7 days a week, you need contingency plans to minimize the effects of system downtime.

If you are implementing a fault-tolerant network sensitive to site failures, there are different ways of designing and implementing the servers of the network. In many cases, organizations are leveraging WAN technologies, including Internet virtual private networks (VPNs), to create redundancy in multiple sites. When identifying servers for redundancy, it helps to have organized datasets in groupings that make replication of information easier. It is a lot easier replicating an entire server of mission-critical information than loading up a large server mixed with both mission-critical and noncritical archived information. This is the key to managing data when considering fault tolerance.

If your business can sustain a couple of days of information systems downtime, and you do not have a remote site data center for redundancy, your plan should include a way to rebuild servers in your main site location. The installation and configuration document you created when you built the original server can be very useful as a template. This type of disaster recovery is very similar to the total disaster recovery of a lost server.

Testing Your Plan

How much confidence do you have in your plan when you don't have proof for yourself that the plan will work? When you perform daily backups, you may be missing files. Those are typically locked files—files used by a user or application when the backup is occurring. However, without ever testing your recovery plan, you may never realize this or understand why backing up those files (possibly manually) is very important.

By creating a test lab and testing your recovery plan against it, you will quickly see the weak points. You can then evaluate whether the recoverable portion is sufficient for your operation. If not, you will have to change your plan.

If you have an alternate site, schedule a couple of days every six months or so to visit the alternate site and test your recovery plan. There may be changes to your infrastructure that will have to be reflected at your alternate site. By visiting the alternate site from time to time, as well as testing your disaster recovery procedures with the alternate site, you can proactively validate your recovery plan as well as practice the procedures.

SERVER CLUSTERING

Clustering technologies offer an additional layer of protection and high availability for data and certain applications. For your mission-critical and 24×7 requirements, consider clustering.

How Clustering Works

Basic clustering employs a primary server and a backup server. In the event of a primary server failure, the backup server takes over. Depending on which applications are being identified as failover applications, the failover process can take as long as 10 minutes. This needs to be taken into account when you are creating a system recovery plan.

In an active/active cluster scenario, the primary server runs and manages some services, and the standby server runs and manages other services. Both servers are active, but they split the active services. If one of the servers fails, the services on the failed server are transferred to the other server. You need to make sure each of the servers can provide reasonable performance when failed over. The most crucial resource is memory, followed by processor power. In most cases, you cannot cluster two servers running the same application on an active/active scheme, because most of the current applications are not cluster-aware. Active/active clustering of two instances of the same application requires applications to be cluster-aware.

Cluster-aware applications are emerging, such as IIS and Proxy running with Windows 2000 Load Balancing service. You can set up a virtual server with up to 32 nodes. All instances are running and dynamically load balancing. If one of the servers fails, the rest will pick up the demands of the failed system. Dynamic load balancing also provides minimal failover times, since all services are already running on the backup server(s). Dynamic load balancing, however, generally requires applications to be cluster-aware or have add-on components that make them cluster-aware.

Clustering Topologies

Before an application can be failed over from one server to another, both servers, in their respective active states, must be able to access a common set of data. For active/standby and active/active installations, you will need to install the operating system on a nonclustered drive. This is typically a simple boot drive designated as the C: drive. This drive houses only the information required to boot and configure the system as well as to start up the appropriate services. You will then have an array drive for the application and application data. The boot drive typically cannot be a partition on this array, since most clustering solutions lock at the clustered logical drive level, not the partition level.

One approach to making your data available to both servers is to have an array of the backup server constantly update the array in the primary server. In an active/standby setup, each server will have a boot drive and an array. The array of the active server will be active, and the array of the standby server will be inactive but constantly updated with changes of the active server's array. When failover occurs, the array on the second server activates.

In the active/active scenario, each server has a boot drive and at least two arrays. The first array is active on the first server and inactive on the second server, and the second array is inactive on the first server and active on the second server. The first array on the first server constantly updates the first array on the second server, and the second array of the second server constantly updates the second array on the first server. If the first server fails, the first array on the second server is activated. If the second server fails, the second array of the first server activates.

If your application requires multiple arrays, such as a separate array for a transaction logs on a database server, the servers must have an additional array installed and configured for clustering.

An alternative to the data replication model is the shared bus model. In this scenario, there are two servers, each containing only a boot drive. They both access an external array through a shared SCSI or Fibre Channel bus. Only one of the servers has exclusive use of the array at any given time. For databases that require very massive arrays of transaction logs and data, the shared bus topology offers cost savings because you do not have to purchase two arrays. Another advantage is that both servers will be accessing the identical data with no replication latency—because there is no data replication.

One advantage of the data replication model is severability. Where the shared bus topology limits the placement of the server at a distance limited by the physical bus length (in meters), the data replication model can have both servers on two ends of a WAN link. Coupled with the alternate site disaster recovery, your alternate site can be up and running before you even get into your car and drive there. Remember that the arrays of a shared bus model are a single point of failure. If the arrays are in a building inferno, neither server can access them.

LEVERAGING REMOTE STORAGE IN WINDOWS 2000

New to Windows 2000 is integrated hierarchical storage management (HSM), called Remote Storage. Some administrators are beginning to feel that server storage arrays are getting out of hand, because they deal with servers containing 80GB, 150GB, 300GB, or more. The challenge is to back up and restore that much information. Remote Storage provides the ability to archive old information and keep only active information on the primary servers.

How Remote Storage Works

With Remote Storage, you can identify that point at which information on a server is automatically migrated to a removable storage device as shown in Figure 9-5. A primary server can have information that is less than 6 months old and the remote storage device can have information that is older than 6 months. Since information stored on the primary server is less than 6 months old, the server storage can potentially contain less than 16GB or 32GB of space. Clustering a server with this amount of data is a lot easier than trying to cluster a server with 300GB of information. In the event of a primary server fail-

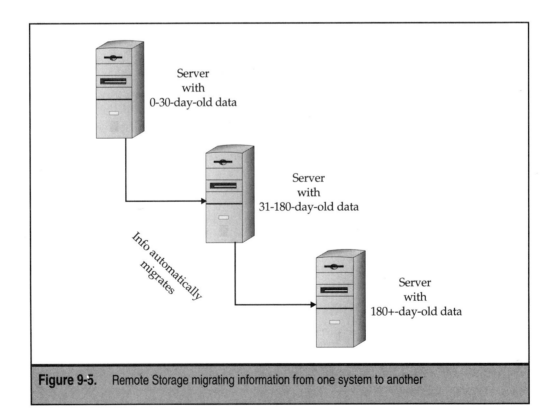

Figure 9-5. Remote Storage migrating information from one system to another

ure, information can be restored from a 16GB server in an hour or two, compared to the 24+ hours it would take to restore a server with 300GB.

In operation, when a user requests a file that has been remotely stored, there will be a time lag while the Remote Storage system retrieves the requested file. In effect, the file has to be restored from the tape library. This is a small price to pay, especially if this is a relatively infrequent event.

NOTE: Windows 2000 supports up to two levels of Remote Storage, but depends on third-party add-ins to support more than two levels.

CHAPTER 10

Designing and Planning Thin-Client Terminal Services

Terminal Services, which provides thin-client access to Windows, is an add-in to the Server and Advanced Server editions of Windows 2000. In this chapter, I'll discuss the ways Terminal Services might fit into your networking environment and offer some suggestions for designing and implementing this service.

Windows 2000 Terminal Services evolved from two products: Citrix Systems OS/2 WinTerm, and the Microsoft Windows NT 3.51-based Citrix Winframe product. These products provided low-bandwidth remote access to the look and feel of the Windows environment. Winframe's popularity led Microsoft to develop the Windows NT 4 generation of the product. Realizing the value of a thin-client offering, in 1997 Microsoft invested in Citrix Systems. In 1998, Windows NT 4 Terminal Server edition was released, providing a Windows 9x look and feel for desktop, NetPC, and terminal-based devices. Citrix Systems developed support for the same environment for DOS, Mac OS, UNIX, and Web-based clients.

TERMINAL SERVICES

Terminal Services is a built-in component of Windows 2000 Server. The server provides multiple virtual sessions for remote thin-client users who run Windows-based applications from the server. Unlike other remote access technologies that require proprietary hardware or multiple computer systems, Terminal Services works on any Windows 2000 server, providing dozens of simultaneous sessions on a single-server system.

Basic Operations

Windows 2000 Terminal Services works very much like a host/remote software application, such as pcAnywhere or Carbon Copy. The client runs a small program (typically taking up less than 1.5MB of disk space), and the CPU, RAM, and processing capabilities are run on the server.

The server captures and sends keyboard and screen images to the remote user as shown in Figure 10-1. This arrangement provides fast performance even over a relatively slow dial-up Internet connection.

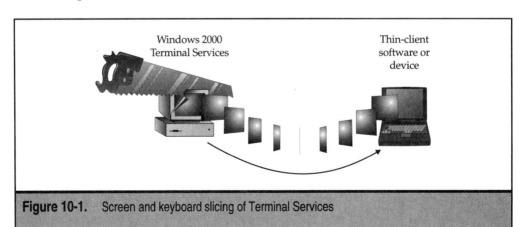

Figure 10-1.   Screen and keyboard slicing of Terminal Services

Technical Operations

From a technical perspective, the terminal server is running Windows 2000 Server as the core infrastructure setup, and the Terminal Services component converts information between the remote and the Terminal Services systems. As shown in Figure 10-2, Windows 2000 acts as a multiuser core operating system, and a new layer adds the Terminal Services communication subsystem. This subsystem, built on the T.120 Remote Desktop Protocol (RDP), provides a high performance, encrypted, multiple virtual channel architecture. T.120 is the same conferencing and communications system used by the Microsoft NetMeeting product.

Each instance of the replicated desktop runs in its own protected memory space, called a Winstation. Each Winstation accepts keyboard and mouse input from the remote client, and returns screen output to the remote system. Typically, a Windows 2000 server has only a single session (the Windows console session), but the principal remains the same. Each user that logs into the terminal server receives an individual protected session, complete with a unique desktop setup (selectable video background, screen saver, and icon placement, individual registry setting, dedicated home drive, and so on).

Because each Winstation runs in protected memory mode for each instance of user access to the system, if one user session "locks up" or has an illegal memory or system fault, other users are not affected. Users in a single session can open multiple applications and share memory space between applications, within the session. This means a user can cut and paste information between applications.

The hard drive of the terminal server can be configured to lock and protect drive space, preventing multiple users from sharing the space. Chapter 17 has more information on configuration and settings for Terminal Services.

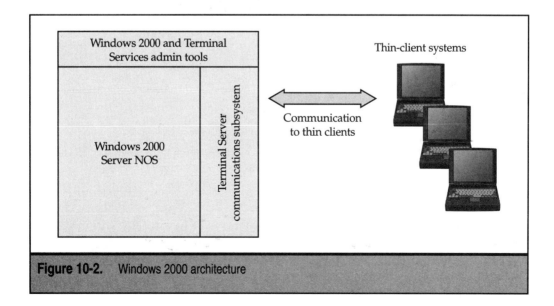

Figure 10-2. Windows 2000 architecture

In addition to managing memory and disk space, Windows 2000 Terminal Services also manages video screen displays. Each Winstation receives its own Win32 desktop look and feel, and all desktops receive rendered output for graphics, text displays, and screen redraws. Any application written for standard Windows video-display-mode graphics will work on Terminal Services.

Windows 2000 Terminal Services supports Windows 9x, Windows NT 4, Windows Terminals, and NetPCs, and each station is a recognized client on the Windows 2000 network. On the client side, the remote station, running Windows 2000 client access, uses the RDP protocol to access and log on to the Terminal Services system. All logon sequences, system policies, and user profiles are based on Windows 2000 network processes, so Terminal Services dedicated functions stop right before the user logs on. After that, it's just regular Windows 2000 logon controls.

USING THIN-CLIENT TECHNOLOGIES IN A NETWORK INFRASTRUCTURE

Many computer professionals shudder when they hear the term "thin-client," because the history of the technology has been one of limited functionality, proprietary software, and restricted performance. Windows 2000 Terminal Services is far superior to these older technologies.

Windows 2000 Terminal Services provides the user with the exact same interface (the Windows 9x desktop, complete with the Start button) that millions of computer users are already familiar with, as shown in Figure 10-3. Most Windows programs (and even most legacy DOS-based applications) will run without any reprogramming or configuration changes. In fact, most of the time you can install the standard Windows applications just as if the terminal server were a Windows 9x workstation. Today's powerful microprocessors, along with Windows 2000 support for 16 or more processors in a single server, and load-balancing and clustering technologies, help Windows 2000 Terminal Services deliver fast performance to every user logging in to the Terminal Services environment.

Some of the major benefits of this technology include:

▼ Centralized administration

■ Easy software distribution and license management

■ Support for existing desktop hardware without costly upgrading

▲ Fast access to "fat" applications that traditionally have been impossible to run on slow dial-up or frame-relay connections

Centralized Administration

Years ago, computer professionals recognized the benefit of a mainframe environment that let administrators put the mission-critical computer equipment in a "glass house." That glass house was protected with a lot of redundancy, and provided 24×7 user access. Terminal Services provides the same benefits.

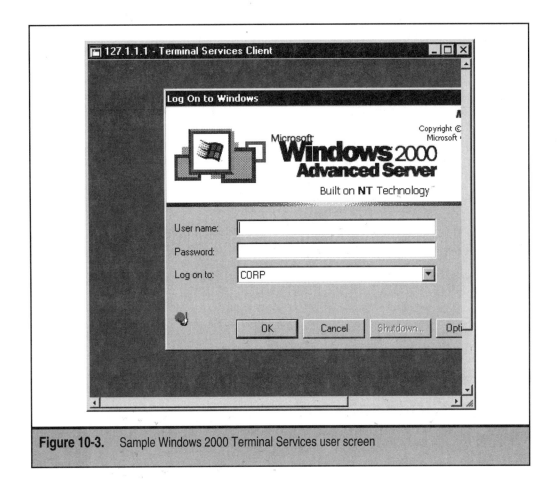

Figure 10-3. Sample Windows 2000 Terminal Services user screen

As your organization grows (or merges), the attempt to distribute technology to multiple points around the country or around the world can become a logistical nightmare. In some cases, organizations have small sales offices or manufacturing facilities in corners of the globe where it is difficult to find personnel to manage and administer a system. If the users in these remote offices access a centrally administered and managed terminal server, all the applications and mission-critical technology reside in the central office. You can even implement low-cost and low-maintenance terminals in the remote locations that boot directly to Windows 2000 Terminal Services. If a remote terminal fails, replacing it is a simple matter of plugging in a connector.

Controlled Software Distribution

Software installation, including upgrades, is a server-only procedure, controlled by the IT staff. It takes only a short time to upgrade all the servers in a Terminal Services cluster, minimizing the effects of system downtime.

If there are software or hardware failures, the centralized location makes it easier for IT administrators to provide support and maintenance to the system. If a software problem is detected, the fix is applied to a handful of centrally stored terminal servers, instead of deploying the fix to hundreds, if not thousands, of individual hard drives on scattered PCs. Users are prevented from installing other software onto their system, which could cause negative effects on the performance of the client machine.

Terminal Services has been welcomed by hundreds of companies fed up with trying to keep current with this year's version of the Pentium processor desktop, this year's release of the desktop operating system, and this week's assortment of software patches and fixes.

Controlled Software Licensing

With Windows 2000 Terminal Services, remote users cannot install software on the terminal server, providing tight controls on licenses. Additionally, Terminal Services has successfully passed home license rules, so that as long as you own enough licenses to cover the total number of users who run the software, employees can run the software at their office desktop or remotely, over Terminal Services, from home.

WARNING: If you don't configure your system properly, a user could download executable code from the Internet and "install" the software on the terminal server.

Reuse of Older Hardware

Another big benefit of Windows 2000 Terminal Services is the ability to reuse old equipment (the computers you tossed into a closet). The Terminal Services client will run on a client system with a 80486 processor running as slow as 60MHz, with as little as 1MB of RAM and 6MB of disk space. In fact, with the Citrix Metaframe add-in running the DOS version of the client software, you could use an 80286 processor running at 6MHz with as little as 512K of RAM on a single 1.2MB floppy disk.

For those software applications that require a minimum of 32MB of RAM, 100MB of disk space, and a high-speed Pentium computer system, use a terminal server with 1GB of memory and an 8GB hard drive on a super fast system instead of upgrading desktop computers.

Companies that have adequate desktop computers can let users run most software from the desktop. If there's a new application that requires more resources than the desktop computers offer, that software can be run via Windows 2000 Terminal Services.

For applications that require high levels of security, such as payroll or human resource applications, loading the software on a Terminal Services system is better than installing it on individual desktops.

High Performance for Remote-Access Clients

Windows 2000 Terminal Services provides excellent performance levels over low bandwidth, which is important for remote or mobile users. Large database or graphical applications are extremely difficult to use over low-bandwidth connections. Terminal Services is a better solution than the typical sophisticated replication schemes needed to move data across a WAN connection in order to provide server access to remote users.

With Windows 2000 Terminal Services, you don't need to move the data. Both the program and data can reside on the centrally administered and managed terminal server. Users connect through a dial-up connection, over a low-bandwidth frame-relay connection, or even through a secured Internet connection. Because only keyboard and screen images pass from the terminal server to the remote user, the traffic is low and performance is excellent.

WINDOWS 2000 TERMINAL SERVICES VS. CITRIX METAFRAME

Windows 2000 Terminal Services has a companion product, made by Citrix Systems, called Metaframe. As Table 10-1 shows, you can use the features in Windows 2000 Terminal Services alone, or add the features included in the Citrix Metaframe add-in. Metaframe is not a stand-alone product; it requires Windows 2000 Terminal Services.

	Windows 2000 Terminal Services	Citrix Metaframe
Product-line fit	Core functionality	Enhanced add-in features
Communications protocol	Remote Desktop Protocol (RDP)	Independent Computer Architecture (ICA)
Supported clients	Windows 95, Windows 98, Windows NT, Windows 2000, Windows Terminals, NetPC	DOS, Windows v3.1, Windows 95, Windows 98, Windows NT, Windows 2000, Windows Terminals, NetPC, Windows CE, UNIX, Mac OS, Web browser, Java
Local printer support	Yes	Yes
Local hard drive support	No	Yes
LPT and COM Port Redirection	Yes	Yes

Table 10-1. Windows 2000 Terminal Services vs. Citrix Metaframe Add-In

In releases of the Windows Terminal Server and Citrix Metaframe products prior to Windows 2000, the Citrix Metaframe product provided functionality that most organizations needed, thus most organizations bought the Metaframe add-in. However with Windows 2000 Terminal Services, Microsoft has included most of the features that organizations require for thin client computing.

Windows 2000 Terminal Services

Windows 2000 Terminal Services provides core functionality to users running Windows 9*x*, Windows NT, Windows 2000, WinTerm terminals, and NetPCs, using the Remote Desktop Protocol (RDP). This is a good solution for LANs, where desktop computers are running standard business applications, but other applications would work better from a centralized terminal server. For example, an application that requires constant updates to code or data is a good candidate for a Terminal Services solution.

Citrix Metaframe

Adding Citrix Metaframe to Windows 2000 Terminal Services provides additional remote client support and additional administrative tools.

The additional support is for computers running DOS, Windows 3.1, Mac OS, Java, and UNIX. In addition, the Citrix Metaframe add-in supports Windows CE and Web-based clients.

SIZING AND SCALING THE TERMINAL SERVER

Terminal Services utilizes the CPU, memory, disk, and LAN connection of the servers much differently than does a standard file and print server or a general application server.

CPU

The Windows 2000 terminal server divides the processing speed of each concurrent terminal session among the client sessions. If you have a dual-processor Pentium III, 500MHz server with only one user logged on to the system, that user receives the power of the server. When a second user logs on, the processing speed is split between the two users (each user receives the equivalent speed of a single processor Pentium III, 500MHz system).

If you do not want the equivalent processing speed to be slower than a Pentium 133MHz system, you can split a dual-processor Pentium III, 500MHz system approximately 25–30 times before you get to a session speed that would be regarded as "slow" by the users. However, because you can put 4, 8, or even 16 processors in a single server, you can easily split the fastest Pentium II or Pentium III server 50, 100, or even 150 times.

Remember, this division is based on the number of concurrent online users. Even if you have a single server that can handle 100 concurrent sessions, you don't always have that many people working on the system at the same time. If you have users that are on-line to the terminal server for an hour a day, this single server could handle a daily population of 400–500 users, and probably no more than 100 users will be on the server at a time.

Rather than adding processors to a single server, though, consider splitting processors across multiple servers to create a load-balancing environment. This way, instead of having a single 16-processor server that is a single point of failure, you have two 8-processor or four 4-processor servers. The load between the servers provides the same performance per user, and the enhanced fault tolerance and redundancy in the terminal server group is an enormous advantage.

RAM

Windows 2000 Terminal Services requires 64MB of RAM. For each user session, you should have the amount of memory that the average user will require. Therefore, if you have 20 users logging onto the system, and each user requires 32MB of memory to run applications, you will need the 64MB of base memory plus 640MB for the users. It's best to plan for 768MB or even 1GB of RAM.

Disk Storage

The disk-storage needs of a terminal server are not as extensive as those of a typical server, which may require a full RAID configuration with 16–32GB of space. Terminal Services needs only one copy of an application on the hard drive of the terminal server, so you only need 2–4GB of disk space for the system. In mission-critical environments, you should mirror a couple of drives for the terminal server, so that in the event of a drive failure, a backup drive is available.

LAN

The LAN adapter is the common bottleneck in a terminal server environment. The adapter is the channel for all data communications, so if 50 users are logged in to Terminal Services, and all of them want to surf the Internet, this single network adapter has the burden of supporting them all. Even if the chance that all users will require LAN adapter communication at the same time is limited, there is always a large possibility that users will require some form of LAN or WAN I/O that puts a demand on the adapter. Be sure to install the fastest LAN adapter your infrastructure can support.

ADVANTAGES OF LOAD BALANCING

There are significant benefits in distributing processing capabilities across multiple systems. Even though the processing performance and the cost of necessary hardware and software will be approximately the same per connected user, the benefits of load balancing are significant.

Creating Fault Tolerance and Redundancy

Load balancing, which used to only be available if you bought the Citrix Systems Metaframe product and Load Balancing Add-in, is now included as a standard component of Windows 2000 (see Chapter 12 on Network Load Balancing). Load Balancing allows multiple severs to distribute incoming user requests to a terminal server that's experiencing lower processing demands. As shown in Figure 10-4, when a user attaches to a load-balanced group of terminal servers, the server with the most system utilization available accepts the connection. Users experience no difference in system interaction, because all the servers in the load-balanced group are configured identically. Roaming profiles or Group Policy technologies (covered in Chapter 16 of this book), provide users with the desktop and software choices regardless of the server.

Load balancing is a way of keeping users operating at good levels of productivity. In addition, load balancing carries the additional benefit of providing redundancy in the event of a server failure.

Load balancing is not the same as server clustering, so if a server fails, the users connected to that server lose their connection and must reconnect to a new server. At that point, the load-balanced group will ignore the failed server and will connect the user to a new server.

If a server in the load-balanced group fails, the demand on the other servers increases. If you need six servers to maintain an appropriate user-to-server ratio for applications, you should add a seventh server. This keeps the user-to-server ratio at the appropriate level if one of the servers fails.

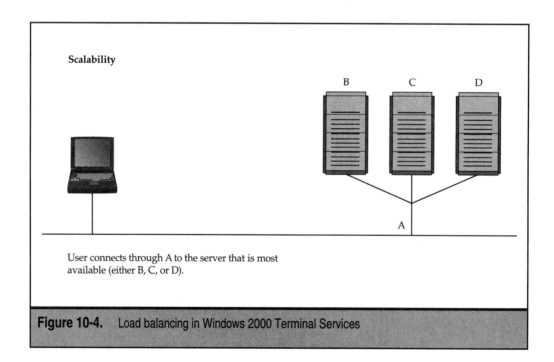

Figure 10-4.   Load balancing in Windows 2000 Terminal Services

After a failed terminal server is repaired and brought online, user connection requests will automatically include that server. In a short time, load balancing will relieve the workload on the other servers, restoring your system to an appropriate user-to-server ratio.

DEFINING USER AND APPLICATION REQUIREMENTS

When you plan for load balancing, your analysis must take a number of elements into consideration: the number of users, the applications accessed by the users, and the resource demands of those applications.

Evaluating the Demands of the Application(s)

Every application has resource demands, such as the amount of RAM required, the average amount of CPU processing time required, and the disk space requirements (both initial and dynamic). In addition, some applications may need access to other resources, such as SQL servers or intranet servers.

Application sizing is accurate only if you use data based on actual usage patterns, instead of the required minimums specified by the manufacturer. There are a number of tools available to determine application resource requirements (this was discussed in Chapter 9).

Quantifying and Grouping User Types

As part of the server-scaling analysis, in addition to knowing the resource demands of the individual applications, you must have information about user access. Some users may access only one application, while others may access multiple applications (perhaps simultaneously). You can use this information to determine the aggregate resource demands of your Terminal Service environment.

DEFINING THE EXPECTATIONS OF THE PROOF OF CONCEPT

When implementing a new technology like thin client service in an enterprise, most organizations want to conduct a proof of concept test to validate whether the solution and technology will meet the organization's needs. The validation typically includes an analysis of verifying software application compatibility, scalability, ease of implementation, fault tolerance, user and administrator training requirements, and evaluating the bandwidth demands on the existing infrastructure.

In this first section we will define the expectations and test criteria for the proof of concept phase of the implementation project. It is this documentation that an organization undergoes to outline whether the solution meets the needs of the organization.

Terminal Services Proof of Concept

While I have referred to Terminal Services for things like application software installation as being "workstation-like" as opposed to "server-like," it takes installing software and testing the software on Terminal Services to realize that Windows 2000 Terminal Services operates just like a desktop workstation.

During the initial installation of application software on Terminal Services as well as conducting initial user administration, the administrator of the Windows 2000 Terminal Services will gain valuable product experience and knowledge of the technology to understand which tools to use to conduct user management, and which tools to use to perform application management.

Another basic expectation of Terminal Services proof of concept is how Terminal Services performs for a single user as well as multiple users accessing Terminal Services at the same time.

It is these basic tests that will give the administrator the ability to understand the core functionality of Terminal Services in the enterprise environment.

Validating Software Compatibility

While most applications can just be installed on Windows 2000 Terminal Services straight out of the box, there are a number of old applications that do not run on Terminal Services, and even some newer applications require special user settings and configuration to make them run properly. It is important to run a series of software application compatibility tests on Terminal Server prior to a full organization-wide deployment to understand the intricacies of application installation and support.

Applications That Write Directly to Screen

One of the things to look for in testing software compatibility is whether the application writes directly to the video. Any application written to the standard Windows screen specifications writes to a relative position on screen, that way a window can be resized, set as the primary screen, set as a background window, etc., and still display information properly on screen. However during the early implementations of DOS based applications, since an application was the only program running on the system at any one time, some applications wrote directly to the video BIOS. It is rare to see these types of applications these days as most have been rewritten or replaced in the past 10 years, however there is still potential for old legacy applications that exist that may not work properly with Terminal Services.

Single-Instance Application Operation

Another thing to look for in testing software compatibility are applications that are not network compatible or network aware that only allow a single instance of the application to run on a system. Sometimes these applications are programs that are copy protected to only allow a single version of the software to run on a system or on the same network.

These applications typically work fine if you launch a single instance of the application on the sever or from a remote session, however the minute you attempt to launch a second or subsequent session of the application, you get an error that tells you the application cannot run. This message may be in the form of a copyright violation of multiple instances of the same application running, or an application program code error saying that the application requires a multiuser version of the software to be installed.

Typically the solution is buying the multiuser version of the software and using that version. Even if you install the multiuser version on the local C> of the Windows 2000 Server, while you are not physically sharing the software over a network, you are effectively allowing multiple users to share the same copy of the software on the network.

16-bit Applications Requiring INI Files

During your software compatibility testing, if you are installing any 16-bit Windows applications that use INI files stored typically in the c:\windows subdirectory of a workstation, these applications need to be closely reviewed and tested. While most 16-bit Windows applications can be made to work with Terminal Services, the critical factor is whether the application can share an INI file among all users accessing Terminal Services or whether the INI file can be distributed to multiple "home" directories so that each user can have a unique INI file for the application. If the application supports one of these two functions, the application will run on Terminal Services. If the application requires a unique INI file for each user but does not allow multiple INI files to run on the system, the application is likely not to work on Terminal Services.

For many applications where the INI file only notes the location of data files of the system configuration of the application (such as location of a CD-ROM, system protocol, etc.), having a single INI file for the application for all users typically works without a problem. This is quite common for CD-ROM-based databases where the INI file points the application to the location of the CD-ROM.

You typically know you have a problem requiring a unique INI file, if you launch the application for one user and it works fine, but when you launch the application for another user, the same user settings are configured for the subsequent user. This typically indicates that each user needs his own configuration settings.

Applications that require unique configuration information in the INI file, such as location of a users home directory or even the default user name and user characteristics similar to information that might be found in an electronic mail program, require a unique INI file for each user. For applications of this type, since Terminal Services provides the ability to specify a unique home directory for each user, the application icon can frequently be set to specify the "initial directory" of the users home directory while launching the application from a different directory. For example, typically when you launch an application, you specify the directory and filename of the program (ex: m:\msmail\mail.exe) and Windows will automatically look in the c:\windows directory for the MS-Mail configuration file. However, if you set the "initial directory" for the applications such as f:\homedirs\{user home directory) and specify the full path and the executable application program name, this frequently enables the application to be run with multiple INI files. For example, the initial directory setting could be something like f:\homedirs\rand and the full path name of the file as m:\msmail\mail.exe. In this example the application would launch the msmail.exe program and look for the unique INI file in the users home directory.

Applications That Lock Files

Some applications lock files on the local hard drive or on a data share drive for each user running the application. In many of these cases the file that gets locked is a software licensing tracking file that provides a way for the application to know whether a single user application is being run by multiple users.

Typically to solve this problem, you would install and run a multiuser version of the software as noted in the previous section on *Single Instance Application Operation*. A multiuser version of an application will allow multiple users to run a program. If the lock files still conflict, other settings such as "temp drive" settings in an INI file or "Home Directory" settings for the application need to be uniquely set for each user. These setting changes typically allow you to avoid lock file conflicts.

Applications That Require Temporary Files

Similar to the lock file problem are applications that write temporary files to a drive. Some applications write cache files to disk or create temporary storage files to designate a particular function or request. The applications typically need the temporary files redirected to unique subdirectories for each user running the application. For many 16-bit Windows applications, a "temporary directory" setting frequently solves the problem, or on 32-bit Windows applications, a registry setting in Hkey_Current_User for the application typically can redirect the applications write of information to variable drives.

Highly Graphical Applications

Lastly, while not necessarily a configuration problem but rather a product limitation is trying to run very graphics-intensive applications on a terminal server. Terminal Services effectively sends screenshots to the remote system, so with an application where the screen changes extremely frequently (such as full motion video), the performance of Terminal Services may not be acceptable.

For these types of applications, sometimes you can disable a video portion or highly graphical portion of the application without affecting the characteristics of the application—and thus drastically improve the performance of the application. If this can be done, the application can be effectively run with Terminal Services. In some cases, the graphical function is critical to the operation of the application and may be deemed unfit for use in a Terminal Services environment.

Modeling the Average Server Demands

During the prototype analysis phase of evaluating Terminal Services, you should model the performance demands of the users and the users' applications to ensure that the sizing and scaling of equipment being implemented will be adequate for the demands of the organization. While we've reviewed the basic server characteristics of Terminal Services, we now need to move from theoretical to actual server demand analysis.

Gathering Application Demand Information

To model the demands of the user's application there are basically five things we need to know about the application:

1. How much memory does the application need to run (minimum and average)?

2. How much processor speed does the application require?

3. How much disk space does the application take plus disk I/O demands of the application?

4. What are the demands the application places on the LAN and WAN?

5. What is considered relative acceptable performance for the application?

While it is very tempting to pull the manufacturer's "minimum requirements" information together for an application and do your modeling based on that information, the information from the minimum specs is typically not accurate enough to multiply by ten, fifty, or a hundred times to come up with realistic aggregate system demands. You can no doubt start with the information provided by the manufacturers, but then you need to actually test the application live to come up with more accurate information.

The first four items of the list can be derived from actual system performance monitoring statistics such as Performance Monitor (perfmon.exe) that comes with Windows NT4 or the Performance Monitor snap-in to Windows 2000. You can measure the statistical demands of the CPU, RAM, Disk I/O, and LAN/WAN I/O to determine workload on a per-use basis. There are a number of third-party applications available, such as Dynameasure (made by a company called Bluecurve Software), that do similar performance demand analysis on system operations. I am covering application performance analysis and third party tools in detail in Chapter 18 of this book, so refer to that chapter for more details on how to specifically monitor application demands on a server.

Analyzing Application Demand Information

After you gather the demand requirements for an application, you now need to analyze the information to determine how it will scale on the server based on the number of concurrent users you expect to add to the server. One of the critical factors when analyzing the information is noting that the demands of the application are not necessarily linear. There is a fudge factor called "think time" that is the amount of time that it takes for a user to interact with an application that spreads out resource demands on the server. Even during the most intense data entry processes people stop to flip a page, pause to review the information they just typed, take scheduled breaks as well as periodic breathers as opposed to sequentially entering information nonstop. This think time creates a buffer that allows more users to access a system simultaneously than pure linear calculations between user demands, and adds to a system's capacity.

Taking into account the minimum acceptable performance requirements for each user's access to an application against the CPU, RAM, Disk, and LAN demands of each application, you can now estimate the number of simultaneous sessions you can have on a single server.

CASE STUDY   After running a series of Performance Monitor tests you determine that a database application used in the organization requires the performance of a Pentium 133MHz system with 20Mb RAM per session, requires 1MB of disk space per user, and transfers 450Kbps of data when a database record is committed to the database every 45-60 seconds. You validate this information by testing the application on a series of computers, including a 486/66MHz system, Pentium/133MHz system, a Pentium II/300MHz system, and a Pentium III/550MHz system. You find that the application is unacceptable using the 486/66MHz system, but is relatively fast on the Pentium/133MHz and Pentium II/300MHz systems. While launching the application on a Windows 95 or a Windows NT system, you run Task Manager (pressing CTRL-ALT-DEL and selecting Task Mgr from the menu, selecting Processes, and looking at memory used for the database application and its associated support drivers), and determine that the application takes 18-20Mb of memory when in use. You notice that the entire program takes 26Mb to install on the hard drive (however, installation occurs only once). Every additional session of the application takes 1MB of disk space for temp files and unique configuration files. Finally, a test using PerfMon (Network Statistics, Sent/Receive transmissions) and NetMon (Sent/Received Packets) shows that the application adds 450Kbps of data any time information is requested or posted to the database. With these figures, and the organization's expectation of having 35 people accessing the application over Terminal Services (with no more than 20 simultaneously accessing the system at any one time), you multiply the demands of the application by 20 to determine the size of the server you require. Twenty times Pentium/133MHz performance will require the equivalent of a 2660MHz Pentium system (divide by two for a Pentium III, so the equivalent of a 1330MHz Pentium III—or a 2-3 processor Pentium III 550MHz system). Twenty times 20Mb puts the memory requirement over 400Mb. Disk and LAN I/O are well within the normal limits of a 4G hard drive and 100Mbps Fast Ethernet. So a 2-3 Processor Pentium III/550MHz system, 512Mb RAM, mirrored 4G hard drives, and 100Mbps Fast Ethernet will meet the requirements for twenty simultaneous users of this application.

This analysis is an initial estimate, and needs to be validated on Terminal Services; however, it is a place to start in sizing the server required to meet the demands of the organization.

Conducting Scalability Testing

Once you have estimated the size of the server required, the next step is to actually conduct a scalability testing of the application on a server in the lab.

Proof-of-Concept Testing

Some organizations want to test their application on Terminal Services before committing capital budget to purchase the hardware and software. This process is typically called the *proof of concept phase*, and is intended to provide the organization with the ability to confirm both software compatibility as well as performance. For organizations interested in conducting a proof of concept, renting a server and requesting an evaluation (or pilot) of the Windows 2000 Server or Advanced Server will allow you to install the system to validate your assumptions about scalability and performance. Some organizations have spare servers to install and test applications that could be used during this proof of concept phase.

Testing Criteria

To make the testing worthwhile, a series of testing criteria should be defined so you know exactly what you plan to install, how many simultaneous sessions you want to test, and what criteria you are using to determine the success or failure of the test. A sample test criteria is as follows:

- ▼ Does the application run at all?
- ■ Do multiple versions of the application run at the same time in different sessions?
- ■ As multiple sessions are launched and tested, at what point does the performance of each session drop below acceptable limits?
- ▲ Validate other application functions such as printing or report processing to confirm performance degradation and effects on system performance.

DOCUMENTING THE CLIENT CONFIGURATION

Part of the installation process of Terminal Services is to implement the user component for each user needing access to Terminal Services. This involves both the installation of a client software application on the remote system as well as configuring the client interface (or user profile) on the Terminal server. These two functions must be configured for each user to have a unique configuration for each user session.

Desktop or Terminal-Based Software Installation

There are a number of different client components available for various systems for installation dependent on the type of remote system. The client component can be either a Microsoft RDP client or a Citrix ICA client. The various options are discussed here.

RDP Client

The RDP client needed to access a terminal server comes in two different versions: a 16-bit Windows version and a 32-bit Windows version. The most common RDP client is the 32-bit client that works with Windows 9*x*, Windows NT, or Windows 2000 systems. The code for the RDP clients is installed in the \winnt\system32\clients\tsclient directory of the system where Terminal Services is installed. The two different subdirectories that exist include win16 for the 16-bit version of the Windows client software and win32 for the 32-bit version.

To install the client software, you have the option of copying the software onto diskette and installing the software from disk, or you can copy the software to a network share and install the software from the network. Either option has the same result.

To copy the installation files to disk, do the following: Click on Start | Programs | Administrative Tools | Terminal Services Client Creator. The Terminal Services Client Creator utility will prompt you for the version of the client software you want to create a diskette set for. You will have the option of specifying the destination drive that you wish to install the software to and to format the diskettes during the process. An option on the screen will notify you whether you need one, two, or three diskettes to get the appropriate software onto diskette. Selecting OK will create the installation disks required.

Once you create the installation diskettes you can install the client software by running the setup.exe program on the first diskette. You will then be prompted to specify the destination where you want the software installed.

WinTerm / NetPC RDP Terminal

The Terminal Services RDP client is typically a ROM-based client component that is installed in the WinTerm or NetPC based terminal. When you boot these types of terminals, they will effectively boot to a ROM chip that has the terminal server RDP client on it. The RDP client will search the network for the available terminal servers and will connect to either the default server defined on the WinTerm or NetPC, or the system will attach to the first available terminal server it finds.

A WinTerm or NetPC is designed to specifically run the Terminal Services client and launch a Terminal Services session. This drastically simplifies the boot process of one of these devices. No software needs to be installed on local resources (like floppy drives or CD-ROM drives) that allow users to install or copy off unauthorized files or information.

Occasionally the manufacturers of these terminal devices will release a boot ROM or BIOS update that would need to be installed or applied. This is effectively the way the manufacturers issue updated versions of the client software that over time will improve performance, add functionality, or increase compatibility with other client services functions.

ICA Client

For those implementing the Citrix Metaframe product and deciding to use the ICA Client software for a PC-based desktop system, you have the option of installing the DOS, Windows 16-bit, or Windows 32-bit version of the client software. The client software is stored on the Metaframe CD in the \clients directory. Within each client version directory is a listing of disks that are used for the installation of the software designated as disk1, disk2, or disk3 dependent on the number of diskettes required to install the software.

The files from each of the subdirectories can be copied to diskette. When the first disk is inserted in the floppy drive of a system, a SETUP program can be run to complete the installation of the software.

Web-Based ICA Client

For organizations wishing to use a Web browser as the front-end client to a Terminal Services environment, the use of the Citrix Metaframe WEB ICA client can be used. The client comes in either an Active-X client for Microsoft Internet Explorer or as a Plug-in for Netscape Navigator. The remote user requires only one of these two browsers to operate.

The client component can be installed manually by the browser user, or in the case of the Active-X client, it can be set in the HTML file to be automatically downloaded and installed at the time the user connects to the Web server.

The bandwidth between the remote user and the Web server can range from dial-up speeds through full DSL or Frame connection speeds. If the connection is 56kb or faster, the remote user experiences a terminal session that is equivalent to being live on the network. Speeds in excess of 19.2kb are considered acceptable WEB based terminal server performance, and while 9600 baud is functional, the experience is sluggish.

Macintosh ICA Client and Java Client

Organizations with Apple Macintosh computers and Java Virtual Machine enabled systems can launch the Citrix ICA clients for either of these environments. Just as with all of the other client components with access to Terminal Services, the Macintosh and Java clients will load the necessary code to launch an operational terminal server session.

Standard User Profile Configuration

Key to the success of installing and configuring the Terminal Services client is understanding the individual settings required to make the client application software operate. Just as we identified the need to have an appropriate INI file for Windows 16-bit applications to run properly, for 32-bit Windows applications, the appropriate registry settings need to be set and configured to ensure the applications run properly.

When Are Registry Settings Used?

Registry settings are configured and used by Windows 32-bit applications. Standard Windows registry settings include screen colors, default screen saver, or background image to be used. For a common application like Microsoft Word, the users' configuration for their default document folder or how frequently their documents are auto-saved are stored in the registry setting for Microsoft Word. When a user makes changes to their configuration settings, those charges are stored in the registry. If the registry is not saved, the next time the user launches Windows or the application, they would need to make the customized modifications again.

Configuring Individual User Registry Settings

To configure and save the registry settings for each individual user, the user must log on to Terminal Services, launch the applications desired to be customized, and make the necessary changes. This can be done manually for each individual user who will access

Terminal Services, or it can be automated through the use of tools such as Microsoft System Management Server (SMS) or the Microsoft Zero Administration Windows (ZAW) utilities. Organization-wide system configuration settings can be set using system policies to automatically configure or automatically limit profile settings and changes by user, group, site, or organization settings. Registry settings and system policies are covered in more detail in Chapter 16.

Storing Individual User Profiles

By default these registry settings and configurations are stored in the users profile on Terminal Services itself. The problem with profiles and settings stored on the server is if the server fails and a new Terminal Services system is installed, all of the users individual settings would be lost. Also if the organization wants to expand its Terminal Services implementation through the addition of servers in the environment, the additional terminal servers will not have a copy of the users registry settings or profile.

The best way to store user profiles is through the use of *roaming profiles*. Roaming user profiles are stored in a separate location on the network. This might be a common network share, so that when a user logs onto the network, it pulls the user's profile setting from this common location. Any changes made by the user will be automatically stored back to the common network share. This allows a user to log on to any Terminal Services system on the network and get the same registry settings and profile settings. It also prevents the settings from being lost by the failure of an individual terminal server. (You'll learn more about Roaming Profiles in Chapter 16 of this book.)

DOING A TOTAL-COST-OF-OWNERSHIP ANALYSIS

The initial investment required to implement a Terminal Services environment is relatively expensive, and, in fact, implementing a Windows 2000 Terminal Services solution is not cheaper than buying a brand new PC (and legal software licenses) for each remote user.

However, offsetting the costs of a Terminal Services solution are savings that accrue from minimized maintenance costs. There's less maintenance involved with the remote machines, resulting in a large reduction in network administration costs. And, you eliminate the need to upgrade computers or purchase new computers.

The best approach to an analysis of total cost of ownership is a comparison of the two sets of costs: the cost of implementing Terminal Services against the cost of not implementing those services (and instead, implementing a solution that involves distributed PCs on every desk). The analysis includes the cost of remote servers, administration, and maintenance contracts for the PCs, and so on.

Cost of Traditional Network Services

The cost of a traditional WAN-based network includes remote desktop computers, servers, network administration expenses, and so on. Over a three-year period, you can expect to purchase and upgrade your equipment, including software updates at least every 18 months.

Desktop Computers

The first cost to consider is the upgrade or replacement of PCs. Many organizations replace computer systems every three years, using a rotation scheme that includes one-third of all the PCs each year. Even though the price of computers continues to fall, the cost of state of the art technology seems to remain the same over time. You must invest in advanced technology to ensure that your equipment will remain viable for its expected three-year cycle.

If you have 300 computers, using this scheme means you'll replace 100 computers each year, for the next three years. The average cost is about $1,500 per computer (including hardware, core operating system, and labor to configure and install these computers). This puts $450,000 on line 1 of Table 10-2.

Servers

Servers such as file and print servers, electronic mail servers, data warehouse servers, and so on, are needed whether you're implementing a WAN or a Terminal Services system, so for this study on total cost of ownership, we'll eliminate those particular servers from our analysis.

The servers we'll consider are those that provide services at remote site locations. In order to accommodate the need for a domain controller, local file storage, email, and database replication, you should plan on two servers at each location.

For this case study, assume that of the 300 employees, 250 of them are in the main office, 30 are in a second office, and two additional offices have 10 users each. At an average cost of $5,000 per server, with two servers for each of the three additional offices, you reach a total expense of $30,000 for additional servers. Assuming a life span of three to five years, over a three-year period you can plan on $15,000 for ongoing replacement costs, bringing the total cost to $45,000 in server expenses over the next three years, which we'll add to line 2 of Table 10-2.

Licenses

Some software license costs are the same regardless of whether they're used in a traditional network or a Terminal Services network. These licenses typically include word processing software, email client licenses, file- and print-server licenses, and other similar software. For this study on total cost of ownership, we'll eliminate those licenses from the analysis.

You will need licenses for the remote servers in the field offices, as well as a fraction of licenses for home users who need to do work from home (telecommuting part-time) where home use licensing does not extend outside of the organization.

We'll make a guess on the cost for server licensing, including three-year renewal or upgrade costs (since server licensing varies based on the function of the server). For the three small offices, each of which has two servers, let's plug in $2,000 per server for the cost of local server licensing over three years. We can assume that 20 percent of the organization will need to work from home or on the road, extending software licensing by approximately $250 per system for 60 users. This brings line 3 of Table 10-2 to $27,000.

LAN Costs

The cost of implementing a traditional network is typically the same as the cost of implementing a Terminal Services–based network. However, many companies are finding it necessary to increase the network's power, moving from a shared 10-megabit, hub-based network to a switched 100-megabit system. This is especially critical for large data warehouses with large sets of data or graphics.

Switched 100-megabit LAN technology is not much more expensive than standard 10-megabit, shared hub technology, so for the remote sites that may be purchasing new equipment when the sites are installed, the cost is close to the same. For the purposes of this study, we'll ignore the cost of implementing 100-megabit switched technologies in our small remote locations. However, for our main office with 250 users, let's add in the cost of switched 100-megabit technology plus any incremental costs in network adapters and cabling. It's safe to add $50,000 to line 4 of Table 10-2.

WAN Costs

Many companies are investigating alternatives to their existing WAN connectivity solutions (such as virtual private networks over the Internet) in order to improve performance and reduce the monthly cost of WAN connections. Older frame-relay connections aren't efficient for server-to-server database replication, server-to-server user authentication, or electronic messaging replication between sites.

WAN costs vary based on the distance between sites and the type of bandwidth. Rates vary based on the carrier and the services. These costs need careful analysis. I've worked with organizations that have saved $30,000 a month in frame-relay costs by tuning and optimizing their network instead of buying additional bandwidth.

For this case study, we'll assume that the organization will invest $5,000 per site (for the three sites in this scenario) in upgrading communications equipment, and then pay an incremental $500 per month per site for increased bandwidth. Over our three-year study period, this means a total of approximately $69,000 in incremental WAN costs, which we'll add to line 5 of Table 10-2.

Help Desk Costs

In any network environment, you need people to respond to user needs and hardware problems. This core help desk cost does not vary between traditional network and Terminal Services–based networks, so we'll omit this in the overall cost comparison.

In a traditional network, when a user's problem cannot be solved over the phone, the fallback is to implement some form of remote administration tool that allows an administrator to take control of the employee's computer desktop. If that doesn't solve the problem, an onsite visit is required.

Even if you implement system policies that prevent users from installing their own software, or making configuration changes that damage the system, it's normal to expect an onsite visit to a desktop computer at least three times each year. However, in a remote site with 10–20 users, the cost of a full-time resource person can't be justified. You can hire a support person at a full-time rate for the part-time work, or split the job between support and other responsibilities. Another option is to outsource support services.

For our scenario with 250 users in the main office, we'll assume that two people will support that site, and assume the cost of the remote control software that allows them to assist users without physically going to each desktop. Let's allocate $30,000 for the software program and licenses for the three-year case study for this functionality. Personnel or contractual services will be needed for the remote sites. We can allocate $450,000 over the three-year period to line 6 of Table 10-2.

Software Updates and Upgrades

Even though software licensing costs are similar for traditional networks and Terminal Services networks, the cost of distributing software or updates to each desktop can be significant in a traditional networking environment.

There are typically four ways to deploy software or updates:

▼   Install software in one desktop computer at a time, using the software
    CD-ROM, along with instructions to ensure that the installation and
    configuration options are identical throughout the system.

■   Use automated software installation tools, such as Microsoft System
    Management Server (SMS). An administrator creates a script that automatically
    installs the software as users log on to the network (or during the night). Scripts
    have to match systems and configurations, and if there is a large mix of
    computer types, the time needed for scripting can be equal to the time
    needed to install without the script.

■   Use a semi-automated system that creates a common script that is run by users
    who select installation and configuration options during the process. This
    requires less time than preparing multiple scripts, but requires a level of
    user knowledge that may not exist.

▲   Buy new computers with the software preinstalled.

The average cost of software installation for organizations over a three-year period runs $500–$750 per computer. This includes the cost of initial installation as well as periodic updates over the three-year period. For automated processes, the figure is the distributed cost of the software distribution system and scripting costs. For our scenario of 300 computers, $200,000 has been added to line 7 of Table 10-2.

Time-to-Market Applications

Time to market for hardware and software deployment is hard to quantify, because it differs from company to company. A database that contains current interest rates, price mark-up rates, or tax rates must be kept up-to-date on each desktop. Updated files for antivirus software are equally important. Keeping hundreds or even thousands of computers updated is a challenge (if not an impossibility).

I'm going to leave the value of this component blank on line 8 of Table 10-2, although the benefit of ensuring that current information is available to every user could be worth hundreds of thousands, or even millions of dollars.

Cost of a Terminal Services Structure

For Terminal Services, the categories remain the same, including desktops, servers, software licenses, network administration, and so on. However, Terminal Services requires centralized purchases of servers (instead of remote desktops) to manage users on an ongoing basis, which saves money on remote site maintenance.

Desktop Computers

If you run Windows 2000 Terminal Services, the life of desktop computers can be extended to 5–6 years. You can even purchase lower-cost terminals in place of full-blown desktop PCs, since the horsepower of the desktop computer is really not used in the Terminal Services environment.

For our scenario of 300 users, half the computers and half of the laptops need to be replaced over a three-year period. The computers could be replaced by low-cost terminals at less than $600each, and the laptops would run around $1400 each. For 150 computers at $1,000 each, $150,000 is added to line 1 of Table 10-2.

Servers

With Windows 2000 Terminal Services, the cost of the servers is the largest expense. The servers provide all the processing speed, memory, disk access, and network I/O, so these systems need enough capacity to support those demands.

For our case study, let's assume a need for six servers to manage 300 users. There should be an extra server to provide load-balancing fault tolerance, which minimizes downtime. Given the amount of memory and processors needed to service user demand, plan on a per-server cost of $30,000, for a total server cost of $210,000. With assumed upgrades every three to five years, the total is incremented by $100,000. That brings the cost of investment in servers to $310,000, which is placed in line 2 of Table 10-2. (Server sizing and capacity planning is covered later in this chapter).

Licenses

Initial license costs for Windows 2000 and Metaframe for the seven terminal servers and 300 users are $15,000 per server. Assuming additional costs for the three-year period could double that total, we'll allocate $210,000 to line 3 of Table 10-2.

LAN Costs

Terminal Services communication between servers and the clients takes place over extremely low bandwidth, so the cost of implementing fast LAN technologies is really limited to the server farm. Existing file servers and terminal servers should be updated to the fastest technology available. Over a three-year period, assuming upgrades for the seven terminal servers, file and print servers, email servers, database servers, and so on, the total cost should be about $15,000, which we'll add to line 4 of Table 10-2.

WAN Costs

Just as LAN demands decrease with the implementation of Terminal Services, so do the demands on the wide area network. Because only keyboard and screen image information are sent across the communication link, there's no need to increase bandwidth.

The actual bandwidth demands may decrease enough to reduce the monthly expense of maintaining existing WAN connections. However, because Terminal Services depends on the connections, redundancy for the WAN connection becomes extremely important.

For this case study, we will plan on a redundant, Internet-based, virtual private network (VPN) as a fallback for connectivity. In the event of a failure of the primary frame-relay connection, the backup Internet VPN will be available immediately.

For this case study, we'll allocate $10,000 in maintenance costs for equipment and services to maintain the existing WAN infrastructure. In addition, we'll allocate $300 per month, per site, for an Internet connection, and $10,000 per site for the VPN equipment. This means $72,400 is added to line 5 of Table 10-2.

Help Desk Costs

A Terminal Services environment doesn't eliminate the need for technical support. However, Terminal Services includes a feature called shadowing, and it allows an administrator to view and support remote users from a central location. This software actually assists help desk personnel provide support.

There's no immunity to hardware problems, regardless of the equipment. We must assume that over the course of a three-year period there will be a need to repair or replace equipment.

However, with Terminal Services, the application software, drivers, icons, desktop configurations, and so on, reside on the servers. This provides a way to switch over to new hardware without the long and complicated setup and configuration processes involved when replacing PCs. In fact, keep some spare terminals in a closet, and if a desktop computer fails, a replacement terminal can be set up by almost anyone in the office.

For this case study, we'll budget a full-time person in the main office who can provide ancillary desk side support. In addition, we'll allocate time for a person in each remote office to provide technical assistance when necessary. The total cost of $250,000 is entered in line 6 of Table 10-2.

Software Updates and Upgrades

Because the servers contain the software, the need to distribute software to multiple desktop computers is greatly minimized. Any method of software installation is efficient: individual installations on each server, or scripts that install software automatically on all servers. The process can be completed in a fraction of the time it would take to install software on hundreds of desktop systems.

For seven terminal severs, upgrading every six months (including patches) still requires less time than traditional software upgrades. Over the three-year period, expect to incur no more than $15,000 in labor costs, and that amount is entered on line 7 of Table 10-2.

Time-to-Market Applications

For companies that must be sure that time-sensitive information is sent to each computer system, that require software updates to maintain productivity, or that need to provide an updated user interface to clients through a Web application, Windows 2000 Terminal Services provides a distinct advantage. Software updates are much faster than the traditional network environment. Because the value of this benefit varies from organization to organization, I'm going to note line 8 of Table 10-2 as "varies."

When comparing the three-year costs in Table 10-2 between a traditional versus a Terminal Services network, the Terminal Services configuration is at least 20 percent lower in overall costs. In our scenarios for the cost comparison, we have even included the cost of a redundant server as well as a completely redundant WAN backbone to minimize downtime. If we took out the costs of this redundancy, the Terminal Services solution would be more than 25 percent lower in overall three-year costs. Our numbers also don't include some of the less tangible figures of time to market for the implementation of software applications, or the shear complexity that most organizations have in trying to roll out new software to computer systems and laptops distributed across the country or around the world.

	Normal Three-Year Purchases	Implementing Terminal Services
1. Desktop computers	$450,000	$150,000
2. Servers	$45,000	$310,000
3. Licenses	$27,000	$210,000
4. LAN	$50,000	$15,000
5. WAN	$69,000	$72,400
6. Help desk costs	$450,000	$250,000
7. Software distribution	$200,000	$15,000
8. Time-to-market delivery	Varies	Varies
Total three-year cost:	**$1,291,000**	**$1,022,400**

Table 10-2. Three-Year Cost Comparison (Traditional Network vs. Terminal Services Network)

CREATING A NEW SET OF MAINTENANCE LEVELS

IT departments are setting and meeting very high service levels. Service agreements have guarantees about the maximum downtime and outage time. Terminal Services makes it easier and cheaper to provide redundancy and maximize service goals.

Shift from Desktop to Infrastructure Service

The big paradigm change in a Terminal Services network is the shift of emphasis from the desktop environment to an infrastructure environment. An advantage of PCs is the ability to install software applications locally, so that when the network is down, users can continue to work.

However, against that advantage is the challenge of supporting the complexities in PC systems. Replacing a PC is not just a matter of plugging in a new computer. There are configuration options for hardware, user preferences, user profiles, and other complications.

Terminal Services takes the focus away from the desktop to the infrastructure. Because the desktop system does not store data or configuration information, a user can roam to any computer or terminal, log on to Terminal Services, and have full access to data, applications, and customized configuration information.

However, a focus on the infrastructure means reliable connections and unconditional uptime are essential on the terminal servers. Rather than depending on the existing organizational frame-relay WAN, provide redundancy with parallel WANs through the use of an Internet-based virtual private network (VPN). The Internet becomes the backup backbone.

Other alternatives include wireless technologies that allow office-to-office communication over wireless connections, eliminating the phone company or land-line connections as possible points of failure. As we saw in our scenario in the previous section, even with the purchase of a redundant WAN infrastructure, the total cost of a Terminal Services solution over a three-year period is less than a traditional network with no WAN redundancy.

Need for Clustering and Load Balancing

One part of redundancy is the ability to ensure that the terminal servers are also set up to provide backup operations in the event that one or more of the terminal servers fails. By implementing Load Balancing, you can provide an environment in which servers automatically add users to the servers with the least usage. Rather than assigning each user to a specific terminal server, the logon process ends in an automatic assignment to the server best able to handle another user. With this type of load balancing, if a server were to fail, users would have fewer servers to randomly attach to, but operations would continue as usual.

Having an extra server or two to balance the workload in the event of a failure improves protection against downtime.

FINALIZING THE FUNCTIONAL EXPECTATIONS OF THE TERMINAL SERVICES DESIGN

After taking all the cost analysis into consideration, we can finalize the expectations for implementing Terminal Services. All that remains is to define the method of implementation.

Dial-up Access

Dial-up remote user access, as shown in Figure 10-5, is typically implemented early on in a Terminal Services environment. Remote and mobile users are an excellent fit for the advantages of this paradigm.

Remote and mobile access can be implemented with a variety of devices. For a PC running Windows 9*x*, a laptop running Windows NT workstation, a Mac OS computer, a DOS-based computer, a Windows terminal, or even a NetPC, all that's needed is an asynchronous dial-up modem or ISDN modem.

When a remote user dials into Windows 2000 Remote Access Services (RAS), Windows 2000 Terminal Services provides the communications transport over standard Terminal Services RDP communications.

NOTE: Dialing directly into a modem attached to the terminal server with the performance benefits of the Citrix ICA communications protocol makes the purchase of the Citrix Metaframe add-in to Terminal Services cost-effective.

Because fat applications run on low bandwidth, Windows 2000 Terminal Services provides a perfect medium for dial-up users to use all the company's applications.

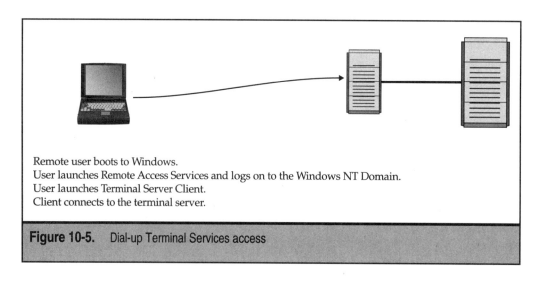

Remote user boots to Windows.
User launches Remote Access Services and logs on to the Windows NT Domain.
User launches Terminal Server Client.
Client connects to the terminal server.

Figure 10-5.   Dial-up Terminal Services access

Network Blueprints

Table of Contents

1. Native Windows NT4 Domains

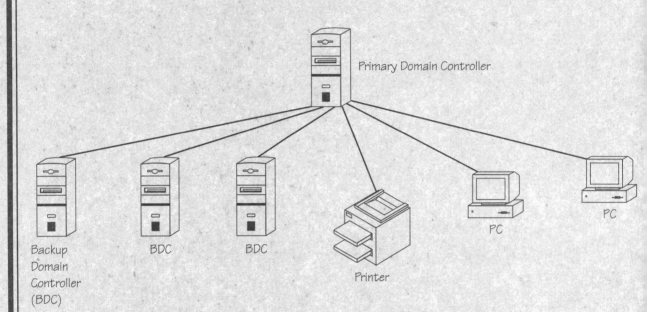

Primary Domain Controller

Backup
Domain
Controller
(BDC)

BDC

BDC

Printer

PC

PC

2. Migration of the PDC to be both the NT4 PDC and Windows 2000 GC

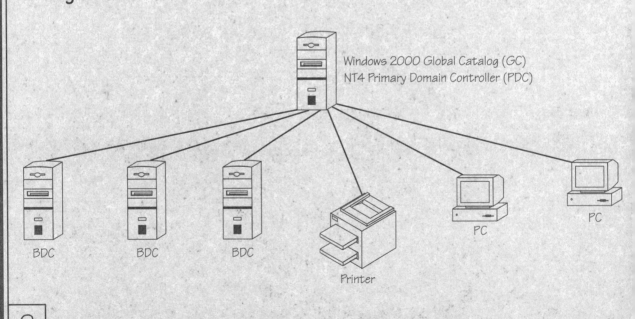

Windows 2000 Global Catalog (GC)
NT4 Primary Domain Controller (PDC)

BDC

BDC

BDC

Printer

PC

PC

3. Migration of the NT4 BDCs to be Windows 2000 DCs

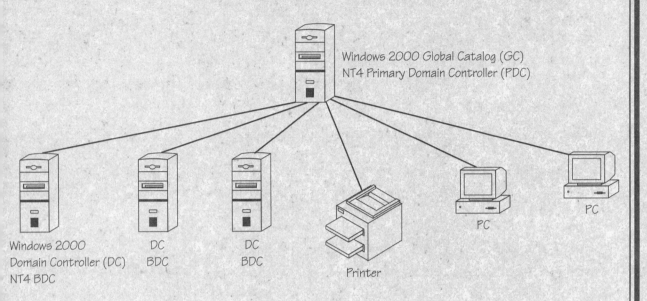

Windows 2000 Global Catalog (GC)
NT4 Primary Domain Controller (PDC)

Windows 2000
Domain Controller (DC)
NT4 BDC

DC
BDC

DC
BDC

Printer

PC

PC

4. Native Window 2000 GC/DC model

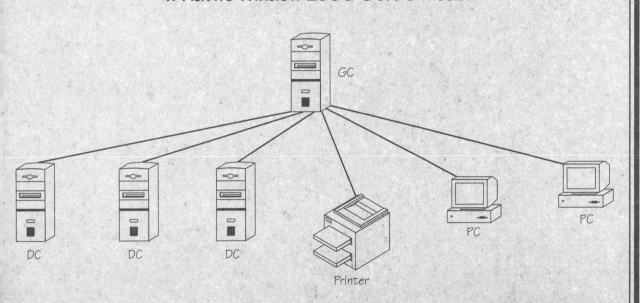

GC

DC

DC

DC

Printer

PC

PC

"Migrating from WINS to a Native DNS Name Resolution" (Chapter 7)

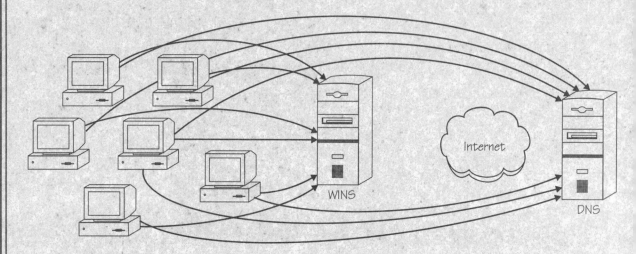

An NT4 environment uses WINS for local name resolution and DNS for Internet name resolution.

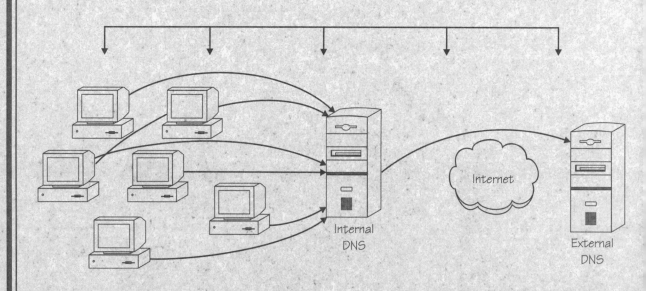

With Windows 2000, an organization can implement DNS for local name resolution and forward DNS requests to a external Internet DNS server.

Leveraging Thin Client Technologies with Terminal Services (Chapter 10)

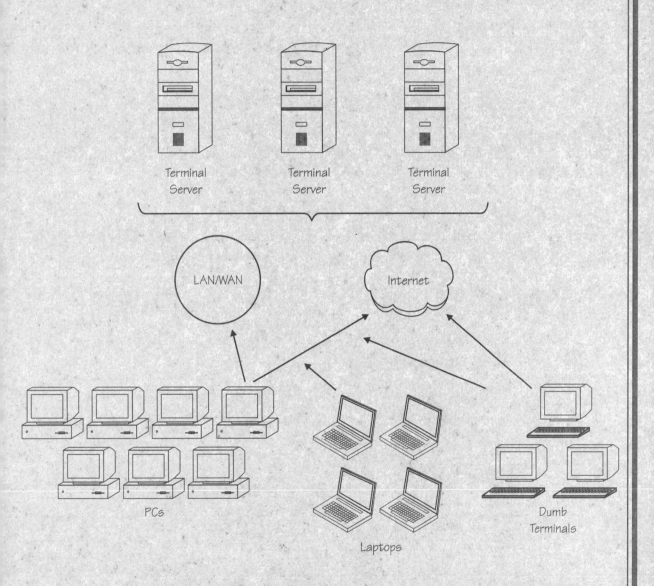

Decreasing the total cost of ownership in computing using thin client technologies of terminal services.

	Task Name
1	⊞ **Evaluate the Features/Benefits of Windows 2000**
17	⊞ **Organize the Windows 2000 Design/Deployment Team**
25	⊞ **Document Existing Orgs Domain, DNS, and LAN/WAN Structure**
46	Document Complete Milestone
47	⊞ **Design the New DNS Structure**
58	DNS Design Completion Milestone
59	⊞ **Design the Organization's Active Directory Structure**
66	Active Directory Design Completion Milestone
67	⊞ **Create/Implement the Windows 2000 Lab**
88	Windows 2000 Lab Status Mtg
89	Windows 2000 Lab Completion Milestone
90	⊞ **Upgrade the Existing Administrative Domain PDC to a Windows 2000**
99	Admin Domain PDC Upgrade Complete
100	⊞ **Upgrade Existing Resource Domain PDCs to Windows 2000 DC**
121	Resource Domain PDC Upgrades Complete
122	⊞ **Upgrade BDCs to Windows 2000 DCs**

Duration	Start		Sep	Oct	Nov	Dec	2000		Ma
							Jan	Feb	
14 days	**Fri 9/17/99**		▰▰▰						▲
5 days	**Wed 10/6/99**			▰▰					
14 days	**Wed 10/6/99**			▰▰▰					
0 days	Tue 10/26/99			◆10/26					
				▱▱					
14 days	**Wed 10/27/99**				▰▰▰				
0 days	Mon 11/15/99				◆11/15				
7 days	**Tue 11/16/99**				▰▰				
0 days	Wed 11/24/99				◆11/24				
30 days	**Thu 11/25/99**					▰▰▰▰▰			
0 days	Wed 1/5/00						◆ 1/5		
0 days	Wed 1/5/00						◆1/5		
7 days	**Thu 1/6/00**						▰▰▰		
0 days	Fri 1/14/00						◆1/14		
21 days	**Fri 1/14/00**						▰▰▰▰		
0 days	Mon 2/14/00							◆2/14	
5 days	**Mon 2/14/00**							▰▰	

Creating an Indestructible Networking Environment (Chapter 12)

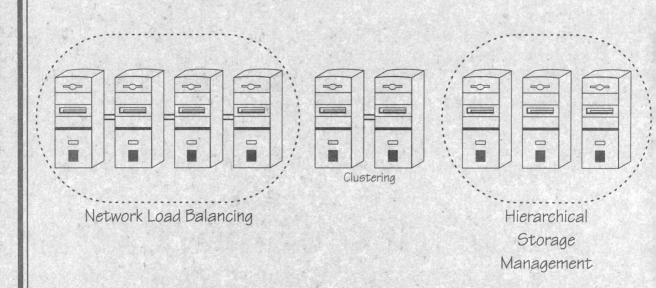

Network Load Balancing

Clustering

Hierarchical Storage Management

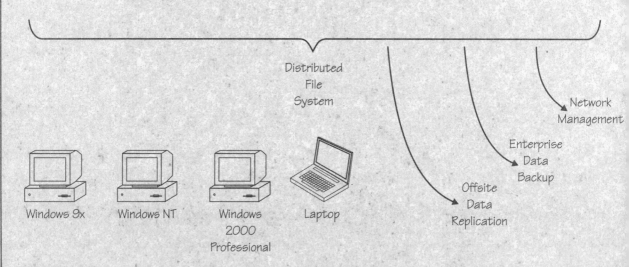

Distributed File System

Network Management

Enterprise Data Backup

Offsite Data Replication

Windows 9x   Windows NT   Windows 2000 Professional   Laptop

Integrated technologies within Windows 2000, when properly designed and implemented, can create a high availability, mission-critical, 24x7 enterprise environment.

Supporting hardware, software, and complicated user configurations is simplified with the centralized Terminal Services solution, which makes dial-up access easier to support, administer, and manage.

LAN/WAN Access

Terminal Services technology can be leveraged for LAN and WAN-based users as shown in Figure 10-6.

Limiting the Need to Support Remote Servers

Many organizations have small remote offices that traditionally require a file server or messaging server to provide data and communications links back to the main office. Typically, those remote servers are put in place to avoid the high cost of the bandwidth for a WAN connection. The low-bandwidth transmission required for Terminal Services means remote servers can be eliminated, along with the need to administer and support them. In fact, the low bandwidth demands of Terminal Services can be securely streamed over an Internet connection.

LAN-Based Implementation for Selected Applications

Thin-client technology for a LAN-based implementation can also mean extending the life of a desktop computer that can no longer meet the needs of high-powered applications. Using Terminal Services for the applications that require more processor speed and system memory means the desktop computer can continue to be useful for another 12, 18, or 24 months.

The ability to run a specialized application over Terminal Services for a selected group of LAN-based users can yield significant benefits. This is especially true for business applications that require code changes based on changing laws, regulations, in-house ap-

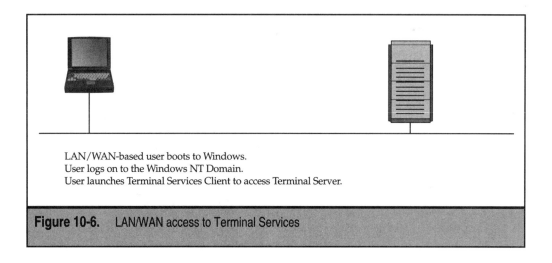

LAN/WAN-based user boots to Windows.
User logs on to the Windows NT Domain.
User launches Terminal Services Client to access Terminal Server.

Figure 10-6.   LAN/WAN access to Terminal Services

plication improvements, or changing data. Updating the application and its data at the organization's data center is far easier than updating every single remote system.

For applications that require high levels of security and should be accessed by a limited number of users, safety and efficiency is improved with centralized implementation instead of desktop installations.

Ability to Maintain Existing Low-Bandwidth WAN Connections

WAN connections tend to require upgrades every three to five years, as bandwidth demands increase. Terminal Services lets you decrease WAN bandwidth demands because you're not pushing application data between locations, you're sending only the keyboard and screen images. You can delay or eliminate planned upgrades and their associated expenses.

Minimizing the Need to Have Remote Administrators

A notable cost reduction is realized in the reduced need for administrative and support services in remote locations. Moving data-management responsibilities to the centralized data center improves administration response times.

Internet/Web Access

The availability of access to the Internet has greatly expanded the options and alternatives for new technologies. Users can connect to a terminal server halfway around the world through the Internet, as shown in Figure 10-7.

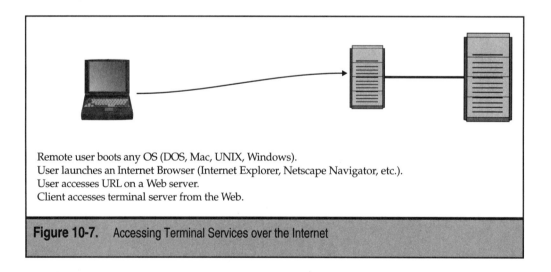

Remote user boots any OS (DOS, Mac, UNIX, Windows).
User launches an Internet Browser (Internet Explorer, Netscape Navigator, etc.).
User accesses URL on a Web server.
Client accesses terminal server from the Web.

Figure 10-7.   Accessing Terminal Services over the Internet

Access from a Web Browser

Thin clients no longer require the installation of a proprietary application. Browser-based access to Terminal Services is a viable alternative and provides services for non-PC systems, such as UNIX workstations, Mac OS computers, and Web terminals.

Access from Any Internet Station

Web-based access is becoming ubiquitous. Hotels have Web stations available in business centers and guest rooms. Airports and train stations have Web kiosks for users who pay an hourly fee. Even in cities and countries where online communications are frequently difficult to find, Internet cafes exist on street corners to provide access to the Internet for an hourly fee.

In many cases, Internet access may be the primary method for a traveling employee to access the company's servers.

Internet-based access is also effectively a fault tolerant backup system.

Leveraging the Bandwidth and Support of the Internet

With the Internet as the on-ramp to the data information system, the responsibility of supporting and administering the Internet connection is in the hands of the Internet service provider (ISP). If a remote user has problems connecting to the Internet, the ISP can assist.

As your point of presence expands to include portals via the Internet, the ongoing cost of private WAN connections, remote administration costs, maintenance and support costs, and never-ending requests for increasing WAN bandwidth diminishes.

CHAPTER 11

Building a Microcosm

W e set up a microcosm environment for Windows 2000, and in this chapter I'll explain how we planned and designed that laboratory environment. We used the microcosm environment to test application compatibility, server implementation, workstation deployment, system security, and other core network validation components.

WHAT IS A MICROCOSM?

Webster defines "microcosm" as:

▼ A little world; especially the human race or human nature seen as an epitome of the world or the universe

▲ A community or other unity that is an epitome of a larger unity

Building a microcosm (as shown in Figure 11-1) that is an epitome of a larger production environment enables you to test the environment under controlled conditions. A microcosm project paves the way for deployment, making the deployment smooth and more effective. This can reduce the uncertainty and risks associated with the actual deployment of Windows 2000. To get the most out of a microcosm, you need to plan it carefully.

After defining the details of your microcosm, the next steps are to determine the microcosm strategy, complete the microcosm design, prepare the microcosm plan, and, finally, build the microcosm. After the microcosm has been built, it will need to be managed according to the plan defined, and the postdeployment fate of the microcosm will need to be set.

Laboratory

Microcosm, as used in this context, refers to a subset of an existing environment and/or an environment that will be in existence in the future. In essence, it is a laboratory with equipment that is representative of the environment that you are moving from and/or migrating to.

The laboratory equipment is dedicated to testing and prototyping. It is self-contained, so that the work that takes place in the microcosm will have no impact on the actual production environment. In this way, you can provide a flexible setting that lets you run tests using all necessary resources without impacting the existing user community.

Environment for Testing

The microcosm can be used to simulate a new environment. Test cases can be developed for migrating to the new environment, and the results documented. The results can be used to validate the original design assumptions, which provides assurance that the new environment will function as anticipated.

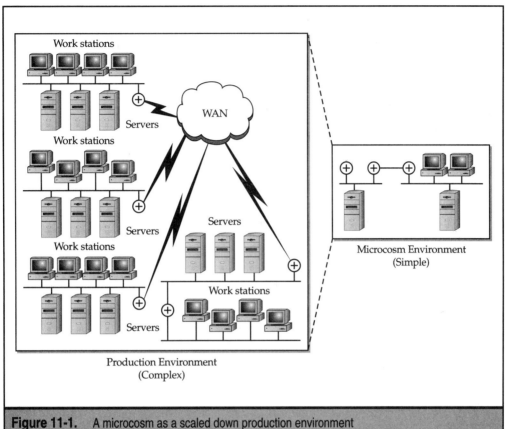

Figure 11-1. A microcosm as a scaled down production environment

In addition to validating the new environment, you can also test migration procedures, which identifies any coexistence issues you need to take care of.

Validation of Strategies, Plans, and Processes

Use the microcosm to evaluate alternative design strategies and determine which should be pursued. The processes you've planned to build and deploy in the final environment can also be validated with your microcosm. For example, you can test your plans for backup and disaster recovery.

Production of Build Documents

Another use of the microcosm is the creation of documentation for the build configuration of servers, workstations, routers, hubs, switches, and any other associated equipment. This documentation can be used to rebuild after tests, as well as to build the real production environment.

Your documentation may be approached in an "as-built" manner, which consists primarily of configuration parameter settings. Or, you may prefer to document the step-by-step procedures, laying out the steps for re-creating the environment.

It's important to validate your documentation with multiple test iterations, especially if you're planning any special, or extreme, scenarios.

Careful testing produces bulletproof documents, because they've been validated by real-life situations instead of relying on theory.

Production of Training Documents

In addition to documenting the building of your environment, use your microcosm to create documents that will assist in the training process. Create validated instructions for the processes and procedures your administrators will use. End-user training documentation can be prepared as well.

Test the documentation in the lab environment before using it in your production environment. The lab environment is also a great place to generate screen shots and exercises that can be used in the training process.

Since the lab is representative of the new environment, trainers will have more lead time for developing and testing training materials. If you wait until the actual environment is created to produce training materials, the shorter timespan allotted for this process will result in material of lower quality, or you may have to turn to "canned" generic material that doesn't quite match your environment.

Reduction of Risk

By validating configurations, processes, procedures, and documentation prior to implementation in a production environment, you minimize the risk of encountering problems. Any issues related to the migration to the new environment or coexistence with the existing environment can be identified and solutions prepared.

Reduction of Project Timeline

The lab environment can be used to determine how long it takes to perform the steps involved in a deployment. Generating accurate time estimates is an essential part of planning.

In addition, the lab provides an environment to test what tasks can be run in parallel and which steps can be combined. Mass production techniques for minimizing the rollout time (such as automated deployment processes) can be developed and tested.

Sample of All Functional Components

The lab needs to include all relevant components of both the current environment and the proposed environment. Enough resources need to be allocated to validate and test migration and coexistence issues. The lab does not necessarily need to be an exact duplicate of what will be used in the product environment, but it must be similar in functionality.

Postdeployment

Since the microcosm was created to represent the production environment, it can also be used to test any postdeployment changes and/or additions in functionality. Keep your lab functional so you can test patches and updates before you deploy them.

Justification of Microcosm Costs

While the microcosm may appear to be an expensive process, the cost is justified because overall deployment costs are reduced. Problems and issues related to the deployment are worked out ahead of time in a smaller controlled environment rather than in a time- and pressure-sensitive production environment.

Downtime, always a considerable expense, is reduced because an environment exists for testing changes before applying them in the production realm.

THE MICROCOSM STRATEGY

A carefully planned approach for setting up, maintaining, and using the microcosm includes, at minimum:

▼ Overall use of the lab

■ Identification of the tests that will be conducted in the lab

■ Training role of the lab

▲ Long-term utilization of the lab (postdeployment)

After determining the microcosm strategy, you can begin to design the microcosm.

Usage Phases

Throughout the life of the lab, you may find a variety of useful purposes. Overall, the lab serves as a strategic element in your decision-making process. It can also be used to evaluate alternative strategies for reaching a goal.

Prior to deployment, the microcosm serves as a test ground for development of the production environment and its implementation. It is also used to validate design assumptions. Performance and stress testing can be done prior to implementation so that any necessary tuning or optimization can occur. Migration and coexistence issues can be identified in the lab. Equipment configurations and implementation procedures can be developed, tested and validated.

In addition, the microcosm provides a training environment for both end users and administrators. It assists in the creation of documentation in the following areas:

▼ Build/configuration

■ Test parameters

■ End-user training

▲ Administrator training

After deployment, the microcosm can be used for the following:

▼ Testing the effects of proposed changes to existing environment

▲ Validation of disaster/recovery procedures

Some examples of the lab's usage include infrastructure and connectivity, integration and coexistence, performance and stress testing, migration testing, deployment testing, disaster recovery testing, training preparation, administration training, and documentation. It is not necessary to include all types of usage. Not all labs will contain all the phases and some lab situations will require additional phases, such as development.

An important consideration is whether the lab should exist specifically for the life of the project or be permanent. The decision affects space allocation, equipment, documentation detail, etc. Making the decision early avoids wasted effort (if the lab is to be temporary), or the cost of rebuilding the lab at a later date because you've made a decision to make it permanent.

Infrastructure and Connectivity

Infrastructure and *connectivity* within the microcosm refers to the base hardware and software necessary to emulate the existing environment. The hardware includes the backbone of the environment, such as servers, LANs, WANs, hubs, routers, and switches. The connectivity element includes the hardware and software necessary to connect to outside resources, such as remote locations, the Internet, and service bureaus. For the purposes of the lab, samples of clients for testing also need to be included.

The lab is a step toward building the future. It includes hardware and software that represent the environment that will exist at the end of the project. In addition, it must contain the elements needed to test the steps that move you from the current environment to the proposed environment.

Of significant importance is the use of the lab to determine whether a specific solution works as envisioned or as it's designed. Do all of the features work? Have all of the necessary patches, updates, and service packs been applied and tested? Is there a smooth migration path, and have coexistence strategies been validated?

The design can then be modified to fit the real world, based on the work performed within the lab.

Problem areas, bugs, and discrepancies in design can be identified. Proposed solutions for issues and problems can be tested and validated. Any "show stopper" bugs or problems can also be identified prior to implementation.

Integration and Coexistence Testing

Integration, as used in the context of this book, is the movement from the old environment to the new. The steps and procedures for getting from the current environment to the new environment must be planned, documented, and validated. There will be a period of coexistence, when both environments (the existing and the proposed) are in use at the same time. You need to determine how the technological past will be bridged to the future.

Without testing, it is difficult to predict how integration will work in each unique environment. The testing procedures you develop must expose any problems that can arise as you integrate legacy systems with new systems. Also, be sure you test and verify manufacturer claims. The goal is to minimize the unexpected, and your lab is the best vehicle for discovering problems and troubleshooting connectivity issues.

Any limitations that will be imposed by coexisting environments must also be identified. There are almost always limitations on connectivity, and these limitations—along with any features that will be "lost" during the implementation process—need to be documented. In addition, you must investigate and document any process that may work differently during the implementation phase than it will after full migration.

Performance and Stress Testing

Performance testing predicts how well the new environment will handle the average load placed on the environment. Performance can be defined as response time, hardware utilization, network utilization, etc.

Stress testing is used to establish the maximum load that can be placed on a system before it "breaks." Stress testing can be used to test peak usage areas. It's important to test how well the environment performs under real-world peak loads in the lab environment, where you can also identify potential areas for optimization.

You must establish a baseline—a starting point for comparison purposes when performing tests. The baseline includes the normal behavior of the environment under a normal load. If the project involves testing for changes in an environment, the baseline is the point at which the environment currently stands, before any changes are made.

You must also define the response time needs, and those needs should be specific to the elements in your project. Response time differs, depending on the type of project, and could include measurements of elements such as (but not limited to) the following:

- ▼ The amount of time an end user has to wait for a response from an interactive application
- ■ The time required to complete a specific project (e.g., report generation) in a "batch" type of system
- ■ The time required to process a transaction
- ▲ The system response time, such as disk access time, throughput on the network, etc.

Response time is typically measured in seconds. Service level agreements, influenced by response time, are determined by the user's threshold for pain.

You need to determine the response time under a normal system load, and in order to do this you must define a normal load. Then, you can measure the response time with the new environment.

Measure the performance and response time of the system at peak usage times, noting whether the performance and response degenerate quickly or slowly as the peak is reached.

Identify the system break points, those points at which the system can no longer handle the load. At what point are you outside of the service level agreement? What are the limiting resources? What would it take to increase the capacity? Is the cost of increasing the capacity justified when considering the probability of the system breaking?

Performance and stress test results should include the following:

▼ Documenting what the baseline was.

■ The criteria and scripts used to create a normal load.

■ The criteria and scripts used to create a heavy load.

▲ At what point the system reached the break point.

Your reports should include raw data, an explanation of the results, and an explanation of the methodology used to create the test. Any limitations of the tests should also be documented.

Migration Testing

Migration is the series of steps and procedures involved in moving from the current environment to the new environment. Migration testing is the validation of those steps and procedures.

You must develop a strategy to move end users across the bridge and into the future environment. Determine whether there will be a period of coexistence, or a one-time migration. End users need to be prepared for the things they might face. It's important to involve end users in the decision-making process as you consider these options.

As you consider the timing of the migration, remember that it's important to plan for a minimum amount of impact on the end-users. Training requirements also need to be identified.

The plan for moving to the new environment needs to be developed long before the migration actually occurs so that a "dry run" of the migration can be performed. The plan should include scheduling and timing for the various elements involved in the migration. For example, you might be able to migrate the infrastructure (servers and other equipment) before migrating the users. You must plan the timing, considering after-work hours or weekends. Don't forget to consider the impact on offsite resources such as service vendors or customers. You must make provisions to give sufficient notification to all affected parties prior to the implementation.

Your plan needs to include documentation for any external systems that might require changing. You must coordinate each step with outside parties that are affected by the migration. If your project involves a large end-user community, your plan needs to specify the assignment of responsibilities for end-user migrations, perhaps considering one of the following options:

▼ **Using IS resources**   Having internal IS staff conduct a migration.

■ **Outsource**   Contracting an external organization to either completely conduct the migration or supplement your existing IS staff to add resources to the process.

- ■ **End-user initiated**   Providing instructions to the end users to conduct a series of migration tasks themselves.
- ▲ **Automated**   Scripting a migration process to be automatically launched and executed.

Consider providing extra support during the migration to handle issues that may occur. Have a fallback plan for an unsuccessful migration. And don't forget to include end-user training and admin training in the plan!

Procedures for implementation can be validated prior to beginning that implementation, and modified if necessary. Numeric targets (e.g., performance results) need to be verified, and processes can be ironed out and streamlined.

Document any exceptions to your migration plan, including any workarounds for the exception cases.

Document the load that the system is capable of handling, including things such as volume limitations, procedure limitations, and data transfer limitations. Document any limitations with regard to features (or lack thereof) related to the new environment.

Deployment Testing

Deployment testing is the process of simulating the implementation of the new environment. The testing includes both infrastructure (e.g., servers) and end-user deployment. This provides validation of the deployment procedures that have been developed. This is also an opportunity to uncover any issues that may occur during the deployment process. Sometimes a deployment test consists of actually deploying a subset of the new system using a pilot group of users.

The deployment test is a way of determining what the end users will experience after the new environment is deployed.

A large-scale deployment test includes a simulation of the deployment of the majority of components in the new environment in a test mode. While this can be a time-consuming and expensive process, it provides assurance that deployment will go as planned.

A small-scale deployment test involves testing the deployment of a subset of the environment. While this approach is less time-consuming than a large-scale test, it limits the exposure of problems. In the end, you may face some additional problems during the actual deployment.

Try to automate as much as possible in the deployment to avoid human error. Ensure that any automated deployment procedures are thoroughly tested and documented. Remember to include in your plan a fallback procedure in case the automated procedure fails.

Disaster Recovery

Disaster recovery is the ability to reestablish the environment that was in existence before the disaster occurred. Disasters can include things such as:

- ▼ Computer hardware failure
- ■ Software failure

■ LAN infrastructure failure (e.g., cabling, hubs, etc.)

■ WAN infrastructure failure (e.g., data lines, routers, CSU/DSUs, etc.)

■ Loss of connectivity to outside services (e.g., Internet, dial-up)

▲ Inability to access resources due to physical limitations (e.g., destruction of the building)

Your plans must include both a recovery procedure for the existing environment and a recovery procedure for an existing environment that is not accessible (e.g., the use of offsite facilities). When you create your plan, include the following elements:

▼ The level of service required during a disaster

■ The minimal level of applications, features, and functionality

■ The likelihood of the disaster occurring and the cost to recover from the disaster

▲ Acceptable recovery times vs. cost associated with the recovery

Use the microcosm to develop and test your strategies. Your lab can also test recovery times, and test to ensure that the procedures that have been developed work as planned.

Data recovery is to the ability to get back the information that existed before the disaster. You must determine the level of recovery that is acceptable, such as:

▼ Previous day

■ Last completed transaction

■ Prior hour

▲ Other levels, specific to your environment

Depending on the level of recovery you require, hardware fault tolerance may need to be considered, such as redundant hardware. In addition, software features such as transaction logging may be necessary.

Component failure is the failure of a specific hardware component, such as a disk drive, a network card, or a port on a hub. Identify what happens when the component fails, and provide for redundancy if it's possible and cost-effective. Document and test recovery time in the lab so accurate service levels can be determined. Use the lab to document and test procedures for replacing failed components.

System failure is the failure of an entire entity in the environment, such as a server, a router, a hub, or a communications line. Identify what happens when the system fails and provide for redundancy if possible. Generally, it is a high-cost solution to provide for complete redundancy for system failures. If complete redundancy is not possible, at least document what features are lost and the recovery time needed.

The lab can be used as a test bed to ensure that procedures work as expected. The lab can also be used to identify the amount of time necessary to recover from a disaster. If absolutely necessary, the lab can be used as the platform for disaster/recovery. However, this is not the recommended approach.

Training Preparation

The training plan consists of elements such as:

▼ Who needs to be trained

■ The level of training necessary

■ The type of training required:

  ■ Hands-on

  ■ Lecture

  ■ Onsite

  ■ Offsite

■ The timing of the training:

  ■ Before implementation

  ■ Concurrent with implementation

  ■ After implementation

■ Who will be doing the training:

  ■ IS resources

  ■ Outsource

  ■ End-user or departmental representatives

The type of materials required also needs to be determined, such as:

▼ Lecture notes

■ Lab assignments

■ How-to documentation

▲ Tutorials

Determine the format of the training materials, such as:

▼ Hardcopy hand-outs

■ Online tutorials

■ Intranet-based

▲ Media-based (e.g., CD or diskette)

Your training plan needs to be verified with the customer and/or user community. An outline of what will be covered in the training as well as the type and level of documentation should be covered. A pilot group can be used to validate that the training meets user requirements. Feedback surveys should be performed after the training to get input on areas that need to be modified for subsequent training sessions.

The training lab can be a subset of the microcosm, or the microcosm can also be used as the training lab. You can use your lab to develop the actual training program, the amount of time required for training, and the development of the training materials.

Administrator Training

Administrator training ensures that the appropriate personnel have the knowledge necessary to manage the environment on a daily basis after it has been implemented. The level of knowledge necessary needs to be defined for each situation. Develop a breakdown of administrative tasks, for instance:

▼ Daily management, such as adding users, changing configuration information, and first-level troubleshooting.

■ Maintenance, such as backup and restore procedures, or installation of software updates and patches.

■ System installation/configuration, such as installing and configuring subsequent instances of the environment.

■ Advanced troubleshooting, including hands-on learning to gain experience about the common problems that may occur during deployment.

■ Optimization techniques, including the ability to monitor the performance of the system and tune parameters to provide optimum performance.

▲ Disaster/recovery procedures.

The lab environment can be used to determine the level of expertise necessary to manage the environment. Document the knowledge level that exists and determine the level of training necessary to meet the demands of the new environment. Consider the format of the additional training, such as:

▼ **Onsite, using the lab**   This option provides training in the environment that the administrators will be dealing with. It can be customized to include only what is required and is usually performed by personnel that have been using the systems in a business environment. However, it may be difficult to get a commitment for uninterrupted time to do the actual training.

■ **Classroom training at a certified training facility**   This option forces personnel to take uninterrupted time to learn the material. However, material that is irrelevant to the individual's environment is often included. The quality of the training is dependent on the instructor—some have only textbook knowledge vs. the few that have actual hands-on experience in a business environment.

■ **Online tutorial**   This is performed at the user's convenience. It generally costs less, and can be used for several individuals. However, there is no instructor present to answer questions or explain difficult concepts. It may also be difficult to get committed uninterrupted time to complete the training.

- ■ **Customized for the environment**   This option provides a way to include only what is relevant, and you can include the appropriate level of detail. However, the cost is generally higher than the other alternatives.

- ■ **General textbook**   This option is readily available for major applications and solutions. While it carries a lower cost, it may include areas that are not relevant to your environment, and may lack items that are necessary to your environment.

- ■ **Vendor provided**   This option takes advantage of the knowledge base the vendor possesses, including "inside info" not generally available. However, sometimes the vendor is not in tune with the real world.

- ■ **Integrator provided**   This type of training is taught by personnel familiar with the environment. It can include details relevant to the environment that will be supported and tailored to the level of detail necessary. A potential disadvantage is that it is not necessarily taught by a trainer, but by an engineer.

- ▲ **Third-party provided**   Third-party training is generally taught by a trainer rather than an engineer. It is usually general in nature, and may cover areas not relevant to your environment or lack information needed for your environment.

Documentation

Documentation is an extremely important part of any implementation. It should include the following:

- ▼ Business parameters driving the project
- ■ Assumptions/limitations of the environment
- ■ Design specifications
- ■ Build/configuration documentation
- ■ Testing parameters
- ■ Training requirements
- ■ Maintenance procedures
- ▲ Disaster/recovery procedures

The level of detail required is dependent on the situation:

- ▼ Is it a necessity to communicate information to management?
- ■ Who is responsible for doing the actual design/implementation (inside personnel, third party, or combination of the two)?
- ■ What is the knowledge level of personnel that will be supporting the environment?

- ■ Is there a knowledgeable and well-trained internal staff?
- ■ Is the documentation for internal staff that has minimal training and knowledge in the environment?
- ▲ Is there a reliance on outside parties for support?

Build Documents

Build documents are used to re-create the environment and include items such as server installation parameters and configurations, router configurations, line configurations, etc. They generally include screen shots from actual builds. This documentation can be specific step-by-step instructions or just enough information necessary to re-create the environment by a knowledgeable person familiar with the environment.

Training Documents

Training documents are used to transfer knowledge to parties not familiar with the environment. The level of detail required is dependent on the environment.

Testing Results

It is generally impossible to test for every situation and case that may occur within an environment, therefore test cases need to be documented so they can be repeated if necessary. Test cases that validate functionality as well as things not tested need to be documented.

Design Modifications

Any changes to the approved design need to be documented, along with the reasons for the modifications. This will assist those people who are responsible for maintaining the environment in the future.

Recommendations

The microcosm is used to validate recommendations, based on hands-on development work. Any issues or concerns uncovered in the lab can be identified, and recommendations for handling these issues and concerns documented.

DESIGNING THE MICROCOSM

Now that the microcosm strategy has been set, the next step is to design the microcosm. There are a number of factors and associated issues to take into account when designing the microcosm, all of which can impact the design.

The factors to consider when designing the microcosm include the scale of the microcosm, the space allocation, the components to incorporate, the tools, and the deliverables that will be produced.

After the design of the microcosm is complete, the plan can be prepared.

Scaling the Microcosm

When designing the microcosm, you must first decide how big and how detailed you want the microcosm to be. In some cases, the microcosm may be a couple of servers and a couple of workstations, and in other cases the microcosm may be a dozen servers and several dozen workstations. There are a number of deciding factors, discussed in this section.

The larger the lab, the more completely it mirrors the real environment, but a large lab is harder to manage and fund. Smaller labs provide a less than complete view of the overall environment, but can be deployed faster and more cost-effectively.

For any particular deployment, the pros and cons of the level of effort required to build the lab have to be weighed against the need to drive out uncertainties in the project. Some of the factors to consider are the previous experience level of your organization with the technology, similarity to previous projects, experience of the partners involved with the project, the level of technology being deployed, and so on.

How Big Is Enough?

The size of the lab is determined by the number of elements you need for each component of the environment. For example, how many servers are needed to represent the server component, or how many switches are needed to accurately reflect the LAN component? The size of the lab is less important than ensuring that all components are represented. However, the size of the lab is key for some aspects of testing, including scalability and performance.

The lab should be large enough to reflect all the key components of the environment, so that every aspect of the environment can be tested to some degree. If funding, time lines, or resources do not permit a full-scale effort, then the lab should reflect any areas where there is uncertainty. For instance, if the performance of the technology over slow links is an area of uncertainty, the lab should include a WAN component with the appropriate link speeds.

Major Components

The major components of a complete lab should include WAN, LAN, routers, servers, workstations, enterprise applications, desktop applications, NOS, and peripherals shown in Figure 11-2. The components should be as close to the actual technology as possible. For example, if the environment includes a switched infrastructure, the LAN component should be built in an analogous manner. This will ensure that the results generated by the lab reflect the results that can be expected in the real environment.

Frequently, the project time line and budget cannot justify the installation of fully functioning WAN or Internet infrastructure for testing purposes alone. Some of these can be simulated, such as WAN links. Simulating the environment lets you get close to the objective with a reasonable level of effort. You could use null modem cables between routers and clocked T1s between CSU/DSUs to simulate a wide area network or slow links. You could use a combination of domain name servers and Web servers across a

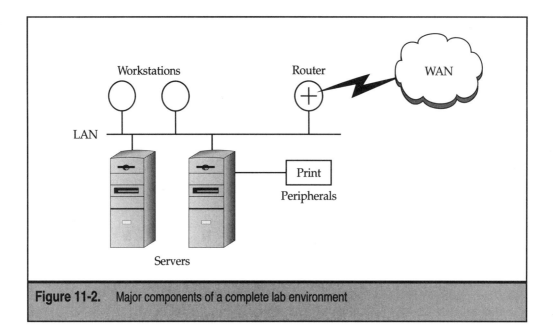

Figure 11-2.   Major components of a complete lab environment

slow link to simulate the Internet. Having an experienced partner is critical to developing these creative solutions.

Areas of Uncertainty

Any areas of uncertainty must be included to reduce your risk. It is frequently a temptation to create a showcase for the project, but this is more appropriate for a proof of concept stage rather than the lab stage. A lab should not be a showcase of the vendor products in an ideal environment, but rather a tool for highlighting problems and resolving them.

Conducting a careful review of the environment, the technologies being deployed, and the project goals will ensure that the areas of uncertainty are clearly identified.

Cost and Time Boundaries

As a practical matter, costs, time, and resources bind all labs. There is always some level of compromise needed as you draw the line that determines where the lab will stop. This line represents your comfort level with the risks and knowledge gained from the lab, after which the lab returns begin to diminish.

An experienced consultant can be invaluable in helping you draw that line. Consultants who have experience setting up laboratories, and experience with the technologies, can make the decisions about where to draw the line much easier.

Space Allocation

A lab should be built in a space that is separated from the rest of the IT infrastructure. It is important that the lab not impact existing operations, but it is equally important that the existing environment not impact the lab results. Failing to allocate the proper space can impact lab productivity and result in contamination or attrition, where the lab environment can accidentally be connected to the real environment or lab components can mysteriously disappear or migrate to the real environment due to emergencies.

It is often difficult to obtain additional space for the IT lab, because most organizations are already packing IT into close quarters. Space allocation is often one of the most contentious topics in creating a lab, so it's important to address and plan for it early on in the project.

Space allocation can frequently be one of the last requirements taken into account, as it's taken for granted that "we'll find somewhere to put it." This can result in unexpected political wrangling when a department finds out that "somewhere" is in their backyard. However, if space is made available for a lab, a sample lab layout is shown in Figure 11-3.

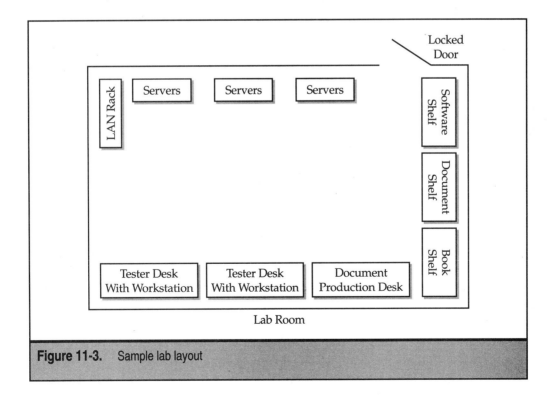

Figure 11-3. Sample lab layout

Area for Equipment

You must know the minimum level of space needed for the equipment. The lab components can take up quite a bit of physical space, considering all the different parts. This includes routers, servers, workstations, printers, racks, cabling, etc. It is important to remember that engineers will be working with this equipment more often than they would in a production setting, because they will be modifying configurations constantly in order to test and optimize the systems. If the lab environment is packed too tightly, these important steps will be more difficult to perform.

Often overlooked are the additional power and cooling requirements, which can be considerable. The heavy power requirements of servers, workstations, and infrastructure equipment can impact the local power circuits and potentially blow circuit breakers. The power used by the systems leads directly to heat dissipation, which can overload air-conditioning systems. You must have sufficient resources to avoid uncomfortable working environments, long-term equipment degradation, or even catastrophic equipment failures in extreme cases.

Area for Testers

The next level of allocation is for the staff conducting the tests. Their requirements include space to sit while conducting the tests, desk areas to record the test results, and areas for transitory equipment such as laptops with power and network and printer connections.

You'll also need shelf space for books—manuals, software, and other documentation. There will be significant quantities of these materials, some of which can be quite bulky. It is important that these materials be readily available to the testing personnel. The more difficult it is to access these valuable reference guides, the less likely it is that they will be used.

Area for Document Production

Document production is also a key element of space requirements. Although the space does not need to be colocated with the lab equipment, it's certainly beneficial for the documentation staff to have quick access to the laboratory when they need to verify information, produce screen shots, etc.

Documentation productivity often hinges on the quality of the equipment (such as screen size and system performance) and the quality of the environment (such as background noise and other distractions). It is important to take those factors into account when allocating the documentation area.

Components

A component of the microcosm is a logical segment of the environment that can be configured, tested, and documented independently of other components. For example, the servers are a component, as they will be configured, tested, and documented as a group.

The rules for defining components are not set in stone, and should be flexible to accommodate different needs. In some environments, servers may be divided by role, such as infrastructure servers and applications servers.

A quick list of components includes the following:

▼ Local area network infrastructure (LAN)

■ Wide area network infrastructure (WAN)

■ Server infrastructure

■ Workstation infrastructure

■ Internet infrastructure

▲ Legacy infrastructure

Through the rest of this section, we will look at the details of the different components.

Server Infrastructure

The server infrastructure component is very meaningful. It is important to use the models and configurations that will be used in the production environment to ensure that the lab results accurately reflect what can be expected during deployment.

Frequently, labs are configured with the "extra" servers that are available from previous upgrades. They can be either slower-performance systems, come configured with less memory, or be an entirely different platform than is currently in production. While this arguably saves dollars up front, it results in a potential disaster for the lab. If the lab test results are successful, the actual production deployment might require a complete rewrite of the installation guidelines due to platform differences. You might also face problems as a result of incorrect tuning and load-balancing parameters, or deceptively low performance ratings, forcing the deployment of more servers than are needed.

If the lab results are unsuccessful due to a substandard lab server infrastructure, the project could be viewed as a failure or technically unfeasible. This is particularly true where the lab server infrastructure is older and prone to hardware glitches, causing time to be spent maintaining the lab environment instead of producing test results.

Key Servers

The key servers to include in the infrastructure are active directory servers, domain controllers, file servers, print servers, domain name servers, application servers, etc. If the purpose of the lab is not specifically to test the scalability of those servers, then multiple servers can be consolidated into a single physical server within the lab environment. If that is done, then it is important to monitor the consolidated servers while conducting tests to ensure that they do not become overloaded and distort the lab results.

When conducting scalability tests on specific applications, it is important to have those application servers installed with the same server platforms and configuration as in production. If the application servers are loaded down with additional services or configured differently than they would be in production, then it can become difficult to compensate for those differences and extrapolate the results. This is particularly true when the test results already require some extrapolation due to the methodology being used, such as increasing the transaction frequency to simulate a larger number of users or workstations.

LAN Infrastructure

It is important to duplicate the production LAN environment from a functionality standpoint, but not from a scale standpoint. If the production environment is 10BaseT to the desktop with a switched 100BaseT backbone, it is important to configure the lab in the same manner.

If the lab is configured as a 10BaseT network, the lab bandwidth could be too low and generate worse than expected performance results. If the lab is instead configured with a switched 100BaseT, the lab bandwidth could be unrealistically high and generate better than could be expected performance results. Either scenario is not optimal.

WAN Infrastructure

Along with Internet infrastructure, the WAN infrastructure can be one of the trickiest parts of the lab to accurately represent. At almost any level, some assumptions and extrapolation will be necessary.

The problem is that it is often difficult or impossible to justify the expense of installing wide area network links for the purposes of lab testing. Even if the expense is warranted, the time needed to order and install wide area network links usually exceeds six weeks, which might be the time line allotted for the entire lab project. These hurdles often result in a decision to forgo the WAN portion of the project and simply extrapolate the results obtained locally. There is quite a bit of risk attached to that decision.

Because one of the main goals of the lab is to reduce the uncertainty and ensuing risk to the implementation phase of the project, this section outlines some techniques for getting the results needed with less uncertainty.

Communications Links

It is important to understand the performance characteristics of different wide area network technologies, such as Point-to-Point Protocol (PPP), packet switched, or Fiber Distributed Data Interface (FDDI). Each of these technologies performs differently and has different limitations during peak loads. When creating the lab WAN infrastructure, it is important to take any differences between the production links and the lab links into account when designing the tests and interpreting the results.

If the lab project has funding and a time line sufficient to incorporate production-equivalent communications links, the testing and subsequent results will be much easier to interpret. This is more likely to be the case in large organizations that are establishing permanent laboratories that will be used for long-term change management and upgrade testing.

However, in most cases neither the budget nor the time line will permit a full-fledged set of tests. In those cases, simulating the communications links is an attractive alternative.

Simulating Communications Links

Simulating the communications links can be an inexpensive and timesaving method of facilitating wide area network tests. The basic concept is to place CSU/DSU units back to back, or place routers back to back as shown in Figure 11-4.

If the CSU/DSU units are back to back, then a specially configured crosslink cable is configured between the units. One of the CSU/DSUs provides the clocking signal normally provided by the telco carrier. The units are configured for the proper link speed, which can be varied depending on the tests being performed. These units then operate as a "cloud," like the one shown in Figure 11-5, and are completely transparent to the respective routers on either side of the simulated link.

If even the expense of the pair of CSU/DSU units is not feasible, then routers can be placed back to back, using a null modem cable between their serial ports as shown in Figure 11-6. The routers then must be configured specially for the link. One of the key disadvantages of this method is that the routers may not be able to throttle down the link performance, depending on the router capabilities.

Routers

The routers used in the WAN infrastructure are not as critical as communications links are, unless you depend upon specialized features. The routers within the infrastructure will not typically be a limiting factor, although the link speeds, LAN infrastructure, or

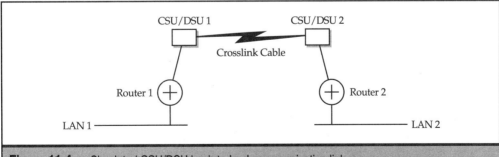

Figure 11-4.   Simulated CSU/DSU back-to-back communication link

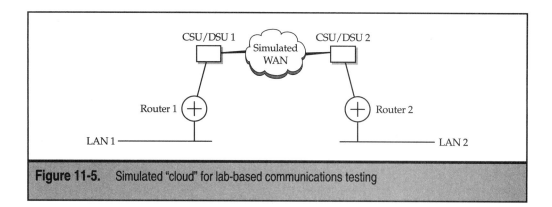

Figure 11-5. Simulated "cloud" for lab-based communications testing

server infrastructures are likely to be. Thus, different models, hardware configurations, or even brands can be used effectively. That said, it is important to monitor performance of the routers during testing to ensure that they do not become a limiting factor.

It is important that routers be configured in an equivalent manner. Pay close attention to particular routing parameters, priority settings, or other tuning mechanisms.

Weighing the Results

It is important to take into account the differences in technologies. For example, there are important differences between a frame relay packet-switched production network, and a point-to-point simulated lab network. Both technologies exhibit very different performance characteristics during loads, and your analysis of the results should take these differences into account.

Internet Connectivity

Building a representation of an Internet infrastructure can be quite tricky, but it is difficult to justify the expense of installing an Internet link for the purpose of lab testing. Even if the expense can be justified, the time required to order and install an Internet link usually exceeds that of a communication link, because after the communication link to the ISP is in place, further configuration is required to establish the Internet connectivity.

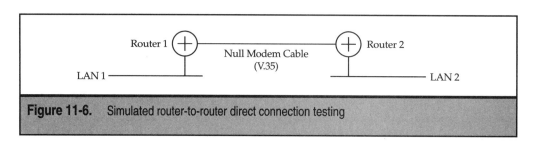

Figure 11-6. Simulated router-to-router direct connection testing

These hurdles often lead lab planners to skip the Internet portion of the project. This section covers some techniques for getting the results needed with less than a complete Internet infrastructure.

Another important issue to consider when building a lab for Internet connection is security. It may be possible for unauthorized persons to gain access to the lab through the link. Because it is possible that the lab environment might be working with "live" data, the lab connection needs to be protected with the same stringent security measures that would be applied to the production Internet connection. On the other hand, you might decide to provide a simulated Internet connection to avoid any possible security breaches. Security personnel should carefully review the design to ensure full compliance with your security policies.

Dedicated Microcosm Connection

A dedicated connection can simplify the lab planning. Some organizations use a dedicated Internet connection in a permanent lab as a fallback link. Often, the IT group can justify the expense of the connection on that basis alone.

Even if there is a dedicated connection, it is still important to take into account the differences in link speeds and technologies. For example, the main Internet connection may be a full T1 frame relay link, while the lab Internet connection is a 384Kpbs ADSL link. Also, remember that performance can vary from ISP to ISP.

Linking Through Existing Connections

It might be possible to use your organization's existing Internet connection in your lab. This should be approached with caution, because it can have an impact on the production environment. This is especially true if there will be significant stress placed on the Internet infrastructure, such as remote access to organization sites through the Internet.

Security also becomes more of a concern when linking to the production network, even if the link is only to the external portion of the network. Security personnel should carefully review the design to ensure full compliance with your security policies.

Temporary Microcosm Connection

It is often convenient to establish an Internet connection on a temporary basis, perhaps using a switched technology to allow the connection to be brought up quickly for testing, and then shut down when testing is completed.

Some examples of technologies that facilitate this approach are asynchronous dial-up connections, or Integrated Service Digital Network (ISDN) connections. Both of these can be configured to establish temporary connections and can be provisioned quickly. The connection may already be available within the organization and would simply need to be reallocated for lab use.

Once again, care should be taken to analyze the technologies being used and the results being generated. Typically, temporary access technologies will not provide the performance that could be expected from permanent connections to the Internet.

Simulating the Internet

An alternative to providing a dedicated Internet connection is to simulate the Internet. This eliminates the need for a communication link and allays many of the security concerns associated with the Internet.

The key to simulating the Internet infrastructure is in determining the Internet services needed. These could include domain name services, Web services, or remote access services, among others.

Using a Microsoft NT server with domain name services, Web services, and remote access services can effectively simulate the Internet. Place this server on the other side of a simulated communications link, as shown in Figure 11-7, that has been set to the speed needed to duplicate the production Internet link. The Internet server should be configured to use sample domain information, and Web sites for simulated browsing.

This simulation permits browsing from the lab across the simulated Internet to the server, using domain lookups and browser access to the Web site. The infrastructure also allows remote users to dial up to the remote access services on the Internet server, simulating ISP access to the Internet. These remote users access the lab through the simulated lab Internet infrastructure, providing valuable performance and functionality results.

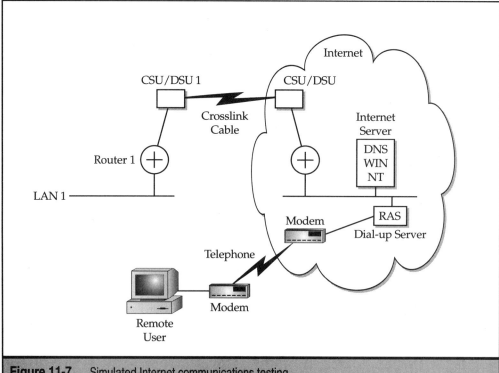

Figure 11-7. Simulated Internet communications testing

Legacy Integration

The integration of legacy systems can be one of the most difficult portions of the microcosm. Many legacy systems are complex and poorly understood, having been developed by staff members that are no longer available. These systems may have expensive platforms that are difficult to duplicate or simulate in the lab.

Even so, it is important to perform legacy integration testing. This is often a key success factor in new projects, because a smooth transition from the legacy systems to the new systems is imperative. Also, there may be an element of long-term coexistence.

Level of Effort

Analyze the efforts required for the various levels of integration for your legacy systems early in your planning, including a cost-benefit analysis. The three main levels of integration are to duplicate the legacy system in the lab, connect to the existing legacy system, or possibly provide no legacy integration.

After looking at the cost-benefit analysis, you can decide on the level of integration required, and plan for it appropriately.

Lab Duplication

Duplicating the legacy infrastructure within the lab is the most beneficial method of testing, because your tests can be faithfully run and the effects evaluated accurately. As might be expected, this also requires the most effort and expense.

There are, however, some effective strategies for minimizing the costs. For instance, you could duplicate and test only critical systems, reducing the scale of your testing. This approach requires a much smaller platform, and usually takes less effort to install. Sometimes it is possible to use existing spare equipment, which might have been underpowered for a full-scale legacy production environment, but could be well suited to the reduced functionality required by the lab.

In reality, this level of legacy integration is rarely performed. This is especially true where the legacy systems are massive in comparison to the systems being deployed, such as mainframe environments. It becomes more common where the legacy systems are microcomputer-based systems, such as email or network operating systems.

Connection to Existing Legacy Systems

It might be possible to connect to the existing legacy systems with little or no impact to the user community. Focus on a narrow time span to conduct legacy testing, perhaps connecting the existing legacy systems to the lab over a weekend or during nonpeak periods.

This is typically the most common approach to legacy integration. It is important to be careful when this type of integration is planned, as there is the potential for the lab environment to impact the production environment through this connection. Take care to design tests with this in mind.

No Legacy Testing

You could decide to omit testing for legacy integration. This is acceptable if the expense of the integration would be high while the benefits are perceived as low. It is also a good option if there will be little interaction between the new systems being deployed and the legacy systems.

Results/Deliverables

It is important to define early on in the project what results are expected of the lab, and what documentation and reports (commonly called "deliverables") should be produced upon the completion of the project. The documentation provides information about the tests that were successful or not successful in the implementation of your microcosm.

Reporting

After the tests have been performed and the resulting data gathered and collated, you need to report out the results. This is an important part of the process, because the report is typically the only tangible result of the testing for persons outside the team. It is important to convey the information in a way that is accurate, understandable, and not misleading.

There are many methods for presenting data, including tabulation, graphing, reporting, and analysis. It is important to choose the most effective method, to be careful about extrapolating the results, and to present any necessary caveats. A report should include several key elements, including an executive summary, background, data collected, analysis, and conclusions.

Executive Summary

The executive summary is a one-page overview of the rest of the report, providing a single-page view of the project background, data collected, analysis, and conclusions. The executive summary is designed to give busy, high-level executives all the information they need to make a decision.

Background

The background section provides readers who are not familiar with the project a high-level view of the reasons for the project, what is being done, and the methods used. It is often the case that a reader has no prior knowledge of the project, so the background section provides a context for understanding the report and its conclusions.

Data Collected

A simple way to present data is to tabulate it, creating a table of the collected values, usually with no interpretation. This is helpful for presenting raw information, which should be followed by analysis.

Another useful method of presenting data is to create a graph. Graphs are very useful for presenting large quantities of data in an easily understandable form, rather than a mass of numbers. Graphs can take a variety of formats, including bar charts, pie charts, line graphs, etc.

It is very important to provide a full list of the data collected during the process, either within the report or as an appendix. This allows readers to verify the facts, giving them confidence in the results.

Analysis

Analysis is very critical in a report, because it provides expert interpretation of the data that was collected. This data is often very detailed and very technical, making it hard for others to absorb easily. The analysis brings meaning and relevancy to the data. The analysis portion is usually in narrative form.

Conclusion

The conclusion section is the "so what" of the report. The data has been collected and analyzed, so what were the final results? This may take the form of a recommendation, a call to action, or a confirmation of position. The conclusion should be short, clear, and specific.

PREPARING THE MICROCOSM

When the design of the microcosm has been completed, you can prepare to build the microcosm. This involves assembling the team, allocating hardware and software, allocating resources, and creating the microcosm plan. The microcosm plan includes the test plan, the project plan, and the test scripts.

The Microcosm Team

The team assembled to create and run the microcosm should have members with a variety of skills. Some of the key roles (as depicted in Figure 11-8) include the following:

- ▼ Consultants
- ■ Project managers
- ■ System engineers
- ■ Technology experts
- ■ Testing technicians
- ▲ Technical writers

Not all members are needed for all labs, and some labs will require expanded teams. Some roles can be combined—multiple individuals can fill some roles and some labs will have full teams for different components.

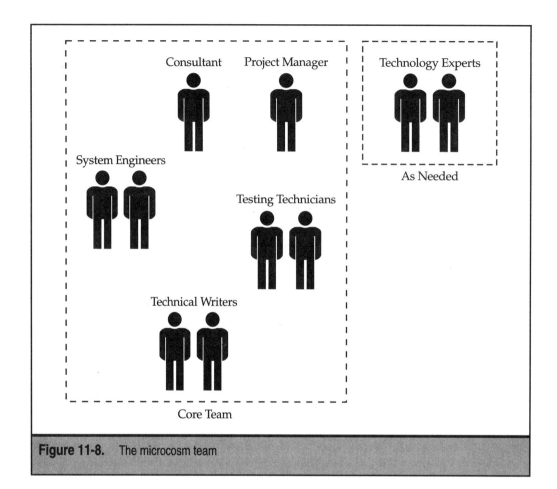

Figure 11-8. The microcosm team

Consultant

A consultant provides overall guidance through the microcosm process, producing the lab design and deliverables. This requires a person who has experience with labs of similar scale. It is also critical that the consultant be experienced with the technology being implemented, especially when the technology being deployed is cutting edge.

Project Manager

The project manager provides project management for the lab project, allocating resources, scheduling resources/equipment, etc. The project manager produces the project plan from the lab design, deliverables list, test scripts, etc. The project manager also facilitates communication, produces status reports, and conducts status meetings.

System Engineers

The engineers are responsible for building the lab, troubleshooting lab problems, and documenting the build steps. Since the purpose of the microcosm is to identify and clear up any areas of uncertainty within the implementation of the technology, there will be times when the system engineers will need to resolve technical issues, develop workarounds, etc.

This can be a time-consuming process that has the potential to set the project back. Experienced system engineers can resolve those problems quickly and effectively, dramatically reducing the time line for the lab project and providing better results for the implementation.

Technology Experts

Technology experts are high-level experts on specific technologies, brought in to build specific components, resolve technical issues, and provide expert advice during the design, build, and testing phases.

Due to the specialized knowledge requirements, technology experts are almost always drawn from outside the organization. These persons are usually expensive, so it's important to utilize their resources effectively.

Testing Technicians

Testing technicians conduct the tests specified by the test scripts, and also document the results. Typically, these technicians are not required to troubleshoot (that chore is usually assigned to system engineers). It's usually effective to employ entry-level engineers for this role.

Technical Writers

Technical writers compile information generated by activities of other team members. They also produce the structured documentation of builds, procedures, and possibly training manuals.

Qualified technical writers are important for the success of the project. They provide the visible portion of the deliverables, by which the results of the project are judged.

Test Plan

The test plan provides the details of the lab tests and their scope. It is important to state the scope of the tests clearly, as well as your goals. These tests could include functionality tests, performance tests, and feasibility tests.

Functionality tests determine whether key functions work in the proposed environment. Performance tests determine the bottlenecks and scalability of a system. Feasibility tests reveal whether a proposed system is feasible from the perspective of cost, supportability, or level of effort. These tests are often matched against the theoretical limits advertised by manufactures or vendors.

Methodology

The methodology section of your test plan describes how the lab will be conducting the tests. This might include how many times a series of tests will be conducted, how the data will be gathered, and if the lab should be reset during any given series of tests. Include technical and statistical information, because that data will be extrapolated to the larger production environment.

The methodology section should be very detailed, because the people who design the lab are typically not the people who implement the plans.

Results

Specify the format of the results so that the entire team knows what they are expected to produce.

Test Scripts

Test scripts provide detailed step-by-step instructions for conducting specific tests. These detailed instructions typically take effort and time to produce, but help ensure the repeatability of the results.

Repeatability

Consistency across multiple repetitions is critical to the success of tests. The tests might be run on multiple platforms and at different times, with the goal being to compare the results. If the tests performed are not exactly the same and conducted in the same order and manner, then the results could be meaningless. Test scripts ensure the consistency of the testing process.

Format

A test script is typically a sequence of steps, along with the initial conditions needed for the tests. The step-by-step sequence ensures that the tests will be conducted in exactly the same way each time they are run. The initial conditions are critical to ensure that the results are consistent. It is also important to specify what data values need to be collected as part of the test and how to collect them, as the test results will be compared to each other.

Expected Values

It is frequently helpful to state what you expect the final values to be. Values well outside the expected range can therefore be scrutinized for systemic problems within the testing environment.

One area in which the initial conditions are critical is database testing. The size of a database can frequently affect the performance dramatically. If a series of performance tests were performed to find an optimal hardware platform, the databases would need to be set to the same starting data before each test to ensure that the size of the database was not impacting the performance.

Project Plan

The project plan takes the "what" will be done and the "how" it will be done, and maps it to "when" it will be done. Putting the plan into a time line is the efficient way to allocate resources and time. Be sure to allow for float and also to set milestones.

Resources

Resources can be personnel, space, hardware, software, or any other aspect of the project that needs to be allocated. Planning for when they will be needed and how much time commitment is required is critical.

Float

Float is the window of time that's acceptable on either side of a start date, and it is important to allow some float in a project. For example, if a server is scheduled to arrive on week 4 of the project and is not absolutely needed until week 6 of the project, then it is said to have a two-week float.

Float gives you an ability to adjust to potential problems, and avoids the common problems that result from scheduling a project too tightly.

Milestones

It is important to set clear milestones for your plan. These milestones set the pace of the project by giving the team minigoals to shoot for, like "Workstation Testing Complete." They can work with the nearest milestone in mind, rather than working with the final project complete goal to motivate them.

During any project, it is normal to have some tasks slip and some run ahead. The milestones allow the project manager to see if the overall project is on schedule or slipping. The milestones also help communication outside of the team, as they provide clear signposts that nonteam members can understand and orient themselves to. A milestone schedule can be distributed to the organization or to the sponsors.

Allocating Resources

After the time line has been set, resources can be allocated, including personnel, space, hardware, software, communications links, and so on. This typically involves getting approvals and commitments, and may include adjusting the plan to accommodate constrained resources.

Another aspect of resource allocation is politics. This is usually the first major commitment that nonteam members will be asked to provide, and there could be resistance.

Timing of Resources

To schedule resources effectively, work out the entire schedule in advance and look for the most constrained resources first. It is also important to get alternative times, so that scheduling can be flexible.

Delivery of Equipment

Arrange for delivery of equipment well in advance of its actual need. A good rule of thumb is to have equipment delivered at least two weeks in advance of its need. This prevents personnel from being allocated and available, but unable to perform tasks. Set up and test hardware as soon as it arrives so that any problems can be resolved before the equipment is needed.

Building in Breathing Room

Above all, build breathing room into the scheduling of resources. Murphy's Law dictates that if something can go wrong, it will. Build in the time to accommodate these problems.

MANAGING THE MICROCOSM

To manage your microcosm effectively, you must supervise its use, its stability, and the tests being conducted. You also have to keep in mind that you must generate results.

Guidelines for Microcosm Use

Without clearly stated guidelines for the use of the microcosm, there is a potential for conflict and confusion. Some examples of potential usage conflicts are nonteam members connecting to the Internet via the lab, testing nonproject applications, or removing software from the lab.

Be sure to make it easy to identify the point at which the lab is reset following a series of tests, so that testing conducted by different team members does not conflict and team members don't feel that they are cleaning up after other members.

Appropriate Usage

One of the key guidelines for the microcosm is what constitutes appropriate usage of the lab. This can include what can be tested, as well as what cannot be tested in the lab. Testing applications that are part of the project is appropriate, while testing other applications is not. Certain data is inappropriate for testing, such as private information in the files of the Human Resources department. Document both appropriate usage and inappropriate usage clearly to prevent problems.

Authorized Users

Specifying and enforcing the notion of authorized users should be part of your guidelines. As part of the authorization process, ask users to sign a copy of the guidelines indicating that they have read and understood them.

Lab Procedures

Documented lab procedures are critical to ensure the orderly and effective use of the lab, and prevents long-term degradation of the infrastructure.

Users of the microcosm will benefit from documented procedures to coordinate their efforts and prevent conflict. Some of the procedures to be considered include restoring the test environment after a series of tests, cleaning up the testing areas after working, and keeping lab material in the lab area.

If the lab infrastructure is changed during use and not restored, the inconsistent environment causes problems. Some procedures to consider include the regular "reset to ground state" of the lab or routine documentation updates as the lab is modified.

Stability in the Microcosm

To ensure the success of the lab, you must work to prevent common procedural failures such as unauthorized or undocumented modifications, changes to the microcosm environment, loss of crucial equipment, and undocumented additions of equipment.

Unauthorized Modifications

Changes to the configuration without regard to the function of the lab or the current usage phase impact stability. This can be the result of users playing in the lab, or not following the microcosm plan.

For stability to be maintained, specify either a hands-off policy for the lab or specific spans of time for users to play in the lab, with a rollback plan to restore the lab to its original state after user access.

Equipment Shrinkage

Equipment shrinkage can occur due to equipment moving back into production from the lab due to emergencies, growth needs, or simple convenience. It can also occur due to equipment failing and not being replaced in good time. Equipment disappearing with no explanation is another cause of shrinkage in the lab.

The loss of equipment over time affects the stability of the lab. Microcosm equipment should not be viewed as a pool of spare parts.

Equipment Additions

The microcosm stability can also be adversely affected by additions of equipment. Unplanned equipment can create confusion. Equipment should be added in a controlled manner and removed in the same fashion. Addition and removal of any equipment must be documented.

Replication

Replication of the lab allows an orderly rollback to the original working state. This maintains consistency and aids in recovery from unforeseen problems.

For transitory labs with few phases, it might not be necessary to create a replication strategy. In those cases, the time required to rebuild the lab may be short and the level of effort required to put replication in place might not be justified.

For long-term labs, it is essential to create a replication plan. Over time, the staff involved with the original build will be reassigned and no longer available to rebuild the lab. Also, the number of times that the lab will be rebuilt on a long-term basis usually justifies the effort required to create the replication plan.

Ability to Recover

Prepare a method of replicating the lab in case you need to recover from equipment failures. For example, a hard drive failure can bring down a laboratory and halt testing completely. A replication plan allows rapid recovery of the lab to its original state rather than spending the time to rebuild.

You may also face the need to recover from catastrophic testing, or changes in the configuration (such as damage to the registry during testing).

Ability to Duplicate

The replication plan must also include methods to duplicate the environment to other sites, if needed. This also allows repetitive testing from identical initial states, which is useful for build documents, deployment testing, etc.

Templates

A template is a general-purpose build replica. It differs from the backup replicas in that it is designed to assist in deployment, allowing customization and/or automatic deployment. A template lets you use a single build to generate multiple systems by modifying key parameters that make the systems unique.

Templates can be completely automated—prompting for the key values and automatically generating unique systems—or manual, with a replication stage followed by manual customization. Templates are also useful for rapid recovery, or to make large-scale changes to the microcosm environment.

Methods

There are a variety of methods for replicating and creating template builds, including the following:

▼ Build images

▲ Backups

Build Images

Build images are complete images of the physical hard disk, permitting rapid restoration to the original state. There are tools available for this task, including Ghost. Build images are necessary for complex labs that need to scale, because they provide rapid system replication and flexibility.

Backups

Backups are essentially just file backups of the builds after they are created. Use them to restore critical components and data as needed, including single files. However, restores are slow and the systems need to be rebuilt to a minimum state in order to start restoring. Consider backup platforms that include image rebuilds from the backups.

Conducting Tests

Testing is the process used to verify functionality, performance, and procedures of the platform and project. The platform could include hardware, software, systems, or any other component. The project could include installation procedures, maintenance procedures, usage guides, and other process-oriented documentation.

All aspects of the platform and project should be tested and verified in the lab prior to general release. This is also true of changes to the platform after it is placed into production.

Test Scripts

Test scripts are typically prepared during the planning stages and need to be executed faithfully during the project. These test scripts ensure that results are repeatable, consistent, and complete.

Test Script Verification

As testing is being completed, verify results to ensure that test scripts have run correctly. This might include checking the volume of data copied, messages transferred, pages printed, etc. This is especially true when conducting automated tests, where there might be little or no human intervention during the testing protocol. Methods for verifying could either be by a complete review or by spot-checking to save time.

Adjusting During Testing

Sometimes test results can be way off the expected results that are outlined in the test scripts. This is one of the reasons that the test scripts should explicitly state what the expected results are for each test being conducted.

It is important to review preliminary test results while conducting the tests, measuring them against the expected values. Then, you can adjust the testing protocols to make sure you're testing properly.

Extrapolated Results vs. Actual Results

It's rare to have the luxury of creating a laboratory that can scale to simulate production. Given that limitation, some interpretation and extrapolation will be required to map the lab results into the production environment.

Once the preliminary lab results have been generated through actual tests, extrapolation calculations can be performed. Use valid statistical methods to provide plus/minus ranges to the extrapolated results. Clearly state the methodology used to arrive at the extrapolated values. It is also important to state the known limitations of the extrapolated results.

While it saves time to estimate or extrapolate results, there is a risk to the credibility of the project if you don't take the time to document your methodology.

Reset to Ground State

Ground state refers to a known good, documented checkpoint in the lab development. This state provides a common point from which to test performance, try out maintenance procedures, test disaster recovery, and create documentation.

At a particular ground state, replication builds should be created to permit the lab to be rapidly restored to that ground state following tests or catastrophic configuration changes. This process of restoring the system is often referred to as a *reset to ground state*.

Clean Slate

During builds, it is desirable to be able to completely wipe the lab and test the build documents as if the system were brand new.

Steady State

After the lab has been built and configured, it is said to be at a *steady state*. This is the long-term configuration and is good for testing production activities, such as stress testing or changing management testing.

You need to be able to come back to this steady state at regular intervals to eliminate incremental corruption of the test environment.

Reset After Testing

For comparison purposes, it is best to run tests from the exact same starting condition. This provides the most consistent results and eliminates much of the uncertainty that can arise during testing. If the tests are conducted sequentially, the testing environment changes after each successive test. For example, when file access times are being tested, the file storage can become fragmented after a series of tests. The fragmentation causes degradation of performance, even though the same tests are being run each time. To ensure the validity of the test results, it is strongly recommended that a reset to ground be conducted after each test or series of tests.

Test Order

The process used for testing the implementation of the test lab can be done in order (or serially) or concurrently (or in parallel), as shown in Figure 11-9.

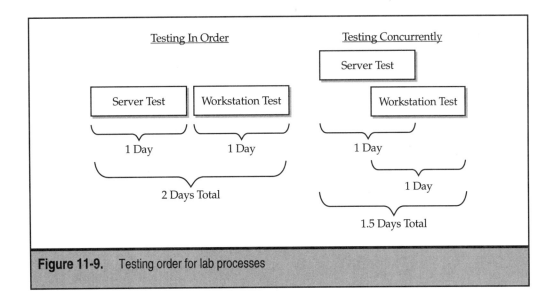

Figure 11-9. Testing order for lab processes

Testing in Order (Serially)

One way to approach testing is to conduct each test in order, or serially. This is the most straightforward testing method, because after completion of each test the lab is reset to ground state. Results are all obtained from the same initial state.

However, this can be time-consuming, and it stretches the schedule out to the maximum. In addition, some tests don't require this method because they can be run in parallel.

Testing Concurrently (Parallel)

Some tests can be run concurrently, in parallel. For example, you could conduct server and desktop tests at the same time. Or, you can test different desktop or server tests at the same time. This reduces the overall testing time and works well if managed properly.

However some tests interact, such as server disk stress testing and workstation response time tests, and parallel testing can lead to potentially ambiguous results. For example, sever tests that place a load on the processor could affect the throughput of a desktop test.

THE MICROCOSM POSTDEPLOYMENT ROLE

After deployment, the microcosm can provide valuable services to ensure the long-term health of the production environment. The benefits of a well-designed microcosm post deployment plan are significant.

The microcosm provides facilities for change management, testing upgrades, performing disaster recovery, assisting with troubleshooting, training, and testing updating procedures.

Change Management

The lab is very useful for previewing changes to the production environment. Any changes to the production environment can first be applied to the lab and the effects evaluated.

Validate Strategies

The postdeployment lab is an invaluable tool for validating strategies and refining change plans. Rollout procedures can be tested, rollback plans can be verified, and time lines can be checked.

Validate Proposed Changes

The lab allows validation that proposed changes would have the proposed effects, which is not always a foregone conclusion. You can verify manufacturer claims of functionality or performance gains, which can be slightly exaggerated at times.

Another powerful benefit of using the lab postdeployment is to preview the unintended consequences of any proposed changes. Many upgrades or service packs succeed in delivering the feature enhancements or bug fixes they target, but either eliminate features, modify operations, or even break other areas.

Testing Hotfixes, Patches and Service Packs

Vendors frequently release hotfixes, patches and service packs. These are modifications to their software and hardware, and are typically released in response to problems or issues identified by the customers during production use.

The modifications are frequently complex and have numerous caveats. Additionally, they are not always tested extensively, resulting in unexpected results or side effects.

Disaster Recovery

Disaster recovery is a topic of critical importance. Organizations frequently invest heavily in backup subsystems, offsite storage of tapes, redundant platforms, etc., to ensure the survivability of the infrastructure. However, too few organizations invest in creating a recovery plan. This results in unpleasant surprises when an actual disaster occurs. It's not uncommon to learn that your recovery systems were designed incorrectly, or that they'd failed during use without notification. The lab provides a platform to test disaster recovery procedures to ensure that they are working, and also provides spare hardware to replace failed production equipment.

Drills

It is important to conduct disaster recovery drills to ensure the integrity of your disaster recovery procedures. The lab has the equipment to perform the drill. It is important to conduct drills exactly as they would occur during a real disaster.

Rebuild and Reintroduce

During an actual disaster recovery situation, the lab provides a place to rebuild and test equipment. The recovered systems can then be reintroduced into the production environment.

Troubleshooting Problems

After deployment, the lab provides an excellent environment for troubleshooting problems that crop up in the production environment. The lab moves the problem resolution process from a stressful production environment with limited diagnosis options to a low-stress environment with many diagnosis options. Problems can be diagnosed at length, without concern for the impact on the production environment. This allows the resolution of issues in a calm environment and makes it possible to test solutions without concern for impact on users, with the full use of tech support from the manufacturer and during normal business hours.

Training

Organizations frequently invest in end-user training, providing complete access to all production applications and extensive training classes. This helps ensure that end users understand the productivity tools that are at their disposal and make the best use of them.

This concept is equally important for information systems administrators, but is often overlooked. After deployment, the microcosm provides a very attractive training facility for administrators.

A lab environment provides administrators with hands-on experience for rarely used procedures such as disaster recovery or database rebuilds. The lab also allows entry-level administrators to become familiar with processes and options, accelerating their learning experience without jeopardizing the production environment.

Use the lab for disaster simulation, giving administrators a chance to practice recovery procedures. Within the microcosm, various failures can be simulated during training sessions, and the staff can perform the disaster recovery procedures as they would in an actual emergency. Be sure to run through variations on the recovery procedures, such as partial restores. You should consider experimenting with incorrect recovery execution. For example, the staff could intentionally skip a database repair step and then see the effect it has on the overall recovery process.

Documentation Updates

When changes occur in the production environment, they should be mirrored into the microcosm environment. This ensures the one-to-one mapping of all aspects of the two environments, which is critical for the successful use of the lab postdeployment. It's important to update the documentation when changes occur.

During the normal evolution of any complex information systems environment, software is upgraded, hardware is upgraded, configurations are adjusted, and new systems are brought online. It is important to keep your documentation updated, and the lab provides a platform for this.

When new systems are introduced into the environment, start them in the laboratory. While they are being tested in the lab, create new documentation or modify existing documentation to reflect the new systems.

PART III

Deploying Windows 2000

I n the first two parts of the book I highlighted the features and functions of Windows 2000, and explained how to plan and design a migration or new implementation of Windows 2000. Those two parts should have prepared you with enough information to begin installing the software now.

In this third part of the book I will focus on actually implementing the Windows 2000 software for servers, desktops, and terminals. I have a chapter specifically on migrating from Windows NT4 to Windows 2000, including how to migrate from domains to Active Directory. I cover software distribution and upgrade tools to deploy Windows 2000 to desktop systems. I address policy management tools to help manage desktops and users in the Windows 2000 environment. Finally, I cover techniques for tuning, optimizing, and debugging Windows 2000 to maintain the environment operating reliability on an ongoing basis.

CHAPTER 12

Installing and Managing Windows 2000

Installing Windows 2000 is not simply a matter of running Setup, because you will face a lot of decisions during the process. In this chapter, I will walk you through the various options available for installing Windows 2000 Server (Server, Advanced Server, and DataCenter editions), as well as file, print, and Web services. See Chapter 14 for information about installing Windows 2000 Professional.

BEFORE YOU BEGIN . . .

Whenever you install a new operating system, there are many decisions that have to be made. Microsoft has provided you with several tools to help you make these decisions as quickly and easily as possible.

Ensure That Your Hardware Meets the Minimum Requirements

You need to verify that the hardware you plan on using for your Windows 2000 server is compatible and meets the minimum requirements for a Windows 2000 server. Check your hardware against the Windows 2000 Hardware Compatibility List that Microsoft posts on their Web site, and also check for updated drivers with the manufacturer of the hardware you will be using.

Should You Perform a New Installation, or Simply Upgrade?

If you have an existing Windows NT Server, you have to decide whether you are going to upgrade it to Windows 2000 or perform a new installation. This section explains the differences.

Performing a New Installation

A new installation ignores (and loses) any previous configuration settings, software registry settings, or parameters set in a previous installation of the operating system. You can perform a new installation on a disk or partition that does not currently have any operating system, or in a different directory on the same hard drive of a previous installation of Windows NT Server.

During a new installation of Windows 2000, you have the option of retaining existing drive partitions or completely repartitioning and reformatting the drive.

If you currently have applications on a partition where you want to do a new installation of Windows 2000 Server, you should first make a full backup of all the data on the drive (you'll have to reinstall the software).

Upgrading an Existing Server

An upgrade is a method of taking a current installation of certain versions of Windows NT and converting them to Windows 2000. The upgrade application accomplishes this by installing Windows NT into the same folder as your current operating system.

Upgrading to Windows 2000 enables you to keep your existing users, settings, groups, rights, and permissions (including file- and folder-level security for the files retained on the server during an upgrade during the upgrade). Additionally, you will not have to reinstall your existing applications and restore your data from backup (assuming your existing applications will run under Windows 2000).

Only certain versions of Windows NT can be upgraded to Windows 2000, as shown in Table 12-1.

When performing an upgrade, there is the possibility that the upgrade of the operating system will not be successful, as is the case when any significant work is being done to

Previous Operating System	Can You Upgrade to Windows 2000?
Windows NT 3.51 Server	Yes.
Windows NT 4.0 Server	Yes.
Windows NT 4.0 Terminal Server	Yes.
Windows NT 4.0 Server, Enterprise Edition	Yes, but only to Windows 2000 Advanced Server.
Windows NT Server, prior to version 3.51	No. You must first upgrade to version 3.51 or 4.0, and then you can upgrade to Windows 2000.
Windows 95, 98	No. You can upgrade to Windows 2000 Professional (see Chapter 14), but not to Windows 2000 Server.
Novell NetWare	No, but migration tools are available from Microsoft to migrate NDS information to a Windows 2000 domain. (See Chapter 15.)
Banyan VINES	No, but migration tools are available from third-party companies to migrate Streetalk information to a Windows 2000 domain.

Table 12-1.   Upgrade Compatibility to Windows 2000

a server. You should back up your existing server prior to attempting an upgrade so that you have a fallback position in case you have to reinstall your previous version of the operating system.

Determining What Type of Server to Install

In previous versions of Windows NT, a server could be designated to perform one of four roles:

▼ Primary domain controller (PDC)

■ Backup domain controller (BDC)

■ Member server (of a domain)

▲ Stand-alone server (of a workgroup)

Windows 2000 Server, however, does not differentiate between a PDC and a BDC. You have the choice of making a system a domain controller or a member server (or a stand-alone server if the server is part of a workgroup instead of a domain). Depending on the role this server will play in your network, you can decide which of these roles your server will fill.

Unlike previous versions of the Windows NT operating system, where a member server could not be promoted to a domain controller, or a domain controller could not be demoted to a member server, with Windows 2000 you have complete flexibility on the promotion and demotion of server functions at any time. A member server can be promoted to a domain controller using the DCPromo utility (see Chapter 13 for details), and merely uninstalling the Active Directory service from the server turns a domain controller into a member server.

Information to Gather

During a Windows 2000 installation, you will be asked for information about the way you want your server configured. The program will take the information you provide and customize the installation of your Windows 2000 server so that it meets your requirements. (A number of these decisions have been discussed in previous chapters.)

The Computer Name

Each computer on a network must be given a unique computer name. The computer name can contain up to 63 characters, but it is important to note that pre-Windows 2000 computers will only recognize the first 15 characters.

It's best to use only Internet-standard characters in the computer name. These characters consist of the numbers 0 through 9, the letters A–Z (both upper and lower case), and the hyphen (-).

The use of the Microsoft DNS service on your network will allow you to use some non-internet standard characters in your computer name. Examples of this include Unicode characters and other non-standard characters such as the underscore (_), however the use of such nonstandard characters may cause compatibility problems with non-Microsoft DNS servers on your network, so you may want to refer back to Chapter 6 on naming conventions for clarification.

Name of the Workgroup or Domain

During the installation process, you will be asked for the name of the workgroup or domain that the server will be installed into. You can enter in the name of an existing workgroup or domain (if this computer is part of an existing organizational structure), or you can enter in a new name (effectively creating a new structure).

A domain is a collection of computers that share a common security database. This is important for establishing centralized security and administration. A workgroup, on the other hand, does not share a common security or administration structure, and each server individually manages security and administrative tasks.

NOTE: You can select a workgroup installation (picking any name for your workgroup) and then join a domain at a later date.

If you are joining an existing Windows 2000 domain, you will need to have the administrator of the domain add your server name into the Active Directory Tree to allow you to join and participate as a member of the domain. See Chapter 13 for detailed information on setting up a Windows 2000 domain controller for the first time, as well as joining an existing Windows 2000 domain.

IP Address of the Server

During the installation of Windows 2000, you will be prompted to provide an IP (Internet Protocol) address and DNS server address to be used by your Windows 2000 server.

There are three methods of assigning an IP address in Windows 2000: static IP, dynamic IP, and Automatic Private IP.

Assigning a static IP address is the common decision, and it means that a predefined IP address has been assigned to the server. A static address is important, because a server is accessed by multiple users who need to know the address of the server in order to access it. If the address of a server changes frequently, systems would have a hard time consistently finding the server. Also, if the server is going to be exposed to the Internet, you must assign a static IP address, because the DNS servers on the Internet require a fixed address. See Chapters 2 and 7 for more on DNS and IP addressing.

If you want to dynamically assign an IP address, you can rely on DHCP (Dynamic Host Configuration Protocol) to assign the IP address of a server during boot-up. Dynamic DNS and DNS name resolution are built into Windows 2000, making it possible for a server to have its IP address change within the domain and still have users find the server. Because there's a chance that a workstation may not be configured to find the DNS server that can locate the target server, this is not a preferred option. Remember that dynamic IP addressing will not work for servers addressed from the Internet.

Automatic Private IP Addressing (APIPA) allows Windows 2000 to automatically assign itself an IP address from a pool of IP addresses. Unlike previous versions of Windows NT, which required an IP address to be enabled on a server for the system to function on the network (either statically assigned or assigned by a valid DHCP server on the network), Windows 2000 can temporarily assign itself an IP address and complete its boot cycle, and the server administrator can then statically assign or request DHCP to assign an IP address of the system without a server reboot.

This is especially important for an organization that configures its servers in a lab environment where IP addressing is different from the production environment, or in the case of a faulty LAN adapter driver or configuration that prevents the adapter from activating during installation. Rather than stopping the installation, fixing the problem, and then restarting the installation from scratch, APIPA allows the installation to continue and the IP address setting to be resolved after the installation is complete.

NOTE: While Windows 2000 does not require the server to be rebooted when an IP address is dynamically changed after the initial system boot-up, applications on the server such as SQL, IIS, and Exchange typically require the server to be rebooted to republish the application service with the new IP address.

Backing Up Your Existing Files

If the computer you are using for your Windows 2000 installation has any data that you wish to keep, it is important that you back up your files prior to installation. Even if you are performing an upgrade, a backup of your data can be invaluable if there are any problems with the installation.

WINDOWS 2000 INSTALLATION OPTIONS

When installing Windows 2000, you have the option of installing the software from several different devices. In addition, you can choose an automated installation, a command-line installation, or an unattended installation.

Choosing a Source

Windows 2000 can be installed by booting to diskette, booting to a Windows 2000 CD-ROM, or installing from a network share or a non-bootable CD-ROM after establishing a connection to the non-bootable device.

Installation from Diskettes

Windows 2000 can be installed by booting to specially created floppy diskettes, called Setup disks. If your Windows 2000 package didn't include the four diskettes, you can create them from the Windows 2000 CD-ROM. Typically you would use this diskette method if you do not have a bootable CD-ROM drive to boot directly to the Windows 2000 CD or if you do not have the DOS drivers for the CD-ROM drive to launch the Windows 2000 installation application directly from the CD itself.

If you need to create the diskettes, take four blank, formatted 3.5-inch diskettes, and follow these steps:

1. Label the diskettes as follows: Setup Disk 1, Setup Disk 2, Setup Disk 3, and Setup Disk 4.

2. Insert the Windows 2000 CD-ROM into a computer running Windows NT or Windows 95/98. Insert the disk labeled Setup Disk 1 in the floppy disk drive.

3. From the Start menu, choose Run, and enter **x:\bootdisk\makeboot.exe A:** where *x* is the drive letter of your CD-ROM drive. You should see a screen similar to Figure 12-1.

4. Follow the prompts to insert the remaining diskettes.

After you have created the four Setup diskettes, go to the server on which you want to install Windows 2000, and boot the computer with Setup Disk 1 in the A drive. As the system is booting, insert the Windows 2000 CD into the CD-ROM drive of the server.

Follow the prompts to insert the remaining diskettes. Assuming your CD-ROM drive is Windows 2000–compatible, the diskette boot process will eventually load the CD-ROM driver for the system and complete the installation from the Windows 2000 CD.

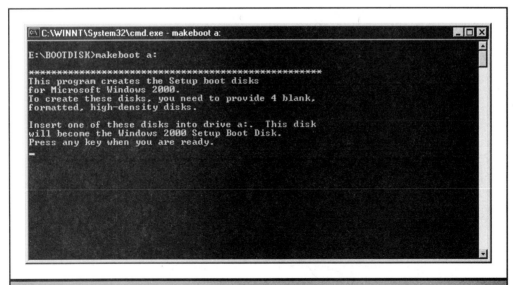

Figure 12-1.   The makeboot.exe utility creates bootable Windows 2000 diskettes

Installation from a Network Share or a Non-Bootable CD-ROM Drive

If you want to install Windows 2000 from a network share or a non-bootable CD-ROM drive, you will need to establish access to the files.

To install Windows 2000 from a network share, you need to have access to the share. This can be established using networking commands or functions from MS-DOS or an existing Windows-based system. The network share is either a shared CD-ROM drive, or a shared directory that holds the files from the Windows 2000 CD (\i386 for Intel-based systems).

To install from a non-bootable CD-ROM drive, you must be able to access the drive, either by loading DOS drivers or through your existing Windows operating system.

TIP: You can also copy the \i386 directory to the local hard drive of the server on which you are installing Windows 2000.

Use the Run command to get to an MS-DOS command prompt to begin the installation:

▼ Type **winnt32.exe** from a computer running Windows NT 3.51, Windows NT 4.0, or a previous release of Windows 2000.

▲ Type **winnt.exe** from any other operating system.

NOTE: For the best performance during Setup from MS-DOS, you should have Smartdrive running to provide disk caching. To accomplish this, add the command **device=himem.sys** to the config.sys file and add the command **smartdrv 8192 8192** to the autoexec.bat file on the boot drive of your MS-DOS system.

Installation from a Bootable CD-ROM Drive

The easiest installation of Windows 2000 is to boot straight to the Windows 2000 CD-ROM disc. Insert the Windows 2000 Server CD-ROM into the CD-ROM drive and boot the computer. Setup will start automatically.

Some computers require a change in the BIOS configuration to boot to a CD-ROM drive (if a bootable CD-ROM drive is present), rather than booting to the hard drive. This option is frequently designated as "boot priority" or "boot sequence." Access the BIOS setup using the appropriate keystrokes during boot-up.

Automated Windows 2000 Installation

The automated installation of Windows 2000—using the Setup wizard—is the most common method for installing Windows 2000. The wizard prompts you for information and automatically installs applications and files onto the server.

The Setup wizard greatly minimizes the number of questions asked during the installation process by selecting the most common settings by default. If you want to change the default settings, there are a number of options in the command-line installation process in the next section that allow you to override the default settings. As an example, one of the defaults assumed in the automated Windows 2000 Setup wizard is that the Windows 2000 software will be installed in c:\winnt. Rather than prompting the user to enter another directory, this question has been eliminated from the installation process. See the "Command-Line Installation" section later in this chapter for the override options for the wizard defaults.

This section will walk you through the installation process of the Windows 2000 Setup wizard. The screens in the Windows 2000 Setup wizard have a look and feel that are familiar to anyone who has used Windows applications. Use the Next button to continue, and use the Back button to return to a previous screen (if you want to change the information you entered).

Welcome to Setup

When the Welcome screen appears, you will see the following prompt: To Set Up Windows 2000 Now, Press Enter. Press ENTER when you are ready to continue.

If you are installing from the startup disks, you will be prompted to insert the Windows 2000 CD and press ENTER when ready.

Windows 2000 Server License Agreement

The first screen you will see is the Windows 2000 Sever license agreement screen. You are shown a copy of the agreement on the screen, and if you accept the terms of the agreement, press the F8 key to continue.

Configuring the Disk Partitions

Before Setup can install Windows 2000, it must know which disk partition you want it to install the system files to. A disk partition can be any size from 1MB to the entire volume of the drive(s) in the server. However, the disk partition that contains the Windows 2000 system files must be on a bootable partition with enough available disk space to hold the Windows 2000 operating system files (approximately 400MB for the operating system and minimum page file). Refer to Chapter 5 on disk sizing to ensure that your computer has enough unused disk space for the installation of the Windows 2000 files.

Select a partition that meets these requirements and press ENTER to continue.

Selecting a File System for the Windows 2000 Partition

Setup needs to know which file system you wish to use (FAT or NTFS). Information on selecting the appropriate file system can be found in Chapter 5 of this book.

A member or stand-alone server can use FAT as the file system, but a domain controller must use NTFS. If you are upgrading your system and the current file system is FAT, you will be asked whether you want to keep the FAT partition or to upgrade the partition to NTFS. If your current file system is an older version of NTFS (for example, NTFS4 from Windows NT 4), the partition will automatically be upgraded to NTFS5. If you wish to retain dual boot capability between Windows 2000 and Windows NT 4, you need to have Windows NT 4 Service Pack 4 or greater to support the new NTFS5 file system.

Once you have selected the type of file system, Setup will configure the partition and begin copying files to the Windows 2000 default installation folder (\winnt). After the installation files are copied, you'll be instructed to remove disks from their drives. Setup automatically restarts the computer to continue installation.

Setup's Detection Phase

Setup detects and installs drivers for system devices, such as audio and multimedia adapters, network adapters, special communication controllers, and so on. During this process you will see product names flashed on the screen one at a time as Windows 2000 checks your system to see if it can detect the product in your system. If Windows 2000 does not automatically detect a component that you have on your system, you will have the opportunity to manually add the item later.

Regional Settings

You can customize Windows 2000 for different regions and languages, as shown in Figure 12-2. Unlike previous versions of Windows that only configured the time zone and

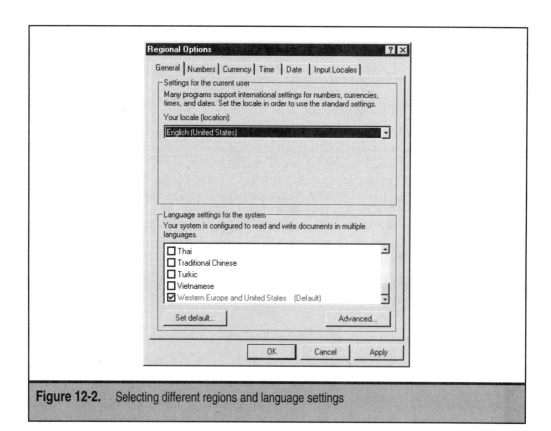

Figure 12-2. Selecting different regions and language settings

keyboard language, the Windows 2000 regional options configure all international settings for the operating system.

Select the appropriate locale to control how numbers, currencies, and dates will appear on the server. The default is English (United States). Scroll through the list of languages and select the checkbox appropriate for the default or an additional language you desire to add. Select one of the tabs on the settings screen to change the way numbers, time, date, or currency is displayed.

The input locales tab provides an ability to change the keyboard layout that controls the characters that appear when you type. The default is the US keyboard layout. Select Customize to change the default.

For any of these settings, you can install a number of different language sets, choosing one as the default.

Personal Information

Setup uses the information you provide on the next few screens to personalize your Windows 2000 software. You are asked for information about yourself, your organization, the licensing mode you are selecting, and the computer name.

PERSONALIZE YOUR SOFTWARE   The Setup wizard asks for your name and the name of your organization, and this information is used during and after Setup for many operations. You must enter this information for Setup to continue. Many organizations have a policy where the name that is entered is not necessarily the name of the person installing the software (like John Smith) but rather a derivative of the business name (such as IT Operations or Corporate Office). The information entered in this screen will show up on the "registered to" section of the Windows 2000 server screen. This information is difficult to change, so it should be set to something the organization is willing to live with. (See Chapter 18 to learn how to change the registered name.)

The information you enter has no effect on the actual server name, Active Directory organizational domain name, or other security, administration, or management functions of the server.

LICENSING MODE   Windows 2000 Server supports two licensing modes: Per Server and Per Seat.

When you select the *Per Seat* licensing option, each computer that accesses the Windows 2000 server requires a separate Client Access License (CAL). With one CAL, a networking client can connect to any number of Windows 2000–based servers. This is the most common licensing option, since most companies have more than one Windows 2000–based server. While the cost of the CAL is more expensive than a Per Server client license, you only pay once for the user to access an unlimited number of Windows 2000 servers.

When you select the *Per Server* licensing option, each connection must have its own CAL. This option is typically preferred by small organizations with only one Windows 2000 server, since a small organization with just one server has a limited number of users connected to the system. It is also useful for Internet or remote access servers where the client connections may not be licensed as Windows 2000 networking clients. You can specify a maximum number of concurrent connections and reject all additional logons. If you are unsure which mode to use, choose Per Server, since you can change once from Per Server to Per Seat at no cost. If you select Per Server, enter the number of concurrent connections you are licensed for.

NOTE: To avoid violation of the license agreement, you can use Licensing in Administrative Tools to record the number of CALs purchased and accessed on the server.

COMPUTER NAME AND ADMINISTRATOR PASSWORD   You are next prompted to provide a computer name and an administrator password for your server. Setup suggests a name for the server based on the name you provided earlier in this chapter, in the "Information to Gather" section. You could (and should) enter your own designated server name (if you are joining an existing Active Directory tree, you must use the server name assigned by the domain administrator, or have had the domain administrator add the name of this server into the tree before you can successfully join the domain).

The Setup Wizard creates a default account for the Administrator. This account is granted local administrative rights and privileges for managing the configuration of the computer. Specify the password for this account in the Password box. Passwords are case sensitive and can contain up to 127 characters. Enter the password again in the Confirm Password box.

It is important that you enter a password that you can remember, because all administration on the server needs to be done with this administrative password. The password can be changed at any time.

Windows 2000 Components

The next step in the Setup wizard, shown in Figure 12-3, is the addition and removal of components. Windows 2000 includes a wide variety of components you can install. For example, you can make the server an IIS Web server, a DNS name resolution server, a terminal server, an Active Directory domain controller, and so on.

When you click a component, a description is displayed below the components section. You can also see the total disk space required to install the components you have selected and the total space available on the disk.

NOTE: You can add or remove components at any time after the server has been installed, so unless you specifically know what components you want to install, you can proceed with the installation and add components later. See "Adding Components to Windows 2000" later in this chapter for details.

DNS AND DHCP COMPONENTS   The DNS component installs the services needed to make the server a Domain Name server, allowing address translation using industry standard DNS. The DHCP component installs the services needed to make the server a DHCP

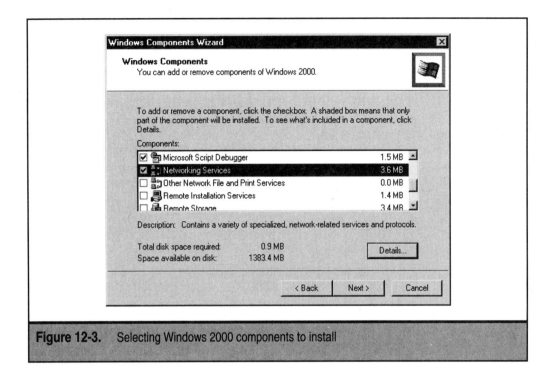

Figure 12-3. Selecting Windows 2000 components to install

server, providing dynamic IP addressing for workstations connecting to the network. Both of these components are covered in depth in Chapter 13.

MANAGEMENT AND MONITORING TOOLS The management and monitoring tools components are tools that allow you to monitor and improve network performance. These are typically installed on management servers that monitor the entire network, and they notify and alert the network administrator of potential system problems. (See Chapter 18 on performance optimization and management for more details.)

TERMINAL SERVICES Windows Terminal Server technology is included with Windows 2000. This technology provides a multisession environment for clients to access Windows-based programs on the computer. (See Chapters 10 and 17 for more information on this component.)

Modem Dialing Information

To dial calls correctly, Windows needs information about your current location so it knows whether to add international dialing strings or domestic United States area codes. Enter this information on the screen shown in Figure 12-4.

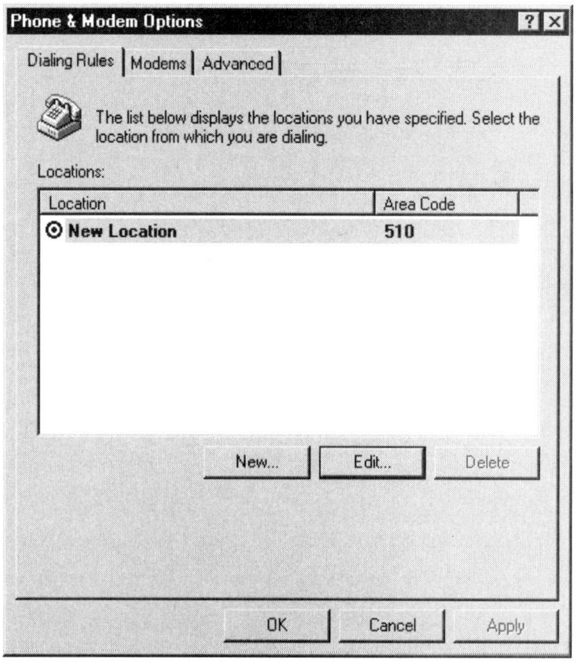

Figure 12-4. Windows 2000 modem dialing options

During this process, you need to select your country or region (United States is the default). You are prompted to enter your area or city code. If you must dial a number to get an outside line (such as 9), specify that number. Select either tone or pulse dialing.

Date and Time Settings

Set the correct date and time for your Windows computer, as well as the appropriate time zone (see Figure 12-5). If your area uses Daylight Savings Time, ensure that the box for that option is checked.

Network Settings

The next section of the Setup wizard verifies information about your networking configuration. Windows 2000 selects a series of defaults, including the client for Microsoft Networks, file and print access, and Internet TCP/IP as the protocol. Most organizations find these default settings adequate. The only thing you may want to change is the IP settings for TCP/IP, to set a static IP address for the server.

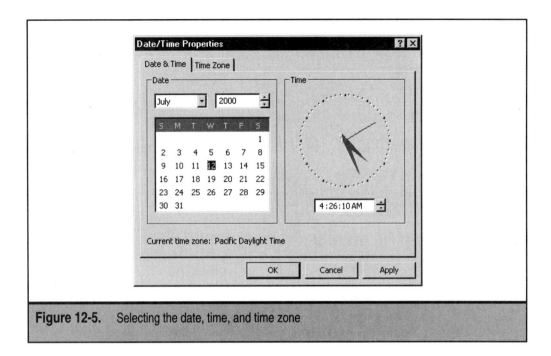

Figure 12-5.   Selecting the date, time, and time zone

When you select the properties option of the TCP/IP setting, you see a screen similar to Figure 12-6. By default, the IP address will be dynamically assigned. As noted earlier in this chapter, the address for servers on a network should be statically assigned. It is here that you can enter the static address for the server. If a DNS server has been set up on the network, you should enter the DNS server address in this screen as well. If you are unsure of the settings for both of these options, see Chapters 2 and 7 on DNS and IP addressing.

CUSTOM SETTINGS   If you need to add additional configuration settings beyond the client for Windows, file and print services, and Internet TCP/IP protocol, choose the Install option button, which allows you to manually install additional services and protocols. Select Install if you need to add any of the following:

▼   Clients, such as Gateway (and Client) Services for NetWare

■   Services, such as SAP Agents

▲   Protocols, such as AppleTalk, NetBEUI, or IPX/SPX

Workgroup or Computer Domain

Now you must enter the name of the workgroup or domain you wish to be a part of. Although you can change the setting after installation, it's preferable to establish these settings now.

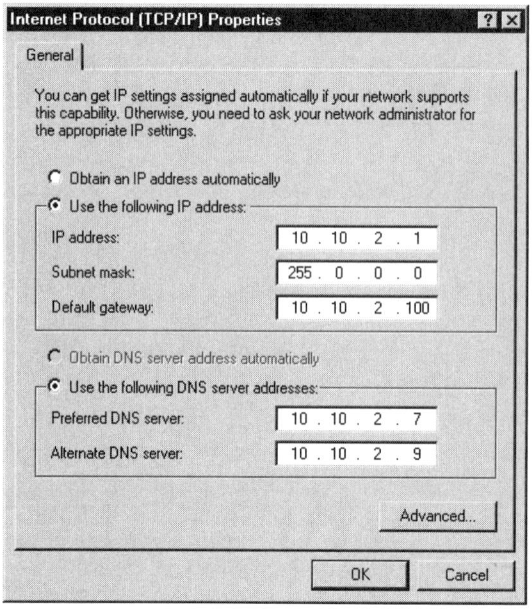

Figure 12-6. Setting a static IP address and a DNS setting for the server

Completing the Installation

The balance of the Setup wizard steps install Start Menu Items, register the components, save the settings, and remove any temporary setup files. Then you are prompted to remove the CD (if any) from the CD-ROM drive and select Finish to continue.

After the operating system has loaded, press CTRL-ALT-DEL to log in. Your default administrator name should be entered for you. Type your password (remember, this is case sensitive) and click OK to continue.

Command-Line Installation

You may want to change the default installation options with customized parameters. This could include changing the default directory in which the Windows 2000 operating system files are stored (the default is \winnt), selecting and implementing unattended installation, adding commands to be executed after the Windows 2000 installation is complete, and so on. All of these optional functions can be activated from command-line parameters when you execute winnt.exe or winnt32.exe.

Winnt.exe Installation Parameters

During a new installation of Windows 2000, you can select a handful of slash (/) command-line options. The various parameter options are listed in Table 12-2.

Winnt.exe Slash (/) Parameter	Function	Example
/s:*sourcepath*	Specifies the source of installation files (x:*path* or *servershare*[*path*]).	winnt /s:c:\windows
/t:*tempdrive*	Specifies the location of temporary files and Windows 2000, unless otherwise specified.	winnt /t:d:\tempdir
/u:*answer_file*	Specifies unattended setup using the answer file. (Requires /s.)	winnt /u:ansfile.txt /s:c:\winnt
/udf:*id,udf_file*	Indicates the identifier that Setup uses to specify how a uniqueness database file modifies an answer file. /udf overrides the values in the answer file, and the *id* determines which value in the *udf_file* is used. If no *udf_file* is specified, Setup prompts you to insert a disk that contains the $unique$.udb file.	winnt /udf:12,udffile
/r:*folder*	Indicates an optional folder to be installed. (The folder is kept after setup.)	winnt /r:c:\OptFolder
/rx:*folder*	Indicates an optional folder to be copied. (The folder is deleted after setup.)	winnt /r:c:\TempFolder
/e:*command*	Specifies a command to be executed at the end of the GUI-mode setup.	winnt /e:showbanner.exe
/a	Enables accessibility options.	winnt /a

Table 12-2.   Winnt.exe Command-Line Installation Parameters

Following is a list of situations in which you might use these parameters.

▼ **/s (Source Location)**   When you execute winnt.exe, the installation program assumes that the installation files are located in the same directory as the winnt executable file. If you locate the installation files elsewhere, such as on a network share, use this parameter to specify the location.

■ **/t (Temporary File Location)**   When you install Windows 2000, about 300MB of files are temporarily copied to the hard drive of the system you are installing Windows 2000 onto. When installing on a small drive with limited storage capacity, you may want the temporary files stored on a different drive partition.

■ **/u (Unattended Setup)**   An unattended installation of Windows 2000 allows all of the questions that are asked during the installation of Windows 2000 to be scripted before installation. This allows an administrator to type **winnt /u**, along with the name of the answer file, and walk away from the system. See the "Unattended Windows 2000 Installation" section later in this chapter.

■ **/udf (Modifying UDF Options)**   When installing Windows 2000 in an unattended mode, some options may need to be changed from system to system (such as the server name or IP address). Rather than editing the unattended script file, the unique options that need to be changed can be modified from the command line. This can allow an administrator to create a common unattended script file and just make the modifications through simple command-line changes.

■ **/r (Optional Folder—Remains After Installation)**   During the installation of Windows 2000, some organizations create home directories for their users, or other folders not normally installed during a standard Windows 2000 setup. The /r parameter automatically creates these folders during the installation process.

■ **/rx (Optional Folder (Deleted After Installation))**   During an unattended installation of Windows 2000, some organizations have a series of programs and scripts run. To speed up the execution of the applications and scripts, rather than running them from a network share, the organization may elect to push the files to the system. Through the use of the /rx command, the organization can temporarily create a folder, push the temporary files to the directory, and after the installation of Windows 2000, the system will delete this temporary folder.

■ **/e (Command Executed After Installation)**   The /e parameter is one of the most common optional parameters used by organizations implementing scripted installations of the operating system. The /e command executes a program after installation. The program could be something like a Microsoft Systems Management Server (SMS) inventory run, the execution of a MAPI command-line utility that sends an email or text page to the administrator that the installation has been successfully completed, or an executable file that begins the installation of applications or installs data files.

▲ **/a (Accessibility Options)**   Installs the accessibility features.

WINNT32.EXE Upgrade Parameters

Just as there are command-line parameters to aid in the installation of Windows 2000, there are command-line parameters to assist in the upgrade process from previous versions of Windows NT to Windows 2000. These command-line parameters provide options to the winnt32.exe upgrade application. The options are listed in Table 12-3.

Winnt32.exe Slash (/) Parameter	Function	Example
/s:*sourcepath*	Specifies the source of installation files (x:*path* or *serversharepath*).	winnt32 / s:c:\windows
/t:*tempdrive*	Specifies the location of temporary files and Windows 2000, unless otherwise specified.	winnt32 / t:d:\tempdir
/u:*answer_file*	Specifies unattended setup using the answer file. (Requires /s.)	winnt32 /u:ansfile.txt / s:c:\winnt
/udf:*id,udf_file*	Indicates the identifier that setup uses to specify how a uniqueness database file modifies an answer file. /udf overrides the values in the answer file, and the *id* determines which value in the *udf_file* is used. If no *udf_file* is specified, Setup prompts you to insert a disk that contains the $unique$.udb file.	winnt32 / udf:12,udffile
/checkupgradeonly	Checks your computer for upgrade compatibility with Windows 2000. For Windows NT 3.51 or 4.0 upgrades, it saves the report to the winnt32.log in the installation folder.	winnt32 / checkupgradeonly

Table 12-3.   Winnt32.exe Command Line Installation Parameters

Winnt32.exe Slash (/) Parameter	Function	Example
/cmd:*command_line*	Executes a specific command before the final phase of Setup (after Setup has collected the necessary configuration information and rebooted twice, but before Setup is complete).	winnt32 / cmd:runprog.exe
/cmdcons	Adds a Recovery Console option for repairing a failed installation to the operating system selection screen.	winnt32 /cmdcons
/copydir:*folder_ name*	Creates an additional folder within your Windows 2000 operating system folder.	winnt32 / copydir:MyFolder
/copysource:*folder_ name*	Creates an additional folder within your Windows 2000 operating system folder, but deletes the folder after installation.	winnt32 / copysource:Tfold
/debug*level*: *filename*	Creates a debug log at the *level* specified. The default creates a log file (c:\winnt32.log) that has the level set to 2. The log levels are as follows: 0 for severe errors, 1 for errors, 2 for warnings, 3 for information, and 4 for detailed information for debugging. Each level includes the levels below it.	winnt32 / debug1:ErrorLog
/m:*folder_name*	Instructs Setup to copy replacement files from an alternative location. Setup will look in the alternative location first, and if files are present, will use them rather than the files from the default location.	winnt32 /m:AltSetup
/makelocalsource	Copies all installation source files to your local hard disk. Use this with an installation from a CD to provide installation files when the CD is not available later in the installation.	winnt32 / makelocalsource

Table 12-3.   Winnt32.exe Command Line Installation Parameters *(continued)*

Winnt32.exe Slash (/) Parameter	Function	Example
/noreboot	Instructs Setup not to restart after the file-copy phase of winnt32 is completed, so that you can execute another command.	winnt32 /noreboot
/syspart:*drive_letter*	Copies Setup startup files to a hard drive, marks the drive as active, and then allows you to install the drive in another computer. When you start that computer, Setup automatically starts with the next phase. You must always use the /tempdrive parameter with the /syspart parameter.	winnt32 /syspart:d / t:d:\tempdir
/unattend	Upgrades your previous version of Windows 2000 in unattended Setup mode. All user settings are taken from the previous installation, so no user intervention is required during Setup.	winnt32 /unattend
/unattend*num*: *answer_file*	Performs a new installation in unattended Setup mode. The *answer_file* provides your custom specifications to Setup. *Num* is the number of seconds between the time that Setup finishes copying the files and when it restarts. You can use the *num* option only on a computer running Windows 2000. *Answer_file* is the name of the answer file.	winnt32 / unattend10:ansfile

Table 12-3.   Winnt32.exe Command Line Installation Parameters *(continued)*

Unattended Windows 2000 Installation

You can script the installation process in order to install the operating system multiple times without any need for user intervention. You need an answer file (unattend.txt) to hold information about unique system configuration settings, such as computer name, IP address, default installed components, and so on.

Common Uses of Unattended Installation

Anyone who has to install more than one Windows 2000 server, or Windows 2000 Professional workstations, should take advantage of unattended installations. This feature is commonly used to create consistent installations throughout an organization, to assist remote sites as they install Windows 2000, and as part of creating a disaster recovery process.

SIMPLIFYING BASIC INSTALLATIONS   The basic installation of Windows 2000 in any organization has the same characteristics regarding registered name/company, licensing options, networking protocols used, and so on. A default answer file uses this data to install multiple instances of the operating system.

INSTALLING REMOTE SYSTEMS   Another use for an answer file is to deploy Windows 2000 in remote locations. The systems being configured in a remote location will be set up just like all other servers in the organization.

PROVIDING DISASTER RECOVERY ASSISTANCE   In the event of a server failure, you don't want to have to guess how to configure a server. Many network problems are made worse when you rebuild a server on the network, whether after an emergency rebuild of a system crash or after the reinstallation of an updated system. By inserting all common organizational information into a scripted answer file, you can achieve consistency.

Sample Unattend.Txt

The unattend.txt script file can be as simple or as complex as you require, and these files can range from 15 lines to 200 lines. There are dozens of parameters to select. A full list of the option parameters is found on the Windows 2000 CD in the \i386 subdirectory. There are options as simple as setting the default directory in which you want to install Windows 2000, to more complex options that cover detailed parameter settings for a network adapter.

The following is a sample unattend.txt file with comments (when you create your unattend.txt file, you can leave the comments out).

```
[Unattended]
TargetPath=winnt    ; leaves the install directory to c:\winnt
Filesystem=LeaveAlone   ; keeps the file system as what it is now (assuming NTFS)
[GuiUnattended]
OemSkipWelcome = 1   ; knows to skip the Welcome screen
AdminPassword = *   ; sets the password to no password
TimeZone=04      ; sets the time zone to -8 (Pacific time zone)
AdvServerType=servernt   ; specifies this is an upgrade to Windows 2000
[LicenseFilePrintData]
AutoMode=PerServer      ; sets licensing to Per Server mode
AutoUsers=250        ; specifies that you have 250 CAL licenses
[UserData]
FullName="Rand Morimoto"   ; specifies the Name of the registered individual
OrgName="Inacom Oakland"   ; specifies the Company of the registered individual
ComputerName= NT-Srv-01   ; provides a new name for the server
```

```
[Display]
BitsPerPel=16            ; 16 bits per pixel equals 65536 colors
XResolution=1024         ; 1024x768 resolution
YResolution=768
VRefresh=60              ; video refresh speed of 60hz
[Networking]             ; no networking options means leave the same as current
[Identification]
JoinDomain=INACOM        ; specifies the domain to join
[NetAdapters]
Adapter01=params.Adapter01    ; identifies the network adapter in the system
[params.Adapter01]
INFID = "pci\ven_0e11&dev_ae32"    ; specifies the plug and play ID type
[NetClients]
MS_MSClient=params.MS_MSClient    ; installs the MS Client for Networks
[params.MS_MSClient]
[NetProtocols]
MS_TCPIP=params.MS_TCPIP         ; installs TCP/IP as the main protocol
[params.MS_TCPIP]
AdapterSections=params.MS_TCPIP.Adapter01,params.MS_TCPIP.Adapter02
[params.MS_TCPIP.Adapter01]
SpecificTo=Adapter01
DHCP=no
IPAddress=1.1.1.1        ; specifies the IP address for the adapter
SubnetMask=255.255.248.0   ; specifies the subnet mask
DefaultGateway=2.2.2.2   ; specifies the default gateway
WINS=no                  ; no WINS server
[NetServices]
MS_Server=params.MS_Server
[params.MS_Server]
```

As you create and prototype test the unattended script file, you'll find that unattended installation makes it easy to install Windows 2000 on multiple computers on an ongoing basis.

ADDING COMPONENTS TO WINDOWS 2000

After you install Windows 2000, you can install additional components, perhaps making a server a domain controller, adding terminal services, DNS services, DHCP services, and the like. These additional services are called components. To add a component, use the following steps:

1. Choose Start | Settings | Control Panel.
2. Double click Add/Remove Programs.
3. Click Add/Remove Windows Components.
4. Select the components you wish to install.

NOTE: When you click a component, a description is shown below the components section, along with the total disk space required for the component and the disk space available.

5. Click Next to continue. You will then be prompted to insert your Windows 2000 installation CD.

6. Click Finish when prompted.

DELETING COMPONENTS FROM WINDOWS 2000

There are times when you want to delete a component from Windows 2000 that you had previously added. This may be caused by a change in the role of the server where the system used to act as a domain controller, DNS server, DHCP server, and the like. You can delete a component as simply as you add a component. To delete a component, follow these steps:

1. Choose Start | Settings | Control Panel.

2. Double click Add/Remove Programs.

3. Click Add/Remove Windows Components.

4. Deselect the components you wish to uninstall.

5. Click Next to continue.

6. Click Finish when prompted.

IMPLEMENTING IMPROVED SERVER-MANAGEMENT TECHNOLOGIES

Windows 2000 includes a number of product-enhancement tools focused specifically on improving the manageability of the Windows 2000 Server environment.

Distributed File System

The distributed file system (DFS) in Windows 2000 provides the ability to create a single file directory that is made up of the files spread across multiple servers throughout the organization. Rather than having users point to files on a single server, which opens up the potential of a server failure resulting in loss of access to all files by all users, the files the organization accesses can be distributed across multiple systems. If one server fails, only the files physically residing on that server are inaccessible. All other files in the directory that reside on other servers are fully accessible. One of the other benefits of implementing DFS is that all users can have the same drive letter to access common files. So, if K is assigned as the drive letter for shared files, rather than some users accessing K on one server, and others accessing K on another server, all users can access the same K list of files. The files may physically be distributed across multiple servers for scalability purposes. The distribution of files across multiple servers also lets you create multiple 16GB or 32GB servers that can be easily backed up and restored, instead of one huge 360GB server that creates a huge risk of system failure.

Earlier versions of DFS had a centralized DFS directory, which could be a single point of failure. The directory resided on a single server, and if that server failed, even though the files were physically available on other servers, the directory was inaccessible. With Windows 2000, the DFS directory is automatically published to the Active Directory, creating built-in redundancy. A DFS directory can also be directly hosted by multiple servers, creating server-based redundancy. Additionally, DFS directories can now be created and torn down without the need to reboot and disrupt users.

The volumes that users add to a DFS root are the leaves or branches that represent the shared network directories. Shared resources can be distributed using either a single tree or multiple DFS trees. By using Windows 2000 Active Directory security, including group access rights, access to DFS directory shares can be limited. A DFS tree is a single DNS namespace. The DNS names for the DFS volumes resolve to the host server(s) for a DFS root. The Active Directory manages volume references between multiple hosting servers for a DFS tree.

Installing DFS

DFS is built-in to Windows 2000 and only needs to be activated through the DFS Microsoft Management Console (MMC) snap-in. The snap-in can be installed at any time. To install the MMC snap-in, do the following:

1. Choose Start | Run and type **mmc.exe** to open the MMC utility screen.
2. Click Console.
3. Click Add/Remove Snap-In.
4. Click Add to open the Add Standalone Snap-In screen shown in Figure 12-7.
5. Select Distributed File System.
6. Click Add, click Close, and then click OK.

Once the snap-in has been installed, you can create DFS directories. If you have just added the MMC DFS snap-in, you are already in the DFS Administrator. Otherwise, open the DFS Administrator from the Administrative Tools folder menu item.

Configuring DFS (First-Time Installation)

If this is the first installation of DFS on your system, select the option to create a new DFS root volume to launch the Create a New DFS Root wizard. The first wizard option is whether or not to configure a fault-tolerant DFS root (see Figure 12-8). If you are using Windows 2000 Active Directory, it's best to select Create a Fault-Tolerant DFS Root. This places the DFS information in the Active Directory so that file management information

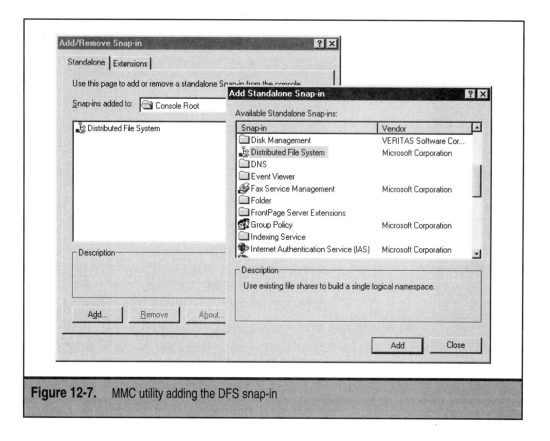

Figure 12-7. MMC utility adding the DFS snap-in

is replicated to other domain controllers on the network. If you are not running Active Directory, or you elect to skip a fault-tolerant DFS root, you will be asked to select a single server on which to install the DFS root. If that server fails, you will lose the directory information of the DFS share stored on that system (unless you backup and restore). The whole goal of DFS is to distribute load, functions, and file services, so inherently, a fault-tolerant DFS root is very important.

In the next screen, you are asked to select the domain where the DFS root should be created. Select the branch of the Active Directory tree that is managed and administered by the person overseeing the security of the file services.

You are asked to specify the server that will host the DFS root, and then you are prompted to provide a new logical name for the DFS root. Instead of specifying c$, you can create a logical name for the DFS directory, in which you will consolidate a number of c$, d$, e$ physical drives to the DFS logical configuration. Upon completing the DFS installation, a screen summarizing the installation of your DFS root is displayed, as shown in Figure 12-9.

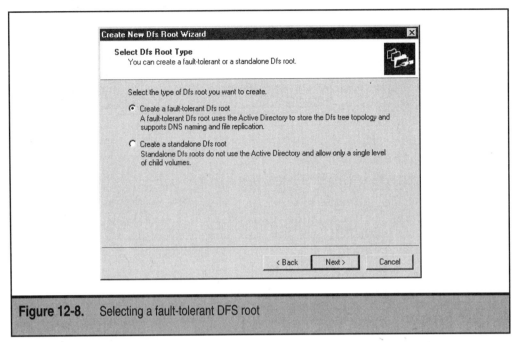

Figure 12-8.   Selecting a fault-tolerant DFS root

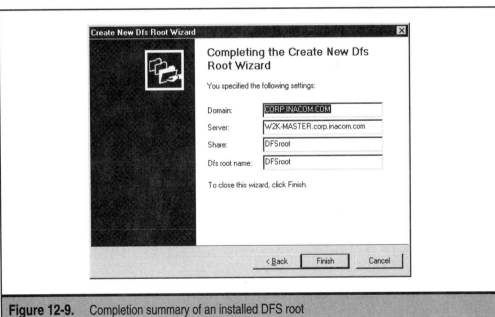

Figure 12-9.   Completion summary of an installed DFS root

Configuring DFS (Updating an Existing Installation)

If you have already created a DFS root, you may want to add branches (or child nodes) to it. The child nodes can be used to create branches that correspond to different shares on new servers in the DFS tree, or to create branches that further break down a very large volume of an existing share on the network. In both cases, the DFS child nodes build the DFS root to create logical boundaries that extend the physical storage mapping beyond just a single drive storage share.

To create a child node, open the DFS Administrator (Start | Programs | Administrative Tools | Distributed File System), and connect to the DFS root (select Action | Connect to Existing DFS Root). A list of the DFS roots available on the server or in the Active Directory will be displayed. Select the DFS root to which you want to add child nodes, and click OK. To add a child node, select Action | New DFS Child Node and you will see an Add to DFS screen, similar to the one in Figure 12-10. You are prompted to enter the child node reference (the logical name you want represented on the screen when accessing the DFS root) and to enter the network path of this logical child node (enter the UNC address for the share).

Accessing Your DFS Share

After you have successfully created your DFS root, and possibly added child nodes, you can mount the share from any Windows device by simply entering the UNC address of the DFS root or child node. For example, if I created a share called DFSRoot and the mas-

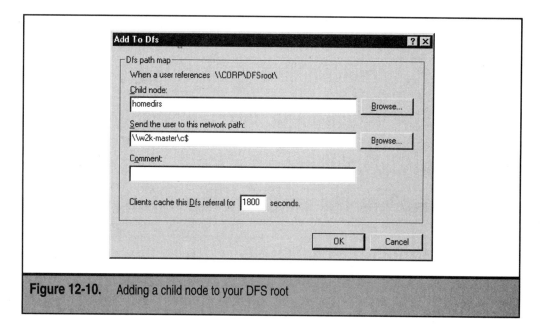

Figure 12-10.   Adding a child node to your DFS root

ter server name is W2K-Master, I would mount the \\w2k-master\dfsroot share to access the files assigned to this DFS logical share.

Dynamic Volume Management

Windows 2000 has dynamic volume management that provides a way to conduct administrative tasks without shutting down the system or interrupting users. A volume can be created, extended, or mirrored without rebooting the system. Disks can also be added without rebooting. This is achieved through the introduction of a logical disk manager (LDM) in addition to the current fault-tolerant disk manager (FT Disk).

FT Disk

FT Disk is carried forward from previous versions of Windows NT for managing partitions and fault-tolerant volumes. FT Disk mounts basic disks and partitions created with MS-DOS and previous versions of Windows NT, and provides the functionality for creating (and signing) basic disks and volumes. FT Disk provides full backwards compatibility with older Windows disk-partitioning systems.

Logical Disk Manager

The new logical disk manager extends fault-tolerance functionality, improves system recovery, encapsulates system metadata, and provides improved management functionality. The LDM creates a 4MB "soft" system partition at the end of a physical disk. Any disk containing a volume managed by the LDM contains this partition. The LDM system partition stores metadata that is replicated among other dynamic disks in the system.

Dynamic disks can contain basic volumes and dynamic volumes. Basic volumes are managed by FT Disk functionality, and dynamic volumes are managed by LDM functionality. Dynamic volumes offer features such as volume extension and fault tolerance configurations. Operations on dynamic volumes do not require machine reboots to implement configuration changes.

Installing Volume-Management Utilities

The volume-management utilities for Windows 2000 are automatically installed with Windows 2000 and do not require special installation. To configure, modify, or update volumes on your Windows 2000 server, you need to make changes in the Storage section of the Computer Management MMC snap-in. This can be done by launching the Computer Management tool from the Administrative Tools menu.

When you select the Storage option in the snap-in, you will see a screen similar to Figure 12-11. Through this window, you can administer and manage removable storage volumes or logical drives on the network. You can also run disk defragmentation from this screen.

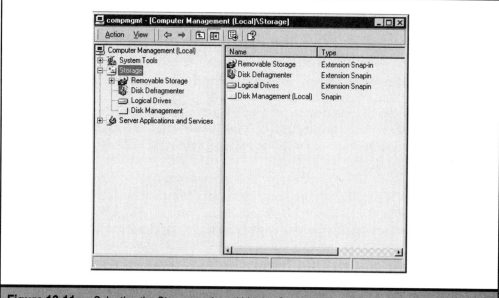

Figure 12-11.   Selecting the Storage option within the Computer Management snap-in

Disk Management

With the Disk Management option in the Storage section of the Computer Management snap-in, you can create new partitions, delete partitions, stripe datasets, format partitions, or add new drive space to an existing logical partition. For those familiar with Windows NT 4, this is the same as the Disk Administrator utility that provided the ability to manage and administer physical and logical drives on the network.

Disk Defragmentation

A basic disk defragmentation utility is built into Windows 2000. You can manually invoke, or automatically schedule, the defragmentation of disks. The defragmentation utility screen (shown in Figure 12-12) allows you to select a volume, analyze the volume to determine whether the volume requires defragmentation, and invoke the defragmentation command. It is recommended that you defragment a file and print server once a week (more frequently for a very highly used server). Typically, defragmentation has little effect on application servers, such as SQL, Notes, or Exchange.

Disk Quotas

Windows 2000 provides disk quota support for volumes formatted with NTFS5. Administrators can use disk quotas to monitor and limit the use of disk space. In addition to user

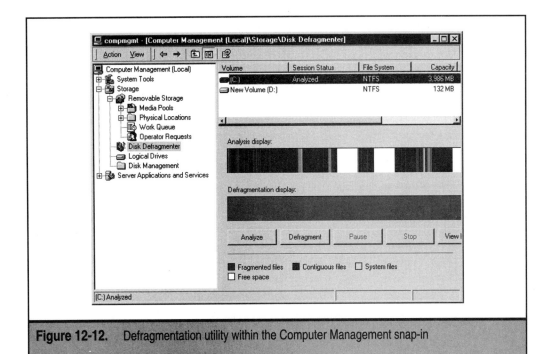

Figure 12-12.   Defragmentation utility within the Computer Management snap-in

notification when disk quotas are exceeded, events are automatically logged when users exceed warning thresholds and quota limits. Quotas are tracked on a per-user, per-volume basis, and users are charged only for the files they own.

NOTE: For security reasons, when a member of the local computer's Administrators group creates a new file, the file is owned by the Administrators group, not by the individual user. Therefore, to track disk quotas on an individual basis, users must log on under separate user accounts that are not members of the Administrators group.

Quota information can be saved along with other volume information during backup. When the administrator restores files from tape, the files being restored do not go against the tape administrators' personal quota but rather get applied to the quota for the users who originally owned the files being restored.

Setting Quotas

Quotas are set and administered as part of the Properties settings of the physical and logical drive. To get to the quota administrator, right-click the drive, choose Properties, and click the Quota tab.

The Quota tab offers a series of options. First, check the Enable Quota Management checkbox to enable quota functions and provide the ability to specify disk space allocation, default quota limits, and quota logging. You can set the default quota limit for all users that access the drive share, or you can click the Quota Entries button to select individual users or groups in order to vary the quotas. When you select the quota entries button, you will see a screen like the one shown in Figure 12-13.

It is typically suggested that you set the warning level to 75 or 80 percent of the maximum disk storage limit. This lets users know far enough in advance that they are reaching disk quota maximums, so that they can do necessary housecleaning or request more space.

Internet Printing Protocol

The Internet Printing Protocol (IPP) provides print services to a URL over an intranet or Internet connection. Rather than having a specific printer defined on the systems print console or printer manager, a user simply prints to a URL. Two services are included with Windows 2000 to provide IPP: the server publishes a printer as a URL, and the client prints to a URL.

TIP: Printing service bureaus are offering Web-based printing so that customers can gain access to high-speed and high-quality color printers.

Through IPP, a user can view print-queue status from any browser, including printer and job information of public service as well as internal Windows 2000 server–based printers. Drivers for the remote printers are automatically downloaded and installed over the Internet.

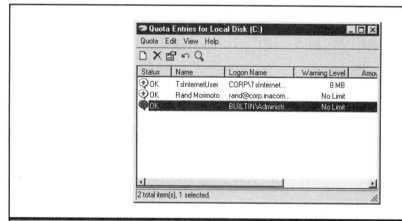

Figure 12-13.   Selecting quotas for drive space access

Publishing a Printer IPP Host Sharing

The publishing of a printer is controlled by the Listed in the Directory checkbox on the printer's Sharing tab (Start | Settings | Printers, right click on the printer, select the Sharing tab). If the List in the Directory option is checked (as shown in Figure 12-14), then the printer is published. If you deselect the checkbox for a published printer, the printer is deleted from the Active Directory (AD).

The Add Printer wizard does not allow you to change the listing in the Directory setting. You must manually open the printer's Sharing tab to change the default printer listing. The default behavior (set in system policies) is to turn the List in the Directory checkbox on by default and to publish printers that are added using the Add Printer wizard. Only shared printers can be published.

The printer is placed in the print server's Computer object in the directory store. There is no way to change this behavior. However, the object can be moved or renamed once it has been placed in the DS. The print servers are the masters, the DS is the slave.

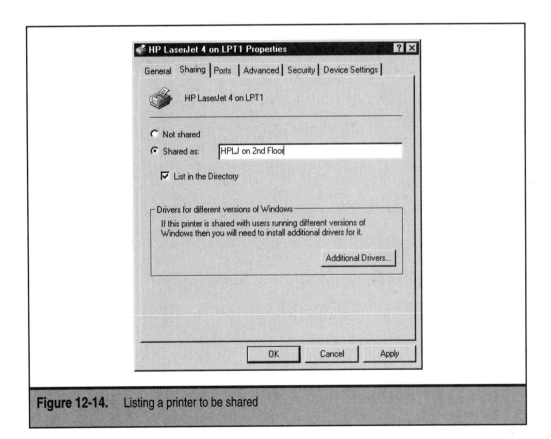

Figure 12-14. Listing a printer to be shared

Each print server is responsible for its own printers being published in the DS. There is no centralized printer publishing service. The print servers do not have an affinity to any specific domain controller—they dynamically find a domain controller in the appropriate domain.

Invoking IPP Client Printing

To print to an IPP host, access the IPP host by entering http://servername/printers in an Internet browser or Windows Explorer (for an intranet-based connection) and press ENTER.

The All Printers on *Server Name* page displays information about the printers, including the printer name, status of print jobs, location, model, and any comments entered when the printer was installed. This information helps users select the correct printer. The *Printer Name* on *Server Name* page displays multiple options. Only those options the user has permission to use are visible.

IMPLEMENTING HIGH-AVAILABILITY SERVER TECHNOLOGIES

Part of any server implementation strategy is to establish high-availability servers to maintain system operation and system reliability. This section covers the Windows 2000 functions that improve system availability.

Clustering

Windows 2000 includes server clustering in the Windows 2000 Advanced Server and DataCenter editions of the operating system. When many administrators think of clustering, they think of a more robust server fault tolerance, where every server has a completely redundant system take over full server operations on all server features and operations. However, Microsoft's current implementation of clustering creates redundancy on Windows NT services. For example, for a Microsoft Exchange e-mail server cluster if one server is running a mail routing service that forwards mail messages to the Internet, in the event that server fails, the other server in the cluster will assume the responsibility for routing mail when the router service is moved from the failed to the operational system.

For example, if the cluster is providing inbound and outbound email message transfers to the Internet as part of an Exchange messaging cluster, the Internet Mail service is running on just one of the two servers. That server assumes 100 percent of the responsibility and server utilization for that service. If that server fails, the Internet Mail service is automatically started on the secondary server, and messaging communications is assumed by the secondary system.

For functions that are not cluster-aware, if a primary server fails, the secondary server can be configured to pick up the function of the service, but there may be an interruption in server function to the user. In some cases, the interruption is significant enough to cause the application to fail. Server clustering in a Windows 2000 environment needs to be thoroughly tested to ensure that the operation of the cluster in situations of server or cluster failure meets the expectations of the organization.

Implementing Clustering

Windows 2000 Clustering can be installed on any Windows 2000 Advanced server or DataCenter server. The hardware should be verified for Windows Clustering compatibility. To install the Windows 2000 clustering component, do the following:

1. Choose Start | Settings | Control Panel.
2. Double click on Add/Remove Programs.
3. Click on Add/Remove Windows Components.
4. Select the checkbox for Cluster Services.
5. Select Next to Continue.

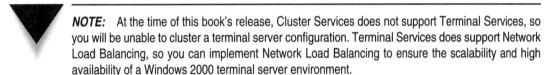

NOTE: At the time of this book's release, Cluster Services does not support Terminal Services, so you will be unable to cluster a terminal server configuration. Terminal Services does support Network Load Balancing, so you can implement Network Load Balancing to ensure the scalability and high availability of a Windows 2000 terminal server environment.

The Cluster wizard takes you through the steps of creating a cluster. The first screen prompts you to validate whether the hardware you have has been certified by Microsoft as being cluster-compatible. Since clustering implies high availability, the equipment that a cluster runs on must be equipment that has been tested by Microsoft to meet the requirements of a valid cluster.

The next wizard screen asks whether you want to form a new cluster or join an existing cluster. Since Windows 2000 only supports a cluster of two servers, you are either creating a new cluster with the first server, or you have already setup the first server in the cluster and you are joining it with the second server. For the first server, select the Form a New Cluster option. You are then prompted to give the cluster a name, using any name you wish. While each server in a cluster has its own physical name (such as server-right and server-left), the cluster name is the logical name that users access.

If you have already created the first cluster server and you are joining that server with the second server, select Join an Existing Cluster. You are prompted to enter the name of the existing cluster, along with a valid user name and password to connect to the cluster, as shown in Figure 12-15.

Once the cluster component has been installed, you can administer your cluster by launching the Cluster Administrator. Select Start | Programs | Administrative Tools | Cluster Administration.

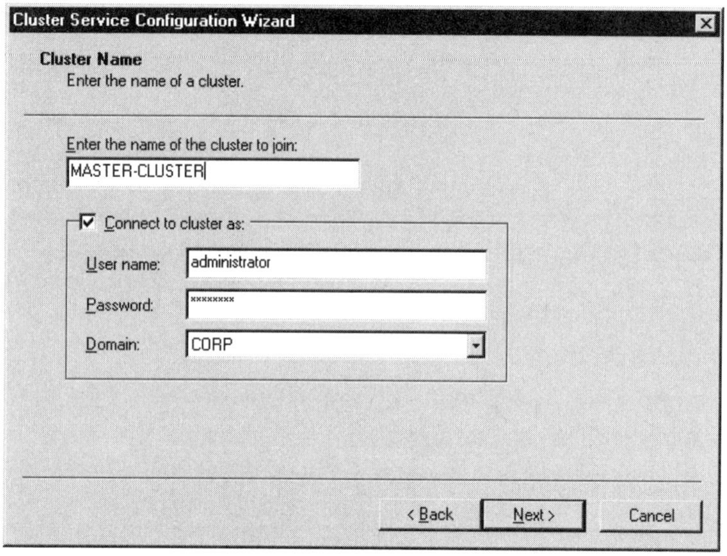

Figure 12-15. Joining an existing cluster

Configuring Clustering Parameters

You can change the parameters of a cluster to define the operational functions of applications and services running on the cluster. Some of the functions that can be modified with the Resource Properties dialog box include the ability to view or change the name of the cluster resource service, to change the owner of the resource, and to automatically restart a failed service.

Another parameter lets you run a resource in a separate memory space. Some applications within a Windows environment are intended to run most efficiently in the general memory space allocated for the applications. Some applications, however, misbehave when other applications or services are loaded on the server, and they should run in their own memory spaces.

You can also view and modify resource dependencies. As failover occurs on a cluster, certain services or functions must be activated on the redundant system before a resource service can be activated on the backup server. Specify the dependent resources, so that those services are activated before the main resource is shifted over to the backup system.

There are two options for validating whether a cluster is operational; one is a "looks alive" validation and the other is an "is alive" validation. Not only can you select which of the two validation models to use, but you also have the ability to specify the polling interval on the checks between the systems. The "is alive" validation is more bandwidth intensive. It conducts a check of the server to make sure the other server in the cluster is alive and operational. The "looks alive" validation can be set more frequently since it does a less intensive validation of the operation of the other server in the cluster, but it is aware enough to know when there is a system failure.

One of the key resource parameters is the function that defines the amount of time that a resource is in a pending state. The options are: The Server is Online Pending or The Server is Offline Pending. This is what tells a server in a cluster whether the other server is offline and in a failed status. It is during this counter that the other server determines when to issue a failover status command to switch services to the operational server within the cluster.

Network Load Balancing

The Windows 2000 Load Balancing service is an enhanced extension of the Windows Load Balancing service (WLBS) in the Windows NT 4 Enterprise edition. Network Load Balancing uses a distributed algorithm to statistically map the workload between the nodes of the load-balanced workgroup. Network Load Balancing moves incoming TCP/IP traffic across all the hosts in a workgroup. Running a copy of the server program on each load-balanced host enables the load to be partitioned among them in any manner you choose. Load-balancing services transparently distribute the client requests among the hosts and lets the clients access the cluster using one or more virtual IP addresses. Up to 32 hosts may operate in each cluster, and hosts can be added transparently to a cluster to handle increased load. Load-balancing services can also direct all traffic to a designated single host, called the default host.

Load Balancing Provides True 24×7 Operations

Load balancing provides high availability and scalable performance by distributing the client workload to multiple parallel servers. Load balancing can also be used to provide rolling upgrades and updates to a 24×7 network operation. Since servers can be added and deleted from the load-balanced workgroup at any time, a server can be taken offline while the rest of the workgroup maintains 24×7 operation of client services. The server brought offline can be upgraded or updated and then brought back online into the load-balanced workgroup.

Implementing Network Load Balancing

The Windows 2000 Network Load Balancing service is a network protocol that can be installed on any Windows 2000 server. To install the Windows 2000 Network Load Balancing protocol, do the following:

1. Choose Start | Settings | Control Panel.
2. Double click on Network and Dial-up Connections.
3. Right click on the Local Area Connection you wish to add Network Load Balancing.

4. Select Properties.

5. Click on Install.

6. Click Add and Choose Protocol.

7. Choose Network Load Balancing.

8. Click OK to Continue.

Configuring Network Load Balancing Parameters

Once the protocol or service has been installed, you need to configure the Network Load Balancing properties. You do so in the Local Area Connection Properties dialog box (Start | Settings | Control Panel | Networking and Dial-up Connections | right click on Local Area Connection) by selecting the Network Load Balancing option and clicking on Properties. You will see a screen that looks like Figure 12-16.

There are three tabs in the Network Load Balancing Properties dialog box: Cluster Parameters, Host Parameters, and Port Rules.

In the Cluster Parameters tab, you can specify the options for the cluster parameters, but you have to think about the effect on the entire cluster. For example, the first option is

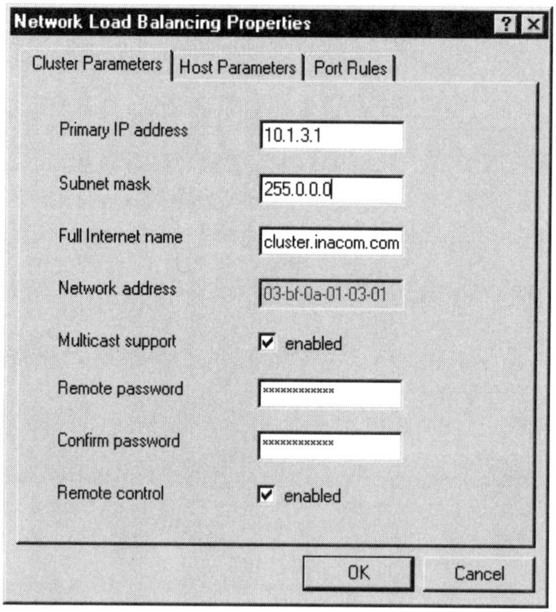

Figure 12-16.   Configuring network load balancing properties

the Primary IP Address for the cluster. This is the IP address that all the servers in the network load-balanced cluster group share. It is what the cluster is known by to all resources wishing to access the cluster. (The subnet mask and Internet name are similarly viewed by the rest of the cluster).

You have the option of enabling or disabling multicast. This cluster parameter determines the compatibility of the cluster in a routed or switched environment. If a cluster is on a flat single-segmented network, multicast mode (the default) works best, since the cluster only services a single subnet on the network. However, if the cluster services multiple segments (routed either through a switch or through a routed network), then unicast enables the server to operate across other segments on the network.

You also have the decision of whether to use a single network adapter or multiple network adapters. For the best performance, you should have two network adapters in each server. Configure one adapter as the host adapter for all clustering communications, and the other adapter can facilitate noncluster communications (such as maintenance and support services) directly with the server itself. In either case, if you provide direct support to the server through either a separate network adapter or through a multihomed configured single adapter, you can enable remote control services and define a password that can be used for remote management and administration.

In the Host Parameters tab, you can specify a priority for each server in the cluster, ranging from 1 to 32. Each server in the cluster group must have a unique priority number. When a user requests information from the cluster, it first accesses the server with the lowest priority number and then works its way up the priority list based on the load of each server. The Host Parameters tab also contains the dedicated IP address and network mask setting for network traffic that is not associated with the cluster communication.

The Port Rules tab is where you specify the weight associated with each server in the cluster. By default, the filter mode is set to multiple hosts with single affinity and equal load weight. The following are parameters in the Port Rules tab that designate the filtering mode that needs to be set for the Network Load Balancing cluster. Depending on how the filtering is set determines how the cluster will respond to client requests.

▼ **Multiple Hosts Filtering Mode**   This parameter specifies that multiple hosts in the cluster handle network traffic for the associated port rule. This filtering mode provides scaled performance as well as fault tolerance by distributing the network load across multiple host servers. You can specify that the load be equally distributed among the hosts or you can directly specify that each host handle a specified load percentage. Network traffic is distributed across the servers on a per-connection basis for TCP, where the combination of source IP address, and source and destination port numbers determine a unique client connection.

■ **Single Host Filtering Mode**   This parameter specifies that the network traffic for the associated port rule be handled by a single host in the cluster. This filtering mode allows the administrator to set the handling priority parameter for each host. This filtering mode provides fault tolerance for the handling of network traffic.

■ **Disabled Filtering Mode**   This parameter specifies that all network traffic for an associated port rule will be blocked. This filtering mode lets you build a firewall against unwanted network access to a specific range of ports.

■ **No Client Affinity**   The None option for Client Affinity specifies that Network Load Balancing does not need to direct multiple requests from the same client to the same cluster host.

■ **Single Client Affinity**   The Single Client option for Client Affinity specifies that Network Load Balancing should direct multiple requests from the same client IP address to the same cluster host. Network Load Balancing will only forward a client's request to a specific server in the cluster.

▲ **Class C Affinity**   The Class C option for Client Affinity allows client requests to multiple hosts within the cluster. This feature ensures that clients that use multiple proxy servers can access the cluster and have their TCP connections directed to the same cluster host each time. The use of multiple proxy servers at the client's site allows requests from a single client to appear to originate from different computers.

Enabling either single or class C affinity ensures that only one cluster host handles all connections that are part of the same client session. This is important if the server program running on the cluster host maintains the same session state (important when security cookies are used). However, disabling client affinity improves performance, because it allows multiple connections from the same client to be handled concurrently by different cluster hosts. To maximize scaled performance, disable client affinity by clicking the None option for affinity.

Remote Storage

Remote Storage is a component of Windows 2000 that grooms old information from a primary disk on a server to secondary disk systems. The local disk is frequently a high performance RAID drive configuration, and the remote storage device is typically a tape drive or magneto-optical drive subsystem. Since removable optical disks and tapes are less expensive per megabyte than hard disks, this can be an economical way to provide both maximum storage and optimal local performance.

Windows 2000 includes a technology called Remote Storage Management (RSM), a subset of the Remote Storage Services (RSS) component. RSS makes it easy to increase disk space on a server without adding more hard disks. RSS automatically monitors the amount of space available on the local hard disk, and when the free space on a managed primary hard disk dips below the desired level, RSM automatically deletes any files that have been previously groomed to a remote storage device by the Remote Storage system.

Remote Storage can be configured to automatically groom information from the primary disk volume to the remote storage device, based on a series of administrator-defined rules. The rules are typically based on date and time of file storage.

As far as the users of the network are concerned, the files still reside in the same directories in which they were originally saved. The users never know the files were groomed from the primary disk to the secondary disk subsystem.

Implementing Remote Storage Services

Windows 2000 Remote Storage Services is a component that can be installed on any Windows 2000 server. To install the Windows 2000 Remote Storage Services component, do the following:

1. Choose Start | Settings | Control Panel.
2. Double click on Add/Remove Programs.
3. Click on Add/Remove Windows Components.
4. Select the checkbox for Remote Storage.
5. Select Next to Continue.

Configuring Remote Storage Services

You can configure and administer Remote Storage using the Remote Storage Administrator. Start the administrator by choosing Start | Programs | Administrative Tools | Remote Storage.

When configuring remote storage, you can set the volumes for which you want to define management properties. The parameters that need to be set include the source (the network share being managed for analysis and grooming) and the destination (the target location). In addition to specifying source and destination, the definition for the trigger to migrate information needs to be defined. This specifies when information will be migrated from the source to the destination.

Creating High-Availability Networking

While each of the three high-availability technologies provide a specific type of fault tolerance to improve the availability of networking services on a network, it is the combination of these three technologies that gives you true high-availability solutions. The variations include:

▼   A focus on performance with a secondary focus on uptime availability

■   A focus on uptime availability with a secondary focus on performance

■   A focus on fast data recovery in the event of a failure

▲   A priority focus on all of the above

The choice is really dependent on cost.

A Focus on Performance

If your focus is on performance, the best components are Network Load Balancing and Remote Storage Services. If you manage all users from a single server, and then add more servers to the network and load-balance them, you can add more users or distribute the additional bandwidth to the current user group.

Remote Storage can groom the files stored on the server to minimize unnecessary overhead in administering and managing unnecessary files. By keeping the number of managed files under control, overall system performance is increased.

A Focus on Uptime Availability

If your focus is on ensuring high availability, use clustering to provide failover from a primary to a secondary system. To create an environment that provides virtually no downtime, run both clustering (for failover) and load balancing (for redistributing the load).

A Focus on Fast Data Recovery

If your goal is to minimize the downtime caused by a system failure, use Remote Storage to create a system that is much easier and quicker to restore. Adding RSS means that information can be easily migrated from one server to another.

A Focus on All of the Above

If you want all of it: high availability, flexible scalability, fast recovery, and fault tolerance, you need to avail yourself of all three high-availability technologies. While there is a considerable cost associated with this level of redundancy, you can quantify the cost of a system that is down and allocate that cost to the implementation of a fully clustered and load-balanced system.

WINDOWS 2000 BACKUPS

Windows 2000 includes a backup software application that provides full backup and restoring of files, and provides the ability to back up the Active Directory. The utility, ntbackup.exe is a GUI-based utility complete with a Backup wizard to help you configure your backup process. You can back up the entire server, or back up portions of the server on a folder-by-folder basis.

The Ntbackup utility is automatically installed in Windows 2000 with the basic software installation. Unlike previous versions of the Windows backup utility, the Ntbackup that comes with Windows 2000 can back up to a variety of media, including streaming tape, digital tape, magneto-optical hard drive, or even over the LAN/WAN to other server shares.

Executing a Backup

The Ntbackup utility can be invoked by launching the application:

1. Choose Start.
2. Select Run.
3. Type ntbackup.exe and then click OK.

Once you launch the Ntbackup utility you will see a welcome screen that provides some wizards to walk you through backing up your system. The Backup wizard steps you through the options of backing up everything on your local computer, backing up everything on a remote system, or backing up just critical system files. You also must select the target device for the backup file.

You can also manually back up the system by selecting the Backup tab on the Ntbackup utility screen, which displays a window similar to the one in Figure 12-17. As

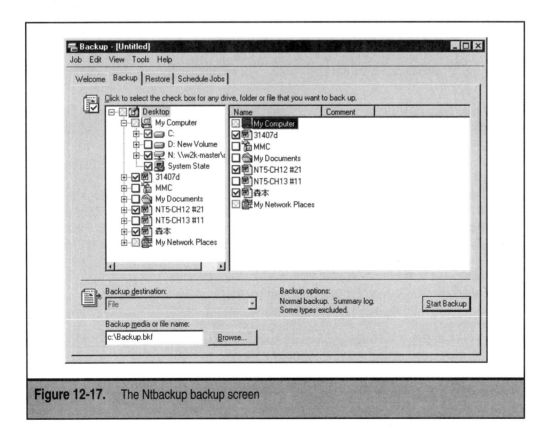

Figure 12-17.   The Ntbackup backup screen

you can see in the figure, the left pane shows the devices that can be backed up, the right pane shows the files specified for backup, and at the bottom you can specify the backup device and media or file name.

Ntbackup uses a very sophisticated compression algorithm that compresses information before it is transferred to the backup device, speeding the process.

Restoring from a Backup

Restoring from a backup is as simple as creating the backup. In the Ntbackup utility, use the Restore wizard, which will walk you through selecting your source device (tape drive, drive share, removable media, and so on) and your destination. Just as with the backup function, you can manually restore information by selecting the source, destination, and the files you wish to restore.

IMPLEMENTING INFORMATION-MANAGEMENT SERVICES

Windows 2000 includes a series of information-management services that help you manage the information in your system. Traditionally, this has meant database information and desktop application documents, but now information also includes electronic messaging information and information stored on an intranet or the Internet.

Index Services

One of the biggest challenges organizations face is the ability to store and then easily find information stored on the network. Index Services is a Windows 2000 core component that makes information accessible to users, whether the data is stored on a Windows 2000 server, or on the Web.

With Index Services, users can query indexes and documents stored on a Windows 2000 Server. The search engine can find documents in almost any format, including text in a Word document, statistics on an Excel spreadsheet, or the content of an HTML page. Once set up, all the services are automatic, including updates, index creation, and optimization.

Implementing Index Services

Windows 2000 Index Services is a component that can be installed on any Windows 2000 server. To install the Windows 2000 Index Services component, do the following:

1. Choose Start | Settings | Control Panel.
2. Double click on Add/Remove Programs.
3. Click on Add/Remove Windows Components.
4. Select the checkbox for Index Services.
5. Select Next to Continue.

Using Index Services

The Windows 2000 Index Services component is an add-in service for a number of application services, including IIS, Exchange, and SQL. To manage and administer Index Services in Windows 2000, the configuration components are integrated into the other applications.

Distributed Authoring and Versioning

The Windows 2000 Web-Based Distributed Authoring and Versioning service (WebDAV) lets you publish, manage, and share information over the Web. An Internet Engineering Task Force (IETF) working group known as WebDAV has developed a set of extensions to HTTP 1.1 that enable distributed authoring. This protocol extends the current HTTP 1.1 commands to include commands you can use to manage resources, manipulate properties, and lock information.

Distributed authoring and versioning (DAV) support is enabled via Internet Information Services (IIS) technology. The implementation of DAV is based on version 8 of the WebDAV protocol specification.

CHAPTER 13

Installing Domain Controllers, DNS Servers, and DHCP Servers

Three very important services are installed in a Windows 2000 environment: domain controllers, DNS servers, and DHCP servers. As I have explained in the planning and design section of this book, the domain controllers authenticate users to the network, the DNS servers provide name resolution necessary to find servers on the network, and DHCP simplifies the dynamic distribution of IP addresses to systems on the network necessary for the systems to participate in the Windows 2000 environment. This chapter covers the installation of these components.

PREPARING FOR DOMAIN CONTROLLER INSTALLATION

A Windows 2000 domain controller is a server that is configured to manage a replica of all of the Active Directory, or a portion of it, storing directory data and domain-user information. Domain controllers also process user logons and authentication.

Problems with the configuration of a domain controller can corrupt the Active Directory, and can replicate an unreliable copy of the Active Directory throughout the domain.

When you are preparing for the Windows 2000 Domain Controller installation, you need to verify that the hardware you plan to use meets the hardware and compatibility requirements as specified by Microsoft. You should also ensure that you have all of the latest updates for the Windows 2000 software. Having compatible hardware and software updates will minimize the chance of system failures on a very important component in a network.

Review Hardware Requirements and Compatibility

As I described in Chapters 5 and 12, the three most crucial sources that should be reviewed to determine hardware compatibility and suitability for your Windows 2000 environment are the Microsoft Windows 2000 hardware compatibility list, Microsoft's technical knowledge base, and the compatibility and knowledge base resources of the hardware vendors' products. Although the hardware compatibility list of both Microsoft and the hardware vendor of the product on which you intend to install Windows 2000 form the basis of your Windows 2000 systems, it is the knowledge bases from these vendors that may provide insight into any known problems with download patches, updated drivers, or fixes. A domain controller is particularly important to ensure hardware compatibility and reliable operation. Otherwise, the entire user access security system may be rendered inoperatable.

Hardware compatibility is extremely important for the domain controllers on your network. I have experienced serious problems with a noncertified hard drive cache controller that caused inconsistent writing of Active Directory information. Faulty information was replicated throughout the organization unabated, but until user logons failed to operate properly, the organization had no idea of the extent of the problem. The corruption had spread throughout the organization, creating unrecoverable errors.

Obtain the Latest Service Packs and Drivers

Verify the level of your drivers with the manufacturers (typically through a Web site search). Microsoft periodically releases updates and patches for the Windows 2000 network operating system software, so be sure to stay on top of the latest release.

Install service packs for all the domain controllers on a network at the same time. Differences between service pack revisions can cause directory errors or corruption across domain controllers.

Determine the Type of Installation to Be Performed

When installing Windows 2000 for a normal workstation or server there are choices to make such as selecting the type of filesystem (FAT or NTFS) that you want to install, how you want to partition multiple drives in the system, or whether you want the system to dual boot to other operating systems. However, on a Windows 2000 domain controller, because the system is integral to the security and user access to the network, your options are limited (in many cases predefined by the operating system) on how you can configure the server.

▼ **Configuring your file system**   Disk partitioning is a way of configuring a physical disk so that it can operate as separate logical units. These logical drives can all run the same file system, or you can install a different file system on each. Windows 2000 domain controllers must be configured with an NTFS5 partition in order to support the Active Directory (there are currently two versions of NTFS; version 4 and version 5). Windows 2000 domain controllers cannot be installed on a FAT or FAT32 partition. When you attempt to activate the Active Directory, you will be prompted to upgrade your partition to NTFS.

▲ **Boot configuration**   Windows 2000 supports dual boot configurations, as long as each system is on its own partition (which can have its own file system). However, domain controllers should not participate in a dual boot configuration.

Verify Internet Domain Name Registration

When installing a DNS server in an organization that connects with the Internet, verify the domain name with your Internet service provider (ISP) to ensure proper connectivity and access to the Internet.

Determine Key Information

There is some planning required when you integrate a server into a network. Be sure to use a consistent naming convention for servers, be sure you use the correct domain name (use an Internet domain name if the network is connected to the Internet), and be sure you know the Administrator account name and password. Also, be sure the administrator has the appropriate levels of permissions. You need a specific, unique IP address (along with the network subnet mask and default gateway address) if this is the first server on the network, or if you are not using Dynamic Host Control Protocol (DHCP) to assign a TCP/IP address for server communication. If you are not configuring an IP address on your server, then Windows 2000 will install a default DHCP IP address on the server during installation.

If the domain controller you are installing is not the network DNS server, you will need the IP address of the DNS server.

INSTALLING THE FIRST DOMAIN CONTROLLER

The installation of the first domain controller requires some special attention.

Installing from an Automated Windows 2000 Setup

As discussed in Chapter 12, a server is initially installed as a member server, which can be promoted to being a domain controller at any time.

NTFS Installation Partition

During the installation of Windows 2000, one of the first screens asks you to specify the file system you wish to install. Because a domain controller must be installed on an NTFS partition for security purposes, select NTFS during the initial file system portion of the setup. Of course, if you forget and leave the file system as FAT, the file system will be converted to NTFS automatically during the installation process of the Active Directory service.

Computer Name and Administrative Password

During the installation of Windows 2000, you are prompted for the computer name and the administrative password. It is important to specify the correct domain and computer name. While Windows 2000 allows you to change the name of the server and domain at a later date, changing the name requires a complete flushing of the DNS server cache and of all other domain controllers or system-name resolution caches on the network. Depending on the size of the network and the length of time that the name had its previous setting, this can create complications. Design your naming convention and directory structure prior to installing the first server so you don't need to change the names at a later date.

Setup creates a user named Administrator, which is the logon name for administrative rights on the domain controller. The password may consist of upper and lowercase letters and numbers. Ensure that the password is unique, and record this information in a secure location in case the password is forgotten.

Windows 2000 IIS Components

By default, IIS will be installed at the time you initially install the Windows 2000 software on the system, but if you are not planning to access your network from the Internet or use Web server hosting services, you should deselect the IIS installation option. Typically a domain controller is configured just as a logon and security authentication system and not as an application or production server for other services. Disabling IIS adds a higher level of security to this server.

Enable IIS services if you plan to take advantage of the Internet Printing Protocol shared printing services within Windows 2000, or if you plan to use any of the Web-based administration tools that take advantage of Web-based services.

I'm frequently asked whether domain servers can also be configured as application servers, and the answer is both yes and no. For a small organization, or a workgroup with less than 50–100 users, it can be efficient to have the application server participating in replication on the domain. When a user requests authentication to the domain or access to domain resources, such as a database, the security resolution occurs immediately. For a small organization, it can also be excessively costly to have redundant servers on the network. However, if your organization grows and you eventually have hundreds of users accessing an application server, the domain controller services can affect the performance of the applications. Domain security services take priority in processing threads, because it is important that security information is promptly distributed throughout the organization. If you have more than 150–200 users requesting data on the application server and are simultaneously authenticating access on the same server, you will find that distributing those services across multiple systems improves network performance.

Windows 2000 Networking Components

If you've disabled IIS services, when you select the Networking Services component (as shown in Figure 13-1) and view the details, you should also disable IIS support services, such as the COM Internet Services Proxy and the Internet Printing Services. If you will be using IIS, leave these services selected.

Enable DNS Services for a domain controller unless you have a DNS server elsewhere on the network to perform name resolution. If you will be using Windows 2000 DNS Services, having the Active Directory server also act as the DNS server significantly improves the efficiency of Active Directory management.

Date and Time

Configuring the proper date and time is important on all domain controllers. While Windows 2000 does not solely depend on time stamping for domain controller updates, during a domain controller change contention, Windows 2000 uses the time and date as the tiebreaker in determining which change to accept.

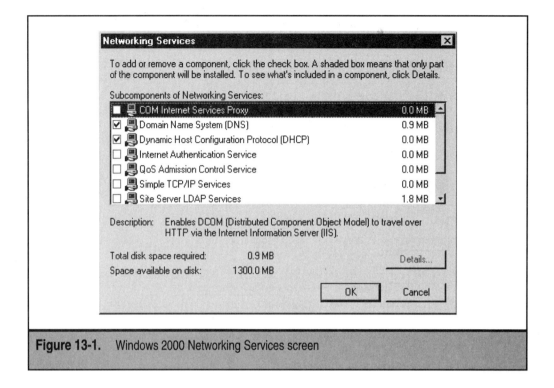

Figure 13-1. Windows 2000 Networking Services screen

Network Settings

The standard installation of Windows 2000 installs basic networking components, such as Windows networking and the TCP/IP protocol. By default, the server installer will select dynamic IP address assignment from a DHCP server. While you can reset this later to a static IP address, it is more efficient to enter the correct server IP address manually during installation.

To change the IP address for the server, use the network properties page (Start | Settings | Networks and Dial-in Connections | Right click the Local Area Connection and select Properties) and select the Internet Protocol (TCP/IP) Component. Choose properties, as shown in Figure 13-2, and enter the static IP address and the DNS server address that this domain controller will use for name resolution.

The Configure Your Server Wizard

After you have completed the initial installation and configuration of your server, the Windows 2000 Setup utility forces a reboot of the server to initiate all server services. Log on as Administrator, using the password you designated during setup.

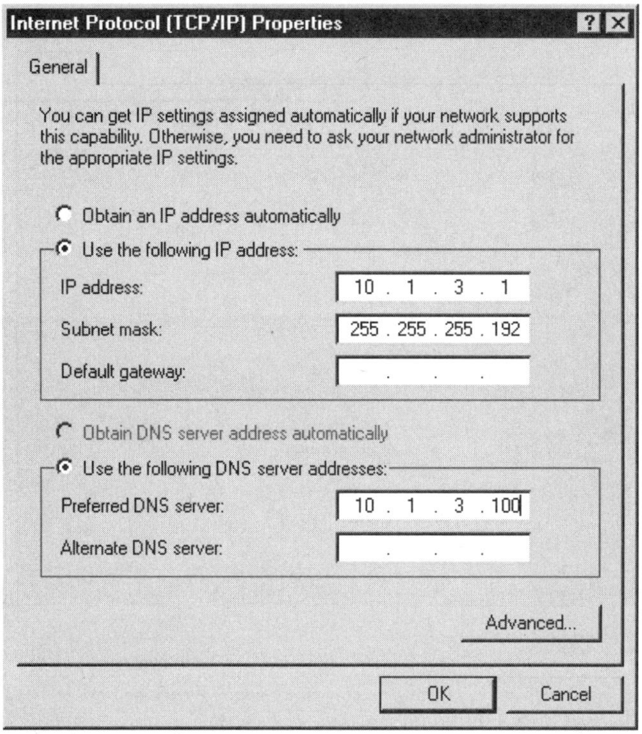

Figure 13-2. Selecting the TCP/IP properties during automated installation

When you first log on, you will see the Configure Your Server wizard, which walks you through the rest of the installation (see Figure 13-3). The wizard should appear automatically, but if not, you can manually invoke the wizard by choosing Start | Programs | Administrative Tools | Configure Your Server.

The wizard guides you through the installation of the Microsoft Active Directory, DHCP, and DNS. Use the information you designed and planned for in Chapters 6 and 7 to create the Active Directory.

Only Server in the Network

If you have a single-server environment, select the option called This Is the Only Server in My Network, and then click Next to continue. You will be prompted with a warning that cautions you to automatically configure the server with Active Directory, DHCP, and

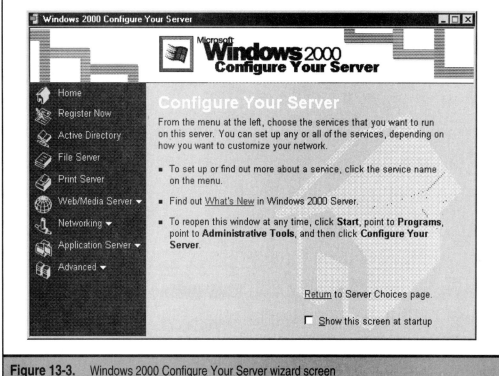

Figure 13-3. Windows 2000 Configure Your Server wizard screen

DNS if an existing server already exists on your network and runs these services. If this is the only server on the network, click Next to continue.

Domain Name

The next screen allows you to initiate your Active Directory tree. There are two fields to fill in. The first field prompts you for the name of the Windows 2000 domain. Recall from Chapter 2 that the Windows 2000 domain name can be the small workgroup you are creating as the initial security zone of the Active Directory tree. Ultimately this domain name can be one of a few different peer-level Windows 2000 domains with independent security administration rules. If you have mapped out your entire Windows 2000 Active Directory, and this server will be the master server for the root of the Active Directory, then the domain name you enter in this screen will be the name of the root of the Active Directory.

The second field contains the registered domain name of the organization. As we determined in Chapter 7, this is the internal namespace you use for your organization. If you are using the same internal namespace as external namespace, enter the registered Internet domain name that you are publicly known as (for example, inacom.com). However, if your organization has different internal and external namespaces, you may be known as inacom.com to the general public, but your internal namespace may be inac.com. Enter your internal namespace in the second field.

If you do not have a registered Internet domain name, enter **local** into the second field.

The bottom two fields on the page are automatically generated, showing you a preview of your Active Directory domain name and the NetBIOS name for the domain. The end result is a screen similar to the one in Figure 13-4.

Scroll down the page and click Next to continue.

A message will be displayed, telling you that Setup is complete and your server will reboot when you click Next. After the computer reboots, you can log on to the server.

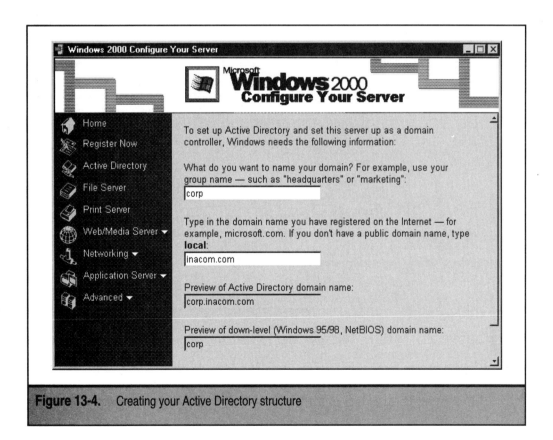

Figure 13-4.   Creating your Active Directory structure

Configuring an IP Address

After your server reboots and you log on as Administrator again, the Configure Your Server wizard returns to prompt you to configure the IP address for the server. This portion of the wizard does not walk you directly through the installation process of the IP address. The system will only prompt you with the steps you need to take to configure a static IP address. The steps are as follows:

1. Right-click My Network Places, and click on Properties.
2. Right-click Local Area Network Connection, and click Properties.
3. Click the Internet Protocol (TCP/IP) component, and click Properties.
4. Check Use the Following IP Address.
5. In the IP Address field, type in the static IP address you want to define for the server.
6. In the Subnet Mask field, type in the subnet mask you have defined for the server.
7. Click OK and OK again to finish.

Once you set a static IP address for the server, you need to authorize the DHCP services on the server, effectively enabling DHCP on the system. The wizard has a link to the DHCP MMC snap-in, however the process is as follows:

1. Launch the DHCP Administrator (Start | Programs | Administrative Tools | DHCP).
2. Expand the DHCP Server service.
3. Right-click the server you wish to edit.
4. Click on Authorize.

After you have completed these steps, reboot the server and log on again.

Configuring Additional Services

When the system reboots, the Configure Your Server wizard continues (as shown in Figure 13-5), giving you the opportunity to install a number of additional services on the server. The options include creating shared folders for network information sharing, creating shared printers for networking printing, implementing Web Server or Streaming Media services, installing remote access or routing services, implementing thin client terminal services, or configuring clustering or message queue services.

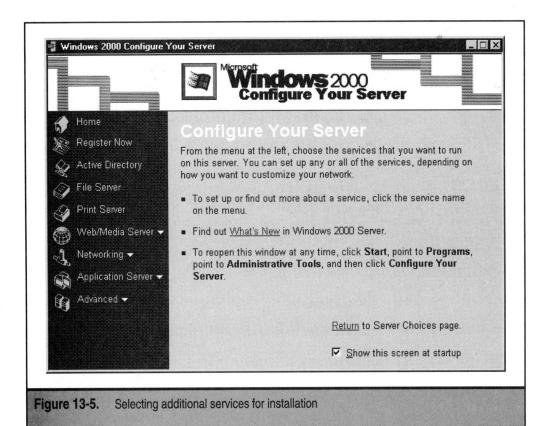

Figure 13-5.   Selecting additional services for installation

ADDING EXTRA DOMAIN CONTROLLERS

If you have an existing domain controller on the network and you are adding another domain controller, the installation process remains the same as outlined in the previous section of this chapter. After Windows 2000 has been installed and the system reboots, log on to the server with the Administrator account and password when prompted at the CTRL-ALT-DEL screen.

When you first log on to the server, you will be prompted with a Configure Your Server wizard that will walk you through the rest of the installation and allow you to add this server as an additional domain controller for the Windows 2000 network.

Already One or More Servers on the Network

Because you have existing servers in your environment, select the There Are Already One or More Servers Operating in My Network option, and click Next to continue. Since an additional server on the network will not require Active Directory, DHCP, or DNS installed by default, you will see a menu of configuration options for manually configuring the server for functions such as an Active Directory domain controller, file/print server, and the like.

UPGRADING A MEMBER SERVER TO A DOMAIN CONTROLLER

Unlike previous versions of the Windows NT operating system, you don't have to decide at the time of installation whether a server is going to be a member server or a domain controller. You can upgrade a Windows 2000 member server to a domain controller at any time, by running the DCPromo utility. Many organizations are choosing this route, adding a server to the network and making sure it's stabilized and tested prior to adding the critical Active Directory services to the system.

Preparing to Upgrade a Member Server

Prior to upgrading a member server to a domain controller, the installer should validate a number of things to ensure the upgrade is completed successfully. While the upgrade process is quite simple, not validating some of the information could result in undesired outcomes. Before conducting an upgrade, validate the following:

▼ *The server meets Windows 2000 compatibility requirements.* Since the server will be a critical component of the security and authentication operation of the network, ensuring the server meets Microsoft's hardware compatibility requirements will minimize the chance of a server problem causing network logon and authentication problems.

■ *The server is operating reliably.* Testing the server's reliability will minimize the chance of a system problem causing interruption or failure of logon and authentication services.

■ *The time, date, and time zone settings are valid.* Since time and date are important to the domain contention resolution, ensuring that the proper time, date, and the time zone are set prior to promoting the server will minimize the chance of a time-related network error.

▲ *Validate the server name and IP address.* As with all core servers on the network, you should ensure the server name is what you want for the server prior to promoting the server. You can easily change the server name or the IP address prior to the server promotion (assuming that there are no other services running on the server that are closely tied to the server name and IP address), and then proceed with the server promotion.

Running the DCPromo Utility

To upgrade a server from a member server to a domain controller you run dcpromo.exe, which is automatically installed on a server during the installation of Windows 2000. To run the software, follow these steps:

1. Boot the server to Windows 2000.
2. Log on as an administrator of the domain that has the rights to manage the Active Directory.
3. Select Start | Run.
4. Enter **dcpromo.exe** and press ENTER.

A wizard opens, and the first screen asks whether you want the server to be the domain controller for a new domain (effectively creating the first server of brand new domain) or whether it will be an additional domain controller on an existing domain.

If you specify that this server will just be an additional domain controller on the network, you are prompted to enter the domain administrator password. Then you are attached to the existing domain and the server is made a replica of an existing domain controller.

If you are creating a new domain with this server, you are walked through the creation of either the root of a new Active Directory domain tree or a new child domain of an existing domain tree. When you create a new domain tree, you are prompted to either create a new forest or integrate the new domain into an existing forest.

You are then prompted to enter the full DNS name of the server. If you are using the same internal and external namespace, then the domain name you enter will be the same as your publicly registered domain name. If you have different internal and external namespaces, enter your internal domain name. When you click Next, it may take a while for the wizard to configure and internally register the domain name for your network. The next screen will prompt you for the NetBIOS domain name that provides backward compatibility with earlier versions of Windows.

In the next screen, you will be prompted to enter the location of the Active Directory database and log files. The default location for the Active Directory is the c:\winnt\ntds directory. The default location for the log file is on the same drive and in the same directory as the main Active Directory file. For performance and fault tolerance reasons, it is best to store the log files on a completely different drive partition than the Active Directory files. That way, if the Active Directory were to get corrupted, you could restore the Active Directory from tape, and then replay the logs stored on the other drive to bring the database back to the same condition it was the morning before.

Lastly, you are prompted to enter the name of the directory where you want to store the server's copy of the domain's public files. This is a fault-tolerant process, and it can take a while, so be patient.

The system then automatically installs RAS and confirms the modifications and settings (which are saved and archived in case you ever need this information). Upon completing this step, the Active Directory is installed. This step can take several minutes to complete. When it is done, you will be prompted to reboot the system.

DEMOTING A DOMAIN CONTROLLER TO A MEMBER SERVER

Unlike previous versions of the Windows NT operating system, Windows 2000 provides the ability to demote a domain controller to a member server. It's a somewhat crude method, but it is highly effective in its end result. The demotion of a domain controller simply involves uninstalling the Active Directory service of the Windows 2000 server.

Preparing to Uninstall the Active Directory

Uninstalling the Active Directory component of a server is a fairly simple task, however it does have irreversible consequences, so you should do a number of things prior to deleting the Active Directory.

Deleting Replica Information

Because Windows 2000 provides a replicated directory service, the information stored on this domain controller may very well be stored in other domain controllers on the network. However, you cannot make that assumption, and you should make sure the information resides elsewhere. If the Active Directory replica information resides on the Global Catalog of the domain, then there is a complete copy of the directory information still residing elsewhere in the domain.

Another factor to consider is where the next nearest domain controller resides. If the domain controller you are deleting is the only domain controller in a site or on "this side" of a WAN connection, you need to realize that authentication will take place over a slow WAN connection. While this does not cause the network to fail, deleting the local domain controller could have significant effects on the performance and operation of the network.

NOTE: When deleting the Active Directory on a server, I have found that if you just take the server "offline" (basically just disconnecting the server from a LAN/WAN port connection), you can see the effect of deleting the system as a domain controller on the network. Within a day, you will see the bandwidth demands on other resources in the organization, as well as the response time to Active Directory requests being made to the domain without this domain controller on the network.

Deleting the Global Catalog

You cannot demote a server if it is acting as the global catalog for the organization. Typically there is only one global catalog in the entire domain and it is the master record of all domain information. Even though the domain information is replicated throughout the domain, all the site servers depend on the main global catalog for the master domain information. Eliminating the global catalog makes replicas invalid.

Uninstalling the Active Directory

To uninstall the Active Directory, run the domain controller promotion utility, DCPromo. To do so, follow these steps:

1. Choose Start | Run.

2. Enter **dcpromo.exe** on the command line, and press ENTER.

The DCPromo utility that typically upgrades a member server to a domain controller will recognize that the server is already a domain controller. A wizard will prompt you to confirm that you want to demote the server, using the screen shown in Figure 13-6.

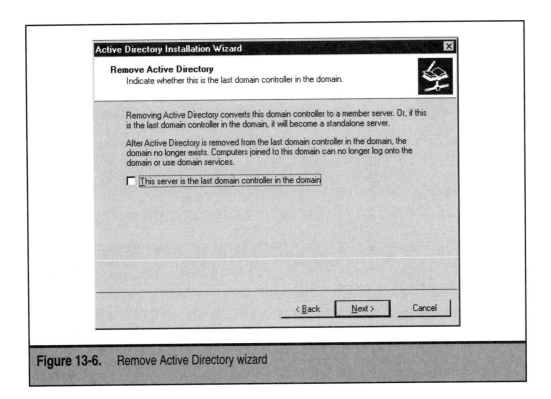

Figure 13-6. Remove Active Directory wizard

If the domain controller is the last domain controller of a domain, select the This Server is the Last Domain Controller in the Domain checkbox, so that the server will be demoted to a stand-alone server. Otherwise the server will think it is part of a domain that no longer exists (since you deleted the last domain controller in the domain). Click Next and enter the password for the domain controller. You will be shown a warning that you are deleting the domain controller services and making the server a member server (or stand-alone server).

INSTALLING DNS SERVERS IN A WINDOWS NT 2000 ENVIRONMENT

Because Windows 2000 is based on DNS for name resolution, you need at least one DNS server on the network. Large organizations with multiple offices and extensive infrastructures design and implement very sophisticated DNS designs.

Preparing for Your DNS Installation

DNS is not a technology that can be installed haphazardly and then tuned and fixed later. DNS is based on a structured hierarchy that requires top-down implementation. Since every Windows 2000 server and workstation depends on a valid DNS server to resolve resource names to physical addresses, implementing DNS properly from the start is important.

Determining the Type of DNS installation

As discussed in Chapter 7, there are three arrangements for utilizing DNS:

▼ Having a Windows 2000 DNS server at the root of the DNS structure for the entire organization

■ Setting Windows 2000 DNS to be subordinate to an existing non-Windows 2000 DNS server

▲ Providing DNS name resolution from a non-Windows 2000 DNS structure

It is important to know the type of DNS implementation you want for your organization as you add a DNS server or multiple DNS servers to your environment.

Gathering Important DNS Information

As you prepare to implement a DNS server in your environment, you should refer to the information you designed in Chapter 7. You will need the following information:

▼ **Name of the domain**   You will need the Windows 2000 domain name, and if you have a registered Internet domain name, you will need that as well.

- ■ **IP address** Since a DNS server is the primary system for name resolution and security, the server should have a static IP address rather than a dynamically acquired IP address.

- ■ **Network subnet mask and default gateway address** The subnet mask and the default gateway address for the segment upon which the server resides should be identified at the same time the IP address is acquired.

- ▲ **DNS forwarding address** If your DNS servers forward unresolved DNS requests to other DNS servers for name resolution, you will need to know the IP address of the target DNS server.

Installing the DNS Component

The Microsoft DNS component can be installed at the time of the initial Windows 2000 installation or from the Windows Control Panel's Add/Remove Programs option.

If DNS was not installed in the initial Windows 2000 installation, you can install the DNS component from the Windows Control Panel using the Add/Remove Programs command. To install the component, follow these steps:

1. Choose Start | Settings | Control Panel.

2. Double Click Add/Remove Programs.

3. Click Add/Remove Windows Components.

4. Select the Networking Services.

5. Click on Details.

6. A list of components will be displayed, with installed components being check marked. If DNS is not checked, you can install the DNS component at this time by selecting the checkbox and clicking on Next to proceed with the installation.

You are prompted to install your Windows 2000 CD if the installation files are not on an accessible network share. Click Finish to install DNS.

Configuring a Primary Name Server

A primary name server acts as a zones point of update where all name servers on the zone go to get a copy of name resolution information. You can configure a zone either as a standard primary zone, or as a primary zone integrated with Active Directory. As noted in Chapter 7, you would want to have the primary zone integrated with the Active Directory to take advantage of the capabilities of Windows 2000 security and resource management functions. However, if the organization decides not to integrate the zone with Active Directory, Windows 2000 supports standard primary zone configurations. The way you integrate DNS depends on whether you use the Windows 2000 Active Directory or a non-Microsoft DNS server.

The easiest way to set up DNS is to use the Configure DNS Server wizard. If you have not configured DNS on the server yet, the first time you launch the DNS Administrator, the Configure DNS Server wizard activates. To launch the DNS Administrator, choose Start | Programs | Administrative Tools | DNS.

TIP: If you have already begun the installation of DNS and decide you want to use the wizard, delete your DNS configuration. This causes the system to prompt you to build the DNS configuration through the wizard.

The first wizard screen asks if this server is the first server on the network, or if DNS is running on an existing server. To create the primary name server on the system, select the first server option, as shown in Figure 13-7.

1. Choose the This Is the First DNS Server on this Network option, and click Next.
2. Choose the Yes, Add Forward Lookup Zone option, and click Next.
   If this server is an internal name server, and you also require external name resolution to the Internet, identify the IP address of a name server that resolves to the general Internet as a DNS forwarder.

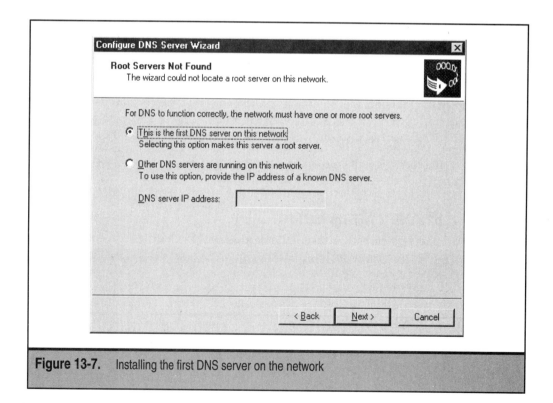

Figure 13-7. Installing the first DNS server on the network

3. Choose the Standard Primary option and click Next
   If this is the first primary server, the wizard creates a master copy of the new zone in the master host text file. If you have other primary servers on the network, opt to create this server as a standard secondary, which causes a replica of an existing zone to be created. For this case, select Standard Primary, since this is the first DNS server on the network.

4. Type the name of new zone, and choose Next.
   Enter a name for the zone you are creating, using the dotted domain format, such as sales.abccompany.com.

5. Type the name of the DNS zone file to be used, and click Next.
   The DNS zone file is the hard file copy of the DNS information gathered by the DNS server. By default, the zone file takes the name of the dotted domain zone created in step 4, adding the .dns file extension (for example, sales.abccompany.com.dns). The file is stored in the %systemroot%\system32\dns folder.

6. Choose the No, Do Not Add a Reverse Lookup Zone, and then click Next.
   If you want to create additional zones under this primary name server, choose Yes to add a reverse lookup zone that will allow requests to resolve IP addresses into names for the zone. (You can also do this later.)

Configuring the Properties for Your New Zone

After you install the basic DNS name server configuration using the Configure DNS Server wizard, you can add, edit, and update the properties for the zone by using the DNS Administrator snap-in (Start | Programs | Administrative Tools | DNS). In the DNS administrator tool when you select Actions | Properties you have a series of tab pages to make modifications to the DNS configuration.

Interfaces

If your server has a second network adapter, you may want to configure a list of the IP addresses DNS must listen to for requests on the Interfaces tab. Perhaps one adapter serves the internal trusted network and the other adapter connects to an external, untrusted network. However, if the DNS server is to resolve names only on the internal trusted network, you only need to configure the IP address of the adapter serving that internal network. (The adapter to the external network may only be an adapter forwarding DNS requests outside of the internal domain.)

Forwarders

The IP addresses listed in the Forwarders tab are the servers that this DNS server will use to forward unresolved query requests. Commonly, internal DNS servers forward unresolved query requests to an external DNS server.

Advanced

Use the Advanced tab to enable or disable the advanced options for DNS properties. These include options such as disabling recursion, enabling round robin, enabling netmask ordering, and so on.

Root Hints

Root hints are IP addresses and host names for other DNS servers on the network. You can add, remove, or edit list entries. A list of Internet standard name server records are already entered into the list for the *A–Z* root servers. In many large organizations, there are a number of root name servers in the organization that distribute the core names throughout the organization.

Logging

There are eleven options for enabling logging for problem solving and troubleshooting DNS. Enabling any of the logging options causes tracking information to be written to the event log in the Event Viewer (Start | Programs | Administrative Tools | Event Viewer).

Monitoring

Use the Monitoring tab to test the name-resolution process. You can conduct a simple query (send a query test to the DNS resolver and see the response), or a recursive query (forward a query to another DNS server). The test results are displayed at the bottom of the screen.

Creating a Secondary Name Server

If you already have a name server on the network, you can add a secondary name server using the same process described previously, but selecting the secondary name server option. This is helpful for distributing the load for name resolution, and for creating redundancy. To create a secondary name server, launch the DNS management console by selecting Start | Programs | Administrative Tools | DNS.

When the DNS management console appears, launch the Create New Zone wizard by following these steps:

1. Highlight Computer.
2. Click on Actions.
3. Select the Create a New Zone option. (The Create New Zone wizard will launch. Click Next to continue.)
4. Click Standard Secondary (which creates a replica of an existing zone).
5. Select either a forward look-up zone (if you want to map names to addresses) or reverse look-up zone (if you want to map IP addresses to domain names). (Chapter 7 would help you understand which option is best.) Click on Next.

6. Enter the name of the zone you are creating and then press Next.

7. Specify the IP address(es) of the master server(s) from which you want to copy zone information. If you enter multiple IP addresses, sort the list by putting the high priority server at the top of the list (the order in which information is transferred is determined by the list priority). Press Next to continue.

Press Finish to complete the installation.

Configuring DNS in Various DNS Environments

As discussed in Chapter 7, there are three possible scenarios for DNS name resolution. This section covers the procedures you must follow for each of those scenarios.

Windows 2000 as the DNS Root

When a Windows 2000 DNS server is at the root of the DNS hierarchy, follow the installation steps listed previously to install Windows 2000 as the primary name server.

Windows 2000 as Subordinate to an Existing Root

If there is an existing DNS hierarchy, you should subordinate the Windows 2000 DNS to the existing DNS structure. When you install Windows 2000 DNS, configure it as the primary name server (assuming it is the first Windows 2000 DNS server in the zone) and specify the new zone you are creating. For example, if the root of the existing domain is abccompany.com, you could create a new zone named w2k.abccompany.com. All Windows 2000 domain information is placed at and below this zone.

No Windows DNS in the Environment

If there is a non-Windows DNS structure, you cannot install the Windows 2000 DNS component. Instead, you must depend on the existing DNS structure for name resolution. See Chapter 7 for information on name resolution in a non-Windows 2000 DNS environment.

Configuring Dynamic DNS and Zone Transfers

Windows 2000 supports dynamic DNS, so you need to configure and enable dynamic updates and transfers between zones. This is accomplished through the Properties option for the zone forwarding section of DNS. You can access the properties option by right clicking on the zone forwarding option in the DNS administrator screen and selecting properties.

Enabling Dynamic DNS

To enable Dynamic DNS, launch the DNS management console by selecting Start | Programs | Administrative Tools | DNS. Select and expand the domain for which you want to enable dynamic DNS, and then select the forward lookup zone, and expand that section. Select the name of the zone for which you wish to enable dynamic DNS, and then select the pulldown menu Actions, then Properties.

On the General tab, select the Allow Dynamic Update pulldown, as shown in Figure 13-8, to display the options:

▼ **No** This is the default, and no DNS updates will be dynamically updated for this zone.

■ **Yes** Dynamic DNS will update requests for this zone.

▲ **Only Secure Updates** The Only Secure Updates option appears if the zone type is Active-Directory Integrated. Secure updates occur when Windows 2000 DNS security is provided by the Active Directory between Windows 2000 DNS servers.

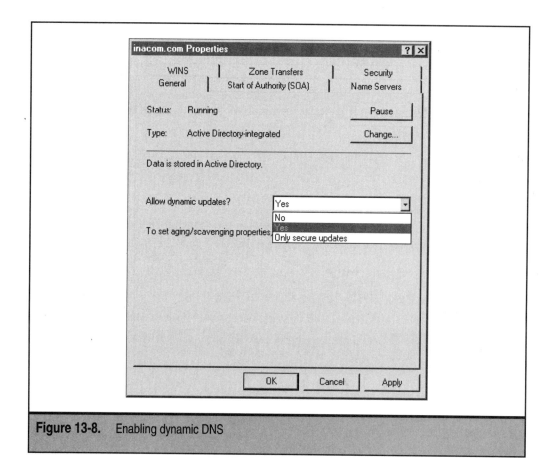

Figure 13-8. Enabling dynamic DNS

Forwarding Zone Transfers to a Secondary Server

If you want to configure your primary name server to allow transfers of the forward lookup zone to a secondary server, launch the DNS management console by choosing Start | Programs | Administrative Tools | DNS.

Select and expand the domain for which you want to enable dynamic DNS. Select and expand the forward lookup zone. Then select the name of the zone and choose Actions and select Properties. You can also select resolve to automatically locate IP addresses.

On the Zone Transfers tab, select Allow Zone Transfers Only to Servers Named in the Name Servers Page, as shown in Figure 13-9. Then go to the Name Servers tab and click ADD. Enter the fully qualified domain name and the IP address of the secondary server to which you are forwarding zone transfers.

This creates a link between the two DNS servers for transfers to the forward lookup zone of the secondary server.

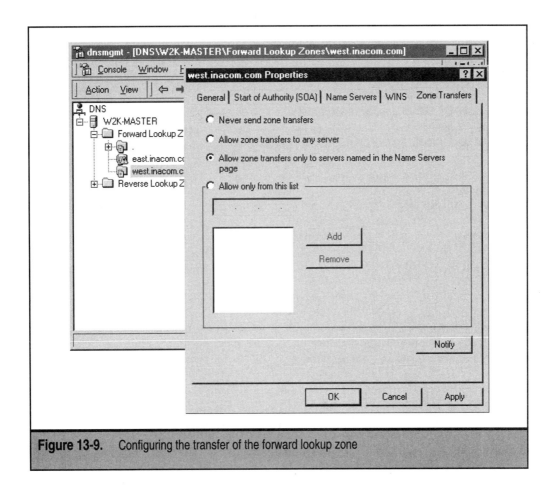

Figure 13-9.   Configuring the transfer of the forward lookup zone

Reverse Lookup Zone Transfers to a Secondary Server

If you want to configure your primary name server to allow transfers of the reverse lookup zone to a secondary server, launch the DNS management console by choosing Start | Programs | Administrative Tools | DNS.

Select and expand the domain for which you want to enable dynamic DNS. Select and expand the reverse lookup zone, and select the name of the zone by choosing Actions and then selecting Properties.

On the Zone Transfers tab, select Allow Zone Transfers Only to Servers Named in the Name Servers Page. Then go to the Name Servers tab and click ADD. Enter the fully qualified domain name and the IP address of the secondary server that you want zone transfers to be forwarded to.

This creates a link between the two DNS servers for transfers to the reverse lookup zone of the secondary server.

Delegating Authority for Subdomains

It is frequently helpful to delegate the administration and management of the DNS servers on your network. In order to assign this authority to an individual, you need to partition DNS into a zone for which authority can be assigned to a user.

The Effect of Delegating Authority

Delegating authority over a subdomain effectively delegates physical access security rights. To administer the subdomain, you must assign administrative rights in the Active Directory that provide full access to the subdomain (including rights for adding users, deleting uses, accessing files or resources, and so on).

Enabling Authority

To delegate authority for a subdomain, launch the DNS management console by choosing Start | Programs | Administrative Tools | DNS.

Select and expand the domain, and then select and expand the forward lookup zone. Select the name of the zone and then choose Actions | New Delegation.

The Add New Delegation wizard will open and prompt you to click Next. The wizard will then prompt you to enter the name of the subdomain for which you want to delegate authority. Enter the name and click Next, then enter the host name and the IP address of the DNS server that will host the delegated zone. Click Add and then OK. Select Next, then Finish to complete the configuration.

INSTALLING WINDOWS 2000 DHCP SERVERS

To simplify IP addressing and create a dynamic IP assignment system, Windows 2000 Server allows you to configure any server with DHCP services. DHCP can be configured either automatically (with wizards) or manually (by configuring parameters).

Preparing for Your Installation

Before you begin your Windows 2000 DHCP implementation, there is information you need to gather in order to answer the questions that are presented during the configuration.

IP Scheme

The first thing you need to know is the IP scheme for your network. Review the IP scheme you created in Chapter 2. You need to know the IP address of the server on which you are installing DHCP (assuming the IP address has already been statically set), and you need to know the segment and subnet mask for the segment that this DHCP server will be servicing.

Reserved IP Addresses on the Segment

Besides the basic range of IP addresses for which the server will provide dynamic IP addressing, you need to know whether any of the addresses are reserved by other static devices. You must enter these reserved addresses when you configure DHCP in order to prevent the DHCP server from allocating an address that conflicts with another core server or device on the network.

Scopes, Superscopes, and Multicast Scopes

Windows 2000 supports scopes, superscopes, and multicast scopes. A DHCP *scope* consists of a range of TCP/IP addresses on the same subnet. This configuration supports a single physical network and one range of IP addresses. Most small networks have only a single subnet and can be serviced by a single DHCP server. To improve network performance, most larger networks break their subnets into groups of 70–80 devices per a subnet (see Chapter 18 for more details on optimizing the Windows 2000 network). When you need multiple subnets, you have to create a scope for each subnet, and combine the scopes into a superscope.

A *superscope* can support multiple scopes, which simplifies the configuration and setup of the scopes. Superscopes can be configured to support a network where multiple logical IP subnets are being used.

A *multicast scope* is used when multicast DHCP (MDHCP) is required. Multicast communication occurs when a transmission is sent to multiple servers on the network. Most network communication is one-to-one, as a specific device communicates with another specific device. However, for group-based communications, you can add a device to enable communications to go to all devices in the group. Multicast addresses are made up of Class D addresses (224.0.0.0 to 239.255.255.255).

IP Scheme Details

Once you determine the scope(s) for your DHCP server, you need to know the basic TCP/IP scheme details, such as the subnet mask, the default gateway address on your network, and an internal or external DNS address. If your network is configured for WINS, the address of the network WINS server is needed as well.

DHCP Scope Name

You need a name for your DHCP scope. This can be any arbitrary name, but it is generally best to select a name that allows you to easily identify the scope (such as SC10-1-x-x).

Lease Duration

Lease duration is the time that the IP address assignment is available to the user before it is made available to another device on the network. If your network rarely changes, a relatively static IP design makes it easy to identify devices on the network. However, the whole purpose of using dynamic IP addressing is to reassign unused IP addresses. If you set the lease duration for 15 days, and then remove a device from the network, the IP address will not go back into the general IP pool for 15 days. If devices change frequently, you can easily run out of IP addresses in your scope.

Conversely, if you set a very short lease duration, perhaps a single day, over the weekend all leases will expire, and on Monday, all systems will request a new IP address. It's quite common for lease duration to be set to three days, which is long enough to maintain leases over an extended three-day weekend, but not so long that leases may never be released.

Adding the DHCP Component to a Server

Before you can run DHCP on a server, it must be installed and configured.

Is DHCP Installed?

You can verify whether the DHCP component is installed by doing the following:

1. Choose Start | Settings | Control Panel.
2. Double Click Add/Remove Programs.
3. Click Add/Remove Windows Components.
4. Select the Networking Service component.
5. Click on Details.
6. A menu of the installed components will appear. If DHCP is not selected, install the DHCP component at this time.

Installing the DHCP Component

To install the DHCP component, continue the steps just described by selecting the DHCP component and clicking Next to continue. You will be prompted to insert your Windows

2000 CD (if the installation files are not on a network share on your local hard drive). Click Finish when prompted.

Configuring the DHCP Service

DHCP configuration is done from the Microsoft Management Console (MMC) DHCP snap-in. This can be launched by choosing Start | Programs | Administrative Tools | DHCP.

In the console tree, select the DHCP server in which you want to create the new scope. Click the Actions tab and go to the New Scope option to launch the Create Scope wizard.

Create Scope Wizard

The Create Scope wizard walks you through the installation of a DHCP scope on your server. It provides prompts as well as recommendations throughout the installation process. The wizard also guides you through the configuration of options such as the default gateway address, DNS server address, and WINS server address.

After clicking Next to get past the welcome screen, you will have to name the scope using a name that allows you to identify the scope easily and click Next to accept it. You must then enter the starting and ending IP addresses for the scope, as well as the subnet mask. Click Next to continue. Enter any addresses, or range of addresses, that need to be excluded and click Next. Specify the length of the lease, which defaults to 8 days, and click Next to continue.

The next wizard screen asks whether you want to configure the most common DHCP options. If you are unsure, just select the default Yes to set up the options for default gateway, DNS server, and WINS setting (you are prompted step-by-step in the next three screens). When you complete these entries, you are asked whether you want to activate the scope. Select Yes, and your server will now respond to DHCP requests. Click Finish to exit the wizard.

Manually Configuring Scope Options

If you don't select the most common options, or if you want to modify the settings of the DHCP management console, you can configure the scope options. From the DHCP management console, select the DHCP server you want to modify, expand the Scope definition, and then select the Scope Options folder. Then select the Action item on the menu bar and scroll down to select Configure Options.

When Configured Options open, you have a series of check boxes you can select to enable or disable. You can configure new options by checking the option you wish to add. When you enable an option, a data entry screen will appear at the bottom of the DHCP Options properties screen so you can enter the information for the selected option. To add a default gateway (also known as a router), fill in that screen (see Figure 13-10).

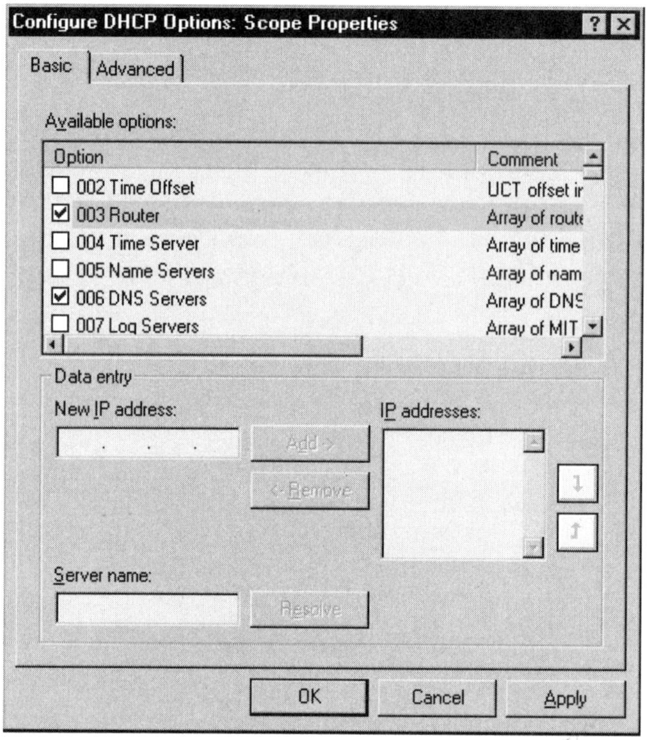

Figure 13-10.   Entering scope configuration options

Creating a New DHCP Superscope

You can also create a superscope, which permits a server to manage multiple network segments and scopes. To accomplish this, follow these steps:

1. Open the DHCP administration console by choosing Start | Programs | Administrative Tools | DHCP.

2. The DHCP administration console will appear. In the console tree, select the DHCP server on which you want to create the superscope.

3. Click the Actions tab, select New, and choose New Superscope to launch the Create Superscope wizard. Click next to get past the welcome screen.

4. You will be prompted to name the superscope you are creating on the first screen, as well as the scope(s) you want to add to the superscope (these are child scopes) on the second screen. Select the specific scopes to add to the superscope, and click Finish to complete.

NOTE: Once a superscope has been configured, additional new scopes can be added to the superscope at any time. Simply add a scope directly to the superscope.

Creating a New Multicast Scope

To create a Multicast Scope, follow these steps:

1. Open the DHCP administration console by choosing Start | Programs | Administrative Tools | DHCP.

2. The DHCP administration console will appear. In the console tree, select the DHCP server on which you want to create the new multicast scope.

3. Click the Actions tab, select New Multicast Scope. This opens the Create Multicast Scope wizard.

4. The wizard prompts you to name the multicast scope you are creating. You are also prompted to select the range of multicast IP addresses (from 224.0.0.0 to 239.255.255.255) to define, along with any address exclusions and the length of the multicast scope duration.

You can then activate the Multicast scope.

CHAPTER 14

Installing and Managing Windows 2000 Professional

During the installation of Windows 2000 Professional, you will face a number of decisions about configuration settings and installation parameters, which I will explain in this chapter. In addition, this chapter covers automated installation processes that help simplify the implementation of Windows 2000 Professional in an organization.

BEFORE YOU BEGIN . . .

Whenever you install a new operating system, you have to make decisions about components and configuration. In addition, you have to have information about your network at hand, because the data is important for the configuration process.

For Windows 2000, you must verify that your hardware is compatible with the operating system. Check your hardware and peripherals against the Windows 2000 Hardware Compatibility List that Microsoft posts on its Web site. Check with the manufacturers of your hardware to see if there are updated drivers that you should use.

An Upgrade vs. a New Installation

If you are installing Windows 2000 on a computer that already runs Windows 9x, Windows NT 3.51 Workstation, or Windows NT 4.0 Workstation, you have to decide whether you are going to upgrade to Windows 2000 Professional or perform a new installation. This section explains the differences.

Upgrading an Existing System

Upgrading to Windows 2000 means installing Windows 2000 Professional into the same folder as your current operating system. Only certain versions of previous operating systems can be upgraded to Windows 2000 Professional, as shown in Table 14-1.

If you have an upgradeable Windows NT Workstation installation, you can keep your existing applications and application settings as long as they run under Windows 2000. Additionally, you can keep the file and folder security settings you've established.

In case things don't work perfectly, perform a backup of your existing desktop setup (programs, data files, and registry settings) prior to attempting an upgrade. This gives you a fallback position. However, if the process goes well (it usually does), your existing data files will survive the upgrade.

Performing a New Installation

For computers that have been in use for some time, a new installation of an operating system is a fresh start, and it is less likely to inherit files and registry settings that can cause problems. However, a new installation ignores (and loses) all previous configuration settings and software settings, including registry settings and parameters that were set in a previous installation of the operating system.

If you currently have applications or data on the drive on which you plan to do a new installation, make a full backup of all the information on the drive.

Existing Operating System	Can You Upgrade to Windows 2000?
DOS or Windows v3.1	No.
Windows 95, 98	Yes.
Windows NT 3.51 Workstation	Yes.
Windows NT 4.0 Workstation	Yes.
Windows NT Workstation, prior to v 3.51	No. You must first upgrade to version 3.51 or 4.0; then you can upgrade to Windows 2000.
Any version of NT Server	No.

Table 14-1.   Upgrade Compatibilities with Windows 2000 Professional

Information to Gather

During a Windows 2000 Professional installation, you will be asked for information about the way you want your system configured. The program will take the information you provide and customize the installation of your Windows 2000 system so that it meets your requirements. (A number of these decisions are discussed in previous chapters.)

The Computer Name

Each computer on a network must be given a unique computer name. The computer name can contain up to 63 characters, but it is important to note that pre-Windows 2000 computers will only recognize the first 15 characters.

It's best to use only Internet-standard characters in the computer name. These characters consist of the numbers 0–9, the letters A–Z (both upper and lower case), and the hyphen (-).

If you are running Microsoft DNS service on your network, you can use some non-Internet-standard characters in your computer name. Examples of this include using Unicode characters and other nonstandard characters such as the underscore (_). However, the use of such nonstandard characters may cause compatibility problems with non-Microsoft DNS servers on your network.

Name of the Workgroup or Domain

During the installation process, you will be asked for the name of the workgroup or domain that the workstation will be installed into. You can enter the name of an existing workgroup or domain (if this computer is part of an existing organizational structure), or you can enter a new workgroup name (effectively creating a new structure).

> *TIP:*   You can select a workgroup installation (picking any name for your workgroup), and then join a domain at a later date.

If you are joining an existing Windows 2000 domain, a domain administrator must add the computer name in the Active Directory tree.

IP Address of the System

You will be prompted to provide an Internet Protocol (IP) address and a DNS Server address to be used by your Windows 2000 workstation. There are three methods of assigning an IP address in Windows 2000: static IP, dynamic IP, and Automatic Private IP.

▼ **Dynamic IP**   Dynamically assigned IP addresses are most common for workstations, where DHCP dynamically assigns the IP address of the workstation during boot-up. Dynamic DNS and DNS name resolution are built into Windows 2000, making it possible for a workstation to have its IP address change and still have the resources on the network find the workstation. Because workstations are regularly upgraded, replaced, or modified, dynamically assigning an IP address minimizes the need to track static IP addresses, or reuse the same IP address on a replacement computer.

■ **Static IP**   Static IP addresses are usually used for servers, but static addressing for workstations is permissible. However, you must create a database to track the addresses for each workstation on the network.

▲ **Automatic Private IP Addressing**   APIPA allows a Windows 2000 computer to automatically assign itself an IP address from a generic pool of IP addresses. Unlike previous versions of Windows NT, which required an IP address to be enabled on a workstation for the system to function on the network (either statically assigned or assigned by a valid DHCP server on the network), Windows 2000 can temporarily assign itself an IP address and complete its boot cycle. The server administrator can then statically assign, or request DHCP to assign, an IP address for the computer without requiring a reboot. This is especially important for an organization that configures its workstations in a lab environment, where IP addressing is different from the production environment. APIPA is also useful if a LAN adapter fails to activate during installation. Rather than stopping the installation, fixing the problem, and then restarting the installation from scratch, APIPA allows the installation to continue and the IP address setting to be resolved afterwards.

Backing Up Your Existing Files

If the computer you are using for your Windows 2000 Professional installation has any data that you wish to keep, it is important that you back up your files prior to installation.

WINDOWS 2000 PROFESSIONAL INSTALLATION OPTIONS

Windows 2000 Professional provides a variety of installation methods: floppy disks, bootable CD-ROM (if your BIOS supports it), a network share, or a non-bootable CD-ROM.

In addition, you can choose an automated installation, an unattended installation, a command-line installation, or a cloned installation.

Floppy Disk Installation

You can install Windows 2000 Professional from specially created floppy disks, called Setup disks. If your Windows 2000 Professional package didn't include the four Setup disks, you can create them from the Windows 2000 CD-ROM. Typically, the floppy disk method is used if you do not have a bootable CD-ROM drive or the DOS drivers needed to access the CD-ROM drive.

If you need to create the diskettes, take four blank, formatted 3.5-inch diskettes, and follow these steps:

1. Label the diskettes as follows: Setup Disk 1, Setup Disk 2, Setup Disk 3, and Setup Disk 4.

2. Insert the Windows 2000 CD-ROM into a computer running Windows NT or Windows 9*x*. Insert the disk labeled Setup Disk 1 in the floppy disk drive.

3. From the Start menu, choose Run and enter *x*:**bootdisk****makeboot.exe A:** where *x* is the drive letter of your CD-ROM drive. You should see a screen similar to the one shown in Figure 14-1.

4. Follow the prompts to insert the remaining diskettes.

After you have created the four Setup diskettes, go to the system on which you want to install Windows 2000 Professional and boot the computer with Setup Disk 1 in the A drive. As the system is booting, insert the Windows 2000 CD-ROM into the CD-ROM drive of the system.

Follow the prompts to insert the remaining diskettes. Assuming your CD-ROM drive is Windows 2000-compatible, the diskette boot process will eventually load the CD-ROM driver for the system and complete the installation from the Windows 2000 CD-ROM.

Network Share or Non-Bootable CD-ROM Drive Installation

In order to install Windows 2000 Professional from a network share or non-bootable CD-ROM drive, you need to establish access to the files.

To gain access to a network share, use MS-DOS networking commands, or an existing Windows-based system. The network share is either a shared CD-ROM drive, or a shared directory that holds the files from the Windows 2000 CD-ROM (the folder named \i386 for Intel-based systems).

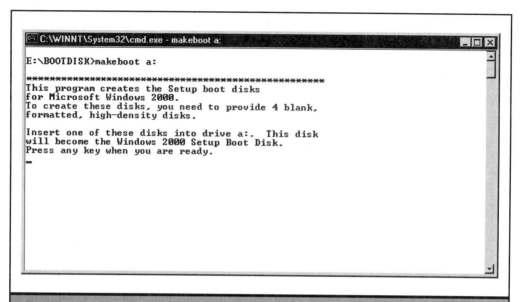

```
C:\WINNT\System32\cmd.exe - makeboot a:                    _ □ X

E:\BOOTDISK>makeboot a:

***********************************************************
This program creates the Setup boot disks
for Microsoft Windows 2000.
To create these disks, you need to provide 4 blank,
formatted, high-density disks.

Insert one of these disks into drive a:.  This disk
will become the Windows 2000 Setup Boot Disk.
Press any key when you are ready.
_
```

Figure 14-1. The Makeboot utility for creating bootable Windows 2000 diskettes

To install from a non-bootable CD-ROM drive, you must be able to access the drive, either by loading DOS drivers or through your existing Windows operating system.

TIP: You could also copy the \i386 directory to the local hard drive of the system on which you are installing Windows 2000.

Use either the Run command or an MS-DOS command prompt to begin the installation:

▼ Enter **winnt32.exe** from a computer running Windows 95, Windows 98, Windows NT 3.51, Windows NT 4.0, or a previous release of Windows 2000.

▲ Enter **winnt.exe** from any other operating system.

NOTE: For the best performance while running Setup from MS-DOS, you should have Smartdrive running to provide disk caching. To accomplish this, add the command **device=himem.sys** to the config.sys file, and add the command **smartdrv 8192 8192** to the autoexec.bat file on the boot drive of your MS-DOS system.

Bootable CD-ROM Drive Installation

The easiest installation of Windows 2000 Professional is to boot straight from the Windows 2000 CD-ROM. Insert the Windows 2000 Professional CD-ROM into the CD-ROM drive, and boot the computer. Setup starts automatically.

Some computers require a change in the BIOS configuration to boot from a CD-ROM drive if a bootable CD is present rather than booting from the hard drive. This option is frequently designated as "boot priority" or "boot sequence." Access the BIOS setup using the appropriate keystrokes during boot-up.

Automated Windows 2000 Professional Installation

The automated installation of Windows 2000 Professional, using the Setup wizard, is the most common way of installing Windows 2000. The wizard prompts you for information and automatically installs the most common applications and files onto the system.

The Windows 2000 Professional Setup wizard greatly minimizes the number of questions asked during the installation process by selecting the most common settings by default. If you want to change the default settings, there are a number of options in the command-line installation process (described in the next section) that allow you to override the default settings. As an example, one of the defaults assumed in the Setup wizard is that the Windows 2000 software will be installed in c:\winnt. Rather than prompting the user to enter the default directory, this question has been eliminated from the installation process. See the section on command-line installation later in this chapter for the override options.

After you boot to the Windows 2000 CD or launch winnt.exe, and the first installation series and system reboot occurs, the Windows 2000 Setup wizard launches. The following explanations walk you through the installation of the Windows 2000 Setup wizard.

Welcome to Setup

When the Welcome screen appears, you will be prompted: "To set up Windows 2000 now, press Enter." Do so when you are ready to continue.

If you are installing from the startup disks, you will be prompted to insert the Windows 2000 CD and press ENTER when ready.

The Windows 2000 License Agreement

The next screen you will see is the Windows 2000 Professional license agreement screen. You are shown a copy of the agreement on the screen, and if you accept the terms of the agreement press the F8 key to continue.

Configuring the Disk Partitions

Before Setup can install Windows 2000 Professional, it must know which disk partition to use. A disk partition can be any size from 1MB to the entire volume of the drive(s) in the system. However, the disk partition that contains the Windows 2000 system files must be on a bootable partition with enough available disk space to hold the Windows 2000 operating system files (approximately 400MB for the operating system and minimum page file).

NOTE: Refer to Chapter 5 on disk sizing to ensure that your computer has enough unused disk space for the installation of the Windows 2000 files.

Select a partition that meets these requirements and press ENTER to continue.

Selecting a File System for the Windows 2000 Partition

Setup needs to know which file system you wish to use (FAT or NTFS). Information on selecting the appropriate file system can be found in Chapter 5 of this book.

While certain types of servers (such as domain controllers) must be configured with NTFS, Windows 2000 Professional workstations can be configured for either FAT or NTFS. If you are upgrading your system, and the current file system is FAT, you will be asked whether you want to keep the FAT partition or to upgrade the partition to NTFS. If your current file system is an older version of NTFS (perhaps NTFS4 from Windows NT 4), the partition will automatically be upgraded to NTFS5. If you wish to retain dual boot capability between Windows 2000 Professional and Windows NT 4 Workstation, you need to have Windows NT 4 Service Pack 4 or greater to support the new NTFS5 file system.

Setup configures the partition for the appropriate file system and begins copying files to the Windows 2000 default installation folder (\winnt). After the installation files are copied, you're instructed to remove disks from their drives. Setup automatically restarts the computer to continue installation.

The Windows 2000 Setup Wizard

The screens in the Windows 2000 Setup wizard have a look and feel that are familiar to anyone who has used Windows applications. Use the Next button to continue, or use the Back button to return to a previous screen (if you want to change the information you've entered).

Setup's Detection Phase

Setup detects and installs drivers for system devices, such as audio and multimedia adapters, network adapters, special communication controllers, and so on.

Regional Settings

You can customize Windows 2000 for different regions and languages, as shown in Figure 14-2. Unlike previous versions of Windows that configured only the time zone and keyboard language, the Windows 2000 regional settings configure all international settings for the operating system.

Select the appropriate locale to control how numbers, currencies, and dates will appear on the system. The default is English (United States). Click on the list bar to select your default language and click to highlight the language to change this default.

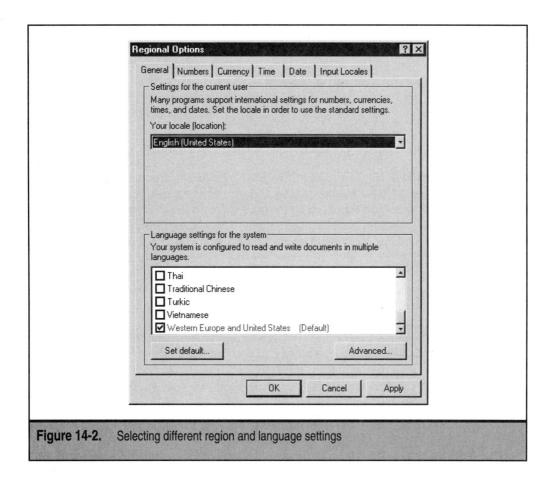

Figure 14-2.   Selecting different region and language settings

On any of these settings, you can install a number of different language sets, choosing one as the default.

Personal Information

Setup uses the information you provide on the next few screens to personalize your Windows 2000 Professional software. You are asked for information about yourself, your organization, the licensing mode you are selecting, and the computer name.

PERSONALIZE YOUR SOFTWARE   The Setup wizard asks for your name and the name of your organization, and this information is used during and after Setup for many operations. You must enter this information for Setup to continue.

Many organizations have a policy that the name entered is not necessarily the name of the person installing the software (like John Smith) but rather a derivative of the business name (such as IT Operations or Corporate Office). The information entered in this screen will show up on the "registered to" section of the Windows 2000 system screen. This information is difficult to change, so it should be set to something the organization is willing to live with. (See Chapter 18 to learn how to change the registered name.) The information you enter has no effect on the actual system name, Active Directory organizational domain name, or other security, administration, or management functions of the system.

COMPUTER NAME AND ADMINISTRATOR PASSWORD   You are next prompted to provide a computer name and an administrator password for your system. Setup suggests a name for the system based on the name you provided in a previous step. You could (and should) enter in your own designated system name. This is the computer name we identified earlier in this chapter in the "Information to Gather" section (if you are joining an existing Active Directory tree, you must use the system name added by the domain administrator).

The Setup wizard creates a default account for the Administrator. This account is granted local administrative rights and privileges for managing the configuration of the computer. Specify the password for this account. Passwords are case-sensitive and can contain up to 127 characters. Enter the password again in the Confirm Password box.

It is important that you enter a password that you can remember, because all administration of the computer is performed by the Administrator account. The password can be changed at any time, and the administration of the computer can be delegated to an administrator of the domain.

Modem Dialing Information

To dial calls correctly, Windows needs information about your current location so it knows whether to add international dialing strings or domestic United States area codes. Enter this information on the screen shown in Figure 14-3.

You need to select your country or region (United States of America is the default), and you are prompted to enter your area or city code. If you must dial a number (such as 9) to get an outside line, specify that number. Select either tone or pulse dialing.

Date and Time Settings

Set the correct date and time for your Windows computer, as well as the appropriate time zone (see Figure 14-4).

If your area uses daylight savings time, ensure that the box for that option is checked.

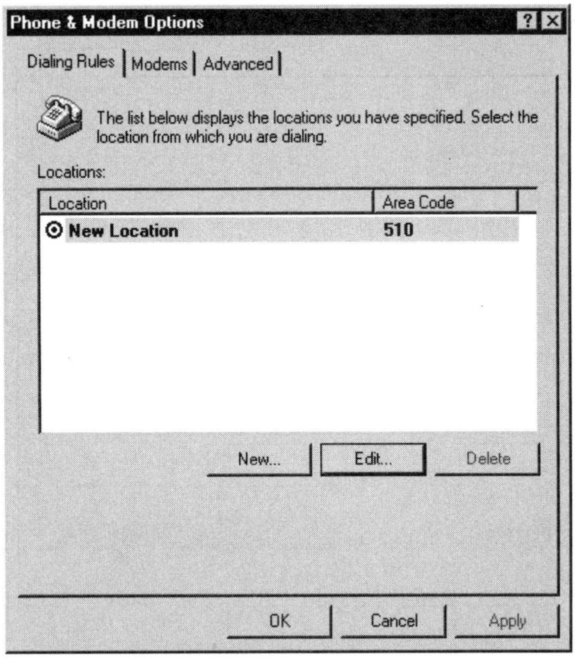

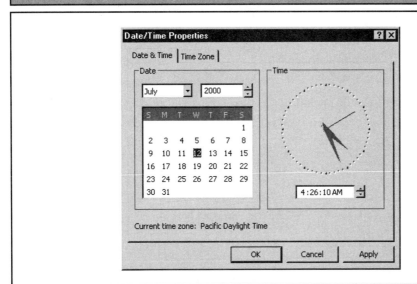

Figure 14-3.   Windows 2000 modem dialing options

Figure 14-4.   Selecting the date, time, and time zone

Network Settings

The next section of the Setup wizard verifies information about your networking configuration. Windows 2000 selects a series of defaults, including the Client for Microsoft Networks and Internet TCP/IP as the protocol. Most organizations find these default settings adequate.

When you select the Properties option of the TCP/IP setting, you see a screen similar to Figure 14-5. By default, the IP address will be dynamically assigned. As noted earlier in this chapter, DHCP is usually preferred for workstations. Enter either the static address for the computer, or accept the default setting for a dynamic address. If a DNS server has been set up on the network, enter the DNS server address in this screen, as well. If you are unsure of the settings for these options, see Chapters 2 and 7 on DNS and IP addressing.

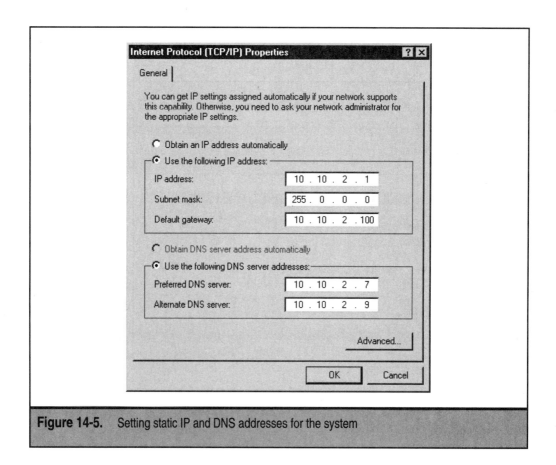

Figure 14-5. Setting static IP and DNS addresses for the system

CUSTOM SETTINGS   If you need to add additional configuration settings beyond the Client for Windows and Internet TCP/IP protocol, choose the Custom Settings option from the main network settings screen. This provides the opportunity to configure additional networking components, such as the following:

▼ Protocols such as NetBEUI or IPX/SPX

▲ Clients such as Client for NetWare Networks

Workgroup or Computer Domain

Now you must enter the name of the workgroup or domain you wish to join. Although you can change the setting after installation, it's preferable to establish these settings now.

Completing the Installation

The balance of the Setup wizard windows install the Start menu items, register the components, save the settings, and remove temporary setup files. Then you are prompted to remove the CD (if any) from the CD-ROM drive and click Finish to continue.

After the operating system has loaded, press CTRL-ALT-DEL to log in. Your administrator name should already be entered. Type your password (remember, the password is case-sensitive) and click OK to continue.

Command-Line Installation

You may want to change the default installation options with customized parameters. For example, you can change the directory where the Windows 2000 operating system files are stored (the default is \winnt), implement an unattended installation, add commands to be executed after the Windows 2000 installation is complete, and so on. All of these optional functions can be activated from a command-line parameter when you execute winnt.exe or winnt32.exe.

Winnt.exe Installation Parameters

During a new installation of Windows 2000 Professional, you can select a handful of slash (/) command-line options. The various parameter options are listed in Table 14-2.

Here are the guidelines for using these parameters.

▼ **/s (Source Location)**   When you execute winnt.exe, the installation program assumes that the installation files are located in the same directory as winnt.exe file. If you locate the installation files elsewhere, such as on a network share, use this parameter to specify the location.

■ **/t (Temporary File Location)**   When you install Windows 2000, about 300MB of files are temporarily copied to the hard drive of the system onto which you are installing Windows 2000. If you're installing on a small drive with limited storage capacity, you may want the temporary files stored on a different drive partition.

Winnt.exe Slash (/) Parameter	Function	Example
/s:*sourcepath*	Source of installation files (x:*path* or *systemsharepath*).	winnt /s:c:\windows
/t:*tempdrive*	Location for temporary files and Windows 2000, unless otherwise specified.	winnt /t:d:\tempdir
/u:*answer_file*	Specify unattended setup using answer file (requires /s).	winnt /u:ansfile.txt /s:c:\winnt
/udf:*id,udf_file*	Indicates the identifier that Setup uses to specify how a uniqueness database file modifies an answer file. /udf overrides the values in the answer file, and the *id* determines which value in the *udf_file* is used. If no *udf_file* is specified, Setup prompts you to insert a disk that contains the $unique$.udb file.	winnt /udf:12,udffile
/r:*folder*	Indicates an optional folder to be installed. (The folder is kept after setup.)	winnt /r:c:\OptFolder
/rx:*folder*	Indicates an optional folder to be copied. (The folder is deleted after setup.)	winnt /r:c:\TempFolder
/e:*command*	Specifies a command to be executed at the end of the GUI-mode setup.	winnt /e:showbanner.exe
/a	Enables accessibility options.	winnt /a

Table 14-2.   Winnt.exe Command-Line Installation Parameters

■ **/u (Unattended Setup)** In an unattended installation of Windows 2000, the answers to all of the questions that are asked during installation are scripted. This allows an administrator to type winnt /u, along with the name of the answer file, and lets the operating system install itself without human intervention. See the "Unattended Windows 2000 Professional Installation" section, later in this chapter, for details.

- ■ **/udf (Modifying UDF Options)**   When you install Windows 2000 in unattended mode, some options may need to be changed from system to system (such as the system name or IP address). Rather than editing the unattended script file, the unique options that need to be changed can be modified from the command line. This allows an administrator to create a common unattended script file and just enter the modifications through simple command-line changes.

- ■ **/r (Optional Folder—Remains After Installation)**   During installation of Windows 2000, some organizations create "home directories" for their users, or other folders not normally installed during a standard Windows 2000 installation. The /r parameter creates these folders during the installation process automatically.

- ■ **/rx (Optional Folder—Deleted After Installation)**   During an unattended installation of Windows 2000, you may choose to run programs and scripts. To speed up the execution of the applications and scripts, rather than running them from a network share, you can elect to push the files to the system. Use the /rx command to create a temporary folder, push the temporary files to the directory, and delete the temporary folder after installation is complete.

- ■ **/e (Command Executed After Installation)**   The /e parameter is one of the most common optional parameters used to implement scripted installations of the operating system. The /e command executes a program after installation. The program could be something like a Microsoft Systems Management Server (SMS) inventory run, a MAPI command-line utility that sends an e-mail or text page to the administrator as notification that the installation has been successfully completed, or an executable file that begins the installation of applications or installs data files.

- ▲ **/a (Accessibility Options)**   This command installs the accessibility features.

Winnt32.exe Upgrade Parameters

Just as there are command-line parameters to aid in the installation of a new installation of Windows 2000 Professional, there are command-line parameters to assist in the upgrade process from previous versions of Windows 9*x* or Windows NT to Windows 2000 Professional. These command-line parameters provide options to the winnt32.exe upgrade application. The options are listed in Table 14-3.

Unattended Installation of Windows 2000 Professional

You can script the installation process in order to install the operating system multiple times without any need for user intervention. You need an answer file (unattend.txt) to hold information about unique system configuration settings, such as computer name, IP address, default installed components, and so on.

Winnt32.exe Slash (/) Parameter	Function	Example
/s:*sourcepath*	Specifies the source of install files (*x:path* or *systemsharepath*).	winnt32 /s:c:\windows
/tempdrive:driveletter	Location for temporary files and Windows 2000.	winnt32 /tempdrive:d:
/unattend	Upgrades your previous version of Windows 2000 in unattended Setup mode. All user settings are taken from the previous installation, so no user intervention is required during Setup.	winnt32 /unattend
/unattend*num:answer_file*	Performs a new installation in unattended Setup mode. The *answer_file* provides your custom specifications to Setup. *Num* is the number of seconds between the time that Setup finishes copying the files and when it restarts. You can use the *num* option only on a computer running Windows 2000. *Answer_file* is the name of the answer file.	winnt32 /unattend10:ansfile

Table 14-3.   Winnt32.exe Command-Line Installation Parameters

Winnt32.exe Slash (/) Parameter	Function	Example
/udf:*id,ubf_file*	Indicates the identifier that Setup uses to specify how a uniqueness database file modifies an answer file. /udf overrides the values in the answer file and the *id* determines which value in the *udb_file* are used. If no *udb_file* is specified, Setup prompts you to insert a disk that contains the $unique$.udb file.	winnt32 /udf:12,udbfile
/checkupgradeonly	Checks your computer for upgrade compatibility with Windows 2000. For Windows 95 or 98 upgrades, Setup creates a report named upgrade.txt in the Windows installation folder. For Windows NT 3.51 or 4.0 upgrades, it saves the report to the winnt32.log in the installation folder.	winnt32 /checkupgradeonly
/cmd:*command_line*	Executes a specific command before the final phase of Setup (after Setup has collected the necessary configuration information and rebooted twice, but before Setup is complete).	winnt32 /cmd:runprog.exe

Table 14-3.   Winnt32.exe Command-Line Installation Parameters *(continued)*

Winnt32.exe Slash (/) Parameter	Function	Example
/cmdcons	Adds a Recovery Console option for repairing a failed installation to the operating system selection screen.	winnt32 /cmdcons
/copydir:*folder_name*	Creates an additional folder within your Windows 2000 operating system folder.	winnt32 /copydir:MyFolder
/copysource:*folder_name*	Creates an additional folder within your Windows 2000 operating system folder, but deletes the folder after installation.	winnt32 /copysource:Tfold
/debug*level*:*filename*	Creates a debug log at the *level* specified. The default creates a log file (c:\winnt32.log) that has the level set to 2. The log levels are as follows: 0 for severe errors, 1 for errors, 2 for warnings, 3 for information, and 4 for detailed information for debugging. Each level includes the levels below it.	winnt32 /debug1:ErrorLog
/m:*folder_name*	Copies replacement files from an alternative location. This command instructs Setup to look in the alternative location first, and if files are present, to use them rather than the files from the default location.	winnt32 /m:AltSetup

Table 14-3. Winnt32.exe Command-Line Installation Parameters *(continued)*

Winnt32.exe Slash (/) Parameter	Function	Example
/makelocalsource	Copies all installation source files to your local hard disk. Use this with an installation from a CD to provide installation files when the CD is not available later in the installation.	winnt32 /makelocalsource
/noreboot	Prevents Setup from restarting after the file-copy phase of winnt32 is completed, so that you can execute another command.	winnt32 /noreboot
/syspart:*drive_letter*	Copies Setup startup files to a hard drive, marks the drive as active, and then allows you to install the drive in another computer. When you start that computer, Setup automatically starts with the next phase. You must always use the /tempdrive parameter with the /syspart parameter.	winnt32 /syspart:d /tempdrive:d:\tempdir

Table 14-3. Winnt32.exe Command-Line Installation Parameters *(continued)*

Common Uses of Unattended Installation

It's typical for an organization to have to install multiple copies of Windows 2000 Professional, which is much easier with unattended installations. This creates consistent installations throughout the organization, and decreases the time it takes to answer system questions during the configuration process for each computer.

SIMPLIFYING BASIC INSTALLATIONS   The basic installation of Windows 2000 Professional in any organization has the same characteristics regarding registered name/company, networking protocols used, and so on, for all computers. A default answer file uses this data to install multiple instances of the operating system.

INSTALLING REMOTE SYSTEMS   Another use of an answer file is to consistently configure Windows 2000 Professional in remote locations. The systems being configured in remote locations will be set up just like all other desktop systems in the organization.

PROVIDING DISASTER-RECOVERY ASSISTANCE   In the event of a workstation failure, you don't want to have to guess how to configure a system again. By inserting all common organizational information into a scripted answer file, you can achieve consistency.

Sample Unattend.txt

An unattend.txt script file can be as simple or as complex as you require, and these files can range from 15 lines to 200 lines. There are dozens of parameters to select. A full list of the option parameters is found on the Windows 2000 CD in the \i386 subdirectory. There are options as simple as setting the default directory in which you want to install Windows 2000, to more complex options that cover detailed parameter settings for a network adapter.

The following is a sample unattend.txt file with comments. (When you create your unattend.txt file, you can leave the comments out.)

```
[Unattended]
TargetPath=winnt    ; leaves the install directory to c:\winnt
Filesystem=LeaveAlone   ; keeps the file system as what it is now (assuming NTFS)
[GuiUnattended]
OemSkipWelcome = 1    ; knows to skip the Welcome screen
AdminPassword = *   ; sets the password to no password
TimeZone=04      ; sets the time zone to -8 (Pacific Timezone)
[UserData]
FullName="Rand Morimoto"    ; specifies the Name of the registered individual
OrgName="Inacom Oakland"    ; specifies the Company of the registered individual
ComputerName= W2KPro-01    ; provides a new name for the system
[Display]
BitsPerPel=16          ; 16 bits per pixel equals 65536 colors
XResolution=1024      ; 1024x768 resolution
YResolution=768
VRefresh=60          ; video refresh speed of 60hz
[Networking]          ; no networking options means leave the same as current
[Identification]
JoinDomain=INACOM      ; specifies the domain to join
[NetAdapters]
Adapter01=params.Adapter01    ; identifies the network adapter in the system
[params.Adapter01]
INFID = "pci\ven_0e11&dev_ae32"    ; specifies the plug and play ID type
[NetClients]
MS_MSClient=params.MS_MSClient    ; installs the MS Client for Networks
[params.MS_MSClient]
```

```
[NetProtocols]
MS_TCPIP=params.MS_TCPIP        ; installs TCP/IP as the main protocol
[params.MS_TCPIP]
AdapterSections=params.MS_TCPIP.Adapter01,params.MS_TCPIP.Adapter02
[params.MS_TCPIP.Adapter01]
SpecificTo=Adapter01
DHCP=yes
[NetServices]
MS_Server=params.MS_Server
[params.MS_Server]
```

As you create and prototype test the unattended script file, you'll find the unattended implementation of Windows 2000 Professional makes it easy to install Windows 2000 on multiple computers on an ongoing basis.

Mirrored Drive Installation

An alternative to creating a scripted installation is to mirror the installation of one system to multiple other systems. This works if all of the systems are identically configured (same hard drive controller, same network adapter, same system board, and so on). Mirrored images can be replicated very quickly, because the installation process does not go through a step-by-step file installation, but rather a track-by-track duplication of a disk. Windows 2000 comes with a drive-mirroring utility called sysprep.exe. Sysprep lets you make an image of a drive, save the image to a network share or other stored media, and then replicate the image on another system.

It is becoming quite common to use drive mirroring on desktop and laptop systems, especially when you purchase systems that are of the same make, model, and configuration. By purchasing numerous similarly configured workstations, you can set up one system and test the configuration and applications, then mirror the configuration to multiple other systems.

Preparing to Mirror System Configurations

There are some preparatory tasks to perform before you run the Sysprep utility:

▼ Make sure you have the most current version of the Windows 2000 Professional software, service packs, and third-party drivers installed on the system. Don't replicate old or outdated versions of software.

■ Install as many of the standard application software programs used by the organization, even if that means over-installing applications and deleting them on the replicated systems. It's a lot easier to delete a subdirectory of software that is not needed than it is to run the installation manually for each individual user.

■ Make as many of the minor changes and adjustments to the system as you can. This includes updating screen colors, video resolution, and default directories, configuring screen savers, and so on. The more details you take care of at this point, the fewer modifications you will need to make to all of the replicated systems after mirroring.

▲ Set default parameters, but don't customize. When configuring the template system, make sure to set default parameters, such as default directory settings or application icons on the desktop that are universal to all users. However, don't customize the template based on a specific user configuration. If you go to the extent of setting a user's home directory, or e-mail application profile, you may find that you will have to delete the profile on the mirrored system and reinstall a new profile for the new user. The rule of thumb is that if you have to enter a user's name, leave it alone.

Sysprep

The sysprep.exe utility that comes with Windows 2000 is a command-line application with very few options. The options are as follows:

▼ **-quiet**   Does not show confirmation dialog boxes

■ **-nosidgen**   Does not automatically generate a unique security ID on reboot

■ **-pnp**   Forces plug-and-play refresh on next reboot

▲ **-reboot**   Reboots the system after Sysprep has completed

CREATING AN IMAGE WITH SYSPREP   By default, when you launch the Sysprep utility, the utility walks you through two sets of options. One set of options prompts you to create an image of an existing system. You are prompted to confirm the drive partition you wish to mirror and the destination of the storage location for the image file.

After the image has been written to a file, the system notifies you that Sysprep has successfully created an image file. You can then copy the image file to a CD-ROM disk or a network share.

While you may eventually want to store your image on a CD-ROM by burning a copy of the image from a CD writer, you should not try to write the Sysprep destination file directly to the CD writer. The Sysprep utility has intermittent write delays when processing the image file that will corrupt a direct write to a CD writer file. To create an image on a CD, first send the image to a network share or another hard-drive partition, and then burn that image to a CD.

RESTORING A SYSPREP IMAGE   To restore an image, run the same Sysprep utility, specifying that you want to restore an image to a partition. You're prompted to specify the source location of the image. The Sysprep utility automatically rebuilds the partition from the image. Upon completion, the system prompts you to reboot, and a new Security Identifier (SID) is issued for the new system. The automatic generation of a SID is an important task, since every computer in the network needs to have a unique identifier.

One of the available switches for restoring an image is -pnp. If the image you are using is being replicated on a system with the exact same hardware configuration, you just need to run the Sysprep restore process. However, if the system you are restoring has a slightly different system configuration (such as a different network adapter), you may want to launch Sysprep with the –pnp command-line option. Then, after the image restoration and a reboot, the system will automatically invoke plug-and-play hardware detection, and new devices will be automatically detected and added.

PERFORMING A DETAILED UPGRADE TO WINDOWS 2000 PROFESSIONAL

Upgrading Windows 2000 Professional over an existing version of Windows (95, 98, or NT) is a process that many organizations are evaluating instead of performing a clean installation. Many organizations planned their installations of Windows 9*x* and Windows NT Workstation very carefully, and would like to leverage that work in the migration to Windows 2000 Professional. Retaining previous Windows configuration settings for applications and system configuration means that the amount of time needed to migrate to Windows 2000 Professional is greatly reduced.

This section takes you through the migration process from a previous 32-bit version of Windows to Windows 2000 Professional.

Auto-Detecting the OS

To upgrade from a previous version of Windows, you can simply insert the Windows 2000 Professional CD. The auto-play CD-ROM will detect the existing version of Windows and offer to upgrade to Windows 2000 Professional automatically, as shown in Figure 14-6. Click Yes to begin the upgrade.

Selecting an Upgrade or a Clean Installation

The next step in the upgrade process is to select whether you want to upgrade the existing system or whether you want to do a clean installation in a separate directory, as shown in Figure 14-7. If you elect a clean installation of Windows 2000 in a separate directory, you are effectively performing a new installation. In this case, we will select Upgrade to Windows 2000 to replace the existing operating system and retain the settings and installed programs.

Preparing the System for Upgrading

The next step in the upgrade process is to analyze your system configuration to identify any potential problems you may run into during the upgrade process. Unlike early upgrade utilities, which sometimes completed the upgrade process but left the system inoperable because of an incompatible system driver or basic application incompatibility, Windows 2000 Professional validates system compatibility before proceeding with the upgrade.

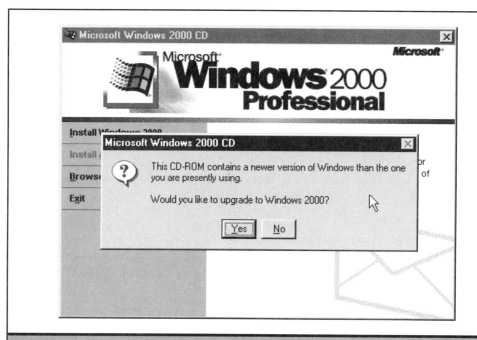

Figure 14-6.   Automatically detecting the option to upgrade

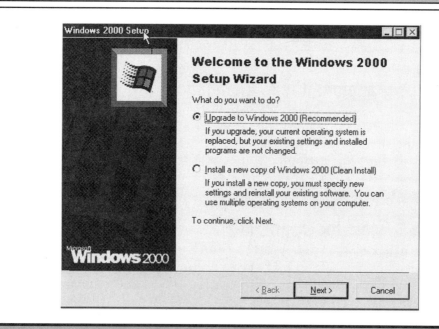

Figure 14-7.   Choosing to upgrade or to conduct a clean installation

The next screen, similar to the one shown in Figure 14-8, informs you that the upgrade process will prompt you for special hardware and software upgrade files that you may have. The installation program then conducts a scan of the system, looking for potential hardware, software, or setting incompatibilities, and creates a report so that you have a printed record before any files are copied to the system.

Detecting System-Compatibility Errors

The scan of the system identifies any system-compatibility errors with existing applications. The most common application-compatibility errors are applications that require real mode drivers, or 16-bit and 32-bit drivers that do not adhere to standard Windows application programming interface (API) specifications. These drivers are missing the appropriate hooks into the Windows 2000 networking environment. It is important that these applications are identified prior to upgrading to Windows 2000, so that you know which applications will not operate properly, or at all, after you have migrated to Windows 2000.

A system compatibility report, similar to the one shown in Figure 14-9, is generated and displayed on the screen. It shows the applications identified by the Windows 2000 Upgrade wizard as those that may not operate after upgrading. You can abort the up-

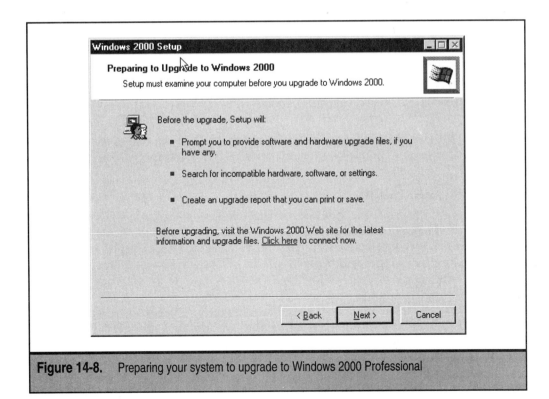

Figure 14-8. Preparing your system to upgrade to Windows 2000 Professional

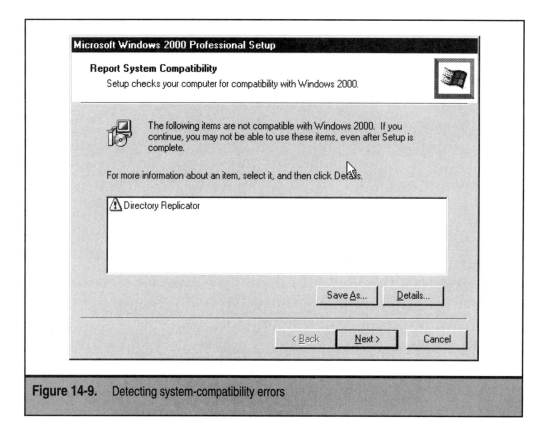

Figure 14-9.   Detecting system-compatibility errors

grade if any of those applications are critical components. You can also elect to ignore the advisory and proceed with the upgrade to Windows 2000 Professional.

Selecting Upgrade Packs

A new concept in the conversion process is installing an upgrade pack during the up-grade process. Upgrade packs can include both hardware and software updates, and they are typically provided by the manufacturer of the equipment or application to patch the drivers during the upgrade process to achieve Windows 2000 compatibility.

During the upgrade process, you will see a screen similar to the one shown in Figure 14-10, which inquires whether you have upgrade packs to correct any of the problems identified in the system-compatibility error report on the previous screen. In many cases, the upgrade packs are downloadable over the Internet and can be copied to floppy disk. If you select Yes, I Have Upgrade Packs, you will be prompted to specify the location of the upgrade pack files.

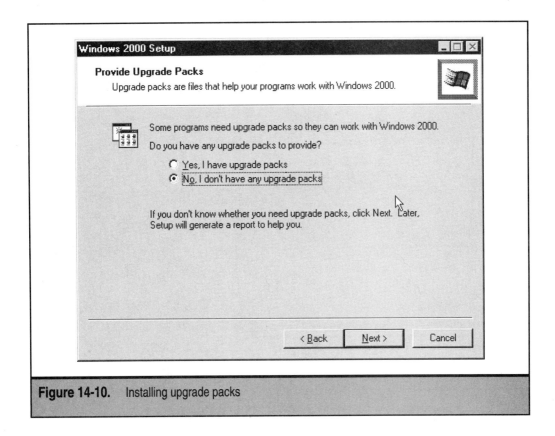

Figure 14-10. Installing upgrade packs

Keeping FAT or Upgrading to NTFS

During the upgrade process, you will be presented with the option of keeping the file system as FAT or upgrading the file system to NTFS (see Figure 14-11). You can update a file system from FAT to NTFS at any time, just by dropping to a DOS prompt and running the Convert program (enter convert.exe c: /fs:ntfs where c: is the drive letter of the Windows 2000 partition you wish to upgrade). However, once a system is converted to NTFS, it cannot be changed back to FAT. Therefore, if you are uncertain whether to upgrade to NTFS or not, just leave the partition as FAT and upgrade it at a later date, if desired.

Reporting Errors and Advisories

Finally, you will be prompted about plug-and-play devices that are detected in the system but for which no Windows 2000 Professional driver is included with the Windows 2000 CD-ROM. A screen similar to the one in Figure 14-12 lists the various devices that require device drivers from manufacturers.

Even though plug-and-play can find hardware devices, you still need a Windows 2000 device driver to make the device work properly. Updated drivers can frequently be

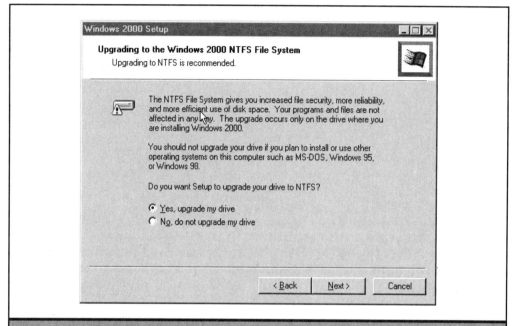

Figure 14-11. Keeping FAT or upgrading to NTFS

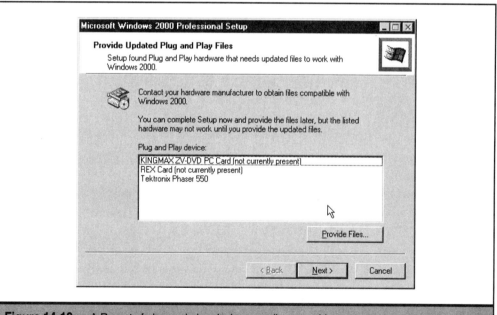

Figure 14-12. A Report of plug-and-play devices needing new drivers

downloaded from the Internet and then installed manually, using the Hardware wizard in the control panel.

Completing the Upgrade

After completing all of the system scans and update prompts, the upgrade process will give you one final chance to abort the upgrade process, otherwise the upgrade proceeds. The time required to complete the installation varies, based on the number of options selected and the type of applications that need to be upgraded. When the upgrade is complete, you are prompted to reboot the system.

IMPLEMENTING SYSTEM-MANAGEMENT TECHNOLOGIES

There are a number of system-management technologies integrated into the Windows 2000 Professional core operating system. These technologies help you manage the computer, and they include disk management, disk defragmentation, and disk quotas.

Disk Management

The Disk Management utility lets you create disk partitions, delete existing partitions, create stripe datasets, format partitions, and add new drive space to an existing logical partition. For those familiar with Windows NT 4, this is the same as the Disk Administrator utility that managed and administered physical and logical drives.

NOTE: As explained in Chapter 18, it is better to use hardware mirroring, data striping (also known as RAID-5), and hardware disk management for faster system performance than to use software based fault tolerance. Therefore, in most cases, the Disk Management utility would not be used for mirroring or striping.

Invoking Disk Management

The Windows 2000 Disk Management utility is executed as snap-in to the Microsoft Management Console (MMC). The utility can be launched by selecting Start | Programs | Administrative Tools | Computer Management.

From the Computer Management tool, selecting the Storage folder provides you with authenticated access to the Disk Management utility. You see three window panes on the Microsoft Management Console screen, as shown in Figure 14-13. The left pane shows the various storage-management utility options available. The upper-right pane allows you to select the specific logical drive partition on the system for administration, and the lower-right pane allows you to see physical drives and physical drive partitioning.

Disk and Partition Administration

To change the partition configuration of a physical drive, select the physical drive in the lower-right pane. To make changes to the physical drive setting, right-click the physi-

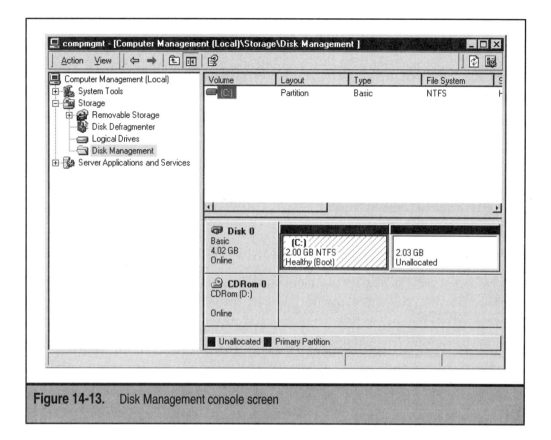

Figure 14-13. Disk Management console screen

cal drive in the lower-right pane to display a menu of choices for changing the drive or partition:

▼   If the drive is not partitioned, the right-click menu offers an option to create a partition.

▲   If the drive is partitioned, a series of options is offered, including changing the drive letter, formatting the drive, or deleting the partition.

After you right click a network share and choose the Properties option, a series of tabs appear, offering you a range of options for the partition. The tabs are: General, Tools, Hardware, Sharing, Security, Quota, and Web Sharing. The available options are not commonly configured in detail, because access to the physical drive is limited by logon access to the server itself. By controlling logon access to the server, you avoid having to limit access to the drive with user or group permissions. (These options are detailed in Chapter 16.)

Disk Defragmentation

A basic disk defragmentation utility is built into Windows 2000 Professional. You can manually invoke, or automatically schedule, the defragmentation of disks.

The disk defragmentation function is integrated in the Computer Management MMC administrator tool. The utility can be launched by selecting Start | Programs | Administrative Tools | Computer Management.

Once in the Computer Management tool, select the storage section. Then select the Disk Defragmenter item. The defragmentation utility screen (similar to Figure 14-14) allows you to select a volume, analyze the volume to determine whether the volume requires defragmentation, and invoke the defragmentation command.

The Disk Defragmenter utility included with Windows 2000 provides basic defragmentation functionality for the system. However, for complete disk analysis, there are third-party add-ins to Windows 2000 that provide enhanced features, such as moving files closer to the inside track of the drive (files closer to the inside track can be accessed

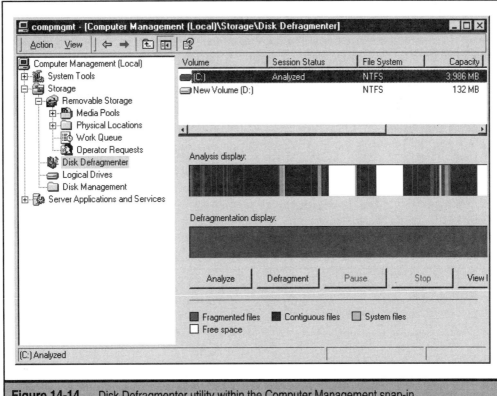

Figure 14-14.   Disk Defragmenter utility within the Computer Management snap-in

more quickly, since drives calibrate to track 0, the track furthest inside), moving associated files together (if you have an index file for a database, having the index file closer to the database file will provide faster results when doing an index lookup), or specifically defragmenting certain files on an automated basis.

Disk Quotas

Windows 2000 provides support for disk quotas for volumes formatted with NTFS5. Administrators can use disk quotas to monitor and limit disk space use. In addition to user notification when disk quotas are exceeded, events are automatically logged when users exceed warning thresholds and quota limits. Quotas are tracked on a per-user, per-volume basis, and users are charged only for the files they own.

NOTE: For security reasons, when a member of the local computer's Administrators group creates a new file, the file is owned by the Administrators group, not by the individual user. Therefore, to track disk quotas on an individual basis, users must log on under separate user accounts that are not members of the Administrators group.

Quota information can be saved along with other volume information during backup. Restoring a backup copy of a file will always be permitted, regardless of quota limits, provided the user performing the restore operation has backup privileges.

Setting Quotas

Quotas are set and administered in the Properties dialog box of a drive. To open the dialog box, double-click the My Computer icon and right-click the drive. Choose Properties from the pop-up menu, and select the Quota tab.

If you wish to place quotas on a share, double-click the My Network Places icon on the desktop of the server, and then select an existing network place or share (or select Computers Near Me or Entire Network). Right-click the file share you wish to modify, choose Properties, and select the Quota tab.

Select the Quota Management option to enable quota functions, which provides the ability to specify disk space allocation, default quota limits, and quota logging. You can set the default quota limit for all users that access the drive share, or you can click the Quota Entries button to select individual users or groups in order to vary the quotas. When you click the Quota Entries button, you will see a screen similar to Figure 14-15.

It is typical to set the warning limit at 75–80 percent of the maximum storage limit allowed for the user. This helps users know that they are reaching their disk quota maximums and gives them enough warning that they can do necessary housecleaning.

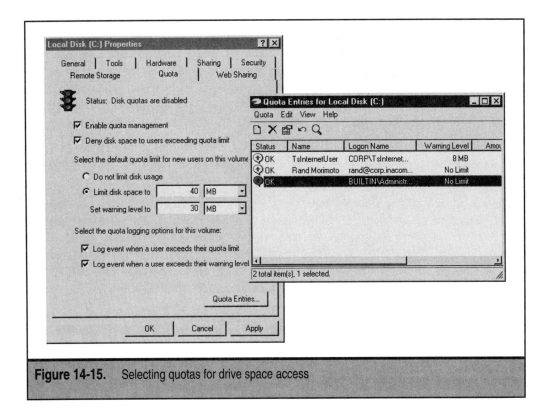

Figure 14-15.   Selecting quotas for drive space access

IMPLEMENTING DESKTOP-MANAGEMENT TECHNOLOGIES

Windows 2000 Professional includes three core desktop-management technologies that help you administer and support the installation, perform ongoing maintenance tasks, and support desktop systems and users in the network. These technologies include Intellimirror, Remote Installation Service, and Windows Scripting Host.

These three technologies have both an infrastructure (server and desktop) component as well as a user/group component. In this chapter, I will cover the installation of the infrastructure components that get installed on the servers and desktop computers. These components provide the network with the functions needed to use the administration and management features. I cover more detailed user and group configuration functions in Chapter 16.

Intellimirror

Intellimirror is a core technology of Windows 2000 Professional and Windows 2000 Server. Intellimirror provides the core structure for the administration of user data management, software distribution and installation, software and driver maintenance, and the management of user profiles and settings. Simply stated, Intellimirror is a series of policies and tools that helps you keep desktop systems running more reliably and eases user access to distributed information.

The Importance of Intellimirror for Organizations

Distributed computer technology has grown. The definition of a network has expanded to include a global environment encompassing thousands of employees around the world, and even vendors and clients connected through the Internet. With this expansion, it's necessary to enhance your ability to manage computers and users easily.

Intellimirror makes it easy for administrators to install the operating system and application files on computer, and to manage those files and applications on an ongoing basis. The initial installation of software on a computer represents only a fraction of the tasks required to keep desktops operational.

When new software is installed on a computer, new or updated drivers may overwrite older drivers, causing the system to become unstable or even causing system failure. Most of the time, the cure is to reinstall the original driver files. Additionally, as new patches or updates become available, the ability to automate the installation becomes important. Intellimirror includes a number of technologies that help reinstall drivers or applications after the software installation is completed.

Windows 2000 also provides a process to help users access applications, data files, and configuration settings, regardless of which desktop they use. This "follow me" function makes user settings and data files available, regardless of the users' logon location.

Intellimirror Components

The components in Intellimirror are divided into enterprise/system components and desktop/user components. The enterprise/system components include the following:

▼ Windows 2000 Active Directory (defined in Chapter 2, designed in Chapter 6, and implemented in Chapter 13)

■ The implementation of Group Policies in the organization (detailed in Chapter 16)

■ Remote Installation Service (RIS) (detailed later in this chapter)

▲ Dynamic Host Configuration Protocol (DHCP) services (implemented in Chapter 13)

The desktop/user components include the following:

▼ Roaming policies (detailed in Chapter 16)

■ Group Policy Editor for user and group configurations (detailed in Chapter 16)

■ Offline folders and Synchronization Manager for data management (detailed in Chapter 16)

▲ Windows installer scripts for applications (detailed in Chapter 16)

Remote Installation Service

The Remote Installation Service (RIS), is a Windows 2000 server component that provides automated installation of Windows 2000 Professional software onto computer systems through either a boot ROM-enabled workstation adapter, or a floppy-disk booting workstation.

RIS has both a server component and a desktop component. The server component is the RIS server software that holds copies of images of the Windows 2000 Professional software that can be pushed to a desktop computer. The desktop component of RIS is the boot component that invokes the installation from the RIS server.

The ability to automate remote installation of the operating system can save hundreds (if not thousands) of hours a year.

Prerequisites for Implementing RIS Server

Before you begin installing and implementing the RIS, you need to ensure that a number of prerequisites have been met—otherwise RIS will not work properly.

REVIEWING HARDWARE REQUIREMENTS AND HARDWARE COMPATIBILITY   Installing RIS on a server requires standard Windows 2000 hardware compatibility. (The list is maintained on the Microsoft Windows 2000 home page.) The system needs high processing speed and memory configuration, similar to a file and print server (detailed in Chapters 5 and 12 of this book) because remote computers log on to the RIS server to access image files for downloading. The RIS server should have ample disk storage space to hold the installation files for the Windows 2000 Professional operating system.

RIS cannot be installed on the same drive or volume you use for booting Windows 2000 Server. Therefore, you need a second drive and volume for RIS. Since Windows 2000 Professional uses approximately 400MB of disk space, the second drive in the system should be 4GB or greater. All drives should be formatted with the NTFS file system.

The network adapter typically is the bottleneck in an RIS implementation. If your organization is serious about implementing RIS, upgrade the network to 100MB or gigabit Ethernet.

PLANNING FOR RIS SERVERS   For upgrades, updates, and rebuilding individual workstations, a single RIS server usually suffices. However, if you add 50 new computers to the network and need to install the operating system on each, a single RIS server creates a burden on the server that diminishes its efficiency.

In my early implementation and testing of RIS, I found that a single Pentium III server with 128MB of RAM and fast mirrored 8GB drives could handle 24 simultaneous remote installation sessions at the same time. As I pushed that limit to 50 simultaneous installations, the process took two and a half times longer for each workstation. Installing a second processor didn't help, because the bottleneck was not the speed with which the processor could service requests, but rather the performance of the disk subsystem and the LAN adapter bandwidth. The best way to perform large-scale rollouts is to use multiple RIS servers.

While RIS can be used over a WAN connection, the performance (even over a T1 line with full capacity allocated to the RIS session) took 15–20 times longer than a LAN-based implementation. For frame-relay networks or networks where existing traffic takes up a portion of the available bandwidth, remote installation can take even longer. For remote offices, you can use a domain controller as an RIS server.

OBTAINING THE LATEST SERVICE PACKS AND DRIVERS FOR YOUR IMAGES   Microsoft, hardware vendors, and software vendors all release updates and patches for their products, so be sure to stay on top of the latest release when doing a distributed release to multiple systems.

ENSURING THAT YOUR WORKSTATIONS SUPPORT RIS   In order for RIS to work, the target workstations must have either a Preboot Execution Environment (PXE) remote boot ROM adapter, or a network adapter that is supported by the RIS boot floppy disk you create (if you do create a disk).

The PXE boot ROM is a special ROM chip that many network adapters support as an add-in to an open ROM socket on the adapter card. At the time of this writing, a company called Bootware (http://www.bootware.com) sold PXE boot ROMs for standard network adapters made by companies, including 3Com and Intel. The boot ROM needs to be PXE (LSA) version .99C or greater, and some systems require the .99L or greater version of the remote boot ROM. Check the compatibility notes for Windows 2000 RIS on Microsoft's Windows 2000 home page for updated information.

For systems that do not have open sockets for the addition of a boot ROM, the RIS server software provides the ability to create a floppy disk that supports a handful of network adapters. Verify that your network adapter is supported by the RIS boot floppy by checking the Microsoft Windows 2000 home page.

CHECKING THE NETWORK FOR AN ACTIVE DNS AND DHCP SERVER   In order for RIS to work, you need to have an active DNS and DHCP server on your network. The remote workstation must acquire an IP address from your DHCP server to establish a valid physical connection to the RIS server. DNS is required to locate the RIS server and other devices on the network.

NOTE: You can configure your RIS server to act as the DNS and DHCP server.

Installing the Remote Installation Service (Server)

As mentioned earlier, RIS is an optional component that can be installed at the time the server is installed, or the component can be added on a Windows 2000 server at any time. The RIS server does not need to be a domain controller nor a member of the domain. RIS's sole function is to work at the hardware and OS level. When a workstation or laptop requests a remote installation of the OS, an RIS server delivers it. The process is intended to be fully automated, so no logon or validation is required, or even expected, for invoking an RIS session.

ADDING THE RIS COMPONENT TO A SERVER   If you did not install the remote installation service at the time of server creation, you can add the component at any time by doing the following:

1. Choose Start | Settings | Control Panel.
2. Double-click Add/Remove Programs.
3. Click Add/Remove Windows Components.

Scroll down to the Remote Installation Service option, select the option by clicking the checkbox, and click Next to begin the installation of the RIS server service. After the installation is complete, you will be prompted to reboot the system.

SETTING UP RIS FOR THE FIRST TIME   When your system reboots after installing RIS server services, log on as the administrator. The Configure Your Server screen will be displayed, prompting you to complete the installation and configuration of RIS, as shown in Figure 14-16. If the Configure Your Server screen is not displayed automatically, you can also configure the component by doing the following:

1. Choose Start | Settings | Control Panel.
2. Double-click Add/Remove Programs.
3. Click Add/Remove Windows Components.
4. Select Configure Remote Installation Services and click the Configure button.

After you click Configure in the screen shown in Figure 14-16, the next screen asks for the server drive and directory onto which the RIS files should be installed. This must be a second drive, because you cannot install RIS on the same drive as your Windows 2000 Server software.

The next screen asks whether you want the RIS server enabled at the completion of the installation process. Typically, it's safe to answer in the affirmative, because it's un-

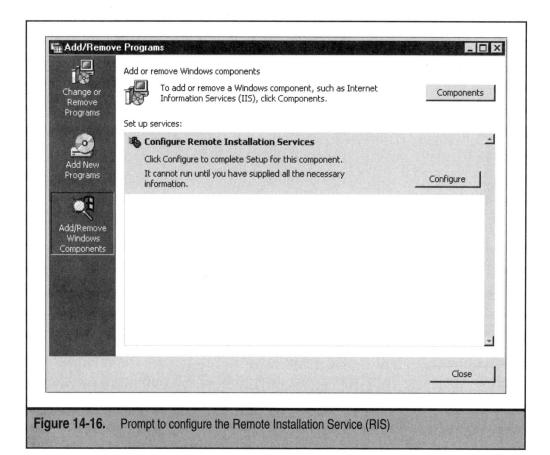

Figure 14-16.   Prompt to configure the Remote Installation Service (RIS)

likely that remote clients will be requesting sessions. However, if you are installing an additional RIS server on an existing network currently using RIS, you may not want to have RIS enabled until you have had a chance to test the installation of the configuration software.

You are also asked if you want RIS to respond to a system that is unknown on the network (a known system is one that is in the Active Directory). For security purposes, you should not permit an unknown system to be activated as an RIS client. Even if the network is secured through firewalls, internal users can place a workstation on a network connection and purposely (or accidentally) install Windows 2000 Professional through an RIS session. To retain control of the remote installation process, configure RIS to ignore unknown clients on the network.

The next screen asks for the location of the Windows 2000 Professional source-code files. These are the files stored on the Windows 2000 Professional CD in the \i386 subdirectory. Since RIS installs the operating system using the standard setup sequences, a copy of the Windows 2000 Professional program files need to be available.

The next screen asks for a name for the image folder. Unless you are installing multiple versions of the Windows 2000 Professional configuration files, just give the folder a descriptive name, such as win2000.wks.

Lastly you will be asked to enter a common description for the installation. Something simple like "Windows 2000 Professional" can adequately describe the installation.

After all these steps, you will see a screen similar to the one in Figure 14-17, summarizing all the settings you have defined for your RIS setup.

AUTHORIZING THE RIS SERVER IN THE ACTIVE DIRECTORY   After you've installed the remote installation services, you need to add the RIS server to the Active Directory so that client systems will be able to see and access the server. This is both a function of matching the right RIS servers to the right branches of the Active Directory tree, and also of a security function that ensures that RIS servers are not installed by users (which could permit unauthorized operating system installations).

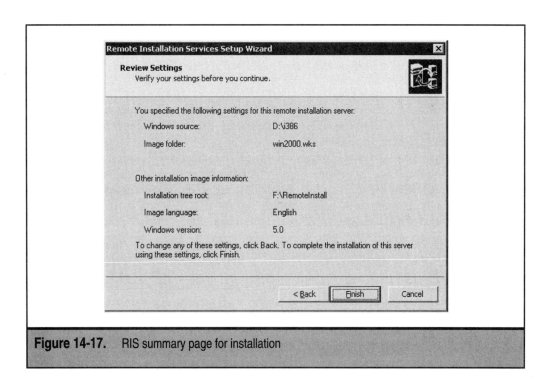

Figure 14-17.   RIS summary page for installation

To authorize an RIS server in the Active Directory, do the following:

1. Log on to the Active Directory as an administrator that has access to the portion of the domain where your RIS server will be servicing client computers.

2. Start the DHCP Management MMC snap-in by selecting Start | Programs | Administrative Tools | DHCP Manager.

3. Right-click DHCP and choose the Browse Authorized Servers option.

4. Click Add and enter the IP address of the RIS server.

After you confirm that the address is correct for the server, the new RIS server will be authorized within the Active Directory and will respond to client computers requesting remote installation service requests.

CONFIGURING REMOTE INSTALLATION SERVICES   The RIS server is administered from the Directory Management MMC snap-in. You can invoke the Directory Management administrator by choosing Start | Programs | Administrative Tools | Active Directory Users and Computers.

Depending on whether the RIS server was set up as a domain controller or just as a member or stand-alone server, you'll find the RIS server in either the Computers or the Domain Controllers section of the Active Directory Users and Computers administrator.

When you find the computer you wish to administer, right-click the server and choose Properties. A Properties page with six tabs will be displayed. To administer the RIS server functions, select the Remote Install tab. This tab provides the options to enable or disable the RIS server functions (effectively allowing or disallowing computers from being connected to the RIS server), as well as to enable or disable advanced settings for RIS configuration. If you want the RIS server to service RIS client requests, enable the Respond to all Clients Requesting Service checkbox.

The Advanced Settings dialog box is the place to define what happens when a computer invokes the RIS server functions. The first tab provides the ability to select the name of the new Windows 2000 Professional system. The name of the system can be the name of the user (first name, last name, or combination of the first/last names), or it can be customized. For example, you might want to use an automatic incremental naming process where the default name is WS and the first system is WS-001, the second system is WS-002, and so on.

Also in the advanced settings is the ability to set the computer account location. This allows you to define a default directory-services container where all remote-installation client computer accounts are created. You can select from one of three options:

▼ **Default directory service location**   This creates the new RIS computer account in the same location where all computer accounts for the Active Directory are created.

■ **Same location as the user setting up the computer**   This creates the new RIS computer account in the location of the Active Directory where the user's information is stored.

▲ **A specific directory service location**   This allows an administrator to set a specific Active Directory container where all client computer-account objects are installed.

Of the three options, the most common are the first and third. The first option adds the system into the container where all other computer accounts are located. Using the third option allows the administrator to go into that container and ensure that all of the computers are valid systems and are known to the administrator. After each system is identified and authorized by the administrator, the computer account can be moved from the temporary RIS container into the computer account container of the Active Directory. This is an additional step for the administrator, but it provides validation of the systems added to and managed by the Active Directory.

The Images Tab displays the images that are available for installation by remote client systems. By default, the image created during the setup of the RIS server is shown. This is typically a full image of the Windows 2000 Professional CD-ROM. Many organizations would rather install not only an image of the core Windows 2000 Professional software, but also a fully customized desktop. By using the RIPrep utility (covered later in this section) you can create an image of a standard configured workstation that can then be replicated to new systems using RIS.

The Tools Tab is available for third-party add-ins that install maintenance and troubleshooting tools related to automated remote installations of desktop systems. Some of the tools in development include utilities that automatically format, RAID stripe, and format a drive, so the remote system is prepared prior to the installation of the Windows 2000 Professional image. Other tools are post-installation utilities that invoke system documentation and image backup processes to take a snapshot of the system for information lookup or system restoration in the future.

Creating RIPrep Images

You can add images to the RIS server and install them onto remote systems. Many organizations create a series of images based on the type of target systems. For example, you may need three different images: one for the standard desktop user, one for the power user, and one for managers.

NOTE: RIPrep does not require that the master computer be identical to the target computers, because plug-and-play can handle hardware differences. However, you should test images against the target systems, especially those that are unique.

To launch the RIPrep utility, do the following:

1. Choose Start | Run.
2. Type **\\RISServerName\Reminst\ riprep.exe**, and then click OK.

In this example, RISServerName is the name of the RIS Server. Reminst is a share on the RIS server, which must point to the \winnt\system32\reminst directory on the server where the riprep.exe utility resides.

The RIPrep utility launches a wizard to help you create a new image. On the first screen, enter the name of your existing RIS server and click NEXT.

Enter the name of the folder in which you want to locate the files for this image. You may want to name this descriptively, using w2ksales.img or w2koff2k.img. Click Next to see a window in which you can enter a descriptive phrase about the image (perhaps "Windows 2000 Professional Image for the Sales Staff").

Choose Next to see a summary page that will review the image configuration settings you entered. If you don't have to change anything, click Next to have the system prepare and copy the image to the RIS server you specified.

Installing the Remote Installation Preparation (Workstation)

For a workstation to take advantage of the RIS server functions, it must either have a DHCP PXE-based remote boot ROM, or a network adapter that is supported by the Boot from Floppy option for RIS access.

Additionally, the user logging in from the workstation needs to have a user account that has Logon as a Batch Job enabled. This allows the user to log on and launch RIS batch-processed services. To grant a user the Logon as a Batch Job privilege, follow these steps:

1. Choose Start | Programs | Administrative Tools | Directory Management.
2. Right-click the Domain Controllers container, and select Properties.
3. Select Group Policy.
4. Select the Default Domain Controllers Local Policy, and click Edit.
5. Locate the user's rights and then open the Computer Configuration folder.
6. Open Windows settings, security settings, local profiles, User Rights Assignment.
7. Right-click the Logon as a Batch Job right, and choose Security. Add the Everyone account or the specific user accounts that will be allowed to initiate an RIS client service. (The Administrator account is not granted the Logon as a Batch Job right by default, so even the Administrator account needs to be added to the list.)

Security on a domain controller that is configured through the Group Policy Editor will not take effect for the users or the group accounts immediately (sometimes this can take several hours, depending on the number of domain controllers and the replication scheme of the network). To have the rights applied immediately, you can either shut down and restart the server or you can do the following:

1. Drop to a DOS prompt by choosing Start | Run | cmd.exe.
2. Type **secedit /refreshpolicy machine_policy**.

Invoking a Remote Client Installation (PXE Remote Boot ROM)

With a DHCP PXE remote boot ROM in your system, when your system boots you will be prompted on some systems to press <F12> and on other systems to press the spacebar within a five second countdown to choose to boot to the PXE remote boot ROM instead of to the local hard drive.

Invoking a Remote Client Installation (Boot Floppy)

If you do not have a DHCP PXE remote boot ROM in your system, you can create a boot floppy diskette that boots to an RIS server and invokes the installation services. The remote installation boot floppy is created at the RIS server (with a blank floppy diskette available) using the following steps:

1. Choose Start | Run.
2. Type **\winnt\system32\reminst\rbfg.exe**, and then click OK.

This invokes the remote-boot floppy-generator utility and shows you a screen similar to the one in Figure 14-18. Click Create Disk to create the boot disk. Click Adapter List to see the list of adapters currently supported by this utility.

Windows Scripting Host

Windows Scripting Host (WSH) is a scripting system that supports a variety of scripting agents. These agents provide scripts that are executed directly on a Windows computer without embedding those scripts in an HTML document. Scripts are run by executing the script file. WSH provides a low-memory script process that has the ability to script logon processes, administrative tasks, software installation, or other functions, without installing a script-execution applet.

At the time of this writing, WSH for Windows 2000 supports VBScript as well as JavaScript scripting agents. Other agents are expected to be provided either by Microsoft or by third-party companies, including agents for Perl, XML, TCL, and REXX.

The Importance of Windows Scripting Host for Organizations

As you automate processes and tasks, sometimes the utility or application you want to install is actually an updated script generator. For example, to support XML, you need to support Internet Explorer 5.0 (IE5). If IE5 is not installed, XML scripts fail. By using WSH

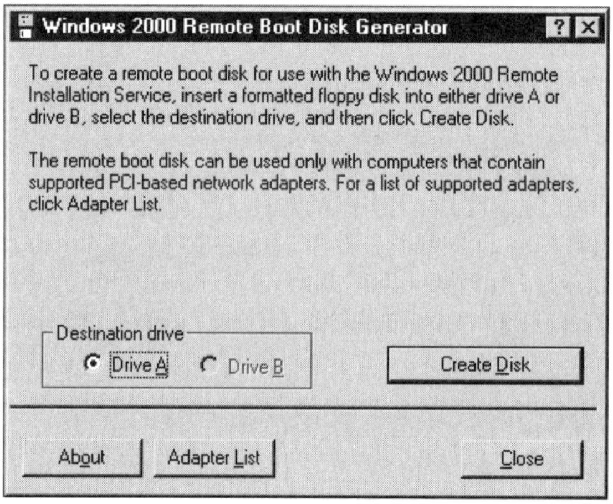

Figure 14-18. Remote boot floppy generator

with the WScript engine and XML support on the host system, a Windows 2000 Professional workstation can run the XML application installer to install IE5 onto the system before IE5 XML support is loaded.

For those scenarios where an agent needs to be installed prior to running a script, the workaround is to install the scripting agent on WSH, and then have the remote client launch the script from the WSH system.

Invoking Windows Scripting Host

Windows Scripting Host has two components: a server component and a client component. The server component is invoked by running the wscript.exe utility on a Windows 2000 server that is acting as the scripting host. When wscript.exe is launched, a screen similar to Figure 14-19 allows you to configure host parameter settings. It's usually best to accept the default setting to let a script run until completed (as opposed letting it run for a finite number of seconds).

On the client side, scripts are executed with the cscript.exe utility, where the syntax is as follows:

CScript *host_parameters script_name script_options*

Host parameters either enable or disable WSH options. The host parameter options are listed here:

Option	Function
//B	Specifies batch mode, which suppresses script errors and prompts from displaying.
//D	Enables active debugging.
//E:engine	Uses engine for executing script.
//H:CScript	Changes the default script host to cscript.exe.
//H:WScript	Changes the default script host to wscript.exe (default).
//I	Specifies interactive mode (default, opposite of //B).
//Job:*xxxx*	Executes a WS job.
//Logo	Displays logo at execution time (default).
//Nologo	Prevents the logo from displaying at execution time.
//S	Saves the current command-line options for this user.
//T:*nn*	Specifies the script will stop running in *nn* seconds.
//U	Use Unicode for redirected I/O from the console.
//X	Executes the script in debugger.

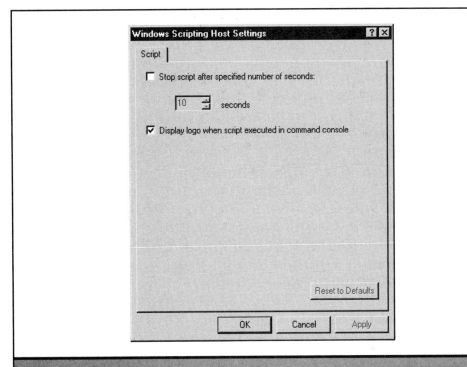

Figure 14-19.   Wscript.exe host parameter settings

The script name parameter on the command line identifies the file that holds the client script that is to be executed by WSH. The script parameters are command-line modifications to the script (similar to an environment variable), and they are passed to the script. Command-line script parameters are always preceded by a single slash (/), whereas the host parameters are always preceded by a double slash (//).

CHAPTER 15

Implementing and Migrating to an Active Directory–Based Network

In this chapter, I'll discuss how to create a fully hierarchical Active Directory–based network. In addition to covering the implementation of an Active Directory environment, I'll cover the process of migrating from previous versions of Windows NT as well as from Novell NDS.

IMPLEMENTING THE ACTIVE DIRECTORY

For organizations with more than 50–100 users, fully implementing an Active Directory environment involves a number of steps. To create a true enterprise environment, you must create organizational units and groups, add users to those units and groups, delegate administrative authority to others, and set up trusts or parent/child domain structures with other domains.

Creating Domain Trees and Forests

Active Directory domains are linked together in a hierarchical manner, forming a tree structure with parent and child relationships. The parent domain is the domain at the top, and the child domains are the domains under the parent domain. Since administrative security flows from the parent to the child, it is important that the hierarchical relationships are established properly. A single parent domain can spawn multiple child domains, which creates multiple domain trees. Multiple parent domains can also be linked to form a trust, which creates a forest.

Creating Parent and Child Domains

Linking domains together in parent and child relationships creates trusts between the domains. When domains are linked in this hierarchical fashion, there is a transition trust established among them. If Domain A trusts Domain B, and Domain B trusts Domain C, then there is a transitive trust between Domain A and Domain C.

This structure is created as domain controllers are added to the network. When a member server is promoted to be a domain controller, one of the questions you must answer is whether the new domain controller will create a new domain tree, or whether it will be a child domain in an existing domain tree. Your answer to that question determines whether a parent and child domain relationship is created.

CREATING A PARENT DOMAIN When promoting a member server to a domain controller (running the DCPromo utility), you are prompted by two screens that determine whether the domain controller will be the domain controller of a parent domain. The first question is whether the domain controller is for a new domain or an existing domain. If the domain controller is for a new domain, you are creating either a new parent domain or a new child domain, but in either case you are creating a new domain. To create a parent domain, select "Domain Controller for a New Domain" and click Next. The next question is whether you want to create a new domain tree or create a new child domain in an existing domain tree, as shown in Figure 15-1. To create a parent domain, select "Create a New Domain Tree" and click Next.

You are prompted to specify the location of files, including the sysvol folder. See "Running the DCPromo Utility" in Chapter 13 for detailed information on answering the rest of the questions. When you click Finish, the parent domain is created and you are prompted to reboot the server. When the server starts again, it will be the domain controller for the parent domain.

CREATING X.509 TRUSTS BETWEEN DOMAINS   To link domains together securely, you can create an Enterprise Certificate of Authority server, which issues certificates to authenti-

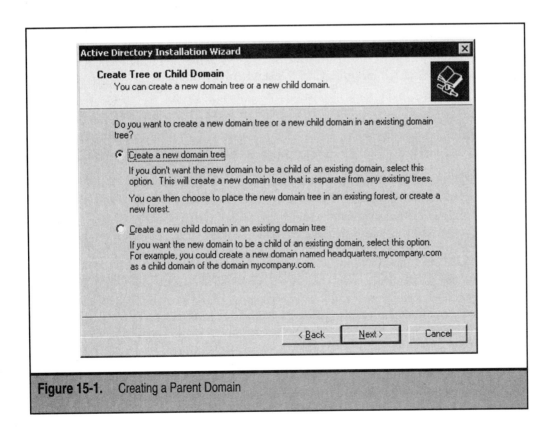

Figure 15-1.   Creating a Parent Domain

cate the trusts between domains. To create an Enterprise Certificate of Authority server, do the following:

1. Select Start | Settings | Control Panel, and then double-click Add/Remove Programs.

2. Click Add/Remove Windows Components, and then click the Components button.

3. Select the Certificate Services checkbox, and click Next.

4. You are prompted to select the type of certificate authority (CA) you wish to install—select Enterprise Root CA, and click Next to continue.

5. Enter identifying information for the CA. Most of the fields are self-explanatory, such as organization name, locality, and email address. These fields are for informational purposes only. The two key fields are the CA name (enter a description that identifies this CA Server service) and the validity duration (how long the certificate for the server is valid). Click Next to continue.

6. Enter the location of the certificate database and log. Typically, it's okay to accept the default location. Click Next when you are done.

7. Click Finish.

After you create your CA, validate its operation by doing the following:

1. Select Start | Programs | Administrative Tools | Certification Authority.

2. Double-click the name of the CA server you created, to expand the container.

3. Click the Issued Certificates folder.

4. Double-click the certificate in the right pane of the Console screen.

5. A copy of your certificate will appear on screen, similar to the one shown in Figure 15-2.

CREATING A CHILD DOMAIN   When you create a child domain by promoting a member server to become a domain controller (by running the DCPromo utility), you will see two screens that provide the options for setting up a child domain. The first option is whether the domain controller is for a new domain or for an existing domain. Select "Domain Controller for a New Domain" and click Next. The next option is whether you want to create a new domain tree, or create a new child domain in an existing domain tree. Select "Create a New Child Domain in an Existing Domain Tree," and click Next.

The rest of the process is similar to that of creating a parent domain, and the details are in Chapter 13. Once you are finished, reboot the server, which starts as the domain controller for the child domain.

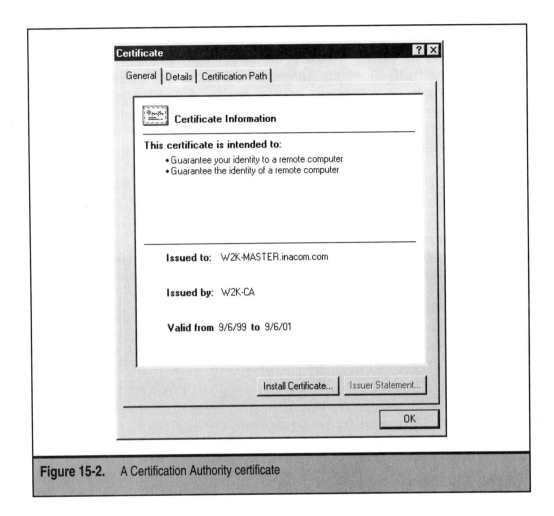

Figure 15-2. A Certification Authority certificate

If you have established X.509 authentication between domains, when the domain controller for the child domain boots, it will request an X.509 certificate from the Enterprise CA. The certificate is installed on the domain controller of the root domain.

Adding a New Domain Controller

As you create domains, do not create a single domain controller. Having a sole domain controller can be a central point of failure for logon authentication to the domain. You should have at least one additional domain controller in each domain on the network. In the event that one domain controller fails, the other domain controller(s) can assume all authentication services.

To add a domain controller to an existing domain, do the following:

1. Run the DCPromo utility on a member server to make it a domain controller. (Select Start | Run, type **dcpromo**, and click OK.)

2. In the first screen of the Active Directory Installation wizard, select "Additional Domain Controller for an Existing Domain," as shown in Figure 15-3.

Using the Active Directory Domains and Trusts Snap-in

The Active Directory Domains and Trusts snap-in is a simple administration tool that tracks and manages explicit and transitive trusts. You can use this snap-in to change a domain mode from a mixed mode to a native mode. You can also create explicit trusts to other domains.

CHANGING A DOMAIN MODE   By default, a Windows 2000 domain is created as a mixed mode domain, which allows for the integration of previous versions of Windows. However, running in mixed mode means you cannot take advantage of the capabilities available in native mode operation. Some of these advantages are multi-master

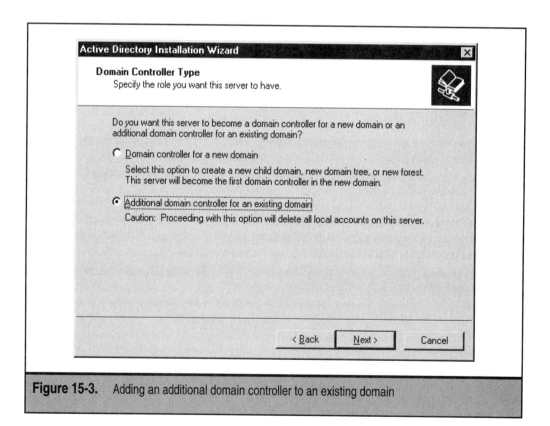

Figure 15-3.   Adding an additional domain controller to an existing domain

replication among domain controllers, the existence of universal groups, and the ability to nest groups.

The ability to nest groups is important for scalability, because group membership is stored in the Active Directory as a single, multi-value attribute. Any changes made to the membership of the group results in the entire attribute being updated and distributed throughout the domain. Rather than create extremely large and unmanageable groups, you can work with subsets of users, nesting them for easier management.

When all the workstations on the network have been upgraded to support Windows 2000 Active Directory and domain-security authentication, the Windows 2000 system should be upgraded to a native mode operation. To do so, follow these steps:

1. Synchronize all domain controllers on the network.

2. Right-click the domain in the Active Directory Domains and Trusts snap-in Console screen, and select Properties.

3. Click Change Mode.

4. When prompted "Are You Sure You Want To Change this Domain to Native Mode?", select Yes.

VIEWING AND MODIFYING TRUSTS   You can use the Active Directory Domains and Trusts snap-in to view, edit, add, and remove trusts on the domain. Right-click the domain in the Active Directory Domains and Trusts snap-in Console screen, and select Properties. Then select the Trusts tab to see a screen similar to the one shown in Figure 15-4. Use this screen to add, remove, view, or edit trusts between domains.

Using the Active Directory Site and Services Snap-in

You can use the Active Directory Site and Services snap-in to administer and manage replication, both within a site and between sites. Replication within a site is the process of keeping domain controllers and replication servers synchronized on a LAN. For WAN connections between sites, the same type of replication and synchronization occurs, but the process uses a slow link. Sites are not the vehicle for authentication services, and that's why the Active Directory Site and Services snap-in is separate from the Active Directory Users and Computers snap-in.

A site contains one or more high-speed connected subnets. A site can span multiple domains, and a domain can span multiple sites. The sites exist to provide replication boundaries. Within a site, the servers replicate information quite quickly over high-speed connections. Between sites, a site link or a site-link bridge is established to provide replication over traditionally slower LAN or WAN link connections.

Building Sites

When you design a site, you do not need to take the administrative or security zones of DNS or your domains into consideration. The only consideration is the physical location of the servers and the type of physical connections. When you use the Active Directory

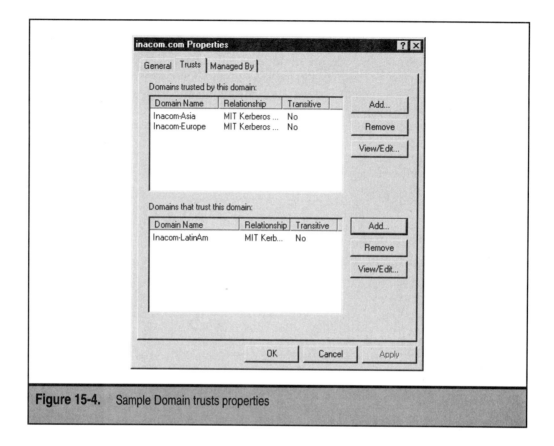

Figure 15-4. Sample Domain trusts properties

Site and Services snap-in, you can create the sites, designate the subnets that make up the sites, add or move servers into the correct sites, and establish the intersite transports between the sites in the physical site structure.

DEFAULT FIRST SITE NAME   When you create the first server in a Windows 2000 environment, the first site is called the "Default-First-Site-Name," and the server is placed within that site. You can rename the site by clicking on the site name, pressing F2, and entering a new name for your initial site.

ADDING A SITE TO YOUR PHYSICAL SITE STRUCTURE   You can add sites to your physical site structure by doing the following:

1. Right-click Sites in the Active Directory Site and Services snap-in tree, and then click New Site.

2. Type in the name of the new site (use a maximum of 63 alphanumeric characters with no spaces or periods, although a hyphen is permitted).

3. Assuming you will be communicating among sites via TCP/IP, click DEFAULTIPSITELINK as your site-link transport, and then click OK.

ADDING A SUBNET TO YOUR PHYSICAL SITE STRUCTURE   When you are creating sites, you need to define the subnets that make up the sites. When a server or computer is added to the domain and is identifiable by its subnet, it is automatically added to the appropriate site in the Active Directory Site and Services snap-in. You can always change or rename subnets, or move systems to other subnets. However, if you planned ahead as suggested throughout this book, your physical diagram will have all of your connections defined, and you simply need to enter the information.

To create a subnet, do the following:

1. Double-click Sites to expand the Sites container.

2. Click to highlight Subnets.

3. Select the Action pull-down item from the Console screen, and select New | Subnets.

4. Enter the subnet and subnet mask information. The description will initially be the subnet address/mask, which can be changed to a more meaningful name by right clicking the subnet after creation.

5. Click the Site list, and select the site that this subnet should be correlated with. Then click OK.

Linking Sites Together

Now that you've created sites, you need to link them together to form the physical structure of your organization. Sites are interconnected through site links. When you designate site links in the Active Directory Site and Services snap-in, you need to be very certain of the type of connectivity you have among sites. If you say that San Francisco is connected to New York as a site link, the operating system assumes the connection is direct from San Francisco to New York, even if San Francisco actually physically routes through Denver and then Denver routes through Chicago before reaching the New York network segment. Mistakes like this can cause performance problems in communicating between sites.

When a site link routes through another site, the Active Directory Site and Services snap-in provides a designator called a site-link bridge that allows you to specify that two links interconnect through a single site.

CREATING A SITE LINK   After you have created all of the sites in the Active Directory Site and Services snap-in, you can link the sites together by following these steps:

1. Double-click Sites to expand the Sites container.

2. Double-click Inter-site Transports to expand that container.

3. Right-click either IP or SMTP, depending on the type of WAN connection you have, and select New Site Link.

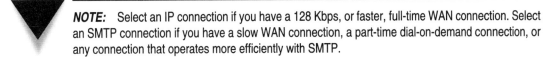

NOTE: Select an IP connection if you have a 128 Kbps, or faster, full-time WAN connection. Select an SMTP connection if you have a slow WAN connection, a part-time dial-on-demand connection, or any connection that operates more efficiently with SMTP.

4. In the Name field, enter a descriptive name for the site link, using any alphanumeric characters, including spaces and punctuation.

5. Select the sites from the left pane and click Add to move the sites to the right pane, as shown in Figure 15-5.

6. Click OK to finish.

CREATING A SITE-LINK BRIDGE   To create a site-link bridge (after you have created the site links in the Active Directory Site and Services snap-in), do the following:

1. Double-click Sites to expand the Sites container.

2. Double-click Inter-site Transports to expand that container.

3. Select either IP or SMTP, depending on the protocol being used by the sites. All of the site links must be running the same intersite transport protocol, so if all of the site links you want to bridge are SMTP, right-click SMTP. If all of the site

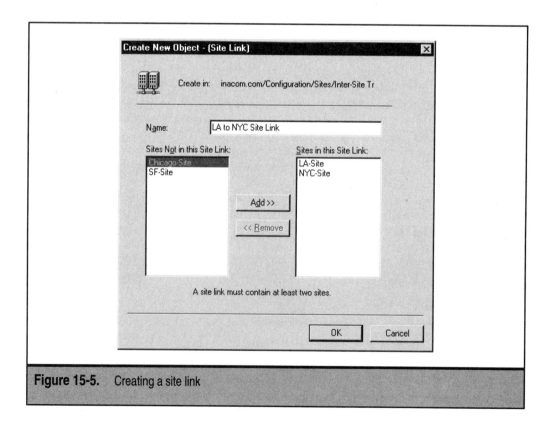

Figure 15-5.   Creating a site link

links you want to bridge are IP, right-click IP. Select properties that will bring up a series of fields to update or edit.

4. Under the Name field, type in a descriptive name for the site-link bridge using any alphanumeric characters, including spaces and punctuation.

5. Select the site links from the left pane and click Add to move the site links to the right pane, as shown in Figure 15-6.

6. Click OK to finish.

EXAMPLE OF ROUTED SITE LINKS AND BRIDGES   Suppose an organization has sites in Singapore, Tokyo, San Francisco, Chicago, New York, London, and Frankfurt. Singapore routes through Tokyo to get to San Francisco, and Frankfurt routes through London to get to San Francisco. Both Chicago and New York link directly to San Francisco. The configuration is shown in Figure 15-7.

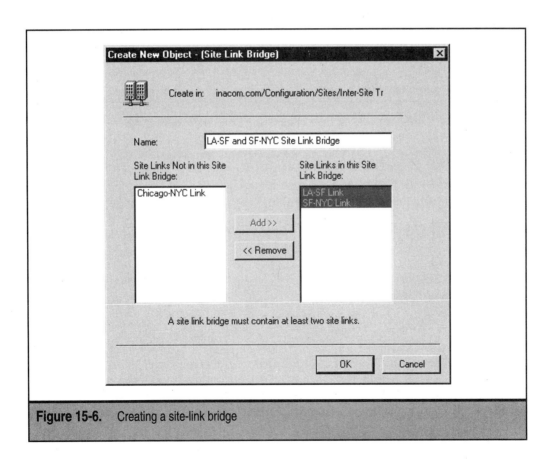

Figure 15-6.   Creating a site-link bridge

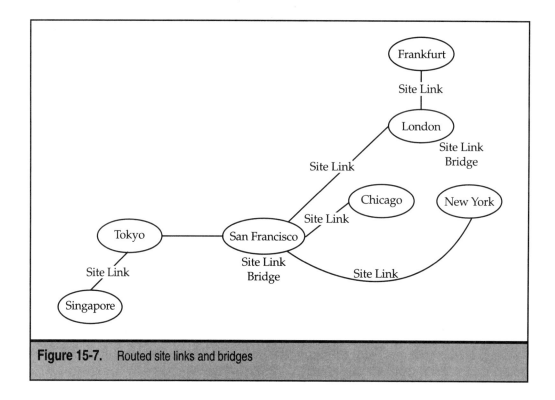

Figure 15-7. Routed site links and bridges

You would have the following site links:

▼ Singapore to Tokyo

■ Tokyo to San Francisco

■ Frankfurt to London

■ London to San Francisco

■ Chicago to San Francisco

▲ New York to San Francisco

You would have the following site-link bridges:

▼ Singapore to Tokyo bridges Tokyo to San Francisco

▲ Frankfurt to London bridges London to San Francisco

EXAMPLE OF A REGIONAL FRAME-RELAY NETWORK   In this example, an organization has sites in San Francisco, Seattle, Los Angeles, Portland, and Denver. As diagramed in Figure 15-8, all of the sites are interconnected through a common frame-relay WAN cloud.

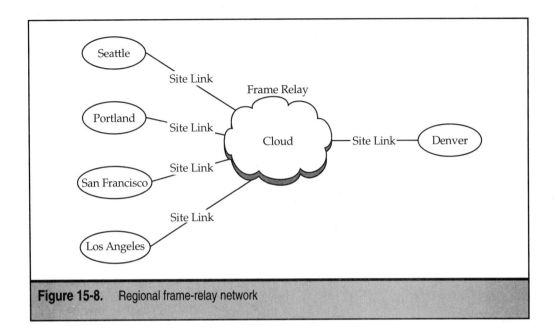

Figure 15-8. Regional frame-relay network

Each site can communicate with another site in the cloud. Therefore, as far as Windows 2000 is concerned, all of the sites are linked together. The configuration looks as follows:

You would have the following site links: Seattle to Portland to San Francisco to Los Angeles to Denver.

You would have no site-link bridges.

EFFECT OF THE SMTP SERVICE ON INTERSITE TRANSPORTS   In order for sites to communicate with each other over the SMTP intersite transport, the SMTP service must be installed on the network domain controllers (which should occur by default). If SMTP site-to-site communication is not functioning, you should verify whether the service has indeed been installed. If not, you can install the SMTP service manually by following these steps:

1. Select Start | Settings | Control Panel, and double-click Add/Remove Programs.

2. Click Add/Remove Windows Components, and then click the Components button.

3. Click Internet Information Service (IIS), and then click Details.

4. Select the SMTP Service checkbox, and click OK.

5. Click Finish to install the SMTP service.

Using the Active Directory Users and Computers Snap-in

The Active Directory Users and Computers snap-in controls the way security and administration is applied within and among domains. This snap-in manages domains, organizational units, groups, users, contacts, computers, shared printers, and shared folders.

Adding an Organizational Unit

You can add a new organizational unit in the Active Directory Users and Computers snap-in. Organizational units are a way of distributing security and administrative tasks. To create an organizational unit, do the following:

1. Right-click the domain where you want to add an organizational unit, and select New | Organizational Unit.
2. Type in the name of the new organizational unit, and click OK.

Adding a User Account

User accounts are kept for users who are authorized to log on and access domain resources. To create a user account, right-click the domain or organizational-unit object you want to add a user to, and select New | User. Then fill in the user information.

Moving a User Account

After you create a user account, you may want to move the account to a different organizational unit. To do so, right-click the account and select Move. Then select the target destination from the browse window.

Creating a Group

You can use groups to create common functions specific to multiple users. This could be users who have access to specific shares, or users to whom you want to apply specific group policies. You can create a group by doing the following:

1. Right-click a domain or organizational unit where you want to add a group, and select New | Group.
2. Type in the name of the group.
3. Specify the type of the group.
4. Click OK to complete the process.

Adding a User to a Group

When you add a user to a group, there is no visual evidence of the group members in the group folder. Groups simply hold users in a members list for administrative and operational purposes. To add a user to the group, you can do either of the following:

1. Right-click the user, and select Add to Group.
2. Select the group you wish to Add the user to.

    or

1. Right-click the Group, and select Properties.
2. Click the Members tab, and click Add.
3. Scroll through the list, click on a user, and click Add.

Publishing a Shared Folder

Shared folders can be published on the network, allowing users to connect to them. To create a shared folder, you can right-click a folder and select Share, or you can do the following in the Active Directory Users and Computers snap-in:

1. Right-click the domain or organizational unit where you want to publish a shared folder, and select New | Shared Folder.
2. Enter the name of the folder you want to publish, and press TAB.
3. Enter the UNC address of the folder you wish to share, and click OK.

Publishing a Printer

Printers can be published by right-clicking the printer object in the printer folder, and selecting Share. However, you can also publish a printer by doing the following:

1. Right-click the domain or organizational unit where you want to publish a printer, and select New | Printer.
2. Type in the name of the printer you want to publish, and press TAB.
3. Type in the UNC address of the printer you wish to share, and click OK.

Moving an Object

While it would be nice to drag and drop objects around in the Active Directory Users and Computers snap-in, unfortunately that level of functionality is not included at this time. In order to move objects around in the utility, you need to do the following:

1. Right-click the object (user, computer, shared printer, shared folder, and so on) and select Move.
2. Click Browse, scroll through the directory tree, highlight the domain, site, or organizational unit to which you want to move the object, and click OK.

Finding Objects

In a large network, it can be a challenging task to find an object among hundreds or thousands of objects listed in the tree. To find an object quickly, do the following:

1. Right-click a domain or organizational unit where you want to begin searching for an object (user, computer, shared printer, shared folder, and so on).

2. In the Name field, type in all or part of the name you wish to search for, and then click Find Now.

The results of your query will appear at the bottom of the screen.

Filtering for Objects

If you need to filter for objects of the same classification or category, such as all users or all printers, do the following:

1. Select View | Filter Options.

2. Select the option "Show Only the Following Types of Objects," and then select the object type you wish filter for.

3. Click OK.

The filtered results will appear in the container you are in, along with an indication ("filter activated") in the description bar that a filter has been applied.

STRATEGIES THAT SIMPLIFY THE MIGRATION PROCESS

As you prepare your existing network for migration to Windows 2000, there are a number of things that can help you simplify the migration process. A simple rule of thumb when migrating to an Active Directory is to create a new directory rather than try to work with an older directory structure.

Understanding New Administration and Security Needs

After reviewing the material regarding directory analysis and planning in Chapter 6, do a last-minute review of the existing domain objects and structure before initiating a migration.

Validating Users and Groups from the Old Domain Structure

Go through the users and groups in your old domain structure to find information that is obsolete. This can be a tedious and time-consuming task, but it is worth doing this housekeeping rather than migrating a lot of obsolete users.

Consolidating Resource Domains

It may be effective to consolidate domains in order to simplify the task of migrating domains into the Active Directory. Typically, all resource domains on the existing Windows NT 4 network are migrated to the Windows 2000 Active Directory. If you created large numbers of miscellaneous resource domains over the years, it could take the Active Directory migration team a long time to analyze and migrate them.

Rather than migrating useless domains and then having to deal with integrating them for administration and management, consolidate as many domains as possible to create a simplified organizational structure.

DELETING UNUSED RESOURCE DOMAINS   It's typical to find resource domains that were created to distribute security privileges or other services on a temporary basis, and those domains are no longer used, nor are they needed. Deleting them decreases the time and effort needed to administer and manage the migration to Windows 2000.

CONSOLIDATING AND RESTRUCTURING DOMAINS   You may find that no matter how much housecleaning you do, you still end up with a number of currently valid resource domains that you now wouldn't create in the current environment (the "if I knew then what I know now" syndrome). There are a number of third-party products available to consolidate and restructure a Windows NT 4 domain model. Fastlane Technologies' DM/Manager (www.fastlane.tech.com) and Mission Critical's OnePoint Domain Administrator (www.missioncritical.com) are good examples of these tools. These products give you a view of your existing domain structure and move objects into new or existing domain structures.

Windows NT does not permit the movement of objects between domains because the operating system cannot perform that task, and also to preserve the SID history of objects. If you delete and re-create an object, the SID is changed, and any preexisting security is no longer valid.

However, the Fastlane Technologies and Mission Critical products allow objects to be moved from domain to domain. You can even create new domains and place objects within them. The SID history of a moved object is preserved, which means that you can restructure and reorganize a domain to make migration to Windows 2000 an easier task.

Preparing for Components That Don't Work in Windows 2000

As you prepare to migrate to Windows 2000, you may discover some components and functions that do not work in Windows 2000. Sometimes this causes organizations to decide not to migrate to Windows 2000 at all. However, sometimes the decision to migrate is made because the features in Windows 2000 are important to your core applications (messaging, databases, thin-client strategies, and so on). You need to analyze any incompatibilities you discover and determine the best way to proceed with migration.

Server Applications That Are Not Compatible with Windows 2000

If you find that a server application is not compatible with Windows 2000, you can run in a mixed mode to provide backwards compatibility. Other alternatives may be available, depending on the specific incompatibility.

For example, in some cases the application services run on a Windows NT 4 server but use other methods of user authentication. This means the system doesn't have to be tied to an Active Directory migration. You could allow this specific server to remain on Windows NT 4 and proceed with a full migration to a native mode Active Directory.

LMRepl Needs To Be Replaced by FRS

One component that does not migrate to Windows 2000 is the LAN Manager Replication (LMRepl) application that is frequently used to copy user profiles and logon scripts from domain controller to domain controller. Since LMRepl is not supported in Windows 2000, you need to use the Windows 2000 File Replication Service (FRS). Any change made to a logon script stored in the sysvol of any domain controller is automatically replicated in a multi-master manner to the other domain controllers in the organization. This conversion process of using FRS instead of LMRepl is not complicated, because the functionality is the same. However, logon scripts and other components replicated between servers must be identified prior to the migration process.

MIGRATING FROM WINDOWS NT 4 DOMAINS

There are a few methods for migrating domains into the Active Directory. The options vary based on the type of existing domain structure, so it is very important to pay attention to the type of model being discussed and to use the right process and right tools to complete the migration process.

Choosing Your Migration Path

The first decision to make is to choose the migration path for converting domains. You can either select a native-mode migration, or you can select a mixed-mode migration. By default, Windows 2000 is configured for a mixed-mode migration, but there are circumstances in which you should use the native-mode migration process.

Native-Mode Migration

A native-mode migration assumes a quick and immediate migration to the Windows 2000 Active Directory. Native-mode migration disables Windows NT 4 Netlogon backwards compatibility with Windows 9x and Windows NT workstations that have not been upgraded to support the Active Directory.

Because workstations can be upgraded by installing new client network drivers, while still retaining backwards compatibility with existing Windows NT logons, many organizations have elected to do a workstation migration first, and then migrate the servers. After the workstations have been updated, it's easy to move to an infrastructure that is based completely on the Active Directory.

The benefits of native mode is the ability to utilize features such as universal groups and group nesting. These are very valuable tools when you are implementing an Active Directory environment. It's a catch-22 for an organization that wants to take advantage of the capabilities of Windows 2000, but that is hindered from doing so because it is running in a mixed mode.

Mixed-Mode Migration

Mixed-mode migration is the common method of converting from Windows NT to the Windows 2000 Active Directory. The biggest benefit of using a mixed-mode migration is the ability to migrate over a period of time. Many organizations just can't prepare all the workstations and servers quickly.

Mixed-mode migration also provides the ability to fall back to Windows NT domains if moving to a native Windows 2000 Active Directory is not possible right away. This is commonly caused by applications that work fine under Windows NT but have not been certified to run on a Windows 2000 server. Until all of those applications have been updated, many organizations will only be able to upgrade part of the infrastructure to Windows 2000.

Options for Migration Strategies

All of the organizations I have worked with on Windows 2000 migrations have had to choose between two migration choices:

▼ Make a direct in-place upgrade to Windows 2000

▲ Create a clean Active Directory and migrate users into the clean
directory structure

No doubt there are minor variations on these two options, such as consolidating domains prior to migration, or creating a process to do some form of consolidation after migration. However, these two options are the foundation for every migration from Windows NT domains to a Windows 2000 Active Directory.

Upgrading a Domain Directly to Active Directory

Upgrading the domain controllers, as is, into Active Directory provides a quick single-step process for migration. For organizations with relatively simple Windows NT domain structures, such as small businesses or organizations that have a single domain model that is very flat, a migration straight to an Active Directory can be the easiest approach.

THE MIGRATION SEQUENCE   The migration sequence for a conversion from Windows NT domains into a Windows 2000 Active Directory is as follows:

1. Force a synchronization of all backup domain controllers (BDCs) in the Windows NT 4 domain so that all of the BDCs are completely updated with the latest version of the SAM database.

2. Upgrade the primary domain controller (PDC) to Windows 2000. If the Windows NT domain model is a master domain model with both administrative and resource domains, upgrade the PDC of the administrative domain first. During the migration process, Windows 2000 recognizes the system as the PDC and prompts the administrator to upgrade the domain information to an Active Directory. When the administrator agrees, the DCPromo utility runs to upgrade the system to a domain controller in the Active Directory.

3. The administrator has the option of creating the first tree in a new forest, creating the first tree in an existing forest, creating a replica of an existing domain, or installing a child domain. Typically, if you are migrating the Windows NT domain directly to an Active Directory structure and upgrading the administrative domain first, you are creating a domain controller in a new domain, creating a new domain tree, and creating the first tree in a new forest.

4. After the DCPromo utility runs, the PDC will appear as a Windows 2000 domain controller to all Windows 2000 systems on the network, and it will appear as the Windows NT PDC to computers still running Windows NT 4 utilities.

5. The next step is to upgrade at least one BDC in the domain to be a Windows 2000 domain controller. In the DCPromo utility, select "Additional Domain Controller in an Existing Domain" and select the first domain controller as the domain controller master.

6. Continue to upgrade the other BDCs in the domain (or administrative domain) and then proceed with the resource domains.

7. Upgrade the PDC of one of the resource domains. To create a hierarchical structure for administration, have the resource domain become a child domain to the administrative domain that you upgraded in step 2. To do so, during the DCPromo utility upgrade, indicate that you are creating a domain controller in a new domain, and you are creating a new child domain in an existing domain tree. Select the original administrative domain as the parent domain.

8. Continue to upgrade the BDCs of the resource domain to create domain-controller redundancy. In the DCPromo utility, select "Additional Domain Controller in an Existing Domain," and select the domain controller created by the resource domain as your master domain controller for replication.

9. After you have at least two domain controllers migrated to Windows 2000, begin migrating computers to support Active Directory logon. Either migrate

the workstations to Windows 2000 Professional, or install the appropriate service packs and service releases to provide Active Directory support.

10. After all domain controllers, servers, and workstations have been upgraded to support the Active Directory security, set the network to native mode.

PROS AND CONS OF MIGRATION   There are, of course, pros and cons to consider when you are deciding on the approach for upgrading a domain directly into an Active Directory model.

One positive aspect in migrating straight from Windows NT domains into an Active Directory is that the task can be performed in a sequential migration process. Domain controllers can be migrated one at a time and can run in a mixed mode while the desktops and servers are slowly migrated to the native Active Directory model. Assuming you are currently operating with a relatively flat administrative model, there's no need to complicate the model in a migration process by creating unnecessary levels of administration or organizational units.

Negative side effects of migrating directly to an Active Directory model from a Windows NT domain model include the possibility that you will migrate obsolete users, groups, or other objects. Additionally, a direct migration may make it more difficult to reconfigure the system to take advantage of organizational units, universal groups, or nested groups.

Creating a Clean Active Directory

You can install Windows 2000 on brand new systems and create an Active Directory tree that is pristine. Once the Active Directory is set up, you can either move users and resources into the Active Directory manually, or upgrade the PDCs of the Windows NT domain to populate the Active Directory with the existing users, groups, and resource objects. Those objects are immediately moved into the clean Active Directory structure.

MIGRATION SEQUENCE   The migration sequence for a conversion from Windows NT domains into a clean Windows 2000 Active Directory is as follows:

1. Install Windows 2000 on a system and run the DCPromo utility to promote the system to become the first domain controller on the network. During the DCPromo process, select the options to create a domain controller in a new domain, create a new domain tree, and create the first tree in a new forest.

2. Create at least one other domain controller in the domain to provide fault tolerance for the Active Directory. When you run the DCPromo utility, select "Additional Domain Controller in an Existing Domain," and select the first domain controller to be the domain controller master.

3. Create your Active Directory tree, establishing organization units within the domain and creating groups that are appropriate for your organization.

4. If the Active Directory structure requires additional domains and sites, create those objects, link the sites, and join the additional domains to form the domain tree.

5. After the entire Active Directory structure is in place, you can manually create users, or you can migrate a domain controller from the administrative domain to a domain controller in the Active Directory.

6. To migrate a domain controller from the Windows NT domain, force a synchronization of all BDCs in the Windows NT 4 domain so that all of the BDCs are completely updated with the latest version of the SAM database.

7. Upgrade the PDC or BDC to Windows 2000, and then run the DCPromo utility. When the domain controller has been upgraded, you can use the Move command to move users, groups, and other objects from the old Windows NT domain server into the new Active Directory. After all of the objects have been moved, you can remove the old PDC system from the network, if you desire.

8. After you have migrated at least two domain controllers, begin migrating computers to support Active Directory logon. You can migrate the workstations to Windows 2000 Professional, or install the appropriate service packs and service releases to provide Active Directory support.

9. After all the domain controllers, servers, and workstations have been upgraded to Active Directory security, configure the network for native mode.

PROS AND CONS OF A NEW ACTIVE DIRECTORY   There are some pros and cons to consider when you want to create a pristine Active Directory from scratch, as described in the preceding section.

On the positive side, starting from scratch means you can design your plan and test the process. Because you create the Active Directory completely apart from the existing Windows NT domain, the operation of the Windows NT servers does not affect the completion of the Active Directory design or implementation. As users are migrated to the Active Directory, they can be moved logically into appropriate organizational unit containers and made members of groups that are appropriate for their group policy rights and access.

On the negative side, there are a lot of steps to take to build the Active Directory separate from the existing Windows NT domain model. You may inadvertently miss some design considerations regarding the way resource domains or groups are set in the current Windows NT 4 environment. If the hierarchy of your Windows NT system is relatively simple, the task of creating the perfect Active Directory and migrating users may be more complicated than a direct migration.

Comments on the Windows NT Domain Migration Process

When given a chance to upgrade account domains, resource domains, or workstations, the order of preference is to upgrade the account domains first, then the resource domains, and lastly the workstations. Account domains are typically the trickiest to migrate, since that's where the users are. When you migrate the account domains first, all user and group planning for the migration must be taken into account early on in the migration process. By upgrading the account domains first, the resources in the resource domains can be migrated into an organizational unit, and then added to the directory tree for down-level administration.

Who Will Be Migrated Where?

When a PDC or BDC is migrated to Active Directory, the users, computers, and groups from the domain are migrated to the top-level folders of the Active Directory domain, using corresponding folders. The exception to this rule is the default groups, such as Domain Admins, which are moved to the Builtin folder. Global or local groups created by the administrator are moved to the Users folder. One item to note in regard to migrations from Windows NT domains is that user rights, account, and audit policies are not migrated to Active Directory because of differences in the way policies are handled within Active Directory. The Active Directory domain controller is installed in a new domain tree and will have the default security policy applied. If it is installed in an existing tree, it will inherit the security policy from the parent domain.

MIGRATING FROM NETWARE NDS TO ACTIVE DIRECTORY

Many organizations with mixed network environments may be considering migrating to Windows 2000 and Active Directory. Earlier versions of Microsoft Windows NT were migrated from NetWare to Windows NT through the NetWare Convert utility (nwconv.exe) that was bundled with Windows NT. Nwconv.exe nondestructively migrated bindery-based users, groups, files, and file security (ACLs) to a Windows NT Server domain controller, but it did not support migrating from Novell's NDS.

For Windows 2000, Microsoft has replaced NetWare Convert with the Directory Service Migration Tool that supports migrating from both bindery and NDS-based NetWare environments. This utility is nondestructive and migrates the NetWare information into an offline database. Administrators can then model the account information before committing it to the Active Directory.

The major benefit of the Directory Service Migration Tool is that you can migrate selected branches of the NDS tree without migrating the entire tree. Because you can model the information to be migrated, you can verify that the changes are exactly what you want, prior to committing them.

Installing the Directory Service Migration Tool

To migrate from Novell Bindery or NDS networks to a Windows 2000 Active Directory environment, you must first install the Directory Service Migration Tool. During the installation process, the Gateway Services for NetWare (GSNW) service will be installed on your Windows 2000 system, if it is not already installed. To install the Directory Service Migration Tool, do the following:

1. Select Start | Settings | Control Panel, and double-click Add/Remove Programs.
2. Click Add/Remove Windows Components, and click the Components button.
3. Select Management and Monitoring Tools, and click Details.
4. Select the Directory Service Migration Tool checkbox, and click OK. Then click Next to begin the installation of the component.

Preparing for a Migration

Because the Directory Services Migration Tool provides you with the ability to migrate your Novell NetWare information into an offline database, you have the ability to do a fair amount of planning and testing. Also, you do not need to migrate your entire environment all at once. Instead, you can select a portion of your NetWare environment to migrate to the Windows 2000 Active Directory. You should start with a small group of users and resources from your NetWare environment, and test the migration process first. As you get familiar with the process (which is quite simple), you can take larger groups of users and resources in subsequent passes of your migration process.

Creating a View of the NetWare Environment

The first thing to do during the migration process is to create a view of the NetWare resources (users, computers, printers, groups) that will be copied to populate the Directory Services Migration database. To launch the initial view process, do the following:

1. Start the Directory Service Migration Tool by selecting Start | Programs | Administrative Tools | Directory Service Migration Tool.
2. Right-click the Directory Service Migration Tool object in the left pane of the Console tree, and select New | Project.
3. Enter a name for this project (use any alphanumeric characters, including spaces and punctuation).
4. Right-click your new project name, and select New | View from NetWare.
5. In the View Name field, enter a name for this particular test run. You can pull in the information from NetWare multiple times, and each time you import the information, you can create a new view that you can use to manipulate information, see how it works, and then perform the actual migration.
6. Select the binderies and/or NDS directories you wish to migrate, and select Next.
7. The migration process imports the resource objects from NetWare into the Directory Service Migration Tool's offline database. Click Finished when you are done.

After you migrate the groups and users from NetWare into the Directory Service Migration Tool, you will see a screen that looks similar to the one in Figure 15-9.

Creating Containers for Active Directory

After you've imported the objects from NetWare, you can create containers to use for your Active Directory. You can opt to keep the containers just as they are, if you wish. Or, if you want to rename containers, this is the time to do it. The changes you make will create the environment you will import into the Windows 2000 Active Directory.

To create containers, right-click any of the containers in the Directory Service Migration Tool, and select New. Depending on where you are in the migration tool tree, you are prompted to add either a new organization or organizational unit, or to create a new user, group, or volume. Typically at this point in the migration process, you only create new organizational units to store users in, and then you can drag and drop users into the organizational units that will be imported into the Windows 2000 Active Directory.

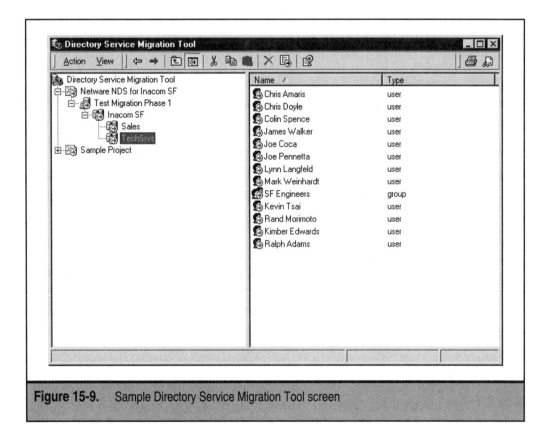

Figure 15-9. Sample Directory Service Migration Tool screen

Rearranging Your Migration Hierarchy

After you've created any new containers for your new directory structure, move objects around within the Directory Service Migration Tool to reorganize the user, group, and resource structure.

Exporting Your Offline Database

After you've created containers and moved users around as needed, export the information out of the Directory Service Migration Tool and into the Active Directory, using the following steps:

1. Right-click the organizational unit you wish to export (all objects below the organizational unit will be exported, as well) and select All Tasks | Configure Objects to Active Directory.

2. In the Pre-Configure Verify Object screen, double-click LDAP to expand the container, and then double-click the name of the domain in which you are adding this organizational unit. Click Next.

3. The export process runs through a series of checks on the objects and logs any errors. You can continue with the migration, cancel the migration, or view the Log Viewer screen. If errors were detected and are noted on the screen, you should view the errors and determine the problem(s) before you proceed with the migration.

4. If you review the log and there are no errors, click Continue. The system runs through a series of Configure Object modifications to change the characteristics of each object from a Novell object into a Windows 2000 Active Directory object. Click OK it is when complete.

You can now go into your Active Directory and view the Active Directory users and computer domain structure to see the objects that were moved from NetWare into the Active Directory, as shown in Figure 15-10.

Validating the Migration

After you've migrated users from NetWare to Windows 2000, validate the users to make sure that the migrated information is correct and that the users can successfully log into the Windows 2000 network.

Verifying User Information

To verify the user information, go into the Active Directory Users and Computers snap-in and double-click any of the users to verify that the username, group distribution, address, and privileges are correct. If there are minor errors, such as an address field migrated to the wrong place, you can safely ignore the error. However, if a user has an

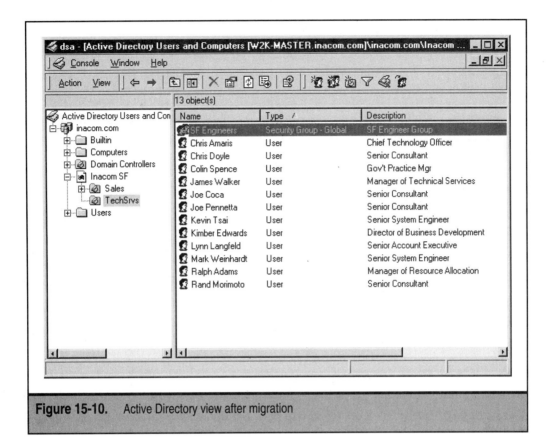

Figure 15-10. Active Directory view after migration

incorrect group membership, or is located in the wrong organizational unit, you must determine the best way to resolve the error.

In many cases, errors can be easily fixed by simply deleting the erroneous objects in the Active Directory, making the changes in the Directory Services Migration Tool, and rerunning the export migration process.

In other cases, the migration modifications required cannot be changed on either the export or the import side. These changes can be handled as separate tasks and in many cases can take advantage of the LDIFDE utility described in the "Migration Using the LDIFDE Utility" section, later in this chapter.

Testing User Logon

If all the information migrated from the NetWare directory to the Active Directory looks correct, verify that users can successfully log on to the network and that they have appropriate access to resources. Check access to shares and printers, proper file- and folder-level security, network administration security, and remote dial-up access security.

Completing the Migration

Assuming you only selected a small portion of your NetWare directory to migrate to Windows 2000 in your initial process, fix any problems in the migration process to prepare for a full migration.

In many cases, the migration process requires a series of tests of small groups of users, or even the creation of test users on the Novell NetWare side. Then watch the results of the migration to determine if there is anything more you need to do to perform a complete migration.

MIGRATION USING THE LDIFDE UTILITY

The LDIFDE utility is a command-line program that comes with Windows 2000. This utility provides the ability to create users in the Active Directory, or to modify existing user information via a text file that can be imported into the Windows 2000 Active Directory. This utility lets you migrate users instead of entering all the users by keyboard. An existing network directory can be exported to a file, manipulated with a text editor or a spreadsheet, and then imported directly into the Active Directory.

The LDIFDE utility is found on the Windows 2000 CD-ROM or is copied to the \winnt\system32 directory during the installation of the operating system.

Importing User Data into the Active Directory

User information can be imported into the Active Directory either by manipulating an export file from a different network operating system or by creating the import file directly.

Using LDIFDE to Create a User Import File

The file structure for the import file is simple ASCII text. A file can be created to meet your organization's configuration, as in this example:

```
dn: CN=Rich Dorfman, OU=BusDev, DC=inacom, DC=com
changetype: add
cn: Rich Dorfman
objectclass: user
samAccountName: Rich
givenname: Rich
sn: Dorfman
```

Save the file as a text file, and then run the LDIFDE import utility. The syntax is:

ldifde –i –f *filename* –s *servername*
    –d" ou=*OU*, dc=*domain*, dc=*com*"

When you execute the command, you will see a screen similar to Figure 15-11.

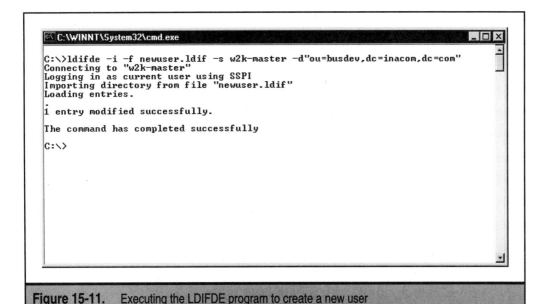

Figure 15-11.   Executing the LDIFDE program to create a new user

Using LDIFDE to Delete a User

You can also delete a user with the LDIFDE utility, as in this example:

```
dn: CN=Rich Dorfman, OU=BusDev, DC=inacom, dc=com
changetype: delete
```

Modifying Existing User Entries with the LDIFDE Utility

You can also use the LDIFDE utility to make modifications to existing entries in the Active Directory. You export information from the Active Directory, manipulate the information using a text editor or spreadsheet application, and then run the LDIFDE utility to import the information back into the Active Directory.

Exporting Information from the Active Directory

To export information from the Active Directory, use the LDIFDE utility with the following syntax:

ldifde –f *filename* –s *servername* –d" ou=*OU*, dc=*domain*, dc=*com*"

The export process produces a screen like the one seen in Figure 15-12.

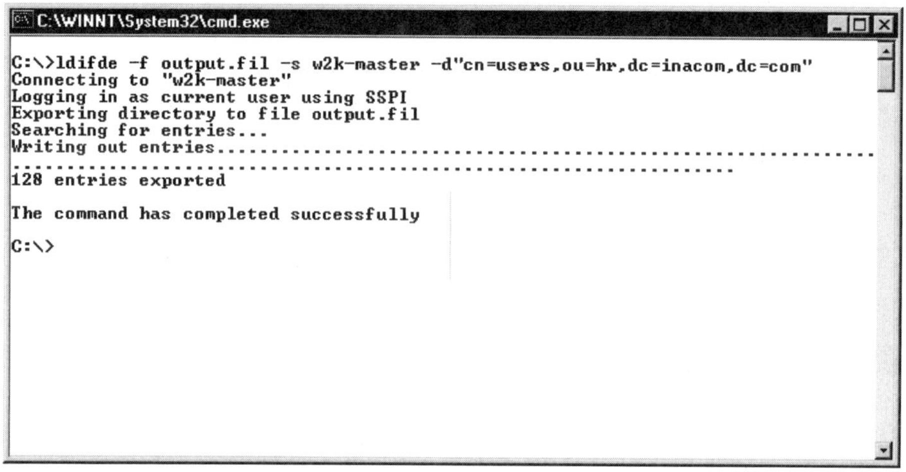

Figure 15-12. LDIFDE export of information from the Active Directory

Changing and Replacing Information

To change or replace information, cut and paste information from the file you exported and use the changetype command to replace information in the file. Then import the file into the Active Directory. This example shows the modification sequence:

```
dn: CN=Bob Cohn, OU=HR, DC=inacom, DC=com
changetype: modify
replace: title
title: Director of HR
-
replace: streetaddress
streetaddress: 399 Grand Ave Ste attn: HR
```

Running LDIFDE to Import Changes into the Active Directory

After you've modified the file, you can import the changes back into the Active Directory. To do so, run the LDIFDE program one last time:

ldifde –i –f *filename* –s *servername* –d" ou=*OU*, dc=*domain*, dc=*com*"

LDIFDE Command Options

Here is the syntax available for the LDIFDE command:

```
LDIFDS v1.0, September 1997.
LDIF Directory Synchronization Bulk import/export tool
General Parameters
==================
```

```
-i                  Turn on Import Mode (The default is Export)
-f filename         Input or Output filename
-s servername       The server to bind to (Default to DC of logged in Domain)
-c FromDN ToDN      Replace occurrences of FromDN to ToDN
-v                  Turn on Verbose Mode
-j                  Log File Location
-t                  Port Number (default = 389)
-?                  Help


Export Specific
===============
-d RootDN           The root of the LDAP search (Default to Naming Context)
-r Filter           LDAP search filter (Default to "(objectClass=*)")
-p SearchScope      Search Scope (Base/OneLevel/Subtree)
-l list             List of attributes (comma separated) to look for
                    in an LDAP search
-o list             List of attributes (comma separated) to omit from
                    input.
-g                  Disable Paged Search.
-m                  Enable the SAM logic on export.
-n                  Do not export binary values


Import
======
-k                  The import will go on ignoring 'Constraint Violation'
                    and 'Object Already Exists' errors


Credentials Establishment
=========================
Note that if no credentials is specified, LDIFDS will bind as the currently
logged on user, using SSPI.

-a UserDN Password          Simple authentication
-b UserName Domain Password SSPI bind method

Example: Simple import of current domain
    ldifde -i -f INPUT.LDF

Example: Simple export of current domain
    ldifde -f OUTPUT.LDF

Example: Export of specific domain with credentials
    ldifde -m -f OUTPUT.LDF
            -b USERNAME DOMAINNAME PASSWORD
            -s SERVERNAME
            -d "cn=users,DC=DOMAINNAME,DC=Microsoft,DC=Com"
            -r "(objectClass=user)"
```

CHAPTER 16

Managing Users, Software, and Data

This chapter covers the way organizations can take advantage of the user-, software-, and data-management capabilities of Windows 2000. Properly managing these elements results in an improved environment for users and administrators.

USER MANAGEMENT

Some of the components in Windows 2000 benefit users, such as the ability to retain individual settings for Internet Explorer favorites, personal links and channels, security cookies, and desktop and background settings. In fact, these settings can follow a user who moves to another computer.

For administrators, there are management components that can restrict users from changing system settings and configuration options, or from installing unauthorized software. While some users see these restrictions as limiting desktop functionality, from an administrative standpoint, the less a user can change (either purposely or accidentally) the less chance the system will require administrative support. The goal of Windows 2000 user management is to improve the administrator's ability to manage the network infrastructure.

Local Policy

Typically in a network environment, systems are controlled by group policies that span an entire domain. However, there may be circumstances that make local policies more desirable. For example, a group of computers may require policy restrictions that are different from those imposed across the organization. This is commonly the case for non-employee computers, such as the computers used by contractors, home computers connected to the network over a virtual private network connection, or application servers.

Local policies are stored in the %SystemRoot%\System32\GroupPolicy folder. You can exclude a computer from inheriting the group policy from the domain by making the following registry modification:

Hkey_Local_Machine\Software\Policies\Microsoft\Windows\System.
Set the DisableGPO object with the Reg_Dword being set to 1.

Group Policy

Group policies can define settings for groups of users or groups of computers. User policies focus on functions that affect users, such as application settings, desktop settings, or menu settings. Computer policies focus on functions that are system-specific, such as hardware component settings or software installed for all users. Group policies are applied and enforced by domains and organizational units.

▼ **Computer settings**   Computer settings are components that affect the Hkey_Local_Machine section of the registry. They include video adapter resolution settings, system processor definition, primary network server provider settings, hard drive and CD-ROM drive controller settings, and computer system name settings. Computer settings are typically the properties for device settings of hardware objects stored in the control panel on a system.

▲ **User Settings**   User settings are components that affect the Hkey_Current_User section of the registry. This includes settings that affect the user desktop settings (application icons and Start button application icons), user application settings (personal folder settings and favorites), user-assigned and published applications (applications available specifically to the user), user security (security privileges for the specific user), and user logon and logoff scripts (scripts executed based on the user).

More specifically, these group policies are applied based on registry settings, scripts, software management options, user files and settings, and security settings as follows:

Group Policy Objects (GPO)

Group policy settings are stored in group policy objects (GPOs). GPOs are associated with Active Directory objects, such as domains and organizational units. Because group policy settings are applied through the Active Directory, the settings are cumulative from the largest grouping (the domain) to the smallest grouping (the individual user or computer). Each security-policy system has its own method for applying policies and establishing inherited rights through the directory tree.

Windows 2000 group policy objects allow subsequent settings to override the previous settings, as each setting gets more granular. There is an option on each group policy settings property page that can be enabled so that lower-level Active Directory containers are prevented from overriding the group policy set by higher-level policies. This blocking of inheritance of group policy from container to container modifies the normal flow of policies, and should be prevented since it makes debugging policy inheritance difficult. I have found it better to design and plan a top-down group policy process, so that the flow of policies through the directory tree can be easily followed.

Group Policy Template

Group policy objects store group policy information in group policy templates. These templates are stored in the container that holds all software policy, script, file, and application-deployment information specific to the policy. It is located in %SystemRoot%\SYSVOL\Sysvol\<DomainName>\Policies\<AppropriateSubfolder>. The subfolder is MachineCLSID or User CLSID of the domain controllers on the network.

Designing Group Policies

Group policies are cumulative, and lower-level, more specific policies can override the policies of previously applied group policy objects. Creating a design that has a broad application at the top and gets more granular as you move down the directory tree makes it easier to implement nesting policies.

The best way to design a simple structured policy process is to map out the policies you wish to apply to the users and computers in your organization. Typically, users can be grouped by roles or departments, and these groups have specific application, management, and security needs. For example, a telesales representative may have a very limited desktop configuration, requiring only a single application, and may have every other PC-based function locked down to limit changes to the system. On the other hand, a field sales representative may need access to a variety of applications, and may also need to access network resources. While their specific needs differ, there is some commonality that can affect the settings at the top domain level. You can set organization-wide policies that limit the ability to change desktop settings or to install new software. Here are a few tips on the characteristics of group policies:

▼ Group policy objects are created and stored per domain.

■ Group policy objects can be associated with a single domain or organizational unit.

■ A single group policy object can be associated with multiple domains and organizational units.

■ When group policy objects span a domain over a WAN connection, the processing of the group policy object may be slow.

▲ Group policy objects can be filtered, based on security group membership and Access Control List (ACL) settings.

Creating a Group Policy Object

Group policy objects are created in the Active Directory Users and Computers administrative tool. To invoke the tool, follow these steps:

1. Choose Start | Programs | Administrative Tools | Active Directory Users and Computers.

2. Right-click the portion of the tree for which you want to create a group policy (either the domain or organizational unit).

3. Select properties, which brings up a properties dialog box.

4. Click the group policy tab.

The group policy tab, shown in Figure 16-1, provides a variety of options:

▼ Create a new policy

■ Add an existing policy to this container

■ Edit an existing policy

■ Set policy options

■ Delete a policy

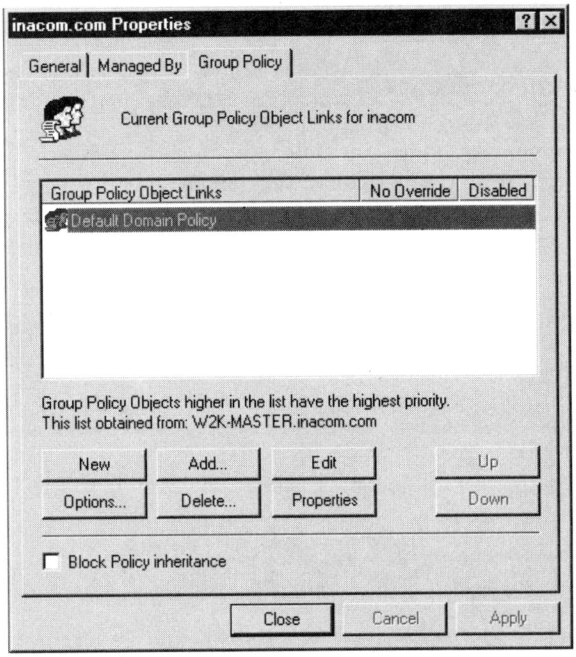

Figure 16-1.   Group Policy tab for domain settings

- View the properties of a policy
- Block the policy inheritance at this level of your Active Directory tree

To create a new policy, click New and enter the name of the new group. Click Add to add an existing policy, or click Edit to create a new group policy setting. When you click Edit you will see a group policy setting screen similar to the one in Figure 16-2.

If you want to apply multiple policies to a container in the directory tree, use the Add button and then use the Up and Down buttons to select the order in which the policies are to be applied. Remember, Windows 2000 policies are cumulative, and subsequent policies override policies applied earlier, so the sequence of the policies is important.

Editing and Applying Group Policies

While group policies are applied on a top-down basis, you have some choices about the way policies are applied to computers and users. On boot-up, computer-configuration policies are applied first, and then the user-configuration policies are applied (after user

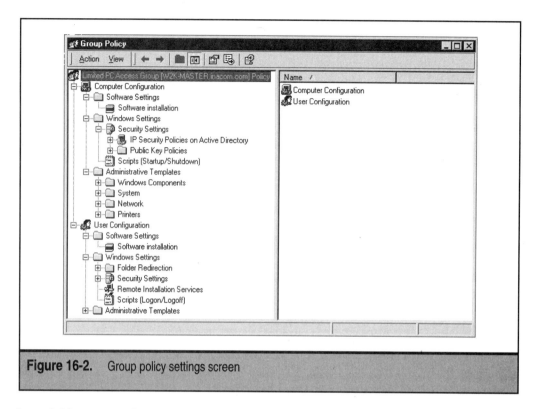

Figure 16-2. Group policy settings screen

logon). You can configure processing variations with logon scripts in the policy-processing modification screen, which is opened as follows:

1. Click on Start | Programs | Administrative Tools | Active Directory Users and Computers.

2. Right-click the portion of the tree for which you want to edit a group policy (either the domain or organizational unit).

3. Select properties, which brings up a properties dialog box.

4. Click the Group Policy tab.

5. Select an existing policy, and click Edit.

6. Select Computer Configuration | Administrative Templates | System | Logon.

You will see a screen of options similar to the one shown in Figure 16-3.

Change the default settings by double-clicking an option and selecting the appropriate checkbox. Here are the guidelines for implementing the available options:

▼   **Run logon scripts synchronously or asynchronously**   By default, logon scripts are executed one at a time, or synchronously. This allows time for functions to be applied and executed before proceeding to the next process. If

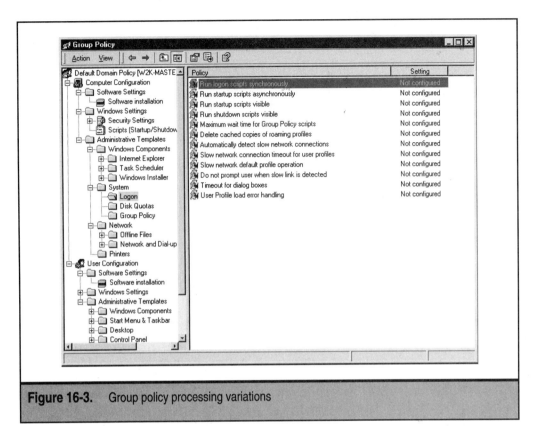

Figure 16-3.   Group policy processing variations

you create scripts that can execute simultaneously, the logon process time is decreased by setting the option to asynchronous execution.

■ **Run startup scripts synchronously or asynchronously**   By default, startup scripts are executed simultaneously, or asynchronously. If your startup scripts should be executed synchronously, change this option.

■ **Run startup or shutdown scripts visible**   You can opt to let users see the display as scripts are processed.

▲ **Processing over a slow link**   When Winlogon detects a slow link connection, it sets the GPO_INFO_FLAG_SLOWLINK software policy flag to an "on" state. Policies can behave differently over a slow link. When the slowlink software policy is turned on it should not be forced off so that large files are prevented from being transferred over a slow network connection.

Overriding Group Policies

Sometimes it is effective to override a user-based policy with a computer-based policy. This is commonly done to enforce a policy regardless of the user who is logged on, which is useful for enforcing higher-level security on a mission-critical server, or for restricting access to system options on a kiosk system. You can set system policy overrides by following these steps:

1. Click Start | Programs | Administrative Tools | Active Directory Users and Computers.
2. Right-click the portion of the tree for which you want to create a group policy (either the domain or organization unit).
3. Select properties, which brings up a properties dialog box.
4. Click the Group Policy tab.
5. Click Properties.
6. Select Disable User Configuration Settings.

When you disable user-configuration settings, only the computer configuration settings are applied.

Software Configuration Management

Group policies let you manage software installation as an assigned application or as a published application. If an application is *assigned*, a shortcut appears on the user's Start menu and the user's registry settings are automatically updated with application-specific information. The first time the user selects the application icon, the application is automatically installed.

Software is assigned in the Group Policy Editor as follows:

1. Double-click on either the Computer Configuration or the User Configuration option.
2. Double-click Software Settings.
3. Right-click on the words Software installation in the configuration tree.
4. Select New | Package.
5. Select the Windows Installer package (*.msi) file you wish to assign.
6. Select Assigned as the deployment method.
7. Click OK to finish the installation.

For *published* applications, the software access and installation is different. Published applications allow users to decide whether they want to install the application or not. If they do, users must open the Add/Remove program tool (Start | Settings | Control Panel | Add/Remove Programs) and select the application (which has been published in the application-installation settings to be installed on request).

Software is published in the Group Policy Editor as follows:

1. Double-click either the Computer Configuration or the User Configuration option.
2. Double-click Software Settings.
3. Right-click on the words Software installation in the configuration tree.
4. Select New | Package.

5. Select the Windows Installer package (*.msi) file you wish to publish.

6. You will then be prompted with a deployment-method screen that will allow you to publish, assign, or configure the package properties. If you will be publishing the package, select Publish.

7. Click OK to finish the installation.

Configuring Security

Security settings for group policies can be set as computer-configuration settings or as user-configuration settings. Most security settings default to computer-configuration settings because the computer connection is the physical portal into the network. By securing the computer configuration, user-security configuration settings play less of a role in creating a secure environment.

Security configurations are accessed as follows:

1. Click Start | Programs | Administrative Tools | Active Directory Users and Computers.

2. Right-click the portion of the tree for which you wish to create a group policy (either the domain or organizational unit).

3. Select properties to bring up a properties dialog box.

4. Click the Group Policy tab.

5. Select an existing policy, and click Edit.

6. Select Computer Configuration | Windows Settings.

7. Select Security Settings.

You can configure the security options to meet your own requirements.

ACCOUNT POLICIES   Account policies let you define security settings for the several password policies, including password change uniqueness, maximum and minimum password age, minimum password length, password complexity, any logon requirement to change a password, the account lockout policy (where lockouts are caused by invalid logon attempts, and the account is automatically reset after a specified number of minutes), and the Kerberos policy (which enforces user logon restrictions and sets the maximum service and lifetime for security tickets, synchronization, and user tickets).

LOCAL POLICIES   Local policies contain the security settings for a number of events. There are policies for auditing events: logon events, account management events, directory service access, object access, policy change, privilege use, process tracking, and system events.

There are also policies for user rights assignments, such as accessing the computer from the network, acting as part of the operating system, adding a workstation to the domain, backing up files and directories, changing the system time, creating a pagefile, debugging programs, forcing a remote shutdown, generating security audits, increasing quotas, loading and unloading device drivers, logging in as a batch job or service, removing a computer from a docking station, restoring files and directories, shutting down the system, synchronizing directory service data, and taking ownership of files and other objects.

Finally, there are policies for security options, such as allowing server operators to schedule tasks, allowing a system to be shut down without having to log on, auditing access to internal system objects, automatically disconnecting sessions, changing the administrator account name, digitally signing client and server-side communications, disabling the CTRL-ALT-DEL requirement for logon, hiding the user name on the logon screen, forcing a logoff when a user's logon hours expire, preventing users from installing print drivers, prompting users to change their passwords before expiration, restricting CD-ROM or floppy-drive access, restricting management of COM and LPT devices, securing a channel for digitally encrypted communications, and shutting down the system immediately if the system is unable to log security information.

EVENT LOG POLICY   The event log policy settings let you specify the maximum log size, restrict guest access, and set the retention time for the log files.

RESTRICTED GROUP POLICY   The restricted group provides policy settings that are specific to the built-in groups.

SYSTEM SERVICES   The system services provide security controls over the configuration of services. This includes configuration options such as whether a service is started automatically or manually, and whether the service is logged on manually or through a service account.

REGISTRY GROUP POLICY   The registry group policy settings let you configure settings for security descriptions.

FILE SYSTEM POLICY   The file-system group policy provides settings specific to security for volume, directory, and file access.

IP SECURITY POLICY   The IP security policy enforces security on a server level (for the server requesting security authentication), on a secured server level (where the server requires security authentication), and on a client level (where the client responds to security requests to the domain controller).

PUBLIC KEY POLICIES   Public key policies provide the ability to modify encrypted data-recovery agents, automate certificate-request settings, modify domain-root certification authorities, and modify certificate trust lists.

Sample Template Files

Windows 2000 provides three sets of sample group-policy template files, and you can use them as guidelines if you want to create template files. You can find the files in the %SystemRoot%\security\templates directory.

The following sample templates can be used for basic system settings:

▼ Basicdc.inf for domain controllers

■ Basicsv.inf for servers

▲ Basicwk.inf for workstations

For secured system templates, which provide tighter controls on the ability to modify services and settings, these sample files are available:

▼ Securews.inf for secured workstations

▲ Securedc.inf for secured domain controllers

For high-security templates, which prevent access to most system settings, as well as access to resources, these template files are available:

▼ Hisecdc.inf for high-security domain controllers

▲ Hisecwk.inf for high-security workstations

Delegating Group Policy Rights

Group policy controls can be delegated to other individuals, and you can limit the level of access the delegated administrators have. To delegate group policy control, create and save group policy functions from the MMC consoles to a container at a branch within the Active Directory. Then, define permissions for the group policy object by using the ACL editor.

To open the ACL editor, right-click the root node of the Group Policy Editor, select properties (which brings up a properties dialog box), and then click Security to open the Security tab (see Figure 16-4). Use the options on the Security tab to add and remove users, and to allow or deny access to the group policy object on a group-by-group basis.

Authenticated users have permission to apply group policy and read ACL permissions. Domain administrators have full ACL permissions but do not have permission to apply group policy. (This is to ensure that an error in policy does not prevent domain administrators from accessing the domain.)

Roaming User Profiles

With a local user profile, when a user makes changes to the configuration, the changes are stored on the local hard drive. If the same user logs on to a different computer, his or her individual settings aren't available and have to be configured anew on that computer.

Roaming profiles allow user settings to be available to the user, regardless of which Windows 2000 desktop the individual uses to log on to the network. With roaming profiles, user-configuration settings are stored on a server, so regardless of which computer the user logs in to, the settings are downloaded from the server. This provides the user with his or her familiar interface.

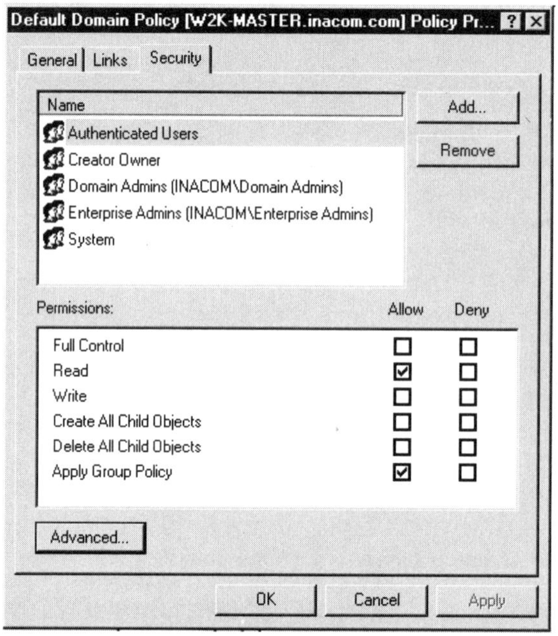

Figure 16-4. Security ACL permissions for group policies

Configuring Server Settings

To enable roaming profiles, you must set up a share on the server to store roaming profiles. Roaming profiles under previous versions of Windows NT were stored on a single server. In the event of a hard drive or server failure, the profiles would not be available and would cause a problem for users trying to log on to the network. However, with Windows 2000, the profiles are stored in the Active Directory that allows for data and directory redundancy, minimizing the change of a catastrophic system failure.

Configuring User Settings for Roaming Profiles

After a server share has been created, enable roaming profiles for users with the following steps:

1. Choose Start | Programs | Administrative Tools | Active Directory Users and Computers.

2. Double-click your domain.

3. Click Users.

4. Right-click a user.

5. Select Properties.

6. Select the Profiles tab.

7. In the Profile Path field, enter the UNC of the share that holds this profile.

8. Click OK.

Typically you would enter *servername**sharename**username* (for example, \\server1\profiles\bob) as the Profile Path, so that each user's profile is stored separately, as shown in Figure 16-5.

SOFTWARE MANAGEMENT

Windows 2000 provides a series of software-management tools that help you distribute and install software, update existing software, and repair software that has become corrupted.

Group Policy Interaction

The Windows 2000 Group Policy Editor plays a key role in defining the ways in which software is made available to users. Within the Group Policy Editor console is a Software Settings option for both computers and users (see Figure 16-6). Some software is best de-

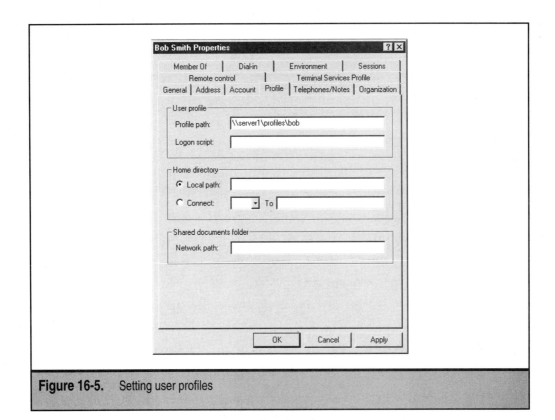

Figure 16-5.   Setting user profiles

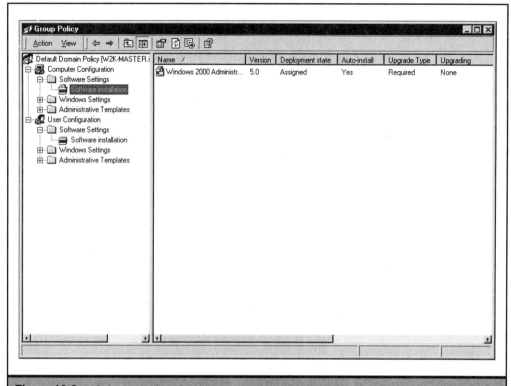

Figure 16-6. Software settings for either computers or users

fined and attached to a particular computer. For example, human resources or payroll software should be installed on specific computers, instead of following a specific user. Service packs and drivers are machine-specific, and need to be installed on a computer-by-computer basis. Software that uploads and downloads data should be available only on systems with modems.

If the application is user-dependent, you need to make sure the application follows the user. If the user logs in to a system where the software has not previously been installed, the software-installation capabilities of Windows 2000 can automatically install the software.

Configuring Package Properties

Besides being able to designate software installation as Assigned or Published, you can configure package properties. These properties provide optional characteristics for deployment. For example, you can uninstall the application, and the group policy for the application will no longer apply to the user or computer on the system. You can also prevent an application from appearing in the Add/Remove Program option in the Windows Control Panel, in order to give the power to install and uninstall to an administrator instead of the user. Other options allow you to write a script that either uninstalls old versions of software before installing new versions, or overwrites old software with updated versions.

Windows Installer Service

The Windows Installer service is new to Windows 2000 and provides a common method for all software installation. Previous versions of Windows provided a variety of different tools to install software, including third-party utilities. The lack of standards meant that occasionally applications overwrote critical system files during installation, and that uninstall utilities deleted critical files used by other applications.

Creating a Software Distribution Point

With the Windows Installer service, software is typically stored in a network share to provide access to users who need to launch the scripts that automatically install software. To create a shared directory for use as a software distribution point, follow these steps:

1. Create a folder on any network server drive (File | New Folder in My Computer).
2. Share the folder (Right click the folder | select Sharing | click on Share as | give the share a name).
3. Click on Permissions and configure security as follows: the Everyone group receives the Read permission, and the Administrators group receives Full Control, Change, and Read permissions.

Using Setup.exe

Applications that are not Windows Installer–aware can only be published as setup.exe application and cannot be assigned. This means users must go into the Control Panel and install the application using the Add/Remove Programs function.

Software that is installed with setup.exe cannot automatically roll back if the installation is unsuccessful. Although there may be an uninstall function for the application, most administrators have found that uninstall utilities work improperly. Frequently files remain in the system and data remains in the registry, and sometimes .dll files are removed that are needed by other applications.

System Management Server

With all of the software-management functions built into Windows 2000, you still need Microsoft Systems Management Server (SMS) if your network includes legacy platforms—it would be unusual for a company to deploy Windows 2000 throughout the organization in one fell swoop. During the transition, SMS can be used to provide software-management support to the systems not based on Windows 2000.

Additionally, SMS provides a number of other functions for both the older Windows operating system and the Windows 2000 systems that are not included in Windows 2000. These functions include providing hardware and software inventory and network management.

DATA MANAGEMENT

Windows 2000 provides the ability to manage data. In the past, file servers were nothing more than depositories for the storage of files. With Windows 2000, file sharing and data access goes beyond just the storage of information.

Through the implementation of offline folders, users can work on files while they're away from the office and synchronize those files with the network server when they reconnect to the network. New indexing technologies make finding files two to three times faster than in previous versions of Windows NT.

For administrators, tools including automatic disk defragmentation and file compression help minimize the task of managing file access and storage availability. File grooming through hierarchical storage management, file distribution through DFS, file-directory redundancy through Active Directory, and file-management scalability through network load balancing can automate many tasks that administrators have historically had to manage on a daily basis.

Data Management Infrastructure Services

There are a number of services included in Windows 2000 that improve the ability to manage files and conduct ongoing data-management services. The services include hierarchical storage management, DFS, Active Directory, and network load balancing. All of these services, along with their benefits, capabilities, and implementation options were covered in Chapter 12 and need not be revisited in this chapter.

File Sharing and Data Access

With Windows 2000, file sharing and data access have been extended beyond simple file and information sharing. There are a number of functions that can be modified to automate and simplify administrative file services.

To access the file-sharing data-administration functions of the network, right-click a network share, and select Properties. A Properties page similar to the one shown in Figure 16-7 appears. You can use the options on the various tabs to modify the parameters and characteristics of the share.

General Tab

On the General tab, you can change the Label of the partition. This is the physical partition name and is not necessarily the name that is published as the share name. It is best to select a label name that describes the physical drive characteristic of the system.

You can also enable disk compression. While compression provides more disk space, it has a large disadvantage in the overhead placed on the CPU. Don't compress disks of primary servers that are heavily used. However, secondary or tertiary archive servers can benefit from drive compression.

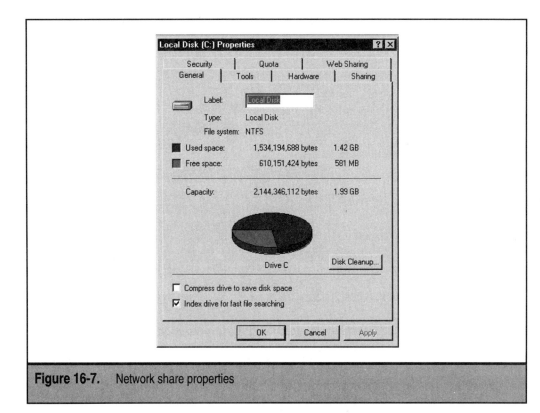

Figure 16-7.   Network share properties

You can also index the drive for faster file searching. By default, fast file searching is enabled, making file searching two to three times faster on the system through the Microsoft Index services.

Finally, you can launch Disk Cleanup. This tool scans the drive and calculates the amount of space that can be saved by invoking a series of options shown in Figure 16-8. The options are displayed on screen, along with an estimate of how much space you would gain if the option were enabled. The first option is to delete temporarily downloaded ActiveX or Java applets that were automatically downloaded from the Internet. Another similar option is to delete temporary Internet files, such as Web pages that were stored on your system to cache the pages for faster viewing. The third option is to delete files being temporarily held in your recycle bin. The fourth option is to compress old files, and you can specify the age of files (in days) that will be compressed. You can set the threshold to compress files anywhere from 1 to 500 days old. The last option is to delete old index catalog files (left over from previous indexing processes on the system).

Tools Tab

The tools tab provides links to three separate utilities:

▼   Error checking (the Chkdsk utility) scans the drive for disk errors and automatically fixes the errors and recovers bad sectors.

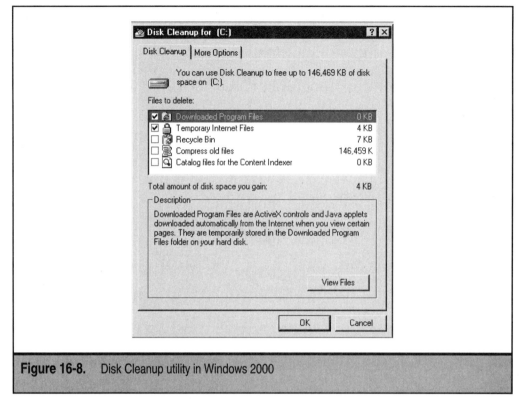

Figure 16-8. Disk Cleanup utility in Windows 2000

■ Backup launches the backup program (Ntbackup).

▲ Disk defragmentation reunites fragmented sections of files (see the section on disk defragmentation in Chapter 12).

Hardware Tab

The hardware tab displays the hardware devices on the system, and you can troubleshoot problems, as well as view the properties of the devices.

Sharing Tab

The sharing tab allows you to create, modify, or delete shares. By default, a share is created for every drive for administrative purposes—C$ for the C drive, D$ for the D drive, and so forth. You can add additional shares along with defining permissions for users and groups to access this share by clicking the Permissions button and adding the Active Directory user, group, or organization that you wish to either include (allow) or exclude (deny). The three levels of permissions you can specify are Full Control (access to all files on the drive), Change (ability to modify files on the drive), or Read (ability to only read files, not to modify them). Typically your selection would be Read, Read and Change, or Full Control.

Also on the Sharing tab is an option for caching. Caching provides the ability to work with files on the network or to store them on a desktop or laptop computer for offline use. This feature will be covered later in the section "Offline Folders."

Security Tab

The Security tab allows you to specify security access to the physical drive, specifically from a logon to the server itself. This option is not commonly configured in detail because access to the physical drive is limited by logon access to the server itself. By controlling logon access to the server, limiting access to the physical drive device based on user or group is not necessarily required.

However, if you wish to, you can specify, by Active Directory user, group, or organization, those who have access to the physical drive for six standard storage options. Those options include full control (access to all information), modify (ability to modify or change files), read and execute (ability to launch an application and run it), list folder contents (the ability to see files stored on the drive), read (ability to only read files), and write (ability to only write to files). Common settings include:

▼ **Allow list folder contents and read permissions**   Allows access to files, but not to modify them

■ **Allow list folder contents, read, and write permissions**   Allows access to files and the ability to add new files to the directory

■ **Allow list folder contents, read, modify, and write permissions**   Allows access to files, the ability to read and modify existing files, and the ability to add new files

■ **Allow read and execute permission**   Allows the running an application stored on the drive, but not necessarily the ability to install new applications or save data files to the drive

▲ **Allow full control**   Allows administrator access

On the Security tab is an Advanced button that enables an even more granular level of file, folder, and drive share privileges. You can allow and deny access and enable or disable information-access auditing for a number of different permission categories, as shown in Figure 16-9. These permissions can be applied to a variety of different characteristics, such as the following:

▼ This folder only

■ This folder, subfolders, and files

■ This folder and subfolders

■ This folder and files

■ Subfolders and files only

■ Subfolders only

▲ Files only

Quota Tab

The Quota tab provides the ability to set disk quotas on the disk space made available to users. By enabling quota management, disk space can be limited using any grouping of

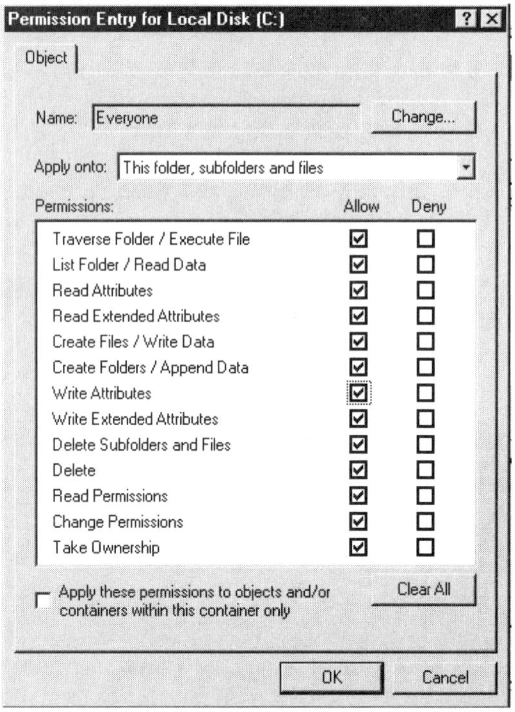

Figure 16-9.   Granular permissions for file, folder, and share access

Active Directory management (by user, by group, by organizational unit, and so on). In addition to specifying a quota limit, a threshold can be set to notify users as they reach a limit level for their storage.

Web Sharing Tab

The Web Sharing tab offers the ability to publish and share a folder to the Web services of the Windows 2000 system. You can publish the folder with access permissions including read, write, script source access, and directory browsing.

Offline Folders

Offline folders give users the ability to replicate files that are stored on a server to their local hard drive, commonly to a laptop or over a remote connection to a home or remote office system. To access offline folder functions, right-click the network share and select Properties. Click the Sharing tab and click Caching.

Enabling Folder Caching from a Share

To enable folder caching, click the Allow Caching of Files in this Shared Folder checkbox option. This displays the options shown in Figure 16-10.

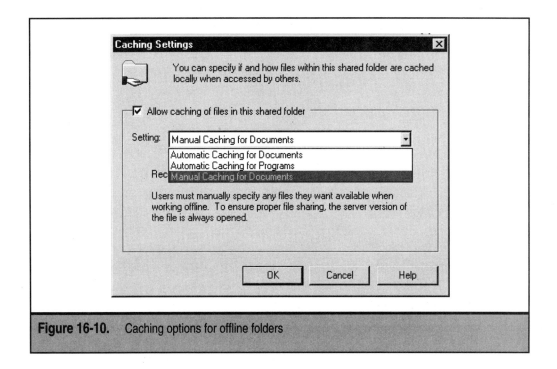

Figure 16-10.   Caching options for offline folders

The Automatic Caching for Documents option specifies that open files are automatically downloaded and made available to the user for working offline. Older copies are automatically deleted and replaced with newer revisions of the files.

The Automatic Caching for Programs option specifies that open files are automatically downloaded and made available when working offline. However, because the files are open, file sharing is not ensured. With this option, older copies of the files are automatically deleted to make newer and more recent copies of the files available. Use this option only if the folders are set with read-only data, so that there is not a contention problem with mismatched file edits.

The Manual Caching for Documents option means that users need to manually specify the files they want available when they are working offline. To ensure proper file sharing, the server version of the file is always opened.

Enabling Folder Replication in Group Policy

You can also invoke folder replication within the Group Policy Editor. By activating folder replication, files and folders can be stored in a remote location. Many users want to back up their local files to a network share to protect crucial files. This requires greater bandwidth between the server and user, however replication maintains copies of the folder in both locations.

To activate folder replication in the Group Policy Editor, do the following:

1. Launch the Active Directory Users and Computers administration tool (Start | Programs | Administrative Tools | Active Directory Users and Computers).

2. Right-click the domain or organizational unit you wish to edit, and select Properties.

3. Select the Group Policy tab, and then select New or Edit.

4. Select User Configuration | Windows Settings | Folder Replication.

5. Select the share you wish to modify, such as My Documents.

6. Click the Action pull-down option and select Properties.

7. On the Target tab, under the Settings drop-box, select Basic—Redirect Everyone's Folder to the Same Location, and then specify the target folder location on the server for replication.

8. Select the Settings tab and check the Grant the User Exclusive Rights and the Move the Contents to the New Location checkboxes.

9. Under Policy Removal, choose either the Leave the Folder in the New Location When the Policy is Removed option, or the Redirect the Folder Back to the Local Userprofile Location When Policy Is Removed option.

10. Select OK.

Invoking Folder Replication for a User

To replicate a folder for offline use, users launch the Offline Folder wizard with the following steps:

1. Right-click the folder you wish to make available offline.

2. Select Make Available Offline.

3. An Offline wizard will appear. Select Next.

4. Click the Automatically Synchronize the Offline Folders When I Log on and Log off my Computer checkbox, and then select Next.

5. Click the Enable Reminders checkbox, and select Next.

6. In the Confirm Offline Subfolder dialog box, select Yes, Make this Folder and All of Its Subfolders Available Offline.

7. Click OK when finished.

CHAPTER 17

Implementing Thin-Client Terminal Services

In Chapter 10, I covered the design and planning of Terminal Services in Windows 2000. In this chapter, I'll discuss the installation and configuration of the software. The installation and configuration of Windows 2000 Terminal Services spans from the installation of the client software for Windows as well as Web access through the installation of the more complex server components of the Terminal Services technology. In addition to just the basic installation steps of the product, I address technology roll-out services including server scalability as well as end-user training.

CLIENT SOFTWARE INSTALLATION

The features and functions you install with Terminal Services must include the services expected by the client computers. In addition, you have to install all the software applications that client users need. As described in Chapter 10, the client computer can use a Microsoft RDP client component or a Citrix ICA client.

RDP Client

The RDP client is available in two different versions:

▼ 16-bit Windows

▲ 32-bit Windows

The code for the RDP clients is installed in the \%SystemRoot%\system32\clients\ tsclient\<*RDP version*> subdirectories of the computer in which Terminal Services is installed. You can install the client software from floppy disks or from a network share point.

If you want to install from floppy disks, you must create the disks first. To do so, choose Start | Programs | Administrative Tools | Terminal Services Client Creator. The

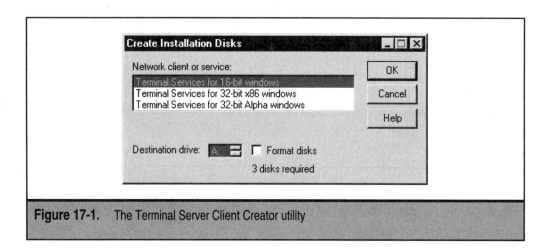

Figure 17-1. The Terminal Server Client Creator utility

Terminal Services Client Creator utility (shown in Figure 17-1) will prompt you for the version of the client software you want the floppy disk set to install. You're told the number of floppy disks needed for the version you're creating (1–3).

Install the client software by running the setup.exe program on the first diskette and specifying the installation destination.

The Terminal Server RDP client is a ROM-based client component that is installed in a WinTerm- or NetPC-based terminal. These machines boot to a ROM chip that contains the Terminal Server RDP client. The RDP client searches the network, looking for Terminal servers, and connects to either the default server or to the first available Terminal server it finds.

A WinTerm or NetPC client is designed to launch a Terminal Services session, which simplifies the boot process. No software or local drives are needed. Manufacturers of these terminal devices release boot ROM or BIOS updates, and you should install these when they're available to improve performance, add functionality, or increase compatibility with other client-services functions.

ICA PC Client

The Citrix Metaframe/2000 ICA client software is available in DOS, Windows 16-bit, or Windows 32-bit versions. The client software is in the \Clients directory of the Metaframe CD, with a subdirectory for each client version. Each of the version subdirectories contains a list of the disks that are needed for installation (named disk1, disk2, and so on, depending on the number of disks required for the version). Copy the files to floppy disk and run the setup program from the first disk.

Web-Based ICA Client

If your users are employing a Web browser as the front end of a Terminal Services environment, use the Citrix Metaframe/2000 WEB ICA client. The software is available as an ActiveX client for Microsoft Internet Explorer, or as a plug-in for Netscape Navigator.

The client component is installed manually by the browser user. For ActiveX users, you can create an HTML file that automatically downloads and installs the software when the user connects to the Web server.

The bandwidth between the remote user and the Web server can range from dial-up speeds through full DSL or frame connection speeds. If the connection is 56 Kbps or faster, the remote user experiences a terminal session that is equivalent to being live on the network. Speeds in excess of 19.2 Kbps are considered acceptable Web-based Terminal Server performance (although a 9,600 bps connection is functional, the performance is sluggish).

NOTE: The Citrix ICA clients include Macintosh computers and systems with an enabled Java virtual machine.

USER PROFILE CONFIGURATION

Key to the success of the Terminal Services client are the individual settings required to make the client application software operate. Many 16-bit Windows applications require .ini files, and 32-bit Windows applications require registry settings.

INI File Configuration

In order to work properly with Terminal Services, 16-bit software must either be able to share its .ini files among all the users accessing the terminal services, or permit multiple .ini files to be distributed to "home" directories so that each user can have a unique .ini file. Software that does not permit the use of multiple .ini files will not work with Terminal Services systems.

Registry Configuration

Windows 32-bit applications write user-specific software information (such as customization choices) to the registry, guaranteeing each user a unique set of data. To configure and save their registry settings, each user must log on to Terminal Services, launch the application, and make user-specific configuration changes. The changes are saved to the registry in user-specific keys.

You can automate registry entries with tools such as Microsoft System Management Server (SMS) or the Microsoft Zero Administration Windows (ZAW) utility. This is useful for setting default system-configuration settings. You can also use system policies to configure or limit changes by user, group, site, or organization. More information on registry settings and system policies can be found in Chapter 16.

By default these registry settings and configurations are stored in the user's profile on the Terminal Services server. However, if you add Terminal Services servers, those servers will not have the user registry settings or profiles. The best way to transfer user profiles is through the use of Roaming Profiles, which stores user profiles in a specific location on the network. When a user logs on to the network, the profile is found and loaded, even if the user logs on from a different client machine. User changes are saved to the network location. More information on Roaming Profiles can be found in Chapter 16.

Determining User Needs

The needs of users determine the applications that must be installed and configured. To make sure you meet all needs, create a list of the users, matching them to the applications they use. An effective way to accomplish this is to create a table similar to Table 17-1.

INSTALLING TERMINAL SERVICES SERVER SOFTWARE

Terminal Services can be installed on any Server, Advanced Server, or Data Center edition of Windows 2000. As with any component, the installation can be performed at the time of the initial installation of Windows 2000, or added later.

	Word	Excel	IE	Home Directory	Printer	32-bit client	Web client
Rand Morimoto	X	X	X	F:\users\rand	HP4	X	X
Jeff Kahn	X		X	G:\users\jeff	HP4L		X
Chris Doyle	X	X	X	F:\users\chris	Lexmark	X	
Martin Brohm	X		X	H:\users\martin	DeskJet	X	X

Table 17-1.   Terminal Server User-Settings Chart

Because of the demands Terminal Services makes on a computer, limit the role of this server. No domain controller, DNS, or DHCP services should be installed on the same server.

Preparing for Your Installation

As with the installation of any core component or service in a Windows 2000 environment, make sure you're using compatible hardware and drivers as tested and published by Microsoft in their Hardware Compability List (HCL).

Terminal Services can be installed on either a FAT or NTFS file system. However, NTFS offers more security and provides a number of logging and tracking components, so that is the preferred file system type for any server on the network.

Using the Automated Windows 2000 Terminal Services Installation

The automated installation of Windows 2000 is the most common method for installing the operating system. The Setup wizard prompts you for information, including whether or not you wish to install Terminal Services.

The Windows 2000 Setup wizard minimizes the number of questions asked during the installation process. If you want to customize your installation, or script your installation of Terminal Services, refer to Chapter 12 for details on the different installation variations.

Adding Terminal Services to an Existing Windows 2000 Server

To add Terminal Services to an existing Windows 2000 server, follow these steps:

1. Select Start | Settings | Control Panel.
2. Click on Add/Remove Programs.
3. Click on Add/Remove Windows Components.

4. Click on the checkbox next to the Terminal Services component to select this option.

5. Click Next to continue (you are prompted to insert your Windows 2000 installation CD).

6. Click Finish when prompted.

7. The system will prompt you to restart to complete the installation.

Installing the Citrix Metaframe/2000 Add-In

After you have installed the core Windows 2000 Terminal Services on a server, you can optionally purchase and install the Citrix Metaframe/2000 add-in. To install the base Metaframe add-in, just insert the Metaframe CD into the CD-ROM drive and execute the setup program. Metaframe is licensed separately from the Terminal Server program, and you must enter the Citrix Metaframe/2000 license number that came with the Metaframe software. The installation takes a couple of minutes.

Setting Up Web-Based Terminal Services

You can provide Web-based access to Terminal Services for users of Internet Explorer or Netscape Navigator. In order to do so, you need a Web server component, such as Microsoft Internet Information Server (IIS), or a UNIX- or Linux-based system. Web server components include an HTML file, a text file, and, optionally, an auto-downloading ActiveX component. (Since Windows 2000 includes the IIS Web server product, I will use IIS in this discussion.)

You must decide whether you want to use your Terminal server as your IIS server, or whether you will set up a separate IIS server for Web functions. For best performance, you should distribute the load between separate systems. Additionally, separate systems allow you to place the IIS server on the untrusted segment of the WAN structure and place the most crucial Terminal server system inside the firewall on a trusted segment of the network. The IIS server becomes the portal from the general Internet to the Terminal server. An HTML file and a text file are added to the IIS server to redirect Web communications to the Terminal server.

Securing Web-Based Communications

The connection from the general Internet through the ICA protocol has built-in encryption that provides basic security from the Web server to the remote client. However, for more advanced security, Citrix sells a product called Secure ICA that enhances the encryption and point-to-point connectivity encapsulation. A virtual private network (VPN) could be created from the remote session to the Terminal server to increase security, but while VPN no doubt provides a higher level of security (through tunneling technology), the Secure ICA technology provides the same level of encryption, encapsulation, and point-to-point security as VPN, so the extra level of security provided by VPN will not add incremental value.

Since the Web server sits on the outside of the firewall, and the Terminal server sits on the inside of the firewall (as shown in Figure 17-2), a tight security link between the two servers is important. This can be achieved by implementing a point-to-point tunnel between the two servers to achieve direct connection security. Tunneling can be achieved through the use of L2TP, which is included with Windows 2000 (open the L2TP port specifically from and to each of the two servers), or by using third-party firewall products that have host-to-host tunneling options. The firewall will also need to be set up to allow all incoming clients to pass through on the ICA protocol ports, which are port 1494 for sessions and port 1604 for browsing/load balancing.

Another form of security between the outside and inside ports on the firewall can be achieved with SSL. To use SSL, the firewall must be configured with the Web server and the Terminal server IP addresses, which ensures validity through the firewall on port 443 (SSL). The firewall will still need to be configured to pass the ICA protocol, as discussed in the previous paragraph.

Adding a Web Page for Terminal Server Access

After you configure the Web server, you must add an HTML page and a text file to redirect communications from the Web server to the Terminal server. The remote user needs the ActiveX ICA component in Internet Explorer, or the ICA plug-in for Netscape Navigator.

As with all ActiveX components, you can automatically install the ActiveX ICA component by downloading it to the client from the Web server. The following HTML file will accomplish this task (I name this file desktop.htm).

```
<HTML>
<HEAD>
<TITLE>Web Based ICA Page</TITLE>
<P ALIGN="CENTER"><A HREF=" desktop.ica"><IMG SRC="clickhere.gif"
BORDER=0 WIDTH=12 HEIGHT=12></A><FONT SIZE=6><BR>
</FONT><B><FONT SIZE=2>Access to a Normal Desktop</P>
<OBJECT CLASSID="clsid:238f6f83-b8b4-11cf-8771-00a024541ee3"
CODEBASE=wfica.cab></BODY>
</HTML>
```

Copy the Citrix Web ICA .cab and .exe files into the same directory as this HTML file. Use a graphic named "clickhere.gif" for users to click in order to launch a Web-based Terminal Services session.

You also must make available the file named desktop.ica, noted in the HTML source. This file specifies the IP address of the Terminal server and the name and location of the

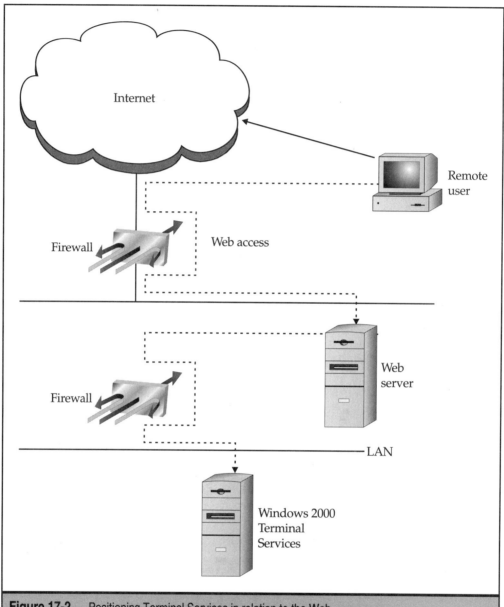

Figure 17-2. Positioning Terminal Services in relation to the Web

executable that the HTML file executes. The desktop.ica file should also be in the same directory as the HTML and the Citrix Web ICA .cab and .exe files.

The desktop.ica file is a text file with the following information:

```
[ApplicationServers]
desktop=

[desktop]
TransportDriver=TCP/IP
Address=xx.xx.xx.xx ;put in the IP address of your terminal server
WinStationDriver=ICA 3.0
Username=   ;you can have users automatically log on with a set name/pw
Domain=
Password=
InitialProgram=c:\winnt\explorer.exe    ;change this to any EXE app
WorkDirectory=c:\winnt

ScreenPercent=75  ;this section determines screen size and color bits
DesiredHRES=640
DesiredVRES=480
DesiredColor=8

[WFClient]
Version=2
```

Netscape Navigator users can download and install the plug-in that provides the code necessary to launch the HTML file and start a Web ICA session using all of the same scripts and pages noted in reference to the Internet Explorer components.

CONFIGURING TERMINAL SERVICES

After you have installed Terminal Services, the core functions need to be configured to provide users with access to the system. You need to set up the protocols that will be used to communicate from the remote sessions to the Terminal server, the default user-connection settings, user application software, and user profiles.

Configuring Connection Protocols

The term "protocol" has two meanings in Terminal Services. There is the traditional transport protocol (such as TCP/IP, IPX, or NetBEUI) and the Terminal Services communication protocol (such as RDP or ICA). Both of these protocol settings are configured in the Terminal Services Configuration utility.

There are two ways to open the Terminal Services Configuration utility:

▼ Open the Terminal Services Configuration snap-in from a Microsoft Management Console (MMC) session.

▲ Choose Terminal Services Configuration from the Administrative Tools folder in the Start menu.

Setting Access Protocols

Terminal Services configures the system to use RDP via TCP/IP (the RDP communication protocol only supports the TCP/IP transport protocol). This means remote clients must run TCP/IP and have the RDP client installed and configured on their system.

If your network is running IPX as one of its transport protocols, or you are running NetBEUI for backward compatibility, clients can access your system using either of these protocols with the Citrix Metaframe/2000 add-in. After you purchase and install Metaframe on the Terminal server, you can add or change the transport protocol.

To add a protocol to the network adapter of the server, use the following steps:

1. Select Start | Settings | Network and Dial-up Connections.
2. Right-click Local Connection.
3. Select Properties.
4. Click on Install.
5. Click on Protocol.
6. Click the Add button.
7. Select the NWLink/IPX or NetBEUI transport protocol. After the transport protocol is configured on the Terminal server, you must add the new transport protocol to the Terminal Services configuration.

Running the New Connection Wizard

The New Connection wizard runs from the Terminal Services Configuration utility discussed earlier in this section. Launch the wizard by selecting Action | Create New Connection. You are prompted to select the Connection Type (either Microsoft RDP or Citrix ICA). If you plan to use a different transport protocol (IPX or NetBEUI), use the Citrix ICA protocol, which was activated when you added the Metaframe/2000 optional add-in.

After you select the connection type, you are prompted for the encryption level. You have three options:

▼ **Low** Provides encryption at the server's standard key strength for all data sent from the client to the server (such as logon information and passwords). However, data sent from the server to the client is not protected.

■ **Medium**   Provides encryption at the server's standard key strength for all data sent and received between the client and the server.

▲ **High**   Provides encryption at the server's maximum key strength for all data sent and received between the client and the server.

By default, low encryption is enabled. If you want to increase the encryption level, going from low to medium encryption adds approximately 7 percent overhead to the communications traffic, and switching from low to high encryption adds approximately 13 percent overhead.

In addition to encryption, you are asked whether you want to use standard Windows authentication, which means the Terminal server will use Active Directory security to authenticate the users to the server.

The next page of the wizard, shown in Figure 17-3, prompts for remote control settings. These settings determine your ability to view and interact with a remote user session. Some organizations feel this privilege is an invasion of privacy, and other organizations utilize the feature to provide help-desk support to remote users who need networking assistance. The default is to use the settings defined in the user's configuration setting (covered later in this section). A second option is to disable remote control, effectively preventing the administrator from viewing a remote user's session. The third option is to set the default parameters.

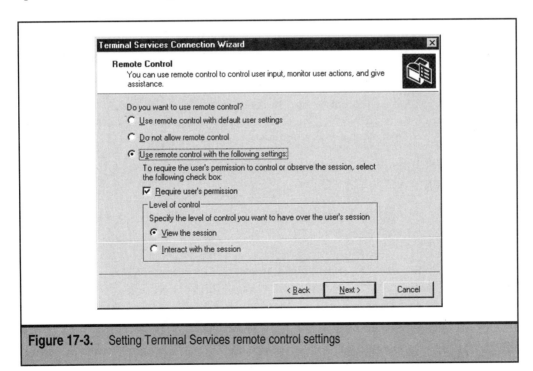

Figure 17-3.   Setting Terminal Services remote control settings

Here are the choices for configuring remote control options:

▼ **Require User's Permission**   The remote user is prompted to approve the administrator's access. This option lets an administrator interact with a remote user session with the user's knowledge, eliminating any concern of a breach of privacy.

■ **View the Session**   This option allows an administrator to view the user's session, but bars any keyboard or mouse activity.

▲ **Interact with the Session**   This option allows the administrator to view the remote user's session and also to have full keyboard and mouse interaction with the user's system.

The wizard asks for a name for the configuration scheme. Use a descriptive name, such as IPX (if you configured IPX), or High Security (if you specified a high level of security).

Assign this configuration to a network adapter. If you have multiple adapters serving multiple segments, you can specify one segment for low encryption (best for an internal segment on the corporate LAN) and one segment for high encryption (for a segment that connects to the Internet). You can also select the number of concurrent connections per adapter.

Manually Configuring Connection Properties

You can manually configure the Terminal Services connection properties in the Terminal Services Connection MMC snap-in. To make changes to the properties, select the connection you wish to edit by either double-clicking the connection or selecting Action | Properties to open the Properties dialog box. In the Properties dialog box, you can set the following options:

GENERAL TAB   In the General tab, select the encryption level—the choices are Low (the default), Medium, or High. If you plan to use Windows 2000 Active Directory security, select the Use Standard Windows Authentication option.

LOGON SETTINGS TAB   In the Logon Settings tab, the default is to allow the remote user to enter their logon name, domain name, and password. However, some organizations use the Terminal server for remote user access to a specific application that requires minimal security. To simplify the process for user logon, the administrator can set the logon name, domain name, and password automatically so that the remote user does not have to enter the information.

SESSIONS TAB   In the Sessions tab, the administrator can elect to override default user settings. The user settings, as shown in Figure 17-4, include disconnect times, limits, status, and reconnection parameters. While these options can be defined on a per-user basis, it is easier to set the default for all users on this tab. The settings on this tab can be set as follows:

▼ **End a Disconnected Session**   This option specifies how long a session should remain active after a user disconnects from the server. A disconnection could

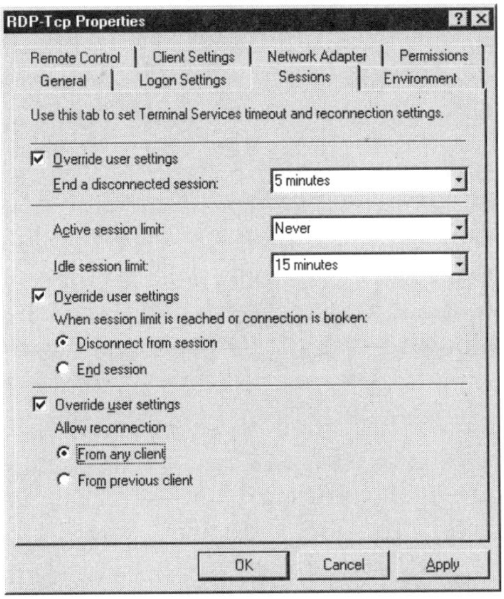

Figure 17-4. Terminal Services session settings

be caused by a bad line connection or accidental disconnection from the server. For convenience, it is nice to provide the remote user with the ability to reconnect to the server and reestablish the session exactly as it was before they were disconnected. Five minutes is generally enough time for the user to dial back in to the network or to reboot their system to reestablish a connection. The only problem with this option is the potential of a security breach. If a user gets disconnected, there is a chance that someone else could reestablish the original user's session. If the original user has access to sensitive information, you may want to set this option to Never.

- **Active Session Limit** This determines how long a user can be online to the Terminal server. Most organizations set the limit to Never. If you want to set a maximum amount of time that a user could or should be online, use this option.

- **Idle Session Limit** This is the amount of time the server will allow a session to have no activity before automatically disconnecting the session. A 15-minute limit provides a user time to step away from the session and return. Beyond 15 minutes, there is a chance the user has forgotten about the session, or is involved in another task and won't return to the session for a long time. If users are dialing into the network through a connection for which there is a per-minute charge, the time online in an idle state causes unnecessary expense. Additionally, disconnecting an idle session frees up resources for other users to access.

■ **When Session Limit is Reached or Connection Is Broken**   This option defines what happens when a session limit is reached (such as the active session limit or idle session limit). If you select the End Session option, the server will disconnect the remote user and reboot the session immediately, in order to clear the resource use from the Terminal server. If you want to provide the remote user with the ability to reconnect within the time limit specified in the first option, select Disconnect from Session. This will disconnect the user from the session but will keep the user's session active on the Terminal server for the time length specified in the first option. If the user logs back into the Terminal server, their session will reconnect automatically where they left off.

▲ **Allow Reconnection**   This option allows the user to reconnect from any client or from the previous (original) client. Every remote system is uniquely identified. If you are concerned about ensuring that the original user is the user connecting to the Terminal server, select From Previous Client. If you select the From Any Client option, the remote user can connect from any computer system.

ENVIRONMENT TAB   The Environment tab allows the administrator to specify a program that the user session will launch automatically. You can combine the option to automatically launch an application with a default logon name and password in the Logon Settings tab, to create a completely automatic connection. The Environment tab also has an option to disable user wallpaper. In a Terminal Services session, wallpaper uses server resources.

REMOTE CONTROL TAB   Use this tab to configure whether an administrator can view or interact with a remote user's session (as discussed in the "Running the New Connection Wizard" section of this chapter).

CLIENT SETTINGS TAB   Use this tab to configure user printers and drive mappings, as shown in Figure 17-5. Users who connect over a dial-up connection cannot print to a network printer at the main office. To configure printing for the user's home printer, enable the Connect Client Printers at Logon option and select Default to Main Client Printer.

For a LAN-based user (such as a Windows Terminal- or NetPC-based workstation on the network) you do not have to enable the options noted for dial-in users, permitting users to select any network printer they have permissions to access.

If you are using the Citrix Metaframe/2000 add-on, you can select the Connect Client Drives at Logon option. This option allows the mapping of the remote user's local A and C drives to accessible drive letters while connected to the Terminal server. Depending on security levels, the user could access the A and C drives on the Terminal server itself. The Connect Client Drives at Logon option maps the drives to the remote user's local computer.

NOTE: If you are using the default Windows 2000 Terminal Services RDP protocol, the Connect Client Drives at Logon option is grayed out. This option is only available in the Citrix Metaframe/2000 add-on.

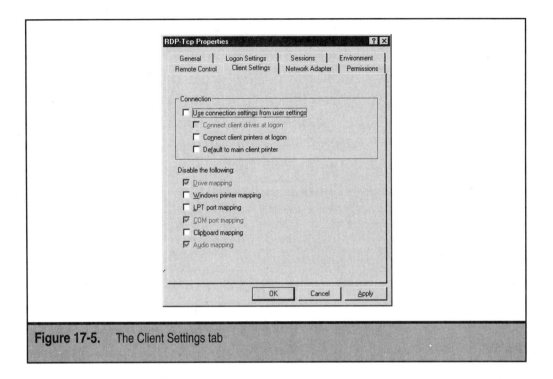

Figure 17-5.   The Client Settings tab

Other settings in the Client Settings tab include the option to disable printer mapping altogether, to disable remote printing, and to disable the ability to cut and paste from the Terminal server to the local machine.

Options that are grayed out without the Citrix Metaframe/2000 add-in include the Connect Client Drives at Logon option, the COM Port Mapping option, and the Audio Mapping option. The COM Port Mapping option provides remote user redirection of access to the COM ports on the remote system, and the Audio Mapping option permits the pass-through of audio from the Terminal server to the remote system.

NETWORK ADAPTER TAB   Use the Network Adapter tab to enable optional settings for the network adapter. You should configure these settings to reflect your security concerns (some settings are more appropriate for an internal LAN adapter that doesn't present the security risk of a dial-in connection).

PERMISSIONS TAB   Use the Permissions tab to define the users who have access to the Terminal server. You can use any combination of Active Directory users, groups, sites, or organization-wide settings. Some administrators create a group specifically for users who have access to a Terminal server.

Installing User Applications on the Terminal Server

Software installation on a Terminal server is exactly the same as software installation on a standard desktop system. Even though the system is operating a version of Windows

2000 Server, applications should be installed and configured as workstation-based applications. For applications that offer both server-based and desktop-based versions (such as virus protection software), purchase and install the desktop version of the software on the Terminal server.

However, some specialized graphics applications, computer-aided design (CAD) programs, accounting applications, and database applications have network versions of the software that allow multiple users to run the same version of the software. In these cases, install the network version of the software onto the C drive of the Terminal server.

Installing 16-bit Applications

DOS-based and 16-bit Windows applications typically run without a problem on Terminal Services, providing the software does not write directly to video and does not require a real mode driver in the Config.sys file. The rule of thumb is that if the application runs in Windows 9*x*, it will run in a Terminal Services session of Windows 2000.

To set up an application, log on to the Terminal server as the user who will have access to the application. Create a shortcut specifying the location of the .com or .exe program file of the application. If the application requires a unique .ini file, be sure to copy and create one for each user. Typically, you can have a DOS or 16-bit Windows application find the .ini configuration file in a different directory by setting the target and default directories specifically within the application shortcut. Set the target file to the actual location of the executable file (for example, c:\application\program.exe), then set the "start in" directory, or "application home directory" to the location of the .ini configuration file (for example, \\server\share\user\bob).

Installing 32-bit Windows Applications

Windows 32-bit applications require the user to log on and set configuration options, which are saved in the registry. To customize 32-bit application settings for a user, log on as the user, launch the application, and create the unique settings for the user. When you log off, the user settings are stored in the user's profile on the Terminal server.

ROLLING OUT TERMINAL SERVICES

Sometimes you can move your prototype lab installation of a server straight into production. However, if the lab-based prototype was put through a number of tests and variations, it is better to start from scratch by reinstalling the server to ensure that the server configuration is clean.

Configuring the Production Server

Configure the Terminal Services component, install application programs, and set up user profiles on the system, as covered earlier in this chapter.

Piloting the First Group of Users

Start your Terminal Services system with a small group of users who can validate the configurations and assumptions made throughout the prototype phase of the installation. While it is sometimes viewed as a good strategy to get key business executives connected to the technology early on in the process, I think it is better to wait until IT users can test the system to make sure all of the configurations and settings are working properly.

The pilot group typically represents 1–5 percent of the total target population for the technology. The group should be small enough to enable administrators to monitor feedback directly. The pilot group should include users who understand how to use the various applications and technologies. This ensures that any problems you encounter are not the result of a lack of knowledge. The pilot phase should run for one to two weeks.

Confirming Application Load

During the pilot phase, make sure that enough users are accessing Terminal Services to determine whether the bandwidth demands and system performance are adequate. If the pilot group is too small to determine whether the performance on the system is adequate, expand the number of users accessing the Terminal server.

Confirm the Need for Training

As more users are added to the pilot group, you should be able to determine whether training is required help users access the Terminal server, log on to the Terminal server, or run any of the applications on the Terminal Services system. While you can usually assume that the use and operation of Terminal Services will be the same as working at a desktop system, there are differences with respect to accessing local printers or drive shares that may require clarification.

If you are introducing new versions of software with the Terminal server system, you may also need to provide application training.

Implementing an Automatic Download of the Client

For Web-based client access, the installation of the Web-based client may require support or assistance, either through the automated ActiveX installation process or by a manual installation of the ActiveX or Netscape plug-in.

Full Roll-out

After the basic pilot has run for a couple of weeks and additional users are being added to Terminal Services with relative ease, you can enable Terminal Services access for all remote client users.

CHAPTER 18

Optimizing and Debugging Windows 2000

P roblem-solving and system-optimization techniques are typically applied after the
network infrastructure has been put into place and problems begin to arise. This
chapter, although at the end of the book, is a section that most designers and imple-
mentors of networks should review early on in their network planning and implementation process. Rather than waiting until users complain that the network is sluggish, or a
server fails, work through these processes before problems arise.

In this chapter, I will highlight some of the core performance-analysis tools and functions available to a network administrator who wants to optimize the Windows 2000 environment. If you take the time to review this chapter before you begin your deployment
of Windows 2000, you'll have a head start on preventing problems.

OPTIMIZING THE WINDOWS 2000 ENVIRONMENT

When you are optimizing a server, your first task is to create a baseline that you can make
comparisons to at a later time. The information you gain from the tools that measure statistics does not automatically flag areas of inefficiency. You need to measure statistics
against the baseline, and against optimal levels for your organization.

Creating a Baseline

A baseline consists of statistics about a networking environment, and they are typically
gathered while the network is operating properly. Many network administrators wait
until the network is experiencing problems and then try to run a series of performance-analysis tools to determine what the problem is. This is like looking for a needle in
a haystack, because you don't really know where to start looking. On one network, a
server running at 50 percent utilization would be a good thing if the system normally
runs at 45–70 percent utilization throughout the normal business day. But on another network, a server running at 50 percent utilization may be a sign of problems if the system
normally runs at 8–10 percent utilization through even the worst days in operation.

What to Baseline

A good baseline is a series of statistics about a network that you can use to compare
against statistics that are collected at some time in the future. The best things to baseline
in a Windows 2000 environment are the following:

▼ **Server processor utilization**   The server processor manages information flow
through the system. When the processor experiences high levels of utilization,
it takes longer for the server to respond to user requests.

■ **Server RAM utilization**   The server RAM is used to cache information,
creating very fast read and write access times. When a system runs out of
RAM, it begins reading and writing requests from and to the hard drive, which
is significantly slower than using RAM.

- **Server disk read/write utilization**   For databases or file information stores, disk read and write times are critical in getting information out to the users. When a disk subsystem is impacted with demands for information access by users of the network, the operation of the system slows. Organizations typically distribute disk read/write requests to multiple drive subsystems, or to multiple storage servers, which provides better service for data requests.

▲ **Network LAN and WAN bandwidth utilization**   Regardless of how fast a server processes information, the information still needs to travel to a user either over a local area network (LAN), or over a wide area network (WAN) connection. These connections link areas impacted by too many user requests on the same LAN or WAN connection for the amount of bandwidth capacity available for communications. You can upgrade the LAN to 100MB or even gigabit speeds to improve performance over older 10MB communication lines, and increase WAN bandwidth from fractional speeds to full data-line speeds.

When to Baseline

Now that we have identified what we need to baseline, you need to begin collecting data. Start by creating a series of reports of the performance statistics at different times of the day, because demand loads may vary in morning, mid-day, and evening hours. Then, if you have a system problem in the middle of the day, you are not comparing system performance against statistics you created one evening when no one was on the network. Also, determine the performance of the servers and the network for various levels of system use during these different times.

Monitor and log system performance in relatively short segments of time (typically over a couple of hours, as opposed to over days or weeks). The reason for this is that performance analysis counters taken over an extended period of time factor in idle time (the middle of the night or over a weekend). When you average out the statistical performance of a network, the idle time skews downward the performance demands of the network during normal business hours.

The best time to monitor a network for analyzing system performance statistics depends on the cycle of the business requirements for the server. If the server you're monitoring runs an accounting application, you'll probably see higher utilization at month and quarter ends. That's usually the time accounting departments do their reporting and reconciliation. If you're monitoring an email server, you might have the heaviest traffic early in the day when everyone opens their email and begins checking messages received at the end of the previous day or overnight. A Web server for a consumer-based organization may find server access to be heaviest in the early hours of the evening, when people log on from home.

One of the best server monitoring techniques is to monitor a 2-hour segment of time throughout a 1–2 week interval. This provides a knowledge base about system operation for specific time windows. You may notice two different system-performance cycles: one during the day when people are using the system, and one during the night when people are not using the system. Or, you may find 5–6 different system-performance cycles, perhaps showing differences among morning, mid-morning, lunch break, early afternoon, late afternoon, and evening time periods.

Updating Your Baseline Statistics

Baseline statistics are dynamic and should be rerun periodically so that they reflect the current status of the network. If users are added to the network, the baseline changes, and new statistical information should be drawn. Additionally, if new applications or services are added to the network, they can affect the state of the network to the point where a new baseline should be created and filed.

Understanding Common Problems that Affect System Performance

There are a number of areas where system performance problems occur without an administrator knowing about them. Some are caused by misperceptions about network performance issues, while others are caused by misunderstandings about the technical design of a network. The net effect is that system performance is affected, creating slowdowns in the operation of the network.

Faster Doesn't Necessarily Mean Better

Adding more processing speed and memory to a computer will not necessarily make the system run better. In many cases, the addition of resources to a server or workstation may only mask an inherent configuration problem. For example, if a server is running slowly because there is not enough memory in the system, Windows 2000 is constantly swapping information from memory to disk. If another processor is added to the system, that will just cause the system to swap data between memory and disk faster. As far as the users are concerned, they may see an increase in performance because of multiple processors in the system, however, as the system swaps more and more to disk, it can cause the hard drives to fail prematurely.

If the system is properly optimized, it can function adequately with a lot less hardware and will actually run more efficiently over time. In fact, the approach of adding more hardware to mask a performance problem can reach a point of diminishing returns, both in performance levels and the operational life of the hardware. It is important to determine the cause of a system's performance degradation so that proper measures can be taken to upgrade the components that are truly bottlenecks in the system.

Comparing the Baseline to a Current Test

A number of factors can cause the baseline statistics to be interpreted in different ways. The factors include changes made to the system, the ways in which the changes affect the baseline, and the analysis of the baseline compared to optimal performance for the system configuration.

The key to analysis is to take a good baseline measurement, make changes to the server configuration, and then determine how those changes affect the performance and operation of the system.

Background Processes in Use

Server performance may not necessarily be affected solely by the number of users logged on to the server, or the size and number of files being read or written to the server. Instead, the culprit may be other background services that the server is managing. Instead of splitting the file and application server functions to multiple system so that the network load is distributed, try to evaluate the background processes on the server to determine whether they are causing negative performance effects. This can occur when a file server is also acting as a domain controller, DHCP server, IIS server, or the like. Also, virus detection and eradication utilities put a heavy load on a server. By reviewing the processor utilization of the server and the amount of CPU time being allocated to various services, you can perform an analysis of the server resources.

To view the server processes, run the Task Manager software by running taskmgr.exe or by pressing CTL-ALT-DEL and selecting Task Manager from the menu. Once in Task Manager, select the Processes tab. A screen of processes similar to the one shown in Figure 18-1 will be displayed. Click the CPU Time column header to sort the processes based on CPU time. In many cases, administrators are unaware that certain applications or tasks (such as virus scanning, DHCP services, or domain controller services) take up quite a bit of system resources.

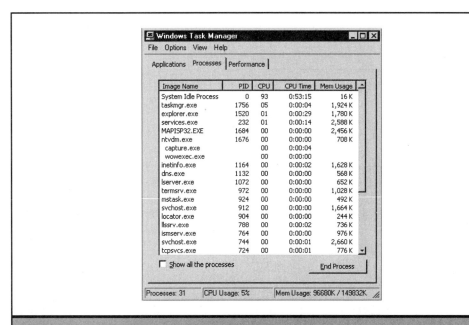

Figure 18-1.   Task Manager showing the CPU time being used on a server

Understanding Server-to-Workstation Communications

When evaluating the performance between a workstation and a server, don't jump to the conclusion that higher bandwidth network adapters are needed. First, evaluate and test the transfer route between the client and the server. Frequently, the speed of the adapter is not as important as minimizing other unnecessary traffic over the LAN or WAN connection.

One of the common client-to-server performance problems occurs when desktop systems have multiple transport protocols installed and loaded (such as NetBEUI, TCP/IP, and IPX/SPX). If the adapter drivers are loaded for all three protocols, the method of communication is not necessarily assured. For example, in a network with a Novell backbone, clients may communicate with the Novell servers with IPX/SPX, and communicate with the Internet with TCP/IP. However, unbeknownst to the administrators, the client may also be communicating with older Windows NT servers using NetBEUI. Every protocol communicated over a network takes additional bandwidth from the entire network communications infrastructure. The addition of extra protocols may decrease the overall performance of the network bandwidth by half for two protocols, or by a third for three protocols, and so on.

Misrouting Information on the Network

With Windows 2000, the default protocol is TCP/IP and, in fact, every desktop, laptop, and server in a Windows 2000 environment can run TCP/IP as the single protocol. Organizations that are running TCP/IP as the only protocol on their network may have multiple routes between segments or sites in their organization. One route may be over a LAN connection and another may be a redundant link over a slower WAN connection. Although administrators would probably assume that the client systems are communicating with the servers over the faster communication link, the client may in fact be communicating by default over the slower WAN connection. It is important to remember that most devices communicate over the same route that they have previously used, and if there was an interruption in the higher speed communication link between the client and the server, and the client defaulted to the slower link, the client may not automatically switch back to the faster link when it becomes available.

In TCP/IP networking, each route is given a "cost," and the communications route is determined by the lowest-cost route for the communication link. However, when many organizations configure TCP/IP networking in a Windows 2000 environment, they do not properly assign the costs for the various communication links, which can cause the organization to have the same cost on all routes, regardless of their actual performance. Thus, the default communications path from the client to the server will be based on the last successful route of communications, regardless of its level of performance.

There are a number of tools you can use to help validate the path between a workstation and the server. First, determine the appropriate protocol for communication between the client and the server. The only way to ensure a constant link between the client and the server over a given protocol is to set up the workstation so that it will only

communicate over a predefined protocol configuration. To view and configure the protocols that are used, do the following:

1. Choose Start | Settings | Control Panel.
2. Double-click Networks and Dial-Up Connections.
3. Right-click the Local Area Connection icon.
4. Select Properties.

If the network will communicate solely over TCP/IP, that protocol should be selected, and in most cases it would be the only protocol listed in the components section of
the Properties page. If the client cannot communicate with the server, run standard
TCP/IP communication link tests, such as Ping.

Once the client software is configured to communicate over a specific transport,
perform a trace to confirm that the route the client is using to communicate with the
server is correct. Under TCP/IP networking, this can be accomplished using the
tracert.exe utility that comes with Windows and is installed simultaneously with TCP/IP
networking. The Tracert utility can run a trace between the client and the server to check
whether the route that the link is actually taking and the one the administrator assumes it
is taking are the same. Figure 18-2 shows how Tracert can determine the actual route of an
assumed link.

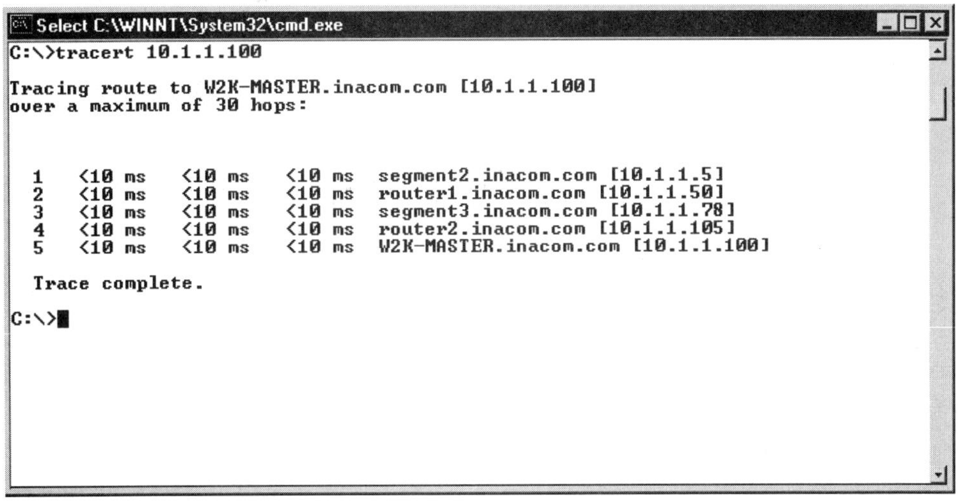

```
Select C:\WINNT\System32\cmd.exe                                          _ □ ×
C:\>tracert 10.1.1.100

Tracing route to W2K-MASTER.inacom.com [10.1.1.100]
over a maximum of 30 hops:


  1    <10 ms    <10 ms    <10 ms    segment2.inacom.com [10.1.1.5]
  2    <10 ms    <10 ms    <10 ms    router1.inacom.com [10.1.1.50]
  3    <10 ms    <10 ms    <10 ms    segment3.inacom.com [10.1.1.78]
  4    <10 ms    <10 ms    <10 ms    router2.inacom.com [10.1.1.105]
  5    <10 ms    <10 ms    <10 ms    W2K-MASTER.inacom.com [10.1.1.100]

  Trace complete.

C:\>█
```

Figure 18-2.   Using Tracert to confirm an assumed TCP/IP link

MONITORING PERFORMANCE USING THE PERFORMANCE TOOL

The main tool that comes with Windows 2000 to conduct baseline analysis and performance monitoring is the Performance snap-in tool for MMC. The Windows 2000 Performance tool includes a series of administrator-definable functions that help analyze processor, RAM, disk, and LAN/WAN performance statistics. While the Performance tool provides a rich set of indicators you can monitor and analyze, the downside is that there are so many indicators to choose from that selecting the correct ones becomes a challenge.

To simplify the process, in this section I have broken down the performance monitoring processes into four major areas, and I have made a series of recommendations about the components to monitor and how to set the monitoring components to monitor the right sets of information, and I have indicated what would be considered normal (or abnormal) for a particular statistic.

Launching the Performance Snap-In Tool

There are two ways to launch the Performance Console snap-in MMC monitoring tool. The easiest is to launch the tool from the Administrative Tools menu from the Start button. To do so, select Start | Programs | Administrative Tools | Performance. This will launch the performance Console tool with no predefined monitoring components set.

The other way to load the performance tool is to manually add the Performance Console snap-in to an MMC session. To do so:

1. Choose Start | Run.
2. Type **mmc** and click OK.
3. After the MMC has loaded, select Console.
4. Select Add/Remove snap-in.
5. Click Add.
6. Choose ActiveX Control.
7. Click Add.
8. Click Next.
9. Select System Monitor Control.
10. Click Next.
11. Click Finish.
12. Choose Performance Logs and Alerts, and then click Add.
13. Click Close.
14. Click OK.

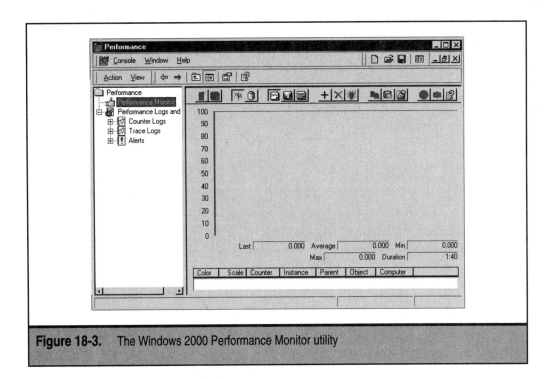

Figure 18-3.   The Windows 2000 Performance Monitor utility

After installing either option, you will see a performance monitoring screen similar to the one in Figure 18-3.

Capturing and Analyzing Processor Performance

The first component to analyze is processor performance. As discussed previously in this chapter, to increase the performance of a Windows 2000 system, the conclusion most organizations leap to is to upgrade the server to a faster processor (550MHz instead of 300MHz) or to add another processor to the system. Although this will increase the performance of the server, the decision to upgrade or add a processor should be systematic and planned.

The key components to view in the System Monitor, as graphed in Figure 18-4, are the following:

▼ **Processor Utilization**   % Processor Time (Click the + button on the System Monitor screen, select the Processor performance object, select the % Processor Time in the Performance Counters screen, select _Total#0, and then click the Add button)—The % Processor Time counter shows the percentage of time that the system processors are being utilized. It is calculated by measuring the time that the processors spend executing the thread of the Idle process at each

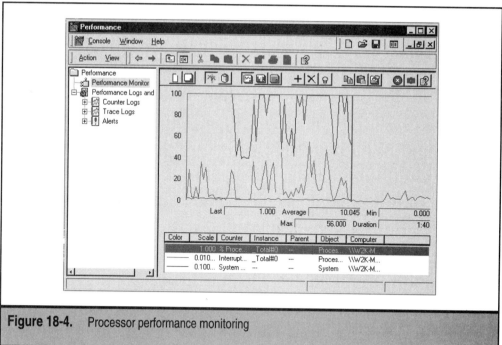

Figure 18-4.   Processor performance monitoring

interval, and then subtracting that number from 100 percent. In effect, this statistic shows the average percentage of time that the processor was busy during the sequence interval. When processor time is utilized in excess of 70 percent, the system processor may be a bottleneck.

■ **Hardware Interrupts**   Interrupts/sec (Click the + button on the System Monitor screen, select the Processor performance object, select the Interrupts/sec in the Performance Counters screen, select _Total#0, and then click the Add button)—If the % Processor Time counter is excessively high, the next thing to check is the interrupts per second on the processor. This will reveal whether the CPU activity is being caused by hardware interrupts, which is a hardware problem, not a software problem. When there are more interrupts per second than system calls, this confirms that the hardware devices are generating more demand on the system processor than the software calls to the Windows 2000 services. When over 1,000 interrupts per second are being generated, hardware devices in the server that are CPU-intensive should be evaluated. These devices include 16-bit controllers and PIO devices that require a processor cycle to manage the hardware adapter. Many older network adapters, IDE or 16-bit SCSI hard drive controllers, or even video adapters require these processor cycles. Devices that do not require PIO processor interrupts, such as PCI network adapters or bus-mastering controllers, can minimize the demand on the processor.

▲ **System Calls**   System Calls/sec (Click the + button on the System Monitor screen, select the System performance object, select the System Calls/sec in the Performance Counters screen, and then click the Add button)—The number of system calls per second is the frequency of calls made to the Windows 2000 services. This will reveal whether the CPU activity is being caused by an application request (such as an application server function in Microsoft Exchange, SQL Server, or IIS). An application server should generate more system calls per second than interrupts per second.

Faster processing speeds provide the ability to add more users to a single server. Microsoft Windows 2000 can be scaled to add more processors if processor performance is a severe problem.

Capturing and Analyzing Disk Performance

The second series of statistics to analyze is disk-storage performance. In previous versions of Windows NT, running diskperf -y activated disk-performance tracking and counter monitoring, Windows 2000 requires no action to begin capturing and analyzing disk performance. The key components to view in the System Monitor, as graphed in Figure 18-5, are the following:

▼ **Paging File**   % Usage (Click the + button on the System Monitor screen, select the Paging File performance object, select % Usage in the Performance Counters screen, select \??\C:\pagefile.sys#0, and then click the Add button)—The paging-file-usage percentage reports how much of the paging file is being used at any given time. When the paging file exceeds 90 percent, it is dynamically increased, which requires server resources. Also, the file is increased in a noncontiguous disk configuration. The paging file is initially a single contiguous block of disk space that can be efficiently used.

■ **% Disk Time**   % Disk Time (Click the + button on the System Monitor screen, select the PhysicalDisk performance object, select % Disk Time in the Performance Counters screen, select _Total#0, and then click the Add button)—The physical-disk-percentage time is the amount of time a disk read or disk write takes to be conducted on the server. When the percentage of disk time is in excess of 65 percent, the disk subsystem may be a bottleneck on the server. A number of options can be invoked to improve disk performance caused by excessive disk access, and these are discussed later in this chapter.

■ **Disk Read/Write Transfers**   Disk Bytes/Sec (Click the + button on the System Monitor screen, select the Physical Disk performance object, select Disk Bytes/Sec in the Performance Counters screen, select _Total#0, and then click the Add button)—The disk-bytes-per-second figure is the volume of

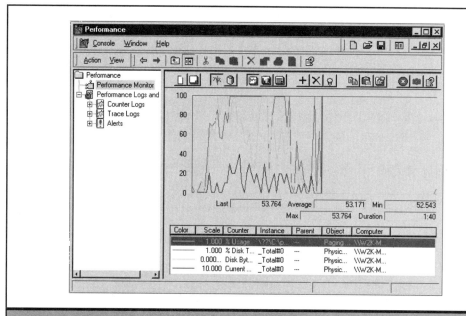

Figure 18-5. Disk performance monitoring

information being read or written to the disk at any given point in time. By tracing the amount of information that is read from and written to disk, you can evaluate whether the demand for disk throughput (whether it be a Fast SCSI-2, Fast Wide SCSI, or a cached disk subsystem) is necessary for the actual disk throughput demands made on the server.

■ **Current Disk Queue Length**   (Click the + button on the System Monitor screen, select the PhysicalDisk performance object, select Current Disk Queue Length in the Performance Counters screen, select _Total#0, and then click the Add button)—The current disk queue length shows how many disk I/O requests are pending processing. When the disk queue length exceeds two, the pending request transactions for the server may indicate the need for a faster controller card or a distributed subsystem.

▲ **Average Disk sec/Transfer**   (Click the + button on the System Monitor screen, select the PhysicalDisk performance object, select Avg Disk sec/Transfer in the Performance Counters screen, select _Total#0, and then click the Add button)—The average disk transfer shows how many seconds a read or write request takes to complete. When the average disk transfer exceeds .05 seconds, a caching disk controller may improve disk read and write performance on the server.

Disk-Caching Controllers

Disk-caching controllers can significantly improve the performance of a server with heavy disk reads and writes. A server with high activity manages information transfers from user to user, as well as the transport of information in and out of directory and information stores. When the System Monitor snap-in thresholds are excessive, a disk-cache controller can minimize the bottleneck on the disk subsystem. A caching controller typically handles more transactions and user requests on a server than a system with just a standard hard drive controller, thus improving overall system performance.

Capturing and Analyzing RAM Usage

The third series of statistics to capture and analyze in a Windows 2000 system is RAM usage. The analysis lets you determine whether the amount of memory in the server is adequate for the demands of the environment. Key to server memory management is sufficient caching power to minimize the number of times the server needs to read information from disk. The components to view in the System Monitor, as graphed in Figure 18-6, are the following:

▼ **Available Memory**   (Click the + button on the System Monitor screen, select the Memory performance object, select Available Bytes in the Performance Counters screen, and then click the Add button)—The available-bytes figure is the amount of memory available for use. When this figure drops below 4MB, paging is occurring on the server and the system may require more memory to minimize the number of times it needs to page to disk.

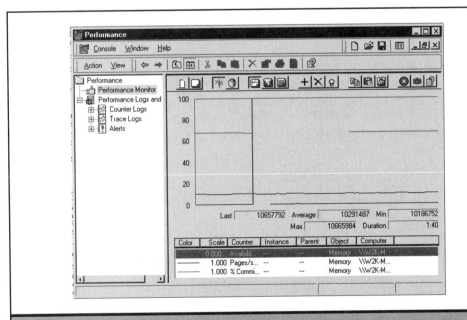

Figure 18-6.   RAM management monitoring

■ **Memory**   Pages/sec (Click the + button on the System Monitor screen, select the Memory performance object, select Pages/sec in the Performance Counters screen, and then click the Add button)—The memory pages per second value reflects the number of memory pages being read from and written to disk that were not cached in memory at the time of request. When this value exceeds 15 pages per second, the system is most likely destroying the disk, and either more RAM or a cached disk controller should be added to the server.

▲ **Committed Bytes in Use**   % Committed Bytes in Use (Click the + button on the System Monitor screen, select the Memory performance object, select % Committed Bytes in Use in the Performance Counters screen, and then click the Add button)—The percentage of the committed bytes in use is the ratio of committed bytes to the committed limit, which is the amount of virtual memory that is in use. When the committed percentage exceeds 90 percent, the server may reallocate memory for the paging file, causing a decrease in performance while the paging file is updated.

Capturing and Analyzing LAN/WAN Performance

The fourth and last series of statistics to capture and analyze in a Windows 2000 system is LAN and WAN performance. The analysis lets you determine whether the LAN and WAN configurations are adequate for the demands of the environment. The key components to view in the System Monitor, as graphed in Figure 18-7, are the following:

▼ **Bytes Transferred**   Bytes Total/sec (Click the + button on the System Monitor screen, select the Network Interface performance object, select Bytes Total/sec in Use in the Performance Counters screen, select your network adapter setting #0 option, and then click the Add button)—The total bytes per second is the rate at which information is sent and received on the network adapter, including framing characters.

■ **Current Bandwidth**   Current Bandwidth (Click the + button on the System Monitor screen, select the Network Interface performance object, select Current Bandwidth in Use in the Performance Counters screen, select your network adapter setting #0 option, and then click the Add button)—The current bandwidth is an estimate of the network adapter's current bandwidth, in bits per second.

▲ **Queue Length**   Output Queue Length (Click the + button on the System Monitor screen, select the Network Interface performance object, select Output Queue Length in Use in the Performance Counters screen, select your network adapter setting #0 option, and then click the Add button)—The output queue length reflects the total number of packets that are waiting. If there are more than two, delays are occurring on the network adapter, and a bottleneck needs to be eliminated.

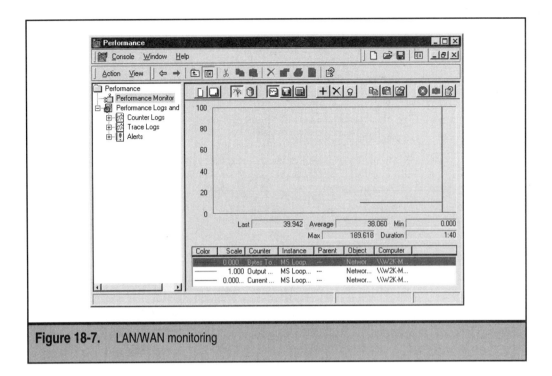

Figure 18-7.   LAN/WAN monitoring

CONFIGURING HARDWARE FOR OPTIMAL PERFORMANCE

Monitoring and analyzing hardware performance helps to determine where the bottlenecks are. Then, reconfiguring the hardware configuration optimizes system performance.

Processor and RAM Configuration

The first thing to check when optimizing the server processor performance is whether the server is configured to maximize throughput for network applications, rather than for file and print management. This option can be set by following these steps:

1. Choose Start | Settings | Control Panel.

2. Double-click System.

3. Click the Advanced Tab.

4. Click Performance Options.

A screen similar to the one shown in Figure 18-8 will be displayed. Select Applications to ensure that a foreground application is given system priority. In addition to processor priority, this also optimizes the amount of memory allocated to functions including paged memory, thread counts, free connections, and in-process items. For most file and

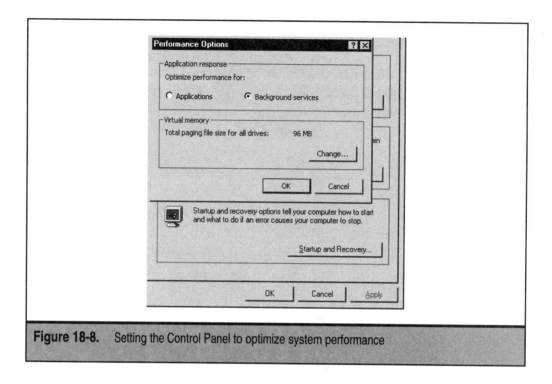

Figure 18-8. Setting the Control Panel to optimize system performance

print servers or application servers, select the Background Services option. This balances system resources equally across all running services, which is appropriate for most server-based applications.

Although every operating environment is unique, there are some rules of thumb to use when determining the size of the server and the amount of RAM.

In a Windows 2000 environment, server RAM plays as important a role as processor speed in determining the capabilities of the server to manage network resources. More memory in a Windows 2000 server means more caching, which improves performance.

Additionally, as more components are added (such as messaging, Web, DNS/DHCP, and so on), the demand on file server RAM by the applications and add-ins is increased.

Typically, the rule of thumb for memory in a file server in a highly optimized server configuration is 64MB of base memory plus 10MB of memory for each add-in application, plus 8MB of RAM for each 1GB of disk storage in the system. Thus, a server with 12GB of disk storage and with DNS installed on top of Windows 2000 should have approximately 170MB to 192MB of memory installed. File servers that are used as archived data stores or small office servers with large disk-space needs create less demand on server resources, so the amount of memory can be significantly lower.

Table 18-1 indicates common baseline configurations appropriate for a Windows 2000 server depending on the number of users.

Run your own capacity-analysis utility (described in the "Capacity Planning for a Windows 2000 Environment" section of this chapter) to determine the server performance capabilities for your organization.

For large and very large workgroups or organizations, you may want to consider splitting users or services across multiple servers as described in the "Network Load Balancing" section in Chapter 12. This is frequently more efficient than adding more RAM or processors.

Hard Drive Configuration

In Windows 2000, the disk-storage demands of the file server have a direct relationship on file and application-storage requirements. Variations in the type of hard-drive hardware (Fast/Wide SCSI, SCSI-2, PCI or EISA controller, cache controller, and so on) can increase the performance of server access (see Chapter 5 for hardware recommendations on these items). Obviously, the faster the drive speed, the faster the disk transfer speed, and the better the hardware performance.

Users per File Server	File/Print Server	Application Server
20 users	Pentium processor, 8GB disk space, 96MB RAM	Pentium processor, 8GB disk space, 128MB RAM
50 users	Pentium II processor, 16GB disk space, 128MB RAM	Pentium II processor, 16GB disk space, 160MB RAM
100 users	Pentium II processor, 32GB disk space, 192MB RAM	Pentium II processor, 32GB disk space, 256MB RAM
200 users	Dual-Pentium II, 64GB disk space, 256MB RAM	Dual-processor Pentium II, 64GB disk space, 384MB RAM
500 users	Dual-processor Pentium III, 96GB disk space, 384MB RAM	Dual-processor Pentium III, 96GB disk space, 512MB RAM
1,000 users	Dual-processor Pentium III, 128GB disk space, 512MB RAM	Dual-processor Pentium III, 128GB disk space, 768MB RAM
1,500 users	4-processor Pentium III, 140GB disk space, 768MB RAM	4-processor Pentium III, 160GB disk space, 1GB RAM

Table 18-1.   Sample per-Server Configurations for Windows 2000

Boot Drive

The boot drive is the typical location of the \winnt directory for Windows 2000 executables and DLLs. The boot drive is commonly the location of application programs, as well. Having both the Windows 2000 files and application program files on the boot drive of the server does not drastically affect server performance. It is common to have boot drive storage space of 2 gigabytes or 4 gigabytes to store all of this information.

The boot drive also becomes the default location for the Windows 2000 *pagefile*. You can move your pagefile to a different drive location, but if the drive you put your pagefile on is not accessible at boot-up, the system will not boot.

Data Drive

The data drive is typically the storage location for data files, such as documents, spreadsheet files, SQL databases, or mail-server message databases. By default, database files and message database files are stored on the same drive where the application program files are stored. The default location for these files can typically be changed by going into the Administrator utility for the application and specifying the directories in which various files should be stored.

Log Drive

Most database applications and enterprise messaging systems automatically log all transactions in separate message logs as a way of providing for recovery of lost information in the event of a system failure. The log files are typically stored in the same directory as the main application and message databases. However, because information is simultaneously stored in both the database and the log files on the server, extensive disk write sequences are performed.

Drive Configuration Recommendation

With the three drive definitions just noted, the optimum configuration for the server is to have the Windows 2000 system files and pagefile on a dedicated boot drive, the application data files and information databases on a dedicated data drive, and the log files on a third hard-drive subsystem. A Windows 2000 server can run more efficiently reading and writing information to multiple drive units instead of bottlenecking on a single drive.

Disk Fault Tolerance

Disk fault tolerance is critical in minimizing the loss of information caused by system failure. You can implement disk fault tolerance either through hardware or software management. Microsoft Windows 2000 provides software disk fault tolerance for disk mirroring and disk striping, but hardware disk fault tolerance requires a disk controller that supports hardware fault tolerance.

When possible, consider hardware fault tolerance over software fault tolerance management. The advantages of hardware fault tolerance over software fault tolerance include the following:

▼ **Faster performance**   Because hardware fault tolerance is managed by a controller card or other hardware device, processing performance is not compromised in order to provide the fault-tolerance functions.

▲ **Error trapping**   If there is a hard-drive subsystem failure, a system that uses software fault tolerance may be affected by the subsystem fault, which potentially can cause the server to halt network operating-system functions. A hardware fault-tolerance system can usually isolate the disk failure from the operating system functions and prevent the operating system from halting processing operations.

If the file-server hardware vendor provides utilities to create fault-tolerant disk configurations for the server, it is preferable to use the hardware fault-tolerance options for disk mirroring, duplexing, or data striping, rather than the software options included in the Windows NT disk administrator.

Within an optimized Windows 2000 environment that has a separate boot drive, data drive, and log file drive, the fault tolerance suggestions for each of these three separate physical drives are as follows:

▼ **Boot drive**   Drive mirroring is a good solution to ensure protection of system boot processes. Since Windows 2000 cannot boot without a valid boot drive, mirrored boot drives provide redundancy.

■ **Data drive**   The data drive in a Windows 2000 environment is typically the largest volume on the server. The implementation of RAID5 provides an N+1 fault tolerance scheme, where one backup drive is added to the entire array of data drives to provide the necessary fault-tolerance capabilities.

▲ **Log drive**   Since the log drive only stores message logs, the log drive can simply be a mirrored drive. By definition, the log drive is a backup of the primary data-drive information, so it provides redundant services anyway.

CAPACITY PLANNING
FOR A WINDOWS 2000 ENVIRONMENT

Capacity planning for a Windows 2000 environment goes through three different phases in the life of a server. The first occurs prior to the purchase and installation of the Windows 2000 software and is when the size and capabilities of the new server are determined. The second occurs after the server has been installed and users are accessing the system, at which point an analysis is conducted to confirm that the server configuration is adequate for the demands of the environment. And lastly, as the demands of the server change (addition of users, addition or changes in add-in applications being used, increased traffic), an incremental capacity analysis will ensure that the server can continue to meet the needs of the organization.

Sizing a New Server Configuration

Before an organization deploys Windows 2000 for their file and print or application server environment, basic (and sometimes advanced) analysis is usually conducted to determine what size server is appropriate. The analysis determines the appropriate server processor, amount of memory, and size of disk storage. For organizations already using network file servers, much of the historical information about system usage is readily available. For organizations new to networking, or those that will be using some of the advanced server functions of Windows 2000 (such as DFS, network load balancing, Intellimirror) you must estimate the usage and demands for the server.

There are a few different ways to come up with a suggested system configuration. One method is to work with Microsoft's recommendations of a minimum server configuration and do guesswork to build the final system configuration. If you already have a server providing networking services to users, the second method is to use the performance monitoring tool that comes with Windows 2000 to measure the current usage of the existing server and extrapolate that information to estimate the size of the Windows 2000 server. The third method is to use a third-party capacity-analysis and planning tool to do formal modeling and come up with a recommended system configuration. I will address all three methods in this section.

Capacity Planning Based on Microsoft's Recommended Minimums

In Chapter 5, I outlined Microsoft's recommendations for the suggested minimum configuration for a Windows 2000 system. In that chapter I also discussed a few variations on the Microsoft minimums, which I believe to be better minimum system requirements.

Surprisingly, most organizations take these minimums and use a form of guesswork to come up with a system configuration. Some take it to an extreme by estimating what they think they need, and then they double that to come up with the configuration specification.

So, while the guesswork method for determining the configuration of a system tends to be the most common, the next two options are preferred methods for configuration analysis.

Using the Performance Console for Capacity Planning

The Performance Console snap-in can also be used for capacity planning when you are specifying the configuration of a new server or a replacement server. The Performance Console snap-in captures a lot of information that you can use to analyze a server or networking environment. The trick is to understand how to use the information. The statistics that are gathered from the System Monitor snap-in only tell you that a problem exists. You must then use those statistics to identify which specific object is at the root of the problem. In most cases, problems occur in improperly configured hardware components (such as caching, LAN adapter performance, or the like). These components affect the extendible performance components of the Windows 2000 environment. When properly used, the System Monitor snap-in can alert you about impending problems in Windows 2000 or other server components.

Monitoring and analyzing the performance of an existing server on the network provides historical information about the demands on the server and the type of bottlenecks on the system. Use this information to project the demands on the Windows 2000 server.

Sometimes, the network is running slowly, or it appears that the network halts for a few seconds before responding to a query. You need to determine whether there is a bottleneck in the network, and if there is, where the bottleneck resides. As the discussion in this chapter indicates, bottlenecks can occur at the processor, memory, disk capacity, and network adapter. Bottlenecks can also be the result of Internet connections, gateway or host servers, WAN connections, third-party add-in applications, and so on.

Using a Third-Party Tool for Capacity Planning

There are a number of third-party utilities available for performance and capacity analysis of a Windows 2000 environment. The program that provides the best analysis to Windows 2000 (at the time of this writing) is Dynameasure from Bluecurve Software (http://www.bluecurve.com). Dynameasure provides graphs, charts, and reports, as well as options for input and information measurements, providing flexibility in simulating user activities.

Dynameasure provides user-defined input criteria, based on dozens of variable options, as shown in Figure 18-9. Measurements of the time and duration variables defined by the administrator and measured against system response time can be tested against an existing Windows 2000 server that is in production use. The results of the measurements provide the network administrator the ability to determine the actual characteristics of users, and test these characteristics against the server. Tests are conducted in a controlled state, where the administrator can put as much load or as little load on the production server as needed, without affecting the usage of the server. The advantage of testing an existing server is that the results provide an exact analysis of capacity and capabilities.

During any server capacity analysis, the component being tested (in this case Microsoft Windows 2000) should not be the one tested. Just as other applications (such as domain controller processes, file and print access, and data warehouse interaction) affect the performance of Windows 2000, the use of Windows 2000 can affect other existing applications. Testing should include other demands on the network to ensure that a new messaging system does not negatively affect the performance of the rest of the environment. Dynameasure analyzes and measures file and print access, as well as SQL and database access. These measurements can be conducted independently, or as part of the entire testing process of Windows 2000. Figure 18-10 shows a sample graph that provides information about the demands of a Windows 2000 server's CPU utilization, disk utilization, and network I/O.

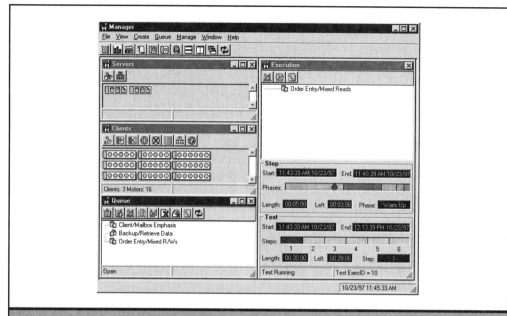

Figure 18-9. Dynameasure capacity-planning and analysis tool

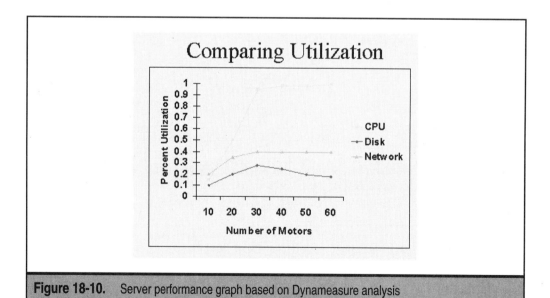

Figure 18-10. Server performance graph based on Dynameasure analysis

Planning for Additional Load on an Existing Server

Beyond determining server utilization, you should analyze what effect an increase in the number of users or server functions will have on performance. This focus on the maximum capacity of the server helps you justify the acquisition of additional servers to support the growth of the organization. The goal is to determine the existing operations, determine the growth requirements, and then model the growth to determine whether the server will be sufficient.

Modeling Performance Requirements

If changes are planned for the network, a solid, up-to-date baseline will help you project the future with relative accuracy. For example, if the organization has added 20 new users to the network twice before, and each time a new baseline was taken, you have solid information about the effect of adding 20 more users to the network. If the network performance was affected by 3 percent each time 20 new users were added, then you can safely assume that this new addition of 20 users will also impact the network by 3 percent.

To confirm this expectation, you can conduct actual modeling of performance. First, be sure to have a baseline of the existing system performance. Then, determine what the expected additional increase in demand or growth will be on the network. Set up a performance-modeling utility like the System Monitor snap-in or Bluecurve's Dynameasure to model the additional load. The utility will be able to determine the effect of the new load on the capacity and capability of the environment.

DEBUGGING SYSTEM PROBLEMS

While I have done everything I can in this book to help you plan, prepare, and implement Windows 2000 properly, there comes a point in the implementation or migration where the network just doesn't behave properly and you turn some or all of your resources from implementation mode to problem-solving and debugging mode. Some problems are small, and therefore don't affect more than a handful of users. Other problems are enterprise-wide, and they require the cooperation and support of dozens of IT resources to try to resolve them. This section focuses on techniques to help you identify, isolate, and resolve system problems.

Problem-Solving Procedures

Sometimes resolving a network problem means weeks or months of effort spent chasing a problem with no resolution in sight. Many times, the problems are embedded in the application or in the operating system (commonly called "bugs"). Other times, the problem is something that is publicly known or easily fixable, but the organization has been unable to match up the problem with the fix. Key to improving the ability to debug a problem and fix it is a methodical analytical process.

Following is a 10-step process to help you identify, isolate, and resolve a problem in a Windows 2000 environment.

Step 1: Document the Problem

The first step in trying to debug a problem is to document it clearly. Some of the key questions to answer in your documentation process include:

▼ *When does the problem occur?* or *What is the time, date, and/or frequency of the problem?*   In many cases, knowing the time and date of the problem reveals a lot of information. If the problem occurs at a particular time every day, that is an important clue. For instance, one network problem occurred every afternoon at 4 P.M. It turned out that a large security vault system was activated every day at 4 P.M., requiring a great deal of electrical power. Because of the drop in power throughout the facility, hubs, switches, workstations, and other devices that were not on a supplemental power backup system failed every day at 4 P.M. In another instance, an organization had a server failure every night, requiring a reboot every morning. The administrator tracked down the failure time, and found it occurred between 2 A.M. and 3 A.M. in the morning. The tape backup system backed up this server every morning between 2 A.M. and 3 A.M. It was found that a problem during the backup process caused the system to fail.

■ *Is there any specific event that triggers the problem?*   Another organization was required to document the entire configuration of the organization's network before a solution to its problem was found. This was a very large network, so it took a few days just to gather the information about the network design. The problem was that every now and then the network server would be extremely sluggish at responding to user requests. By documenting the network configuration, and tracking the problems that occurred, the organization found that virus-protection software installed on the system caused the server to pause for a few seconds whenever a large number of files were added or modified on the system.

■ *What is the exact wording of the error?*   Documenting the exact wording of information about the problem is absolutely critical. The phrases and error codes you see can be investigated in knowledge bases.

■ *Does anything make it worse, or does anything make it better?*   Knowing the history of a problem, and whether certain actions make the problem worse or better, sometimes indicates the general characteristics of a system problem. For example, if adding more users causes the system to fail, then the problem may be specific to the number of user connections on the system, or to a workload level that a specific number of users imposes. These problems can be debugged by identifying those characteristics.

▲ *Does this occur on one server or client or all of them? Are all systems similarly configured?* Sometimes a problem is specific to a user's workstation or to a specific user. You don't have to investigate the entire system if only one person is affected. Additionally, some Windows 2000 computers may be configured identically, and other computers are not. If the problem occurs on one computer, but another computer with an identical configuration is not experiencing problems, the problem is probably related to a user.

Step 2: Create a Problem-Resolution Checklist

The second thing to do during the debugging process is create a problem-resolution checklist, effectively taking guesses about the cause of the problem and listing all of the potential solutions. Far too often, problem-solvers focus on a single fix to a problem, blinding them to other solutions. (This is commonly the approach that problem solving on the phone with a manufacturer takes.)

It is better to list *all* the possible sources of the problem, and write down any potential guesses for the solution, including those solutions that seem unlikely. At worst, you will have to cross off some options on the list.

Once you have your core list, order the list by the likelihood of this being the problem or solution. Some problem solvers work on the easiest possible fix, even if that fix offers the least likely chance of solving the problem. If the most obvious and most probable solution is also the most complicated, you should start prepping for time to attempt this more complicated fix. Even the easy fixes can take several days, because you have to run through all of those tests, letting precious days elapse before trying the solution that works. Also, sometimes the simple fixes change the system configuration and make it less stable. Then, when you apply the more complicated fix, the system may fail because of new problems that were introduced in the simple, low-impact solutions that were applied.

As you rate each fix by level of complexity, determine whether any of the easy fixes may make the problem worse. If so, apply only the easy fix that you believe won't make the problem worse.

The bottom-line rule to fixing a problem is that the fix should not take more than one-half the time or cost of a new system. While it sounds absurd that a fix could cost more than buying and building a brand new system, think about the cost of spending two weeks working through a variety of fixes, bringing the network up and down throughout that two-week period, keeping the IT staff working through the night over a long period of time (including a couple working all weekend running problem-solving tests). Spending one weekend rebuilding from scratch is probably more effective.

Step 3: Conduct Initial Knowledge-Base Validation

Before diving into the first fix and applying service packs and updates randomly, call the manufacturers of the hardware and software that you have (or surf the Internet) to see if there are known fixes to your problem. Sometimes the manufacturer is already aware of the problem and has the solution. More and more companies have a database available to their technical support people. Some of the people on the phone are good at finding information in their knowledge-base, and others are not. Providing technical support personnel with a complete description of error codes or error messages helps them search the database.

For problems related to Microsoft products (including Windows 2000), Microsoft has a subscription-based CD-ROM service called TechNet that provides a huge knowledge-base about Microsoft products. As you search the database, you may find a number of possible fixes. Rather than implementing each of them, go back to your resolution checklist and determine the likelihood that a particular fix will solve the problem you are experiencing. Match the database information against your ideas of the problem's cause.

Resist the temptation (and manufacturer's suggestions) to load service packs, patches, and fixes unless you know the suggestion offers a likelihood of solving your problem. In fact, your decision to install service packs and fixes should be connected to the fact that the service pack explicitly says it will fix your problem. If you apply patches and fixes randomly, you could create a whole new series of problems on the system.

Step 4: Test Your Solutions One at a Time

Before you start applying patches and attempting fixes for your problem, do a full backup of your system and document any settings you plan to change during the process. Most importantly, apply one fix at a time. Resist the temptation to apply two or three fixes at the same time, trying to shorten the time it'll take to fix your problem. While you might hit the problem on the nose, you may find that something else stops working. Having too many things changed all at once makes it very difficult to isolate the new problem when you work backwards to determine which fix solved the problem and which fix created the new problem.

In addition to testing one fix at a time, documenting the changes that were made before and after making modifications is important, because you may need to work backwards to remove fixes or changes. If you keep a diary of modifications, you can avoid breaking other things along the road to fixing the current problem. This is extremely important when several people are working on the same problem. Sometimes different people attack the same problem from different angles, or a night shift works to solve a problem that the day shift wasn't able to fix. With a lot of different people working on the same problem, documenting every effort prevents more problems.

Only as a last resort (prior to doing a complete system rebuild from scratch) should you "shotgun" all fixes at the same time in an attempt to see if any of the fixes will solve the problem. Sometimes you can replicate the problem in a lab or controlled environment. Use that to see if a solution results from applying *all* of the patches, and fixes. If the problem is solved, you can try to determine which fix provided the solution. If the problem persists, you know that you need to be working on the problem from a different angle. You also know which fixes don't work.

Step 5: Identify and Isolate Timing Factors

Try to determine the last time the system was working. Sometimes, knowing that the system worked perfectly until last week and then all of a sudden the problem occurred, is an indicator that something that occurred in the past week caused the problem. If you track system changes, you can go back through your actions over the past week and find the items that may have caused the problem. It could be something as simple as the installation of virus-protection software.

Step 6: Determine Scope of Problem

A quick test for isolating the problem is to determine whether it arises from a single workstation, server, or user, rather than occurring across the system. If the problem is only occurring for one user, figure out what's unique about this user compared to all the other users. If the problem is not organization-wide, applying a server or network-wide fix is unlikely to provide a solution.

Sometimes, installing or recreating the problem on a completely different system or on a different version of the software can help isolate the problem. If the exact same user walks to another system and does business as usual and never experiences the problem again, the problem may have been the previous computer system. Sometimes the problem can be traced to a specific version of a software application, and you can try a different version. The more things you can examine to isolate the possible problems, the better.

Step 7: Check for Human Factors and Settings

You need to check to see if the problem is a user-error situation. This may be as simple as determining whether all users are experiencing the problem, just a selected group of users, or just a single individual. If a group or individual is experiencing the problem, evaluate the differences between their use of the system and that of others who are not experiencing the same problem. Sometimes you will learn that the problem is caused by user error. However, a problem that has affected a single user or a group of users may be caused by system settings, such as access levels or permissions.

Step 8: Review Event Logs

Windows 2000 keeps event logs to track system problems. It's always helpful to monitor the logs for major events and minor events, as well as for recurring events that may indicate a problem. Some administrators stop viewing event logs because the information in the logs isn't always useful, especially for a system that is running properly. The key is to view the logs on a regular basis so that you can easily identify what a normal event-log entry looks like, and what may be new or different.

The challenging part for many network administrators is that they don't know what an event log for a normally operating system looks like. Then, when problems occur, they look at the event logs without being able to determine which information is related to the problem. I've found it helpful to go into the event logs when the system is operating properly, and capture and annotate the logs (much like doing a baseline on system-performance monitoring). This exercise results in a good understanding of common network events.

When a problem arises, the best thing to do is filter all of the events so that only problematic events are displayed. By going through the exercise of noting common events, you already have a list of events that can be excluded, and when you have excluded them, you'll have a list of new events that have not occurred on a regular basis.

Often a system is not properly configured to trap and enter events in the event logs. If the logging level is set too low, events that may be important to note during problem-solving procedures aren't available. If the level of detail is set too high, minor events may cause confusion during problem-solving procedures. Event-logging options can be enabled and disabled, and many applications provide the ability to set logging at a minimum, medium, or maximum level. Typically, the minimum level of logging tracks only major or critical events, which are those that commonly occur just before a server fails. The medium level typically tracks critical events, as well as some minor events. It isn't until logging is set to maximum that most applications will track minor events. Those events may seem inconsequential during normal network operations, but when you are trying to isolate and analyze system problems, those minor events can indicate a failing state of system operations, leading to major events, and eventually to a system fault. By setting error-logging traps properly, you will have more information when you need to isolate a system problem.

Another tool that is extremely helpful when analyzing the event logs is Veritas Software's Crystal Reports. The Crystal Reports product provides a way to create reports or automatically filter information in a customized fashion. A basic version of the Crystal Reports product comes with Windows 2000, and it generates standard reports. However, the full product provides a number of filtering and report-generation tools that make the use of the product even more valuable when doing problem solving and debugging.

Step 9: Compare Current Data to Baseline

After you've gathered information about the operation of your network environment, you can compare that information with the baseline you took when your network was operating properly. Use the System Monitor snap-in statistical information, as well as log files, to search for differences that may indicate the source of the problem.

In most cases, system faults do not occur out of the blue, but are the result of a series of failures that occurred over time. If you track statistical information about the system, and monitor the information over time, you will see a trend of slowing or bottleneck performance on the system. This can be an indicator that the system is about to fail and gives you a chance to fix problems before they arise. However, if serious problems are occurring and there is no historical data, the best thing to do is check the current system against the original baselines to determine whether there is anything obvious that is indicative of the problem.

Step 10: Contact an Expert for Assistance

When all else fails, outside assistance is needed. Far too many organizations wait too long before calling for assistance. Finding expert help isn't easy, because there is a substantial difference between skill levels among all the experts who claim to be able to solve system problems. Keys to finding a true expert are references and recommendations from other business associates. Sometimes the manufacturer of the product you are using can lead you to someone who knows how to fix problems.

It's important to find someone who has years of experience specific to the problem you are trying to solve. Many times the best experts are those who have been working with the product during product development (in beta development cycles).

Try to find a person or company with broad enough experience to have a deep understanding of the product and knows the product "under the hood." Such experts have information that goes beyond knowing the standard response to error messages, and extends to knowledge that interprets an error message in terms of the way the product was written or designed. The more knowledge a person has about the basic design of the product, the better they are at problem-solving.

Lastly, a true expert is someone who is willing to escalate their problem-solving efforts to a higher source. Experts who say they know everything, and can figure out the problem with no assistance from anyone else, may be too short-sighted to know when additional assistance is necessary. Additional assistance is frequently sought by contacting experts at the manufacturer. The expert in the field can actually work on the problem, and the expert at the manufacturer will have internal knowledge and resources to information about the problem. As a team, the two sets of experts can work together to solve the problem.

Windows 2000 Problem-Solving Tools

Windows 2000 provides tools that administrators can use to identify system faults and network problems. We have already covered the Performance Monitor snap-in as one such tool. There are other tools built into Windows 2000 that I'll discuss in this section. Additional tools are available in the Windows 2000 Resource Kit, which is available for download from the Microsoft Web site.

Secondary Logon Service

Key to problem-solving is the ability to get administrative access to log files, system services, and other components on the system. However, in the normal course of a day, the system is in use by a non-administrator, so in order for the administrator to resolve problems, the current user must log out of the system and the administrator must log on since only the administrator typically has access to the management functions of the systems. Windows 2000 solves this problem by providing secondary logon access to a system. This service provides the administrator the ability to log on and conduct administrative tasks while the original user remains logged on.

To be able to use secondary logon services, the service must be enabled on the system. To accomplish this, do the following:

1. Log on for the first time to a system on which you wish to conduct secondary logon services.

2. Right-click the My Computer icon on the desktop, and select Manage.

3. Under Computer Management, select Services and Applications, and then Services.

4. Scroll through the list of services until you come to the Secondary Logon Service. If the service is not set to automatic, double-click the service to access the service properties.

5. Under Startup type, select Automatic (this will set the service to start every time the system is booted in the future).

6. To enable the service immediately, select Start on the Current Status option.

Then, when you want to use a function that the current logged-on user can't access (because of permission levels), hold down the SHIFT key as you right-click the function's icon (perhaps a Control Panel applet). The shortcut menu will display the command Run As. Selecting Run As displays the dialog box shown in Figure 18-11, into which you must enter the appropriate user name and password in order to use the component or service.

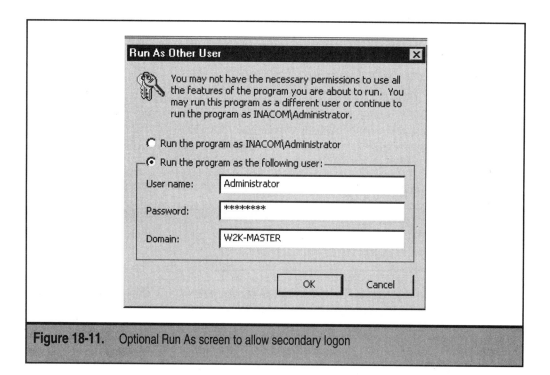

Figure 18-11. Optional Run As screen to allow secondary logon

To enable a secondary logon function for access to a command prompt, do the following:

1. Choose Start | Run.

2. Enter **runas /user:{machine/domain}\{username} cmd**.

This creates a command-prompt session with a logon as the user you designate in the command line.

The Run As function is useful, because it prevents the need to log off and log on again as a user with higher permission levels.

Boot with the F8 Key to Run a Directory Repair

New to the Windows NT family of products (but not to Windows 9x) is the ability to press F8 during system boot-up to access administrative repair tools. Pressing F8 during the boot process displays a menu with several options:

- ▼ **Safe Mode** Safe mode boots the system without loading operational services on the server. Operational services include anything that allows the system to boot as a server, such as enabling the network adapter, invoking logon services, virus protection or detection utilities, or other add-in services to the network. You can modify the configuration of any of these services in Safe Mode, and then boot normally.

- ■ **Safe Mode with Networking** This is the same as Safe Mode, except networking functions are enabled. This means you can log on to a network to download files or replace corrupted files before booting normally.

- ■ **Safe Mode with Command Prompt** This mode boots to a command prompt to provide access to the boot drive. This is a common practice when drivers need to be manually copied onto the system, or command line–based functions need to be executed.

- ■ **Enable Boot Logging** This enables logging of the individual steps involved with booting, which can be important for debugging boot problems. If the computer fails to boot properly, you can then boot to the command prompt and access the boot log to determine which driver or function caused the system to fail. Reinstalling the appropriate files should permit a normal boot.

- ■ **Enable VGA Mode** This mode boots the system with full services, but uses the standard VGA display adapter driver that comes with Windows 2000. Use this option to correct display options after a driver upgrade or configuration change makes the boot process fail.

- ■ **Last Known Good Configuration** This option allows the system to boot to the last configuration that booted properly. Use this function after you add or reconfigure devices and thereafter the system failed to boot properly. The last known good configuration mode uses a copy of previous settings that are stored in the registry. This used to be the only way to boot the system during a faulty boot cycle, but Windows 2000 provides the additional options discussed here.

■ **Directory Services Restore Mode**   For servers that are domain controllers, the directory services restore mode allows the rebuilding of the directory service from a server that has a valid copy of the directory. This mode is used if a domain controller is taken off the network for a period and requires an updated copy of the domain-directory information, or if the domain-directory information becomes corrupt.

▲ **Debugging Mode**   The debugging mode walks you through the boot process, allowing you to view the boot functions of the server so you can see what is causing the boot failure (such as a driver that doesn't load, or a system hang while a driver is trying to load).

COMMON OR KNOWN SYSTEM PROBLEMS IN WINDOWS 2000

Some of the common system problems I have run into during implementations of Windows 2000 include a server or domain controller failing to find a valid DNS server exhausting the resources of an existing server, causing the network to operate sluggishly. I have highlighted these problems in this section.

Can't Find Server

One problem that I've found quite common in new Windows 2000 installations has been the inability of a workstation or server to find a domain controller or another server on the network. The most common cause is the failure to use DNS. Many organizations with Windows environments in the past ran the NetBEUI protocol to find severs and Windows devices on the network. With Windows 2000 systems using DNS as the naming and look-up system, it frequently happens that a system cannot find a server on the network.

If a workstation is configured to look at an external DNS (Internet based) for name resolution, the system will not be able to find the internal servers on their network. The fix for this problem may simply be to point the workstation DNS look-up to an internal DNS server on the network. With Windows 2000 dynamic DNS, look-up can be changed to internal devices.

If changing the IP address of the internal DNS server still doesn't solve the problem, make sure the DNS host configuration on the workstation has the right name-resolution address.

Running the nslookup command on the computer that is having a problem provides information that may be helpful. The first thing to look at is the DNS server the computer is using as the default. In the following example, the system is defaulting to dsn.inacom.com. I know this is an internal DNS server, so that setting is correct.

```
C:\>nslookup
Default Server:  dns.inacom.com
> set type=soa
>
> dns.inacom.com
dns.inacom.com
        primary name server = dns1.inacom.com
        responsible mail addr = mailadm.inacom.com
> server dns1.inacom.com
Default Server:  dns1.inacom.com
Address:   10.1.100.5
```

If I run the NSLookup command and the first default server prompt identifies a server I am not familiar with as an internal server on my network, I need to find out whether that server is a valid internal DNS server. If the server noted as the default server is an external DNS server, change the DNS setting for the system. To accomplish this, follow these steps:

1. Choose Start | Settings | Control Panel.
2. Double-click Networks (Win 95/NT) or Networks and Dial-Up Connections (Windows 2000).
3. Select the TCP/IP Protocol (Win 95/NT) or Internet (Windows 2000).
4. Select Properties.
5. Select the DNS settings, and ensure that the setting is for a valid internal DNS server on the network.

If the system is using DHCP to acquire an IP address as well as receive definition of the DNS settings for the network, and there seems to be an invalid DNS server setting, the DNS setting on the DHCP server may be incorrect. This is a common problem when organizations that have multiple DHCP servers on the network forget to upgrade or modify a DHCP server. This causes users who get IP addresses from a DHCP server to receive an improper DNS server setting.

After validating that the server is getting a DNS address from a valid default server, the next thing to check is whether the DNS server is entered properly in the internal DNS server table. In the following example, typing the name of the DNS server that I believe to be my valid DNS server should result in the IP address of the DNS server I should be resolving and addressing. If the address that returns from the DNS lookup is an address I do not recognize as a valid DNS server on my network, I would flush the DNS tables on the server and have the tables rebuild themselves. This is covered in detail in Chapter 7.

When a network goes through multiple changes because of updates, upgrades, or system modifications, and IP addresses and server names are changed, sometimes the

DNS table does not properly update itself. Manually flushing the DNS tables forces a rebuild of the tables, creating valid name and IP address settings.

Exhausting the Resources of a Single Server

Another common problem I've found in Windows 2000 implementations is when a server fails to respond consistently to query requests for file, print, or application access. It's interesting situation that this problem occurs inconsistently. Sometimes the server responds without difficulty, and other times there is either an extensive delay or no response at all.

I frequently find that the trouble is a result of overloading of the server. While Windows 2000 scales significantly better than previous versions of the Windows NT operating environment, there comes a time in any server configuration when demands exceed the system's capability. When a server is overtaxed by requests and queries, the system is slow to respond, and at times appears not to be present on the network. In these cases, I find that implementing load balancing (allowing server processing to be distributed across multiple servers) results in better response times. This is particularly important for application servers, such as mail servers, database servers, and Web servers facilitating services to thousands, if not tens or hundreds of thousands, of simultaneous users. (Network load balancing is covered extensively in Chapter 12.)

Changing the Registered Name

The following function is more a trick than a debugging or problem-solving technique: changing the registered name of a Windows 2000 system. This is a trick that many organizations need, however, because sometimes a network administrator who no longer works for the company has entered his or her name as the registered owner of all the servers, or sometimes the registered name is inappropriate for the name of the organization.

The key to changing the registered owner name and company is in the registry of the server. The registry key that holds the name is:

```
Hkey_Local_Machine\Software\Microsoft\Windows NT\CurrentVersion
```

The two strings are RegisteredOrganization and RegisteredOwner. By double-clicking each of those strings, you can change the name of the registered company and owner of the system.

APPENDIX A

ISO-3166 2-Letter Country Codes

I addressed DNS and Active Directory naming conventions in Chapters 6 and discussed how you need to be careful about using certain two-letter combinations in your naming scheme. For example, if you use the postal codes for the U.S. states in your naming scheme, you need to be careful with using .ca in your DNS address because .ca is an Internet-wide recognized country code for Canada. You will find two-letter conflicts for Massachusetts, Missouri, Colorado, Indiana, and the like. The following is a chart of the ISO-3166 registered two-letter country codes. You can also refer back to the "Naming Convention" section of Chapter 6 for Active Directory naming and the "Naming Convention" section of Chapter 7 for DNS naming.

ad	Andorra	ch	Switzerland	gn	Guinea	lk	Sri Lanka	nz	New Zealand	sz	Swaziland
ae	United Arab Emirates	ci	Ivory Coast	gp	Guadeloupe	lr	Liberia	om	Oman	tc	Turks & Caicos Islands
af	Afghanistan	ck	Cook Islands	gq	Equatorial Guinea	ls	Lesotho	org	Organization Domain Name	td	Chad
ag	Antigua, Barbuda	cl	Chile	gr	Greece	lt	Lithuania	pa	Panama	tf	French Southern Terr.
ai	Anguilla	cm	Cameroon	gt	Guatemala	lu	Luxembourg	pe	Peru	tg	Togo
al	Albania	cn	China	gu	Guam	lv	Latvia	pf	Polynesia	th	Thailand
am	Armenia	co	Colombia	gw	Guinea Bissau	ly	Libya	pg	Papua New Guinea	tj	Tadjikistan
an	Netherland Antilles	cr	Costa Rica	gy	Guyana	ma	Morocco	ph	Philippines	tk	Tokelau
ao	Angola	cs	Czechoslovakia	hk	Hong Kong	mc	Monaco	pk	Pakistan	tm	Turkmenistan
aq	Antarctica	cu	Cuba	hm	Heard & McDonald Island	md	Moldavia	pl	Poland	tn	Tunisia
ar	Argentina	cv	Cape Verde	hn	Honduras	mg	Madagascar	pm	St. Pierre & Miquelon	to	Tonga
as	American Samoa	cx	Christmas Island	hr	Croatia	mh	Marshall Islands	pn	Pitcairn	tp	East Timor
at	Austria	cy	Cyprus	ht	Haiti	ml	Mali	pr	Puerto Rico	tr	Turkey
au	Australia	de	Germany, Deutschland	hu	Hungary	mm	Myanmar	pt	Portugal	tt	Trinidad & Tobago
aw	Aruba	dj	Djibouti	id	Indonesia	mn	Mongolia	pw	Palau	tv	Tuvalu
az	Azerbaidjan	dk	Denmark	ie	Ireland	mo	Macau	py	Paraguay	tw	Taiwan

ba	Bosnia-Herzegovina	do	Dominican Republic	il	Israel	mp	Northern Mariana Island	qa	Qatar	tz	Tanzania
bb	Barbados	dz	Algeria	in	India	mq	Martinique	re	Reunion	ua	Ukraine
bd	Bangladesh	ec	Ecuador	io	British Indian, Terr.	mr	Mauritania	ro	Romania	ug	Uganda
be	Belgium	ee	Estonia	iq	Iraq	ms	Montserrat	ru	Russian Federation	uk	United Kingdom
bf	Burkina Faso	eg	Egypt	ir	Iran	mt	Malta	rw	Rwanda	um	US Minor Outlying Island
bg	Bulgaria	eh	Western Sahara	is	Iceland	mu	Mauritius	sa	Saudi Arabia	us	United States
bh	Bahrain	es	Spain	it	Italy	mv	Maldives	sb	Solomon Islands	uy	Uruguay
bi	Burundi	et	Ethiopia	jm	Jamaica	mw	Malawi	sc	Seychelles	uz	Uzbekistan
bj	Benin	fi	Finland	jo	Jordan	mx	Mexico	sd	Sudan	va	Vatican City State
bm	Bermuda	fj	Fiji	jp	Japan	my	Malaysia	se	Sweden	vc	St.Vincent & Grenadines
bn	Brunei Darussalam	fk	Falkland Island	ke	Kenya	mz	Mozambique	sg	Singapore	ve	Venezuela
bo	Bolivia	fm	Micronesia	kg	Kirgistan	na	Namibia	sh	St. Helena	vg	Virgin Islands, British
br	Brazil	fo	Faroe Islands	kh	Cambodia	nc	New Caledonia	si	Slovenia	vi	Virgin Islands, US
bs	Bahamas	fr	France	ki	Kiribati	ne	Niger	sj	Svalbard & Jan Mayen Island	vn	Vietnam
bt	Buthan	fx	France, European Terr.	km	Comoros	net	Network Domain Name	sk	Slovakia	vu	Vanuatu
bv	Bouvet Island	ga	Gabon	kp	Korea North	nf	Norfolk Island	sl	Sierra Leone	wf	Wallis & Futuna Islands
bw	Botswana	gb	Great Britain, UK	kr	Korea South	ng	Nigeria	sm	San Marino	ws	Samoa
by	Bielorussia	gd	Grenada	kw	Kuwait	ni	Nicaragua	sn	Senegal	ye	Yemen

bz	Belize	**ge**	Georgia	**ky**	Cayman Islands	**nl**	Netherlands	**so**	Somalia	**yu**	Yugoslavia
ca	Canada	**gf**	Guyana	**kz**	Kazachstan	**no**	Norway	**sr**	Suriname	**za**	South Africa
com	Commercial Domain Name	**gh**	Ghana	**la**	Laos	**np**	Nepal	**st**	St. Tome and Principe	**zm**	Zambia
cc	Cocos Island	**gi**	Gibraltar	**lb**	Lebanon	**nr**	Nauru	**su**	Soviet Union	**zr**	Zaire
cf	Central African Rep.	**gl**	Greenland	**lc**	Saint Lucia	**nt**	Neutral Zone	**sv**	El Salvador	**zw**	Zimbabwe
Cg	Congo	**gm**	Gambia	**li**	Liechtenstein	**nu**	Niue	**sy**	Syria		

Index

D

G

▼ **H**

▼ I

Q

 R

T

X

Z